Romania Between East and West
Historical Essays in Memory of
Constantin C. Giurescu

Edited by
Stephen Fischer-Galati, Radu R. Florescu
and George R. Ursul

EAST EUROPEAN MONOGRAPHS, BOULDER
DISTRIBUTED BY COLUMBIA UNIVERSITY PRESS
NEW YORK

1982

FOREWORD

The present volume honors the memory of Constantin C. Giurescu, the man and the historian.

It was conceived as news of his death reached his friends, disciples, and admirers in the United States in 1977. As in the case of most collaborative works there were delays in readying the book for publication. But, thanks to the efforts and support of those close to Constantin C. Giurescu we are able to give the so-called *"bun de tipar"* this month of October 1981 when we would have celebrated his eightieth birthday.

The following pages contain many a recollection and reflection on the stature, work, and role of Constantin C. Giurescu in the history of Romania. It seems fair to say that he has not only placed the Romanians in the history of the world but also, and foremost, that he has placed Romania in the history of the twentieth century. And he has done that with authority and elegance.

Stephen Fischer-Galati

CONTENTS

Foreword   v
Stephen Fischer-Galati

Introduction   1
Radu R. Florescu

I.   Constantin C. Giurescu, 1901-1977: Romanian Historian
and Historian of Romania   9
Dinu C. Giurescu

II.   Recollections of Constantin C. Giurescu   15
J. Constantin Drăgan

III.   The Master of Synthesis: Constantin C. Giurescu
and the Coming of Age of Romanian Historiography
1919-1947   23
Paul E. Michelson

IV.   Professor Constantin C. Giurescu and the Mass Media   109
Cristian Popișteanu

V.   The "Dark Millenary" in the History of the Romanians
as Seen by Constantin C. Giurescu   115
Virgil Cândea

VI.   Origins of the Slavic Narrative About the
Historical Dracula   127
Raymond McNally

VII.   Hetman Ivan Mazepa in Romanian Literature   147
Demetrius Dvoichenko-Markov

VIII.   Social Classes and Revolutionary Ferment in
Nineteenth Century Bucharest   159
Radu R. Florescu

IX.   Balcescu as an Economic Historian and Theorist   169
Bruce C. Fryer

X.   The Jewish Question During the Period of the Romanian
National Renaissance and the Unification of the Two
Principalities of Moldavia and Wallachia, 1848-1866   195
Lloyd A. Cohen

XI.   From Political Freedom to Religious Independence:
The Romanian Orthodox Church, 1877 to 1925   217
George R. Ursul

XII.	Some American Observers of the Russo-Turkish War *James F. Clarke*	245
XIII.	Origins of Romania's Oil Policy *Gh. Buzatu*	259
XIV.	The Adaptation of a Western Political Theory in a Peripheral State: The Case of Romanian Liberalism *Victoria F. Brown*	269
XV.	Constantin C. Giurescu, Promoter of Romanian- American Scientific and Cultural Relations *Paul Cernovodeanu*	303
XVI.	The Diplomatic Career of Charles J. Votipka in Romania, 1913-1920 *Glenn E. Torrey*	319
XVII.	Romanian-Americans and the Union of 1918 *Gerald Bobango and Ion Stanciu*	337
XVIII.	The Romanian-American Press as a Source of Information on Romania *Stephen Fischer-Galati*	359
XIX.	The United States and the Problem of Transylvania During World War II *Paul D. Quinlan*	369
XX.	Romanian-American Economic Relations, 1947-1975 *Robert Forrest*	385

Radu R. Florescu

INTRODUCTION

Brought up on Constantin C. Giurescu's History of Romania textbooks with the whole interwar generation of secondary school students, I never had the privilege of meeting the renowned scholar until 1967, when I spent a year in Romania as a Fulbright scholar after an absence of 28 years. Somewhat isolated in the new environment of socialist Romania I needed friends, contacts, above all, guidance to help focus on a suitable research topic during my sabbatical year.

I shall long remember my first meeting with Giurescu in the Fall of 1967 at his small second floor apartment located in the old mint house of Bucharest, off Kiselev Avenue. He knew of me through my family which had since the 15th century served their country in the shadows of history. Having just written a biography on Alexander John Cuza, the unifier of Romania, Giurescu began the conversation praising the accomplishments of General Ion Emanuel Florescu, the creator of the modern Romanian army, and a close collaborator of Cuza, whose career needed a good monograph. As a member of the family, I told him it was perhaps more fitting to have one of his doctoral students undertake the task. "In that case," answered Giurescu, "there is another subject connected with the period, equally rewarding. Why don't you research the career of Cuza's French secretary Baligot de Beyne. I have come across his voluminous correspondence with the eminent men of the day which is located at the Romanian Academy. If you need the manuscript room which is always crowded, feel free to take my reserved seat." I needed little further encouragement and the first three months of my stay were spent compiling notes and photostats on that topic. Fate changed the course of my research (and my career) in the form of a letter of enquiry from my Boston College colleague Raymond T. McNally concerning possible connections between the mythical Count Dracula and the historical Vlad the Impaler.

The story of our combined research leading to the publication of the best seller, *In Search of Dracula*, in 1972 has been the object of extensive

1

publicity. What is not generally known is the significant role Giurescu had in ensuring the completion of our work. Giurescu had been intrigued with Vlad the Impaler's career since his student days in 1924 when he discovered the inscription of a church dedicated by the redoubtable "Impaler" on June 24th, 1461 at Tîrgşor, which proved among other things, that Vlad III was also a man of God. When I told Giurescu of the new direction of my research, he introduced me to Matei Cazacu, one of his brilliant students whose thesis he was directing focusing precisely on Vlad the Impaler's career. During the weeks, the months, in fact the years, that were to follow until the publication of *In Search of Dracula*, it would be difficult to acknowledge sufficiently the extent of my and Professor McNally's indebtedness to the great scholar, though we payed him a tribute in the preface of both our works (*Dracula a Biography of Vlad the Impaler*) and in an article published in May 1969 in *Magazinul Istoric*. He was most generous of his time in numerous conferences at his house, at the Romanian Academy, at *Casa Oamenilor de Ştiinţe* (the Academy faculty club which was his favorite dining place); he introduced us to numerous scholars in fields connected with our study: literature, folklore, archeology, linguistics; he would accompany us on field trips to locations associated with Vlad the Impaler. As it turned out the most dramatic was our visit to Dracula's famous castle, at the time still abandoned—an old ruin—sitting on a mountain overlooking the river Argeş at Poenari. Apart from Giurescu, the expedition consisted of my son John, Horia Nestorescu (currently director of the Bălcescu Museum), and my uncle, George Florescu, distinguished genealogist and former Director of the City of Bucharest Museum. Watching Giurescu spryly escalate the rather abrupt incline towards the summit of the mountain, my uncle ten years Giurescu's senior, attempted to do likewise. However, he slipped, lost his balance, fell several feet and was unable to move. He was carried off the mountain on an improvised stretcher, Giurescu at one end, an impressive demonstration of his shear physical power and mountain climbers ability. My uncle was rushed back to Bucharest. The diagnosis: a broken hip from which he never fully recovered. The incident was embellished by the western sensation-seeking press under the headline: *The Dracula Castle Curse*, an oblique reference to Dracula's hatred for one of Florescu's forebearers Vintilă, who had defected to his political enemies: the Turks.

Giurescu was the obvious choice for writing the introduction to a projected collaborative monograph on "the Impaler" with the help of half-a-dozen specialists. The proposed book never got under way, but Giurescu's introduction was delivered as a lecture during his American tour and later appended in his published *Journal of Travels* to America.

Although Dracula provided the focus for mutual interests, my conversations with Giurescu extended over the full range of Romanian history, which included his own career so closely intermeshed with contemporary events. He spoke affectionately of his father and regretted his premature death, which had changed his whole career; he was saddened by the stir which his polemics with Iorga had caused among historians; imprisonment during the Stalinist persecutions had strengthened his charater—his greatest punishment was that of being deprived of pen and paper during a period of seven years; he loved the city of Bucharest "a city of churches" we would say, as we visited many of them together. A precious lesson Giurescu taught me for life was the value of self-discipline. In his eyes, history was less a matter of poetry than good organization and hard work. "I am at my desk daily at 8 a.m." he once told me on the porch of the cottage he rented at Mangalia "and I will continue to work until 1 p.m. until I complete my ten pages of manuscript." Then followed a copious lunch, the siesta, a swim or mudbath and socializing.

It was late in the early Fall of 1968 on the eve of my return to America that our conversation focused on the well known journey that Nicolae Iorga had undertaken to the United States in the nineteen-twenties, and on the reminiscenses the historian had written subsequently. Half seriously, I asked Giurescu whether it would interest him to indulge in a similar experience at half a century's distance of time. From the gleem in his eye I could perceive he had not taken my suggestion lightly. "How would we set the ball rolling," he asked. I explained to him that initially I could ask the Dean of Boston College—the largest Catholic University in America— to extend an invitation to lecture on some aspect of Romanian history. I would then write colleagues at other universities with East European interests: to Professors Charles and Barbara Jelavic at Indiana University (my alma mater); James Clarke at the University of Pittsburgh; Stephen Fischer-Galati at the University of Colorado. We would apply to the International Research and Exchanges Board (IREX) for funds. On Giurescu's way back to Europe, I could arrange for him to lecture at Oxford Univesity, at my old college, St. Antony and would write to Hugh Seton-Watson for an invitation at the School of Slavonic and East European Studies at the University of London. Giurescu then told me that he had collected a number of invitations from various friends at American universities, which included Peter Sugar at the University of Washington, but had never given serious thought to the realization of such an ambitious program. If I took the necessary initiatives, he would be tempted to accept. This is in essence the manner in which Giurescu's American career was born. We agreed to have three lectures prepared in English: *Transylvania in the History of the Romanian People*, *The Life and Exploits of Vlad the Impaler: Drăculea* and *The History of a Capital: Bucharest*, allowing each college or university to make the final choice.

Giurescu's arrival at Logan airport in Boston on that beautiful last day of September 1969 marked an important stage in his career as "the ambassador extraordinary" of Romanian culture. Even on our journey back from the airport and later during that first week that he spent in the spacious home that I had rented on the shores of the Atlantic in the village of Cohasset, I could see that the relatively modest schedule we had established at Bucharest was mushrooming into something far more ambitious, with additional lectures at Columbia University, the University of Illinois, the University of Arizona, in addition to official visits to the centers of the Romanian community in Detroit and Cleveland, all this to be accomplished within a single month, with complex plane schedules, changes of climate and time zones, little time for rest. A program such as this, I thought to myself would tax the energies of a far younger man. He would not heed my entreaties to scale down the number of activities, nor limit them to purely academic pursuits. He was in the United States to see as much of the country as was possible. With regards to the Romanian communities, he wished to lend the prestige of his name in an attempt to effect a reconciliation between the two wings of the Romanian Orthodox church in America.

From the hectic pace of Giurescu's Boston week, I realized what was in store for him. Lectures at Boston College, Wellesley, at the Russian Research Center at Harvard, a moving address to the Romanian community, a day trip by car to Columbia University, returning in the small hours of the morning, sightseeing excursions in Boston and its vicinity, not to forget our daily exercises in English pronunciation.

Giurescu's natural curiosity and thirst for accurate knowledge was truly insatiable. Sometimes with pad in hand like a youthful newspaper stringer, he would fire the questions at me: "When was Wellesly College founded? What was the nature of the success of the Christian Science church in the Boston area? How much would it cost to paint the frame house I rented?" Every evening he would retire to his bedroom after dinner and meticulously jot down the varied experiences of each day, which later provided the substance for his best selling *Journal of Travels*, printed in two separate editions.

The physical, mental and moral strains of this whirlwind journey from coast to coast had overtaxed the physical strength of a man who had overcome the rigors of prolonged imprisonment and my worst forebodings were confirmed, when Giurescu called me from Washington on October 30th at the tail end of his trip. Judging from the strained expression in his voice he was clearly in great physical distress. Upon his return to Boston, Giurescu stayed with my colleague, Anghel Rugina, Professor Emeritus at Northeastern University. We were both concerned as we noticed his languid state reflecting pain and fatigue, and took him to a doctor who diagnosed sciatic problems in his left leg recommending most of all, rest. We advised Giurescu to give up the remaining portions of his lecturing tour in the United Kingdom and fly directly to Romania to seek further medical treatment. He argued with us and became obdurate, demonstrating his stoicism and his belief that an engagement must be honored "even if he had to lecture in a wheel chair." These were more or less his last words as we bade farewell at Logan Airport on November 3. We took the precaution of ordering a wheel chair to await his arrival at Heathrow Airport. He lectured in England, but it took weeks of hospital care following his return to Bucharest for Giurescu to recover his strength and health.

There can be no question that Giurescu's American travels, coupled with extensive European lectures, sponsored in part by the Drăgan European Foundation, represented a real turning point which furthered Giurescu's successful second career. The experience also acted as a catalyst, buoyed his spirits and created countless international contacts which enhanced his prestige. Back in Romania, he plunged with renewed intensity in the publication of specialized monographs centering on social and economic problems. Together with his son Dinu, he wrote the *History of the Fatherland*, began his memoirs and embarked upon the republication of the first two volumes of his successful prewar five volume history. In collaboration with Virgil Cândea and others, Giurescu was one of the cofounders of the Romanian Associations, a society aimed at promoting and restoring the links between Romania and the Romanian communities overseas throughout the world. He encouraged Christian Popisteanu's uniquely successful formula of creating a popular historical journal, *Magazin Istoric* containing articles written by first-rate historians, but directed essentially to the popularization of history, a concept always close to his heart. Giurescu supported Contantin Drăgan's research stressing the significance of Thracian history, among others, as a means for stressing the continuity of the Romanian people. He also fought hard to preserve the importance of history in the scale of national values, whether by cultivating research, preserving historical monuments and churches, indulging in dialogues with historians of other nations, or insisting upon the historian's role in the making of films, or cultivating the masses in the press and the media. Giurescu's prestige was great enough to have a weighty voice in the highest councils of the state. Activities such as these however, in no way shortchanged Giurescu's handful of doctoral students whose dissertations he continued to guide personally with the kind of meticulous concern for detail that was his wont.

Completely rehabilitated, the historian reaped numerous honors and awards, some of them denied to him during his first career. He was given back half of his house at 4 Berza Street; he became a member of the Academy of Social and Political Sciences; finally, he had the satisfaction of being elected a full member of the older, more prestigious Romanian Academy, a prize denied him by his enemies during the interwar years. During the spring term of 1972, Giurescu was nominated—ironically in the eyes of some—to the recently created Iorga Chair at Columbia University. Both the manner in which his formal invitation to the inaugural lecture, and his delivery on the occasion was characteristic of the man and a formal style of lecturing of an era gone-by, no longer fashionable on the American campus. The subject matter: *American-Romanian Cultural Relations*, paced with information, was a model for the extensive research, the precision, and rather formal, well recognized exposition it reflected. Giurescu had adjusted well during his second extended American visit, initially in a small hotel, then in a riverside apartment placed at his disposal by the University. He admired America, enjoyed it and led a fully adjusted American academic life, fostering new personal contacts, approaching American publishers to translate his books into English and lecturing nationwide—I was to meet him again at the University of Washington in Seattle and at Ohio State University in Columbus.

It was an extraordinary privilege for me to get to know Giurescu the man in the course of the years which had ellapsed since our first meeting in 1967. Inevitably, the facade of the scholar, the lecturer, the educator was so powerfully stamped upon his whole personality that it is the first image that comes to mind: Giurescu at the podium lecturing with authority in his slow, deliberate tone of voice which bound your attention and commanded respect. His knowledge of subject matter, erudition, his memory and mastery of detail on all aspects of Romanian and East European history was little short of uncanny. Rarely did he emit an opinion that was not solidly anchored in fact. He expressed himself well, always choosing his words carefully, factors well evidenced in his writings. Giurescu should be best remembered as "the educator of a nation," historically speaking half-educated until his time. He was *the* pedagogue and writer of history books *par excellence*. In this respect he owed his style and erudition to no one but himself.

The personality of the scholar was so pervasive and overawing that it was difficult to get to know Giurescu the man. One character trait I admired in his life was his adherence to the golden mean ideal of the Ancient Greeks; "nothing in excess" could have been his motto. Giurescu was above all measured in all things. Overindulgence in food and drink, keeping late hours (he would invariably retire at 10 p.m.), ribald conversation, vulgar jokes, excessive speed on the highway (Dinu his son was instructed not to exceed 50 mph when driving in Romania) were anathema to him. In society he was the traditional image of the gentleman, somewhat formal in his manners and always galant to the ladies.

Whether at work or at play Giurescu was first and foremost a family man, only truly happy when surrounded by his loyal clan. His wife was the daughter of the well known geographer Simeon Mehedinti. He was inordinately proud of the artistic and architectural accomplishments of his younger son, Dan, whose talents were well recognized in Paris. He was extremely fond of his daughter Mona, whom he saw frequently when living in New York. His oldest child Dinu, however, was more than just a son, he was his confident, his collaborator and above all represented the third generation of historians in the family. He was constantly by his side and part of the intimate family circle.

Both his profound knowledge of Romanian history and his ancient roots in the squirearchy of the land contributed to an intense love of the countryside, which was best evidenced during his vacation retreats. He was truly happy fishing at Cheia in the scenic Carpathian valley of the Teleajen, his mountain retreat, or admiring a sunset on the *pridvor* (porch) of the quaint peasant cottage he had rented for years at Mangalia. Of the nationalized properties confiscated by the regime, he regretted most his beautiful villa at Predeal, which he explained had been "earned" with the royalties of his books. His "passion" for Romania filtered through the historian's dedication to impartiality whenever the nation's rights to its historic lands were challegened, as happened occasionally in the course of his American lectures. They had a traumatizing effect.

Giurescu was, of course, ambitious, both for himself, and the advancement of his family, factors which impelled him to tackle a political career during the interwar period which caused him more harm than good in the long run. This acquaintance with power accounted for a certain imperiousness and an air of authority. He was impatient with underlings, could not tolerate mediocrity and was incensed with incompetent bureaucrats whom he characterized as "des imbéciles." He personally was most unforgiving not so much towards those who had crossed him, but the many personalities he had helped in difficult moments and who later made manifest their total ingratitude towards the man who had saved their jobs and in some instances their very lives. Given his meteoric rise both as a historian and a national figure, it was inevitable that Giurescu should have enemies, both during the first and second careers. The label "careerist" and "opportunist" were affixed to his name by those who reproached him his tergivesations and acceptance of the values of Socialist Romania. Giurescu's repartee might have been: "the only principles which he recognized were the eternal values of the continuity of the Romanian state in its struggle for independence through the ages, and that no matter what the regime, the character of a nation does not change. Besides, it is everyman's prerogative to change his opinions with the times."

I happened to be in Bucharest in the late Fall of 1977 (October) at the time of Giurescu's sudden, premature death at age 76. I had just returned to Romania from Paris on a IREX grant enabling me finally to complete the research initially proposed to me by Constantin C. Giurescu a decade before, on General Ion Emanuel Florescu which none of his students had undertaken. Following an excursion in Moldavia on my arrival in Bucharest, I called Giurescu's house, as was my wont, to resume the dialogue we had interrupted for some months. I will long remember Dinu's grim tone of voice at the other end: "s'a prăpădit tată." It seemed Giurescu died, as he had lived throughout his life, at work at his desk. It was an extraordinary testimony to the greatness of the man to witness people of all ranks and professions and trades filing by his body which lay in state in the hallway of the history faculty at Bucharest. At the center stood guard at each corner of the coffin, representatives of the government, officials of the city, the delegates of the Romanian universities, history institutes, members of the academies, the family, close friends and collaborators. In the hallway, the crowd which overflowed into the street outside—many people in tears—was so dense that one could hardly move. In the afternoon we all left for Bellu cemetary where the last rites were administered by three officiating priests including the Reverend Cazacu, from the Batişte church, and old friend and former secretary to three patriarchs, the father of Giurescu's former student.

Dinu C. Giurescu

CONSTANTIN C. GIURESCU: 1901-1977
ROMANIAN HISTORIAN AND HISTORIAN OF ROMANIA

Constantin C. Giurescu* took his degree in History and Geography (1922) and subsequently his doctor's degree (1925) at Bucharest University. He became reader in the History of the Romanians at the same University in 1926; associate professor in 1927 and full professor in 1930. From 1923 to 1925 he was on the staff of the Romanian School in France (Paris), carrying on research work in record offices and libraries. He was professor at Bucharest University until 1948 and from 1963 to 1971, and subsequently consulting professor at the History Department of the same University (1971-1977). From 1948 to 1950 and from 1956 to 1963, he worked in the capacity of scientific researcher at the *N. Iorga* History Institute of Bucharest. He became a member of the Academy of Social and Political Sciences in 1971 and of the Academy of the Socialist Republic of Romania in 1974. For 17 years (1930-1947), he directed the *Revista Istorică Română* (The Romanian Historical Review).

Professor Constantin C. Giurescu began his scientific activity at the age of 18, when he published a critical review; by the time of his death in November 1977, he had published a total of 376 works including: surveys, collections of documents and chronicles, monographs, synopses, reviews, bibliographical notes, interviews, popular articles and memoirs.

Until 1947, his research focused on the study of the high officials in Wallachia and Moldavia in the 14th and 15th centuries; the financial organization of Wallachia during the period of Mircea the Old (1386-1418); a course on the History of the Romanians delivered at Bucharest University: to lithographed volumes published from 1927 to 1937 inclusive; an edition of Grigore Ureche's *Chronicle;* an edition of the volume: *Ion C. Brătianu, Acte şi Cuvîntări* (Documents and Speeches); two

---

* Born at Focşani, 13/26 October 1901; died in Bucharest, 13 November 1977.

handbooks on the History of the Romanians, for the 4th and 8th year high-school grades; "The History of the Romanians," a synopsis in 5 volumes published from 1935 to 1946—from the first prehistoric settlements to the end of the Phanariot Period (1821); a synopis on the history of the Romanians in a single volume (1943); contributions to the publication by the Hungarian professor Dr. Andrea Veress, of 10 volumes of "Documents Concerning the History of Transylvania, Moldavia and Wallachia" (Bucharest, 1929-1938).

During the second part of his professional career (1956-1977), Constantin C. Giurescu encompassed a broad spectrum of subjects on Romanian histioriography. The most important are the follow (in chronological order):

1. *Principatele române la începutul seculului al XIX-lea. Constatări istorice, economice și statistice pe temeiul hărții ruse din 1835* (The Romanian Principalities in the Early 19th Century. Historical, Economic and Statistical Findings. Founded on the Russian Map of 1835) (1957, 318 p.).

2. *Istoria pescuitului și pisciculturii în România* (The History of Fishing and Fish-breeding in Romania) (1964, 389 p., awared the Nicolae Bălcescu Prize by the Academy of the Socialist Republic of Romania).

3. *Viața și opera lui Cuza Vodă* (Prince Cuza's Life and Work) (1966, 469 p.; second edition revised and enlarged, 1970).

4. *Știri despre populația românească a Dobrogei în hărți medievale și moderne* (New Facts Concerning the Romanian Population in Dobrudja from Mediaeval and Modern Maps) (1966, 64 p. + 2 maps).

5. *Istoria Bucureștilor din cele mai vechi timpuri pînă în zilele noastre* (The History of Bucharest from the Remotest Ages to Date) (1967, 465 p.; second edition revised and enlarged, 1979; a summarized version in English, French and German, Sport-Turism Publishing House, Bucharest, 1976, 203 p.).

6. *Tîrguri sau orașe și cetăți moldovene din secolul al X-lea pînă la mijlocul secolului al XVI-lea* (Moldavian Boroughs, Towns and Citadels from the 10th to the Mid-16th Century) (1967, 379 p.).

7. *Transilvania în istoria popurului român* (Transylvania in the History of the Romanian People) (1967, 159 p.); French, English, German, Russian, Hungarian and Spanish editions, Meridiane Publishing House, Bucharest; an English edition entitled *Transylvania in the History of Romania. An Historical Outline*, London, Gaston Press, 1969, 138 p.; a German edition *Transilvanien. Ein Beitrag zur Geschichte Rumäniens*, Köln, Schäuble Verlag, 1970, 142 p.; a Portuguese edition: *A Transylvania na história do povo romeno*, Grifo Publishing House, Rio de Janeiro, 1977, 125 p.

8. *Istoricul oraşului Brăila. Din cele mai vechi timpuri pînă astăzi* (The History of the Town of Brăila. From the Remotest Ages to Date) (1968, 373 p.).

9. *Istoricul podgoriei Odobeştilor. Din cele mai vechi timpuri pînă la 1918* (This History of the Odobeşti Vineyards. From the Remotest Antiquity to 1918). With 124 documents hiterto unknown, 1624-1864 + 8 manifolds (1969, 551 p.).

10. *La formation de l'Etat unitaire roumain* (1971, 170 p.); English, German and Spanish editions (Meridiane Publishing House, Bucharest); second edition in English, Spanish and French (Meridiane Publishing House, Bucharest, 1974); Japanese edition published in Tokio in 1972, to be followed by a new edition, in Tokio again, in 1978; Hindi edition published in India (Delhi, 1978); Chinese edition (Beijing, 1978).

11. *Contribuţiuni la studiul originilor şi dezvoltării burgheziei române pînă la 1848* (Contributions to the Study of the Origins and Development of the Romanian Bourgeoisie up to 1848) (1972, 296 p.).

12. *Contribuţii la istoria ştiinţei şi tehnicii româneşti în secolele XV— începutul secolului XIX* (Contributions to the History of Romanian Science and Technique from the 15th to the Early 19th Century) (1973, 268 p.), Academia Publishing House, Bucharest, 226 p.

13. *Formarea popurului român* (Formation of the Romanian People) (1973, 172 p.); English, French and Spanish editions (Meridiane Publishing House, Bucharest, 1972).

14. *Istoria pădurii româneşti, din cele mai vechi timpuri pînă astăzi* (The History of the Romanian Forests from the Remotest Ages to Date), (1975, 388 p.); second edition, revised and enlarged, 1976; English edition (summarized version): *A History of Romanian Forests*, Bucharest, 1980, Academia Publishing House, 260 p.

15. *Probleme controversate în istoriografia română* (Controversial Issues in Romanian Historiography), (1977, 176 p.).

Moreover, Constantin C. Giurescu wrote and published jointly with his son, Dinu C. Giurescu, the first two of eight projected volumes of a synopsis of the history of the Romanians in 1974 and 1976 at the Ştiinţifica şi Enciclopedica Publishing House, and a compendium of the same history published in two editions (1971 and 1975). Furthermore, he directed the teams who compiled *Istoria României în date* (Romania's History in Dates), with English and French editions and *Istoria învăţămîntului în România* (The History of Education in Romania), to which he contributed 60 pages of his own.

During 1965-1977 Constantin C. Giurescu attended numerous scientific meetings and conferences at several university centers in Austria, Great

Britain, Bulgaria, France, Greece, Italy, The Federal Republic of Germany, Spain, Switzerland, Turkey, the United States of America and Yugoslavia, in keeping with his conviction that the maintenance of continuous relations with the historians of other countries was indeed indispensable.

Constantin C. Giurescu visited the United States on six occasions: in 1968; in 1972, as visiting professor at Columbia University; twice in 1975 and again in 1976 and 1977. His lectures and papers took him from Cambridge and Boston, to Portland and Seattle by way of New York, Rochester, New Brunswick, Philadelphia, Washington, D.C., Pittsburgh, Detroit, Chicago, Bloomington, Champaign-Urbana, Dallas, Denver, Boulder, Phoenix, Tuscon, Los Angeles, Santa Barbara, San Francisco, and other centers. He described and reflected upon his American travels in his *Jurnal de Călătorie* (Travel Diary), which he published in 1971. The second edition, which comprised his later travels through 1976, come out in April 1977 in 35,000 copies.

In 1977, Constantin C. Giurescu continued to work as assiduously as before. Apart from his current work which included meetings with colleagues of all generations, weekly consultations at the University of Bucharest, radio, television and press interviews, participation in various symposia and the like, he was also engaged in writing or delivering lectures on the following—the second edition of his Travel Diary; *Scurtă istorie a românilor pentru tineret îndeosebi* (A Short History of the Romanians mainly for the Young), written jointly with Dinu C. Giurescu and published in May 1977; on the second volume of *Amintiri* (Recollections), with 120 pages written; on the third volume of the synopsis of the History of the Romanians, with about 100 p. written; on *Istoria Bucureştilor* (The History of Bucharest), second edition; on a paper read at Bucharest University on the Centenary of Romania's State Independence (3 May 1977); and on a paper read at the Bucharest University History Department on Fifty Years since Vasile Pîrvan's Death (24 June). In addition, he also travelled abroad during that year for lectures, symposia and dissertations to Switzerland, the United States and France.

On 26 October 1977, Constantin C. Giurescu turned 76 years of age. Three days later, he delivered a lecture in the town of Piteşti; the following days he continueed his work on the second edition of his History of Bucharest; on 5 November he read a paper at the section of Ancient Romanian law at the Academy of Social and Political Sciences. On Friday 11 November, he went to the History Department for his consultation (with post-graduates); in the afternoon I spent some time with him in his study, as usual; among other things he spoke of the 15th International

Congress of Historical Sciences to be held in Bucharest in August 1980. He was also thinking of adding a second volume to Controversial Issues in Romanian Historiography, the first volume having just been printed. The week after that he was to have lectured at Slatina, on the ancient origin of the town, and his other scheduled activities included a doctoral examination, a meeting at the History Museum of the Bucharest municipality, a call on Dr. Gh. Constantinescu, Director of the Sport-Turism Publishing House . . .

The following day, Saturday 12 November, we both leafed through his Controversial Issues in Romanian Historiography. We all had lunch, and around 3:30 in the afternoon, I saw father go into his study after a short rest. In the evening, at about 6:30 I found him in his study, senseless; the victim of a sudden, violent stroke. He was taken to the Elias hospital but to no avail.

He had completed his journey on earth. A journey during which he had experienced the great joy of creation but also pain and much suffering. He had known people and everything that was good in them, but also everything that was bad. He had believed in the power of science, in truth —even when truth was dangerous to tell—and he had believed in work— the daily work he went through methodically, perserveringly, putting all his heart into it. He was a true father to his family. He never failed his friends but he also answered those who assailed him. He made it his goal, even when circumstances were adverse, to defend the major interests of his homeland.

Through the medium of his works, he continues his journey in the ranks of the greatest, the permanent founders of Romanian historical science.

RECOLLECTIONS OF CONSTANTIN C. GIURESCU

Some years ago, Professor Alexander von Randa spoke to me about Giurescu and suggested his giving a series of lectures at one of the branches of the Drăgan Foundation. I had endowed two chairs in Romanian Culture and Civilization at the University of Palma di Mallorca, and von Randa was one of the incumbents. Since he had completed an initial introductory cycle of lectures he proposed Giurescu to collaborate with him in the sequel which focussed on Romanian history. Giurescu accepted my offer and his presence in Spain marked the first time he had been abroad since World War II. This invitation and subsequent lectures in Western Europe contributed in strengthening Giurescu's position and was helpful in securing his nomination at the Romanian Academy of Social and Political Sciences. From his election onwards he could be introduced as "Academician" to his audiences in Athens, Rome, Palma, Paris and Vienna. In the course of these visits Giurescu's distinguished and imposing personality struck most of his audiences and he was far more appreciated than other eminent Romanian historians.

Reviewing the totality of Giurescu's career one is impressed by his extraordinary accomplishments. The premature death of his father, the historian Constantin Giurescu impelled him to give up the study of mathematics, to devote himself entirely to prepare for a historian's career, with the through of continuing the work of his father. His brilliant studies earned him a univeristy appointment at Bucharest at the early age of 27. Among the members of the committee responsible for the appointment was Nicolae Iorga. When Giurescu was barely 30 years old, Alexandru Rosetti, a pioneer in the study of Romanian language and linguistics and editor of a number of cultural reviews, entrusted him with the awesome task of writing a history of the Romanian people—a synthesis aimed a filling a void in Romanian culture at the time. Giurescu undertook this crucial task and concluded it brilliantly, writing five volumes on *The History of the Romanians from the Earliest Times to the Revolution of 1821.*

Giurescu's father belonged to "the critical school" which believed that historians should only formulate interpretations based upon solid documentation, and that the student of history should invariably stay close to his sources. Having been nurtured on mathematics and science, young Giurescu found little difficulty in following the methods instilled into him by his father. This is the reason why Giurescu could not tolerate hypotheses which were not rooted in fact. He applied this method in writing the history of the Romanians, which he modestly described as a textbook, as it is labelled in the subtitle. The originality of the work consists in the manner in which the material unfolds. Up to this time historians had generally laid the emphasis on political history and invariably on a chronological treatment of events. Rare indeed were the number of monographs which tackled economic, social or cultural history.

Constantin C. Giurescu was the worthy successor of a father who had pioneered writing basic studies highlighting the importance of social and economic phenomena. This approach enabled him to devote considerable attention to all past human endeavours, whether they affected feudal institutions, military and ecclesiastical establishments or cultural and intellectual pursuits. His work thus marked a new phase in Romanian historiography which placed Giurescu among the leading national historians of his time with a broad and comprehensive vision of the past. Each chapter in his *History of the Romanians* is followed by an updated bibliography which enhances the scholarly character of each volume. In summary, the sober and precise manner in which the facts were narrated under the various chapter headings provides an indispensable tool for students and scholars alike. Another unusual merit was Giurescu's flawless style. The concise and logical flow of events was pleasurable reading even to a non-specialist and contributed greatly to the instant literary success and broad mass appeal of Giurescu's history. This success unfortunately provoked the resentment of a few scholars, including Nicolae Iorga.

Speaking of that feud, Giurescu told me at one time that Iorga or some of his friends printed roughly 700 articles criticizing his work—a fact which embittered him. He used an amusing anecdote to illustrate his point. One of Giurescu's friends who happened to be a bookseller by trade hearing of the historian's unhappiness with Iorga's attacks told him: "Professor listen to an old Jew who is world wise in the book trade, professor Iorga has rendered you an enormous service." Seeing Giurescu perplexed by his remark, he continued: "Had you spent 1,000,000 lei advertising your work you would not have sold as many copies or occasioned as much public interest as resulted from professor Iorga's persistent attacks." Although amused by the anecdote, it is clear that reflections such as these provided little consolation for Giurescu who was saddened by the lifelong emnity of a great man.

However paradoxical it might sound, the publication of Giurescu's history had a further merit: namely that of provoking Iorga to respond within two years by writing his own synthesis on Romanian history in 11 volumes, dictated by the author in French and Romanian. It is highly unlikely that Iorga's monumental history would have been written at all had Giurescu not challenged him with the success of his own work.

Giurescu's academic career unfolded interlaced with a political career which continued until the abdication of King Carol II in 1940, following the surrender of Transylvania and Bessarabia to the Hungarians and Russians. In spite of his political and administrative activities however, he found the time to write specialized monographs as well as to revise his five volume history of Romania. (The first volume reached five editions by 1943.) This generated renewed controversy. Some of his detractors objected that Giurescu was prolific because he had inherited his father's notes and index-cards. Statements such as these were little less than slander when one recalls that this giant of Romanian history was thrown in jail during the years of Stalinist persecution and that both his personal library and that of his father, together with manuscripts, cabinet files, index cards, many of them written in his own hand, were confiscated. When finally freed, Constantin C. Giurescu, former university professor, former correspondent member of the Romanian Academy and renowned historian had neither function nor title. In the end the authorities condescended to allow him to work at the History Institute as a mere research assistant whose task it was to fill index cards for others. He was labelled "historian with a bourgeois mentality" and accused of refusing to be indoctrinated in the new official Marxist ideology. For a number of years the History Institute withheld permission for Giurescu to write books requiring "interpretative analysis." His first opportunity came quite by chance. Giurescu was assigned the job of compiling and cataloguing all the documents in Alexander John Cuza's voluminous archive which was located at the Romanian Academy. Grudgingly, accepting Giurescu as a capable researcher, he was also encouraged to write a biography of the Prince who had united the Principalities of Moldavia and Wallachia to commemorate in 1966 the 100th anniversary of his fall. No one else in Romania had undertaken this task. It was in this fashion that Giurescu, while cataloguing the Cuza documents managed to complete a first rate updated biography. The celebration of Cuza's centennial helped speed the publication of the volume which greatly contributed to the consolidation of Giurescu's reputation and ultimately to his rehabilitation. Needing books for his particular research and other historical writings, Giurescu rebuilt his library, put together new notes and index cards and embarked upon a second professional career writing a number of broad syntheses and specialized monographs both of which contributing to fill voids in Romanian historiography. Among these were: *The History of Bucharest;* the *History of Brăila;* the *History of the Odobești Vineyards;* the *History of Fishing* and many other titles which covered gaps in Romanian social and economic history.

In response to a number of critics abroad challenging the historical continuity of the Romanian people in the Carpatho-Danuabian area, Giurescu took up the challenge and wrote *Transylvania in the History of the Romanians* and *The Formation of the Romanian People and its Language.* Similarly Giurescu exposed the theories of Professor Lazarev and other Soviet scholars who had deliberately misinterpreted the history of the lands between the Dniester and Pruth, claiming that this area constituted a separate nation from the beginning of the 16th century, and was not a part of Romania. Giurescu pointed out that this theory lacked documentary proof and that its sole aim was to provide a theoretical justification for the extension of the Soviet Empire beyond its Slavic ethnic limits and the inclusion of Bessarabia and Bukovina in the Russian state. One of the most important works in Giurescu's second career is *The History of Cities and Market Places in Moldavia.* The result of painstaking research and rigorous detailed analyis, this crucial work deals with the beginnings of socio-economic and political institutions and the earliest state formations in the Moldavian territories, a most difficult endeavor given the paucity of written sources.

With the help of extensive archeological finds, Giurescu was able to trace and prove the existence of social and political institutions before the written history of Moldavia begins. There were cities, townships, boroughs, market-places, some of them fortified, veritable administrative, political and even military entities which *de facto* represented political formations before the existence of a unified Moldavian state. Aided by his research Giurescu challenged the mistaken theories which had been inserted in official textbooks by pro-Russian historians in the early period of Stalinist control, which suggested that "Slavic Cnezates" extended within Moldavian territory.

In his major treatises on Romanian history, Giurescu had alloted only limited space to the history of the Thracians, who were not a subject of special interest to the great historian. In my conversations with him, I always endeavored to trigger his interest, stressing the importance of

Thracian civilization in the History of the Ancient World. In the end my comments and the research in which I was involved sparked Giurescu's interest and help expose some of the prejudices which existed on this subject among Romanian historians. In fact, Giurescu was sufficiently convinced to encourage me to continue the research I had undertaken saying: "Mr. Drăgan, you have seized a golden thread with these Thracians of yours see that you do not loose it and persevere on this path." He supported my Thracian studies in public and lent official support in his lectures when he made frequent references to my published work *Noi Tracii* (We the Thracians). I was grateful to Giurescu for having had the kindness and patience of reading the two volumes in manuscript and making observations on the margin which deepened my insights and helped highlight problems which had not received sufficient attention. When the first volume of my autobiography *Through Europe* was published, Giurescu complemented me for having minutely described and stressed the importance of the guilds in my native city of Lugoj in the Banat—a good source for the social historian.

When we met later in Rome at the Drăgan Foundation which lies across Trajan's column, we discussed in some detail the problem of revising certain preconceptions that had grafted themselves in Romanian historiography. One to which I most objected, I told him, was the arbitrary manner in which most history textbooks separated the history of Moldavia and Wallachia from the history of Transylvania, the oldest and in some ways the most important Romanian state. Transylvania, the region bounded by the Danube, the Carpathians and the Tisa river had in the course of its 1000 years of history, always been Romanian. It belonged to the Romanians and that population represented the overwhelming majority of its people. The Principality of Transylvania was originally established by the unification of various duchies, cnezates and townships. At certain times the state was ruled by Romanians; at other times by Hungarians. This in no way implies that Transylvania was Hungarian, anymore than that the rest of Romania should be considered Greek, just because Greek princes were appointed by the Turks from 1711 to 1821. It was most important to stress, I told him, that Transylvania had always been an autonomous Romanian state (Hungary itself was occupied by the Turks from 1526 to 1699). I finally concluded my appeal by stating: "Professor Giurescu, from now onwards all Romanian textbooks should integrate the history of our three provinces in a comprehensive whole, even if it requires an effort for our students to remember the names of certain foreign princes who ruled on the Western side of the Carpathians.

Not only did Giurescu agree with my point, but he assured me that he had already begun to rewrite some important chapters in his history dealing with Transylvania. This structural revision of Romanian textbooks stressing the unity of the Romanian people, not only influenced Giurescu, but also had an impact on other contemporary historians. As his second professional career evolved, Giurescu found renewed energies, for his spirit had never been broken by adversity. In Western Europe, he was continuously sponsored by the Drăgan Foundation. New possibilities also opened in America where he was greeted officially and invited to lecture at many universities from coast to coast. He was also the first incumbent of the Iorga chair at Columbia University. Subsequently he described his travels and experiences in the United States in a volume of essays and travel diaries written with a lively spirit of observation and penetrating intuition. In his contact with the student body at many universities, he was astonished at the manner in which the authentic and heroic ruler Vlad the Impaler had been deformed and transformed into the mythological vampire, Dracula, rendered particularly gory by a sensation-seeking movie industry. Later Professors Radu Florescu and Raymond McNally in their bestseller *In Search of Dracula* were able to separate historical fact from fiction. I first heard of that book from Giurescu, who had been helpful to the two authors and in turn read it with interest.

My relations with Giurescu led to a deep friendship which honored me and gave me the opportunity of acquainting myself with his plans for the future, with his work methods, and finally with his family and the atmosphere of his household. He was endowed with an extraordinarily strong physical constitution which helped him overcome the rigors of imprisonment, and other adversities. Here was a man who witnessed the confiscation of his personal library, material goods, burning of invaluable family archives and dispossession of other belongings. He overcame all these frustrations and humiliations, rebuilt his physical and moral strength and set out on a new career which in a way equalled the first, in terms of scholarly activities. Hard work was the religion of Giurescu's life. Keenly aware of the importance of time he did not allow a moment to pass unexploited. Very methodical, wise, prudent, weighing each sentence or action with care, Giurescu had accumulated the kind of experience that few Romanian historians could boast of both as a historian, scholar, teacher, as a politician who held important posts which included the Ministry of Education and Culture, and as an academic ambassador to the world. Through his influence he was able to encourage and help the careers of a number of Romanian intellectuals, among them Mircea Eliade, who later attained world wide fame as Professor of Comparative Religion at the University of Chicago. By this opeing the frontiers of the world to gifted young men, Giurescu was directly instrumental in infusing a new liberated spirit among the younger generation of Romanian intellectuals. Giurescu's outwardly severe countenance, betrayed a warm accessible man with a keen sense of humor which reflected his social and cultural origins rooted in the proud landed tradition of the country's squirearchy. He was equally known for his gallantry and charming manners which endeared him to the ladies who looked upon him as the image of a perfect gentleman. A well-balanced sense of national and patriotic feeling permeated the many facets of his career. He cultivated this sentiment particularly within his family circle, aided by his wife, the daughter of a distinguished Romanian geographer, Simeon Mehedinţi, and enriched it by transmitting it to his three children, brought up in the solid traditions of landed families.

Whenever I was in Bucharest, I visited Giurescu frequently either at his apartment at Monetariei 4, located within the courtyard of a church, or else more recently at his home given back to him by the government, at 47 Berza Street. He once showed me the courtyard where some of his books, papers and family archives were burned during the Stalinist persecutions. He was also proud to show me his new library, which among many volumes contained a book I had given him by Indro Montanelli, an Italian author, who stressed a point upon which both I and Giurescu agreed, namely that history must be written in a pleasing style and for the public at large, and that mythical personalities must be reduced to human proportions, intelligible to contemporary man.

Following the International Marketing Congress at Timişoara in 1971, Giurescu came to Bucharest accompanied by Professor Dumitru Berciu, one of his former students and a specialist in Thracology. This meeting proved particularly meaningful to me and loaded with consequences. Berciu the archeologist had made a sensational discovery at Hamangia in southwestern Romania (Dobrodja): in the course of a dig he had uncovered an extraordinarily beautiful piece of sculpture "the thinker of the neolithic age," which enhanced his career as a historian of Antiquity. It was with Berciu's help that I completed the documentation for my two volumes on the Thracians, and Berciu wrote the preface to the first edition. My last meeting with Giurescu took place in 1978 on the occasion of the celebration of the centenary of Romania's indepedence, when my new "Thracian idea" was commended in Giurescu's presence as a contribution to Romanian historiography and as a useful argument in defense of Romanian continuity. We both later attended a session of the Titu Maiorescu Society where on my initiative, Giurescu was elected a member.

Viewed in its totality, Giurescu's career is closely intertwined with the destiny of his fatherland during the stormy interwar years and those following World War II. His success and his failures, his satisfactions as well as his sufferings stemmed from the flow of events which criss-crossed his country's history, during an eventful period, with Romania the guardian at the gate defending Western civilization against untoward forces. Giurescu the historian made his own personal contribution in this fateful confrontation, defending his nation's right to exist as an independent state and helping ensure the survival of its ancient civilization.

Paul E. Michelson

THE MASTER OF SYNTHESIS:
CONSTANTIN C. GIURESCU AND THE COMING OF AGE
OF ROMANIAN HISTORIOGRAPHY
1919-1947

"Cel răposat nu poate fi mai drept prețuit și mai
sincer plâns decât trecatorul stie cine-a fost el și
ce-a fost, în viața de aici."

V. Pârvan[1]

I. INTRODUCTION

The life of Constantin C. Giurescu (1901-1977)[2] covered and mirrors
the complex, sometimes tragic, modern history of Romania. He grew up
in the old Romanian kingdom of King Carol I. He reached adolescence
during the trying days of World War I, an era capped in 1918 by the premature death of his father and the achievement of the unified Romanian
national state, *România Mare*. In the booming 1920s of King Ferdinand's
reign, young Giurescu developed into erudite manhood, becoming a professor at the University of București in 1927 and, for a time (1927-30),
director of the Ion C. Brătianu Foundation. In the 1930s, he was a leader
in the coming of age of Romanian historiography as a founding editor of
the *Revista Istorică Română* (1931) and author of the first truly comprehensive post-World War I synthesis of Romanian history, the multi-volume
Istoria Românilor (1935+).

Intellectual maturity brought a thirst for involvement in the maelstorm
of politics under King Carol II. Constantin C. Giurescu won election to
the Romanian parliament (1932-1940) as a member of Gheorghe Brătianu's
dissident wing of the National Liberal Party. In 1939, he was named Royal
Resident of the Dunărea de Jos and in September, 1939, a cabinet minister charged with the organization of Carol's one party creation, Frontul
Renașterii Naționale. In 1940 he also served briefly as Minister of Propaganda. The abdication of Carol II in favor of young King Mihai and the
advent of the Legionary-Military regime in 1940 terminated his political

activity. He narrowly escaped physical and other reprisals that this epoch brought upon many Carolist figures. His scholarly work continued unabated with a one-volume synthesis of Romanian history (1943) and the official founding of the Institute of National History (1942). These activities continued following the ouster of the Antonescu regime in 1944 until the abdication of Mihai in 1947.

Dismissed from his university posts, in 1947-1950, Giurescu served as a researcher at the new Institute of History set up by the Communist regime. Stalinization of Romanian intellectual life accelerated in 1950 and as a leading cultural and political figure of the old era, he was incarcerated at Sighet from 1950-1955. His personal distaste for the new regime was less than his unflagging devotion to Romanian nationalism, and in 1956 he began to work as a temporary researcher for the Romanian Academy's historical institute. As Romania's communist rulers began more and more to play the nationalist card, the survivors of the prewar era once again rose to prominence. In 1965, Constantin C. Giurescu was restored to his university post, and an amazing flood of works soon flowed from the scholarly presses. By the late 1960s, he was one of Romania's chief cultural ambassadors abroad—a trip to the United States in 1968 was only the first of many. In 1974, he was elected a member of the Romanian Academy itself, the same year that a new edition of his multi-volume synthesis (in collaboration with his son Dinu) began to appear. He died in 1977, a few weeks after his 76th birthday, still actively engaged in the historical work to which he had devoted more than half a century.

As this rapid survey of the life and work of Constantin C. Giurescu indicates, his career falls into two distinct phases demarcated by his period of imprisonment in the early 1950s. The study that follows focuses on the first half of Giurescu's career, from his student days following World War I, through his emergence as leader of Romania's younger historians and master of synthesizing Romanian history, to his temporary eclipse.

I have decided to forego an account of the amazing second career of Constantin C. Giurescu (1956-1977) for a number of reasons. The first of these is the lack of sources; they are simply too scanty at this juncture to permit a full study. The second problem is caused by the first: in lieu of information about his career, the focus would fall on his works. However, cool analysis and evaluation of these is not yet really feasible. Such an account would more likely be an annotated bibliography than a study. The reader will therefore have to be content for the time being with a memoir by Professor Giurescu's son and intellectual heir, Dinu C. Giurescu, included in this *Festschrift*.

This restriction in scope of the present study does not make our task unproblematic. The eras of Romanian history in which Constantin C. Giurescu lived and worked are controverted and poorly understood. Many archival sources are still closed, restricted, or in need of exploration. Many strong personal feelings are involved. Truly, the historian of contemporary events is always on a shaky footing as a result.

In light of this, I am aware that not all who read what follows will be pleased. Inevitably there will be errors. Certain interpretations and views will touch unhealed wounds or challenge unadmitted predispositions. The study is written *"Sine ira et studio"* (Tacitus); the reader is requested to take from it what is useful or interesting and to disregard the rest.[3]

II. THE FORMATIVE YEARS:
FROM THE OLD TO THE NEW, 1901-1929

Constantin C. Giurescu was born on October 13/26, 1901 in the Romanian city of Focșani, the son of Constantin and Elena Giurescu. The senior Giurescu (1875-1918) had just begun a career—at one of the oldest and best provincial secondary schools in Romania—and came to be ranked, by 1914, among the foremost of Romanian historians.[4] In 1903, the Giurescu family left for a three year study and research sojourn in Vienna, funded by the Casa Școalelor, where the elder Giurescu participated in the well-known seminars of Konstantin Jireček and collected documents on the reign of Constantin Brâncoveanu[5] and the 18th century Austrian occupation of Oltenia.[6] For the younger Giurescu, it was the start of a cosmopolitan educational experience as the family, enlarged by the birth of Horia in 1904, hired a German nursemaid, and the children learned to speak German fluently.[7]

1906 saw Constantin Giurescu named teacher at the Dimitrie Cantemir secondary school in București when the family returned to Romania. His reputation was rapidly growing as a series of original studies cast new light on a number of significant historical problems,[8] and he continued to participate in the discussion and work of Titu Maiorescu's Junimist review *Convorbiri Literare*. His affiliation with Junimea was natural because of his own views and because the review was mainly led at the time by personal friends and professors: historians Ioan Bogdan (director, 1900-1907), Dimitrie Onciul, and Simion Mehedinți (director, 1907-1923).[9] In 1908 he was appointed chief of the Romanian Foreign Ministry's archival service.[10] Further advancement came rapidly. In 1909, he was the first doctoral candidate in Romanian history at the University of București; he was named to the 5-man Romanian Historical Commission (with Ioan

Bogdan, D. Onciul, and soon D. Russo) under whose auspices he published a series of significant critical editions; and he was elected a corresponding member of the Romanian Academy (in 1914 a full membership). In 1912, he assumed a newly-created lectureship in Romanian history at the University of Bucureşti, a post never raised to full professorship.[11]

Young Constantin C. Giurescu began his formal schooling in 1908, and in 1912, was admitted first in his calss to Liceul George Lazăr, a ranking he held during most of his high school career.[12] As he later recalled, his formative years were spent in the patriotic fevor and turmoil of, first, the Balkan wars and, then, World War I.[13] A favorite uncle's death on the Bulgarian front in 1916 was a significant moment in the young man's development: the uncle remained etched on his memory as "one among many who gave their lives so that the country could live and be unified."[14] This experience was followed by the other disasters of 1916-1917, the retreat of the government to Moldova, and the occupation of Bucureşti by the Germans—events which also made a strong impression on Constantin C. Giurescu.[15]

He continued his schooling during this period, though part of the time at a private school when the state schools were closed down. Despite a touch of typhoid fever (along with his father in 1917), he was able to advance a year ahead of his class. His career interests were as yet unsettled, but moving toward becoming an engineer.[16]

In 1918, the senior Giurescu was appointed secretary general of the Ministry of Public Instruction for the German-occupied areas of Romania. This important but exhausting task left him an early victim, when the Spanish influenza epidemic of 1918 struck; he died October 15, 1918 on the eve of Romanian unification and the end of the war.[17]

The unexpected death of his father was the crucial event in young Constantin C. Giurescu's decision to pursue a career in history.[18] Though he had excelled in his mathematical and other pre-engineering studies, he felt an increasing inclination and apititude for history as he entered the eighth and final year of the liceu. In later years, his regret was that he had not confided his growing decision to his father before it was too late, for his father was also his model and historical guide, as we shall see below.[19]

The change in career aim implied a change in preparation, but not in the speed with which the neophyte historian moved toward a university post. His first step—though still in the liceu—was to obtain permission from Vasile Pârvan, the Professor of Ancient History at the University of Bucureşti and a friend of his father's, to audit Greek. At the same time, he plunged into intensive study of Latin.[20]

Secondly, he embarked on his initial efforts in published historical study (interestingly, a polemic!). His first article, in a 1919 issue of *Convorbiri Literare*,[21] was a critical review of a book dealing with Mihai Viteazul's peasant legislation. In the same year, he prepared for publication his father's seminal study of medieval Romanian nobility, an undelivered Academy address entitled: "Despre boieri." This appeared in 1920.[22] The project also entailed controversy as the Academy (i.e. Ion Bianu) had refused to publish the lecture because of the influential Nicolae Iorga's opposition to the senior Giurescu's revisionist thesis.[23]

The final move in 1919 toward a career as a historian was taken when Constantin C. Giurescu entered the Faculty of Letters of the University of București in history and geography, focusing on Romanian history as his primary area and on Slavistics and Byzantine history as secondary areas. The group of students entering in the fall of 1919 was the first to begin their studies in the newly formed Greater Romania and, though the rigors of the war were still being felt, there was a certain exhilaration and feeling of "a new beginning."[24] The sentiment had its justification for this new generation was to bring to maturation Romania's cultural development . . . and Constantin C. Giurescu was to be a key figure in that growth. We turn now to his education as a historian.

The most important and influential of young Giurescu's teachers was, by his own assessment, his deceased father. "The greatest influence on me, though I did not have him as a professor, was exercised by my father," he recalled near the end of his life. "To him I owe not only my conception concerning historiography, the worship of historical truth, strict method, care for clear form, but also that the work should be accessible to the multitude."[25] The obvious question concerns how Constantin C. Giurescu was instructed by his father, given the latter's death prior to young Giurescu's decision to become a historian. This may be explained in several ways.

First, we have the corpus of scholarly work and the reputation left by the senior Giurescu. It was fairly obvious that once the young man embarked on a career as a historian he would immerse himself in his father's publications. Simultaneously, he would be increasingly influenced by what he remembered and what others told him about his predecessor. Emulation was a natural consequence (and perhaps even a cause) of the original decision.[26]

Secondly, Constantin Giurescu influenced his son through the first-rate library, the manuscripts, and the papers he left to him as intellectual heir. This influence was demonstrated almost immediately when Constantin C. Giurescu published his father's posthumous essay in 1920. Some of the

young man's foes, e.g., Nicolae Iorga and Ion Vlădescu, later asserted
that he profited excessively and illegitimately from the unpublished
work (notes, copies of documents and the like) left by his father along
with his extensively annotated historical library.[27] It appears rather
absurd and petty to quibble over the use of these papers and notes by
the son, who in any case gave credit and notice to his father's work when
he used it.[28] The implication that the young man was simply living off
the intellectual capital so laboriously accumulated by his father is un-
tenable in light of the consistent and rich work Constantin C. Giurescu
produced over the span of fifty years. This said, the wealth of work left
by Constantin Giurescu, Sr. was of immense influence, use, and benefit
to his son.

Not only did the older Giurescu's books and papers provide ideas and
materials for the incipient historian; they also provided models. Constantin
C. Giurescu's article "Cum lucra Constantin Giurescu,"[29] stresses this
value of his father's work, while underlining the key elements: thorough
bibliographic investigation, critical annotation, attention to the documentary base, careful structuring of the work in progress. The style was
clear and sparse, given to careful argumentation rather than evocative
persuasion. And after a work was published, he continued to annotate
and update. The discipline and rigor of the father no doubt made a deep
impression on the son.

As a historian, Constantin Giurescu followed the lead of the critical
school of D. Onciul and Ioan Bogdan, which in turn was tributary to the
Junimist movement and Titu Maiorescu. Maiorescu's seminal attack on
slip-shod Romanian cultural currents, "În contra direcţiei de astăzi în
cultura română," (1865)[30] sounded as a fundamental note the need for
avoidance of nationalistic falsifications in the supposed service of the
nation. This goal was paramount to Constantin Giurescu's work; the note
was often sounded by his son.

In short, Constantin Giurescu's scholarly temperament was a synthesis
of the critical approach of Onciul, the methodical rigor of Ioan Bogdan,
and the intiutive grasp of Iorga—all his teachers. To these he added an
objectivity which none of the others had and the courage to express his
findings.[31] To Vasile Pârvan, the senior Giurescu's temperament was
distinctive in its combination of careful preparation, calm self-assurance,
willingness to attack the most controverted problems and tasks, powerful
argumentation, and a stubborn sense of scholarly and personal propriety.[32]
These traits can be seen displayed in the son, though perhaps because
the latter's life was full and tumultuous, not nearly as consistently as in
the father.

As a final inheritance received by Constantin C. Giurescu, we can consider the good will and assistance of his father's friends and colleagues. D. Onciul was his father's mentor as a historian; D. Russo, S. Mehedinți, and Vasile Pârvan were his friends. Each also played a significant role in the education of the son, to which we now turn.

Giurescu's seminar professors were the recognized "greats" of the prewar era: Dimitrie Onciul (1853-1923; Romanian history), Vasile Pârvan (1882-1927; Ancient history and eipigraphy), Demostene Russo (1868-1938; Byzantine history), Nicolae Iorga (1871-1940; World history), and Simion Mehedinți (1869-1962; Geography). He also participated in the Slavistics seminar of Petre Cancel and that of Ramiro Ortiz in Italian.

Dimitrie Onciul was one of those tireless, amazing phenomena of Romanian intellectual life, the single individual carrying out the career of a dozen and doing it well: prolix scholar and speaker, professor and dean of the Faculty, Director of the State Archives, President of the Academy.[33] His first series of students had included the senior Giurescu; his last included the younger. A vigorous adherent of the no-nonsense Germanic approach to history (educated in Cernăuți and Vienna) and creator of what may be called the critical school in Romanian historiography, Onciul impressed upon Constantin C. Giurescu a respect for and adherence to sound documentation, precision, and vigor. It was in Onciul's seminar that the future master of synthesis practiced the precise, clear style that characterized his work. At the same time, Onciul—a Bucovinian immigrant to București—communicated to Giurescu a deep patriotism and a conviction of the importance of history for the Romanian people.[34]

Vasile Pârvan was perhaps even a greater influence and support to Giurescu in this period, especially following the death in 1920 of Giurescu's mother. He was for Giurescu "the personification of *The Master*, a learned man who was at the same time educator and patriot."[35] Pârvan's activity also bordered on the unbelievable: one of the dominant figures of the University and Academy (serving as secretary-general); Director of the National Museum of Antiquities; co-founder of the South-East European Institute of București, the Romanian School in Rome, the Romanian University in Cluj, numerous scholarly journals, and a publishing house. The creator of the Romanian school of archeology, Pârvan's monumental and pioneering work and scholarship have withstood the test of time.[36] Meanwhile, he inspired a virtually mystical respect and adherence among students and colleagues that only increased following his sudden death in 1927 at the age of forty-four.[37] This adherence was fostered especially by Pârvan's striking memorial addresses, one of which may have influenced Giurescu's turn to history and certainly warmed his nationalistic feelings.[38]

Pârvan had been of the same scholarly generation as Giurescu's father and, as his eulogy quoted above shows, felt a deep respect, friendship, and sympathy for him. This friendship seems to have been transferred to the younger man. On the death of Giurescu's mother, which led to the dispersal of the family in 1920, Pârvan immediately offered Giurescu an assistantship at the National Museum which not only saved him financially, but furthered his academic preparation through field work (at Histria) and work on epigraphy. Later, Pârvan participated in Giurescu's doctoral, docental, and professorial commissions, writing favorable reports on behalf of the candidate in the latter two steps toward Giurescu's university post.[39] The moving passages in Giurescu's evocation of Pârvan (also reflected in his memoirs) attest to his respect and recognition for the influence and assistance of the "Master."[40]

Pârvan was for Giurescu "a model of conscientiousness. . . his lectures were the product of systematic preparation, not easy improvisation. . . the succession of ideas was always logical and the structure of the lectures well-balanced."[41] In addition, he admired and emulated Pârvan's skill in combining erudition (detail and exhaustive investigation) with the gift of synthesis and harmony.[42] Finally, as with Onciul, Pârvan's patriotism also made a key impact on the young Giurescu.[43]

A third major influence on the budding historian was Demostene Russo. Russo, a Greek in origin, had been at the Foreign Ministry the same time as Giurescu's father and moved on to join him at the University in 1915. He was legendary for his attention to detail, critical methodology, bibliomania, and learning.[44] Unfortunately, his passion for detail prevented him from ever completing his master work on Greek influences in Romania, *Elenismul în România*, a short sketch of which was published in 1912.[45]

Russo's scholarly influence reinforced that of Onciul in the formation of Constantin C. Giurescu's historical position. In addition, Giurescu always felt a particular support and affection from Russo, whose home was the scene of a weekly gathering in the late 1920s and 1930s (including Giurescu, P. P. Panaitescu, Al. Rosetti, Scarlat Lambrino, Nicolae Cartojan, and others) that was at the core of Giurescu's academic life.[46]

The fourth of Giurescu's university mentors was the Professor of Geography and Ethnography, Simion Mehedinţi, likewise a prolific scholar, writer, publicist, politician, and academician.[47] Founder of the modern school of geography in Romania (following a German doctorate), he was

an editor of *Convorbiri Literare*, a disciple of Titu Maiorescu, and the
Minister of Education in 1918 who appointed Giurescu's father to his
government post. He heavily influenced young Giurescu's views in regard
to the importance of geography and ethnology in historical study. Asked
in later years what the most important factors for the understanding of
Romanian history were, Giurescu's response was "knowledge of the geographic situation of Romania,"[48] a remark attested by his practice.[49] To
Giurescu, geography not only "helps the *understanding* of historical fact,
often it *determines it*,"[50] a view Mehedinți promoted.

Giurescu's relationship with Nicolae Iorga, perhaps the giant of Romanian scholarship and intellectual politics during this period,[51] is a bit
more problematic. The controversies between them that embroiled Romanian historiography in the 1930s (discussed below) undoubtedly color
recollections and later assessments. In appearances, the two were close in
the 1920s: Giurescu was a student of Iorga's seminar between 1919-
1922; he was a member of Iorga's Romanian School in France from 1923-
1925; he published more than a dozen pieces of Iorga-edited journal
prior to 1928.[52] Iorga, for his part, encouraged and praised the work of
the young Giurescu;[53] served on his doctoral and docental committees,
writing the laudatory report on the thesis;[54] and supported his university
appointment.[55] However, the contacts between Iorga and Giurescu were
never really warm, owing in the first instance to the rivalry which had
existed between Iorga and the elder Giurescu.[56] The son was aware that
because of his father's refusal to accept the Iorga line in certain scholarly
debates, the latter had prevented him from becoming a full professor at
the university despite his impressive work and his Academy membership.[57]
Understandably, filial piety prevented more than a superficially cordial
relationship.

A second factor was Iorga's personality, which was such that this fragile
relationship was not likely to last anyway. In Giurescu's words, "Iorga
had the temperament of a great feudal lord; he would allow no contradictions and if you have the daring to affirm in writing other opinions
than his, he considered you a personal enemy."[58] As long as the younger
Giurescu could be patronized, their relationship remained amicable. But
when he began to go his own way, the break appeared.

Iorga's temperament was in other ways—volatile, romantic, impetuous,
poetic—unlike that of his junior colleague; this was Giurescu's own explanation for Iorga's lack of direct influence on him.[59] In Al. Zub's view,
there was no greater contrast between the two men than their temperaments, which were "made, it seemed, to enter into collision."[60] Iorga's

bibliographer and biographer, Barbu Theodorescu gives a comparison between Iorga and Titu Maiorescu that is equally apropos for Iorga and
Giurescu:

> Diametrically opposed to the concise academic style—abstract and
> linear—however, of great impressiveness, conquering through the
> solidity of thought of Maiorescu; the style of Iorga is that of the
> fighter, the polemicist, the *philosophe* . . . preserving the spontane-
> ity and vehemence, the power of conviction and self-sacrifice, the
> bewitching graphicness, the elan which calls to action.[61]

Thus, the clash between Giurescu and Iorga was not only a confrontation
between two generations, it was also a clash between temperaments and
between conceptions rooted in those temperaments.

A final aspect that played a role in the relationship between Giurescu
and Iorga was the fact that Iorga was on uneven or bad terms with Giurescu's mentors.[62] Mehedinți was a long-time political, cultural and academic rival.[63] Pârvan had been a student of Iorga's and Onciul's prior to
World War I, but had independently established himself in the archaeological field. He had often joined Iorga in various causes, most notably
the Liga Culturală campaign for unity of Transylvania with the Romanian
kingdom. Subsequently, occasion disputes erupted between the two.[64]
Pârvan's support and friendship with Constantin Giurescu, as mentioned
earlier, displeased Iorga. He was further irked in 1922 when Pârvan, rather
than himself, was elected vice-president of the Academy. From June,
1923 to May, 1924, Iorga actually "resigned" from the Academy and refused to participate in its activities because his candidates for vacancies
were rejected, because Pârvan was now elected Secretary-General, and
because he felt that Pârvan's memorial evocation of Constantin Giurescu
in 1923 was a direct personal attack.[65]

March, 1926 found Pârvan writing a close friend that "there was no
abuse" that Iorga had not hurled at him "for the old motive, that I per-
secute him and want to destroy him; in fact an idiotical and hysterical
jealousy."[66] He added, no doubt with some satisfaction, that Iorga still
did not know that he, Pârvan, had been invited by Cambridge University
for a series of lectures,[67] an invitation Iorga had coveted. One possible
reason for Iorga's failure to be invited? "The English cannot abide him
because of his mad outbursts. . . . " It seems fair to say that Giurescu's
links to Pârvan were no asset in Iorga's eyes.

Even more damning from Iorga's point of view were Giurescu's ties
with Demostene Russo. Barbu Theodorescu's biography of Iorga makes

a conscious and on the whole successful effort to avoid detailing the many personal feuds, polemics, and vendettas engaged in by Iorga against his historian colleagues (and vice versa).[68] The one exception to this is a direct attack on Russo, who is depicted as the organizer "with diabolic patience" of a cabal against Iorga and his work.[69] In this, Theodorescu is only following his mentor, who devoted an entire article denigrating Russo after his death.[70] The reason, besides temperaments, was that the methodical and meticulous Byzantinist Russo was one of Iorga's peers in this field and his recognized command of textual and critical problems, far superior (albeit far less productive) to that of Iorga's, was irritating to the master.[71]

Thus it was that the young scholar had made all the wrong friends from Iorga's point of view. Their relationship, however, was acceptable, for the time being, though Giurescu found Iorga's seminar to be of minimal value in his scholarly development.[72] (It should be noted that Iorga's emphasis was at this time on world history, while Giurescu was focusing more and more on Romanian history.)

With regard to intellectual impact, Iorga was more of a stimulus to Giurescu than an influence. Thus, he was impressed by Iorga's ability to elucidate historical epochs and events through association of ideas and allusions: "His lectures were sometimes veritable fireworks displays, impressive through their brilliance and color."[73] Certainly the older man's charisma and power for work were a challenge to the ambitious younger man; his subsequent career and efforts were tailored to production of the master synthesis of Romanian history that would make "Giurescu" rather than "Iorga" the standard. But as far as a mentor goes, I think we can accept Giurescu's own analysis:

> I did not take from him (Iorga) either a method or a conception of history. . . . I owe the greatest part of my formation to my father, though I could not attend his university lectures; I am next in debt to Vasile Pârvan, Dimitrie Onciul, Simion Mehedinți, and to Demostene Russo, from each of whom I received something. I do not see, however, anything that I could have received from Niculae (sic) Iorga.[74]

As a student, Constantin C. Giurescu showed immediate talents for research and writing, winning three prizes for seminar papers, and as a scholar, finishing the four year course in three "magna cum laude," in 1922.[75] At the same time, his university days were the source of friendships and acquaintances that continued into maturity. Many of these classmates were to become significant leaders in Romanian letters and culture, including Alexandru Rosetti, Ioachim Crăciun, Victor Papacostea, and Radu Vulpe.[76] In addition, he published critical reviews of the work of Giorge Pascu,[77] an article on Byzantine art in Iorga's *Revista Istorică*,[78] and an important paper on the Phanariot Prince Caragea.[79] Clearly, he was moving toward an eventual doctorate and a future university post—perhaps even that held by the ailing Onciul.[80]

On the advice of Pârvan, Giurescu followed graduation with the qualifying exams for secondary teaching in history and geography in early 1923. This led to an appointment to a post at his father's former school in Focșani.[81] However, he was not to begin his career in the provinces as his father had done, because in the fall of 1923 he was chosen to pursue graduate study at the Romanian School in France, founded by N. Iorga in the Parisian suburb of Fontenay-aux-Roses in 1922.[82]

France was the final step in Giurescu's educational preparation, and he now quickly fixed on a definite personal plan of action. Decided that completion of the doctorate at Paris was out of the question,[83] he began to enlarge his undergraduate study of Romanian institutional history into a thesis to be defended at the University of București, using Parisian resources to develop comparative aspects and sources of influence. His archival work also included study of documents for the two papers required for the *Melanges de l'Ecole Roumaine en France*.[84] Lastly, he embarked on an extensive program of reading, lecture attendance, and travel. Thus, while interacting daily with other future luminaries of Romanian scholarship—Scarlat Lambrino, Grigore Nandriș, Ion Mușlea, Basil Munteanu, and P. P. Panaitescu among others—he was able to absorb French culture, tradition and learning in depth and to complete the work for his doctoral thesis.

In the fall of 1925, Constantin C. Giurescu returned to the University of București and presented his study of 14th and 15th century Romanian political institutions[85] to a doctoral commission composed of Vasile Pârvan, D. Russo, P. Cancel, Dean of the Faculty Charles Drouhet, and N. Iorga, who served as "raporteur." The report gave his work high praise and the doctorate was awarded "magna cum laude."[86]

The final piece of this meteoric career fell into place almost simultaneously with the death of Ioan Ursu in October 1925 which left vacant the chair of Romanian history at the University of București. To be able to apply for a university post, Giurescu needed to pass the docent examination. This required submission of a printed docent thesis as well as an oral examination. Giurescu was able to round into publication the manuscript of a further study on medieval Romanian political institutions[87] in a week and then pass the examinations with flying colors.[88] At the beginning of 1926 (January 1), Constantin C. Giurescu was named "conferențiar suplinitor" in Romanian history; his university career had begun.[89]

Constantin C. Giurescu's rapid advancement to a post at the University of București and two adjunct professorships at the age of twenty-four were owed partly to fortunate circumstances, but mostly, as we have already seen, to his already impressive productivity. In addition to his teaching posts, he was chosen in 1927 as the first director of a new private cultural foundation created to study 19th century Romanian history, the Așezământul Ion C. Brătianu. Positions such as these not only sharpened his skills as an organizer, writer, and editor, but also further broadened his command of Romanian history and its auxilliary disciplines.

Despite his achievements, C. C. Giurescu was only at the start of a vigorous scholarly career and still continuing his development into a mature historian. He was about to embark on intensive self-preparation for the production of a new history of the Romanians. At the same time, he would emerge as leader of Romania's younger historical generation. His university work was purposely organized to lead him to write a synthesis of Romanian history.[90] This he began with his inaugural lecture on February 15, 1926; an extensive review of Romanian historical study in the previous twenty years[91] in conscious emulation of Ioan Bogdan's famous and influential 1906 survey of the state of Romanian historical scholarship.[92]

The stated purpose of the lecture was "to show how far the program enunciated then (by Bogdan) has been carried out and, as a logical consequence, to show what . . . remains to be completed from here on out."[93] The Giurescu agenda for the Romanian historical profession that resulted from this review stressed the following needs: more and better document collections and repertories; increased monographic elucidation of key periods, people and problems;[94] greater and more systematic study of medieval Romanian institutions; and improved scholarly coordination and collaboration.[95] The article concluded with some points that are extremely interesting in retrospect: an appeal for more collective works to overcome excessive Romanian intellectual "individualism;" and two assertions: "Only through the coordinated efforts of the younger historians, under the supervision and guidance of those with the experience of a long career, will the desiderata of contemporary Romanian historiography be realized. Only through this route can we prepare the necessary material from which our successors will create the complete synthesis of our historical development."[96]

Giurescu's first university course followed the path thus outlined; he gave a series of lectures on medieval Romanian institutions.[97] However, in his own mind, the goal of his writing the definitive synthesis he had left to a later generation in his inaugural lecture was now established. In order to prepare the way, his lectures would have to deal with the entire scope of Romanian history over the course of several years.[98] This was something he could not do unless he was promoted from "conferenţiar," to holder of the chair of Romanian history.

Again circumstances were favorable. In February 1927, the Faculty of Letters decided to hold a competition for the chair in Romanian history, vacant since 1925. Giurescu was the only candidate; his impressive *Memoriu*[99] and previous successes; probably intimidated all competitors. The committee (Pârvan, Russo, Cancel, Minea) was again outspoken in its commendation of the candidate[100] and on March 1, 1927, at the age of twenty-five, he was named "professor agregate."[101]

Giurescu was not able to embark on the planned series of courses and seminars he had contemplated as precedent any attempted symthesis: [102] 1927/1928—Curs de Istoria Românilor (Course on the History of the Romanians);[103] 1927/1929—a study of Dimitrie Cantemir's *Descriptio Moldaviae*;[104] 1929/ 1930—Curs de Introducere în Studiile Istoria (Introductory Course in Historical Science);[105] and back to Curs de Istoria Românilor in 1929/1930.[106] The staggering amount of work displayed in the preparation of these courses was an investment which would pay off in 1935. The discipline and method that produced them had already been long formed.

At the same time, varied articles from the pen of Constantin C. Giurescu continued to appear regularly, numbering twelve between 1926 and 1930. The most significant of these (apart from his doctoral and docental theses of 1926 given above) were two lengthy papers published in the Annals of the Romanian Academy in 1927, one on medieval financial organization under Mircea cel Bătrân (the Old)[107] and one on Nicolae Milescu.[108] Other items included a specialized linguistic study[109] and five documentary pieces.[110]

Between 1927 and 1930, as previously mentioned, Giurescu also directed the Ion C. Brătianu Foundation. In addition to initiating and supervising the extensive publication program of the Foundation (fourteen volumes by 1930), he was the editor and compiler of two books issued under the aegis of the Foundation: a volume of Ion C. Brătianu's papers (the first to appear in a series of nine)[111] and a collection of papers on the 50th anniversary of the Romanian acquisition of the Dobrogea in 1928.[112] In 1929-1930, he assumed directorship of the second Brătianu

Foundation as well—that established in honor of Ion I. C. Brătianu (1864-1927) with its own publication series.[113]

The young professor also began to promote activities among Romanian historians. Thus, in 1927, Giurescu was named secretary of the newly-created Romanian Historians Committee, presided over by Iorga, and was active in the organization of international contacts, especially in connection with the 1928 Oslo meeting of the International Committee of Historians.[114]

In his private life, numerous changes were taking place as well. In April 1926, he married his long-time sweetheart, Maria Mehedinţi, daughter of Simion Mehedinţi. They had three children: Dinu (February 15, 1927); Dan (November 21, 1928) and Mona (December 2, 1930). In 1976, they celebrated their 50th anniversary.[115] In 1929, the Giurescus re-modeled and expanded their home at Strada Berzei Nr. 47 and were also able to buy a small vineyard at Odobeşti in Putna. During the Christmas vacation of 1927, they travelled to France and Italy and to Istanbul in 1929.[116]

III. C. C. GIURESCU AND THE COMING OF AGE OF ROMANIAN HISTORIOGRAPHY

The turning point in C. C. Giurescu's career (and in Romanian historiography of the interwar period) was the Third Congress of Romanian history professors held in June 1929, at Sibiu, with N. Iorga as president. Despite Iorga's nominal leadership, the congress was dominated by the younger generation, prominently Constantin C. Giurescu and P. P. Panaitescu.[117]

Panaitescu's speech set off most of the fireworks. Noting that, since national unification had been achieved, Romanian historians were now freed from continual production of nationalist propaganda, Panaitescu called upon his colleagues to direct their attention toward more profound studies of cultural, economic and social life, with truth as the only objective. He further called for the establishment of a new historical journal to lift Romanian historical scholarship to this new plane of candor.[118] Since Panaitescu mentioned only Bogdan, Onciul, C. Giurescu, and Pârvan as "honorable exceptions" to his charge that previous historical work had been more or less nationalistic propaganda,[119] the speech was rightly taken by Iorga, the dean of Romanian historians and editor of two major journals, as a direct personal affront—and he walked out of the meeting.[120] The congress nevertheless proceeded to endorse the idea of a new journal (and by implication, the attack on Iorga and the older generation).

The fat was now in the fire. Iorga began to openly attack Giurescu and Panaitescu in his university lectures, though he was not able to prevent Giurescu from being promoted to "profesor titular" (Full Professor) in March, 1930. Giurescu, for his part, offered a course in 1929-1930 on historical methodology which drew upon the works of Iorga (and others) for illustrations of error.[121] The June, 1930 historian's congress in Iaşi was the final breaking point, as the decision to publish a new journal was reiterated.[122] However, virtually simultaneously, another bombshell burst on the Romanian scene. This was the illegal return of Prince Carol to the country to take over as king, which altered Romanian politics and opened up to Constantin C. Giurescu the potential vistas of political power.

Carol's return was a blow to the National Liberal Party which had forced him to renounce his position as Crown Prince in 1926. However, Gheorghe I. Brătianu—son of the late Liberal Prime Minister Ion I. C. Brătianu, professor of history at the University of Iaşi, and a friend of Constantin C. Giurescu's—broke with the party to support Carol's return and on June 9, 1930, was expelled from it to form his own National Liberal Party (Gh. Brătianu), known as the "Georgists."[123] Brătianu (and for that matter most Romanians) expected the new king to pull Romania from its political and economic doldrums. As N. Iorga wrote, "the population expected the new thing, the radical change, the miracle: miracles of honor, of order, of initiative which would pull . . . the country out of chaos and misery."[124] Giurescu, too, was captivated by the opportunity for a new politics in which intellectuals could play an influential role.

In Bucureşti, following the parting of the ways between Gheorghe Brătianu and the National Liberal Party, Constantin C. Giurescu took the initiative of creating an organizational force among intellectuals for the Georgists. He published an appeal calling for adherence to the leadership of Brătianu. The appeal was signed by 32 scholars, including Al. Rosetti, Scarlat Lambrino, G. M. Cantacuzino, Vintilă Mihăilescu, P. P. Panaitescu, Victor Papacostea, Radu Vulpe, G. Potra and Ion Conea.[125] Iorga, a long-time independent politician, who fancied himself the leader of Romanian intellectuals in politics, was angered and annoyed at the action of "my former students at Fontenay-aux-Roses, under the leadership of Giurescu."[126] The parting of the ways between Giurescu and Iorga was now complete, though the heavy artillery had not yet begun to fire.

The political gap increased in 1931 when the King called Iorga as Prime Minister heading a government of technicians. The new cabinet (as was customary) proceeded to hold elections in May, 1931, in coalition with the old National Liberal Party (i.e., against the Georgists). Giurescu lost his first election return in Putna, where he headed the Georgist organization, a defeat he attributed to fraud and intimidation by the government. (In the elections of 1932, 1933, and 1937, however, he won parliamentary mandates from the same district.)[127] No doubt to Giurescu's delight, the Iorga government was generally unsuccessful and lasted only until May, 1932.[128]

The political and scholarly break between Iorga and the younger generation of historians led by Giurescu was solidified in March, 1931, when the voice of the younger generation, the *Revista Istorică Română* was published for the first time.[129] The journal had been planned since the 1929 Sibiu congress. It made its formal appearance under the auspices of Giurescu's newly-created (1931) Institute of National History attached to the University of Bucureşti. The committee of direction was listed alphabetically on the cover of the first issue: Gh. I. Brătianu, G. M. Cantacuzino, Nicolae Cartojan, C. C. Giurescu, Scarlat Lambrino, P. P. Panaitescu, and Al. Rosetti. The journal was, despite this long list, obviously Giurescu's. In the credits, he was named editor-in-chief and the program statement was clearly his responsibility. His second-in-command and book editor was P. P. Panaitescu (1900-1967), who was "conferenţiar" in Slavic history at Bucureşti and a brilliant, productive historian. Except for Giurescu's synthesis of Romanian history, Panaitescu was his equal as a writer and scholar.[130] His work was sometimes marred by striving for originality, but his interpretations were always provocative and well-marshalled. (Panaitescu eventually sympathized with the Legionary movement, becoming the Legionary Rector of the University of Bucureşti in 1940, one reason why Giurescu broke with him in 1939 or 1940.)

Another close collaborator was Giurescu's lifelong friend and colleague Alexandru Rosetti (1895-), a remarkable man who was a linguistics specialist at the University of Bucureşti, probably *the* historian of the Romanian language, and one of the great editors of the interwar period (*Cultura Naţională* and the *Fundaţia Regală*).

Gh. I. Brătianu (1898-1953) was the only non-resident of Bucureşti being professor of world history at Iaşi. He was also the political leader of most of those on the board. Like Giurescu and Panaitescu, he was well-educated, widely-published, and already at the height of his considerable scholarly powers in his late 20's and early 30's.[131] As we shall see below, he too broke politically with Giurescu after 1937.

The foreword described the aims, scope and philosophy of the new journal in succinct, direct phrases.[132] The aim was to deal with the past of the Romanian people. This was seen as spanning the entire history of the regions occupied by Romanians in the past and the present, not merely national or political history. Secondly, the study of this past was to embrace all aspects of existence (social, economic, and so forth), both separately and as an "organic whole."[133]

Compared to preceding statements about other schools, the preface is somewhat more diplomatic than Panaitescu's 1929 speech for instance. The prewar generation is described as having had as its "central preoccupation the problem which formed the idea of the entire Romanian society: national unity." Their work, however, is not to be denigrated; it is now completed. With national unity an achieved ideal, new historical problems and concerns became imperative. A vague reference to controversies stemming "sometimes from certain political interests" is followed by an appeal for "strict respect of the truth." Truth should not be feared by Romanian patriots because:

> From the national point of view as well as the individual, the truth can never bring loss; it always brings, on the contrary, real usefulness. Between patriotism and objectivity there is no antinomy. This scientific direction signifies nothing more than a continuation of the struggle begun in 1890 [i.e., when Ioan Bodgan came on the scene] by our forerunners, who began then a reaction against the romantic currect in our historiography. Their work must be a guide to the activity which will be carried out in this journal.

Promising a comprehensive critical approach, which would be honest, severe, yet urbane, the editors lament the fact that much Romanian historical work lacks the requisite rigor, though these works are unidentified. Finally, the journal undertook to provide comprehensive and systematic bibliographic information; both foreign and domestic, for the specialist and for the teacher.

Revista Istorică Română was expertly and attractively laid out and the first bibliographical section contained over 330 annotated items in a carefully developed classification scheme. In these respects, it was clearly a generation ahead of Iorga's *Revista Istorică*. In the substantive sense, the contribution of *Revista Istorică Română* was impressive and considerable. The note of vigor injected into Romanian scholarship by the journal's critiques and articles was a decided achievement with a salutory effect across the board. The accent on more than political history and the solid analysis of important questions connected with Romanian history led to a considerable deepening of the work of Romanian historians without sacrificing accuracy. As a source of information, the journal was and is indispensable. Finally, the journal led to a temporary attenuation of the romantic/nationalist tone that pervaded Romanian historiography (and society).

Revista Istorică Română's programatic statement was issued at what now appears to be a unique juncture in Romanian history, one in which nationalist talismans briefly lost their complete dominance. This period reaches back at least to Panaitescu's 1929 statement, but probably does not reach forward much past 1933. The distinctiveness lies in the bold (for Romanians) statements by the editors giving priority to historical fact regardless of its impact on the nationalist approach to history. Not only did Panaitescu call for this in 1929 and in the foreward written in 1931; so did Giurescu in his 1929-1930 university course which criticized the patriotic blind spots of earlier Romanian historians, including Iorga's nationalist predilections which were well-known.[134] Giurescu even cited as an example his own mentor. Dimitrie Onciul, for his refusal to recognize the existence of any but very limited regional Magyar political suzerainty over the Romanians in the medieval era. Such refusals, however laudable for a patriot, Giurescu told his students, must be rejected by the true historian.[135] In his 1931-1932 critique of Iorga, quoted below, Giurescu emphasized the same note, while Panaitescu published an article exposing pious frauds by the 19th century Romanian historian Bogdan Petriceicu Hasdeu.[136]

In the post-1933 era, all this began to totter. Although Panaitescu and Iorga still polemicized over the former's revelations of what the latter considered "unfavorable" information concerning Mihai Viteazul in 1936,[137] the *Revista Istorică Română* group had already beaten somewhat of a retreat on the "national" front, as Panaitescu gravitated ever more toward the ultra-nationalistic Iron Guard. With respect to patriotic blind spots, Giursecu's own *Istoria Românilor* in 1935 followed exactly the line for which he had earlier criticized Onciul.[138] In the same year, Gh. I. Brătianu himself called for a "policy of demographic defense" espeically in the cities and border regions" and advocated "proportionaltiy in eduction "to insure the superiority of the Romanian element."[139] By 1941, Giurescu was writing effusively on "the European role of the Romanian people," which was that of a shield against invasions from the East—from the Tartars, the Turks and the Soviets.[140] And 1943 found him explaining to his readers that Romanians were the hiers of a number

of historical legacies which, along with numerous others, made "the sentiment of *national pride* and *absolute faith* in the future of our people and
state totally natural. . . . "[141]

Given the nature of the evidence available, it is not clear why or even
when this transition back to the nationalist approach took place. Certainly the radicalization of Romanian politics which occurred after 1933 was
to blame. So, too, was the increased politicization (and disillusionment)
of Romanian intellectuals that the Carolist regime had fostered. The
renaissance of an agressive Germany under Adolf Hitler after 1933 and
the prospect of Stalin's outward-looking Soviet Union also colored Romanian intellectual and political life in ways not present during the Franco-
British twenties. Perhaps the group around *Revista Istorică Română*
deserves recognition for their objectivist thrust, even if they were not
able to sustain their laudable efforts against nationalist blind spots.

The excitement generated by the new rival to Iorga's publications
was soon magnified. In the fourth issue of 1931, the veil of anonymity
thoughtfully placed over Romanian "nationalist" historians and writings
was lifted, through Giurescu's astonishing critique of N. Iorga's recently
published synthesis of Romanian history: *Istoria românilor și a civilizației
lor*,[142] under the title "O noua sinteză a trecutului nostru."[143] The review
was astonishing because of its scope—a 122 page treatment of a 300 page
book[144] —and its relentless assault on Iorga's work, method, and rigor,
listed under 63 main headings.[145]

The plan of the Iorga book is subjected to intensive scrutiny and is
judged to be full of "numerous and grave slips and errors," as well as
inconsistance (355). The only real virtue shown is Iorga's dominant idea:
considering the history of the Romanian people as a unity across time
and space (348).

Moving on to the information base and methodology of Professor
Iorga, Giurescu called into question Iorga's knowledge of geography and
geology (357-364), points out internal contradictions between assertions
made concerning word origins ("the presence of these two opinions
which contradict each other, in the same book, is characteristic for the
manner in which the author works, for the method which he uses,")
(375-376). Other Iorga errors are attributed to "the haste, therefore the
superficiality with which Mr. Iorga works," (9) "dispositions of the moment and subjective considerations determined by contemporary circumstances. But, once more, what scientific value can such a historical synthesis have?" (45; cf. 169-171: on Iorga's somersaults relative to Junimea,
Giurescu makes the scathing observation: "The scientific evolution of Mr.

Iorga has occurred in reverse: his best works were written in his youth and his weakest now, toward the end of his career.")

A further source of a remarkable series of errors is the chronological tables at the end of the book. Giurescu shows that these sometimes contradict the text (16-17), sometimes vary from well-known documents published by Iorga himself (175-177), sometimes ignores texts and accepted conclusions of others (175). Giurescu throughout shows a staggering command of Iorga's own works, which is put to extensive use in dealing with inconsistencies or controverted points.

Giurescu's conclusion takes Iorga to task on several counts:

> 1) His use of materials is subject to "considerable and surprising lacunae" (182-187). Surprising because he ignores significant sources, even those that he published himself, and considerable because he ignores most or much of the monographic work done in the last 20 years, even works which he had reviewed and commended on their appearance, and even his own works.
>
> 2) His knowledge of geography, ethnography, and philology display not even a "minimum of elementary notions" (186-187).
>
> 3) His interpretations are hasty, inexact and often incoherent: "Whatever the explanation is, the fact remains the same: the synthesis of Mr. Iorga includes a series of errors of historical interpretation, which produce in the mind of the reader a deformed image of our past" (187-192).
>
> 4) His methodology is suspect in that he often makes totally unfounded assertions, presents hypotheses as fact, and overgeneralizes (192). In the end, "Mr. Iorga's synthesis not only fails to summarize the productive results of his predecessors and even his own, but in a number of significant questions, constitutes a regress" (193).[146]

Perhaps sensing the sensation that his book-length review was causing, Giurescu concluded with a further rationale and a credo. The need for such an airing of scholarly dirty linen was due to the fact that Iorga, at age 60, was considered within and without Romania as the leading, most authoritative, representative Romanian historian. To allow his multitudinous errors to pass unheeded would both misinform specialists abroad and undermine the efforts of Romanian historians to attain world scholarly standards. Even worse, if Iorga's work was allowed to remain "normative," students of history would either follow it or become cynical about the gap between historical theory and practice (194-196).

This led to a lengthy restatement of Giurescu's historical and scholarly credo:

> We think that, in truth, 'historical romanticism'. . . needs to be definitively eliminated. It has lived. Explainable—not, however, excusable—in the nineteenth century . . . when 'historical' arguments and justification had an especial value; today in our time of realism, of general verification and strong scientific interdependence, it can no longer be tolerated. We need, consequently, in historiography, as in all other disciplines (and, in general, in all areas of our spiritual and material existence) to build on a healthy basis. Leaving aside chauvinism, vanity, class or party interest, as well as self-importance, approximation, and hastiness, we need to build soundly. We will work perhaps more slowly, but our building will be from true stone. It will have less luster of facade perhaps, but it will be with certainty more lasting. Because only the truth lasts. . . . Our conviction is that only by working in this manner can we bring the maximum of service to the people in the midst of which we live and to humanity of which we are an integral part. (196)[147]

Beyond these polemical fireworks and professions, Giurescu's critique was also important because it set forth his views on the nature of historical synthesis. There are three types of historical work, he wrote: documentary publications, monographs focussing on a single problem or question, and syntheses. All three are closely related and interrelated. Syntheses are designed "to sum up the results of diverse monographs, establishing at the same time links and comparisons which can shed new light on certain problems, and, in the end, signal lacunae, indicating questions or domains which still require special studies." (337)

Secondly, the would-be author of a synthesis faces certain conditions: 1) the need for a adequate grasp of the monographic base; 2) a plan or system of exposition; and 3) a superior written style is desirable, but not necessarily required (337-338).

The need for works of synthesis in Romanian history is now a pressing one, Giurescu tells us; surprisingly enough considering that just five years earlier his survey of Romanian historiography between 1905-1926 had indicated a vast terrain yet to be covered before an adequate synthesis could be undertaken.[148] This changed position was probably due to his pedagogical experiences of the past five years which had convinced him both that syntheses need not be the grand culmination of the historical craft and that he himself could achieve a synthesis on the basis of the Romanian historiographic status quo. He now emphasized the role of syntheses in carrying out a number of intermediate functions (i.e., establishing a balance sheet for further documentary and monographic work), functions that in 1926 he appeared to delegate to historiographic surveys (338).

The plan of a synthesis is important, in Giurescu's view, because it must provide an organic link between the facts presented as well as a clear understanding to the reader of what is being covered (347). The stress is on the organic rather than the formal nature of the plan. This is because the plan should flow out of the internal logic of the work in question (355).

The heart of any synthesis is the information base, which is composed of primary and secondary sources. The information gathered must be complete, not in terms of facts, but in terms of essentials, which are defined as "that which determines the conclusion in its general lines" (355-356). The next step is to group and confront the materials in order to see linkages, significance, and inconsistencies of data. This raises the usual methodological questions; however, in Giurescu's view, these are generally resolved by historians' rules scuh as are laid out by Langlois and Seignobos or Bernheim's manuels (356-357). Two rules are singled out for particular attention. The first is that affirmations need to be based on conclusive documentation, all other results needing to be labeled "hypotheses" or "supposition." Failure to distinguish is not only misleading but retrogressive (357). The second emphasizes the necessity of avoiding any conclusions but those issuing from the material. Personal opinions must be avoided, and the habit of adding preconceived ideas to the material in order to confirm them, eschewed. "When our views. . . come into contradiction with the conclusions drawn from detailed study of the documentary material, they must be sacrificed without hestitation." (357)

Finally, by implication, there are the historical circumstances in which the synthesizer is working. In a period in which a particular people's history is not yet written, a synthesis has a different role than in a more developed era. The need for Romania in the 1930s was, as we have seen Giurescu state above, to objectivize the foundations of Romanian historiography and consolidate gains already made. This would require a work that concentrated on accuracy and clarity, rather than spectacular theses and poetic declarations. We shall see shortly how Giurescu's own work measured up to his desiderata.

Giuresuc's massive public attack on Iorga was not unprecedented in Romanian historiography or intellectual life. For example, Iorga himself was a vociferous, not to say a harsh, critic of his own colleagues in the early 1900s.[149] However, Giurescu was not only attacking an intellectual rival; Iorga was also prime minister of Romania, Rector of the University, and being feted at home and aborad on his 60th birthday (1871-1931). The motives of the younger man were undoubtedly mixed (by reason of loyalty to his affronted father, academic aspirations, and political interests among other factors). Nevertheless, the courage he showed through this forthright attack speaks well for him and his concern for an improved presentation and interpretation of Romanian history. In many ways, it would have been more prudent and politic for Giurescu to have avoided or blunted the confrontation; the fact that he did not, lends credence to his expressed intellectual purposes.[150]

Iorga's response to Giurescu's unpleasant birthday gift was, temporarily, a dignified silence. *Revista Istorică* had briefly noted the appearance of the new *Revista Istorică Română* and its program "containing unjust, cutting remarks." "We will not follow on this path, but continuing in the modest conditions imposed upon us by the country and the times," Iorga concluded, "we will praise that which is to be praised and, in calmness, dismiss—if they are mistaken—the attacks which they promise us."[151] And, in fact, Giurescu's critique was simply dismissed as "exceeding the bounds of observations to which one can respond seriously."[152] In this Iorga was also being consistent with the 1908 preface of his synthesis of Romanian church history: "I do not wait for praises, and I have no need of them. But there is one thing I wish to be spared, that of trial by minute observation, which does not diminish a book, but rather shows the lowered point of view of the specialist who improvises himself into a judge."[153]

Another reason for a lack of response was that Giurescu's review appeared in the midst of Iorga's difficult (perhaps impossible) labors as prime minister during a deepening world economic crisis. Following his fall from office in June, 1932, Iorga was preoccupied with the July elections and subsequently with the production of massive apologia for his political career (several thousand pages of memoirs, pamphlets, and *pro domo sua* political works).[154] Then, too, Giurescu's attack seemed to have little immediate effect on those not already disposed to view Iorga one way or the other: Iorga was honored on his 60th birthday with a vast memorial volume;[155] this was followed in 1933 by a French festschrift which affirmed Iorga's place of honor in the world's cultural capital, Paris.[156]

This is not to say that Iorga was inactive or undefended. One of his followers, Emanoil Bucuța, initiated a series of brief rebuttals to Giurescu in his cultural journal, *Boabe de Grâu*.[157] Bucuța's not overly powerful reply was to minimize the seriousness of Iorga's "little omissions and lapses," and to deny that Iorga's book was either his last word or even intended to be a synthesis. Giurescu's withering rejoinder was unsparing of these "arguments" of a "literary critic," and concluded with a rehearsal of Iorga's primary errors once more.[158] In May, 1933, Giurescu was proposed for corresponding membership in the Academy. Iorga, outmanuevered in the voting, was able to prevent his election by a stratagem.[159] Iorga and his followers were also carrying out extensive efforts to give Giurescu his comeuppance.[160] However, public recriminations were few in 1932-1934.

"Speaking frankly," Giurescu wrote toward the end of his long Iorga piece, "it is not a pleasant thing to write critiques. Life is too short for what we have to build to dissipate on peripheral matters. On the other hand, I don't have a particular temperamental inclination for such activity either." (194) That this disclaimer must be taken with a grain of salt is clear when we look at Giurescu's other writings during this period. His major article, "Despre Vlahia Asăneştilor," was a revisionist attempt to establish (contra Xenopol and Iorga) the location of these medieval Romanian princes in the Balkan mountains. This brought charges of plagiarism from C. Brătescu and a scathing rebuttal by Giurescu that successfully refuted the charges.[161] (A second article, "Bucoavna basarabeană din 1815"[162] was a slight piece on a 19th century Russo-Rumanian grammar.)

Four of Giurescu's five book reviews in the first volume of *Revista Istorică Română* mince no words over the uselessness, poor writing, and the general inadequacy and incompetence of the works in question.[163] Unfortunately a note of polemical sarcasm often intrudes on otherwise sound observations. His final publication in 1931, was a review of proposed changes in secondary history education, changes which he found less than satisfactory.[164]

1932 was a hectic year for Giurescu as well and less productive on the publication side.[165] The fall of the Iorga government brought another election, and Giurescu was back to the polls in Putna as a candidate and judeţ (district) party leader. In July, 1932, he won his first mandate as the Georgists increased their number of deputies from 12 to 14. The Georgists' 16.6% share of the vote in Putna was their largest share in any judeţ.[166]

He was also charged by the Romanian delegation to the Third Balkan Conference (October, 1932) with preparation of a draft project for the creation of a Balkan Institute for Historical Studies.[167] This institute was to be located at Istanbul and funded by the Albanian, Bulgarian, Greek, Romanian, Turkish and Yugoslav governments as well as private

donors. It was to focus research on Balkan commonalities and influences
and to promote a vigorous publication/research program. The draft was
approved, with modification, by the Conference, but was never acted upon
by the respective governments.[168]

At the university, interestingly enough, Giurescu was encountering
difficulties with the conferenţiar appointed to his chair, I. Vlădescu.
Vlădescu, a former student of Giurescu's father and unsuccessful rival
for Giurescu's university posts, assumed the mantle of Iorga's defender
in 1932-1933 since Iorga had chosen not to respond. The clash between
Giurescu and Vlădescu remained out of public print, while a move to get
Vlădescu dismissed in 1933 failed.[169] A more decisive struggle would
ensue in 1935-1936.[170]

The fall of 1932 was a further milestone for Constantin C. Giurescu
as it marked the beginning of his numerous radio broadcasts on historical
subjects.[171] A significant aspect of these lectures is that Giurescu's willingness to introduce complex historical problems to a popular audience
never forced him to relent on his high standards of accuracy and documentation. The broadcasts are rich in citation, but never pedantic or beyond the grasp of the general listener. The early lectures (there were eight
in 1932-1934) show the sure grasp of his material and the clarity of exposition that he had outlined as necessary to the synthesizer of history.

It was toward that synthesis that Giurescu clearly directed his activities
in 1931-1935. By now he was certain of his ability to achieve his goal,
despite his extremely varied schedule of editorial, pedagogical, polemical,
and political involvements. His courses minutely explored the vast length
and breadth of Romanian history, his seminars and discussions with students serving to iron out problems and sharpen his presentation.[172] Because of his focus on his courses and the press of other activities, 1933
and 1934 were slow years in terms of publications.[173]

The long preparation paid its dividend in January, 1934, when he was
called to the Royal Foundation office of Al. Rosetti and asked if he could
prepare a synthesis of Romanian history in a new series of scholarly works
for mass consumption. Giurescu was not only able to present a comprehensive plan for such a work, but to feel that the basic groundwork was
accomplished.[174] He had already set forth a set of theoretical goals for
a synthesis of Romanian history in 1931 in his critique of Iorga. He now
specified a program for his own synthesis[175] which in general followed
the 1931 guidelines. It was to be a book that summarized the accumulated
study of Romanian history (including more than just political/diplomatic
events) to that point, while focussing on accuracy of presentation, detail

and bibliography. This was to be done in the context of a clearly understood and rigorously followed plan of organization. The book needed to
be useful to the specialist, but accessible to the general reader. This would
be achieved by the orderliness of presentation and through a stress on adequate illustrations, maps, and indices. At the same time, clarity of language
and simplicty of style would be pursued. Finally, the volume needed to
cover all of Romanian history; therefore, it would be a "history of the
Romanians," not a "history of Romania."[176]

A year later, the first volume (of a projected four) was completed.
Alexandru Rosetti predicted it would "sell like warm bread," and on
May 15, 1935, "Book Day" in București, the new *Istoria Românilor* was
launched on the Romanian reading public. There were two results: 1)
sales of the book far exceeded Rosetti and Giurescu's hopes; the former
informed Giurescu on the first day of release that a second edition would
be necessary by fall. 2) N. Iorga was roused with a fury from his "calm
dismissal" of his foe. Stage two of the Giurescu-Iorga controversy had
opened.[177]

Constantin C. Giurescu's *Istoria Românilor*. Vol. I. *Din cele mai vechi
timpuri până la moartea lui Alexandru cel Bun (1432) (From the Earliest
Times to the Death of Alexander the Good (1432))* was a volume worthy
of its reception. Carefully edited and graphically attractive, the book was
a triumphant demonstration of the possibilities of the younger generation.
The preface outlined some of the objectives of a synthesis, discussed
above, and revealed a little more of Giurescu's multi-causal view of history.
He rejected both the idealist and the materialist approach, concluding:
"In order to understand the extremely complex development of humanity, and therefore of the fragment of humanity which is a nation, we
need to take into account both factors—spiritual and material. They co-
exist at every moment of history; that which varies is only their intensity."[178] The nature of a synthesis is once more signaled in Giurescu's
preface in his explicit recognition of the debt owed to preceding historians
and their works.[179]

As one would expect, the book proper began with a description
and survey of "Pământul Românesc," the geographic factor in Romanian history. This factor was seen as significant both in terms of location
(at the eastern margin of Europe) and in terms of resources. The book
also contained seven excellent maps. A favorite theme of Giurescu's that
received emphasis here, is the importance of the Romanian forests, most
of which had long since vanished.[180]

The story of the Romanians commenced with the pre-history of the
Dacians, followed them through the Roman conquest and evacuation. The

narrative's task is to show what happened between the Romanian exit
and the establishment of the Romanian principalities of Muntenia and
Moldova. The emphasis is given to continuation of the Daco-Roman elements, but Giurescu also stressed the influences of various invading groups
especially the Slavs whose mixing with the native population between
the sixth and tenth centuries is seen as crystallizing the Romanian nationality. Finally, the principalities emerge and the work concluded with
two significant chapters on Mircea cel Bătrân and Alexandru cel Bun.

The natural question that arises is "How successful was Giurescu's
Istoria Românilor? "[181] This question may be examined from three points
of view: 1) in the terms of his own goals and principles; 2) from the
assessment of his critics; and 3) from the vantage point of his general
readers and subsequent generations of users. On the basis of his own
criteria (cf. pp. 44ff. above) the effort was a success. The work through
its exhaustive review of Romanian history and the literature produced
by modern historians did indeed synthesize and summarize the existing
state of the art. Giurescu's command of the literature and usually un-
erring eye for the essential combine to produce a text that is rigorous
yet unencumbered. At the same time, the reader gets a reasonably clear
and candid idea of controverted or unresolved problems.[182] There were
a few slips in the bibliography of the first edition of the first volume,[183]
but these were generally resolved by the second edition. On the whole,
Giurescu succeeded in his assignment of communicating with both specialists and the general reader. Romanian history had never been presented
so fully, so accurately, and so clearly to so many. Giurescu's synthesis
also succeeded in avoiding the common military/political emphasis. By
his own count, less than half (48%) of the work was devoted to the traditional political staple of syntheses. The means by which this was achieved
was to devote separate sections of each volume to politics and to institu-
tional/cultural matters. This accomplished the task, though the integration
of these aspects was not as full as might have been desired.

Giurescu had stressed the necessity of an organic plan of organization
for a synthesis. Organization is particularly important given the cross-
disciplinary range and the scope in time and space that a "history of the
Romanians" needed to cover. The *Istoria Românilor* is an easy book to
read and follow, something made the more convenient by extensive indices and careful chronological organization. It is not clear, however, if
this was owed to the nebulous idea of "organic plan" or to Giurescu's
intuitive gifts as a synthesizer. The illustrations (over 130 of them) also
conformed to Giurescu's previous specification in that they are well
chosen and usually relevant to the text.

The public response to the new synthesis was, as noted, impressive. By 1946, the first volume had gone through five editions, volume two (appearing in 1937) through four editions, and volume three (part one, 1942) two editions. It is safe to say that to the general public, the Giurescu history became, indeed, the standard work of reference on Romanian history.

The critical response, the reactions of specialists, was varied, but falls generally into three categories: Giurescu's advocates; Iorga and his followers; and subsequent students of Romanian history. The former, as could be expected were enthusiastic (and probably relieved) over the new work. In December 1935, over 100 colleagues attended a gala dinner at the Athénée Palace in Giurescu's honor.[185] The latter's views are a bit more subjective to assess. It seems fair to say that, in general, Giurescu's volumes were and remain indispensable for the student of Romanian history to 1821. Obviously, no serious study of Romanian history can ignore what has been published since 1935 or be satisfied with only a synthesis, but it is the place to start.

To account for the success of *Istoria Românilor* we must go beyond Giurescu's mere adherence to a set of principles. Al. Zub pinpoints the matter concisely and suggestively: "that which Iorga wrote about his [Giurescu's] dissertation can be said about his work in general: 'Perfectly versed, of a critical approach, as penetrating as it is level-headed. . . . ."[186] The now mature historian C. C. Giurescu was able to apply the characteristics he had exercised in specialized studies to a much broader field, that of synthesizing the entire span of Romanian history. This work of synthesis was at the same time the product of C. C. Giurescu's intensive development as a historian since 1919 and the most representative work of the younger generation that rejuvenated Romanian historiography in the 1930s and brought it to a new level of maturity. The man, the training, the power of mind and work, and the times all came to fruition at the moment in which *Istoria Românilor* appeared, and as a result left an indelible mark on Romanian historiography and letters.

That moment in time also continued a conflict which was to reverberate in Romanian intellectual life far beyond the 1930s. We turn now to the response of N. Iorga to *Istoria Românilor* and the subsequent debate which constitutes the heart of the second stage of the Iorga-Giurescu dispute.

Iorga's reaction was outrage and possibly chagrin over the public "invasion" of his turf by the upstart Giurescu. He proceeded to launch a flurry of newsprint. His newspaper, *Neamul Românesc*, carried articles, reviews, unfavorable allusions, and snide references to Giurescu and

Istoria Românilor daily for the next two years. Iorga himself published
a twenty page review in *Revista Istorică*, deriding the book as a "manual,"
a dry compilation of facts lacking literary skill.[187] He also implied that
C. C. Giurescu's work contained numerous plagiarisms. Giurescu responded with a fifty page counter-blast in *Revista Istorică Română* which was
then republished as a pamphlet.[188] Secondly, Iorga announced that he
himself would write a ten volume history of the Romanians.

One result of this increased scholarly bombardment and counterbomb-
ardment is that the outlines of the Giurescu-Iorga clash became a little
clearer on the intellectual plane. What Zub calls the parascientific elements—temperament, political loyalties and ambitions, personal factors—
lie at the heart of the confrontation and have been given detailed attention
above.[189] The sound and fury of the polemic should not obscure the fact
that a number of substantive claims and counter-claims, particularly of a
methodological nature, also lie close to the heart of the matter as well.
The parascientific aspect, by its very nature, is always just a little beyond
our grasp; this should engender analytical caution. However, we will fail
to understand the conflict if we ignore or deny either substance or the
personal element.

Giurescu's response highlighted some of the key issues, apart from the
obvious ill-will that lay between the two men. To Iorga's complaints
that his work lacked any "poetry" or "literary characterization," Giurescu reaffirmed his basic goals: the establishing of historical fact and the
explanation of causal relationships. In sum, "Poetry, for me, enters precisely in *the most exact and truest* re-establishment of the deeds of our
forerunners. I do not deem it necessary to add exterior poetic elements
to these deeds."[190]

The quotation points to a basic difference of view (and some unfair-
ness to Iorga's conception). While it is true that Iorga's historiographical
views shifted and re-shifted drastically over his long career (as even a
cursory reading of his methodological essays show), it is also true that he
always held to the necessity of historical imagination and the effort to
"re-live" the time about which a historian writes.[191] "In a work of history
there are four elements," he wrote in 1897, "sources, criticism, organization, style." The romantic historian, argued Iorga, was wrong in ignoring
documentation and critical methodology, but the "literary fantasy" of
the romantic and his style, are imperative. Without it, the scholar remains
an erudite, a digger-out of minutiae, not a historian. The contrast is between a great painter and a scientific sketch artist: both depict trees with
accuracy, but the one's trees "live" and the other's do not.

In another essay in 1911,[192] Iorga outlined what can be called a nationalist view of history. In this view, historical facts exist and find their meaning only in the life of the nation (or nationality). The historian's task is to unravel this life, a task which involves "reliving" and poetic imagination. He specifically upholds this view over that which restricts itself to "establishing the facts and seeking their most immediate and viable connection," (i.e., exactly what Giurescu set out to do two decades later).

The Giurescu emphasis on simply "finding the facts" leaves a variety of complex problems untouched.[193] Certainly Iorga's assertion that the historian is not the analogue of the natural scientist relating "facts" is true; however, Iorga's solution (for the historian to relive the past as a poet)—goes too far. It overlooks the key point that what the historian is "reading" is not past literature or poetry, but past documents and monuments of past people, most of whom were rather prosaic. The task of symbolic reconstruction involved is, thus, not one of finding the poetry of the past, but of reconstituting whatever message was "sent" by the people of the past. The kind of historical reconstruction which helps us grasp that past is symbolic, as Iorga saw, but not necessarily (or even usually) poetic (as Iorga, with his powerful imagination and literary sense, would have had it).[194] Giurescu's point was that with inaccurate documents and fragmentary monuments, no amount of imaginative skill will be either adequate or even useful. In such a situation, the more pragmatic (simpler ?) aim of a Giurescu appears to serve us better than the more imaginative (complex ?) approach of a Iorga.

Giurescu's reply to Iorga besides those of a general or methodological nature was to show that Iorga misattributed to him numerous statements; that a number of Iorga's points flatly contradict the most recent findings; and that a number of Iorga's criticisms not only differ from Giurescu and the sources, but also from previous Iorga writings themselves. The tone of the debate is highlighted by the following example from Giurescu:

> I said that after the fall of Sarmizegatusa, Decebal decided to attempt a final stand with the remainder of his army 'in the mountains around the capital.' (*Istoria Românilor*, p. 70). Mr. Iorga, dictatorially decrees 'around Sarmisegetuza there are no mountains.' (*Revista Istorică*, p. 123). Very insolently these mountains continue to exist nevertheless. I recognize it is very annoying for Mr. Iorga, but that's how it is.

Giurescu then prints a photograph to illustrate his point.[195]

Iorga and Giurescu were not the only participants in the debate, however. One of Giurescu's most bitter critics was none other than I. Vlădescu, his "conferențiar" at the university. Vlădescu published a series of articles in *Adevărul* and *Curentul* in 1935-1936[196] accusing Giurescu of plagiarism, stealing his father's work, general discourtesy, and activities inconsistent with the professional ethics of the university. He charged that Giurescu's advancement had owed less to his merits and more to the sympathy and perhaps recompense of Iorga to the young Giurescu.[197] He also invoked a number of criticism of the text and arguments of Giurescu's *Istoria Românilor*, particularly of a bibliographical nature.[198]

The exact facts of the Vlădescu-Giurescu disputes in 1932-1936 are hard to determine. The charges of an ethical nature that he made against Giurescu were taken up by the university along with countercharges by Giurescu. The net result was Giurescu's vindication and Vlădescu's permanent expulsion from the faculty in 1936 (and the abolition of his post in 1937).[199]

On the scholarly side, some of Vlădescu's critique did influence the second edition of *Istoria Românilor*, though he was not credited for it. These included the adding of a general bibliography (p. xvi of the second edition) which the first edition had surprisingly omitted; and the citations in the chapter bibliographies of certain standard works obviously used by Giurescu (and referred to in the text in passing) but not given at the end of all appropriate chapters.

Another Giurescu critic was Anton B. Balotă, a Balkan specialist, whose approach was to compare the Giurescu volume with a new volume by Iorga *Le place des Roumains dans l'histoire universelle.*[200] Balotă contrasts Giurescu's view, history as establishment of the truth, with Iorga's view: "history is not enumeration but explication."[201] His first criticism of Giurescu is well taken in that, indeed, the historian's task is considerably more problematic than Giurescu seems to allow. Balotă's contention that the choice of any historical method or position is in itself an a priori element, is equally unexceptionable, though his conclusion that this makes all choices and historians equally subjective does not follow.

The main point of difference that Balotă sees between Iorga and Giurescu is that Giurescu's book, though of real merit, is merely a manual of sorts designed for the average person, whereas Iorga's works are true syntheses created from the breathtaking perspectives of philosophical-historical explanation. In concluding, Balotă faults Giurescu because his approach is out of date, by which he means Giurescu's analysis and explanation are not situated in a positive philosophical world view that focuses on collectivities and not individualities.[202]

These attacks on Giurescu were reflected not only in the columns of Iorga's *Neamul Românesc*, but also in unprecedented debates carried by the large dailies *Adevărul* and *Curentul*, which Giurescu attributed to personal animus.[203] The intensity and magnitude of the counter-Giurescu assault did occasionally dishearten Giurescu, he recalls, but in the end he took consolation in the free advertising that the published vendettas were giving him.[204]

Matters did not improve in 1936. The conflict now entered into its final stage, the "Şcoala Nouă" debate. Giurecus's success with *Istoria Românilor* had been further enhanced in 1935 when he was asked to head up the Fundaţia Regele Carol I and inaugurate a monograph/document series.[205] These series included two works by P. P. Panaitescu: *Documente privitoare la istoria lui Mihai Vitcazul*[206] and a monograph on *Mihai Vitcazul*.[207] Their publication helped precipitate the third stage of the clash between Giurescu and Iorga.

The other precipitatory event was connected with the April, 1936 meeting in Bucureşti of the International Committee of Historical Sciences. During this meeting offprints of Giurescu's reply to Iorga's review *Istoria Românilor*[208] went on sale in Bucureşti.[209] Iorga judged this to be a direct provocation and published a pamphlet entitled *"Şcoala nouă" de istorie*[210] that for the first time directed most of the debate toward the personalities involved.

The pamphlet was addressed to the Romanian National History Committee and announced that Iorga could no longer work with them. He then launched into a detailed personal recollection of his relationship with Giurescu since 1923. Giurescu was charged with a number of specific personal affronts toward Iorga, who continued nevertheless to support his advancement all the way to full professorship. The result of his patient and unstinting encouragement of the younger generation was ingratitude, insults, and worse. First came Panaitescu's 1929 speech, then the adhereence of his former students to Gh. I. Brătianu's political party, finally *Revista Istorică Română* and Giurescu's review, a veritable manifesto of ill will. The criticisms aduced by Giurescu are beside the point, Iorga asserted, since the 1930 book was merely a translation of a wartime work produced in the service of the country without access to materials, a work based largely on Iorga's first youthful synthesis of 1905.

Iorga moved then to Giurescu's *Istoria Românilor:*

> an act of courage, without doubt, at such an age and in the middle of electoral and political preoccupations. . . . It did not cross my

mind to concern myself with this audacious work, whose value we
could guess based on the patent lack of preparation of the author,
his few courses unable to substitute by a long shot for the necessary experience of an entire life of study. (p. 14)

However, receiving an insulting challenge from Giurescu, Iorga decided
to read the book, much to his amusement:

the style is completely inferior, the ideas childish, the attempt to
popularize inept beyond all measure . . . [a book full of] material
ready-made for a comic newspaper, but presented with the buf-
foon-like gravity which the solemn professor of "objectivity" takes
so well to. (pp. 14-15)

The result was Iorga's decision to write "a calm, impartial review" of the
book for *Revista Istorică*. (15)

Then came the international historians' gathering and Giurescu's
counter-critique, a "response of his usual insolence and unmatched bad
faith to my calm and just evaluation of his historical work." (16) The
last straw was the creation of the King Carol I Foundation's Historical
Section under Giurescu and the publication of the Panaitescu volumes.
These Iorga saw once more as a direct attack since Panaitescu's documents criticized errors in Iorga's document publications and his monograph called into question several points in Iorga's own history of Mihai
Viteazul[211] ("on which I worked an entire life"). (16-17)

Iorga's "definitive explanation" was not entirely clear as to what constituted the characteristic features of the new school and in truth his
criteria seem to be mainly personal: Giurescu is "a professional insulter;"
Panaitescu's works are based on "denigration of the labors of half a century;" (17) and so forth.

The Iorga pamphlet unleashed a new barrage of paper. In Dumitru
Bodin's rejoinder, *Şcoala nouă de istorie, Răspuns d-lui N. Iorga*,[212]
he defended himself successfully against Iorga's charges that Bodin had
joined the Giurescu faction because of poor grades from Iorga and because of a desire to advance his career.

Panaitescu likewise responded: *Şcoala nouă de istorie. Un răspuns*.[213]
He affirmed the essence of his appeal in 1929, but rejected Iorga's comments about possible material motivation. He further disputed Iorga's
remarks concerning his work on Mihai Viteazul, concluding that Iorga's
anger was less owing to Panaitescu's interpretation and more to his tres-
passing on Iorga's proprietary claim to the history of Mihai.

Iorga next dealt a blow at Panaitescu's *Mihai* in a May 1936, Academy lecture[214] that contrasted with earlier polemics in the more substantial nature of the critique. The conclusion, however, revealed an interesting aspect of Iorga's approach:

> I feel obligated. . . to oppose these shocking conclusions of Panaitescu's which denigrate a great figure of our people and provide arms against us for our enemies, who, far from decreasing and quieting after the realizations of our national unity, are on the contrary, all the more numerous and more irreconcilable. Where more than here [the Romanian Academy] is it appropriate to defend the treasure of honor and glory which the studies of many generations have put at the disposal of their heirs, called to add to it, not to reduce it.[215]

Still in May 1936, Iorga issued his third blast, in the form of yet another pamphlet, *O şcoală nouă istorică,*[216] this time running to 50 pages. The pamphlet comprised two speeches Iorga gave to public meetings of the Liga Culturală in Bucureşti and reiterated the charges made in his earlier pamphlet. Iorga's motivation is clarified: history is "an essential element in the formation of the soul of a people" and the job of the university history professor is to be a "means of strengthening the power of the people." (4) Instead, the "new school" devotes itself to destructive activities. The new school is "a school of negation, a school of fault finding, a school of offensiveness." (50) It was in fact not a new school at all, but a throwback (or continuation) of the detested (by Iorga) Junimea school.[217]

What are the characteristics of this school? Besides their anti-national tendencies, the basis aspects are "the use of the adroit syllogism, of unbending rationalism, of the search for contradiction, of pettifogging details. . . ." (50) The "new school" is thus situated by Iorga in the ranks of those whose contribution to the nation is at best doubtful and at worst destructive.

A similar view is taken by Anton Balotă in a critique of Panaitescu's book.[218] Many of his historical observations are judicious or well-taken. However, a more sinister note than mere personalities or scholarly debates also appears. Panaitescu's book is primarily dangerous, Balotă declares, because it undermines national values and encourages "pretended human values. . . internationalism." (28) Balotă's thesis is that the book is part of a general cultural struggle in Romania to undo the work of the national poet Eminescu and the national historian Iorga. The main vehicles

of this insidious effort are "scientific" books and "criticism." (4) The
works of the Giurescu-Panaitescu group, put forth under the pretense
of objectivity and humanitarianism, are the tools of an unnamed but
"foreign" force that seeks "to tear down national values in order to
raise itself. . . on the ruin of the past." (30).

Panaitescu and Giurescu responded more ferociously than ever. Panaitescu's reply in *Revista Istorică Română*[219] did not back off of his positions in the detailed rebuttal. However, some effort is devoted to showing
that the conclusions advanced in his book are not unpatriotic, but rather
the contrary, give more credit to Mihai.

Giurescu's response was the most detailed of all, a 70 page pamphlet,
Pentru "Vechea şcoală" de istorie. Răspuns d-lui N. Iorga,[220] that analyses the charges and assertions made in Iorga's two "şcoală nouă" pamphlets. The first 20 pages are devoted to rectifying Iorga's history of his
relations with Giurescu. Some of these matters are hopelessly subjective
and unjudgeable with any certainty. However, where the facts are a matter
of public record, Giurescu is able to show that Iorga is invariably in error,
misinformed, or misleading.

Next, Giurescu points out the feebleness of Iorga's attempt to excuse
the shortcomings of his *Histoire des Roumains et de leur civilisation* (and
its various translations) as a wartime work written in difficult circumstances. What rationale could there be for a world circulation of such a
work ten years after the war? What excuse could there be for failing to
revise errors in the interval? (23-24) He also notes with some wryness
Iorga's adoption in later works of many of the corrections Giurescu had
suggested in 1931-1932. (20)

Moving on to Giurescu's *Istoria Românilor* and Iorga's charge that
Giurescu (at age 34 with nine years of courses in manuscript) was too
young and inexperienced to attempt a synthesis of Romanian history,
brought the rejoinder that this had been attempted by others previously:
B. P. Haşdeu in 1872 at the age of 34. . . and Iorga in 1905 also at the
age of 34 after ten years of courses. (32-33) Giurescu also finds it interesting that at least nine of the points Iorga challenged in *Istoria Românilor*
in 1935 are now taken as fact in Iorga's own new synthesis.[221] (35-36)

Giurescu turned next to Iorga's second pamphlet and its placing of the
conflict in the context of Giurescu's link to Junimea (47-70) This connection was probably a tactical error on Iorga's part. First of all, it gave
Giurescu a chance to clarify the "new school—old school" debate on his
terms. He accepts Iorga's affirmation that there existed in 1936 two
schools of history, the "new," composed of the younger generation,

and the "old," that of Iorga. The new school is seen as evolving in the 1920s-1930s through the same key events depicted by Iorga (though with numerous amendments and rectifications) culminating in the fury of 1936. This leads to a discussion of why the cleavage between Iorga and the younger generation occurred. It is because of fundamental differences in methods and concepts.

How do the two schools differ in method and conception? These are plentiful, Giurescu finds. Iorga's view of the character of historical fact is shown to vary between a belief that historical laws are impossible to a belief that historical events are rarely "now." The new school is firmly individualist: "historical facts never repeat themselves exactly." (51) This being the case, the best we can expect are "conclusions of a more or less general nature." (57) Iorga gives little attention to the geographic factor; the new school finds it critical in the understanding of historical fact which geography often determines. Iorga seems to disregard or takes methodology lightly; thus, his many inconsistencies and mistakes. On the other hand, Iorga seems to regard documents and memoirs so highly subjective and prone to error that intuition is the only sure avenue. Giurescu quotes Iorga's 1935 and 1932 course inaugurals in this regard, e.g. "infinitely more is required, that which cannot be provided by any method, that whic is inborn in the true historian: divination, the intimate sense which without passing through the steps of rationalist and syllogistic thought helps to find, sometimes instantaneoulsy, the truth which being an expression. . . . is no less true."[222]

To the new school, this is simply unacceptable. Some sources give precise and indubitable information (e.g. certain records); other sources (e.g. memoirs) can be evaluated and used according to accepted principles. The problematic nature of historical evidence is precisely the reason for strict rules and method; not, as Iorga would have it, for escape into intuition and complete subjectivity.

The purpose of history is also controverted. Iorga's view of the use of history again varies from essay to essay, but seems to move more and more toward history as "an instrument, a weapon of struggle, a means of propaganda or justification, often times even of a personal nature." (56) This, too, explains numerous Iorga contradictions as his views of the past vary according to his present inclinations and needs. For the new school, history "has but a single preoccupation: that of *the truth*." (59) The truth may be hard to find, but we have a moral obligation to search. This turns out to be practical anyway because only the truth will last.

Might not this emphasis on the truth cause harm to the country in some cases? The new school's credo is "there does not exist and has never existed an antinomy between truth. . .and the real interests of the nation." (59) As for Iorga's insistence that history shapes a nation's soul and spirit, the new school agrees; but this can only be done through a search for and presentation of the whole truth. "Cheap patriotism" and pious frauds can only harm the nation.

Finally, turning to the Junimea linkage proposed by Iorga, Giurescu enthusiastically accepts the filiation, especially Maiorescu's stress on strict objectivity and truth.[223] Further, he showed that the Junimist heritage included the recognized greats of Romanian historiography of the post-romantic stripe: Xenopol, Onciul, Bogdan, C. Giurescu, and Pârvan.[224] The conclusion which Giurescu's rebuttal drives us toward is that the "new school" really is the "old school" of Maiorescu and Junimea, that the upstart younger generation is in reality the continuation of the healthy trends begun by Maiorescu and his followers seventy years earlier.[225]

Was there really a "școală nouă" and a Iorga school? The question is exceedingly ambiguous and can truthfully be answered "yes," "no," and "somewhat." In several senses, the answer is "no." One of the results that issued out of the "școală nouă" debate was that Giurescu group was simply a continuation of the critical Junimist turned which had encompassed the generation of Onciul, Bogdan, Pârvan, and Giurescu's father in the two decades preceding World War I. Iorga himself had been a part of that current.[226] The older generation had died off just after World War I, leaving Iorga as the only remaining commanding figure in București historical circles.[227] As Iorga diverged farther and farther from the Onciul-Bogdan approach and as the younger generation reached maturity in the 1920s, a schism appeared, with the younger men harking back to Onciul, Bogdan, Pârvan, and C. Giurescu (most completely in the case of Constantine C. Giurescu).[228] Such a harking back would in no way constitute a "new" school, while the content of their emphases was largely methodological and therefore not the stuff of which "schools" are made.

The answer is "no" in a second sense, that in the usual sense of a specific philosophy (as, say, in the *Annales* school).[229] In a curious way, the "sides" were analogous to Romanian political groupings: they were organized around personalities and personal aims rather than a theory or thesis or philosophy. They dealt more with temperaments and generations than with programatic exchanges. This is not surprising since Giurescu was not by inclination given to philosophy, while the mercurial Iorga's point of view was constantly in flux. Both men had their devoted and proteges; even today there are among Romanian historians and scholars who knew both, quite strong feelings of loyalty and antipathy dating back to this era. However, neither man had a distinct enough philosophy of history that could fuel a school of historical study in more than a personal fashion.

Part of the reason lay in the rapid transformation of Romanian political and cultural life in the 1930s which effectively prevented these views from coalescing into a sufficient basis for a "school." The time and the focus necessary for the creation of distinctive "camps" in the philosophical sense was simply not available to Romanian scholars in the decade preceding World War II. Iorga was perhaps moving toward such a well-defined position in his "historiology of humanity" work, but of course his murder in 1940 terminated the attempt.[230] Whether the kind of positivist, methodologically-oriented approach of Giurescu could ever become a school in the philosophical sense is problematic.

On the other hand, this is not to say that the issues involved were unimportant or merely personal. It is unquestionable that Giurescu and Iorga had fundamentally different views of the historian's task, as discussed above. These methodological differences were important in the work that they produced. The literary/intiutive bent of Iorga made his work often unreliable from the factual standpoint and questionable from an interpretative angle, but always suggestive and stimulating. This, unfortunately, makes his work mostly of use to the knowledgeable specialist seeking inspiration, insights, or felicitous phrasing. Giurescu and his associates, in contrast, eschewed the dramatic and soaring for the factual and straightforward. In the long run, this has proven to be of the most abiding value.

Thus we have two factions, but the one is not really "new" and the other not really a school. Study of the question "was there a 'școală nouă' in the 1930s" leads to an equivocation: "Yes" in the sense that groups formed around certain powerful and productive personalities; "No" in the sense that neither group had a new, completely distinctive, or extensively developed point of view.

Despite the energy dissipated in the "școală nouă" debate both Giurescu and Iorga were productive in the 1936-1937 period. The major event for Iorga was the appearance of the first volumes of his own *Istoria Românilor*.[231] It may have been that his satisfaction over the appearance of his synthesis and a lack of suitable appreciation for it at the Academy[232] were goads to the May 1936 flurry of activity on the polemical front. For Giurescu, the fall of 1935 had seen the second edition of volume one; in 1936 he completed work on the second volume which appeared in 1937 in two parts as *Istoria Românilor* II. *De la Mircea cel Brătrân și Alexandru cel Bun până la Mihai Viteazul.*[233] (From Mircea the Old and Alexander the Good to Michael the Brave.) He also prepared his last three courses at the university[234] and delivered eight more radio lectures.[235]

The second volume of Giurescu's *Istoria Românilor* was an eagerly awaited event, especially given the controversy stirred by the first volume. The period covered, the 15th-17th centuries, was Giurescu's specialty, and this probably accounts for the much more muted critical response (in fact from Iorga, no response at all).[236] The volume's two parts signal a slightly different approach from the first volume, with much more space being devoted to special topics and institutional history such as a chapter on Romanians in the Balkan peninsula, a chapter on the princes and another on administrative organization. Particularly distinctive were chapters on geographical topics, many never before explored in a synthesis: the name of the Romanians and their principalities; cities, markets, and villages; regional units. Also important were chapters on the two great medieval Romanian princes Ștefan cel Mare and Mihai Viteazul. The volume was accompanied by an extremely detailed one hundred page index.

The appearance of volume two was also interesting because of a restatement of the purposes of *Istoria Românilor*, especially for the specialist, that a critical review elicited from Giurescu.[237] "*Istoria Românilor* is an attempt at synthesizing the Romanian past," Giurescu wrote. "I wrote it not only for students and the cultural public, *but also for specialists.*" The specialized nature of the volumes is based on three characteristics: 1) the coalescing of a large monographic base (several hundred) into a unified, organized presentation; 2) the publication of synthetic treatments of many aspects never before covered in such a work; and 3) the presentation in the text of dozens of new contributions and conclusions based on published and unpublished documents. (He lists more than twenty of these.) In these claims, despite a somewhat peevish tone, Giurescu is quite right, and we have a further explanation for the rapid dissemination ("like warm bread") of what is not after all a popularization or typical nightstand work.

With the close of 1937, the public phases of the Giurescu-Iorga debate was more or less over.[238] The exhaustive polemics of 1937 had evidently satiated the appetites of both men for personal combat. The effort that both now devoted their academic energies toward was the same: the continuation, improvement, and completion of their monumental syntheses. Iorga clearly triumphed in respect to completion; the tenth and final volume of his *Istoria Românilor* appeared in 1939.[239] The French translation was appearing at the same time, though not completed until 1944.[240] For Giurescu, the focus was on improvement and continuation, while completion eluded him, as we shall see. This delay was caused by the conception which lay behind his work, a conception that made his task more difficult than Iorga's.

1938 makes, therefore, a suitable summing up point for the Giurescu-Iorga debates and an assessment of the results and impact of the conflict. On the balance, the Giurescu-Iorga debate goes strongly to Giurescu. The younger man's sarcasm sometimes exceeded the bounds of normal discourse, and some of the controverted issues do not appear as unproblematic as he seemed to think. On the other hand, he clearly established that Iorga was remarkably unreliable in matters of detail and recollection; that the older man's great output was seriously vitiated by haste, preconception, and dogmatism; and that much of his critical work appears dominated in a negative sense by the personal element.

If Iorga's olympian mantle appeared a bit more tattered as a result, the clash clearly established Constantin C. Giurescu as a power in Romanian historiography, as the true twentieth century master of synthesis. The merits and achievements of his work in this area have been sketched above and need not be reiterated here. Suffice it to say that if Giurescu the students had aimed at attaining the first rank of Romanian historians he had handsomely accomplished the goal by 1935.

The critical approach taken so boldly and a bit imprudently by Giurescu and his associates also had a great impact on their own work. It is clear that one reason Giurescu's *Istoria Românilor* is a much more cautious, careful, and accurate work than any previous such attempt is that he knew the same critical and methodological weapons could be turned back upon him. On the whole, he came off rather well on this count, though it may have prevented him from completing the synthesis.

For Romanian historiography, the debate lifted the standards of individual works to a new level as far as documentation and accuracy are concerned. It is debatable whether the level of critical discourse was always what it should have been in terms of the tone and scholarly give and take, but perhaps that, too, is part of the maturation of a historiography. It also might have been healthier if the issues had not become so personalized.

For N. Iorga, the clash had important results as well. In the 1920s and especially the 1930s, one characteristic feature of Iorga's historiographical thought was the description of the true historian (as opposed to the mere "erudite" or "specialist") as a person of vast literary and cultural, as well as historical background—a description that increasingly came to describe him alone.[241] It seems clear that the dispute with Giurescu and his friends played a significant role in this process, as Iorga gradually moved toward a philosophy of history in which accuracy, lucid narration, and sober synthesis—all of which were better cards in Giurescu's hand—play a secondary role. The final statement of this view (which, it should be stressed, was not solely developed as a reaction to events of the 1930s) was the preface to his vast project "Istoriologia umană"[242] where Iorga declared his "dynamic conception of historiology, opposed to that of a static presentation which informs but which does not interest or explain except through cheap artifices."[243] The final published statement of Iorga's historical views concludes: "I wish, on my part, that I had more 'poetic' talent in order to be closer to the truth,"[244] a statement that shows how far Iorga had traveled since his first lecture of 1894. Given the influence and impact that Iorga continued to have on post-World War II Romanian historians, this development indeed had a critical effect.

The conflict of the 1930s also had as a result the production of N. Iorga's *Istoria Românilor*. Iorga was 64 when Giurescu's synthesis began to appear. The challenge was one which could not be dismissed if Iorga was to maintain his near-legendary image. And in truth, for all its defects, Iorga's ten-volume reply was impressive, valuable, and face-saving. It is likely that without Giurescu's burr under the saddle, Iorga would not have embarked on a project which required, in his own words, "an uncommon effort" and took him away from his intended tasks.[245] The loss of this highly idiosyncratic and rich work would have been a serious one for Romanian historiography.

1937-1940 was a critical and fateful period for Constantin C. Giurescu's political involvement. The National Liberal Party (Gh. I. Brătianu) which had formed in optimistic support of the return of Carol II and potential new politics, had become increasingly disillusioned, especially its leader. At the end of 1934, Gh. I. Brătianu was proclaiming that "above all, before all, the system of government needs to be radically and profoundly modified."[246] By 1935, Brătianu was openly attacking the government and the king's entourage.[247] The party was also moving toward a more and more strident tone on the nationalistic front. The 1936 party program[248] called for a policy of "ethnical defense. Nationalization of the frontier towns and areas by means of Roumanian settlements, Roumanians from the outside of the frontier being preferred for this purpose."

The motto of the part was now: "National dignity, political social integrity, and true realism," and its thrust was: "It is time to make it known that in Greater Roumania it is not the foreigner by the Roumanians who must take the lead."[249] In parliament, Giurescu was chosen as point man for the colonization-nationalization of border regions program. In February and March, 1937, he delivered a lengthy interpellation on this issue in the chamber on behalf of the party.[250] The speeches also were connected with a less than creditable performance on Giurescu's part. In the course of the interpellation he mentioned that there were opponents to the view he was developing, such as a Romanian politician who actually recommended that Jews in Romania be allowed to take up farming and become like everyone else. To the astonishment of all, particularly Octavian Goga who asked in disbelief if the maker of this recommendation could possibly be a Romanian, Giurescu responded, "He is a Romanian; unhappily, he is Professor Nicolae Iorga."[251] Giurescu was pleased to report later in 1937 that "subsequently—comprehending the error committed by his post-war attitude in connection with the Jewish problem—Mr. Iorga returned, in a series of articles and declarations, to his former [i.e., anti-Semitic] attitude. I believe that I had a merit in this: . . . the discussion in the chamber contributed to his return to reality."[252] Both the attack and the response probably tell us a great deal about the times into which inter-war Romania was now moving.

Giurescu was, however, gradually falling out with Brătianu over the latter's growing anti-monarchialism, to the point of threatening resignation in 1937 if this did not attenuate.[253] The split came rapidly. At the end of 1937 Brătianu formed a fateful electoral coalition with the National Peasant Party and Corneliu Codreanu's Legionary front group *Totul pentru Țară*. The "non-aggression pact" denied the government its expected election triumph and precipitated the eventual collapse of the Romanian political system. It also meant the end of Bratiănu's party: their vote in December 1937, fell to less than four percent, and in January 1938, his group reunited with the majority Liberal Party.[254]

In February 1938, King Carol II abruptly proclaimed an end to the parliamentary regime and installed a royal dictatorship.[255] Though a new constitution was quickly instituted, 1938 was a year of political realignment in Romania as Carol endeavored to solidify his position. This involved, internally, action against the Legionary Movement and efforts to coalesce a personal faction composed of royalists, anti-rightists, and pro-French/English elements.[256] There were also a fair number of mismatched idealists (those taken by yet one more appeal for "new"

politics and a "new era") and "fripturiștii" (those whose interest in political power or influence drove them to the nearest attraction). Carol's
new cadres were drawn from these major sources: his camarilla of followers, a group of defectors from the National Peasant Party led by
Armand Călinescu, and a group of defectors from the National Liberal
Party led by Gh. Tătărescu.

Constantin C. Giurescu was unable to follow Gh. I. Brătianu's anti-
Carolist line and threw in his lot with the new regime.[257] Brătianu, in
turn, resigned in 1938 from the board of *Revista Istorică Româna;* two
years later he took up Iorga's posts and became a defender of the Iorga
tradition.[258]

Giurescu's sympathies for Carol's regime were fostered by his own
ambitions and by the congeniality of the "new era." Already in 1933,
he had given a radio lecture on "Desvoltarea României moderne și noul
ideal national"[259] in which he called for strenuous efforts to justify the
Romanian national state through concrete achievements: "That which we
need, at the present time, is a methodic plan of action in all directions, for
a prolonged time and leaders with a high ethical sense who can apply this
plan." As with many another young man in the 1930s, Giurescu grew impatient with the slowness of free processes in devising, let alone carrying
out, such a plan and at the same time was impatient with the incompetent
efforts of others.[260] The new regime presented an excellent opportunity,
he thought, to advance these ideals as well as his own fortunes.[261]

His big political chance came in February 1939, when he was appointed the Royal Resident of the Dunărea de Jos ținut (Lower Danube district),[262] one of ten such regional governments set up by King Carol
in an effort to reorganize the economy and state. In this post he both
proved his political usefulness and drew nearer to the king's inner circle
dominated by Armand Călinescu.

An even greater opportunity came in September 1939. Armand Călinescu had endeavored to root out the Legionary movement in 1938-1939,
starting with the arrest and subsequent murder of its leader, Corneliu
Zelea Codreanu (November 1938) and followed this by the arrest and
sometimes execution of numerous others.[263] In return, the Legionary
underground finally avenged their "Căpitanul" by assassinating Călinescu on September 20, 1939.[264] This resulted in re-shuffling the cabinet
and the state apparatus to face additional shocks. Giurescu was named
cabinet minister for the organization of the Frontul Renașterii Național
(FRN—Front of National Rebirth) on September 28, 1939.

The FRN was Carol II's monopoly political formation, launched in
December 1938, to replace the now-abolished political parties.[265] "The

need to create and organize elites, to watch over the founding and development of new institutions," were a few of the declared tasks of the FRN which was to provide the cadres of "the parliamentary, administrative, and professional establishment on which the entire life of our state will be supported in the future."[266]

The FRN was thus conceived by Carol and Călinescu as the organizing and staffing mechanism for the king's new authoritarian state. It was also the resident symbolic structure of the royal dictatorship with absurd uniforms that became required garb for parliamentarians and government ministers.[267] It is probably this latter function that was most successfully filled by the FRN. On the political side, the Front was a failure largely because of its artificial nature. Savu's scathing description is a bit exaggerated but apt: "a 'national' party, of social harmony, in which the oppressors and oppressed, the exploiters and exploited, the robbers and the robbed will live in a holy brotherhood as on a veritable Noah's ark under his majesty's command."[268]

Giurescu's efforts in 1939-1940 to resuscitate the FRN were unavailing, but led to his further advancement when he was named Minister of Propaganda in March 1941, in the cabinet of Gh. Tătărescu. The Tătărescu government[269] was to be Carol's final attempt to rally the major political forces of Romania behind his dictatorship, and the Minister of Propaganda obviously had a key role to play in that process.

However, time had run out for Carol and for Giurescu's political ambitions. The external situation had rapidly changed complexion and by 1940 Romania was starting the reap the consequences. Hitler's rapid advances east and west led Carol to reverse his Anglo-French policies, and cabinet re-shuffling brought in a more Germanophile element (e.g., Ion Gigurtu). France's disastrous fall occurred on June 22; the same day the FRN was dissolved and replaced by the Partidul Națiunii and an explicitly totalitarian state under Carol established. The June 26, Soviet ultimatum to relinquish Bessarabia and northern Bucovina occurred shortly thereafter. To Giurescu fell the task of making the public announcement of Romania's capitulation to the U.S.S.R.: "There must have been a hundred of us present at the second conference as Minister of Propaganda Giurescu read the full communique," an American journalist wrote. "There were tears streaming down his face before he reached the end."[270] The Tătărescu cabinet fell on July 3, and Giurescu's political career was over, though not all its consequences.

Politics was probably not the wisest choice made by Constantin C. Giurescu. In later years, he reflected on this both directly and indirectly. In his memoirs, he noted the Delphic inscription: "Know thyself," and commented that searchers for oracular advice could "avoid a host of errors, rash decisions, and unpleasantnesses" if they merely would have applied the inscription to themselves.[271] In 1972, he told me that in looking back on his life he would change very little; but one of the changes he would have made would have been in his political interests and involvements. He wished he had not succumbed to the lure of political ambition and had stayed with his history.[272] Perhaps this is one of the things he had in mind in his later reflection on the Delphic "Know thyself." No doubt he was right in retrospect. His political activities had hardly the anticipated results, served to divert his time and effort from scholarly concerns, and precipitated further enmities. In the end, he also paid with considerable personal hardships.

In the scholarly realm, the effects of political involvement were quite evident. In 1937 he had published the second volume of *Istoria Românilor*. Volume three, part one would not appear until 1942, though he did publish the third edition of Volume one in 1938 and the second and third editions of Volume two in 1938 and 1939. These editions involved minimal revisions, however. Political activism also prevented Giurescu from producing a foreign language edition of his history, or even of a foreign version of a one volume synthesis (as he had hoped).[273] The result was that he never got the foreign reception that his works truly deserved and his reputation abroad never approached that of Iorga or even Xenopol. Perhaps this price was also on his mind when he weighed the utility of his political career.

Constantin C. Giurescu's other activity in 1938-1940, while not insignificant, was not of the quantity and quality one had come to expect. He was able to assist in the editing of the *Enciclopedia României* (1938-1943, four volumes), to which he contributed three articles;[274] and to publish two textbook condensations of his synthesis in 1939.[275] His only major articles were his biographical piece on D. Russo and a study of Putna in 1820.[276] He also gave six radio lectures.[277]

1940-1941 was a frightening period in which to live in Romania as Carol's proclamation of a totalitarian state was followed by his ouster in September 1940, the establishment of a National Legionary State, and then an unsuccessful Legionary coup against their military ruling partner General Ion Antonescu in January 1941. This was capped in June 1941, with Romania's entry into World War II on the Axis side. The era was one of the bloodiest in Romanian internal history, including the shocking murder by the Legionaries of N. Iorga and a number of their political enemies.[278]

We know a little about this period in Giurescu's life because he published a brief memoir about the Legionary regime.[279] One of the key events was a final break with his associate P. P. Panaitescu. Panaitescu was the sole full professor in the Faculty of Letters who belonged to the Legionary movement and became their rector of the University in 1940. (He also was named director of the Legionary newspaper, *Cuvântul*, when it reappeared in October 1940.)[280] Panaitescu had survived in 1938-1939 only because Giurescu, Mihai Ralea, and Al. Rosetti had come to his aid: Ralea, close friend of the Minister of Interior Armand Călinescu, spent more than three hours arguing with Călinescu to get Panaitescu's name off a list of Legionaries to be interned. Many of those interned were later killed.

Giurescu spent several days in hiding in 1940 during a period of murderous visits by legionaries. In November, he, along with Ralea and Rosetti, was summoned for an interview in connection with a move to "purify" the University now headed by Panaitescu. Giurescu was questioned about the newspaper article he had written about Călinescu, though not about his other connections.[281] The dismissal was a foregone decision, he felt. He, then, went to see Panaitescu for help on his (and Rosetti's and Ralea's) behalf. His erstwhile colleague and friend would not look him in the face: "I can't do anything; there are others higher than me." The decision to dismiss Giurescu and Rosetti (but move them to other scholarly posts) and to fire Ralea outright stood. However, the Legionary regime fell before action could be taken.

The attempted Legionary coup in January 1941, was a last period of terror for Giurescu. He recalled waiting with two friends and guns ready for nearly two days in his home for an attack that could easily have come as the Legionary Movement spent itself in one last bloody throe.

With the new military dictatorship, Giurescu landed on his feet again. He was restored to his post and resumed his historical labors.[282] The fact that the new vice-premier, Mihai Antonescu, had been a political associate and friend of Giurescu's in the early 1930s facilitated "normalizing" his position.[283] With 1940, Giurescu had taken over the sole direction of *Revista Istorică Română* and had resumed serious work on his *Istoria Românilor*. He was also involved in academic politicking at the Royal Foundations in 1941-1942, becoming for a time director of the Historical Section of the reformed Union of Royal Cultural Foundations and then a rival for the job of his one-time friend Al. Tzigara-Samurcaş in 1942.[284]

At the University, Giurescu's Institute of National History (founded and conducted on an informal basis and connected with *Revista Istorică Română* since 1931) became a recognized and funded state institution in March 1942.[285] Apart from the obvious research and publication purposes, the Institute now had as part of its official charge "scientifically combatting the erroneous affirmations of foreign historians of our history." The Institute had a staff of twenty and was charged also with expanding its public conference series and book program. This unleashed an impressive series of lectures and publications that included eleven volumes and nineteen lecture programs (involving forty-eight presentations) between 1941-1944. In general, the Institute and the *Revista* can fairly be said to have contributed significantly to the creation of a greater body of substantive Romanian historical work and to the spreaking of the results of that work. At the same time, a higher regard for historical accuracy and truth was created through the group's extended polemics with "historical sentimentalists." Finally, the format, appearance, and technical aspects of Romanian historical work were raised to a new level.[286] In all of these, Constantin C. Giurescu was the initiator and leader, and he deserves credit for the devotion of time and effort he made to these ends and to the work of others.

Giurescu's scholarly efforts in 1941-1944, apart from reviews and notes in *Revista Istorică Română*, fall into four main categories: *Istoria Românilor*, Volume III, part one, and the one volume synthesis; articles, mostly brief items related to *Istoria Românilor;* editing; and preparing works connected with his father. The major achievement, of course, was *Istoria Românilor*, Volume III, part one: *Dela moartea lui Mihai Viteazul până la sfârșitul epocei fanariote (1601-1821)* (From the Death of Michael the Brave to the End of the Phanariot Period, 1601-1821). The organization of this volume was parallel to that of Volume II: a first section on rulers and events followed by a second part on institutions and special topics. This volume highlighted the reigns of Prince Matei Basarab and Prince Constantin Brâncoveanu and was written in the same style and manner as the preceding two volumes. In connection with the Phanariot princes, Giurescu advanced the thesis that Al. Ipsilanti was the most significant ruler in a period of general decline. Three extensive chapters are devoted to the political and religious life of Transylvania. The volume included 143 illustrations and seven maps.

1943 saw the publication of *Istoria Românilor din cele mai vechi timpuri până la moartea Regelui Ferdinand I.* (The History of the Romanians from the Earliest Times to the Death of Ferdinand I.) This work, based to a substantial degree on his 1939 high-school textbooks, is a synthesis of his *Istoria Românilor* in process and is an excellent compendium of Romanian history for the general reader not concerned with the detail provided in the larger work. It is a bit weaker, both in narration and analysis, on the post-1848 period, which shows that his projected volume four was still in the formative stages.

Giurescu's output of articles was again less substantial than earlier. The 1941 piece on *Die europäische Rolle des rumänischen Volkes*[287] reflected more the political concerns and circumstances of the period than anything else. The same might be said for studies of Moldavian Romanians between the Nistru and the Bug Rivers (i.e. "Transnistria") in the 17th and 18th centuries and between the Prut and Nistru.[288] An article on Alexandru Ipsilanti (1942) made an important geographical contribution,[289] as did a piece on a map by Constantin Cantacuzino (1943).[290] The rest were brief notes.[291]

In the editorial sphere, Giurescu's efforts included a number of quite noteworthy projects. He published his collection of radio speeches, *Din Trecut* (Out of the Past), which included three delivered in 1941-1942. He wrote the preface to Iulian Ştefănescu's *Opere istorice*,[292] which appeared under the auspices of the Institute of History along with several other volumes edited by himself. In 1943, he as the editor of a massive work on Transylvania designed to counter Magyar efforts of the same stripe.[293] Giurescu wrote the foreword to "Geschichtlichen uberblick," which was also published in several other languages.[294]

His final editorial chore as of a filial nature. In 1943-1944, he produced three works connected with his father who had died so prematurely twenty-five years earlier. In 1943, his father's classic social history articles were published as *Studii de istorie socială*.[295] In 1944, he published and prefaced the final two volumes of his father's *Material pentru istoria Olteniei supt Austriaci*,[296] still one of the key Romanian documentary collections. Finally, he compiled and contributed a number of articles to the memorial volume for his father that appeared in 1944, *In amintirea lui Constantin Giurescu*.[297]

The year 1944 brought a dramatic turn of events in Romania. The military dictatorship was ousted on the initiative of King Mihai on August 23, and Romanian troops were soon fighting on the allied side against Germany. 1945 brought not only peace, but also a new communist-dominated government to Romania. Constantin C. Giurescu, however, was not present to see the beginnings of what eventually became the Romanian People's Republic. He had managed to depart from Romania for a sojourn in Turkey under the auspicies of a Romanian institute. He took a leave of absence from his electoral and university posts,[298] and thus found himself faced wit a bit of dilemma in 1945 when it became obvious that Romania would not soon leave the orbit of the Soviet Union, whose troops occupied the country.

The question of remaining in Turkey was no doubt a big one for the former Royal Minister of Propaganda. However, he was persuaded by Gheorghe Tătărescu to return to Romania to take part in his fusionist National Liberal political group.[299] Tătărescu was Foreign Minister (March 6, 1945-November 7, 1947) under the Petru Groza (communist-dominated) cabinet; his party held its first congress in July 1945. As part of this effort, Giurescu published an article "Un nou ciclu istoric,"[300] which argued for a version of what became known in the 1970s as "convergence," the idea that the systems of the U.S.S.R. and the U.S.A. would move closer and closer together.

Resuming editorial command of *Revista Istorică Română* (July 1945), Giurescu also continued the publishing and lecturing program of the Institute of History. Between 1945-1947, an additional half-dozen volumes appeared under the auspices of the Institute as well as the last three volumes of *Revista Istorică Română*.[301] Polemics continued with D. Bodin's "Priviri generale asupra istoriei Românilor,"[302] which took up Giurescu's 1937 discussion of the development of Romanian historiography from Bogdan and Onciul, and aroused considerable reaction.[303] There was one final blast in 1946 by Giurescu on the Iorga front.[304] This was a response to Mihai Berza's "Metodă istorică şi falsă erudiție" that raised a number of issues from the "şcoală nouă" debate of the 1930s.[305] Berza's charge is that contemporary Romanian historians are too much under the baneful influence of Giurescu. The result? "Romanian historiography finds itself in full regress compared to the times of Xenopol, Onciul, Bogdan, or Nicolae Iorga." The quantity is greater and so is the effort, but the quality is deplorable. This was due to the method of the "new school" and to its narrow outlook. He had harsh words for collections of "documents" which include every scrape of paper and every debatable secondary source. Articles and monographs fared no better; they are a desolation devoid of ideas (often capable of being summed up in a sentence instead of pages) and buried under a mountain of irrelevant notes and references. The culprit was D. Russo, whose emphasis on method won out over Iorga's emphasis on spirit and broad horizon. This fatal intoxication with method must be overcome, Berza concludes, if Romanian historiography is to advance and see things in proper perspective.

Despite the overall unjustness of his claims about the poverty of the Giurescu group's scholarly production, some of Berza's remarks certainly had substance, for example, his critique of relentless source publication, however minute. Giurescu ignored all that with a summary rejoinder: "Considerations lacking in value on the current status of Romanian historiography by an incompetent." Berza is scored for having the never to critique the work of others despite scanty publications of his own. (Giurescu apparently forgot that his 1931 critique of Iorga preceded his own first major book.) Giurescu's review note concludes with a bit of uncharacteristic irony and self-commendation.[306]

Giurescu continued to work on *Istoria Românilor*. The fourth and fifth editions of Volume I appeared in 1945 and 1946, while the second part of Volume III finally saw the light of day in 1947.[307] It was a massive achievement: 600 pages of text on the most complex institutional, economic, social, and cultural questions; 100 pages of indices; 3 maps; 90 illustrations. The amount of original work needed to unravel the institutional history of this confusing era was truly impressive and the work remains more important on these aspects than most specialized monographs. The story of the Romanians was not completed to 1821; Volume IV carrying the tale to 1914 was already well underway when events intervened.

Giurescu's decision to return to Romania in 1945 proved to be tragic for him in the short-run. The election of November 1946 decisively isolated all non-collaborationist parties from Romanian political life. By November 1947, Tătărescu's group was itself excluded from the Communist-led government and on December 30, 1947, the Romanian People's Republic was proclaimed. In 1947, Giurescu's last major article appeared in the final number of *Revista Istorică Română*: "Relațiile economice dintre români și ruși până la Regulamentul Organic."[308] This article was also a part of his effort to ameliorate Russo-Romanian ties in the postwar era as well as his own position.[309] These efforts failed. The *Revista Istorică Română* would appear no more. C. C. Giurescu, at age 47, was soon relieved of his university posts and transferred to the reorganized Institute of History of the new Academy.[310] There he remained until 1950, publishing nothing, waiting beyond hope for the result of the increasing Stalinization of his country.

IV ECLIPSE (1948-1956)

The end of the Romanian monarchy in December 1947 obviously signalled significant changes in Romanian cultural and intellectual life.[311] For Constantin C. Giurescu, these changes began in July 1948 when he was dismissed from his university post and transferred to the new Institute of History and Philosophy under the aegis of the reconstituted Romanian Academy.[312]

The most prominent manifestation of the "new era" was the Sovietization of Romanian scholarly life, an at first dreary and then increasingly deadly trend.[313] State control of intellectual activity and production was facilitated by the new academic system, including the establishment of monopolistic publishing concerns, such as the Editura de Stat and the new "review of science, philosophy and art," *Studii*.[314] The extent of the change was reflected in such *Studii* "features" as an extensive "Bibliography of Soviet Science,"[315] an article on the "scientific work" of the late lamented Soviet genius and polymath Andrei Alexandrovic Zhdanov,[316] translations of Soviet masterworks,[317] and learned statements by J. V. Stalin.[318] Astonishingly, *Studii*'s toadying to the Soviets took a back seat to the egregious *Analele Româno-Sovietice*, whose avowed purpose in the intellectual sphere was analogous to that of the Sov-Roms in the economic.[319]

In the historical field such errors as "factology," mere narration or objective reports, "cosmopolitanism," and "objectivism" came under heavy fire.[320] At the same time, a vast program of reorientation of Romanian historiography was instituted.[321] This was, of course, necessary as the Communist Party organ *Scînteia* pointed out since

> During the transition period between capitalism and socialism the working class has not only to conquer political and economic positions from the hands of the exploiters. It struggles at the same time to destroy capitalist positions in men's minds. The red-hot iron must burn out all the rot planted in people's minds by centuries of capitalist slavery.[322]

The pace of "cultural" change quickened. *Studii*'s masthead served as a convenient barometer: by September 1948 (nr. 3), the newly-minted Marxist academician Mihail Roller had taken over as editor-in-chief replacing the editorial committee.[323] In March 1949 (Vol. II, nr. 1), the list of collaborators disappeared entirely (shortly after some of them had done so physically, e.g., Anton Golopenția). Roller became, in effect, historical commissar and his Russophile-Marxist interpretation of the Romanian past became normative.[324] With the purging of nationalist elements sympathetic to the Communist regime—followed by widespread trials in all the Soviet satellites—it was only a matter of time before those intellectuals who had been active under the old regime, such as Constantin C. Giurescu, were dealt with more severely.

In May 1950, Constantin C. Giurescu, as a prominent figure of the old political and cultural regime, was arrested and sent to the prison camp at Sighet in Northern Transylvania where he spent the next five years. His entire library, including autographed copies, annotated works, and his manuscripts, were confiscated never to be seen again.[325] Giurescu's sturdy constitution and will to live enabled him to survive (while Sighet became a death camp for numerous others including Gh. I. Brătianu who died in 1953).

July 1955 brought Giurescu's release, but only to an additional five months of forced domicile in the inhospitable Baragan region along the

Danube. Finally, in November 1955, he was able to return to Bucureşti and his family.

Meanwhile the Romanian intellectual scene was in transition as well. Though the years 1955-1960 were still grim, the Romanian element was reasserting itself over the Soviet inundation of the early 1950s.[326] The Roller era of relentless "self-criticism" and self-abasement was moving toward and end.[327] Roller was shifted from vice-president of the Academy (1949-1954) to adjunct director of the history institute (1955-1958), then fell into complete disgrace and was forced to commit suicide in mid-1958, much to everyone's relief.

Recently, Romanian historians, themselves, have explicitly recognized the barrenness of this period as dominated by intellectual parasites,[328] decrying the fettering of scholarly effort by "dogmatic rigors" and "schematization and impoverishment of native creative imagination."[329] The poverty of the Roller approach was manifest, both in quantity and quality as well as in its subservience to Soviet views. As a more national trend ensued, more and more pre-1948 scholars re-appeared.

For Constantin C. Giurescu, all this was to the good. The change in Romania's internal political and cultural policies and the failure of the new scheme of things to produce scholars of the power and productivity that had typified the prewar era meant the gradual rehabilitation of people like himself. In February 1956, he was given a temporary appointment at the Institute of History. The month-to-month nature of this post symbolized the insecurity of his status, but his assiduous academic habits and long-honed skills were soon manifest. Despite the tremendous psychological and physical trauma of the previous six years, the scholarly shock of lost papers and manuscripts, and the necessity of adjusting to a totally new cultural/political environment, Constantin C. Giurescu was able at age 55 to embark on a second career.

V. CONCLUSION

An evaluation of the work of Constantin C. Giurescu's first career (1919-1948) must be set in the context of the development of Romanian historiography in the period in which he functioned. That was the task of what has preceded. Let us consider now, briefly, some of the limitations and contributions of C. C. Giurescu's work.

Two major limitations of his work reflect the context in which he worked. His abrasiveness sometimes retarded intellectual advance in areas he valued. The circumstances as well as Romanian historical traditions, however, were seldom condusive to irenic tendencies. It is difficult to see how some of the bitterness and strife could have been avoided, given the issues and temperaments involved. Nevertheless, many evident and not so evident schisms in Romanian historical studies date back to the wounds opened in this era. Giurescu never exhibited a great deal of interest in mitigating these counter-productive effects.

Methodologically, Giurescu's emphasis on simply letting the facts speak for themselves, while salutary in some respects, obscured a number of problems. That this *sine qua non* does not resolve all controversies was most evident in the increasing nationalism that appeared in his work (as well as others) as Romania moved from constitutional monarchy, to royal dictatorship, to fascist regime, to military rule, and finally to Communist control. His eventual belief that the "essential characteristic of Romanian history is the ceaseless struggle of the Romanian people for *survival* and for the *maintaining of the state* in conditions that are particularly difficult" is only one example of a position derived from more than just facts.[330]

These limitations, however, by no means outweigh C. C. Giurescu's positive contributions. He was without doubt the greatest synthesizer of Romanian history ever to attempt the difficult feat of essaying the vast span of time and space covered by the Romanians in history. Synthesis requires a powerful command of the literature (in all relevant languages) combined with the research ability to solve the problems and fill the lacunae that inevitably exist in any historical literature. At the same time, the synthesizer needs sufficient preparation and depth to comprehend and marshal the cross-disciplinary approaches (geographical, economic, and so forth) vital to a true synthesis. Lastly, the successful synthesizer needs to be clear, accurate, and tightly organized.

These desiderata seem beyond the capabilities of any single person and explain why syntheses are often collective enterprises. C. C. Giurescu, however, met the high requirements of the modern historical synthesizer. The distinctive traits displayed by his writing, especially its lucidity and precision, coupled with a unity of plan and vision no collectivity can have, were foremost. If prior to his work, approximation in *quotation and citation* was tolerated and common, after it, Romanian historical craftsmen evidenced a much greater degree of the scholarly maturity such accuracy entails.[331] His clarity was matchless and his ability to communicate the findings of the best scholarship (including his own) is confirmed by the appeal and ease of access his syntheses have had for the educated public.

Giurescu's expertise in other areas, especially geography and the study of institutions, was of the highest level, while his grasp of the literature relevant to his task unsurpassed. He was, therefore, not a political historian in the usual sense as his syntheses stress the importance of geographic and economic factors in addition to the traditional fare of the historian.

Here, again, his command of his material is demonstrated as the clarity of the narrative is seldom obscured by his inter-disciplinary approach. Nor is the reader subjected to the tedium that seems to plague works which attempt to deal more fully with the social and other aspects.

Istoria Românilor is a monument to his skills and to Romanian historiography. For several generations, students of Romanian history have relied on "Giurescu" when they wished to ascertain the facts of the matter or comprehend the environment of a particular era of Romanian history. They will continue to do so.

C. C. Giurescu's second great contribution to the historical profession of his country was *Revista Istorică Română* and the methodological emphasis articulated and displayed in its pages. Romanian historiography came of age in the 1930s as historical accuracy and critical method became important in themselves. This is not to denigrate the work and contributions of those who came before; as Giurescu himself was the first to acknowledge, no synthesis can be built except out of the materials and monographs so painstakingly developed by the synthesizer's forerunners. It is simply to point out that in almost every way (except, perhaps, polemical courtesy!) the writing of history advanced in Romania during this period. *Revista Istorică Română* played the key role in this process of advance. From bibilographical facility and methodological rigor to marked improvement of graphic appearance and ever more solid critical studies and reviews, *Revista Istorică Română* set the pace which others emulated to the benefit of all.

Constantin C. Giurescu was the driving force and sustainer of *Revista Istorică Română;* to him goes the largest share of the credit for its contributions. At the same time his teaching and organizational activities (the Institute of National History and several publication series, to mention just a few) contributed mightily to the improvement of the work of the Romanian historical profession. In the end, however, C. C. Giurescu's most lasting place in Romanian historiography is secured by his *Istoria Românilor,* as the master of synthesis.

NOTES

1. "Laus vitae," in Vasile Pârvan, *Memoriale* (București: Cultura Națională, 1923), p. 40.

2. Relatively little has been published thus far on the life and work of Constantin C. Giurescu. The most comprehensive study is Al. Zub's "Constantin C. Giurescu: Perspectivă istoriografică," *Anuarul Institutului de Istorie și Arheologie A. D. Xenopol,* Vol. 16 (1979), pp. 480-500. Briefer

sketches include: Florea Stănculescu, "Academicianul Constantin C. Giurescu," *Studii și Articole de Istorie*, Vol. 35-36 (1977), pp. 217-219; Florian Gheorghe, "Constantin C. Giurescu (26.10.1901-13.11.1977)," *Analele Academiei Române*. Memoriile Secției de Științe Istorice, Series IV, Vol. 2 (1977), pp. 163-164; and my "Constantin C. Giurescu; A Historical Memoir," *Romanian Bulletin*, Vol. 7 (1978), Nr. 7-8, p. 3. For comprehensive bibliographical coverage of C. C. Giurescu's works, see Matei Cazacu, "70e anniversaire du professeur Constantin C. Giurescu," *Revue Roumaine d'Histoire*, Vol. 11 (1972), pp. 547-563 (covering publications between 1919-1971) and Ștefan Andreescu, "Le 75e anniversaire de l'académicien Constantin C. Giurescu," *Revue Roumaine d'Histoire*, Vol. 16 (1977), pp. 375-379 (covering 1972-1976). The notes below contain full coverage of publications between 1919-1947, including several items omitted in the above bibliographies. My thanks to Dinu C. Giurescu and Matei Cazacu for helpful responses to a number of questions that arose in connection with this study. They are, however, in no way responsible for any of my conclusions or opinions.

3. Twentieth century Romanian historiography needs further elucidation, especially for the rich and critical interwar era, a study that is just beginning to flourish. The most useful works are: Pompiliu Teodor, *Evoluția gîndirii istorice românești* (Cluj: Editura Dacia, 1970), an anthology with lengthy introductions; Lucian Boia, *Evoluția istoriografiei romane* (București: Tipografiei Universității, 1976), a multigraphed university course that hopefully will appear in book form; and Ștefan Ștefănescu, ed., *Enciclopedia istoriografiei românești* (București: Editura Științifică și Enciclopedică, 1978). All of these include materials on the whole of Romanian historical effort as well as bibliographical information.

4. On the older Giurescu, see Constantin C. Giurescu's "Note biografice," in C. C. Giurescu, *et al.*, *In amintirea lui Constantin C. Giurescu la douăzeci și cinci de ani dela moartea lui (1875-1918)* (București: n. p. 1944), pp. 7-17 (pp. 18-97 are also on the older Giurescu); and C. C. Giurescu, *Amintiri*, Volume 1 (București: Editura Sport-Turism, 1976), pp. 19-22 (hereafter cited as *Amintiri*). A recent study of Constantin Giurescu's work is Pompiliu Teodor, "Erudiție și istorie la Constantin Giurescu," *Studia Universitatis Babeș-Bolyai. Historia*. Vol. 22 (1977), Nr. 1, pp. 66-73. The most comprehensive bibliography of the older Giurescu's work is Constant Gresescu, "Bibliografia lucrărilor lui Constantin Giurescu," in Giurescu, *et al.*, *In amintirea* (1944), pp. 19-21. See also Ștefănescu, ed., *Enciclopedia* (1978), pp. 155-156 and Sanda Cândea, ed., *Bibliografia lucrărilor științifice ale cadrelor didactice Universitatea București*. Seria Istorie: Volume 1 (București: Biblioteca Centrală Universitară, 1970), pp. 256-260. To avoid confusion in what follows, the

older Giurescu is always referred to as "Constantin" and the younger as "Constantin C.," unless this is clear from the context.

5. Published as *Documente şi regeste privitoare la Constantin Brânco-veanu* (Bucureşti: Carol Gobl, 1907), in collaboration with N. Dobrescu.

6. Published as *Oltenia sub Austriaci.* Volume I: Documente (Bucureşti: Voinţa Naţională, 1909) and *Material pentru istoria Olteniei supt austriaci,* three volumes (Bucureşti: n.p., 1913-1947), the last two volumes published by Constantin C. Giurescu in 1944, the index in 1947.

7. Cf. *Amintiri,* p. 11. The youngest child in the Giurescu family was Elena, born in 1910.

8. Particularly his work on Muntenian and Moldovan chroniclers and on Moldova's capitulations with the Ottoman Empire. (Consult the bibliographies in note 4 above for details.)

9. Cf. Z. Ornea, *Junimea şi Junimismul,* 2nd edition (Bucureşti: Editura Eminescu, 1978), pp. 130-143. Regretably, the journal's turn from literature to history marked its slide into comfortable dullness.

10. The appointment was under the patronage and friendship of the Liberal leader D. A. Sturdza, then Prime Minister and Foreign Minister. For his work in archival organization, Constantin Giurescu was twice decorated by the Conservative Prime Minister (and Junimist friend) Titu Maiorescu in 1913. Cf. C. C. Giurescu, "Note..." in C. C. Giurescu, *et al., In amintirea* (1944), pp. 12-13.

11. C. C. Giurescu, "Note..." in C. C. Giurescu, *et al., In amintirea* (1944), pp. 13-16.

12. *Amintiri,* pp. 50-51. Much of what follows is based on Constantin C. Giurescu's *Amintiri.* Unfortunately, only Volume 1, dealing with events up to 1938, was completed before the author's death. About 100 pp. of manuscript for the second volume, dealing with 1938-1940, were written, but were unavailable to me for this study.

13. *Amintiri,* pp. 82-107.

14. *Amintiri,* pp. 90-91. The importance of nationalism in the biographical as well as political/cultural histories of East Europe is a subject that still needs analysis and exploration. For the generation of Romanians who lived through the events of World War I, the near death of their nation, which preceded the triumphs of 1918 was a powerful formative experience. Cf. Simion Mehedinţi, "Locul Junimei în istoria neamului românesc," *Convorbiri LIterare,* Vol. 70 (1937), pp. 47-48 reflecting on 1917. The same trauma was involved after World War II and after; no doubt this contributed to a good deal of otherwise dubious behavior by Romanian cultural and political leaders.

15. *Amintiri,* pp. 93-105.

16. *Amintiri,* pp. 100-101.

17. *Amintiri*, pp. 105-107 and C. C. Giurescu, "Note. . ." in C. C. Giurescu, *et al.*, *In amintirea* (1944), pp. 16-17. There are comments in *Amintiri* which indicate that this event had a powerful negative religious influence on young Giurescu.

18. Written interview with Constantin C. Giurescu, July 30, 1973. Manuscript in my possession (hereafter cited as "Interview").

19. *Amintiri*, p. 112 and "Interview."

20. *Amintiri*, pp. 112-115.

21. *Convorbiri Literare*, Vol. 51 (1919), pp. 744-749. The target was Ştefan Longinescu's *Aşezământul şi legătura lui Mihai Vodă* (Bucureşti: 1919) which was approached from the basis of Constantin Giurescu's study of the same problem (*Amintiri*, pp. 115-116). Longinescu replied without mentioning Giurescu's name [*Curierul Judiciar* (1920), Nr. 4-5] and Giurescu riposted in *Convorbiri Literare*, Vol. 52 (1920), pp. 370-380. In 1931, Giurescu published a warmly commendatory obituary of Longinescu [*Revista Istorică Română*, Vol. 1 (1931), p. 333].

22. Constantin Giurescu, *Despre boieri* (Bucureşti: Cartea Românească, 1920). A revised edition appeared in 1943, including two other key papers as C. Giurescu, *Studii de istorie socială*, 2nd edition revised and augumented by Constantin C. Giurescu (Bucureşti: Universul, 1943).

23. *Amintiri*, pp. 123-124.

24. *Amintiri*, p. 127. On his university career, cf. pp. 127-158 and also C. C. Giurescu, *Memoriu de titluri şi lucrari* (Bucureşt: Cultura Naţională, 1926), pp. 3-4.

25. "Interview;" cp. *Amintiri*, p. 148.

26. Typical remembrances of his father can be found in C. C. Giurescu, *et al.*, *In amintirea* (1944) by a student (Constantin Marinescu), pp. 61-63, and twó colleagues, S. Mehedinţi, pp. 65-78, and Vasile Pârvan, whose "Pomenirea lui C. Giurescu la Academie," of 1923 is reprinted on pp. 95-97.

27. Cf. N. Iorga, *"Şcoală nouă" de istorie. O lămurire definitivă* (Bucureşti: Datina Românească, 1936), p. 6 (hereafter cited as Iorga, *Şcoală nouă* (1936); and I. Vlădescu, *Plagiatorul:* In legătură cu„ Istoria Românilor," I, de C. C. Giurescu (Bucureşti: Datina Românească, 1936), pp. 57 ff. These charges, suspiciously enough, surfaced only in the 1930s controversies. Also, it should be noted that copies of Constantin Giurescu's unpublished courses were available in lithograph form for anyone to see.

28. E.g., "Organizarea financiară a Ţării Româneşti în epoca lui Mircea cel Bătrân," *Analele Academiei Române*. Memoriile Secţiunei

Istorice, Seria III, Vol. 7 (1926-1927), pp. 1-58, which is specifically based on four documents analysed and copied by Constantin Giurescu.
29. In C. C. Giurescu, *et al.*, *In amintirea* (1944), pp. 23-28. Cp. Vlădescu, *Plagiatorul* (1936), pp. 43-47, 57-71 on C. Giurescu's methods. (Vlădescu was a former student of the older Giurescu.)
30. Titu Maiorescu, *Critice*, 2nd, complete edition (București: Minerva, 1915), Vol. I, pp. 151-164. The best book on Junimea is Ornea, *Junimea* (1978). On Junimea's role in the objectifying of Romanian historiography in the early period, see Al. Zub, *Junimea. Implicaţii istoriografice. 1864-1885* (Iaşi: Editura Junimea, 1976).
31. Aurel Iordănescu, "Opera istorică a lui Constantin Giurescu," in C. C. Giurescu, *et al.*, *In amintirea* (1944), p. 30.
32. Pârvan, "Pomenirea. . ." in C. C. Giurescu, *et al.*, *In amintirea* (1944), pp. 95-97. Pârvan attributed Constantin Giurescu's slow advancement to his refusal to play the toady even in an academic/cultural system that often rewarded "sub-mediocrities. . . and those lacking in scruple." (p. 96).
33. On Onciul, see Aurelian Sacerdoţeanu, "Viaţa şi opera lui Dimitrie Onciul," in: Dimitrie Onciul, *Scrieri istorice*, critical edition edited by Aurelian Sacerdoţeanu (București: Editura Ştiinţifică, 1968), Vol. I, pp. 13-86; Teodor Bălan, *Dimitrie Onciul 1856-1923* (Cernăuţi: Tip. Mitrop. Silvestru, 1938); and Ştefan Ştefănescu, "Concepţia şi metoda istorică a lui Dimitrie Onciul (1856-1923)," *Studii*, Vol. 12 (1963), pp. 1237-1251.
34. "Interview;" *Amintiri*, pp. 132-133. For an example from Giurescu's student days, cf. D. Onciul, *Cuvânt la deschiderea cursului de Istoria Românilor in 26 Aprilie 1918* (București: Socec, 1918). Bălan, *Onciul* (1938), pp. 29-32, describes Onciul's mentor, Ottokar Lorenz, as a blend of Rankean methodology (the critical note in Onciul) and moderate romanticism (the nationalist side).
35. *Amintiri*, p. 134.
36. For Pârvan, see the excellent bibliographical work by Al. Zub: *Vasile Pârvan 1882-1927. Biobibliografie* (București: Editura Ştiinţifică şi Enciclopedică and Editura Militară, 1975) and his biography of Pârvan, *Vasile Pârvan—Efigia cărturarului* (Iaşi: Editura Junimea, 1974). Two earlier treatments of value are Em. Condurachi, "Vasile Pârvan (1882-1927)," *Dacia*, new series, Vol. 1 (1957), pp. 9-40; and Radu Vulpe, "Activitatea ştiinţifică a istoricului Vasile Pârvan," *Studii*, Vol. 10 (1957), nr. 3, pp. 7-39. A useful study in English that focusses on Pârvan is Em. Condurachi's *Rumanian Archaeology in the 20th Century* (București: Editura Academiei, 1964).

37. Cf. Al. Busuioceanu, *et al.*, *În memoria lui Vasile Pârvan* (București: Asociația academică Vasile Pârvan, 1934), *passim;* and Șerban Cioculescu, "Comemorări," *Revista Fundațiilor Regale,* Vol. 1 (1934), pp. 405-410.

38. Cf. Zub, "Giurescu," 1979, p. 497. The address was "In Mortem Commilitonum," delivered on 7/20 November to open the course on Ancient History at the University of București in 1918, reprinted in Pârvan, *Memoriale* (1923), pp. 95-103. (*Amintiri,* p. 113 is slightly inaccurate on this lecture.)

39. Pârvan's "referat" appears in *Buletinul Oficial al Ministeriului Instrucțiunii,* Vol. 29 (1927), pp. 439-442. It is quoted below in note 100.

40. See Giurescu's memorial address at the Academy on the 50th anniversary of Pârvan's death: "Personalitatea lui Vasile Pârvan," *Analele Academiei Române.* Memoriile Secției de Științe Istorice, Series IV, Vol. 2 (1977), pp. 121-126; and also *Amintiri,* pp. 132-144.

41. Giurescu, "Pârvan," 1977, p. 122.

42. Giurescu, "Pârvan," 1977, p. 123.

43. *Amintiri,* p. 126.

44. Cf. *Amintiri,* pp. 148-152 and "Interview." On Russo, see C. C. Giurescu, "Necrologul D. Russo,"*Revista Istorică Română,* Vol. 8 (1938), pp. 1-18.

45. D. Russo, *Elenizmul în România. Epoca bizantină și fanariotă* (București: Göbl, 1912), reprinted in D. Russo, *Studii istorice Greco-Române* edited by Constantin C. Giurescu and published by Ariadna and Nestor Camariano (București: Fundația Pentru Literatură și Artă Regele Carol II, 1939), Vol. II, pp. 487-542. The same edition contains a reprint of Russo's classic study "Critica textelor și tehnica edițiilor," (Vol. II, pp. 543-637), first published in 1912 (dated 1915).

46. *Amintiri,* pp. 150-151.

47. *Amintiri,* pp. 153-155. On Mehedinți, see the excellent studies by Vintilă Mihăilescu, et al., "Studii asupra vieții și operei geografice," in: S. Mehedinți, *Opere alese,* edited by Vintilă Mihăilescu (București: Editura Științifică, 1967), pp. 11-104.

48. "Interview."

49. Cf. the extensive chapters devoted to geography in his synthesis.

50. Constantin C. Giurescu, *Pentru "Vechea Școală" de istorie. Răspuns d-lui N. Iorga* (București: n. p., 1937), p. 53 [hereafter cited as Giurescu, *Vechea Școală* (1937)].

51. The amount of material on Iorga is nearly as staggering as his own output, reputed to be 1,250 books and 25,000 articles. In English, the following are helpful: William O. Oldson, *The Historical and Nationalistic*

Thought of Nicolae Iorga (New York: Columbia University Press, 1973); John C. Campbell, "Nicolas Iorga," *Slavonic and East European Review,* Vol. 26 (1947), pp. 44-59; and Vasile Netea, *Nicolae Iorga. 1871-1940* (București: Meridiane, 1971). For bibliography, see Barbu Theodorescu, *Nicolae Iorga 1871-1940* (București: Editura Științifică și Enciclopedică and Editura Militară, 1976), Volume I.

52. Cf. Constantin C. Giurescu, *Memoriu do titluri și lucrări* (București: Cultura Națională, 1926) for a list [hereafter cited as Giurescu, *Memoriu* (1926)].

53. E.g., a *Revista Istorică* [Vol. 12 (1926), pp. 33-36] review of Giurescu's *Noi contribuțiuni la studiul marilor dregătorii în secolele XIV și XV* (București: Socec, 1925): "An erudite work of painstaking and always sure analysis. . . . A perfect clarity and elegance of style distinguishes the work."

54. "A study which gives the greatest honor to the author and promises our historical science a master. Perfectly versed, of a critical approach as penetrating as it is level-headed. . . . " Iorga, quoted in Giurescu, *Memoriu* (1926), p. 6.

55. Iorga's polemical pamphlet, *Școulă nouă* (1936), pp. 6-7, stakes out a claim for a far larger share of the credit than that, but the Giurescu rejoinder, *Vechea școală* (1937), pp. 13-17, demonstrates convincingly that there is a good deal of mis-statement and inaccuracy in the Iorga account (e.g., Iorga did not stage manage Giurescu's promotion to a professorship in 1927 since he was in fact in Paris at the time). Iorga's charge that Pârvan had favored I. Vlădescu over Giurescu in 1925 is decisively refuted by the recently published letter from Pârvan to Iorga of 30 December 1925 urging Iorga to facilitate Giurescu's docentship so that "our young friend Giurescu . . . (who) I know you like as much as I do" won't be deprived of his university appointment. [Published in Vasile Pârvan, *Corespondență și acte* edited by Al. Zub (București: Editura Minerva, 1973), p. 276].

56. *Amintiri,* p. 144 and Giurescu, *Vechea școală* (1937), pp. 11, 17.

57. An excellent example of this is Iorga's review of the C. Giurescu edition of Miron Costin's *De neamul Moldovenilor* (1914) in *Revista Istorică,* Vol. 1 (1915), pp. 4-9 and C. Giurescu's calm dissection (one might say demolition) of the review in *Buletinul Comisiei Istorice a României,* Vol. 2 (1916), pp. 101-132 which led to a Iorga rejoinder in *Revista Istorică,* Vol. 1 (1915), pp. 226-229. Cf. also Iorga's 1918 obituary notice, "C. Giurescu," [reprinted in N. Iorga, *Oameni cari au fost* (București: Fundația Pentru Literatură și Artă Regele Carol II, 1935), Vol. II, p. 364] which emphasizes C. Giurescu's "powerful critical spirit,"

but accuses his studies of social history of being "mostly dominated by preconceived ideas." Young Giurescu may or may not have been aware in the 1920s that Iorga had also tried to block his father's election to full membership in the Academy in 1914, an attempt that led to a schism between Iorga and Pârvan. Cf. Zub, *Pârvan* (1975), p. LIV and also Gh. T. Kirileanu's unpublished memoirs in the Biblioteca Academiei (Arh. Gh. T. Kirileanu, II.MS.5), cited in Zub, p. 142. The former Liberal prime-minister and secretary-general of the Academy, D. A. Sturdza, was the proposer of Giurescu. See also *Amintiri*, pp. 123-124.

58. "Interview." Compare Valeriu Râpeanu's introductory to the reprint (third) edition of N. Iorga, *Orizonturile mele: O viață de om așa cum a fost* (București: Editura Minerva, 1972), especially pp. xxiv-xxx on Iorga's academic maneuvers and his temperament (e.g., "Iorga interpreted any allusion to himself as an attack . . . . " (p. xxvii)).

59. *Amintiri*, p. 148: "Faptul se explică poate și prin structura deosebită a temperamentului amîndurora."

60. Zub, "Giurescu," 1979, p. 493.

61. Barbu Theodorescu, *Nicolae Iorga* (București: Editura Tineretului, 1968), pp. 334-335.

62. Cf. Zub, "Giurescu," 1979, p. 493: "Significantly, his (Giurescu's) sympathies leaned from the start toward those who, in one way or another, opposed the authority" of Iorga.

63. Cf. Iorga, *O viață* (1972), pp. 398-403; 520-521; 529-530 for a number of remarks uncomplimentary to Mehedinți.

64. Details in the Kirileanu memoirs (cited above in note 57).

65. Zub, *Pârvan* (1975), pp. LXIX; LXXII-LXXV; N. Iorga, *Memorii* (București: Editura Națională S. Ciornei, n.d.), Vol. IV, entries for 31 May and 1 June 1923. Iorga finally returned to the fold (the Academy had no provision for resignation) on the condition that neither himself nor the "school" he represented would be debated (Zub, *Pârvan* [1975], p. LXXV).

66. Pârvan (Rome) to Marin Simionescu-Râmniceanu, 19 March 1927, published in Pârvan, *Corespondență* (1973), p. 434.

67. Published as V. Pârvan, *Dacia: An Outline of the Early Civilization of the Carpatho-Danubian Countries* (Cambridge: Cambridge University Press, 1928).

68. See Theodorescu, *Iorga* (1968), p. 378. For example, the Giurescu-Iorga debates are mentioned only once, without giving Giurescu's name.

69. Theodorescu, *Iorga* (1968), p. 321. He concludes with an anecdote that compares Iorga's position and generosity with Russo's, to the latter's disadvantage.

70. N. Iorga, "Un om, o metodă și o școală," *Revista Istorică*, Vol. 26 (1940), pp. 1-21. The piece served, of course, the dual purpose of attacking Russo and Giurescu (part of Russo's "școală") at the same time. See also Iorga's *O viață* (1972), pp. 637-638 for another attack on Russo.

71. Iorga's close associate, the Byzantinist Nicolae Bănescu and Russo were also deadly enemies. Cf. Bănescu's pamphlets: *O misterioasă reputație științifică* (București: Stroila, 1915); *O "celebritate" a științei românești (D. Demosthenes Roussos)* (București: D. C. Ionescu, 1915); and *Rătăcirile științifice ale D-lui Dem. Roussos* (București: Minerva, 1916); and Russo's reply: *Un bizantinolog improvizat* (București: Socec, 1916). Ironically, Bănescu succeeded to Russo's post in 1938.

72. *Amintiri*, p. 145.

73. *Amintiri*, pp. 144-145.

74. *Amintiri*, p. 148, which is consistent with comments in "Interview."

75. *Amintiri*, pp. 130-132; 153-156.

76. *Amintiri*, pp. 127-131.

77. Both in *Convorbiri Literare*, Vol. 53 (1921), pp. 322-328 and 861-872.

78. "Originea artei byzantine," *Revista Istorică*, Vol. 8 (1922), pp. 64-70.

79. "Legiuirea lui Caragea. Un anteproect necunoscut," *Buletinul Comisiei Istorice a României*, Vol. 3 (1923), pp. 45-74. In the same period, Giurescu also published brief notes in Iorga's *Revista Istorică* ("Documente diverse," Vol. 9 (1923), pp. 43-46; and on "O biserică a lui Vlad Țepeș la Târșor," *Buletinul Comisiunii Monumentelor Istorice*, Vol. 17 (1924), pp. 74-75.

80. Reportedly Onciul's opinion. Cf. *Amintiri*, p. 157.

81. *Amintiri*, pp. 157-158.

82. For Giurescu's experiences in France, see *Amintiri*, pp. 161-196.

83. It would take four costly years, besides which Iorga had expressly prohibited such programs by members of the school (*Amintiri*, pp. 169; 176-177).

84. Published as "Une enquête francaise sur les Principautés roumaines au commencement du XVIIe siecle" in Vol. 2 (1924), pp. 39-63; and "Le voyage de Niccolò Barsi en Moldavie (1633)," in Vol. 3 (1925), pp. 279-330. His Paris work also was reflected in the article "Les manuscrits roumains de la Bibliotheque Nationale," *Revue historique du sud-est européen*, Vol. 2 (1925), pp. 41-54; and in assistance he have to Iorga in the publication of N. Iorga, ed., *Album paleographique moldave*. Documents du XIV-e, XV-e, et XVI-e siècle recueillis par Jean Bogdan, publiés avec le concours de R. Caracaș, C. Marinescu, et C. C. Giurescu (București: Pavel Suru, 1926).

85.   Which appeard as "Contribuţiuni la studiul marilor dregătorii în secolele XIV şi XV," *Buletinul Comisiei Istorice a României*, Vol. 5 (1926), pp. 1-76.

86.   *Amintiri*, p. 196. See note 54 above for the Iorga comment.

87.   See note 53 above.

88.   *Amintiri*, pp. 196-198. The Committee was composed of N. Iorga, Pârvan, Russo, Cancel, and Ilie Minea (of Iaşi). The other candidate at the docental exam was I. Vlădescu who shall be heard from on other matters.

89.   *Amintiri*, pp. 198-202; Giurescu, *Memoriu* (1926), pp. 3-6. As of January 1, 1926, he also became a professor at the Archivist School of the State Archives and an adjunct professor at the University Pedagogical Institute. The course outline for his Archivist School lectures is published as "Instituţiile vechi româneşti. Curs predat de prof. Const. C. Giurescu," in Const. Moisil, "Din istoria Şcoalei Arhivistică," *Hrisovul*, Vol. 1 (1940), pp. 38-40.

90.   *Amintiri*, p. 210.

91.   Published by Iorga, "Consideraţii asupra istoriografiei româneşti în ultimii douăzeci de ani," *Revista Istorică*, Vol. 12 (1926), pp. 137-185.

92.   Ioan Bogdan, *Istoriografia română şi problemele ei actuale* (Bucureşti: Göbl, 1905), 33 pp.

93.   Giurescu, "Consideraţii," 1926, p. 138.

94.   This is an echo of V. Pârvan's discussion of the role and importance of monographic work: "Rolul monografiilor în studiile istorice," *Luceafărul*, Vol. 3 (1904), pp. 132-135.

95.   Giurescu, "Consideraţii," 1926, pp. 170-184.

96.   Giurescu, "Consideraţii," 1926, pp. 184-185.

97.   Continued into 1927, *Instituţiile vechi româneşti*, lithographed, 1927, 288 pp.

98.   *Amintiri*, pp. 210-211.

99.   Giurescu, *Memoriu*, 1926, listing sixteen publications and eight more in preparation.

100.   Pârvan's report noted that "the more difficult the exam, the more prepared the candidate showed himself to be," and listed the following points on which the committee's unanimous recommendation were based: "1. That the scientific works of the candidate produce new results and constitute a significant contribution to the historical literature on the periods of the founding and organization of the Romanian lands; 2. That the author has not limited his studies to a single domain, but has manifested an interest for all problems, old or new, of Romanian history; 3. That he possesses rich and precise knowledge both in his own specialty and in

related disciplines; 4. That he is perfectly equipped to undertake great works of historical methodology, of publication of sources, or of historical synthesis; 5. That he is well-endowed with the gift of clear thought and of fluent speech in a pleasant and convincing manner; 6. That he possesses in the highest grade the calmness and equilibrium necessary for true scientific objectivity; 7. That he demonstrates the will and the power for a continued enrichment and deepening of his qualities as a man of science and as professor." From the official published report as quoted in *Amintiri*, pp. 230-231.

101. *Amintiri*, pp. 229-231.

102. Cf. *Amintiri*, pp. 238-241.

103. Lithographed, 1928, 768 pp.

104. Probably based on his father's lithographed 1914-1915 course on the same topic.

105. Lithographed, 1930, 432 pp.

106. Lithographed, 1930, 1048 pp.

107. "Organizarea financiară a Țării Românești în epoca lui Mircea cel Bătrân," *Analele Academiei Române*. Memoriile Secțiunii Istorice. Seria III, Vol. 8 (1927), pp. 1-58.

108. "Nicolae Milescu Spătarul. Contribuțiuni la opera sa literară," *Analele Academiei Române*. Memoriile Secțiunii Istorice. Seria III, Vol. 8 (1927), pp. 231-284.

109. "Despre *sirac* și *siromah* în documentele slave muntene," *Revista Istorică*, Vol. 13 (1927), pp. 23-43.

110. "Un manuscris miscelaneu," *Revista Istorică*, Vol. 12 (1926), pp. 311-313; "Uciderea viziruliu Mohammed Tabani Buiuc, sprijinitorul lui Vasile Lupu. O scrisoare inedită," *Revista Istorică*, Vol. 12 (1926), pp. 98-103; "Uciderea voevodului Constantin Hangerli. O povestire în versuri necunoscută," *Revista Istorică*, Vol. 12 (1926), pp. 320-327; "Istoria lui Iordache Stavracoglu. O povestire în versuri inedită," in: *Omagiu lui Ion Bianu* (București: Cultura Națională, 1927), pp. 201-216; "Une relation inedite de la campagne de Pierre-le-Grand en Moldavie (1711)," *Melanges d'Histoire generale*, Vol. 1 (1927), pp. 125-132. Another significant labor assumed in 1929 was the editing of the massive publications of Andrei Veress, which he read, corrected, and prefaced: A. Veress, *Documente privitoare la istoria Ardealului, Moldovei, și Țării Românești*, eleven volumes (București: Cartea Românească, 1929-1939); and A. Veress, *Bibliografia româno-ungară*, three volumes (București: Cartea Românească, 1931-1935). On this work, see *Amintiri*, pp. 297-300, and also L. Demeny, "De l'activite historiographique d'-Andre Veress," *Revue Roumaine d'Histoire*, Vol. 6 (1967), pp. 29-30.

111. Ion C. Brătianu, *Acte și Cuvântări.* Vol. III (1 Mai 1877-30 Aprilie 1878) edited with a preface by C. C. Giurescu (București: Cartea Românească, 1930), xvi + 402 pp.

112. C. C. Giurescu, ed., *Dobrogea.* Patru conferințe de Universității Libere (București: Cartea Românească, 1928), which includes a paper by Giurescu, "Din istoria nouă a Dobrogei," pp. 53-73 (given 25 February 1928).

113. On his work at the Brătianu Foundations, see *Amintiri,* pp. 119-120; 206-209; and Zub, "Giurescu," 1979, p. 494.

114. *Amintiri,* pp. 245-246. He also contributed a bibliographical note on Romanian historical bibliography to *The Bulletin of the International Committee on Historical Sciences,* June, 1927, Nr. 2.

115. *Amintiri,* pp. 211-212.

116. *Amintiri,* pp. 259-278.

117. Cf. the program report in *Revista Istorică Română,* Vol. 1 (1931), p. 111 and also *Amintiri,* pp. 246-248.

118. Details in Iorga, *Școală nouă* (1936), pp. 8-9; P. P. Panaitescu, *Școala nouă de istorie: Un răspuns* (București: n.p., 1936), pp. 1-2; Giurescu, *Vechea Școală* (1937), p. 49; Iorga, *Memorii,* Vol. IV, p. 348.

119. Panaitescu's remarks are reflected in his survey of Romanian historiography published in 1930 as Onciul, Bogdan, C. Giurescu and Pârvan are distinguished from Iorga as the "critical" school. Cf. P. P. Panaitescu, *Powojenna historjografja Rumuńska* (Lwów: Zakladu Narodowego Imienia Ossolinskich, 1930), p. 3.

120. *Amintiri,* p. 247. Giurescu's professed astonishment at Iorga's reaction (pp. 247-248) is rather disingenuous, given Iorga's notorious hypersensitivity and Panaitescu's blunt presentation to the meeting.

121. Cf. note 105 for the course. *Amintiri,* pp. 249-250, is a bit unfair in mentioning Iorga's courses, but not Giurescu's own.

122. See *Revista Istorică Română,* Vol. 1 (1931), pp. 111-112. Somewhere along the line, Giurescu's 1926 recommendation that the younger historians work under the guidance and supervision of the older generation seems to have been lost.

123. Cf. *Amintiri,* pp. 250-253. The views of the party were published in an election manifesto of May 1931, called for moral renewal, reduction of governmental budgets and functionaries, and an end to political chicanery; and seemed to have been received with great caution. The platform was published in its paper *Mișcarea,* Vol. 24 (1931), May 13. An excellent sketch of Gh. I. Brătianu's life and career is given in Valeriu Râpeanu's "Gheorghe I. Brătianu, Studiu introductiv," the preface to the reprint edition of Gh. I. Brătianu, *Tradiția istorică despre întemeierea*

statelor româneşti (Bucureşti: Editura Eminescu, 1980), pp. v-lxxvi (cited hereafter as Râpeanu, "Brătianu," 1980). On the new party, see especially pp. xi-xxi.

124. N. Iorga, *Doi ani de restauraţie*, 2nd edition (Vălenii-de-Munte: Datina Românescă, 1932), p. 9.

125. Text and details in *Amintiri*, pp. 253-254.

126. Iorga, *Memorii*, Vol. VI (1939), p. 9. Cf. Iorga, *Doi Ani* (1932), p. 12 and Râpeanu, "Brătianu," 1980, pp. xix-xxi.

127. *Amintiri*, p. 257. Cf. pp. 253-258 on Giurescu's early political career.

128. Cp. *Amintiri*, pp. 278-280: "one can affirm without exaggeration that it was one of the most inefficient of all . . . in the inter-war period . . . "

129. The key references are *Amintiri*, pp. 283-295, which includes Giurescu's reflections on his collaborators; *Revista Istorică Română*, Vol. 1 (1931), pp. 3-6; and Paul Cernovodeanu's excellent *Revista istorică română 1931-1947. Bibliografie critică* (Bucureşti: Editura Ştiinţifică şi Enciclopedică, 1977), which includes an introductory study (pp. 11-24) and then a complete bibliographical description of the contents of the journal with some annotations.

130. On Panaitescu, see Dan Zamfirescu, "Prof. Petre P. Panaitescu," *Romanoslavica*, Vol. 11 (1965), pp. 357-368. His bibliography is given along with key articles in P. P. Panaitescu, *Contribuţii la istoria culturii româneşti* edited by Silvia Panaitescu and Dan Zamfirescu (Bucureşti: Editura Minerva, 1971).

131. Cf. Gh. I. Brătianu, *Memoriu de studii şi lucrări (1916-1941)* (Bucureşti: Naţională, 1942), 22 pp.; Râpeanu, "Brătianu," 1980, *passim*; and Lucian Boia, "Gheorghe I. Brătianu (1898-1953)," *Studii şi Articole de Istorie*, Vol. 37-38 (1978), pp. 169-173. The most complete bibliography of his works is E. Turdeanu, "L'Oeuvre de G. I. Brătianu," *Revue des Études Roumaines*, Vol. 7-8 (1959-1960), pp. 137-152.

132. *Revista Istorică Română*, Vol. 1 (1931), pp. 3-6. The rationale is reminiscent of V. Pârvan's "E nevoie la noi de o revistă istorică? " *Viaţa Romînească*, Vol. 1 (1906), pp. 590-595.

133. In this one can detect the same intellectual influences that are associated with the Annales school in France. Cf. Cernovodeanu, *Revista* (1977), p. 12; Zub, "Giurescu," 1979, p. 497; and Lucian Boia, "L'historiographie roumaine et l'ecole des "Annales" Quelques interférences," *Analele Universităţii Bucureşti. Istorie*, Vol. 28 (1979), pp. 31-40. Gh. I. Brătianu and P. P. Panaitescu were the closest in spirit to *Annales*, Brătianu in fact published a comparative article in *Annales*, Vol. 5 (1933), pp. 445-462.

134. Cf. Oldson, *Iorga* (1973).

135. Cited in Vlădescu, *Plagiatorul* (1936), pp. 110-111.

136. See pp. 44 ff. below. An instance of the kind of frank and honest statement implied by the *Revista Istorică Română* program is Giurescu's conclusion that Iorga's only basis for denying post-Roman inhabitation of Dacia by Germanic tribes is the notion that such a denial is required to uphold the Daco-Roman-Romanian continuity theory (*Revista Istorică Română*, Vol. 1 (1930), pp. 373-374). Giurescu accepts the theory, but points out that it is simply not acceptable (any longer) to let theory dominate interpretation. Panaitescu's article is "Diploma bârlădeană din 1134 și hrisovul lui Iurg Koriatovici din 1374. Falsurile patriotice ale lui B. P. Hașdeu," *Revista Istorică Română*, Vol. 2 (1932), pp. 46-58, which shows how a member of the Romantic school falsified two documents for presumably patriotic purposes.

137. Discussed below on pp. 55 ff.

138. Vlădescu, *Plagiatorul* (1936), p. 112. Cf. C. C. Giurescu, *Istoria Românilor* (București: Fundația Pentru Literatură și Artă Regele Carol, 1935), Vol. I, pp. 357-393.

139. The preface to Gh. I. Brătianu, *Problemele politice noastre de stat* (București: Partidul Național-Liberal, 1935), pp. 6-7.

140. C. C. Giurescu, *Die europäische Rolle des rumänischen Volkes* (București: Die Dacia Bücher, 1941), 26 pp.

141. C. C. Giurescu, *Istoria Românilor din cele mai vechi timpuri până la moartea Regelui Ferdinand I* (București: Cugetara-Georgescu Delafras, 1943), p. 6, emphasis in the text.

142. (București: Fundația Ferdinand I-iu, 1930), 301 pp. The work is, as Giurescu shows, a revision as well as a translation of Iorga's earlier *Histoire des Roumains et de leur Civilisation* (Paris: Henry Paulin, 1920), 289 + VIII pp.; second edition: (București: Cultura Națională, 1922), 266 + XIV pp.; English edition-1925; Italian edition-1928; German edition-1929.

143. *Revista Istorică Română*, Vol. 1 (1931), pp. 337-382; Vol. II (1932), pp. 1-45, 164-220. Bracketed numbers which follow in the text refer to this article.

144. 24 remaining pages of Giurescu's review were a French summary.

145. Giurescu's *Amintiri*, pp. 291-295, provide an interesting (and totally unchanged) backward look. In conversation, he told me that he still (1972) stood 100% behind his statements in the Iorga critiques.

146. Giurescu illustrates the regress further by comparing Iorga's current work with the principles outlined by Iorga to his students in the 1890s (pp. 187; 194).

147. In this statement we once again find Giurescu (and his associates) linked with a broader, more European historiographical tradition. Cp. Jakob Burckhardt, *Reflections on History* (Indianapolis: Liberty Classics, 1979), pp. 41-43 (first published in 1905): "Intentions, however, are particularly prone to make their appearance in the guise of patriotism, so that true knowledge finds its chief rival in our preoccupation with the history of our own country. There are certainly things in which the history of a man's own country will always take precedence, and it is our bounden duty to occupy ourselves with it. . . . Our imagined patriotism is often mere pride toward other peoples, and just for that reason lies outside of the path of truth. Even worse, it may be no more than a kind of partisanship within our own national circle; indeed, it often consists simply in causing pain to others. History of that kind is journalism . . . . Beyond the blind praise of our own country, another and more onerous duty is incumbent upon us as citizens, namely to educate ourselves to be comprehending human beings, for whom truth and the kinship with things of the spirit are the supreme good, and who can elicit our true duty as citizens from that knowledge, even if it were not innate in us.

In the realm of thought, it is supremely just and right that all frontiers should be swept away. There is too little of high spiritual value strewn over the earth for any epoch to say: we are utterly self-sufficient; or even: we prefer our own. That is not even the case with the products of industry, where given equal quality, and due account being taken of customs dues and freight charges, people simply take the cheaper, or, if the price is the same, the better. In the realm of mind we must simply strive for the higher, the highest we can attain."

148. Cf. p. 35 above.

149. See N. Iorga, *Opinions sinceres. La vie intellectuelle des Roumains en 1899* (Bucureşti: L'Independance Roumaine, 1899), and *Opinions pernicieuses d'un mauvais patriote* (Bucureşti: L'independance Roumaine, 1900).

150. Cf. Giurescu, *Vechea şcoală* (1937), pp. 45-46.

151. *Revista Istorică*, Vol. 17 (1931), p. 151. A lengthier (32 lines) summary of the contents of *Revista Istorică Română*'s second number for 1931 concludes "the bibliographical indications are useful, some of them hard-to-find; the judgements, often totally incompetent." [*Revista Istorică*, Vol. 17 (1931), p. 325].

152. *Revista Istorică*, Vol. 18 (1932), p. 182, at the end of a five line note on the fourth number of *Revista Istorică Română* containing Giurescu's critique. It is telling that later, when Iorga broke his silence, the response was mostly attack on Giurescu's work and little actual defense of the 1930 book.

153. N. Iorga, *Istoria Bisericii Românești și a vieții religioase a remâni-lor*. Second edition (București: Editura Ministerului de Culte, 1928), Vol. I, from the preface of the first edition, p. 8. A rather gratuitous means of dealing in advance with criticism.

154. See also Râpeanu's preface to Iorga, *O viața do om* (1972), pp. V-XIII.

155. C. Marinescu, ed., *Închinare lui Nicolae Iorga cu prilejul împlini-rii vârstei de 60 de ani* (Cluj: Institutul de Istorie Universală, 1931), XXXVIII + 440 pp. Giurescu had been earlier listed as a supporter of the projected volume, but did not contribute.

156. *Mélanges offerts a M. Nicolas Iorga par ses amis de France et des pays de langues française* (Paris: Gamber, 1933), LXXIX + 955 pp. It should be noted that Gamber was a Romanian immigrant and collaborator of Iorga's in France.

157. "Istoria la răscruce," *Boabe de Grâu*, Vol. 3 (1932), pp. 299-300; and Vol. 4 (1933), pp. 59-60.

158. C. C. Giurescu, *Revista Istorică Română*, Vol. 2 (1932), pp. 418-421; and Vol. 3 (1933), pp. 279-280.

159. *Amintiri*, pp. 309-313, for Giurescu's version; for Iorga's *Școală nouă* (1936), pp. 12-14.

160. Cp. for a typical comment on Iorga's animosity toward Giurescu in this period Grigore Nandriș' letter (May 29, 1932) to Basil Munteanu: "[Iorga] would burn all of Romania, if he could, just get rid of Giurescu." [B. Munteanu, *Corespondențe* (Paris: Ethos-Ioan Cusa, 1979), p. 57].

161. *Lucrările Institutului de Geografie al Universității din Cluj*, Vol. 4 (1928-1929), pp. 109-124 (which appeared in 1931). Brătescu's analysis is in *Analele Dobrogei*, Vol. 12 (1931), pp. 302-304 (a number dedicated to Iorga's 60th birthday); Giurescu's response: *Revista Istorică Română*, Vol. 1 (1931), pp. 430-436. Some of Giurescu's polemical points are less plausible than his defense.

162. *Revista Istorică Română*, Vol. 1 (1931), pp. 124-128.

163. Of Emil Diaconescu (pp. 83-86), A. Gheorghiu-Friedmann (pp. 86-87), G. Pascu (pp. 135-142), and D. C. Arion (pp. 305-310). The posi-tive review was of V. Radu (pp. 421-424).

164. "Învățământul de istorie în școală secundară," *Revista Istorică Română*, Vol. 1 (1931), pp. 333-336. The proposal was by Iorga's collabo-rator N. A. Constantinescu.

165. Aside from the Balkan Institute project mentioned below, only a piece, "Un nou ideal," *Datina*, Vol. 10 (1932), which I have not seen, and the radio lectures.

166. *Amintiri*, pp. 301-302. Cf. Marcel Ivan, *Evoluția partidelor noastre politice în cifre și grafice 1919-1932* (Sibiu: Kraftt and Drotleff, 1933), p. 23 and table V.c.

167. Text in *Revista Istorica Română*, Vol. 2 (1932), pp. 444-448. Cf. *Amintiri*, pp. 280-282.

168. Giurescu later came to hold that Romania was not a Balkan state at all (*Amintiri*, p. 282).

169. Vlădescu, *Plagiatorul* (1936), pp. 88-92 for Vlădescu's version. His intention was to offer a course on contemporary Romanian historiography.

170. In 1933, Giurescu continued the attack by proxy as well as his assistant Dumitru Bodin who gave a new edition of Iorga's collected essays on historiography, *Generalității cu privire la studiile istorice*, Second edition (București: 1933), a detailed and scathing review in *Revista Istorică Română*, Vol. 3 (1933), pp. 396-403.

171. Published as *Din trecut* (București: Cugetarea, 1942), 265 pp., containing 25 addresses given between 1932 and 1942. These broadcasts illustrated his conviction—inherited, he said, from his father—that Romanian history had to be both scholarly and accessible to the public ("Interview").

172. His courses for the period: 1930/1931—Curs de Istoria Românilor, lithographed, 1931, 720 pp.; 1931/1932—Curs general de Istoria Românilor, lithographed, 1932, 854 pp.; 1932/1933—Curs de istoria contemporană a Românilor, lithographed, 1933, 666 pp.; 1933/1934—Curs de istoria contemporană a Românilor dela 1888 înainte, lithographed, 1934, 663 pp.; 1934/1935—Curs de Istoria Românilor și bibliografia critică, lithographed, 1935.

173. 1933 saw a brief article, "Geneza poeziei 'Speranța' a lui Eminescu," *Revista Istorică Română*, Vol. 3 (1933), pp. 266-268, which traced the source of the poem to Schiller's "Hoffnung;" and an obituary/bibliography for the linguist Al. Philippide, *Revista Istorică Română*, Vol. 3 (1933), p. 317. 1934 produced three brief notes in *Revista Istorică Română*, Vol. 4 (1934): "Despre Vrancea," pp. 280-283;" "Vechimea satelor Star-Chiojd și Chiojdul Mic din fostul județ al Săcuienilor," pp. 283-285; and "Întâlnirea lui Guillebert de Lannoy cu Alexandru cel Bun," pp. 286-287, all on problems of dating. He also edited for the Romanian Classics series of N. Cartojan: Grigore Ureche vornicul și Simion Dascălul, *Letopisețul Țării Moldovei până la Aron Vodă (1359-1595) (Craiova: Scrisul Românesc, 1934), LXXXII* + 216 pp. (2nd edition-1939; 3rd edition-1942). In addition, he delivered five more radio lectures.

174. *Amintiri*, pp. 313-314.

175. Cf. *Amintiri*, pp. 314-317 on the book's preparation and plan; for Giurescu's conceptions of syntheses, see also *Amintiri*, pp. 231-238 and the preface to Volume I of his *Istoria Românilor*. The bibliographical data for his master work is as follows: Vol. I: Din cele mai vechi timpuri până la moartea lui Alexandru cel Bun (București: Fundația Pentru Literatură și Artă Regele Carol II, 1935), XVI + 586 pp.; 2nd edition=1935; 3rd edition=1938; 4th edition=1942; 5th edition=1946, XV + 607 pp.; Vol. II: Dela Mircea cel Bătrân și Alexandru cel Bun până la Mihai Viteazul, Part one (București: Fundația Pentru Literatură și Artă Regele Carol II, 1937), VI + 417 pp.; 2nd edition=1938; 3rd edition=1939; 4th edition=1943; Vol. II, Part two (București: Fundația Pentru Literatură și Artă Regele Carol II, 1937), 419-793 pp.; 2nd edition=1938; 3rd edition=1939; 4th edition=1943, VIII + 803 pp.; Vol. III: Dela moartea lui Mihai Viteazul până la sfârșitul epocei fanariote (1601-1821), Part one (București: Fundația Regală Pentru Literatură și Artă, 1942), VI + 443 pp.; 2nd edition=1944; Vol. III, Party two (București: Fundația Regală Pentru Literatură și Artă, 1946), 451-1154 pp. Hereafter this work cited as *Istoria Românilor*.

176. This and the need to discuss the history and destiny of Romanians outside the boundaries of 1920 Romania are stressed in *Amintiri*, pp. 232-236.

177. On the reception of *Istoria Românilor*, see *Amintiri*, pp. 116-119.

178. See the preface to Vol. I of *Istoria Românilor*. In a radio lecture of 1936, he further emphasized the inadequacy of single-factor views such as historical materialism (which he qualified as "naive"). See *Din trecut* (1942), p. 120.

179. Preface to *Istoria Românilor*, Vol. I.

180. He had taken Iorga to task for neglecting the forests in his 1930 syntheses (cf. *Revista Istorică Română*, Vol. 1 (1931), p. 363). Later in life he published an entire book on "codru-i frate cu Românul": *Istoria pădurii românești*, 2nd edition (București: Editura Ceres, 1976), 391 pp. and an English version in 1980.

181. These remarks encompass all three published volumes of the work.

182. The significance of this can be measures by the virtual flood of historical monographs which appeared thereafter.

183. As a friendly review by Z. Pâclișeanu pointed out in *Revista Fundațillor Regale*, Vol. 2 (1935), Nr. 8, pp. 455-457.

184. *Amintiri*, p. 237. This includes all three volumes.

185. *Amintiri*, pp. 323-324.

186. Zub, "Giurescu," 1979, p. 498.

187. *Revista Istorică*, Vol. 21 (1935), pp. 120-141. An attempt by Iorga to get King Carol to cancel further volumes of Giurescu's *Istoria Românilor* under the auspicies of the Royal Foundation failed. Cf. Iorga, *Memorii*, Vol. VII (1939), p. 263.

188. "In Legătură cu 'Istoria Românilor.' Răspuns recenziei d-lui N. Iorga," *Revista Istorică Română*, Vol. 5-6 (1935-1936), pp. 104-157. References here are to the off-print version (București: Naționala, 1936), 55 pp. [cited as Giurescu, *Legătura (1936)*].

189. Zub, "Giurescu," 1979, pp. 495-496.

190. Giurescu, *Legătura* (1936), p. 7, emphasis in original.

191. For what follows, see Iorga's 1897 piece, "Frumusețea în scrierea istoriei," reprinted in his *Generalități cu privire la studiile istorie*, 3rd edition compiled by Liliana N. Iorga (București: Institutul de Istorie Universală N. Iorga, 1944), pp. 39-57 [hereafter cited as Iorga, *Generalități (1944)*]. On Iorga's views, see the excellent sketch by Al. Zub, "La conception de N. Iorga sur le contenu et la forme dans la maniere d'ecrire l'histoire," *Revue Roumaine d'Histoire*, Vol. 10 (1971), pp. 611-621. Also useful is M. Berza, "Știința și methodă istorică în opera lui N. Iorga," *Analele Academiei Române. Memoriile Secțiunii Istorice. Seria III*, Vol. 27 (1944-1945), pp. 245-308.

192. "Două concepții istorice," in Iorga, *Generalități* (1944), pp. 77-98, especially pp. 88-91.

193. For example, "logically it is not the document that is the point of departure. After all, the historian is not a factory-worker intent upon the transformation of raw materials; nor is the historical method a funnelshaped piece of machinery into which documents in the rough state can simply be poured with a fine and continuous fabric of knowledge emerging from the other end. Our work presupposes original activity resulting from personal initiative. History is the response (obviously elaborated by means of documents, as we shall see later) to a question . . . the process of the elaboration of history is set in motion not by the existence of documents but by an initial step, the 'posed question' inscribed in the choice, delimitation and conception of the subject." (Henri-Irenéé Marrou, *The Meaning of History* (Baltimore: Helicon Press, 1966), pp. 70 ff., which also contains some entertaining comments on Langlois and Seignobos. Cf. also J. H. Hexter, *Doing History* (Bloomington: Indiana University Press, 1971), "One one longer hears about historians merely gathering facts which thereupon obligingly 'speak for themselves'." (p. 140). Apart from the programatic statement in Vol. 1 of *Revista Istorică*

Română and a number of comments in his various polemics with Iorga, only the introduction of his one volume synthesis (*Istoria Românilor* (1943), pp. 9-13, gives us any public statements of Giurescu's views on historiography. A fuller treatment would involve an examination of his 1929-1930 lithographed lectures, *Introducere în studiile istorice* (1930), 432 pp. Cf. Zub, "Giurescu," 1979, pp. 497-498.

194. See Ernst Cassirer, *An Essay on Man* (New Haven: Yale University Press, 1962), pp. 174-189.

195. Giurescu, *Legătura* (1936), p. 28.

196. Collected and published by Iorga's press as Vlădescu, *Plagiatorul* (1936), 113 pp.

197. Vlădescu, *Plagiatorul* (1936), pp. 12-13, a somewhat curious argument since it reflects negatively on Iorga's academic practices.

198. E.g., Vlădescu, *Plagiatorul* (1936), pp. 18-31.

199. See *Anuarul Universității din București 1935-1936* (București: Bucovina, 1937), pp. 9-10 and the volume for 1936-1937 (București: Bucovina, n.d.), pp. 8-9. *Amintiri*, p. 322, has a cryptic mention of the case without giving Vlădescu's name.

200. Iorga's book was Vol. I: Antiquité et Moyen-âge ((București: Édition de l'Institute d'Etude Byzantine, 1935). Balotă's review was published as an off-print: *Marginalii la 'Istoria Românilor' de C. C. Giurescu* (București: Ideea Românească, 1936), 16 pp.

201. The reference is from Iorga's *Istoria literaturii românești contemporane* (București: Editura Adevărul, 1934), Vol. I, preface, which takes a few other indirect shots at Giurescu, e.g., "When those who present them [corrections] do not have proper upbringing or taste, I set someone to collect from the muck of insults that which is usable."

202. Balotă's own preference in this regard was the collectivism of the Legionary movement, the notorious Iron Guard. His ideas, which owe to Iorga's nationalist approach, are analysed in Lucrețiu Pătrășcanu's *Problemele de bază ale României* (București: Socec, 1944), pp. 240 ff., especially pp. 243-251.

203. *Amintiri*, pp. 320-322.

204. *Amintiri*, pp. 322-323. Giurescu also published numerous rebuttals and counter-attacks in newspapers, e.g., in *Facla*, June 5, 1935, p. 2. These tended to be a bit more vituperative than his journal articles and pamphlets, but add nothing new.

205. *Amintiri*, pp. 299-301; Giurescu, *Vechea școală* (1937), p. 44.

206. (București: Fundația Regele Carol I, 1936), 177 pp.

207. (București: Fundația Regele Carol I, 1936), 269 pp.

208. This was Giurescu's *Legătura* (1936).

209. Details in Iorga, *Școală nouă* (1936) and Giurescu, *Vechea școală* (1937), especially p. 45.

210. This is the Iorga pamphlet, *Școală nouă* (1936) referred to previously. It should not be confused with the pamphlet cited in note 216 below. *Revista Istorică*, Vol. 22 (1936), p. 191 (the April-June number) contained the statement that alleged plagiarism by C. V. Dimitriu was "learned from his master, Mr. Prof. C. C. Giurescu." To call Dimitriu a plagiarist "is harsh, but true, and Mr. Professor Giurescu the same."

211. Recently published as *Istoria lui Mihai Viteazul* (București: Ministerul Apărării Naționale, 1935), two volumes, 301 and 227 pp. A dual review of Iorga and Panaitescu by I. Crăciun appeared in *Anuarul Institutului de Istorie Națională din Cluj*, Vol. 6 (1931-1935), pp. 685-697.

212. (București: I. N. Copuzeanu, 1936), 16 pp. Bodin was Giurescu's assistant at *Revista Istorică Română*.

213. (București: n.p., 1936), 3 pp.

214. "In jurul lui Mihai Viteazul," *Analele Academiei Române*. Memoriile Secțiunii Istorice, Seria III, Vol. 18 (1936), pp. 153-168. Cf. Iorga, *Memorii* (1939), Vol. VII, p. 336: "La Academie, despre caricatura lui Mihai Viteazul de P. P. Panaitescu." Iorga gave another paper in June, "Originea lui Mihai Viteazul după o chronică românească," also in *Analele* . . . , pp. 169-185.

215. Iorga, "In jurul," 1936, p. 168.

216. (București: Lupta, 1936), 50 pp.

217. Especially pp. 30-50, of Iorga's second pamphlet.

218. A. Balotă, *Mihai Viteazul după D-l P. P. Panaitescu* (București: Leopold Geller, 1936), 30 pp.

219. "In jurul lui Mihai Viteazul. Răspuns d-lui N. Iorga," *Revista Istorică Română*, Vol. 7 (1937), pp. 1-31.

220. (București: n.p., 1937).

221. Iorga's *Istoria Românilor*, ten volumes in eleven, began to appear in 1936 (București: Datina Românească, 1936-1939). The preface of Vol. I, part one, notes "a monument of scientific manners is the insulting review signed C. C. Giurescu . . . . "

222. Giurescu, *Vechea școală* (1937), pp. 53-54. The quote is from Iorga's "Cultura generală și studii istorice," (1932), in his *Generalității* (1944), p. 168. The whole lecture, given at the University in 1932's opening lecture, is more or less an attack on Giurescu's conception of history.

223. P. 28 above and cp. A. D. Xenopol's "O privire retrospectivă

asupra 'Convorbirilor Literare' (1 Martie 1871)," published for the first time in *Convorbiri Literare*, Vol. 70(1937), pp. 66-73, which lists "Spreading of the spirit of true criticism" and "Encouragement of the progress of national literature and the combatting of literary charlatanism dressed in the mask of false patriotism," as fundamental to Junimen.

224. Giurescu gleefully noted that Vol. I, part one (1936) of Iorga's own new *Istoria Românilor* was dedicated to Bogdan, Onciul, and Şt. Orăşanu—Junimists all! It is curious that Iorga's *Şcoală nouă* (1936), pp. 8-9, has some slightly derogatory remarks on Bogdan and Onciul as "models of objectivity that was sometimes too cold...."

225. And, in fact, the 1937 anniversary edition of *Convorbiri Literare*, Vol. 70, has a plate (no. 3) picturing living collaborators that includes Giurescu and Panaitescu, though by this time Junimea was no longer a coherent grouping. (The volume also had an exercpt from Giurescu's forthcoming Vol. II of *Istoria Românilor*.)

226. A regular contributor to *Convorbiri Literare* prior to 1907 and foe of Romanticism in history. Cf. his lectures of the 1890s in *Generalităţii* (1944), *passim*.

227. Leaving aside the significant groups at Cluj (around Ioan Lupaş) and at Iaşi (around Ilie Minea).

228. Compare Zub, "Giurescu," 1979, p. 498. There is also an interesting 1933 lecture by Iorga in Paris, "Romantism şi naţionalism în istoriografia românească," in *Generalităţi* (1944), pp. 173-187, which passes in review his predecessors and colleagues of the pre-World War I generation and places himself in the French school which he defines as combining the best of Viennese positivism and German spirit.

229. Cp. Al. Boldur, "Ştiinţa istorică română în ultimi 25 ani," *Studii şi Cercetări Istorice*, Vol. 20 (1947), pp. 20 ff.

230. On "historiology," see N. Iorga, *Materiale pentru o istoriologie umană* edited by Liliana N. Iorga with a forward by D. M. Pippidi (Bucureşti: Editura Academiei, 1968), especially the foreword, pp. V-XV.

231. Vol. I, two parts, and Vol. II in 1936; Volumes III, IV, and V in 1937.

232. Cf. Iorga, *Memorii* (1939), Vol. VII, p. 335 for a sour note in this regard.

233. His other publications in 1935-1937 included: "Mormântul germanic de la Chiojdu," *Revista Istorică Română*, Vol. 5-6 (1935-1936); "Din istoricul breslelor bucureştene," *Albumul "Lunii Bucureştilor"*, 1936, pp. 27-35; "Judeţele dispărute din Ţara Românească," *Arhiva pentru Ştiinţa şi Reforma Socială*, Vol. 14 (1936), pp. 842-847; "Despre

iliş," *Revista Istorică Română*, Vol. 7 (1937), pp. 253-257; two pamphlets: *Din trecutul judeţului Putna* (Focşani: 1937), 26 pp., and *Colonizarea românilor de peste hotare. Interdezvoltată în Camera deputaţilor în şedinţele din 25 februarie şi 4 martie 1937* (Bucureşti: Naţionala, 1937, 41 pp.; prefaces to two books: C. Dimitriu, *Doi dregători moldoveni* (Bucureşti: 1935) and C. Căpşuneanu, *Eroul Vasile Chilian* (Bucureşti: Dimitrie Cantemir, 1936); and an obituary for Iulian Ştefănescu in *Revista Istorică Română*, Vol. 7 (1937), pp. 472-474. Several excerpts from *Istoria Românilor* also appeared in a number of journals.

234. 1935/1936—Curs de Istoria Românilor, lithographed, 1936, 756 pp.; 1936/1937—Curs de Istoria Românilor, lithographed, 1937, 350 pp.; 1937/1938—Curs de Istoria Românilor. Dela Mihai Viteazul înainte, lithographed, 1938, 700 pp.

235. Cf. *Din trecut* (1942), *passim*.

236. Among the reviews: Charles Upson Clark, *American Historical Review*, Vol. 44 (1938-1939), pp. 866-868; G. Gundisch, *Jahrbucher fur Geschichte Osteuropas*, Vol. 3 (1938), pp. 680-682; I. Crăciun, *Anuarul Institutului de Istorie Naţională*, Vol. 7 (1936-1938), pp. 731-736.

237. The review was by I. C. Filitti in *Epoca*, Nr. 2615 (October 27, 1937); the response was in *Revista Istorică Română*, Vol. 7 (1937), pp. 398-400.

238. In 1937-1938, Giurescu published two shorter, but still lengthy reviews of Iorga's work: *Revista Istorică Română*, Vol. 7 (1937), pp. 180-184 on Iorga's *Le place des Roumains dans l'histoire universelle* (1935), Vol. I; and *Jahrbucher fur Geschichte Osteuropas*, Vol. 3 (1938), pp. 126-132, on Iorga's *Istoria Românilor* (1936), Vol. I, part one. Iorga, for his part, continued a running battle with Giurescu (though not by name) in his *Istoria Românilor* by categorical attacks on certain well-known Giurescu positions, e.g. Vol 3 (1937), pp. 83-89, rejects Giurescu's 1931 work on the Asăneştii and Vol. 4 (1937), p. 12, rejects Giurescu's 1934 conclusions relative to the meeting place of Guillebert de Lannoy and Alexandru cel Bun.

239. *Istoria Românilor*, ten volumes in eleven (Bucureşti and Vălenii-de-Munte: Datina Românească and Naţională, 1936-1939).

240. *Histoire des Roumains et de la Romanite Orientale*, ten volumes in eleven (Bucureşti: Naţională, 1937-1944). These volumes were published under the auspices of the Romanian Academy.

241. See his "Spiritul istoric," (1929), in his *Generalităţi* (1944), pp. 157-168. Compare in the same volume, "Cultura generală şi studii istorice," (1932), and "Fond şi formă în căuterea adevărului istoric," (1937).

242. See note 230 above. The preface was first printed in *Generalități* (1944).

243. *Generalități* (1944), p. 344. The reference to Giurescu is clear.ˇ

244. *Generalități* (1944), p. 348.

245. *Istoria Românilor* (1936), Vol. I, part one, p. 3.

246. Brătianu, *Probleme* (1935), p. 60.

247. Emilia and Gavrilă Sonea, *Viața economică și politică a României 1933-1938* (București: Editura Științifică și Enciclopedică, 1978), pp. 158-160. Cf. Râpeanu, "Brătianu," 1980, pp. XXII-XXIV.

248. Published in *Politics and Political Parties in Roumania* (London: International Reference Library, 1936), pp. 159-168. Râpeanu's declaration that Gh. I. Brătianu never had "any affinity with chauvinist currents" doesn't square well with his platform. See Râpeanu, "Brătianu," 1980, p. XXXVIII.

249. *Politics* (1936), pp. 170 and 158. The obvious reference to "foreigner" here is to the Romanian Jewish population. Romanian politicians always argued that such programs were not anti-semitic in a religious sense, but merely dealt with a "social" or "economic" problem. Whether this makes a great deal of difference is debatable.

250. The only parliamentary speech his bibliography contains. See note 233 above.

251. Quoted in Giurescu, *Vechea școală* (1937), p. 21.

252. Giurescu, *Vechea școală* (1937), p. 22, note 2. Iorga's recollection [*Memorii* (1939), Vol. VII, p. 403]: "I needed to defend myself against charges of bad faith in the Chamber, by my old calumniator, Giurescu . . . . In the Chamber . . . a dialogue with this unfortunate person, who doesn't know how to keep his mouth shut."

253. Sonea, *Viața politică* (1978), p. 161. Cf. Giurescu's *Amintiri*, p. 283, which compares Gh. I. Brătianu unfavorably with his father Ionel Brătianu because "the negative element predominated" in his political activity.

254. An interesting analysis of the election is C. Enescu's "Semnificația alegerilor din Decemvrie 1937 în evoluția politică a neamului Românesc," *Sociologia Românească*, Vol. 2 (1937), pp. 512-526. One of his tables shows that the percentage of the electorate voting had fallen four straight elections from the high of 77.4% (1927) to 66.1% (1937). This was a sign of both increasing lack of confidence in elections and poll intimidation.

255. The most complete account is Al. Gh. Savu's *Dictatura regală (1938-1940)* (București: Editura Politică, 1970).

256. Savu, *Dictatura* (1970), pp. 155-156.

257. For some observations on Călinescu, Tătărescu, and others in the 1930s, see Giurescu's *Amintiri*, pp. 303-309. His friends Ralea and Ghelmegheanu were Călinescu intimates and cabinet members after 1938.

258. Cf. Gh. I. Brătianu, *Nicolae Iorga (Trei cuvântări)* (București: Institutul de Istorie Universală N. Iorga, 1944); Gh. I. Brătianu and M. Berza, *Institutul de Istorie Universală N. Iorga la zece ani dela întemeiere* (București: Bucovina, 1947); and also Râpeanu, "Brătianu," 1980, pp. XXXII-XXXIV.

259. In *Din trecut* (1942), pp. 141-149.

260. Compare the decree abolishing political parties of 1938 March: "The old party organizations no longer correspond to certain political functions; they no longer have a rationale for their existence and become . . . an obstacle to the normal development of the new Romanian public life." [Given in Savu, *Dictatura* (1970), p. 174].

261. Compare Giurescu's description of Carol's 1938 coup as eliminating a situation blocking Romania's progress and making it possible for "a new era to begin in our country's development." This was published in his highschool textbook of 1939, which then concludes: "our duty, of everyone, is to help with all one's power, through work, discipline and faith, its [the country's] growth and flowering." See *Istoria Românilor pentru clasa VIII-a secundară* (București: Cugetara, 1939), p. 407.

262. Some data for this vague period may be found in Lucian Predescu, *Enciclopedia Cugetaea* (București: Cugeterea-Georgescu Delafras, 1940), p. 363, and Mioara Tudorică and Ioana Burlacu, "Guvernele României între anii 1866-1945. Liste de miniştri," *Revista Arhivelor*, Vol. 47 (1970), pp. 460-461.

263. Still the best survey is Eugen Weber, "Romania," in Hans Rogger and Eugen Weber, eds., *The European Right* (Berkeley: University of California Press, 1966), pp. 501-574.

264. Giurescu's closeness to Călinescu by this point is illustrated by his publishing a strongly favorable article on Călinescu just after his death in the leading daily *Universul* and also serving as editor of Călinescu's speeches, *Noul regim (Cuvântări) 1938-1939)* (București: Națională, 1939). On this see, C. C. Giurescu, "Amintiri de la Facultatea de litere din București privind perioada regimului legionar (septembrie 1940-ianuari 1941)," in Ion Popescu-Puțuri, *et al.*, *Împotriva fascismului* (București: Editura Politică, 1971), p. 208. (My copy of the Călinescu volume does not have Giurescu's name in it anywhere.) Giurescu's *Amintiri*, p. 305, also has a

favorable recollection of Călinescu, who is described as a "convinced democrat." A perusal of Călinescu's 1938-1939 speeches makes it clear that Giurescu uses "democrat" in a special East European sense (cp. "peoples' democracy").

265. See the analysis of the FRN in Savu, *Dictatura* (1970), pp. 192 ff.

266. The decree, quoted in Savu, *Dictatura* (1970), p. 193.

267. The creation of a quasi-paramilitary arm of the FRN was less sinister than for show. The regime has other means of dealing with the population (i.e., Moruzov's secret police and the infamous Siguranța).

268. Savu, *Dictatura* (1970), p. 192. On the FRN, see the conclusion of N. M. Nagy-Talavera, *The Green Shirts and Others: A History of Fascism in Hungary and Rumania* (Stanford: Hoover Institution Press, 1970), p. 342: "Carol's F. N. R. does not deserve to be called Fascist. It was a convenient and seemingly up-to-date structure for the oligarchy, carrying the singularly unliberal policies of the Rumanian Liberals to a logical conclusion."

269. See Savu, *Dictatura* (1970), *passim*, on this era.

270. Robert St. John, *Foreign Correspondent* (Garden City: Doubleday, 1957), p. 130.

271. *Amintiri*, p. 336.

272. In a conversation.

273. Cf. C. U. Clark, *American Historical Review* (1938-1939), p. 867, for Giurescu's plan to complete a translation by 1943.

274. "Istoria românilor," *Enciclopedia Romaniei*, Vol. I, 1938, pp. 51-58 (the choice of Giurescu to write this article must have rankled Iorga); "Judeţele dispărute ale României," Vol. II, 1938, pp. 17-18; and "Vechiul comerţ exterior al Ţării Româneşti şi al Moldovei," Vol. IV, 1943, pp. 456-458.

275. *Istoria Românilor pentru clasa IV-a secundară* (Bucureşti: Cugetara, 1939), 303 pp. and the same for clasa VIII-a, 434 pp. (which reached a 5th edition by 1944).

276. "Necrolog D. Russo," *Revista Istorică Română*, Vol. 8 (1938), pp. 1-18; and "Populaţia judeţului Putna la 1820," *Buletinul Societăţii Regale Române de Geografie*, Vol. 59 (1940), pp. 195-232. Other articles included: "Începuturi de industrie în Ţările Româneşti," *Analele Industriei şi Comerţului* (1938), Nr. 2-3 (which I have not seen); "Dobrogea, vechi pământ românesc," *Buletin Muzeul Militar Naţional*, Vol. 3 (1939-1940), Nr. 5-6, pp. 31-33; "Târguri şi oraşe româneşti dispărute," *Revista Fundaţiilor Regale*, Vol. 6 (1939), Nr. 3, pp. 557-561; "Două portrete ale principelui Carol I, " *Revista Istorică Română*, Vol. 9 (1939),

pp. 78-81; "'Oltenii' și Basarabia. Colonizări muntene în sudul Moldovei în veacurile XIV si XV," *Revista Istorică Română*, Vol. 10 (1940), pp. 130-139; "Rectificări și precizări la cronologia domniilor fanariote," *Revista Istorică Română*, Vol. 10 (1940), pp. 379-384; obituaries for N. Iorga (p. 491) and Vasile Radu (pp. 491-493) in *Revista Istorică Română*, Vol. 10 (1940); "Noi numiri de străzi în Capitală," *Revista Istorică Română*, Vol. 10 (1940), p. 493. He also published a political pamphlet, *Ordonanțe și circulări privind programul gospodăresc al Ținutului "Dunărea de Jos"* (București: Națională, 1939), 42 pp.; edited and prefaced D. Russo, *Studii istorice greco-române* (2 volumes; 1939) in honor of his old teacher and friend; and the same for Carol I, *Cuvântările Regelui Carol I*, two volumes (București: Fundația Pentru Literatură și Artă Regele Carol II, 1939), 467 + 530 pp.

277. Reprinted in *Din trecut* (1942), *passim*. A number of the radio lectures were similar to some of the briefer papers he published in this era. In April 1940, he inaugurated the Romanian pavillions in Milan and also wrote the preface to the exposition catalogue [cf. *România*, Vol. 5 (1940), Nr. 5, pp. 50-51, with some photographs of Giurescu and the pavillions].

278. To his credit, Giurescu published one of the earlier obituaries for Iorga [*Revista Istorică Română*, Vol. 10 (1940), p. 491].

279. Giurescu, "Amintiri, 1971, pp. 206-211 for what follows.

280. The lack of Legionary professors owed less to the movements lack of intrinsic appeal to Romanian intellectuals than to the savage repression of the Legion in 1938-1939. For example, at the University, Nae Ionescu, whose broken health led to his death in 1940, and Vasile Christescu—a collaborator of Giurescu's journal who also published a book in 1937 in a series under Giurescu's editorial supervision—who was co-leader of the Legionary Movement with Horia Sima after Codreanu's murder and who died in a shoot-out with the police in January 1939. Cf. *Almanahul Cuvântul 1941* (București: Cuvântul, 1940), pp. 46-48.

281. See note 264 above.

282. He was able to complete his course: Istoria moderna a Românilor, lithographed, 1941, 902 pp.

283. Antonescu, who was not related to General Antonescu except indirectly on his mother's side, had presided over the 1935 Giurescu banquet along with Gh. I. Brătianu and Al. Rosetti. Cf. *Amintiri*, pp. 323-324.

284. Tzigara-Samurcaș and Giurescu had a falling out in 1939. Giurescu's return was under the aegis of D. Caracostea, who headed the Union

of Royal Cultural Foundations between 1941-1944, and who tried to have Tzigara-Samurcaş "retired." The deails of this fight are in Caracostea's defense of his directorship: *Dare de seamă despre activitatea Fundaţiei Regale pentru Literatură şi Artăşi despre activitatea Uniunii F.C.R.* (Bucureşti): Naţionala, 1944), covering the period April 1, 1941-December 31, 1943; and Tzigara-Samurcaş' rebuttal: *Din viaţa Fundaţiilor Regale. O eclipsă (Bucureştî* Naţionala, 1944). During Giurescu's short tenure at the Historical Section, he tried to get Mihai Berza, the consellor of the section, dismissed and replaced with his man, D. Bodin. This failed, but Berza's post (he was mobilized into the army at the time) was then abolished. This accounts, in part, for the later antagonism between Berza and Giurescu. As to the financial allegations made by Tzigara-Samurcaş against Caracostea, Giurescu, and Bodin, information is lacking.

285. The text of the law signed by Marshal Antonescu is published in *Revista Istorică Română*, Vol. 13 (1943), Nr. 1, pp. 141-145. A report of the activities of the Institute was published by D. Bodin, "Dare de seamă asupra activităţii Institutului de Istorie Naţională din Bucureşti pe anii 1942-1944," *Revista Istorică Română*, Vol. 14) 1944, pp. 547-557.

286. Bodin, "Dare de seamă," 1944, pp. 555-557.

287. (Bucureşti: Die Dacia Bücher, 1941), 26 pp. This later appeared as pp. 425-434 of the book listed in note 293 below. It was one of two Giurescu books banned in 1948. Cf. Ministerul Artelor şi Informaţiilor, *Publicaţiile interzise până la 1 Mai 1948* (Bucureşti: Dacia Traiană, 1948), p. 169.

288. "Populaţia moldovenescâ dela gura Niprului şi a Bugului în veacurile XVII şi XVII," *Renaşterea*, Vol. 20 (1941), pp. 596-601; and "Vechimea aşezărilor româneşti dintre Prut şi Nistru," *Revista Fundaţiilor Regale,* Vol. 8 (1941), Nr. 8-9, pp. 307-319. These items are omitted from post-1948 Giurescu bibliographies for some reason or other.

289. "Canalul lui Alexandru Vodă Ipsilanti," *Revista Istorică Romaâaă*, Vol. 11-12 (1941-1942), pp. 1-8. Due to circumstances, this volume of the journal was not published until 1943.

290. "Harta stolnicului Constantin Cantacuzino," *Revista Istorică Română*, Vol. 13 (1943), pp. 1-28.

291. In *Revista Istorică Română*: "Două ctitorii ale lui Matei Basarab în Bulgaria," Vol. 11-12 (1941-1942), pp. 390-391; "Pentru descoperirea Vicinei," Vol. 11-12 (1941-1942), pp. 530-531; "O cruce pe locul luptei

de la Vaslui," Vol. 11-12 (1941-1942), pp. 540-542; "Movilăul, târg moldovenesc," Vol. 13 (1943), Nr. 3, p. 57; "Târgul Soci," Vol. 13 (1943), Nr. 1, pp. 97-98.

292. (București: Naționala, 1942). D. Bodin prepared the work.

293. *Siebenbürgen* (București: Naționala, 1943), two volumes, 795 pp.

294. Including Romanian, French, Italian, and Spanish. This was tho othor Giurescu work banned in 1948.

295. (București: Cartea Românească, 1943), 349 pp.

296. (București: Naționala, 1944), two volumes, XXVIII + 543 + L + 410 pp. An index volume was compiled and published by Gh. Gheorgescu, Gh. Ionescu, and Fl. Stănculescu in 1947.

297. See note four above. It is worth noting that a number of C.C. Giurescu's arguments against Iorga are simply continuations of his father's debates with Iorga. Cf. Giurescu, "O nouă sinteză," 1931-1932, pp. 20-22; 30-45; 164-168.

298. D. Bodin filled in for him in both posts. Bodin had been secretary of *Revista Istorică Română* since the outset and a prolific contributor and polemicist.

299. It is questionable whether the ardently patriotic Giurescu could have actually remained outside of Romania as long as there was some chance of salvaging national desiderata. Cf. his comments defending those who gave in to political necessities to save Romania for another day in *Amintiri*, pp. 121-122.

300. *Drapelul*, November 3, 1946, pp. 1-2.

301. See Cernovodeanu, *Revista* (1977) for details.

302. *Revista Istorică Română*, Vol. 15 (1945), pp. 1-14. This was Bodin's inaugural at the University.

303. See for instance, Aurelian Sacerdoțianu, *Hrisovul*, Vol. 6 (1946), pp. 160-166.

304. In the 1938-1946 period there had been some passing shots, e.g. Giurescu's comment in *Revista Istorică Română*, Vol. 13 (1943), Nr. 3, p. 99, relative to Iorga that "an evolution of views is normal, but to adopt points of view which are totally contradictory... is inadmissable for anyone who values logic and consistency."

305. Berza's article in *Revista Istorică*, Vol. 30 (1944), pp. 97-107; Giurescu's rejoinder, *Revista Istorică Română*, Vol. 16 (1946), pp. 192-193. Berza also had occasion in 1946 to lump Giurescu, Bodin, and company with the views of the Magyar specialist on Romania, Ladislas Makkai [*Revista Istorică*, Vol. 32 (1946), pp. 152 ff.]. thus "showing" the anti national results of their approach.

306. Berza won the next round when he became a history professor at the University in 1950 while Giurescu was being sent to prison. In 1974, however, the rehabilitated Giurescu outmanuevered Berza to gain membership in the Academy.

307. The title page carries the date 1946, but the printer's note in back gives 1947 and the preface is dated December 1946.

308. Vol. 17 (1947), pp. 1-53. His other articles in this period (1945-1947) included the following, all in *Revista Istorică Română*: "Livres turcs imprimțé à Bucarest (1701 et 1768)," Vol. 15 (1945), pp. 275-286: "Două vechi obligații fiscale românești: cărăturile pe cai și podvoa dele cu boii," Vol. 16 (1946), pp. 229-232: "Despre filiația lui Ștefan Lăcustă," Vol. 16 (1946), pp. 77-78: and a funeral oration for a brilliant student C. Racovița, Vol. 17 (1947), pp. 202-203. The same journal carried two review articles dealing with the work of erstwhile collaborators: one on P.P. Panaitescu's *Mircea cel Bătrân* (București: Casa Școalelor, 1944), 363 pp., in Vol. 15 (1945), pp. 413-431: and one on Gh. I. Brătianu's *Tradiția istorică despre întemeierea statelor românești* (București: Institutul de Istorie Universală N. Iorga, 1945), 263 pp., in Vol. 17 (1947), pp. 107-114. He also published a contribution in I. D. Stefănescu, ed., *Prinos închinat Inalt Prea Sfințitului Nicodim, Patriarhul României* (București: Tip. Cărtilor Bisericești, 1946): "Matei Basarab, cel mai mare ctitor bisericesc al neamului nostru. Știri noi despre lăcașurile lui," pp. 167-176.

309. A note in *Revista Istorică Română*, Vol. 16 (1946), p. 300, on V. Borcea's *Relațiile economice româno-sovietice* (1946), by Giurescu concludes: "I believe that a solid, scientific knowledge of former relations between our people [i.e., the USSR and Romania], in all areas, constitutes a sure, durable basis for their development in the future."

310. The last number of *Revista Istorică Română* contained his "Cuvânt către students (20 VI 1947)," Vol. 17 (1947), pp. 211-212.

311. The sorry tale of the Stalinization of Romanian cultural and intellectual life needs further investigation and description. Scattered details may be found in Ghița Ionescu's *Communism in Rumania, 1944-1962* (London: Oxford University Press, 1964). A general overview is presented in Al. Cretzianu, ed., *Captive Rumania* (New York: Praeger, 1956), especially pp. 128 ff., on culture, and pp. 204 ff., on education. Additional information can be gleaned from the pamphlet *The Perversion of Education in Rumania* (Washington, D.C.: The Rumanian National Committee, 1950).

312. The statutes of organization and functioning of the new Academy are printed in *Studii*, Vol. 1 (1948), Nr. 4, pp. 10-23. On the new Academy, see Traian Săvulescu, "90 de ani de viață academică în țara noastră," in C. I. Parhon, *et al.*, *90 de ani de viață academică în țara noastră* (București: Editura Academiei, 1956), especially pp. 69-77.

313. An excellent summary of the process and effects of "Sovietization" is given in Hugh Seton-Watson, *The East European Revolution*, 3rd edition (New York: Praeger, 1956), pp. 281 ff.

314. Vol. 1 (1948), Nr. 1, with an initial editorial committee including Lucrețiu Pătrășcanu, whose name vanishes from the masthead of Nr. 2 (the April-June issue).

315. Vol. 1 (1948), Nr. 1, pp. 273-306.

316. By Ion Banu, Vol. 1 (1948), Nr. 4, pp. 88-101.

317. Such as the article attacking "the Bourgeois ideology of cosmopolitanism" and American pedagogy in Vol. 2 (1949), Nr. 1, which unmasks the reactionary pedagogue and Wall Street lackey "R. Hotchins" (sic) of the University of Chicago (p. 215).

318. Vol. 1 (1948), Nr. 2, pp. 12-13.

319. Curiously enough, these *Analele* are exceedingly hard to locate in contemporary Romania.

320. *Perversion* (1950), pp. 72-75; 83-86, with ample quotations.

321. An interesting study of this process is Michael J. Rura's *Reinterpretation of History as a Method of Furthering Communism in Rumania* (Washington, D.C.: Georgetown University Press, 1961), organized around a five-fold taxonomy. Though sometimes on shaky ground concerning pre-1948 Romanian history, its liberal use of quotation is most illuminating.

322. July 11, 1948, p. 1, quoted in Rura, *Reinterpretation* (1961), p. 116.

323. Roller first appeared on the scene in 1932 as a leader of an agit-prop section in the Romanian Communist Party responsible for "Stalinist indoctrination' of the party and the intelligensia." Cf. Ionescu, *Communism* (1964), p. 45.

324. Through the infamous "Roller" text-books on Romanian history, for example *Istoria Romăniei* (București: Editura de Stat, 1947), 862 pp., with "corrected" versions appearing periodically.

325. Cf. *Amintiri*, pp. 143, 174. The manuscripts included the completed manuscript for Vol. IV of *Istoria Romănilor*, covering the period 1821-1914. Such confiscations were the basis for the huge new Biblioteca Centrală de Stat.

326. A Survey of the trends in Stephen Fischer-Galati, *The New Rumania* (Cambridge, Mass: M.I.T. Press, 1967). Cp. Ionescu, *Communism* (1964).

327. See *Studii și Referate privind Istoria Romîniei* (1954) for some idea of the humiliation Romanian historians had to undergo during this period, especially pp. 1839 ff. The flavor of this era is nicely depicted in Pieter Geyl's "Soviet Historians make their Bow," in his *Encounters in History* (Cleveland: Meridian, 1961), pp. 341-351, which describes the 10th International Congress of History in Rome, the first attended by Soviet bloc historians after World War II.

328. Cf. Grigore Arbore's interview with Acad. Emil Condurachi, "Istoria ca știință a dezvoltării ordonate," *Viața Studențească*, Vol. 25 (1981), Nr. 8, February 25, p. 3. Condurachi remarks: "a few years ago I even requested a transfer from the Faculty of History... in the faculty there are three 'archeological' strata. One, composed of the eldest, is represented by men with an exact professional training, with serious reputations, titles, and works; another formed of very well prepared younger scholars... now about forty years old. In the middle, there exists, however, a parasitic level composed of those who arrived with hasty training, the authors of skimpy doctoral theses on Romanian history, written miles from the sources... "

329. See Ion Bălu, "Dinamica receptare a trecutului," *Romania Literară*, Vol. 14 (1981), Nr. 19, May 7, p. 19, dealing with literary history. A somewhat more subdued piece on the same general theme is Dan Berindei's "A ne cunoaște și a ne cinsti istoria," *Romania Literară*, Vol. 14 (1981), Nr. 19, May 7, p. 18. Brief comments on this theme are also included in Lucian Boia's preface to Doina Elena Făget, ed., *Theorieuet method dans l'historiographia roumaine (1965-1979)* (București: Biblioteca Centrală Universitară, 1980), p. XXVIII. These and other matters are tellingly discussed in Vlad Georgescu's fascinating and excellent study of Romanian historiographical development in the 1944-1977 period: *Politica și istorie:* Cazul comuniștilor români, 1944-1977 (Munich: Jon Dumitru-Verlag, 1981), a book which was available to me only after my study was complete.

330. "Interview," his emphasis.

331. The absurd criticism of this as mere "factology" hardly deserves serious attention.

Cristian Popișteanu

PROFESSOR CONSTANTIN C. GIURESCU
AND THE MASS MEDIA

> "Many generations of people have
> brought us thus far, many generations
> of hard workers have built up a Ro-
> manian country, and in our turn we
> uplift it for those to come."
>
> C. C. Giurescu

At the time I was born Professor C. C. Giurescu was already the founder and publisher of the *Revista Istorică Română* (The Romanian Historical Review), which soon became the most important historical periodical of interwar Romania. And so, when I met him three decades later, in 1962, I was to benefit by his experience in the publication of historical periodicals designed for academic and university circles as well as for a more comprehensive public.

I was privileged constantly to cooperate with Professor C. C. Giurescu during the last 15 years of his life—a cooperation from which our first more extensive talk, was transferred tot he precincts of a friendship I was honored with to the end. C. C. Giurescu invested friendship (as well as all the relations he kept up, whether general or social), with a classical touch, permeating it with mutual respect, spiritual communion, devotion to work, earnestness in upholding his points of view, and at the same time lucidity in his estimation of the arguments of the person he was conversing with. So I knew him in the capacity of professor, fellow worker and friend. The talks we had might total hundreds of hours; he last visited me at the editorial offices of the *Magazin istoric* (Historical Magazine) on 9 November 1977, four days before he passed away, and I was amazed by the vitality that radiated from his whole being of outstanding distinction and good looks even then, with 76 years of age to his credit. It was often his guest at his home at No. 4 Monetăriei Street and at No. 47 Berzei Street, a family heritage he was very much attached to; I visited him and was visited by him on some distressing occasions when hospitalized for longer spells; we partook in many a scientific debate; I watched him delivering his address at the ceremony of his admittance to the Academy of the Socialist Republic of Romania; I saw him working at a desk in our editorial offices. I will recall here, and make explicit the fascination I experienced throughout our long-lived cooperation which has not been concluded, witness these lines. I was impressed not only and not so much by his earnestness, logic and profound intellect, by the diversity of the fields of research he tackled like a genuine poly-historian, by his method and methodology based solely on the study of documents—features which derive quite naturally from a personality that had made restraint and strictness the pivot of his professional life—but primarily by his extraordinary intellectual eagerness for whatever was *new*. Professor C. C. Giurescu's mind was in love with whatever was innovating, provided it stood the test of social utility. His discriminating mind was bent on joining a high regard for tradition, which he deemed to be *the foundation of any national history*, with an intuition for the new economic, social, scientific, technical and artistic components, which crop up in the life of nations and which he defined as *the oxygen of the onward march of every society*.

Professor C. C. Giurescu's life, activities and works offer those who have known him, and studied and analyzed his writings in many spheres of Romanian history, countless possibilities of showing to the new generations of experts in Romania and abroad, the portrait of a multi-dimensional scholar whose total coalescence with the identity of his nation did not in the least detract from the high regard and generous open-mindedness with which he considered the past and present of other nations. One of his basic beliefs centered upon the necessity and the personality of the national states which should assert itself in a world of interdependence, specific diversity and historic pluralism. Another was an unshaken faith in the universal value of reason, individual creativeness and the *sine qua non* necessity of cooperation among nations and peoples, without barriers or discrimination.

I feel it my particular duty, owing to the common experiences we have lived through, to point to a few landmarks in Professor C. C. Giurescu's views concerning the role played by mass media and its impact in the promotion of historical culture, and the assimilation of new concepts introduced in our life by modern technology.

I do it in the belief that I thus make a novel contribution rounding off the personality of this scholar and patriot, whose presence in the scientific life of his country and of the international community, as witnessed by his works, will further mirror the vigor of Romanian intellectual life.

When in the spring of 1967 Professor C. C. Giurescu learned of a projected review of historical culture, which was later to be entitled *Magazin istoric*—in memory of the revolutionary movement of the militant historians, subsequently leaders of the revolution of 1848, whose review was called *Magazin istoric pentru Dacia* (Historical Magazine for Dacia)—he asked me to come to see him. We then had a long and meaningful talk, the essence of which may be summed up as follows: the age we live through is an age of regeneration; such a periodical will help highlight the truth about our people and about everything they have endured throughtout the difficult time gone by.

Descending from a free-holder family which lived in the border district between Moldovia and Wallachia, Professor Giurescu lost no opportunity of reminding me of the necessity of thoroughly and patiently preparing and clearly thinking out a project as his ancestors did when engaging in ploughing or sowing. He often advised me to take good care, when bringing out the historical truth about the national existence of our people, not to neglect, minimize or ignore the part played by other peoples in our past, whether neighboring or more remote. He may well be said to have given the *Magazin istoric* unqualified support from the very beginning. When the first number came out he phoned me. "Where is our *Magazin istoric*? " he asked, "nowhere to be found." (His son, Professor Dinu C. Giurescu was by then on the editorial board of the magazine). Indeed the first issues had been sold out within a few hours and before long the number of copies published was on the order of hundreds of thousands.

The next time we met he was beaming, as if it had all been an achievement of his own.

"You must admit I was right," he said to me. "Our people need history, scientific truth, the glow of the past. You have found the right formula: science + the journalistic touch + polychromy + memoirs + record office information. The road to the reader's heart is now open. But there should be no curtailment of any one chapter. And always keep in touch with the reader: a constant dialogue."

Professor C. C. Giurescu did not confine himself to proffering advice and—I must confess—delighting me with his exuberance and his confidence in the future prospects of our review. For a decade he was one of the closest and most reliable contributors to the *Magazin istoric*. During those years he wrote 18 articles on many and varied subjects, not even shrinking

from occasionally answering the Editor's Mail. In most instances he phoned after every issue had come out and we would comment on the contents
of the review, not without a critical eye, of course, but always joyful to
make further headway into the path of historic truth. A great many of
the books he published were first made known to the public through
the agency of the digest in our review. "I consider it most important
and encouraging to sound out the readers of a mass-periodical such as
the *Magazin istoric*" he said to me before writing an article for our review
on Romanian forests, a grandiose topic to which he was to devote an
excellent and thus far, unique monograph. The first pages of his memoirs
(and also the last pages of the second volume which he left unfinished)
he entrusted to our review. It was due to our cooperation that he published his celebrated study on *Vlad the Impaler—Truth and Legend about
Dracula* in the reviews *Historia y Vida* of Barcelona and *Hayal Tarih Mec-
muasi* of Istanbul (both of them periodicals with wide circulation), for
which he thanked us in his United States Travel Diary, a best seller in
travel literature.

An historic fact Professor C. C. Giurescu often referred to concerned
the old-time settlement and uninterrupted life of our people in the Car-
patho-Danubian-Pontic expanse reflected in the famous phrase of Romanian peasants quoted in the oldest documents: "We are from these
parts." More than once have I heard him say that it was the task of an
historical and cultural review such as the *Magazin istoric*—the huge circulation of which gives it precedence over the specialized periodicals—
to implant and spread the truth concerning the ancient origins of the
Romanian people.

Our great voivodes, those who laid the foundations of our culture,
the outstanding personalities that have risen from among the Romanians,
had no such instrument at hand. This is more valuable than many trea-
sures, for historical truth about the life of our fathers and forefathers
cannot be suppressed, however hard the cannons might thunder at the
geates of the city. To handle such an instrument is a great honor, a great
responsibility and an overwhelming duty. It should also forge a bridge
of friendship and knowledge with other peoples.

Not infrequently throughout these years, Professor C. C. Giurescu's
signature could be seen (apart from the *Magazin istoric*) in academic
publications as well as in the more outstanding dailies (*Scînteia, România
Liberă, Scînteia Tineretului*) and in the weeklies (*Contemporanul, România literară, Săptămîna, Flacăra*), always tackling the national and
the world historical phenomenon with courage and sagacity.

It was in the autumn of 1968, on his return from his first journey to the United States, when laid up with lumbagosciatica in the clinic of the *N. Gh. Lupu* Institute of Internal Medicine, that we first talked about the role of television.

"It is an almost diabolical invention," he said. "It shortens not only distances but life itself for it turns you into a direct-participant in events taking place at that very moment hundreds and thousands of miles away. Consequently, it is a double strain." I can state that it was then, during the leisurely talk about television that the idea of his Travel Diary was born. And that was in close connection with the mass media. This is what I noted in the interview published in issue No. 1969 of the *Magazin istoric:* "I am even thinking of a number of American impressions to be collected in a volume at a later date. For the present I can briefly say that I doubt that anyone could fail to be struck by some of the dimensions of contemporary America. Primarily, the means of conveyance and communication. The development of aviation, of the famous 3- and 4-lane, two-way motor roads, of the telephone, of wireless and television, is of such proportions that it is hard to grasp it all from the outside."

Professor C. C. Giurescu had delivered lectures over the radio every since the Romanian Broadcasting Station had been created and in recent years he had been one of the most sought after guests on the T.V. services. "Thanks to radio and to television, new prospects are opening up for enriching the human mind," Professor C. C. Giurescu opined. He would dwell on the absolute necessity of assigning an ever more important part to the radio and to television, in the field of education and training, without neglecting, however, the informational and the entertainment sectors. He considered television and radio as a valuable aid for the educational system in all countries, and more particularly in bridging the gaps in public education in the developing countries of Asia, Africa and Latin America. I also remember that in one of his last T.V. interviews Professor C. C. Giurescu eulogized the family, which he considered as the soundest cell of society, and pointed to the danger of television monopolizing the children's attention.

However ingenious T.V. games, cartoons and the like may turn children into uni-dimensional audio-visual addicts. Reading, learning, the intellectual effort made in digesting and thinking things out for oneself, cannot and should not be superseded by anthing. Or we may run the risk of creating little living robots with some of man's fundamental intellectual endowments atrophied."

C. C. Giurescu was a great supporter of historical films, whether documentary or of the fiction type. He acted as a consultant for many cinema and T.V. productions. His last work, which he concluded before the violent and ruthless cerebral-vascular accident which put an end to his life while he sat as his writing desk, was a report on a historical film.

In the course of his research work C. C. Giurescu gave his attention to the Romanian contributions to the history of world science and technology, and because of that he took great interest in contemporary developments in this field. The present succession of discoveries, inventions and innovations in the most varied fields and the newly created technologies, he described as "the great revolution of the human mind." More than once did I find him reading a prospectus on the most sophisticated mechanisms, obviously with a desire to incorporate in history the new world of scientific and technological knowledge.

The revolutionary transformations in the mass communication facilities in the second half of the 20th century were well known to him, but he was also interested in the latest innovations in electronics, aviation, chemistry, and computer technologies. I took note of some of these observations.

"There is a tendency to oust from history these unprecedented gains of mankind's inventiveness, which make people speak of a second scientific and technological revolution (actually the most complete scientific and technological revolution so far) and to place them somewhere between heaven and earth. That is a mistake. The phase we live through is the crowning achievement of everything man has been tenaciously and intelligently devising ever since he was born on earth. Science has now become a direct production factor and the scientist a worker equipped, of course, with tools other than conventional ones. A higher level of knowledge and training of the workers and peasants on the one hand, and the technicians' and scientists' participation in production on the other hand, leads to new alloys—not only technological, but social ones as well.

It is, however, essential to understand that everything, including the swift-paced technological and scientific progress which has taken us to other planets, in part of the history of society; that nothing takes place beyond the scope of mankind's action, that nothing *can* take place beyond it."

In his memoirs, Professor C. C. Giurescu contends that a "pure race exists in theory only and, as proved by scientific research, the addition of foreign blood far from being a drawback is on the contrary an advantage." in our talks he told me that there was no such thing as science *per se*, but only fundamental research followed by social correlations and applications subject to the general law of history in its evolution and development.

I will conclude this micro-portrait by quoting a phrase which I consider to express his intimate conviction: "man is the demiurge and the supreme creation, the finality of life on earth."

THE "DARK MILLENARY" IN THE HISTORY OF THE ROMANIANS AS SEEN BY CONSTANTIN C. GIURESCU

For about two centuries an unfounded view has prevailed in historical research concerning Eastern Europe, namely that there was a gap of a thousand years in the history of the Romanians and of their Daco-Roman forebears—from the time when the Roman army and Roman administration left Transdanubian Dacia under emperor Aurelian (271) to the great Mongolian invasion (1241). This was a view easy to implant at a time when neither archaeological excavations nor the investigation of public records, ethnography and linguistics had revealed material vestiges, medieval hoards, inscriptions and historical documents, or sufficient linguistic and toponymic proof to build up a thousand years' interval in Dacia's past history. It might, however, be interesting to note that though the sources of information were scarce, the scholars in other countries ever since the 15th century, and the Romanian scholars from the 17th and 18th centuries onward had built up a unitary and vertical picture of the essential elements of the history of the Romanian people, vis-a-vis: the Daco-Roman origin of the people, their continued life in Dacia from the 3rd to the 13th centuries, the unity as to descent, language and forms of life and culture, of the Romanians of Transylvania, Moldavia and Wallachia, otherwise said of the whole territory of what had been Roman Dacia. The authors we have in mind relied on the statements of the Byzantine chroniclers, on the irrefutably Latin quality of the Romanian language, on toponymy and on the admirable *consensus omnium* among the Romanians in maintaining that, as their name shows, they were the descendants of the Romans and had been living in their "Romanian country" from time immemorial.

Nevertheless, in the late 18th century the historians' curiosity and exigencies in respect of the "dark millenary" were heightened by two circumstances: the ever more potent assertion of the national consciousness of the Romanians living in the principalities of Moldavia and Wallachia

under the domination of the Ottoman Empire, and in Transylvania under
the domination of the Habsburg Empire, which meant intolerable political, social and economic oppression.[1] Secondly, the fact that in support
of their political claims, they advanced their historical right as the oldest
inhabitants of the three principalities. The stand they took induced a
reaction on the part of certain Austrian, Hungarian and German historians and their attacks, which relied on an over-simple interpretation of
a passage in the work of Flavius Vopiscus, one of Aurelian's biographers,
stating that the emperor "had left Dacia, the province founded by Trajan
north of the Danube, relinquishing all hope of being able to maintain it,
and had withdrawn from it the army and the provincial people," settling
them South of the Danube.[2] An added argument was the absence or the
scarcity of sources of information on the population of Dacia during the
"dark millenary." These historians evolved a new theory: Dacia having
been vacated by the autochthonous population at the end of the 3rd
century, the Romanian nation was supposedly formed South of the
Danube, to settle North of the Danube (on the territory of today's Romania), only in the 12th and 13th centuries. Under the circumstances,
the Romanians were not entitled to claim their historical right as the
oldest inhabitants of Transylvania. Though upheld by the Austrian Franz
Joseph Sulzer (1781), the Transylvanian Saxon Joseph Carol Eder (1791),
the Austrian Johan Christian Engel (1804), the German Robert Roesler
(1871) and the Hungarian Pal Hunfalvy (1877), this theory has been categorically rejected by most European historians, including Jiulius Jung
(1876), Edouard Sayous (1876), Joseph Ladislau Lic (1882), L. Ranke
(1883), Theodor Mommsen (1885), Traugott Tamm (1891), and by all
Romanian historians.[3] Relying on a careful analysis of Latin, Byzantine,
Slav, Arabic, Armenian and Persian statements, on archaeological vestiges,
linguistic evidence and toponymy, the aforementioned authors proved
that only a small part of Dacia's Roman population (the army, the administration clerks, the well-to-do people) had withdrawn South of the
Danube in 271, while most of the inhabitants had remained behind, and
that in consequence the space where the Romanian people was formed
was the whole of Dacia's territory. Thus, the other arguments of what
was described as "Roesler's theory" could not hold their ground. It had
also been proved that the obstinate defense of this theory in the Austro-
Hungarian Empire had no scientific foundations, but relied on subjective
political reasons, for the theory was directed against the struggle for national liberation of the Romanians of Transylvania. But it is just as true
that "Roesler's theory" laid so much stress on the ex silentio argument

that "the dark millenary" image was built up on the minds of many authors (the German historian asserts that it is impossible that the Romanian people should have been formed North of the Danube "for nowhere on that territory are Romanians or Wallachians mentioned, at least not by trustworthy historical sources." Thus, the well-known medievalist, Ferdinand Lot stated in 1935: "Never from the end of the 4th century to the 13th century is there any mention made of a Roman population living in what had formerly been Dacia: an impressive muteness that lasted for ten centuries." Taking up the formula lauched by the Romanian historian Alexandru D. Xenopol (*Une énigme historique: les Roumains au Moyen Age*, Paris, 1885), Lot comes to a conclusion which has given rise to much discussion, namely that the Romanian people were "an enigma and a historical miracle."[5] This statement was elegantly and categorically refuted by Lot's disciple, the Romanian historian Gheorghe Brătianu, in one of his works where stress was also laid on the logical impossibility of the more recent theories evolved by a number of Bulgarian, Hungarian, Russian and other historians concerning the territory where the Romanian people were formed; by accepting such theories we would reach "the paradoxical yet obvious conclusion that this people, which has no history, has no origin and no homeland either. This would indeed be a hopeless conclusion, if it weren't laughable."[6]

The use made of the "dark millenary" as a political argument in the campaigns against the right of the Romanians to their national territory has led to a result that their opponents would gladly have dispensed with, for it stimulated Romanian historiography in its efforts to throw as much light as was possible on Dacia's evolution during the 4th to the 13th centuries. We will not enlarge on the progress made in the historical sciences in Romania, vis.: in archaeology, epigraphy, numismatics, linguistics and other disciplines which adduced new proofs relating to the origin of the Romanian people, to the territory of their formation, thus scattering the darkness put forward as an argument by their opponents of the theory of Roman continuity in Dacia. There is not a single Romanian historian of the last century who has not devoted to this subject at least part of his works, but Constantin C. Giurescu is remarkable in this research sector for initiatives and contributions that have not been sufficiently emphasized so far.

Constantin C. Giurescu was never impressed by the difficulties the "dark millenary" raises for a historian. With a thorough knowledge of documents and a great gift for interpreting significant details, he made use in his reconstructions of plain, sound reasoning founded on common sense rather than on risky hypotheses. This accounts for the feeling of certainty and comfort one has when resorting to his works. From Romanian and foreign historiography he always selected the theses that had been properly checked, the facts relying on profound arguments, the genuine documents.[7] But with his bent for an all-round historical outlook on human phenomena, he extended the area of information resorting to sources that had been seldom or never used previously, launching into reconstructions of material civilization activities that threw light on the economic as well as the political history of the Romanian people.[8]

And so, whenever he is faced with problems to all appearances difficult to solve, the Romanian historian does not waver, and neither does he give up the struggle; never resorting to fanciful hypotheses, he confidently uses his method strictly within the limits of scientific truth. In his compact *History of the Romanians,* he asks a number of questions in relation to the co-habitation of the Daco-Romanians with the Slavs: "What were the relations between the Romanic population of Dacia and the Slav invaders? How numerous were the Slavs and what became of them?" These are questions referring to the darkest period of our history, concerning which there is hardly any document, any evidence, and yet these questions must be answered if we are determined to *understand* historical facts and are not content merely to note them. Our answer will obviously include a hypothesis; this is unavoidable wherever facts are non-existing. The hypothesis will, however, start from *such facts as are known.* The history of the thousand years elapsed between the year 271, the year of the withdrawal from Dacia, and 1247, the date of the Diploma of the Knights of St. John, where the first Romanian political formations are recorded[9]—the history of this long period of darkness—may be made clear by starting from two extremities: Trajan's Dacia and Wallachia. With a thorough knowledge of the state of things in the two political formations at the extremities of the "dark millenary," with a knowledge of their social, administrative and economic organization, we will be able to realize what was the course of events during the intermediary period.[10]

With the information available four decades ago, Constantin C. Giurescu reconstructed the 271-1247 interval in the history of Roman Dacia, thus throwing light on the "dark millenary" in many respects. Archaeological vestiges, the hoards of money, and especially a careful analysis of the words in our language, led to conclusions that revealed forms of life, human relations, institutions, intercourse between the autochthonous population and the migratory peoples, which made it possible to see through the mist resulting from the absence of documents and to figure out with increasing clarity organized productive collectivities with a spiritual life and a counteance of their own; first the Daco-Romans, and subsequently the Romanians, constituting a distinct ethnical formation.[11]

But during the forty years that have elapsed since the last edition of his *History of the Romanians*, research work—especially archaeological research—has made considerable progress, and the author himself enriched and clarified his vision of the life of the Daco-Romans and of the Romanians during the "dark millenary," of their material civilization and their political, military and social organization. It is the vision shown in the first volume of the *History of the Romanians*, which has been revised, enlarged and republished jointly with his son, the historian Dinu. C. Giurescu,[12] and also in his address on the occasion of his reception as member of the Academy of the Socialist Republic of Romania (15 February 1979), titled: *Romania during the Migrations Millenary. Considerations on a Number of Aspects.*[13] This last work conclusively shows Constantin C. Giurescu's stand when facing the problems raised by the "dark millenary," for the historian sets forth here the very essence of the information, arguments and results achieved in his studies, whether of older or of more recent date.

And so, Giurescu states, owing to the progress made in our investigations—especially archaeological investigations—concerning the 271-1247 millenary "even though that interval has not been fully elucidated in every respect, I believe that one thing has been clearly established—and I have said it before on other occasions—namely that the formation of the Romanian people is neither an "enigma" nor a "miracle," as has been stated not only by foreign historians and linguists but also by Romanian ones; it is a normal phenomenon similar to that which gave rise to the French Italian, Spanish and Portuguese nations, that is to the other Romanic nations."[14] There is a typical model in the formation of these nations. Roman colonists settled amidst a basic ethnic element (Gauls, Celtiberi, Daco-Getae), introducing the popular Latin language and Roman civilization and culture. They assimilated the autochthonous element, giving rise to a new ethnical synthesis (Gallo-Romans, Ibero-Romans, Daco-Romans). It was upon these ethnical combinations that the migratory elements (Germanic elements in Western Europe and Slav ones in Southeast Europe) exerted their influence. Everywhere, the migratory populations were assimilated by the Romanic populations amidst which they settled. Secondary migratory elements (Arabs in the Iberian Peninsula and in Southern Italy, Normans in Northern France and Southern Italy,

the Germanic Gepides, the Iranian Alanes, the Petchenegs and Turkic
Cumans in Dacia) were in their turn assimilated, melting away in the
masses of Romanic populations. "There is consequently a perfect paral-
lelism between the formation of the Romanian people and the formation of the other Romanic peoples."[15]

While underlining that it was absurd to suppose that the Romanized
population of Dacia had gone south of the Danube in 271-275, when the
Roman army and Roman administration withdrew, Giurescu supported
the idea of Daco-Roman continuity on Romania's present-day territory,
relying on the analogy with the other Romanic nations. "Has it ever
occurred to anyone," the historian asks, "to deny or to question the
continuity of the French people in Gaul, of the Spanish or the Portuguese people of the Iberian peninsula, and of the Italian people in Italy?
Has any historian admitted as a fact that the Gallo-Romans had left their
homes in Gaul to cross the Alps or the Pyrenees and to return home only
centuries later? Or again that the Spaniards had crossed the Straits of
Gibraltar into Africa to return to their ancient territory centuries later?
Such questions are in themselves proof of their groundlessness, of their
inanity. And things were not different in Dacia. Actually until the end of
the 17th century, nobody had put forth the view that the Daco-Roman
peasants, shepherds and craftsmen of the Carpatho-Danubian territory,
with Transylvania as its center, could have left their ancestral lands to
cross the Danube into the Balkan Peninsula and return many centuries
later. Such an absurd theory was only evolved when political, and not
scientific considerations came to the fore, the purpose being to deny the
Romanian people their right to Transylvania, a right that is founded on
priority, continuity, numbers and work."[16]

Adducing archaeological and linguistic arguments to prove the uninterrupted presence of the Romanic population in Dacia during the migrations millenary, the historian dwells on a number of terms and toponyms
which can only be accounted for by Daco-Roman and Romanian continuity. The term *păcură* (petroleum, from the Latin *picula*) is not to be
found in any Romanic language apart from Romanian for the reasons
that nowhere else in Europe, excepting in Dacia, petroleum had been
exploited in ancient times. The migratory populations (Slavs and Hungarians) had no term for this product; they used the Romanian term,
which they had borrowed from the autochthonous population, whom
they had found over the Carpatho-Danubian area when they reached
that area. The Dobrudjan toponyms—the *Vicina* port (on the Danube),
the *Portita* Straits (on the Black Sea coast), the heights of *Biserica* (from

basilica), for the early Romanians considered the ruins to be found there as ancient places of worship——all of Latin origin—prove that there was here a Romanic population, when the migratory Slavs and Bulgarians came over.[17]

In sifting the information referring to historic geography, ethnography, toponymy and linguistics that had been seldom used before him, Giurescu was able to throw light on the "dark millenary," building up a unexpected picture of the Romanians' *way of life* and *pursuits* during that long historical period. And the fact that during that millenary 70 percent of Dacia's hills and plains were covered with forests (which were only cleared in the comparatively recent past), enables the historian to oppose an older theory according to which the Daco-Romans and subsequently the Romanians had taken shelter in the mountains when the migratory population overran their territory (a theory supported by J. Thunmann, J. A. Vaillant, G. Ubicini, Miletici, Leon Homo and by many Romanian historians, including A. D. Xenopol, and even by an American, James D. Doyes[18]), and to prove that the ideal place of refuge before invasions was the forest, which the migratory populations used to the steppe, avoided. In the shelter of the forests, the Romanians continued in their ancient pursuits, inherited from Roman civilization. Giurescu illustrates this by the persistence in Dacia of *water mills*, a typically Roman grinding installation, described by Vitruvius in *De architectura* (1st century B.C.), which the Romanians could not have come to know only in the 8th or the 12th centuries, as certain authors would have it, but had used it uninterruptedly ever sine the Roman period. In proof of it stands the terminology, which is exclusively of Latin origin, as well as toponymy and the proverbs which include the words *to grind* (*a măcina* in Romanian) and *mill* (*moară* in Romanian, from the Latin *machina* and *mola*).[19]

The reconstruction of the forms of life and work among the Romanians during the "dark millenary" enables us to estimate Giurescu's progress over the last four decades, in lighting up this controversial period in the history of his people. After forty years he opposes to the non-scientific theory claiming that no Romanic population had persisted on Dacia's territory after 271, not only the proofs of the presence of such a population but *the very picture of their material life*, a feat beyond anyone's expectations. The compact picture he gives in the first volume of his *History of the Romanians* (1974) and in his address on being received as a member of the Academy, had been pieced together, with effort and archaeological accuracy, in other fundamental works of his, every detail being justified by material vestiges, documents and arguments, whether ethnographic or linguistic. We have in mind *The History of the Romanian Forest from the Earliest Ages to Date* (1975)[20]—Constantin C. Giurescu's contribution to the history of Romanian technology—which makes the most frequent references to the "dark millenary," mostly in the chapters: "The Carpatho-Danubian Forests in Prehistoric Times in Dacia and in Roman Dacia" and "Forests during the Migration Period."

The author corrects the misrepresentation of Dacia as a plain offering vast arable areas by showing that until a few centuries ago, those areas were covered with age-old forests the clearing of which continued up to the 19th century. No one but the natives of the country could find their bearings in the thick of those forests. Foreign armies were wary of venturing into them. In 75-74 B.C., Gaius Scribonius Curio, Proconsul of Macedonia, reached the Danube but did not venture to cross it, fearing "the darkness of the woods" (*Curio Dacia tenus venit, sed tenebras saltuum expavit*). In 87 A.D., Cornelious Fuscus, another Roman general, *did* make his way into Dacia's forests, but was defeated by King Decebalus. During the two wars waged to conquer Dacia in 101-102 and 105-106, the Romans often fought in thickly wooded areas, as shown on Trajan's Column.[22] The only lines of communication that made it easier for the migratory populations to make their way into Dacia were the river valleys. Being used to the steppe, these populations avoided forests and their misleading thickness. The Cumans named *Teleorman* (mad forest) the extensive forests in the southwest of Wallachia, and the Turks gave the same name (*Deliorman*) to the forests in the south of Dobrudja. The migratory populations were awed by the country's forests and many of the toponymy of foreign origin on Dacia's territory designate varieties of forests and of trees.

Inter-Carpathian Dacia was named *Erdely*—wooded land—by the Hungarians (whence the Romanian term *Ardeal* is derived; *Transylvania*, wich is of Latin origin, means "beyond the forest"); southern Transylvania is named *Sylva Blacorum et Bissenorum* (the forest of the Romanians and of the Petchenegs) in a Magyar document of the year 1224; the Slavs named *Vlasca* (the Romanians' land) the wooded area of Wallachia and Moldavia, and the also named *Vlăsia* (same meaning) the widespread forest north of Bucharest. Rivers, counties and geographic areas bear names of the same family given by the Slav migrators: *Bucovina* (from the Slav *buk*—beech); *dumbravă* (from *dyb*—oak); *Ilfov* (from *elha*—alder); *Tutova* (from *tut*—blackberries); *zăvoi* (river-side woods), and so forth. Forests were natural defense works and, according to testimonies of the 16th century (Verancsics)[23] and of the 17th century (Paul of Aleppo),[24] this was one of the reasons why the Turks decided against occupying the Romanian countries.[25] During the invasions (in the "dark millenary" and also later at the time of the Tatar and the Ottoman onslaughts), the Romanians withdrew into the forests. After a first clash, they would arrive at some peaceful form of cohabitation with the invaders to whom they ceded part of their agricultural produce or of their livestock.[26] Forests not only afforded protection, but also excellent living conditions, considering the stage of the economy in those days, from cattle-breeding and hunting, to tillage, fruit-growing, and bee-keeping (in glades and clearings), also providing materials for housebuilding, fortifications and a varied cottage industry.

Writing the first monograph on Romanian forests and bringing out their role in the history, economy and civilization of his people, Constantin C. Giurescu had increased his own contribution to the lighting up of the "dark millenary," and has provided scientific proof of Romanian continuity in Dacia and of the orign of the Romanians. His efforts to gear historical research towards making use of documents showing a material civilization, towards the vestiges that reveal the evolution of technology, towards the study of old-time pursuits (agriculture, sylviculture, hunting, wine-making, bee-keeping, fishing, and the like) open up unexpected vistas in the reconstruction of past Romanian history. It is always fascinating work to read the books he wrote on the subject, for they reveal hitherto unknown aspects of the history of the Romanian people and suggest to the reader questions, associations and hypotheses which stimulate further investigations.

When describing "the prohibited or reserved areas in which nobody had access for such purposes as cutting wood, making hay, cattle grazing, hunting, fishing or picking forest fruit without the owner's permission"[27] —the so-called preserves (branişti, from the Slav braniti, to forbid)— Giurescu writes about a "preserve law," an institution which the Daco-Romans also had and, most probably, the Daco-Getae too. In that case, it is tantalizing to ask whether the interdiction of entering a preserve did not have reasons other than juridical and economic in Dacian and Daco-Roman antiquity—namely spiritual reasons: the protection of sacred areas such as those reserved for the druids in Gaul.[28]

Forests not only did duty as the Romanians' providential shelter from invasions, on which Giurescu insists with good reason; they also offered the Romanians an advantage they made good use of in their relations with the migrating populations who, without the cooperation of the natives, who knew their ins and outs, could not have travelled easily over the occupied territory. In *Strategicon* (XI, 4, 30 and 38) Mauricius proves that he knows the two functions of the forest for the inhabitants north of the Danube, when he writes about the Slavs and Ants who, living in the vicinty of forests, easily sought refuge in them (obviously those were Slavs who had become sedentary and had adopted the ways of life of the Romanians); then, as a warning against the "refugees" (*rhephougous*) "sent to show us the way"—i.e., the Romanized people who had withdrawn south of the Danube and who were used as guides by the Byzantine forces in their expeditions north of that river, he writes: "even though they are Romans," they may mislead the Byzantines.[29] That the Romanians were employed for such jobs is also recorded by Anna Comnena, who stated that in 1094 the Cumans "had learned from the Wallachians the paths through the forests" and had thus been able to cross the Balkan Mountains and to fall upon the Byzantines.[30]

Finally, to the toponymus *Teleorman* and *Deliorman* mentioned by the great historian in order to show the awe the widespread, impenetrable forests inspired in the Turks, we should add two phrases: *agac denisi* (sea of forests), which Mehment Nesri uses to describe Wallachia, and *cenglistan* (wooded hiding place), whereby Husein describes the inaccessible lands of Moldavia.[31]

Although Constantin C. Giurescu did not mention the above passages and phrases in the Byzantine and Turkish authors, he showed how they could be correctly understood, how they fitted into the picture of Romanian life for the reconstruction of which he devoted so much effort and ingenuity.

NOTES

1.   Two recent works sum up conclusively the "dark millenary" notion in European and Romanian historiography: Adolf Armbruster, *La Romanité des Roumains. Histoire d'une idée*, translated by Cireaşa Grecscu, Bucharest, Publishing House of the Academy of the Socialist Republic of Romania, 1977, 279 p., and Nicolae Stoicescu, *Continuitatea românilor. Privire istoriografică, istoricul problemei, dovezile continuită-tii* (Continuity of the Romanians. Historiographic Outlook, History of the Problem, Proofs of Continuity), Bucharest, Scientific and Encyclopaedic Publishing House, 1980, 247 p. These books enable a survey of the European historians' outlook on the past of the Romanians and of their forebearers of the 3rd to the 13th centuries; on the way it was formed and it evolved; on how it was discussed and came to be credited.

2. *Scriptores Historiae augustae, Aurel.* 39,7, in *Fontes Historiae Daco-romanes,* II, Bucharest, 1970, p. 108, information taken from Eutopius IX, 15, 1 by a hypothetical author, see ibid., p. 38.

3. See the bibliography of the controversy in N. Stoicescu, op. cit., pp. 25-84.

4. Ferdinand Lot, *Les invasions barbares et le peuplement de l'Europe, considérés comme introduction a l'intelligence des derniers traites de paix,* Paris, 1937, 282 p.

5. Op. cit., pp. 278-300. P. Mustafciev, a Bulgarian historian well known for his anti-Romanian stand, had stated in his work *Bulgares et Roumains dans l'histoire des pays danubiens,* Sofia, 1932, p. 279, that the Romanian people were "the only people of Europe not to have had a history of their own up to the end of the Middle Ages." (!)

6. Gheorghe I. Brătianu, *Une énigme et un miracle historique: le peuple roumain,* Bucarest, 1937, p. 281.

7. Constantin C. Giurescu has left "works remarkable for their vesiment: system, organization, right proportions, clarity, communicativeness, information richness, maps, illustrations, technical care. The eloquent testimony of an orderly spirit." (Reply of David Prodan, member of the Academy, in *Academia Republicii Socialiste România, Discursuri de recepție* (The Academy of the Socialist Republic of Romania, Reception speeches), New series, 1975, No. 6, p. 25.

8. See I. M. Ștefan, *Constantin C. Giurescu, a Historian of Romanian Science and Technology,* in "Noesis. Travaux du Comité Roumain d'Histoire et de Philosophie des Sciences," VIII, 1981, pp. 113-118, bibliography of the works the historian devoted to Romanian material civilization.

9. In *Istoria românilor* (The History of the Romanians), fourth edition, vol. I, Bucharest, 1942, p. 288, Giurescu mentions older Romanian political formations dating back to the 9th and 10th centuries. In Constantin C. Giurescu and Dinu C. Giurescu, *Istoria românilor,* vol. I, Bucharest, 1974, pp. 157-162, a whole chapter is devoted to "The First Romanian Political Formations" of the 9th through the 13th centuries.

10. Constantin C. Giurescu, *Istoria românilor,* 4th edition, vol. I, Bucharest, 1972, p. 264.

11. Op. cit., pp. 185-341.

12. Constantin C. Giurescu and Dinu C. Giurescu, *Istoria românilor,* vol. I, Bucharest, 1974, p. 147 (*Our Forebears' Main Pursuits during the 275-1241 Interval*) and 163-209 (*The Daco-Romans and subsequently the Romanians during the Migration Period*).

13. In "Academia R. S. România. Discursuri de recepție," New series No. 6, 1975, p. 27; published in *Discursuri de recepție la Academia Română* (Reception Speeches at the Romanian Academy, edited by Octav Păin and Antoineta Tănăsescu, Bucharest, 1980, pp. 339-351.

14. *Românii în mileniul migrațiilor* (The Romanians during the Migrations Millenary), p. 6-7.

15. Ibid., p. 7.

16. Ibid., pp. 7-8.

17. Ibid., pp. 9-10.

18. See his work *Romania. The Border Land of the Christian and the Turk*, New York, 1857, quoted by Constantin C. Giurescu, op. cit., p. 12.

19. Ibid., pp. 14-17.

20. Bucharest, Ceres Publishing House, 1975, p. 388; second edition 1976; concise English version *A History of the Romanian Forest*, translated by Eugenia Farca, Bucharest, Publishing House of the Academy of the Socialist Republic of Romania, 1980, p. 258.

21. Op. cit., pp. 11-37; English version, pp. 11-24.

22. Op. cit., pp. 19-20; English version, pp. 13-14.

23. Op. cit., pp. 29-30, 263; English version, pp. 221-22, 182. But many toponims for the same notions were derived from Dacian or Latin words ibidem, pp. 22-27.

24. Op. cit., pp. 20-21, 46; English version, pp. 14, 32.

25. Cf. Virgil Cândea, *Sources byzantines et orientales concernant les Roumains*, in "Revue des études sud-est européennes," 16, 1978, p 305..

26. Constantin C. Giurescu and Dinu C. Giurescu, *Istoria românilor*, vol. I, pp. 171, 177.

27. *Istoria pădurii românești*, p. 55; English version, p. 40.

28. Caesar, *De bello gallico* VI, 13; Mircea Eliade, *A History of Religious Ideas*, translated by W. R. Trask, vol. II, Chicago and London, 1980, chap. XXI, 172. Henry Thedenat, *Lucus*, in Ch. Daremberg, Ed. Saglio et Edm. Pottier, *Dictionnaire des antiquités grecques et romaines*, t. III2, Paris, 1904, pp. 1351-1356.

29. *Fontes Historiae Daco-romanae*, II, Bucharest, 1970, pp. 563, 561.

30. Ana Comnena, *Alexias* X, II, 3, in *Fontes Historiae Daco-Romannae*, III, Bucharest, 1975, p. 114; Virgil Cândea, *Conceptul de independență—o permanență a gîndirii politice românești*, (The Concept of Independence—Permanent in Romanian Political Thought), in N. Ecobescu (ed); *Suveranitatea și progresul* (Sovereignty and Progress), Bucharest, 1977, pp. 60-61.

31. Mihail Guboglu and Mehmet Mustafa, editors, *Cronici turcești privind țările române* (Turkish Chronicles Concerning the Romanian Countries), excerpts, vol. I, Bucharest, 1966, pp. 116 and 458.

Raymond McNally

ORIGINS OF THE SLAVIC NARRATIVES ABOUT THE HISTORICAL DRACULA*

This article is an attempt to present a coherent theory about the origins of the Slavic Dracula narratives in the light of recent research in Romanian folklore and Russian history. The Slavic Dracula tales were written down in the late fifteenth century. Copies were made from the fifteenth to the eighteenth centuries in Russia.[1] These tales are not really traditionally acceptable historical sources in the modern sense, nor are they strictly fiction. They are a mixture of both. In fact, the Russian historian Nicholas Karamzin considered the Dracula "story" to be the first "historical novel" in Russian literature.[2] There are some twenty-two extant Slavic manuscripts about Dracula in Russian archives,[3] but the name of the original author is unknown, and the exact motives behind the story are the subject of an intense scholarly controversy.

The original tale was written between 1481 and February, 1486, at which time the first Kirillo-Belozersk manuscript copy was made by the monk Efrosin. This copy comes from the Kirillo-Belozersk Monastery in northern Russia. The extant copy itself was made around 1490 and was itself copied from a manuscipt penned before 1486, as stated in the text. The original may have been written down by a Russian diplomat who had been in Hungary and Moldavia during the 1480s, possibly Fedor Kuritsyn.[4] Since Dracula had lived in Buda for ten years, oral tales about him were probably still circulating when Kuritsyn or some other Russian emissary arrived there. Kuritsyn may been begun writing part of the Dracula story first from such oral tales which he could have heard in Budapest, or else the story could have been written down by some other diplomat to the Hungarian court at some other date.

Less than five years after Dracula's death, Ivan III, Tsar of Russia,[5] sent Fedor Kuritsyn, a good friend and confidant, to King Mathias Corvinus of Hungary as his emissary in 1482.[6] Kuritsyn must have spent at least six to nine months in Hungary.[7] Kuritsyn was one of the leaders of the Muscovite heretics known as "Judaizers." These heretics were against the feudal landowning Church championed by Joseph of Volokolamsk and in favor of the reforms associated with Nil Sorsky. Kuritsyn, like some of the other heretics, had a deep faith in the necessity of a harsh but good ruler.

But the question of the exact authorship of the Slavic manuscripts in Russia is still a matter of unsettled dispute among scholars. For example, it has been claimed that Fedor Kuritsyn could not have written down the story, because he supposedly had not returned to Moscow by 1486, the date which the copyist, the monk Efrosin, gave as the one on the document from which he made his copy.[8] But in fact Fedor Kuritsyn had returned to Moscow by 1486.

Another scholar has attributed the work to Ivan Volk Kuritsyn, Fedor Kuritsyn's brother, and has claimed that this Dracula story came into Russia by means of the Hanseatic trade routes through Novgorod around 1500, like other western importants at the time, such as the *Lusidarios* and *Povest' o Troje*. In support of this thesis, evidence has been presented to show that Ivan Volk Kuritsyn was a friend of Bartolomaeus Gothan, an agent in the Russian diplomatic service who later, according to a theory without any substantial evidence or proof, published one of the earliest Dracula pamphlets in German, at Lubeck.[9] There is not even any solid historical evidence that the Lubeck pamphlet was published before the Slavic tale about Dracula was written.

Furthermore, the German Lubeck pamphlet could not have served as the source of the Slavic Dracula story in Russia, because there are entire important sections in the Slavic manuscripts which do not exist in the German pamphlet. Specifically, the Slavic manuscripts mention events relating to Dracula's death early in 1477, whereas the German pamphlet does not even cite the data surrounding Dracula's death and its historical aftermath. It is, of course, possible that these details could have been added at the end of an imported Lubeck text, but this would not account for the other sections not in the Lubeck pamphlet and the entire tone of the Slavic tales. Furthermore, the entire construction of the Slavic tales and the inherent interpretation of Dracula's reign are different from the German pamphlet, though a fairly common set of anecdotes can be found in both: for example, in the German version, Dracula implaes a cowardly monk who praised his deeds and rewards a monk who condemned his cruelties, but in the Slavic manuscripts the opposite occurs— Dracula impales the monk who condemned his cruelties and rewards the monk who praised Dracula's cruel deeds.

The eminent Russian academician M. P. Alekseev assumed that the Slavic Dracula story could have been brought in 1475[10] to Moscow by the Italian architect Aristotle Fioranti who had been in Hungary in 1467. But in 1467 Aristotle Fioranti could not possibly have known about the second reign of Dracula in 1476 and his death, or the reign of Vlad the Monk—all items which are present in the Slavic manuscript.[11] Since Vlad the Monk came to the throne in 1481, the Slavic tale had to have been written down after 1481. Here one would have to assume that these details were added at the end of the text by some unknown copyist, in order to support Alekseev's theory.

Yet another Russian scholar A. D. Sedel'nikov, considers that the reference to the coming to the throne of Vlad the Monk in 1481 was simply a date when the story was sent off or dispatched. Sedel'nikov contends that a better date could be the reference to the death of one of the sons of Dracula, the one who was living with the bishop of Oradea. The author and his friends could have been in Oradea (Varadin) at the death of Dracula's son, and one of them could have written the entire story there. In discussing this thesis Lur'e states that "this date is unfortunately not known to us,"[12] meaning the date of the death of one of Dracula's sons. It is known to the present author.

From the genealogical research of George Florescu, it is clear that Dracula had three sons: 1) an illegitimate son named Mihnea (or Mikhail) who had been born around 1470; 2) a son named Vlad who was still living in 1498; and 3) another son, whose name is unknown, who died before 1486. It must be the death of this son of Dracula which is referred to in the Slavic manuscript. If so, this evidence also supports the theory that the Slavic story about Dracula must have been written down before 1486, probably between 1481 and 1486.

A general challenge to any Russian authorship of the Slavic tale has been issued by Sedel'nikov and the Romanian scholars N. Smochină, Petre Panaitescu, Alexandru Boldur and Pandele Olteanu. It has been claimed that the original text was written in a South Slavic language, specifically Middle-Bulgarian under Serbian influence and that the text was subsequently russified in the copying.[13] Phonetic, morphological, and lexical pecularities have been pointed out as not characteristic of the Russian written language of the fifteenth century.[14] But these pecularities have been demonstrated as being present in the Kievan and Muscovite written language, and errors of interpretation on faulty historical-linguistic grounds have been cited.[15] Smochină's contention that the Dracula story was written by a Transylvanian Romanian and translated into old Russian

seems very unlikely for the following reasons: As Panaitescu himself
pointed out, the author of the Slavic tale does not even know the name
of Dracula's capital city, Tîrgoviște; in the text he calls it simply "his
city." If, as it is claimed, the Dracula story was written by some Wallachian or a Transylvanian Romanian, such a person would certainly
have known the name of the capital city of Wallachia.[16]

Fortunately there is a way of combining many of these arguments
into a synthesis: On his way back to Moscow, Fedor Kuritsyn stopped
off in Suceava at the court of Stephen the Great (1457-1504). It is known
that Stephen attached some of his envoys to Kuritsyn's entourage in the
summer of 1484. It is possible that these Moldavian envoys influenced
the political tone of the Dracula story, namely, the outrage at Dracula's
conversion to Roman Catholicism. Stephen and his followers wished to
solidify the Moldavian alliance with Ivan III, and what better way than
to show the duplicity of Dracula on religious grounds, and thereby cast
a shadow of doubt over Vlad the Monk, Dracula's half-brother, who was
ruling in Wallachia from 1481 to 1495. Perhaps, Stephen's "humiliation
of Colomea," when he sought Polish aid against the Turks in 1484, may
have caused him to be concerned about maintaining good relations with
Moscow. There is a freeze in diplomatic contact between the two countries from 1484 to 1488, and this may also have caused Stephen to seek
out other means of persuasion, such as the Dracula story.

The author of the Slavic tale, whoever he was, was more critical of
Dracula's abandonment of Orthodoxy than his cruelties. Dracula's death
at the hands of his own men resulted largely because of his "diabolical"
conversion to the Latin heretical Church.[17]

Historical evidence seems to support the thesis that this religious theme
was designed to forward the position of Stephen of Moldavia in his efforts
to gain even closer ties with Ivan III: Moldavia would act as a bulwark
of the Orthodox faith against the encroaching Catholic influence, sponsored by the Hungarians, to which Dracula had fallen prey. Stephen of
Moldavia was related to Ivan III in several ways. Stephen's wife Eudokia,
was Ivan III's first cousin. Stephen's daughter Elena married Ivan III's
son, Ivan the Young, in January 1483. Their son, Dmitri Ivanovich, who
had been born on October 10, 1483, had been proclaimed heir to the Russian throne in 1483. When Fedor Kuritsyn and his entourage came to
Suceava in the summer of 1484, Stephen and his followers were anxious
to insist on strengthening Moldavian-Muscovite relations, since Stephen's
grandson stood to inherit the Muscovite throne.

Subsequent events support this view that the overt "religious" issue,
which probably cloaked political and especially cultural factors, was

important: In 1490, at the very time when the monk Efrosin was making his copy of the Dracula story, a crisis had developed over dynastic succession in Muscovite Russia: Ivan III's eldest son, Ivan the Young, the husband of Elena, Stephen's daughter, died unexpectedly in 1490. The heir apparent, their son Dmitri, was only about six and a half years of age in 1490. But there was a real problem. Ivan III had married another wife, the famous Sophia Palaeologus, and she had produced five sons, of whom the eldest was an eleven-year-old child named Vasili. As Fennell points out in his study of Ivan III, "According to the practice of the house of Daniel, the princes of Moscow left their thrones to their eldest sons. But never yet had an eldest son with male issue predeceased his father and there was, therefore, no precedent for choosing between the son of the deceased heir and the eldest surviving son of the reigning prince. The choice between Dmitri and Vasili rested entirely with Ivan III himself."[18]

By 1497, Ivan III discovered a plot among the gentry to support Vasili. On December 27, 1497, the tsar executed the conspirators, put Vasili under house arrest and sent Sophia into disgrace. Then on February 4, 1498, Ivan III crowned Dmitri, his grandson, as grand prince of Vladimir, Moscow, and all Russia. However, in 1499, a new turn of events took place. New treason was uncovered among the gentry; Vasili was forgiven and Sophia was pardoned.

Vasili was given the general title of Grand Prince in 1501, but Dmitri still retained his position as Grand Prince of Vladimir and Moscow, and so technically seemed to have maintained the upper hand. But not for long—for on April 11, 1502 Dmitri was arrested along with his mother Elena, and three days later Vasili was officially blessed by his father Ivan III and given the title "Autocrat of all Russia" and also "placed upon the throne of Vladimir and Moscow." The formal reasons given for the disgrace of Dmitri was that he was too independent and that his Romanian mother, Elena, had become a heretic of the "Judaist" sect.[19] Actually, it appears that Ivan III was forced to bow to political pressure from the boyars and conservative upper clergy.

This historical background gives us several clues as to the motives behind the writing and proliferation of the Dracula story in Russia at that time, and recent research allows us to clarify this situation: The old historical interpretation, as found in Karamzin, Solov'ev and Kliuchevsky was that Dmitri and Elena were figureheads for the old boyar opposition to the central power of the Muscovite grand prince, supposedly Vasili and Sophia were against the boyars, and hence their success was the victory of the autocracy over aristocracy. But the latest research points in the opposite direction: Elena's political convictions were closer to those of Ivan

III than Sophia's were. Many of the Muscovite group of Judaizers were, in general, proponents of autocracy. Furthermore, Ivan III was definitely in favor of closer relations with Stephen of Moldavia, which would have been fostered by Dmitri's claim to the throne rather than that of Vasili. How does one account exactly for this shift?

When Ivan appointed Dmitri as grand prince in 1497, he forced Sophia's hand. She began to solicit support from the boyars and the conservative upper clergy. So, the victory of Vasili over Dmitri, who was never popular with the boyars, must be seen as a gain of aristocracy over autocracy and not the other way around. It follows then that the theme of autocracy in the Dracula story, if it was indeed written down by Elena's fellow heretic Fedor Kuritsyn, should be read as a tract in support of the principle of one-man rule, the apparently cruel yet just autocrat.[20] The actions of the Romanian ruler, like those of Ivan III, which appeared to be cruel on the surface, were to be understood as necessary for the good of strengthening the state.[21] This would account for the basically positive point of view vis-à-vis Dracula's attempt to secure a centralized government in the Slavic manuscript. In general, the Dracula story became popular in Russia probably for the same reason he was popular in his native Romania—because Dracula was such a fierce fighter against the Infidels.

The most recent significant work of interest to the historian has been done by Slavic linguists on the Dracula stories.[22] The comparative linguistic approach, combined with references to other historical documents, is capable of yielding the best general conclusions about the historical sources. The claim of some Romanian Slavicists that the Slavic texts were of Romanian origin is based largely on the following linguistic arguments: the author of the Slavic manuscript uses the verb "hraniti" (to defend) in the meaning this term has preserved in Romanian, namely, "to feed;" he also knew the meaning of the name "Dracul," meaning "the devil" in modern Romania.[23] Yet the author clearly separates his own language from that of the Wallachian people, so he was clearly not a Romanian. Further proof that the author of the Slavic text was not a Romanian lies in the fact that, though he knews very little about Romanian geographical locations, he does convey a good deal of information about Hungarian places. For example, he gives detailed information about Dracula's place of imprisonment in Hungary, his conversion to Roman Catholicism, his marriage to a relative to Mathias Corvinus, his home in Pest, as well as details about Dracula's son Mihnea and other sons of Dracula and their places of residence.

Almost all of the "stories about Dracula" must have originally formed a series of epic traditions common to the local inhabitants during the second half of the fifteenth century. In fact, some of these traditions have persisted in the area around Castle Dracula up to our own day.

The folklore of southeastern Europe, in general, and of Romania, in particular, is rich in stories about Dracula. There are in this case very specific reasons why the historian cannot afford to ignore those kinds of sources: 1) Dracula's life would remain extremely obscure, if one were to depend only on the few remaining official state documents from his day, and 2) it appears that many of the published Dracula tales were actually themselves based upon an oral tradition. By "oral tradition" here we accept the definition by Jan Vansina: "Oral tradition consists of all verbal testimonies which are reported statements concerning the past. . . . The definition also excludes rumors from oral tradition, for although rumors are oral sources which are transmitted from one person to another, they do not concern the past. . . . They are news."[24]

An example of the necessity for using folkloric sources carefully is the following recent case: One of the earliest such sources is a Serbian folksong about the battle of Varna in 1444; this song speaks about the "Dragulovich" or "Drakulovich."[25] On the basis of this source the Soviet scholar Lur'e incorrectly assumed that Dracula may have fought at the battle of Varna.[26] Dracula could not have fought at the battle of Varna, since he was still in Turkish captivity as a hostage at the time. The reference in that Serbian folksong is actually to one of the other sons of Vlad Dracul, namely Mircea, Dracula's elder brother, who did fight at the battle of Varna and died two years later in 1446.[27]

Many of the early travellers to Romania noticed the existence of ballads related by ministrels, often accompanied by music.[28] A 17th century chronicler, Constantin Cantacuzino, stressed the historical importance of such folkloric tales, which contained a grain of solid historical truth.[29] Since these stories were often told to the young, they usually contained a moral or patriotic motive. There was also a tendency to connect the ballad with a fimilar landmark.

Petre Ispirescu, the first Romanian folklorist who centered on the Dracula legend, suffered from a slight handicap: he was a city boy, a worker in a printing shop, instead of transcribing the native country dialect as it existed, he substituted the slang of his own Bucharest suburb.[30] A far more accurate transcription of Dracula peasant stories was compiled by C. Rădulescu-Codin, a native of the Muscel district in which Dracula's famous castle is located, a village teacher who knew the local dialect well.[31]

In recent years the Institute of Folklore in Bucharest has made a commendable effort at organizing research in the various regions of Romania, but the emphasis has usually been upon music, dances, and peasant art, rather than the historical epics passed down by the peasants. With the movement of the peasants to the cities these narratives run the danger of being lost.[32] Fortunately contemporary historical research has helped to stimulate folkloric expeditions to capture the long-neglected Castle Dracula epic.[33]

Most of the previously published Romanian folk tales coincide roughly with the episodes in the manuscripts and pamphlets from the fifteenth and sixteenth centuries in other languages. But there are two important events which are found only in the Romanian sources—namely, Dracula's construction of the castle of Poenari, along the river Argeș, and the building of Snagov monastery outside the city of Bucharest.[34] In both cases modern scholarship suggests that there is some partial truth to both these claims: Dracula did not actually build the castle. As for the Snagov monastery, the case is similar: Dracula did not build that monastery, but he did rebuild sections of it. In the case of Castle Dracula, there is written testimony to confirm the folklore. Archbishop Neofit II recorded his visit to Castle Dracula in 1747, while he was travelling in Romania.[35] Neofit also tells about Dracula's escape from the Turks by having his horses shod backwards in order to throw the oncoming Turks off his trail—a tale which exists in several variants in Romanian folklore today.[36] The tale of the building of the castle is confused with an account of an architect named Manole who had his wife walled up alive in the castle fortifications—an incident which is still prevalent in the folklore of the region, though it is usually attributed to the princely church at Curtea de Argeș.[37] Another tale relating to Castle Dracula and Dracula's escape from the Turks was printed by the Romanian folklorist C. Rădulescu-Codin.[38] In the northern part of the Argeș region at Suici, Rădulescu-Codin recorded a tale concerning the Turkish attack. According to it, Dracula's nephew helped him to escape from the Turks by having his horses shod backwards. There is also a reference to a "letter of donation" by which Dracula gave to his brave soldiers possession of his castle and all the mountains which could be seen around it.[39] Yet a second version of this folk tale was also recorded by Rădulescu-Codin. In it there is mention of royal treasure hidden at Poenari castle and a gateman who was captured and forced to show the treasure to the Turks, who then killed him.[40]

The Russian Scholar Lur'e postulated an oral tradition at the basis of the Slavic Dracula story as early as 1958.[41] In his definitive book on this same subject Lur'e referred again to oral tradition as the source of the Dracula story: "It is possible to assume that this tradition continued to exist for many centuries after the fifteenth century in the folklore of Romania and of other neighboring people."[42] But Lur'e was not able to prove his interpretation conclusively, since he did not travel to Romania to gather the folkloric evidence and was forced to operate on the basis of very limited evidence, namely, Ispirescu's works and those of Rădulescu-Codin on Romanian folktales.[43] Both Bogdan and Sedel'nikov had also considered that the Slavic Dracula story was based on oral rather than written sources.[44] Lur'e was led to speculate that not only the Slavic stories about Dracula but also the German ones did not go back to any one written source, but rather to oral tradition which had spread throughout central Europe during the second half of the fifteenth century.[45] Unfortunately almost all of the arguments by Lur'e come from internal evidence: But if the Slavic stories about Dracula could not have been a translation from any written German source, and if the German sources could not have been a translation from the Slavic sources, then how can one explain the similarities? Precisely an oral basis to these stories in folklore would explain why there are similar tales but with different endings, as in the case of the story about the two monks, the merchants and his goods, etc.

The first systematic expedition to gather research on the local historical folktales in the villages of the river Argeș at the foot of Castle Dracula was inspired by Radu Florescu and me and carried out with the aid of Romanian folklorists in the autumn of 1969.[46] Before this there had been folklore research into the general songs of the area; but this was the first one to concentrate upon the local historical stories and epics referring to Dracula. This evidence confirms the thesis that oral traditions were probably at the basis of the Dracula stories: these stories are still remembered and recited by ordinary peasants in the region around Castle Dracula. Peasants who know nothing about Mathias Corvinus' defamation of Dracula's character, the novel of Bram Stoker or the horror films of the twentieth century, have kept alive the old Dracula story. As in the case of most folklore, those incidents which refer to places removed from the scene of Castle Dracula are vague.

The newly discovered legends gathered a group of folklorists, Florescu and McNally are:

1) "Construction of Castle Dracula" in five variants.
2) "Treasure of Castle Dracula" in two variants.
3) "Dracula's Flight Over the Mountains into Transylvania and the Donations Made to the Arefu Peasants" in six variants.

4) "Where does the Name Vlad Țepeș Come From?" in three variants.
5) "Dracula's Daughter (or Wife)" in three variants.
6) "Burning of the Lazy, Thieves, and the Lame" in two variants.
7) "Foreign merchants" in three variants.
8) "The Servant Who Could not Endure the Stench of Bodies."
9) "The Woman Who Made her Husband Too Short a Shirt" in two variants.
10) "Dracula's Struggle with the Turks."

Arnold Van Gennep, one of the recognized authorities on folklore, postulated that historical facts do not persist beyond five or six generations in the popular memory, i.e., about 250 years.[47] But the Castle Dracula epic which persists in Arefu, Căpățineni, and Corbeni, contradicts this assumption and demonstrates that one cannot apply such a postulate in a universal manner.

The reason for the persistence of the Dracula castle epic is based on the fact that ruins of the castle dominate the Argeș River valley even today and thus allow the continuity of the legends connected with its construction; especially since the local peasants attribute their status as freeholders to Dracula. This title of "freeholder" was recognized by Mircea Ciobanul about one hundred years after the death of Dracula.[48] There is a document dated April 8, 1546, from the chancellery of the ruler Mircea Ciobanul in which the ruler recognizes the old boundaries of the villages, which had been invaded violently by Radul of Golești. Against this invasion the Arefu freeholders brought in support their own documents "from the days of the death of Dan Voevod and Vlad Vodă Țepeș."[49]

With respect to the legend about the donations given by Dracula to the local villagers, there is a variation on that legend in which the name of the ruler Dracula (Vlad Țepeș) has been replaced by that of Negru Vodă.[50] That particular legend was gathered at the village of Albești situated about 25 or 30 kilometers from Castle Dracula, only 5 kilometers from the city of Curtea de Argeș, with its famous church connected with the name of Negru Vodă in popular legends. It is distinctly possible that this legend really referred to Dracula whose name was replaced by the legendary Negru Vodă due to the popularity of the monastery legend.

As for the legend that Dracula successfully escaped from his castle by having his horses shod backwards, there is a similar legend in Cetățeni din Vale, the Muscel Commune, referring to Radu de la Afumati, evidently

Radu Vodă.[51] In the Stoenești Commune, also in Muscel, which is not far from Curtea de Argeș the legend refers to Negru Vodă.[52]

As for the episode of the girl who threw herself down onto the rocks rather than fall into the hands of the Turks, the names differ: in the legend from Cetațeni din Vale, it is the wife of Radu Vodă,[53] the wife of Negru Vodă in the Stoenești Commune and in the Arefu Commune, Dracula's daughter.[54]

By far the most frequent reference to the construction of the Castle Dracula is the story that boyars from Tîrgoviște, whom Dracula had seized by force directly at the church where they were attending the Easter services were responsible for building it. This corresponds closely with the chronicle accounts and with current historical scholarship.[55] This newly recorded legend corresponds to one which appeared under the title "The Ruins of Țepeș' Castle" in *Prietenul Nostru* (year I, no. 5, pp. 77-78) gathered evidently by Radulescu-Codin, since it was then printed in the village of Prioboieni-Vilcea, where Radulescu-Codin was a teacher. The exact tunnel has never been discovered. The current legends refer to "a leather bag filled with gold" buried at the castle site which has not been discovered because it is "guarded by the devil." Here is, of course, a universal theme in folklore. In the Slavic text in Russian archives there is a similar account of a buried treasure. Such a treasure has never been found.

The most prevalent legends are those in connection with Dracula's escape from the castle across the mountains and his donations to the Arefu peasants. In all cases, Dracula's horses are shod backwards with the help of Arefu peasants. From the historical data it is known that, Dracula fled to Transylvania, where he was held captive by Mathias Corvinus for some twelve years; here the name of the site of his imprisonment is different from that recorded in the Slavic documents, which refer to Vișegrad. (One old informant referred to Feldioara castle as the place of Dracula's imprisonment.)

All informants agreed that Țepeș's name came from his customary practice of impaling people on stakes. For example, Ion Ruxanda said "The name of Țepeș comes from the fact that, being a serious man, he impaled those who did not listen to him, in order to achieve order in the land." It is significant to note that the Romanian peasants, in general, see Dracula's impalings as necessary and just.

The place called Luncă Floarei, in fact now near the central electric plant at Căpățineni, is supposedly named after Dracula's wife. Nothing is really known about Dracula's first wife. The idea of the wife throwing herself on the rocks rather than fall into the hands of the Turks is a very common folkloric theme. It is attributed to the wives of Radu Vodă[56] and in the case of the legend heard from Vasile Chilibaşu it is Dracula's daughter.

Dracula's burning of the lazy, the poor and the lame is well known through the German and Slavic texts, and through the chronicles of Bonfinii and Chalkokondylas. The Romanian folkloric accounts justify this because of the imminent danger posed by the Turks. In effect, Dracula committed every killing in a time of extreme crisis.

The story about the foreign merchant has four variants from the Arefu Commune. They correspond rather closely to the Slavic account, especially the story as told by Vasile Chilibaşu.

The peasant with the "short" shirt legend corresponds with the German text, whereas in the Russian version it is a "dirty" shirt. After executing his wife, Dracula gives the peasant another wife.[57] Here the legend has a definitive moral message, Dracula sees to it that the "lazy" wife is replaced. Concerning Dracula's Battles with the Turks, according to the informant Ion Ruxanda, Dracula impaled 20,000 Turks. Chalkokondyles confirms this event. The German St. Gall text refers to 20,000 Bulgarians.

Most of all, there is a general consistency in peasant appraisals of Dracula. For example, Ilie Cîrstescu from Arefu stated "Vlad Ţeăeş was a good ruler for his time." Peasants put the emphasis upon the extreme crisis of the times in which Dracula lived. This persistent theme in peasant tales is corroborated by Bulgarian verses which state: "the Romanian country is split apart, the people run to the mountains, to the valleys, away from the cruel Turks, away from the Hungarian barbarians. The old men, cut down, they enslave the young ones, they rape the girls, they capture the youth and enlist them in their armies. . . . Wherever they pass, they burn the villages."[58] A note from Antonius Bonfinius about the Turkish invaders also confirms that critical state of affairs which helps explain Dracula's harsh measures, ". . . they so scorched the lands of the Romanian provinces that there was no man left to till the fields."[59] Even the appellation "Drăculea" which the peasants know as the common word for "son of the devil" in their current language, is explained away. "He was called Drăculea only by those against whom he worked, namely, the treacherous boyars," said Vasili Chilibaşu of Căpăţîneni.

The final evaluation of Dracula's life from the peasant folkloric viewpoint around the castle area can best be summarized by the words of Ilie Cîreştescu, a descendant of an old family of freeholders in the Arefu region: "When the ruler Ţepeş governed the country with great understanding, word went throughtout the land that everyone respected the law and all were obedient in his land. . . . "

To the Romanian peasants and especially the freeholders around the castle, however "cruel" Dracula may have been, he was "just" to them, almost a kind of Robin Hood somewhat like the "haiduc" (the robber baron of the Balkans), since he punished rich boyars. Thus, Dracula re mains a hero who fought against the Turks, who laid low the boyars, and, most important, who gave the soil back to some of his brave peasant fighers. The memory of Dracula, the hero, is still alive and well in the oral traditions of the Romanian peasants living near the foot of Castle Dracula.

Given the fact of the survival of these Dracula legends among the Romanian peasants in the castle area, these tales or similar ones must have also circulated among the Romanians in Moldavia during the late fifteenth century. Most recently Ștefan Andreescu has nonetheless continued to hold out in favor of a Transylvanian authorship by stating that the Transylvanian Orthodox Church could have been "the only milieu generating such major cultural production."[60] But as Nicolae Stoicescu pointed out, Andreescu did so only "in the absence of any proof,"[61] and furthermore, "in advocating an author of Romanian origin historians have failed to supply convincing arguments to his aims."[62] In this present article I have filled this gap and demonstrated the specific political aims of a Romanian from Moldavia in this matter.

As for the various linguistic analyses, Stoicescu concludes that ". . . the philological arguments are not convincing for either a Russian or a Slavic original language of the stories so that their original language is still an open question for experts until they can persuade all the supporters of one or another thesis. . . . "[63] But then, strangely enough, Stoicescu gives his own opinion: "It seems to us that by recording Țepeș' deeds in Slavonic—the language used by the Romanians at that time, too—the author was rather concerned to keep alive the memory of a great Prince whom he admired."[64] But if this were so, then why the inclusion of the section describing Dracula's torturing and impaling of mice and birds which are hardly acts destined to inspire admiration in anyone but a madman?

Moreover, Stoicescu himself stumbled on a clue to all this, which he should have pursued: "No matter who the author was, he seems to have gathered part of his information from Moldavia too. A Moldavian influence seems to be also the name by which Wallachia was referred to (Țară Muntenească instead of Țară Românească)."[65] As the present study has shown, it was indeed a Moldavian, who was added to the Kuritsyn entourage at the court of Stephen the Great while on its way back to Moscow, who undoubtedly influenced the writing of the Slavic Dracula narratives.

NOTES

* Among the best, most recent studies are Nicolae Stoicescu in Romanian, *Vlad Țepeș*, București, 1976, then by the same author, *Vlad Țepeș Prince of Walachia*, in English, Bucharest, 1978, containing references not in his 1976 book, and finally a Romanian paperback which is a shortened version of the 1976 book entitled also *Vlad Țepeș*, București, 1979. See also Ștefan Andreescu, *Vlad Țepeș (Dracula) Intre legendă și adevăr istoric*, București, 1976, also by the same author "Premierès formes de la littérature historique roumaine en Transylvanie. Auteur de la version slave des récits sur le voivode Dracula," *Revue des études sud-est européennes XIII*, 4, 1975, pp. 511-524, also "Un nou punct de vedere asupra versiunii slave a Povestirii despre Dracula voevod" *Glasul bisericii*, Vol. 1-2, 1975. Matei Cazacu, "A propos de récit russe Skazanie o Dracule voevode" *Cahiers due monde russe et soviétique XV*, 3-4, 1974, pp. 287-292, also by the same author, "Les biographies contemporaines de Vlad III Țepeș, prince de Valachie (1430-1476)" *Positions des theses a l'Ecole Nationale de Chartes*, Paris, 1977, pp. 41-47. A Fulbright Grant supported my researh.

1. S. Lur'e (ed.), *Povest' o Drakule*, Moscow-Leningrad, 1964; A. Sedel'nikov, "Literaturnaia istoriia povesti o Drakule," *Izvestiia po russkomu iazyku i slovestnosti II*, Leningrad, 1929, pp. 621-659; n. Smochină, *Povestirea slavă despre Vlad Țepeș*, Iași, 1939; P. P. Panaitescu, *Cronicele slavo române din sec. XV-XVI*, București, 1959, pp. 197-214; Pandele Olteanu, *Limba povestirilor slave despre Vlad Țepeș*, București, 1961; Ion Stăvărus, *Povestiri medievale despre Vlad Țepeș-Draculea*, București, 1978.

2. N. M. Karamzin, *Istoriia gosudarstva rossiskogo* . . . , Vol. VII, Moscow, 1903, p. 139, also pp. 230-231, note 411.
The oldest, original manuscript, known as the Kirillo-Belozerski no. II/ 1088, is presently housed in the Manuscript Divsion of the Saltykov-Shchedrin Public Library in Leningrad. This 1490 manuscript mentions that it was copied from an older one dated 1486. The best critical edition of this oldest manuscript is to be found in Lur'e, *Povest' o Drakule*, pp. 117-122. See also Sedel'nikov, op. cit., pp. 621-659.

3. Lur'e, *Povest'*, p. 88.

4. A. Vostokov first made the link between Fedor Kuritsyn and Dracula. See A. Vostokov, *Opisani russikikh i slovenskikh rukopisei Riumiantsevskogo muzeuma*, Sankt-Petersburg, 1842, pp. 511-512. See

the same position taken by Ioan Bogdan in *Vlad Țepeș și narațiunele germane și rusești asupra lui*, București, 1896, pp. 119-120.

5.   J. Fennel, *Ivan the Great of Moscow*, London, 1961, p. 113.

6.   Lur'e, *Povest'*, p. 43.

7.   Ibid., pp. 54-58.

8.   For the claim see A. Sedel'nikov, "Literaturnaia istoriia povesti o Drakule," *Izvestiia po russkomy iazyku i slovestnosti* II, 2, 1929, pp. 637-638. Sedel'nikov knew only seventeen versions of the Dracula Tale, about five less than are known today. He did not utilize Bogdan's valuable study.

9.   H. Raab, "Zu einigen niederdeutschen Quellen des altrussischer Schrifttums," *Zeitschrift fur Slawistik* III, 1958, pp. 323-335.

10.   M. P. Alekseev, "K istorii gumanizma v Vengrii (retsenziia na knigu vengerskogo issledovatelia T. Kardosh)," *Vestnik Leningradskogo universiteta*, no. 14, Seriia iazyka i literatury, no. 3, 1959, p. 134.

11.   Lur'e, *Povest'*, pp. 41-42, note 64.

12.   Ibid., p. 41.

13.   The Russian historian, A. N. Pypin was the first to doubt Kuritsyn's authorship and was inclined to consider the work to be South Slavic rather than Russian. See A. N. Pypin, *Ocherk literaturnoi istorii starinnykh povestei i shazok russkikh*, Sankt-Petersburg, 1857, p. 217. See also A. N. Pypin, *Istoriia russkoi literatury*, Vol. II, St. Petersburg, 1898, p. 495. F. I. Buslaev thought that the manuscript was a translation from some unknown foreign document. (See F. I. Buslaev, "Dlia opredeleniia inostrannykh istochnikov povesti o mut'anskom voevode Drakule," *Letopisi russkoi literatury i drevnosti*, Part II, Moscow, 1863, pp. 84-86). See P. Panaitescu, *Cronicele*, București, 1959, p. 198. See also Lur'e, *Povest'*, p. 9.

14.   See especially Anton Balotă's review of Pandele Olteanu's book in *Studii si cercetări linguistice XIII*, no. 1, 1962, pp. 90-97.

15.   See Emil Vrabie's remarks in *Romanoslavica XIII*, 1962, pp. 227-246.

16.   Lur'e, *Povest'*, p. 37. For the Romanian position which reaffirms the theory that the authorship was a Transylvanian Romanian see Alexandru Boldur, "Un Român Trănsilvănean—autor presupus al 'Povestirii ruse despre Dracula'," *Apulum* VIII, Alba Iulia, 1971, pp. 67-96.

17.   This section of the oldest text is to be found in Lur'e, *Povest'*, pp. 121-122.

18.   J. Fennell, *Ivan the Great*, p. 334. See also John Fine, Jr., "The Muscovite Dynastic Crisis of 1497-1502," *Canadian Slavic Papers* VIII (1966), pp. 198-218.

19.   The heretical sect of "Judaizers" is known only through polemics, as is fairly common concerning most heretical movements of the time. It was probably anti-trinitarian and critical of simony among the upper clergy. Ivan III was at first very tolerant of the movement, since he saw in it a means of justifying the secularization of church property. See J. Fennell, *Ivan the Great*, p. 326. See also George Vernadsky, "The Heresy of the Judaizers and the Polemics of Ivan III of Moscow," *Speculum* 8 (1933), pp. 436-454. See also N. A. Kazakova and Ia. S. Lur'e *Antifeodal'-nye ereticheskie dvizheniia na Rusi XIV-nachala XVI veka*, Moscow-Leningrad, 1955, esp. pp. 127 and 164-169.

20.   The Soviet historian L. V. Cherepnin interpreted the motives of the author to be the glorification of the awesome yet just ruler. See L. V. Cherepnin, *Russkie feodal'nye arkivy XIV-XV v.*, Part 2, Moscow-Leningrad, 1951, pp. 310-312. But the opposite view has been expressed by two other Soviet experts, N. K. Gudzii and A. A. Zimin, who have claimed that it was really a political tract directed against the tzar by the feudal gentry in opposition to any centralizing power. See N. K. Gudzii, *Istoriia drevnei russkoi literatury*, 6th edition, Moscow, 1956, pp. 256-262, and A. A. Zimin, I. S. *Peresvetov i ego sovremenniki*, Moscow, 1958, p. 414. To compare the Dracula Tale with Peresvetov see Werner Philipp, "Ivan Peresvetov and seine Schriften Zur Erneuerung des Moskauer Reiches," *Osteuropäische Forschungen* N. F. Vol. 20, pp. 91 ff. For possible Judaic influence on Kuritsyn's views see John Fine, Jr., "Fedor Kuritsyn's Lao-dikjskoe Poslanie and Heresy of the Judaisers," *Speculum* XLI (July, 1966), pp. 500-504.

21.   Lur'e, *Povest'*, p. 13.

22.   Pandele Olteanu, "Lexicul povestirilor slave despre Vlad Țepeș," *Revista Universității*, seria științe sociale, filologie, Nos. 2-3, București, 1955; *Limba povestirlor slave despre Vlad Țepeș*, București, 1961. See especially the review by Anton Balotă, "Pandele Olteanu, Limba povesti-rilor slave despre Vlad Tepes," *Studii si cercetări Linguistice*, Vol. XIII, No. 1, 1962, pp. 90-97; I. A. Lur'e, "Povest' o munt'ianskom voevode Drakule," *Russkie povesti XV-XVI vv.*, Moscow-Leningrad, 1959, pp. 420-421; *Ideologicheskaia bor'ba v russkoi publitisistike kontsa XV-nachala XVI v.*, Moscow-Leningrad, 1960, pp. 395-397; "Povest' XV v. i fil'my XX v.," *Russkaia Literatura*, No. 2, 1962, p. 266; *Povest' o Drakule*, Moscow-Leningrad, 1964.

23.   See especially P. P. Panaitescu *Chronicele slavo-române din sec. XV-XVI*, București, 1959, p. 198.

24.   Jan Vansina, (translated by H. M. Wright), *Oral Tradition, A Study in Historical Methodology*, Chicago, 1965, pp. 19-20.

25. B. Bogishih, *Narodne pjesme iz starijikh hajvishe primorskikh zapisa*, Kn'iga prva, Vol. X, Nos. 18-21, Belgrade, 1878. See also K. Viskevatii, "O sekule Drakulevice (Dragulevice) iugoslavianskikh narodnikh pesen," *Slavia*, XIV, Nos. 1-2, Prague, 1935-36, pp. 160-163.

26. Lur'e, *Povest'*, p. 134, note 43.

27. See Matei Cazacu, "Un Viteaz Frate a lui Vlad Tepeş," *Viaţa Studenţească*, Bucureşti, Octobei 23, 1968, p. 6.

28. See Al. Piru, *Literatura Romînă veche* (Bucureşti, 1962), pp. 76-77. For these early forms of historical ballads also see: A. Balotă, "Funcţiunea socială a cântecului bătrînesc," *Revista de Folklor*, III (1958), pp. 101-112. Also see: D. Marmelius, *Figuri istorice romîneşti în cîntecul popular al Românilor* (Bucureşti, 1915).

29. "These songs of old are not really rhymed chronicles with concrete documentary value. . . . They are reflections of historic moments. . . . Some concrete historical elements cannot be excluded particularly those which reflect facts and occurrences from the surroundings of the feudal order." *Istoria literaturii Romîne* (Bucureşti, 1964), Vol. I, p. 102.

30. Ispirescu (1830-1887) began collecting Romanian folktales from 1862 onwards and published these in a folkloric gazette called *Ţăranul Român*. Most of the Dracula stories were printed after his death in a review called *Făt-Frumos* published in Cernătuţi. These posthumous writings are difficult to obtain. A comprehensive listing os Ispirescu's work is included in: *Bibliografie generală a etnografici şi folckorului românesc*, nos. 2731-2793.

31. Rădulescu-Codin published some folktales in a review he founded called *Prietenul Mostru*.

32. In 1965 the proportion of peasants to the general population in Romania had dropped to 56.5% In 1930, it had been 76.7%. This movement from country to town is still taking place under the impact of current policies of rapid industrialization. Should this continue it seems almost inevitable that many oral traditions will eventually become extinct. See John Michael Montias, *Economic Development in Communist Rumania*, (Cambridge, 1967), pp. 3-4.

33. Special thanks go to the former director of the Institute of Folklore in Bucharest, Professor Mihai Pop, who organized the expendition, and to his fellow folklorists, Drs. Constantine Eretescu and Georgeta Ene, who helped carry out the task.

34. These events are mentioned in the Wallachian chronicle from the seventeenth century. For the most recent critical edition see C. Gresescu and D. Simonescu, eds., *Istoria Ţarii Romîneşti 1290-1690. Letopisul*

Cantacuzinesc, (București, 1960), pp. 4-5 and 205. P. Panaitescu suggested that the story of Dracula's building of the castle of Poenari came from an oral source. See P. P. Panaitescu, "Inceputurile istoriografiei în Tara Romînească," *Studii și materiale de istorie medie,* Vol. V, 1962, p. 203.

35. This manuscript, the House Ledger of Archbishop Neofit, is at the Academy Library of the Romanian Socialist Republic, București, No. 2606/26.

36. The story of the shoeing of the horses backwards can be found in the legends of Radu Negru Vodă, Stephen the Great, and Michael the Brave, as well as Dracula. See V. Adascalitei, *De la Dragos la Cuza-Vodă. Legende populare românești,* București, 1966, p. IX.

37. See Mircea Eliade, *Comentarii la legende Meșterului Manole,* București, 1943, especially pp. 27-37, 126-146.

38. This tale was first published in *Vremea nouă,* Vol. II, No. 5, and republished in *Ingerul Românului,* (București, 1913), pp. 83-93.

39. See the journal, Copii neamului, *Revista Licelui din Ploiești,* I, No. 1 (January, 1922), and No. 3 (March 1922).

40. *Prietenul Mostru.* 1 vol., No. 5, p. 77.

41. Lur'e, "Povesti o munt'anskim voevode Drakule," *Russkie povesti XV-XVI vv.,* (Moscow-Leningrad, 1958), pp. 420-421.

42. Lur'e, *Povest',* p. 32.

43. Ibid., pp. 32-34.

44. I. Bogdan, *Vlad Țepeș,* pp. 119-120; Sedel'nikov, "Literaturnaia istoriia povesti o Drakule," pp. 636-637.

45. Lur'e, *Povest',* p. 31.

46. Georgeta Ene, "Legendele Istorice despre Vlad Țepeș in commună Arefu-Argeș," M.A. thesis in folklore (Bucharest, 1971) and by the same author "Romanian Folklore about Vlad Țepeș," *Revue des études sud-est européennes,* 4, 1976, pp. 581-590.

47. Arnold Van Gennep, *La Formation des Légendes,* 2nd edition, Flammarion, (Paris, 1917), Vol. V, pp. 156-164.

48. See Aurelian Sacerdoțeanu, "Aref—un vechi sat argeșan" in *Studii și Communicări revista muzeului din Pitești.* See also A. Rădulescu "Din trecutul moșnenilor arefeni" *Convorbiri literare* Vol. XLIV, no. 2 (1910), pp. 683-698; A. Sacerdoțeanu "Note de diplomătica românescă" *Hrisovul,* Vol. VII, pp. 137-146.

49. Aurelian Sacerdoșeanu, "Aref—un vechi sat argeșan," *Studii,* p. 180.

50. O. Densușianu, I. A. Candrea and Th. Speranția, "Texte din toate pârșile locuite de romani," *Graiul nostru,* Vol. I, (București, 1906-07), p. 119.

51. O. Densușianu, I. A. Candrea, Th. Speranția, "Texte din toate părțile locuite de români," *Graiul nostru*, Vol. I, p. 122.

52. C. Rădulescu-Codin, "Negru Vodă fugind în Țara Ungurească," *Folklor din Muscel.*

53. O. Densușianu, I. A. Candrea, Th. Sperantiă, *Graiul nostru*, p. 122.

54. According to the legend gathered by Florescu, McNally, Eretescu, Ene, and Vasile Chilibaus, at Căpățîncni. Title of the legend: "The Treasure of Țepeș' Castle."

55. See Constantin C. Giurescu, *Istoria Românilor*, Vol. II, in two parts, pp. 532-533.

56. O. Densușianu, *Graiul nostru*, p. 122.

57. As in the tale recorded by Petre Ispirescu, *Siedietoarea*, Vol. I, (1880), Budapest, No. 1, p. 4.

58. Miladinov *Bulgarski pessi*, Zagreb, 1862, No. 87. For this reference we are grateful to Anton Balotă.

59. Bonfinius, (1691), p. 331.

60. Ștefan Andreescu, "Un nou punct de vedere asupra versiunii slave a Povestiri despre Dracula voevod," *Glasul bisericii*, Vol. 1-2, 1975, p. 130.

61. N. Stoicescu, *Vlad Țepeș Prince of Wallachia*, București, 1978, p. 165.

62. Ibid., p. 168.

63. Ibid., p. 165.

64. Ibid., p. 168.

65. Ibid., p. 167.

Demetrius Dvoichenko-Markov

HETMAN IVAN MAZEPA IN ROMANIAN LITERATURE

During one of the longest wars in Russian history known as the Northern War 1700-1721, Czar Peter I was facing Charles XII of Sweden who had started his decisive campaign against Russia in January 1708 by moving his army from Grodno across the Vistula river directly towards Moscow. Swedish reinforcements under General Lowenhaupt were in Riga ready to join the forces of their king in Russia. After capturing Mogilev, Charles XII and his army were about sixty miles from Smolensk, where Czar Peter I had concentrated his main forces thus blocking a direct route to Moscow. Shortly before this new invasion the Russian czar managed to put down the rebellion of Conrad Bulavin, a leader of the Don Cossacks, and was continuing his struggle against another rebellion of the Turkish Bashkirs in the middle Volga area which was finally suppressed in 1711. Some historians agree with the well known Russian historian Vasili Klyuchevsky that "had Charles been able to join General Lowenhaupt he would have been invincible" would have won the war if he continued on his way to Moscow.[1] Instead of taking the direct route to Moscow by way of Smolensk, Charles XII turned southward and entered the Ukraine where he wanted to join a valuable ally, Hetman Ivan Mazepa, thus strengthening his army in a rich land untouched by the war. Mazepa had been in contact with the Swedish king and secretly turned against his sovereign seeking to protect his leadership of the ruling oligarchy and the autonomy of his land.

In addition to this, the Ukraine also offered a northward passage above the town and fortress of Poltava which was another way to penetrate into the center of Russia by bypassing the fortifications which barricaded the Smolensk-Moscow route. Swedish reinforcements under the command of General Lowenhaupt were intercepted and defeated with heavy losses on October 9, 1708, at Lesnaia. The Russian czar admitted later that the Russian victory at Lesnaia "was the mother of the battle at Poltava nine months later."[2] Hetman Mazepa was able to bring only about two thousand Cossacks to the Swedish side. Another failure was the fact that the

147

Swedish king was not able to secure an alliance with the Ottoman Empire and the Crimean Tatars, but only succeeded to gain the support of the Zaporozhian Cossacks under Ataman Gordienko who paid for his desertion of Czar Peter I by the total destruction by Prince Mechnikov of the Sech'. their fortified headquarters near the Dnieper rapids. The Russian czar was warned previously by Kochubei and other loyalist Cossacks that Hetman Ivan Mazepa had turned traitor, but for quite some time the czar could not believe it and he was quite shocked when this became public knowledge and his comment was:

> 'for twenty-one years he has been faithful to me and now on the
> brink of the grave he has turned traitor to me and to his people.' The
> Orthodox Church excommunicated Mazepa for dealing with the
> Protestants, Menshikov seized and burned his headquarters at
> Baturin, and a new Hetman, Ivan Skoropadsky, was elected with
> the Tsar present at the ceremony.' 'The people of Little Russia'
> wrote Peter 'stand more firmly than was possible to expect.'[3]

The Swedish army and the allied forces of Hetman Mazepa were destroyed on July 8, 1709, during the famous battle of Poltava. King Charles XII and Hetman Mazepa both managed to find asylum in the Turkish fortress of Bender (Tighina) on the river Dniester in the Romanian principality of Moldavia. There, in the village of Varnitsa, Hetman Mazepa died on October 2, 1709.

Born around 1642, Ivan Mazepa was brought up at the Polish court of King Casimir, educated by the Jesuits, and was granted a Polish title of nobility. There are indications that he had close relationships and participated in some major events in the Romanian principalities of Wallachia and Moldavia and had traveled in Western Europe. With the active assistance of Prince Vasily Golitsin in 1687, Mazepa was elected Hetman of the Ukraine and dreamed secretly to become an independent king of Eastern Europe. Mazepa is mentioned by Voltaire in his *History of Charles XII*, by Lord Byron, Victor Hugo, A. Pushkin, Slovatskii, and Franz Liszt. He is a controversial person who sometimes is presented as a scheming villain and traitor or a national hero of Ukrainian national separatists. This paper is an attempt to present some little known Romanian sources which are translated by me into English for the first time.

In general, the Romanian chronicles and annals mention the Ukrainian Cossacks quite often without any attempt to idealize them. The Cossacks are presented as warriors seeking adventure and war booty. Sometimes, the intervention of the Ukrainian Cossacks is presented as a salvation in the form of trusted allies and friends in tmes of trouble and national emergency when the Romanian principalities were engaged in a struggle for survival against the Turks of the Ottoman Empire and the Catholic forces of Hungary and Poland.[4] Both the Romanians and the Russians of the Ukraine belong to the same *Pravoslavnyi* Eastern Orthodox Church which was introduced into Eastern Europe by the missionaries of the Byzantine Empire. Sharing the same faith and enemies brought the Romanians and the Russians into a close collaboration and often one can find Romanians in the service of Muscovy and of Ukrainian Cossacks, and Russians in the service of Moldavia and Wallachia. In fact, a contemporary of Hetman Ivan Mazepa who lived as a hostage in Constantinople and later became the Hospodar (Voevod, Domn, Duke, Prince, Bey) of Moldavia in 1693 and 1710-1711, Demetrius Kantemir, (Cantemir 1673-1723) informs us that the Moldavian army contained some Ukrainian Cossacks on their payroll:

> Four Cossack captains . . . each was in charge of one thousand men, but now have hardly forty or fifty men of their own origin usually from the Zaporozhian Horde.[5]

According to Hospodar Demetrius Kantemir, the Ukrainian Cossacks "are in the Russian tongue called Cherkassians, but chiefly those who dwell along the banks of the river Donets and live in Slobods or colonies.[6] The permanent homes of the early Cossacks are located in the area around the cities of Kanev and Cherkassy. In fact, in the Moscow czardom of the sixteenth century the Ukrainian Cossacks were called "Cherkasets" (Cherkashenin, Cherkastsy or Charkassy) and the name Cherkassy became the name of all the Ukrainians.[7] It is interesting to note that the *Slavo-Romanian Chronicles* refer to the Ukraine as "The land of Russia." Professor Alexandru V. Boldur, a former professor at the University of Petrograd an the University of Jassy, clearly states:

> First of all during the time of Steven the Great the name of Russia was borne by Galicia and not Muscovy. In the documents of this reign Russia is often mentioned as Galicia, but the distant northeastern state was named Muscovy and its inhabitants were Muscovities.[8]

A similar opinion is also expressed by a Moldavian chronicler, Logofet (Chancellor) Miron Costin (1633-1691), a grandson of the Moldavian Hospodar Eremia Movilă (1595-1600 and 1600-1606), who while a student at the Jesuit school in Bar, Poland, took part in the battle of Berestechko (1651) on the Styr river against the well known Ukrainian Cossack Hetman Bogdan Khmel'nitskii. In fact, the Romanian scholar Ion I. Nistor was of the opinion that Miron Costin "presents more clearly than anybody else the beginning of the Zaporozhian Cossacks."[9] They are also sometimes referred to as the Ukrainian Cossacks:

> The Cossacks are of Russian nationality the remnants of the warwiors of the Russian princes who after a long time were brought under the rule of Polish kings and Kiev, the seat of Russia, having fallen under Polish rule, they lived down the Dnieper river on both sides under Polish rulers free from serfdom, the way of life of warriors, with free food on the Dnieper or as hunters in the steppes, or fishing up the Dnieper rapids where the Dnieper has three places with rapids formed by nature so that the water falls over the rocks down to the bottom of the lower reaches. In these places no boat can pass except their boats. . . and many times they drag their boats overland until they pass those places. And so they lived until the day of King Augustus. That Polish King observing them as men of righteous life, as warriors, attracted them with pay promoting them to positions of leadership with a free will to organize campaigns and fight the Tatars as protection of the Polish Kingdom, since at that time the Tatars were also attacking the frontiers of their land. . . because they were agile and savage men they were called Cossacks i.e., a savage goat. . . or goatkeepers. Which name is also with the Poles, a considerable part of the army especially the detachments that are most agile are named Cossack detachments even today.[10]

Educated at a Jesuit school and a member of the Moldavian and Polish aristocracy, Miron Costin obviously is biased toward the Ukrainian Cossacks and therefore it is not surprising to find many historians who do not agree with the theory of the Moldavian chronicler. So, for example, the Ukrainian historian M. Hrushevsky maintains that the term Cossack was "widely known among the people of Turkish extraction." The earlier Polovtsy (Cumans) tribes used the word Cossack "to denote one who lived on booty." Some nomadic Tatars during the fifteenth century who entered the military service of whoever cared to pay them were also called

Cossacks. The late Professor George Vernadsky of Yale University maintained "that in the Tatar language of the period Kazak meant 'free man,'
'free adventurer' and hence 'frontiersman'."[11] The story about the relationship of the wild goats to the Cossacks of the Ukraine is mentioned
by Hrushevsky as an exaggerated story about the food supplies and wild
game available to the Cossacks:

> Wild goats that migrated to the forests in winter could be killed
> by the thousands; while in the spring boys were able to fill their
> boats with the eggs of wild ducks, geese, swans, and the like.[12]

The British scholar Philip Longworth presents a very interesting comparison between the Russian Cossacks and the Ameican frontiersmen:

> The Cossack was a product of the frontier and he exhibited its
> traits. There are striking parallels between him and the American
> frontiersman; indeed both of them sprang from similar roots. The
> venturers who sought fortune, freedom from poverty or from
> religious and political oppression in seventeenth-century western
> Europe fled to America. Those of eastern Europe fled to the border-
> lands of Tatary to become Cossacks. Nor do the similarities end
> there. If the American frontier encouraged democracy, so did the
> Russian. If the American frontiersman disliked taxation and the
> restraints of law and order, so did the Cossacks. . . . While pioneer
> values influenced the character of the American state, for instance,
> the Russian autocracy eventually harnessed the Cossacks and suc-
> ceeded in channeling their energies to its own military and imperial
> purposes.[13]

The Russian historian V. O. Kliuchevsky points out that the Cossacks
of the Dnieper, who are mentioned for the first time at the end of the
fifteenth century, were preceded by the Cossacks of the Riazan and that

> . . .local geographic and political conditions brought complications
> to the Ukrainian Cossacks. They were caught in the whirlpool of
> international conflicts between Russia, Lithuania, Poland, Turkey
> and the Crimea. The part they had to play in these conflicts gave
> them a historical significance.[14]

Hospodar Demetrius Kantemir of Moldavia, who lived twenty-five years of his life as a Christain hostage in the very heart of the Ottoman Empire in Constantinople gives a very interesting evaluation of Turkish captives on the slave market where the Circassians took the first place and

> The next in their esteem are the Polanders, then the Abazae then the Russians for their hardness of their Bodies and their enduring Labour, which considerations often send them to row in the Grand Signior's Gallies, then the Cossacks, then the Georgians, and last the Mengrelians. . . .
>
> A Cherkassian, Man or Woman, would be sold for 1000 Imperial Crowns, a Polander for 600, Abaza for 500, a Russ or a Cozac for 400, a Georgian for 300, a Mengrelian for 250, a German or Ifrenk for still less.[15]

It is interesting to note that the Russians and the Cossacks commanded the same price on the Turkish slave markets during the time of Hetman Ivan Mazepa. Mazepa was a controversial Hetman of the Left Bank Ukraine during the period covering the years 1687-1708 and according to the late Professor G. Vernadsky:

> Mazepa was a well-educated man and a cunning politician. He belonged to a szlachta family and, while he was popular with the upper class of the Cossacks (the starshina), he did not care much for the masses. Neither was he an admirer of Moscow absolutism.[16]

It is not very clear whether everyone in the family of Mazepa was Roman Catholic. Only his mother seems to have been Eastern Orthodox, the religion of the Russians and Romanians. Mazepa was well educated by the Jesuits and spoke Latin, Polish, German and Russian fluently. Serving as a page in Warsaw, Mazepa received a title of nobility from the Polish king Jan Casimir. To counteract the persistent popular opinion that he was a Roman Catholic and a Pole, he promoted the Eastern Orthodox faith by:

> building of magnificant churches and his donation of money and property to the larger Ukrainian monasteries and churches also impressed the people with his piety and respect for Ukrainian culture, as well as his own glory, power, and wealth.[17]

The Romanian writer of Moldavia, G. Asachi (1788-1869), points out the close relationship of Mazepa with the Romanian principalities of Wallachia and Moldavia and that even his features and physical appearance was more Latin Romanian than Slavic. In this connection Asachi describes the well known adventure of Mazepa, which also inspired Lord Byron, Slovatskii and Franz Liszt. This story takes us back to when Mazepa was a young page at the court of King Jan Casimir became involved in a love affair with a married lady at the court, was caught and punished by being tied naked to a wild horse and carried thus into the steppes of the Zaporozhian Cossacks. This story entitled "Mazepa" was published in Moldavia in *Almanahul* (Jassy 1859) and Asachi stresses the close links of Mazepa with Moldavia. He was saved by the Ukrainian Cossacks, who caught the wild horse, untied Mazepa and set him free. Living among the Cossacks, Mazepa developed a close friendship with Timush Khmel'nitsky, the son of Hetman Bogdan Khmel'nitsky. It seems that Mazepa participated in several attempts to conclude an alliance between the Moldavian Hospodar Vasile Lupu (Basil Lupu, 1634-1653) and Hetman Bogdan Khmel'nitsky of the Ukraine by asking for the hand of the beautiful Moldavian princess Roxandra to marry Timush Khmel'nitsky. The wedding lasted ten days in the Moldavian capital of Jassy and thus a solid foundation for a Moldavian-Ukrainian military alliance was created against a common enemy— Poland. During this war Mazepa was able to save a beautiful maiden from captivity by fighting a duel. On the spot where the duel took place the grateful father of the young maiden erected a convent and Mazepa planted three fir trees. After the battle of Poltava, Mazepa returned to Moldavia with King Charles XII of Sweden and visits the spot where the duel took place. He finds the three seedlings now grown into three mighty fir trees and the Abbess of the convent tells Mazepa her life story, according to which she came to Moldavia from Poland together with her mother seeking refuge from a Tatar raid. Mazepa is deeply shaken by this story because he is led to recognize that the Abbess is actually his daugher, the result of his amorous youthful adventure when he was a page at the court of the Polish king. As a result of this, he decides to go with his daughter on a pilgrimage to Jerusalem in order to gain forgiveness for his sins, but during this journey he and his daughter stop for a short rest in the city of Galați on the Danube. Here, Mazepa unexpectedly dies and is buried by his daughter, the Abbess.[18]

A Moldavian chronicler Logothete (Chancellor) Nicolae Costin, the son of the chronicler Miron Costin, quoted earlier in this paper, was also a contemporary of Hetman Mazepa. It is interesting to note that this Moldavian

Boyar is quite outspoken particularly in reference to the treason committed by the Ukrainian Hetman. Costin points to the treachery of Hetman Mazepa which helped the invasion of the Ukrainian borderlands:

> After this he became opulent and gorged himself together with his advisers the Colonels committing treason against their Lord just like Judas sold our Lord Jesus Christ to the Jews. Mazepa wanted to do the same thing to his master the Emperor as once the Hetman Hamil had committed treason under the Poles; but God has not helped them since He did not want to extinguish the crescent of Christianty: for this he was punished harshly.[19]

Mazepa was forced to bring his double game to an end and went openly to the Swedish side. He was followed, however, by only two thousand men while the overwhelming majority of the Cossacks remained loyal to the czar or took a neutral waiting position. According to *The Moldavian Annals* of Nicolae Costin in Baturin, the Hetman's capital and stronghold, Mazepa left behind a garrison of Cossacks under the command of Colonel Cecel, who judging by his last name might have been of Moldavian origin, and a German General Friedrich Kenicseka. Baturin was attacked and occupied by the Russian troops under the command of Prince Menshikov and:

> This way for the first time was demonstrated the bravery of the Cossacks against the Muscovites and all of them perished because God has punished them as they have committed treason against their Emperor whose bread and salt they have eaten and they wanted to bow to the Swede, to the brother of Mohammed; God has not helped them.[20]

It is interesting to note that the Moldavian Boyar calls the Swedish King Charles XII "brother of Mohammed" thus pointing out the friendly relations of a Lutheran king and the Ottoman sultan, who at that time was the common enemy and oppressor of all Orthodox Christians in Eastern Europe. In continuation, N. Costin also describes how a new Hetman, Ivan Skoropatsky, was elected and installed by the Muscovites in the office Mazepa previously occupied and how the Zaporozhian Cossacks also committed treason and joined the Swedes:

> After the Muscovites sent an army against them and they were not able to withstand the firepower of the Muscovites, many of them

perished and their nest at the rapids, where they had their place since ancient times was destroyed. And those who were able to escape, some in their boats by water, others through the reeds and other places . . . to reunite . . . bowed to the Tatars.[21]

After a short description of the Russian victory at Poltava, the Moldavian chronicler states:

It was the perfidious Mazepa who with a few hours ahead of the Swedish King together with his men in his cunning way crossed the Dniester.[22]

The most important information found in the *Annals* of N. Costin is the exact date of the death of Hetman Ivan Mazepa near the Turkish fortress of Bender (Tighina):

In this year of 1710, in the month of March 18th day, died Mazepa Hetman of the Cossacks at Tighina and they laid him down in the Church in the village named Varnitsa, which is close to Tighina. From there his remains were moved to Galați and buried at the monastery of St. George and even there he did not find any rest. It is said the Turks exhumed him during the revolt of Dumitrașko Voda when the people of Galați were enslaved and his bones ended on the shores of the Danube; after his death even the earth could not stand him.[23]

Asachi gives us some additional details by stating that the Hospodar Nicolae Mavrocordat of Moldavia during his second reign (1711-1715):

upon hearing about the death of Mazepa ordered a pompous funeral in the Church of St. Mary the Immaculate where on a gravestone it was written that after a prolonged wrapping of the corpse, Mazepa found a resting place there . . . . The carved gravestone of Mazepa was in the middle of the Church with the coat of arms and a description, but in 1821 it was broken up by the Turks. It is said that the chancellory of the Russian Consulate made a report about this and the dearly departed Bishop Grigori Ierianopoleos has declared as having seen in 1805 that gravestone in its integrity with a full gilded inscription. This information was obtained from a report of Master Toma Giusca addressed in 1836.[24]

This information about the death and the place of burial of Hetman Ivan
Mazepa in Moldavian primary sources is also supported by a contemporary
American scholar who states quite clearly that the remains of Hetman
Mazepa, who died on October 2, 1709, at Varnitsa, a suburb of the city
of Bender, were transported to Galați and found their resting place in the
St. George Monastery on March 18, 1710.[25] Today, a vistor to the Romanian city of Galați on the Danube will be able to find a residential
district of the city that bears the name of Mazepa. This residential district is now the only reminder that here was the last resting place of a
controversial historical personality admired by some and despised by
others.

Mazepa's ex-secretary, Filip Orlik assumed the title of Ukrainian
Hetman-in-exile and in 1710 led a military invasion of the right bank
Ukraine which ended in a disastrous route. A hard core of anti-Muscovites
remained with Hetman Orlik, but the majority of the Cossacks with their
colonels such as Galagan, Apostol and others drifted back to the Russian borderlands of the Ukraine and concluded peace with the Russian
state.[26] Hetman Orlik followed his ally King Charles XII to Sweden and
when his subsidy was eliminated after the final victory of the Russians,
he came to the capital of Moldavia, Jassy, where according to his biographers, B. Krupnitskii and I. Borshchak, he died in great poverty in
1742. Just like Andrew in the well known story *Taras Bulba* by N. Gogol
(1809-1852), Hetman Filip Orlik abandoned the faith of his ancestors,
the Eastern Orthodox Church, and openly became a Roman Catholic.
It is a strange fact that the Romanian Orthodox Hospodar of Moldavia,'
Constantin Mavrocordat (1741-1743) made the funeral arrangements by
paying the full bill for the funeral of Hetman Orlik. In fact:

> The Catholic Church whose loyal son Orlik was, also did not help
> him because according to the testimony of his most recent bio-
> graphers (B. Krupnitsky and I. Borshchak) he died in poverty in
> Moldavia in 1742 and as a pauper was buried at the expense of the
> Moldavian Hospodar.
>
> On the other hand at present the Galician-Catholics show special
> concern for the memory of Orlik. . . . The Apostolic Inspector,
> Archbishop, Kir Ivan Bichko, in an official letter addressed to the
> entire Galician Catholic clergy in Western Europe reminds them
> that Filip Orlik was a Catholic and orders that each year on the first
> Sunday after the day of St. Filip, a solemn mass should be offici-
> ated. [*Ukraina*, No. 8, 1952].[26]

NOTES

1. Vasily Klyuchevsky, *Peter the Great* (New York, 1958), p. 66. See also B. H. Sumner, *Peter the Great and the Emergence of Russia* (New York, 1969), p. 66.

2. Ibid., p. 67.

3. L. Jay Oliva, *Russia in the Era of Peter the Great* (Englewood Cliffs, N.J., 1969), p. 67.

4. Magdalena Laszlo-Kutiuk, *Relaştille Literare Româno-Ucrainene în secolul al XIX-lea şi la începutul secolului al XX-lea* (Romanian-Ukrainian Literary Relations in the Nineteenth and the beginning of the Twentieth Century) (Bucharest, 1974), p. 78.

5. Dimitrie Cantemir, *Descriptio Antiqui et Hodierni Status Moldaviae* (Bucharest, 1973), p. 218. See also my "Demetrius Kantemir and Russia," *Balkan Studies* (Thessaloniki, Greece, 1971), Vol. 12, no. 2, pp. 383-398.

6. A. Duţu and Paul Cernovodeanu eds., *Dimitrie Cantemir Historian of South East European and Oriental Civilizations* (Bucharest, 1973), p. 46. Cited hereafter as *Cantemir Historian.*

7. V. A. Golubutskii, *Zaporozhskoie Kazachestvo* (Zaporozhian Cossackdom) (Kiev, 1957), p. 51. See also my "Cossacks" *Handbook of World History Concepts and Issues* (New York, 1967), p. 251.

8. A. V. Boldur, *Ştefan cel Mare Voievod al Moldovei, 1457-1504* (Stephen the Great Voevod of Moldavia) (Madrid, Spain, 1970), p. 348.

9. Ion I. Nistor, "Miron Costin. Viaţa şi Opera" ("Miron Costin. Life and Works") *Analele Academiei Române* (Annals of the Romanian Academy) (Bucharest, 1942), Seria III, Tomul XXIV, Mem. 9, pp. 18-19. See also my "The Ukrainian Cossacks in the Early Anti-Ottoman Struggle for Independence of Moldavia," *East European Quarterly* (Boulder, Colorado, 1980), Vol. XIV, no. 2, p. 243.

10. P. P. Panaitescu ed., *Miron Costin. Opere Alese* (Miron Costin. Selected Works) (Bucharest, 1958), p. 52. Hereafter cited as *Miron Costin.* See also E. Russev, ed., *Miron Costin Letopiseţul Ţării Moldovei de la Aron-vodă încoace* (Miron Costin the Annals of the Moldavian State from Aron-Voievod to the Present) (Kishinev, 1972), pp. 166-167.

11. Michael Hrushevsky, *A History of the Ukraine* (New Haven, Connecticut, 1948), p. 153. See also George Vernadsky, *A History of Russia* (New Haven, Connecticut, 1959), p. 95.

12. Ibid., p. 152.

13. Philip Longworth, *The Cossacks* (New York, 1970), pp. 4-5.

14.   V. O. Kliuchevsky, *A Course in Russian History, the Seventeenth Century* (Chicago, 1968), pp. 112-113.

15.   *Cantemir Historian*, op. cit., pp. 52-53.

16.   George Vernadsky, *Political and Diplomatic History of Russia* (Boston, 1936), p. 221.

17.   Hrushevsky, op. cit., p. 353.

18.   E. M. Dvoichenko-Markova, *Russko-rumynskie literaturnye sviazi v pervoi polovine XIX veka* (Russian-Romanian Literary Relations in the First Half of the Nineteenth Century) (Moscow, 1966), pp. 166-167. See als Tr. Ionescu-Nişcov and A. Constantinescu, "Relaţii Politice între Moldova şi Rusia în timpul lui Vasile Lupu," ("Political Relations between Moldavia and Russia during the Time of Basil Lupu") *Relaţii romîno-ruse în trecut* (Past Romanian-Russian Relations) (Bucharest, 1957), pp. 3-30.

19.   Michail Kogalniceanu, ed., *Cronicele României seu letopiseţele moldaviei şi vlahiei* (The Chronicles of Romania or Annals of Moldavia and Wallachia) (Bucharest, 1872), Vol. II, p. 57.

20.   Ibid., p. 58.

21.   Ibid., p. 59.

22.   Ibid., p. 62.

23.   Ibid., p. 70.

24.   Laszlo-Kutiuc, op. cit., p. 76.

25.   Theodore Mackie, *Prince Mazepa Hetman of Ukraine in Contemporary English Publications 1687-1709* (Chicago, 1967), p. 36.

26.   Longworth, op. cit., p. 167. See also Ion Neculce, *Letopiseţul Ţării Moldovei şi o samă de cuvinte* (Annals of the Land of Moldavia and an Introduction) (Bucharest, 1959), pp. 186-187.

27.   Andrei Dikyi, *Neizvrashchenaia istoria ukrainy-rusi* (The Non-Perverted History of the Ukraine-Rus) (New York, 1960), Vol. I, p. 315.

Radu R. Florescu

SOCIAL CLASSES AND REVOLUTIONARY FERMENT
IN NINETEENTH CENTURY BUCHAREST

"The Paris of Eastern Europe," Bucharest, the capital of Wallachia, and from 1862 onwards that of Romania, was known by many epigrams coined by the numerous foreign travellers who visited the city. The city had suffered adversities, perhaps unique even in the stormy annals of southeastern Europe: major conflagrations—the fire of 1847 had destroyed perhaps one-fourth of the city; earthquakes of the intensity of the tremor that took 4000 lives last spring (1980); cholera epidemics which felled close to 100 persons a day in 1831; the unpredictable flooding of the Dambrovitza river which spared neither boyar palace nor peasant hamlet on its banks; it also suffered the brunt of 13 years of Russian, Austrian and Turkish occupation during the 19th century alone. Yet, this was supposedly "the city of happiness," founded according to legend by the peasant Bucur (the word *Bucuric* means happiness in Romanian), an inhabited settlement (the land probably belonged to the Bălăceanu boyars) located on the edge of the Vlasie forest and the steppes of the Bărăgan.[1] Bucharest, known to archeologists since prehistoric times, was first mentioned by Dracula as "fortress,' in 1458 and used as a capital in the later part of the 15th century for strategic and commercial ends.[2]

The historical evolution of Bucharest had little in common with either Western or Byzantine urban traditions; the nucleus of the city was the fortress and princely court, the seat of political and administrative power, surrounded by layers of boyar palaces, churches and monasteries, interspaced by open land, orchards, vineyards and gardens. Even allowing for a more densely populated central market place, which included the citizen's corporations and the merchant's shops located on the narrow, crooked streets in the heart of the town, the city presented the aspect of a large village, or more accurately a number of villages connected with each other, built around a church, a monastery or a boyar mansion.[3] Such clusters used to be called *mahalale*—there were some 123 'mahalale' in

159

1815, most of them bearing the name of a specific monastic foundation. At the beginning of the century the word *Mahala* literally meant, "part of the city." It was only later that the term acquired the perjorative meaning of a Western suburb or slum.

According to the first semi-scientific census, tabulated by the Russian administration in 1831, Bucharest and its suburbs had a population of 58,791 native inhabitants: by adding 1,795 foreigners and some 12,000 peasants who drifted in and out of the city, the total reached 70,000 inhabitants, which gave it the distinction of being the largest city between Vienna and Constantinople and undoubtedly the most populated in southeastern Europe.[4] (Sofia and Athens had little more than 28,000 inhabitants at the time, while the population of Belgrade reached 20,133 inhabitants only in 1866). Even more impressive was the total surface area in proportion to the total number of houses (10,074) monasteries and churches (126). The disproportion between the size of the city and the small density of the population diminished at the beginning of our century. (In 1906 for instance, Bucharest had a total population of 381,000 inhabitants, extended over 5,550 hectares and contained 35,000 houses.) The city had in effect reached the size of Vienna (which had only 200 hectares more) *but* a total population of a million and a half.

Comparing the notes of the late 19th century travellers with those who visited Bucharest during Phanariot times, the historian is bound to note the gradual shedding of Bucharest's oriental mantle and the city council's (there has been a city council since 1813) concern for urban environment.[5] By mid-century the unruly waters of the Dambovitza river was controlled—the last great flood took place under the reign of Prince Charles; the muddy streets and bridges once covered with wooden planks were paved with cobblestone (though as late as 1870 there were no sidewalks). The roads of the inner city were lit with the first oil lamps in Europe (in 1858) later by gas (1867) and at the turn of the century by electricity.[6] In 1880 the inhabitants fortunate enough to live in the center of the city had a filtered water supply, sufficient fountains, sewerage, police and fire protection which was more efficiently ensured from 1842 onwards, by dividing Bucharest into five autonomous administrative units each bearing the name of a different color (red, yellow, blue, black, green).[7] Since Kiselev's time the capital also enjoyed its first well groomed parks, like Cismigiu, by draining surrounding swamps.[8] The traditional aesthetically proportioned native palaces of the establishment with their vast gardens, were replaced by an incongrous array of ambitious western styled "hotel particuliers" with smaller courtyards, in the grandiose style of the Cantacuzino mansion which still survives on Calea Victoriei (today the Enescu museum).[9] With Bucharest officially becoming the capital of Romania in 1862, and the nation graduating to the status of a kingdom 20 years later, the government felt the need of constructing ambitious public, administrative and cultural edifices designed by foreign architects at great expense; as exemplified by the *Romanian Athene* built by Albert Galleron in 1886 the classic Ionian style.[10] The numerous picturesque oriental inns which had done a brisk business during the 18th century were replaced by heavily ornate Victorian hotels of the quality of the Athene Palace, resturants like Capşa, the Sacher of Romania (today Bucureşti) and fashionable clubs. Though little could be done with the maize of narrow crooked streets, which still gives the heart of the city the character of an oriental bazaar, the city planners attempted to Hausmannize Bucharest by cutting wide arteries from East to West and North to South, as well as concentric peripheric boulevards, delimitating the city proper, in order to facilitate communications. Horsedrawn carriages were still the principal means of transportation until 1871, when Bucharesters saw the first tramways on rails pulled by horses provide cheaper transportation for the populace. (Only 75 kilometers of rail were electrified at the end of the century.)[11]

Perhaps no city in Europe so strikingly exemplified the wide gulf existing between rich and the very poor; the incongruity between the ostentacious marble palaces of the establishment and the misery of the mud-built, thatched roofed "bordei" on the city's outskirts—a contradiction that gave even the most superficial traveller ample occasion for moral reproof.[12] The more modest native constructed frame houses of the merchants; even the first apartment blocks that had been built by the end of the century, for professional people and bureacrats somehow failed to blur this all too visible social gap, made even more glaring by the lack of amenities provided by the municipality for the poor. The suburbs which had engulfed the surrounding villages had no paving, no sewerage or city water; nothing beyond an occasional lantern for lighting. There was no police protection to speak of and the humble dwellings continued to be at the mercy of major conflagrations. The poorly constructed homes had few amenities of any kind and even a fireplace was a rare commodity. If there was a cellar, it was usually filled with water during the rainy season. In these conditions, it comes as no surprise that typhus and other diseases were rampant on the edge of the town. The conditions worsened with the growth of the urban proletariat. The mortality rate in the poor sections of Bucharest was high and the excess of births over deaths remained low to the end of our period. Indeed in some years (1866 and 1873 for instance), more people died than were born within the city (838 in 1866 and 1,033 in 1873).[13] Thus, the continued growth of the overall population was entirely due to the influx of peasants from the vicinity and the general magnet of attraction exercised by the capital nationwide.

My late friend, Constantin Giurescu, in his remarkable *History of Bucharest,* distinguished four social classes at the beginning of the 19th century: the *moşieri* (large landed proprietors), the *orăşeni* (the city dwellers), the *Rumâni* (small peasant proprietors) and the *gypsy* slaves, at the lowest end of the social scale.[14] The free servants (*sluji*) were placed under the classification of those whom they served, the members of the clergy were ranked as landed proprietors, and most of the foreign community were represented as *city dwellers* since for the most part they were either artisans or merchants. Though, I suppose these categories would loosely correspond to an upper (*moşieri*), middle (*orăşeni*), and lower (*Rumâni*) estate, it would be difficult even at the time to consider any of these groups as a close-knit and coherent social class.

The landowning class (*moşieri*) was numerically very small; one counted no more than 615 individual boyars, mostly of Greco-Romanian origin in 1831.[15] If one added dependents and the members of the clergy, per haps 2,598 in all. Though representing a small minority, some of these boyars—the Ghiculeşti for instance who owned most of the northeastern sections, still had a powerful economic base within the city and its suburbs at the beginning of the century. Most of them were shrewd businessmen constantly increasing their revenues from the inns and stores that they owned—and complaints against boyars and abbots who upped the rents of their stores were often heard in the boyar or city council. Associated with economic power went political responsibilities—the office of Prince was still elective until 1842—service in the Boyar Council, office in the city government, in the civil, judicial and military hierarchy, all centered in Bucharest. Although the "moşieri" still continued to have a strong voice in the affairs of the state until the end of the century, their power base was to wane considerably during the second half of the century as the monopoly of public offices was challenged by the middle class.[16] They lost their gypsy slaves in 1855; after Cuza no boyar was elected prince; privileges and titles were abolished in 1859, as equality of all citizens was proclaimed; both national and city assemblies were opened to the bourgeoisie. Cuza confronted the boyars with the first land reforms and nationalized the land of the Greek convents. In order to maintain luxurious standards of living and afford palatial mansions, the boyars gave up the distinction of representing the noble class and married into the ranks of the monied bourgeoisie (which they had done a century earlier when they courted the Greek Phanariot plutocracy).

If one were to equate Giurescu's word "Orășeni" with the middle class, these "city dwellers" represented an absolute majority of the total population of Bucharest as late as 1832—46,406 out of 72,591.[17] As the century wore on, however, whatever solidarity may have existed among the citizenry at the beginning of the century broke down and it becomes inconveivable to think of the "orășeni" as a unitary social class. Originally the nucleus of the city dwellers were formed by two categories: the artisans and the merchants. The artisans together with their apprentices were organized in carefully regulated corporations—there were fourteen in existence in 1831—each one administered by a single official. These corporations provided the city with basic articles of consumption such as clothing, houschold goods and building materials and are still remembered by the picturesque streets that bear the name of a particular guild, i.e., soapmaker, coppersmith, cloakmaker, hatter, brewer street. The merchants included the numerous storekeepers in and around Lipscani street (the street where articles from Leipzig were unpacked) in addition to innkeepers and money lenders who acted as bankers for the establishment. Within the ranks of the merchants were many foreigners, Greeks, Jews, Hungarians, and Serbs, many of them under foreign consular protection who lived in individual ghettos within the inner city, on streets that still recall their existence at one time, i.e., (Greek street-Serbian street). The foreign community of Bucharest divided along ethnic lines often in trouble with the authorities but constantly expanding owing to the new states' increasing need for qualified technicians imported from the West. By the end of the century, it may have reached as high as one-fifth or perhaps even one-quarter of the cities' total population.[18]

The opening of the Straits and the Danube to international commerce further helped delimitate specific social stratas within the middle class. For instance the influx of western consumer goods led to the gradual impoverishment of the native artisans who were compelled to close their corporations or move out to the suburbs where rents were less expensive. On the other hand the social and financial status of the merchants was enhanced by their new status of European brokers who sold the boyars' agricultural produce and catered to the expensive tastes of the upper class. Since Bucharest was to be endowed with a state supported industry, a centralized banking system, cultural and artistic facilities, a new category of bureaucrats, professional people and a native intelligentsia was added to the middle class. By the end of the century Giurescu's category of city dwellers was as outdated as his concept of a landowning class. There was indeed a new upper class, but it was composed of bankers, industrialists, the more important merchants, the military, administrative, educational, intellectual and professional elite, which in effect shared political power with the former boyars and represented a fairly coherent plutocracy. The middle bourgeoisie was composed of the rank and file of the bureaucracy and the professional people, while the diminished living standards of the artisan made his lot indistinguishable from that of the working class.

What of the lower class? Since Bucharest had always preserved a rural aspect, the city contained a large number of peasants whose number increased as villages became engulfed in the suburbs. In addition, there was a considerable floating rural population that drifted in and out of town, seeking agricultural employment. In the early history of Bucharest, it would have been difficult to classify the free peasant proprietor, the *Rumâni* who sold the product of his land in the city market, as a lower class, since his living standards were often higher than the lower echelons of the city dwellers. However, with the free peasants gradual impoverishment they were compelled to sell their land and entered into the same category of agricultural workers who migrated to the city.

The official Russian census of 1831, does not recognize the existence of a working class in the Western sense of an industrial proletariat, and there existed no capitalistic enterprise in Bucharest at that time. Even by the mid-century only a few enterprising boyars had established manufactures producing simple articles such as shawls, textiles, beer, employing a handful of workers. From the year 1866 onwards, the industrial needs of a new state, especially the need for military hardware, railroad communications, the birth of credit institutions, the Hohenzollern's tendency to seek capital loans from abroad, the introduction of steam and western expertise, all favored the development of simple capitalistic enterprises, employing at most a hundred workers.[19] Apart from weaponry, most of this effort was directed to the creation of a light industry; sugar refineries, breweries, bakeries, textiles, brick, cement and furniture factories, many of them using steam power and financed by private and state capital. Industrial growth, however, was slow and as late as 1898, Bucharest had only a total of 60 enterprises employing 4,100 workers of whom 2,900 were Romanians, hardly the making of an industrial city. Yet, Bucharest was Romania's most industrialized city containing one-third of the total number of enterprises and 40% of the nation's labor force.[20] No matter how modest, this industrialization had the impact of a suction cup drawing the itinerant rural workers in from the surrounding countryside and crowding them on the northeastern section of the town, which gained the dubious distinction of representing Romania's earliest industrial slum. Due to the abundance of unskilled labor, the high levels of unemployment and the absence of working class legislation, labor conditions in these early factories was abysmally low. Working days often reached 16 hours per day including Sunday (there were no holidays). Women and children were exploited at will and there was little recourse against the hazards of industrial accidents. Needless to add, culture and education was reserved only for the well-to-do.[21]

Given this complex social stratification, tensions ran high in the city throughout the 19th century and one may well describe Bucharest as the ideological and political center of the revolutionary forces not only of Romania but of Southeastern Europe. The presence of a large foreign community straddling social categories helped focus attention on Balkan wars of national liberation. Most historians will agree that the revolution of Kara George in 1804, the Greek revolution of 1821, the Bulgarian and Albanian struggles for independence had deep ideological roots in Bucharest. From the Romanian point of view, Bucharest was the revolutionary city par excellence. The city's ferment reflected in the struggle of a whole nation for social equality and national independence. 1821, 1848 and 1859 are just a few of the crucial turning points when the future of Romania was shaped by events on the barricades of the capital.[22]

It would be unduly simplistic to describe the revolutionary tradition of Bucharest in terms of the Marxist struggle between haves and have-nots, and to consider all these upheavals purely in terms of class conflicts. Both 1821, 1848 and 1859, clearly set the national objective of independence above the goals of social equality, thereby rallying all segments of the population in a common struggle. Tudor Vladimirescu, the leader of the revolution of 1821, knew where to find, "the good boyars," of Bucharest affiliated to his cause. In the same manner, virtually all social categories, the boyars, the merchants, the artisans, the priests and the peasants, rallied to the national ideals of the revolution of 1848 and insured its immediate triumph with only a few conservative landowners defending the status quo.[23] The leadership of that revolution with a few notable exceptions was almost exclusively drawn from the liberal, youthful elements of the upper class. That they misled the masses and the bourgeoisie by substituting social for national programs was noted by some with dismay. Though most of the population of Bucharest which had experienced Turkish and Russian repression accepted the truism that political independence must precede constitutional and social reform. Perhaps the most important victory of Romanian nationalism, the election of Alexander John Cuza to the joint throne of Moldo-Wallachian Principalities in 1859, was a cleverly engineered boyar coterie prepared in Bucharest's upper class lobbies in which the masses played a marginal part. Even Cuza's demise, a bloodless coup d'état which displeased the rank and file, was a plot carried out by members of the establishment.

In the second half of the century the struggle between generations, between the young and old boyars gave way to a confrontation between landowners and the newly enfranchised middle class. The latter won for themselves a place in national and city government. Using the liberal party as a vehicle which best represented their interests, they virtually eliminated the landowners conservative party from politics. This opened the way for a realignment of forces. The upper bourgeoisie (the commercial, banking and intellectual elite) reinforced the ranks of the landowners and gave the new establishment a decidedly conservative character. This tergiversation occurred precisely at the time when the lower echelons of the bourgeoisie and some of the impoverished rural masses sank into the ranks of the industrial proletariat, thus sharpening the class confrontation and dividing the city more neatly between haves and have-nots. Yet, even allowing for strikes and minor social upheavals, Bucharest never really experienced social revolution such as had terrorized the propertied class during the Paris commune of 1871. Even the peasant revolution of 1907 affected mostly Moldavia and awakened very little echo in the capital. The principal reason for the absence of a major social confrontation can be found precisely in some of the circumstances affecting the character of the city outlined above. In spite of urbanization, Bucharest retained down to the end of our period the analytical character of a large rural community with a governmental and commercial center. The inner city was still divided into self-contained districts, most of which represented a cross section of the entire population. Apart from the new mahala or suburbs which had more of a rural than urban character, there were few working class districts in the strict sense, where the industrial proletariat represented an actual majority. The unusually large area occupied by the city thwarted as we have seen the progress of the municipal facilities; it was also a deterent both to efficient organization and concentration of a potential commune. Besides, the rural population on the outskirts, generally was more interested in agrarian than industrial reform. The workers may also have been impressed by the simple fact that in Bucharest were concentrated the overwhelming forces of the establishment with its topheavy bureaucracy, its ruthless police and military establishment which had proven its loyalty to the regime repeatedly by quelling minor disturbances. Even admitting that barricades could hypothetically have been set up on the narrow paved streets of some mahala, the broad boulevards which had been cut through and around the city could transport the forces of reaction, almost to any point with maximum speed and efficiency.

History certainly provides a few instances of "revolutions of despair." The people in revolution, however, will rarely defy authority when they are excessively oppressed. Revolutions generally occur when their leaders perceive no matter how vaguely, the possibility of victory and the dawn of better things to come. Such perspectives simply did not exist for the lower classes in the Bucharest of the nineteen-hundreds. The working class was dispersed, divided and simply too downtrodden to revolt.

NOTES

1. Some scholars have traced Bucharest to the Dacian word "bucurie," meaning pleasure or satisfaction in Romanian.

2. The Dracula document commemorating this site refers to the location "Iuxta Fluvium Acque Dimbovita" and is dated June 13, 1458. Radu Florescu and Raymond McNally, *Dracula a Biography*, New York, 1973, p. 53.

3. Constantin C. Giurescu, *Istoria Bucureștilor din cele mai vechi timpuri pînă în zilele noastre*, Bucharest, 1966, pp. 353.

4. Dan Berindei, "Bucureștii anului 1906 și ai răcoalei din 1907" *l Materiale de Istorie și Muzeografie*, Bucharest, 1965, Vol. II., p. 231.

5. Berindei, "Bucureștii," p. 323 et seq.

6. The poorer section of the city were unlit, and the streets had an occasional lantern. I.C. "Igiena Capitalei" *Protestarea*, nr. 59, 30 April 1906, p. 2.

7. Florian Georgescu, "Aspecte privind împărțirea administrativă ș evoluția demografică din Bucureștii anilor 1831-1848," *Materiale de Istorie și Muzeografie*. Bucharest, 1966, Vol. III, p. 53.

8. Florian Georgescu, *Istoria Orașului București*. Bucharest, 1965, Vol. I, p. 199.

9. A good study on the house bordering Calea Victoriei is Ștefan Ionescu's *Podul Mogoșoaiei Calea Victoriei*, Bucharest, 1961.

10. V. Zamfirescu, V. Cândea, V. Moga Ateneul Român, Bucharest, 1976, p. 65.

11.   Berindei, Bucureștii," p. 232.

12.   Foreign travellers and commentators who wrote on Bucharest are legion. Among the more accurate are J. A. Vaillant, *La Romanie*, 2 vols., Paris, 1844; Fr. Dame, *Bucarest en 1906*, Bucharest, 1937, and Paul Morand, *Bucarest*, Paris, 1935.

13.   Dame, *Bucarest en 1906*, p. 138.

14.   Giurescu, *Istoria Bucureștilor*, p. 275.

15.   Idem.

16.   Georgescu, ed., *Istoria orașului*, p. 185.

17.   Giurescu, *Istoria Bucureștilor*, p. 275.

18.   There were 1,795 foreigners in Bucharest in 1831. Florian Georgescu, *Pagini din trecutul Bucureștilor*, Bucharest, 1959, p. 26.

19.   For the development of capitalistic enterprise in Bucharest, see Matei Ionescu, "Episoade din epoca începuturilor industriei moderne Bucureștene," *Materiale de Istorie și Muzeografie*, Bucharest, 1966, Vol. IV, p. 167.

20.   In 1901-1902 of 39,746 workers in industry nation wide, 40% worked in the Ilfov district, especially in Bucharest. Berindei, "Bucureștii anului 1906," p. 234.

21.   See N. N. Constantinescu (ed.), *Din istoria formării și dezvoltării clasei muncitoare din România pînă la primul război mondial*, Bucharest, 1959.

22.   A good study which sins by overstressing the role of the masses during the revolution of 1848 is: Florian Georgescu, *Participarea maselor populare Bucureștene la revoluția din 1848*, Bucharest, 1961.

23.   Radu Florescu, *The Struggle Against Russia in the Danubian Principalities*, Munich, 1962, p. 179.

Bruce C. Fryer

BĂLCESCU AS AN ECONOMIC HISTORIAN AND THEORIST

Whether one is considering him as an historian or an economic theorist, Nicoale Bălcescu is an outstanding example of a 19th century East-European liberal. In the introduction to his very first article, Bălcescu noted that the true history of the Romanian people had not yet been written. Although there were biographies of the rulers, the history of ideas, customs, commerce, and other social institutions still lay under dusty chronicles and contemporary documents.[1] In an attempt to correct this situation Bălcescu began writing historical articles and collaborating with August T. Laurian on the publication of *The Historical Magazine for Dacia.*[2] His first article dealing with economics, "Concerning the Social Conditions of the Land-tillers in the Romanian Principalities at Various Times," appeared in the second volume of this magazine.[3]

In this article Bălcescu not only recounted the past social conditions of the agricultural laborers of the Danubian Principalities, but also attacked the landowning system existing in his own time. He set the tone of the article by affixing a quote from Mirabeau to it: "Privileges will disappear, but the people will live forever." Next, he made comparative remarks about the condition of farmers in various times and countries. The purpose of these remarks was to demonstrate that, unlike people in certain other areas, most of the earliest Romanians were freeholders, who had since been dispossessed. Finally, he proceeded to a brief history of land holding in the Danubian Principalities beginning with the Roman colonization of Dacia.[4]

Bălcescu theorized that the Romans who colonized Dacia divided the land among themselves, as was their custom, and hence became freeholders. He maintained that the barbarian invaders did not destroy the landholding system since they were not farmers and merely passed through Dacia. Thus, he asserted, the development of feudalism in the Principalities did not begin until the 1320s, when many Romanians living in nearby areas fled to Moldavia and Wallachia to escape the invading Ottoman Turks. Under these circumstances the Romanian princes divided their domains into three parts: two parts became the small holdings of the colonistsî

169

the other was available for cultivation in return for several days work. In this way the corvée system was inaugurated, and Bălcescu felt serfdom was the inevitable result.[5] At first the greater part of the population were freeholders. But as time passed, more and more freeholders were dispossessed because of interest, need, and force. The process was accelerated as the owners of the great estates successfully applied to the princes for exemptions from paying taxes on their villages. The result was that the tax burden increasingly fell on the small landholders, many of whom concluded it was in their own best interest to sell themselves and their estates to the great landholders in order to escape the tyranny of the government and enjoy freedom from taxation. According to Bălcescu, other small landholders gave up their land only because of need and/or force. While defending the freedom of their country against the attacks of neighboring peoples, many of this latter group were unwittingly losing their own individual freedom. Upon returning home from the wars, many veterans were forced to selll their lands and their freedom to pay their taxes to the state. "Thus," Bălcescu concluded, "bondage was the reward of the upper classes to the lower classes who had always fed them, respected them, preserved them in their position and sacrificed their work, money, and lives for their country and for liberty."[6]

Bondage led to the extinction of equality in Romania, Bălcescu asserted, and led to the deplorable situation in which a whole nation was subjected to a few individuals. An aristocracy of wealth and position was established and it proceeded to tighten its grip over the country. Finally, during the reign of Mihai Viteazul (Michael the Brave, 1593-1601), the serfs were formally bound to the soil and the development of a feudal regime in the Danubian Principalities was completed. After the reign of this prince, "the country was divided into two hostile camps with opposing interests."[7] The general populace became unresponsive to the patriotic appeals of the princes and the boyars, no longer desiring to fight for a country in which they had neither rights nor liberties. The result was that soon those "who made bondsmen of their brothers were forced to lower their arrogant heads and to suffer under the yoke of the exploitation of the Phanariotes."[8] In these circumstances, the boyars became more sympathetic toward the lower classes, and on August 5/17, 1746, the General Assembly of Wallachia emancipated the serfs. The Moldavian assembly passed a similar act shortly thereafter.[9]

But Bălcescu asserted that it was the boyars who benefited most from the emancipation decrees of 1746. The serfs just freed were not given the right to become small landholders upon the payment of compensation to their landlords, nor were they given hereditary rights to the use of land in exchange for the payment of dues; moreover, they were forbidden to leave their former master's village without his permission. Furthermore, the General Assembly decreed that they should perform twenty-four days of corvée, give a quitrent in crops and hay, and make still other contributions if they wanted to keep cattle. In reality the ex-serfs's osition worsened in Bălcescu's estimation; they remained subject to their former landlords, yet these were no longer obligated to provide them with tools or give them food in sickness or famine. Other non-nobles also suffered as a result of the emancipation. Up to this time peasants had been divided into three groups: freeholders, who had their own land; serfs or bondsmen; and finally freemen who lived on the land of boyars and monasteries without being bound to the soil. After the emancipation of the serfs, all three of these groups were merged into one and subjected to the same regulations.[10]

Bălcescu insisted that "bondage in an inescapable consequence of the corvée; it is rooted in the absolute dependence in which the poor peasant finds himself in regard to his overlord, who alone possesses and is able to give him the tools of work."[11] The laws proclaiming the serfs to be free did nothing to alter this situation. Romania lacked capitalistic or proprietary cultivators able to finance agriculture independently. "Capital alone is able to assure the independence of the peasant," Bălcescu insisted.[12] As it stood, independence was recognized only in the law. In actual fact, the peasant's position worsened as the proprietor's obligations to them were reduced. Under these circumstances, it is not surprising that many peasants became highwaymen while others became degenerate.[13]

The conditions of the peasants in both Principalities continued to grow worse with the passage of time, until finally those of Wallachia rose in desperation in 1821. Bălcescu felt that a complete and radical reform of all Romanian institutions was needed in that year. Some enlightened philanthropists hoped for these innovations, but they were not effected. It was the upper classes who profited from the rising of 1821, since the princes of the country were once again chosen from among their ranks rather than from among the Phanariotes. The plight of the peasants remained unchanged. "Thus," Bălcescu wrote, concluding his article, "in our day we see our brave and powerful nation. . . mouldering in the grave. . . because an egotistical aristocracy trampled the rights of man underfoot."[14]

Bălcescu noted that many documents, other than those he included in his appendix, supported his arguments and promised that he would return to this subject again in the future and judge the relative positions of the various classes without pity or partiality. In the meantime, he would be happy if this article, along with the acts annexed to it, would make the upper classes realize their errors and awaken in them a sense of justice and humanity. He prophisied destruction for any nation in which the few continued to base their power and happiness on the suffering of the masses. Since the peasants did not succeed in improving their position in 1821, Bălcescu insisted they would surely make another attempt in the future.[15]

Bălcescu's article "Concerning the Social Conditions of the Land-tillers in the Romanian Principalities at Various Times" is significant for several reasons. First, Bălcescu was one of the earliest Romanian historians to concern himself with the actions of the common people as revealed through their social institutions, ideas, customs, and commerce. He was also one of the first Romanians to document his works consistently. Furthermore, Bălcescu not only recorded the past in his articles, he also interpreted it and related it to suggestions for improving the contemporary situation. Finally, in writing this article, Bălcescu began to develop several historical ideas which he professed until he died: the ideas of class warfare and determinism, which in turn led him to the belief that only a violent revolution could bring about the changes necessary to inaugurate a democratic republic.

II

Bălcescu's conclusion that since the peasants did not succeed in improving their position in 1821 they would make another attempt in the future was, in a sense, correct. In reality, however, the next attempt came not as a result of peasant initiative, but as a result of efforts on the part of liberals such as Bălcescu to organize the peasants and gain benefits on their behalf. Thus, conspiratorial societies grew up on the Principalities in he 1830s.[16] Some of these were uncovered with the result that the participants were arrested for varying lengths of time. Other liberals went into exile, mainly to Paris. Bălcescu falls into both groups.[17] The outbreak of the February revolution of 1848 in Paris was the signal for the outbreak of similar uprisings in many areas, including the Romanian lands. Bălcescu and other exiles rushed home to lead these movements.[18]

In line with the views expressed in his article "Concerning the Social Conditions of the Land-tillers in the Romanian Principalities at Various Times," Bălcescu took an active stand in favor of appropriating land for the peasants in the early stages of the Revolutions of 1848. Evidence indicates that he was instrumental in the adoption of Article Thirteen of the Islaz Proclamation of June 9/21, 1848, which provided for the emancipation of bondsmen with indemnification for the property owners.[19] He felt that the Romanian Revolution of 1848 was embodied in this article and that the others merely reiterated the program of 1821. He wanted quick positive action on Article Thirteen to ensure the peasantry's support of the revolution, but he faced much opposition. The provisional government at Bucharest made important concessions to the boyars by signing a decree on June 16/28, 1848 expressly stating that the relationship between the peasants and the proprietors would remain the same until a constitutional convention had been convened.[20]

These actions disturbed Bălcescu and on June 22/July 4, 1848, he wrote to Al. Golescu Negru:

> Our measures concerning property, leaving things in the old condition, are somewhat harmful. . . . The peasants do not believe the promises and say why not give it [land] to them now. We have made an error. . . . Now what must be done? In the first place, I recommend enacting the proclamation wiping out serfdom which was originally submitted to the printer. . . . Next, . . . [I recommend that we] revolutionize the peasantry. Thus, even if the General Assembly should wish to be reactionary, it will be prevented from doing so. . . . The peasants will be elevated to a state in which they are no longer required to fulfull their duties and also [are able to] reclaim their rights. Otherwise, our revolution, which is political and social, is half, perhaps, completely lost. . . . [21]

The revolutionaries, he asserted, could gain the support of the people only by energetic and relentless action toward the conservatives.

Due to Bălcescu's insistence and the growing discontent of the peasantry, the government restored the discussion of Article Thirteen of the Islaz Proclamation to its agenda for June 27/July 9. Not wishing to see the implementation of the article but realizing that action was needed to quiet the peasantry, the government temporized and signed a decree setting up a property commission, whose membership was to be divided equally between representatives of estate owners and representatives of serfs. The commission was supposed to draft a bill for the implementation of Article Thirteen and submit it to the future constitutional assembly. Bălcescu accepted these measures, seeing in them the means of keeping the article under discussion, of bringing pressure to bear on the provisional government and constitutional assembly, and mobilizing large numbers of peasants, since half of the comission's membership would be drawn from this class. Athough a great boyar, Alexandru Racoviță, became president of the commission, Ion Ionescu de la Brad, a noted Moldavian agronomist and friend of Bălcescu, was chosen to be vice president.[22]

Despite the fact that Bălcescu was not actively involved in the work of the property commission, he studied its proceedings with interest.[23] In its first session, held on August 10/22, the property commisison recognized the rights of freedom of labor and property ownership, with the corollary right of expropriation by the state, accompanied by indemnification, for the cause of public utility. It also declared that the need to grant land to the peasants was both urgent and in the public interest.[24] However, when the commission attempted to draw up detailed proposals concerning these resolutions, it became bogged down in acrimonious debates. Neither the peasants actually sitting on the commission, nor Bălcescu writing in retrospect, felt that the proposals drawn up by the boyars would have given them an adequate amount of land to support themselves.[25] On August 19/31, when the commission was to decide on the question of land distribution, Ion Eliade Rădulescu[26] entered the hall and read a decree issued by the *caimacam* suspending the work of the property commission. Hence, the property commission actually sat only a little over a week before, in Bălcescu's words, the privileged classes, seeing that they could not defeat the peasants in open debates, pressured the government to dissolve it.[27]

III

The arrival to Turkish troops in Wallachia and the failure of representatives of the provisional government to gain concessions in Constantinople made it imperative to take concrete steps toward instituting land reforms in order to maintain the support of the peasants for the revolution. In order to impress this on the people, Bălcescu anonymously published an article "On the Alloting of Land to the Peasants" in the four issues of *Poporul Suveran* [The Sovereign People] appearing between August 23 and September 3, 1848 (o.s.).[28] In his estimation the question of making the peasant a proprietor was the most delicate and passionate of those considered since June 11/23; nevertheless, he was convinced that it would be beneficial. According to his criterea a social measure had to meet three requirements in order to be so classified. It had to be national (benefit the institution of the nation), be moral, and, finally, be useful to all citizens.

He proposed examining the question of peasant proprietorship dispassionately on the basis of these three criteria.[29]

Bǎlcescu argued that statesmen and historians, both past and present, accepted as axiomatic the idea that those nations in which land was owned by the majority of their citizens had unlimited advantages over those whose inhabitants were merely simple tenants. He asserted that men who possessed land were more imbued with national spirit and would oppose foreign attacks more vigorously than those who did not possess land. Property owners would defend their country even more vigorously than men of equal wealth whose riches were in money and moveable property, for the latter would be able to flee from invaders and take their wealth with them. For them, as for landless persons, the nation was merely a place where they could obtain their bread; they would be grateful to it only so long as this was assured. If an enemy attack enhanced their positions, they might even take comfor in the public calamity. For the property owners, however, happiness and wealth were contained in their land. To abandon this would compromise their interests and ruin them. Furthermore, Bǎlcescu noted, landed peasants would be more willing to perform labor services and pay dues and would be less likely to rebel than landless persons. The reason for this again centered around the former's possession of concrete property; they would rather serve the government than risk losing their property in a desperate uprising. Hence, he concluded that whereas peasant proprietors are an element of stability and strength, tenants are an element of weakness and disorder in society.[30] He argued that land distribution was essential to the progress and prosperity of a society. Almost sixty years earlier, he admonished, the world had begun to cast off the chains of all types of bondage through the French Revolution, and since then each country had been forced to fulfill the just demands of its people in one way or another.[31]

Next, Bǎlcescu considered the question of "whether it is right and moral to make the peasant a proprietor, in other words, if it is right and moral to expropriate a part of the land from the old possessors, to indemnify them, and to divide the indemnified land among some 375,000 families of peasants."[32] He asked the proprietors and nobles if they had ever asked themselves how they obtained possession of their wealth, why they took such a large share of the harvest each year, or what right they had to the land they occupied. The upper class claimed the land was theirs alone because they had received it from their parents, who had inherited it from their ancestors, and so on back to the time of the conquest.

"Madness, fatal madness," was Bălcescu's reply.[33] Many spirited peasants who had served meekly before were now beginning to reply that "on this land where we find ourselves today, were found also our ancestors; furthermore [they were here] in more distant times, when the greater part of the country was covered with forests and all the fields were full of brambles."[34] The forests died, the brambles were cut, and the lands occupied by the nobles were transformed into good ploughland and hayfields. As this happened, the nobles' intrusion increased and they became rulers. On the other hand, the peasants and their predecessors who worked so hard to improve the fields did not profit at all; they still suffered as much as before.

But, Bălcescu said, this was not just; the peasants had their rights on the land—the rights earned by their labor and the labor of their ancestors accruing from generation to generation, from century to century. He was of the opinion that "in any common operation, if some are useful, the others must similarly be useful; because if you (the nobles) have contributed with your land, we (the peasants) also have contributed with our arms, a property contribution which is just as legitimate and sacred as your property."[35] If the landholders insisted on reaping benefits from the land, then the workers should reap the benefits produced by the labor of their hands, the sole means of their salvation. If these rights had been recognized in the past, the peasants would have obtained enough wealth to purchase their own land and refuse the bits of land some now proposed giving them. Since the peasants were never paid a just price for their labor, Bălcescu felt their rights to the proprietors' land were even stronger than before. The nobles achieved their wealth by siphoning off the surplus value (*prisos de valoare*), which could only be attributed to the labor of the peasants and their ancestors, into their own pockets. Without the peasant's labor, the land of the nobles would "still be uncultivated and in its primitive condition would bring very small returns; this surplus value in your return is our wealth. It is our property."[36] In the past, therefore, the proprietors were disposing of wealth which was only partially theirs. Nevertheless, neither the peasants nor those who made revolution in their name wanted "to gain this illegitimate part of your returns nor to seek the means by which the great majority of nobles have obtained their property."[37] "The revolution," Bălcescu asserted, "is generous, and in its progress to the future, toward perfection, towards God, it forgets all past evils. The true question is whether the state is able, for the general interest, for the happiness of all, to expropriate property from individuals by force and to indemnify them."[38] He

felt that a nation would have to be very backward, very barbarous to hold
a contrary principle. "If," Bălcescu asked, "it is unjust to sacrifice in some
the interests of all, how much more unjust is it to sacrifice the interests of
the many for the few? "[39] But expropriation of the nobles' land was not
a question of sacrifice because some indemnification was provided for.
If these ideas were not accepted it would be impossible for civilization
to progress. It would be impossible to build public transportation such as
railroads and canals, for at every turn interested proprietors would claim
that their property rights were being violated. Barbarous institutions
would still stifle European civilization; peasants in France and Germany
would still be subject to the corvée of their seigneurs; the world would
still be in darkness. In Bălcescu's estimation, a civilized society was separated from a barbarous one because:

> in one the rights of society are proclaimed to be more precious
> than the rights of the individual, but the interest of the individual
> is not left in the shadow; that is to say the one who is expropriated
> through force is indemnified. In the other, the interest of the in-
> dividual is considered to be more precious than the right of society,
> meaning it is better for a societal right to perish than an individual
> one.[40]

Despite the evidence that the interests of society demanded it, reactionary
boyars did not wish to sell part of their land; consequently, two million
men suffered because three thousand would not understand. Bălcescu
felt it was imperative, not only economically but from the vantage point
of justice and morality, to give the peasant land.

Finally, Bălcescu asked if it would be useful to grant land to the peasants, or if it would lead to their impoverishment. If it could be demonstrated that this measure would impoverish the proprietors or decrease
their income, Bălcescu declared that he and his followers would be the
first to oppose it. In an effort to demonstrate that this would not be the
case, he drew a parallel between the international scene and the internal
situation of Romania. For half a century, Bălcescu affirmed, a common
diplomatic policy had been to keep one's neighbors as poor as possible
in order to profit from their poverty, because a nation surrounded by
poor neighbors would appear richer, more powerful, and more terrifying.
However, by 1848 statesmen realized this was only an illusion and were
attempting to enrich their neighbors. And how, asked Bălcescu, could it
be otherwise? How could a nation be rich if its neighbors vegetated in

wretchedness? If countries are impoverished their needs are necessarily very simple; they are unable to buy many goods from other nations because they are poor, and probably they will produce little that wealthier, more powerful countries are interested in buying. But if the wealthier nation helped the poorer to increase its production, its consumption would also increase since "a people which produces little consumes little; similarly, one which produces much consumes much."[41] It is in the interest of every nation to help others become more prosperous; by doing so they really help themselves. As Bălcescu stated it, "One's happiness is immediately tied to the happiness of other people. This is the divine law which calls for solidarity between the rich and the poor of all the nations of the earth. The law seeks, it forces people to wish each other well."[42]

Bălcescu maintained the situation was similar for different classes in the same nation. He did not believe that one class could be truly rich and happy (although he did admit they could be rich) while others were poor and unfortunate, having nothing to buy or sell. He insisted that if the lower classes were enriched, their commerce would increase just as in the case of nations. The result would be that those individuals who were presently rich would become still richer. "Wealth cannot be born other than through wealth; happiness, other than in the midst of the happiness of all. Happiness and wealth are not possible in the midst of sorrow and poverty, not even for the privileged class! . . . It [happiness] will be possible for you only when you make it possible for someone else."[43] Then Bălcescu told his readers, "seek the divine decree, the holy law, the law of love which is served even by the passions of men, by the egotism which is inseparable from the privileged classes, that forces them to work for the happiness of the entire society," because in so doing they further enrich themselves.[44]

Bălcescu thus reached the same conclusion on the issue of granting propety to the peasants regardless of the perspective from which he approached it. He felt the action was necessary from the point of view of national unity, justice, and even of utility; furthermore, he felt the state should indemnify the landlords for similar reasons.

IV

The Wallachian Revolution of 1848 was crushed by joint Turkish-Russian intervention in the middle of September of that same year.[45] Bălcescu was arrested and taken to Ruschuk with some other revolutionaries. Here he was put on a ship traveling upstream to Bosnia where he was to be exiled. Nevertheless, Bălcescu, and some of his compatriots, managed to elude their Turkish guards after having been taken ashore at Orșova. A free man once again, Bălcescu journeyed to Transylvania arriving there at the moment when that province's revolution was in full progress. When this movement also failed he returned to Paris, arriving there on October 5/17, 1849.[46]

Bălcescu continued to press for economic reforms in his homeland even after he was exiled. His last and most important work on economics, *Question economique des Principautes Danubiennes*, first appeared in the form of an unsigned pamphlet, intended as a memorandum to the Sublime Porte.[47] Bălcescu began the article by describing the natural riches of the Danubian Principalities and proceeded by pointing out the absymal conditions under which most of the inhabitants of these provinces lived. He attempted to make it clear that the socioeconomic problems he described did not date from 1848; they were not, as many maintained, diplomatic issues, foreign importations, or echoes of agitation in the West. These problems went back "to the beginnings of our society; they were foreseen from the day when the equality of our ancestors disappeared, from the day when there existed poor and rich by birth, slaves and masters, exploiters and exploited."[48] The situation grew progressively worse with the passage of time becaue the problem was rooted in history. Since the only way to solve it was to understand its origins, Bălcescu gave a brief survey of the history of the Principalities. Thus, in the next section he reiterated and amplified the information presented in his earlier article "Concerning the Social Conditions of the Land-tillers in the Romanian Principalities at Various Times."[49] The new material began with a description of the revolution of 1821. Tudor Vladimirescu,[50] the leader of the revolt, affirmed the devotion of the Principality to the Porte, but required "that they [the officials of the Porte] return the former rights to the country, that they dismiss the Phanariots, that they withdraw power from the rapacious hands of the extortioners, and that they establish a constitution in harmony with the democratic traditions of the ancient institutions."[51]

As soon as native rulers were named, calm was re-established and the princes turned to reforming the administration and drawing up a constitution, but circumstances beyond their control—the war between Russian and the Porte in 1828—prevented them from completing their task. Tsarist troops occupied Moldavia and Wallachia and the Russians inaugurated an era of reforms from without through the *Règlement organique* of 1831.[52]

The *Règlement* followed the time honored three-fold division of the lands. Two-thirds of the lands were set aside for the use of the peasants, who paid the proprietors a rent in either money or services. In these circumstances, Bălcescu asserted, there were two hereditary proprietors on each piece of property, the nominal proprietor (owner) and the peasant proprietor (worker). He felt the property rights of both should have been equal, but they were not. The nominal proprietor had many privileges and immunities which the peasant possessor did not enjoy. In addition to this, the amount of land granted to the peasants was inadequate, so they had to bargain with their landlords for more almost immediately. As Bălcescu noted, the demand for additional land and the offers of more land were not balanced by reciprocal need, and abuses appeared. Abuses occurred because the *Règlement organique* permitted the boyar to convert the corvée into monetary payment and gave him (as opposed to a commission on which peasants and proprietors were represented) the sole power to decide what the sum should be. The result was obvious: the landlords set the sums at impossibly high levels. Bălcescu pointed out that it was physically and economically impossible for many of the peasants to meet their obligations to their landlords, let alone additional obligations due to the communes and to the state. He calculated that if one counted the days in the agricultural year and then subtracted Sundays, holidays, bad weather, and work due the lord, the peasants were left with a deficit of fifty days a year.[53]

"The misery and the slavery, the depopulation and ruin of our country are the fruit of this monstrous legislation that one should have called disorganic; Russia and the Porte maintained it after 1848 against the wishes of the people and in spite of the protests that they raised at its birth,"[54] said Bălcescu. He noted that Russian bayonets had to be used against the Moldavian peasants; the "first day of the reign of the *Règlement* was a day of shooting and carnage."[55] The peasants' attitude toward the Russian legislation finally alerted Prince Ghica to the need for reforms and from 1837 to 1842 he repeatedly asked the boyar assembly to relieve the peasants' condition and thus avert a catastrophe. However, the calloused boyars did not wish to cede anything meaningful. In Bălcescu's opinion the measures Prince Ghica took were poorly conceived, irresolute, and tardy. As his government was already discredited, they merely hastened his fall, which was decided by the boyars in concert with Russia. Nor did conditions improve under the next prince, Bibescu.[56]

The violent debates of the previous ruler, Prince Ghica, and the boyars, and the constant suffering of the people led to the formation of the

National Party which sought a just solution to the problems between the
proprietors and the peasants. In 1840, this party recommended the peasants be made free tenants with hereditary rights to the lands they possessed with the obligation of paying the nominal owners a money rent, as
opposed to a service one, fixed once and for all on the basis of the real
value of the soil. In 1846, this program was submitted to the public
through the publication of Bălcescu's article "Concerning the Social
Conditions of the Land-tillers in the Romanian Principalities at Various
Times." Much to the alarm and stupefaction of the boyars, the liberal
leaders of the Revolution of 1848 attempted to implement it.

Bălcescu believed that Article 13 of the Islaz Proclamation which en-
visaged making proprietors of the peasants and indemnifying the boyars
was the cornerstone of the Wallachian Revolution of 1848. Inquiring
as to whether this reform was just, useful, and possible, he answered by
amplifying and supplementing the material presented in his earlier work
"On the Alloting of Land to the Peasants."[57]

He clearly indicated that he did not wish to abolish private property.
It was not private property, but the abuse of the principle, which had
created the disasterous situation in which the country found itself. Rightly used, property led to the creation of agriculture, commerce, industry,
society, indeed to the creation of all the marvels of civilization.[58] Granting freedom of work and the wherewithal to acquire a productive capital
for everyone would end the abuse of the principle.

Bălcescu's proposals regarding the means of obtaining the money needed to indemnify the boyars were clearly spelled out and economically
sound. He favored the establishment of credit institutions by the state.
As the main source of appreciable capital in Romania was the soil, Bălcescu recommended the establishment of mortgage loan societies, or land
banks. By means of mortgages the soil, fixed capital, would become a
circulatory capital as legal tender without losing its ability to produce
more wealth through crops. This capital could be redeemed through
savings over a period of years and thus the debt would be liquified. Bălcescu pointed out that land banks were not a utopian idea or a novelty.
They had been successful in Silesia and other provinces of Prussia, in
Württemberg, Hanover, Switzerland, Holstein, Bavaria, Belgium, Austria,
Galicia, Russian Poland, and France.[59]

According to Bălcescu's plans the state would organize a mortgage
bank to pay the proprietors for their land in mortgage tickets bearing
interest. These tickets would really be stock in the state; within five years
the bank would be able to retire all the mortgage notes and satisfy the

claims of the stockholders. The bank would obtain the money to redeem the bonds from the peasants who would be paying an annual annuity through which they would complete the buying of the land and become the actual as well as the nominal owners. Since the banking laws in Romania permitted the issuing of tickets for twice the amount being taken in (according to Bălcescu this was low—the Austrian banks could issue notes for up to eight times their intake), the proprietors' bonds could be retired long before the peasants completed their payments. Furthermore, according to his plans, the bank would not limit itself to mortgages but would also become the sole tax collector of the state and its general cashier. In order to prevent abuses which might tempt the executive officials of the government, Bălcescu recommended that the bank be placed under the control of the National Assembly which would elect a commission every three years to administer it. Once the property owners were indemnified, the credit could be used to expolit virgin mines, to develop forests, and to build canals. The safety of the peasant proprietor lay in the creation of credit which made it possible for him to escape the mortgage debt, usury, and expropration. The peasants would also gain from the credit institutions because they would become absolute proprietors of their land after making payments for fifteen years.[60]

But, Bălcescu continued, these measures were not taken in 1848 and the revolution collapsed. After its failure the boyars united with the Russians and took authority once again, imprisoning and exiling the revolutionary leaders, pillaging and torturing the masses, while "Turkey, arms folded, silently contemplated the agony of the people who had risen to save her."[61] The Russians and the Turks did make some attemtps to ameliorate the conditions of the Principalities through the Convention of Balta Liman, April 19/May 1, 1849, which established committees of reform.[62] But Bălcescu lashed out against this convention because the reform committees were limited in their jurisdiction to the property question. Even here he felt the results of their deliberations were selfish projects which would benefit the upper classes only. The Wallachian reform committee went so far as to claim that the peasant, the worker, was an unproductive consumer while the boyar was the sole producer. Nevertheless, the commission's report stood and land was not appropriated for the peasants. Bălcescu was very pessimistic about the chances that the changes he felt were necessary could be made peacefully. He concluded his article by stating that the salvation of the Principalities could not be sought from the boyars. With the record they had established, not even the greatest well-wisher would be able to believe they had

repented, albeit tardily. Thus, by default, the Romanians would be forced
to appeal to two powers, Russia and Turkey, despite their affection for
the second and hatred for the first.[63] The tacit suggestion was that if
these powers did not render the necessary aid, there would be more uprisings in the future.

V

Nicolae Bălcescu was an important economic historian and theorist.
He felt the only way to understand the problems his country faced was to
understand the roots from which the sprouted. Hence in "Concerning the
Social Conditions of the Land-tillers in the Romanian Principalities at
Various Times" he presented acceptable theories concerning the origins of
the Romanian Principalities and more especially the origins of feudalism,
question which are still highly controversial. He concluded that past attempts at emancipation had failed because the Romanian peasants were
given neither the necessary capital nor sufficient legal recourse to guarantee their independence. The article is also significant because of the
importance it assigns to the common people and because of the consistent
documentation of sources. Finally, it is noteworthy because in it Bălcescu
began to develop several concepts—such as the ideas of class warfare and
determinism—which he professed for the rest of his life.

Although the aims of the Romanian Revolution of 1848 were not
immediately realized, it should be noted that Bălcescu, unlike many of
his colleagues, did not shrink from attempting to enact his pre-revolu-
tionary ideas. Hence, he supported Article Thirteen of the Islaz Proclamation calling for the emancipation of the serfs with indemnification
for property owners. When the provisional government temporized on
this point he pressured it and was thus in part responsible for the creation
of a property commission to study the matter further and make concrete
recommendations to the yet unborn constitutional assembly. This property commission established three rights (the right to ownership of private
property, freedom of labor, and expropriation for measures of public
utility); nevertheless, Bălcescu did not feel the proposals drawn up by
the boyars to enact them were adequate. He was further disappointed
when the commission was disbanded after meeting only a little over a
week.

In order to keep the issue alive, both because he believed in it and
because he felt it was necessary to do so if the support of the peasantry
was to be maintained, Bălcescu published the article "On the Alloting of

land to the Peasants" in *Popolul Suveran*. Here he examined the question of distributing land to the peasants on the basis of national advisability, morality, and utility. The article contained justifications for the author's point of view rather than practical recommendations as to how it was to be achieved. Although it is possible to argue with Bălcescu's logic in some instances, it must be conceded that he made some excellent points. In this article he also developed an idea of surplus value similar to that of Karl Marx, but apparently arrived at independently.[64] He also reaffirmed his deterministic view of history in which progress towards perfection is actively being made. As was the case with most of the members of his generation, Bălcescu was a humanitarian; he did not favor the wholesale liquidation of his opponents. Instead he affirmed that the revolution is generous; it forgets all past evils. He was even willing to indemnify people who would lose land as a result of the proposed redistribution.

Although the Revolutions of 1848 collapsed and Bălcescu found it wise to go into exile, he continued to press for reforms in his homeland. *Question economique des Principautés Danubiennes*, his most important work on èconomics, first appeared around May 1850. Although Bălcescu reiterated many of his earlier ideas in this pamphlet, it was not merely an amplification of his previous economic concepts. It contained new historical material and new economic theories as well. Thus Bălcescu held up Tudor Vladimirescu as a great national hero, a symbol around whom the people could rally. Much of the new historical material Bălcescu presented in this treatise concerned the *Règlement organique*, a reform imposed by an external power which, he believed, fell far short of wiping out injustice. Continued abuses led the National Party to formulate Article Thirteen of the Islaz Proclamation which proposed to abolish the corvées of peasants who became proprietors by indemnifying their former landlords. Bălcescu again held this measure up as the crux of the Wallachian Revolution of 1848 and reaffirmed his belief in private ownership of property. It was not private property, he affirmed, but the abuse of the principle, which had created the disastrous situation in which the country found itself. Rightly used, he felt private property led to the creation of all the marvels of civilization.

In this article Bălcescu spelled out economically sound proposals regarding the means of obtaining the money needed to indemnify the boyars. He favored the establishment of credit institutions, specifically land banks, by the state. This step, which had been taken successfully in many of the German states, in Russian Poland, and in France would obviate the need for a foreign loan which might lead to economic imperialism in Romania. He also spelled out feasible means of governing the bank to prevent the development of internal corruption.

Finally, Bălcescu lashed out against the Convention of Balta Liman. Although it did establish committees of reform, Bălcescu complained that they were limited in their jurisdiction to the property question. And even here the results of their deliberations were selfish projects which would benefit the upper classes solely. He complained because the Wallachian reform committees presented the idea that the peasant was an unproductive consumer while the boyar was the sole producer. He was correct in arguing that this conclusion was not justified either factually or theoretically. Factually, the converse of the statement was more nearly true. Theoretically, there is no such thing as an unproductive consumer. According to Adam Smith the mere fact that someone consumes makes him productive. By consuming one increases demand and thus creates the need for further production. But the commission's report stood and land was not appropriated for the peasants. Bălcescu was rightly pessimistic when he believed that peaceful reform would not be forthcoming. In general, if one accepts the idea that the historian's job is to develop a feasible explanation of events, he must also admit that Bălcescu has done an acceptable job of presenting his position, notwithstanding the fact that he may disagree with this 19th century historian on certain particulars.

NOTES

1. Bălcescu's first article was entitled "Puterea armată şi artă militară de la întemeierea principatului Valahei până acum" ("Armed Power and the Military Art from the Founding of the Principality of Wallachia until the Present Time.") It was originally published in "Foaie ştiinţifica şi literară" ("The Scientific and Literary Paper"), a supplement of *Propăşirea* (Advance) between May 21 and August 13, 1844. It has been reprinted numerous times and may conveniently be found in Nicolae Bălcescu, *Opere* (Works), I, Pt. i, *Scrieri istorice, politice şi economice* (Historical, Political, and Economic Writings), ed. G. Zane (Bucureşti: Fundaţia pentru literatură şi artă "Regele Carol II," 1940), pp. 41-88. Hereafter cited as *Opere*, I. The ideas noted in this paragraph are found on page 43.

2. August Treboniu Laurian (1810-1881) was a Transylvanian philologist and historian who had earned his Doctor of Philosophy degree in Vienna. Beginning in 1842 he taught philosophy at the College of St. Sava in Bucharest. Bălcescu and Laurian collaborated on the *Magazinu*

istoricu pentru Dacia (The Historical Magazine for Dacia) from 1845-
1847. Living until 1881, Laurian played an important part in the Transylvania Revolution of 1848. He later returned to Wallachia and became
a member of the faculty of the university in Bucharest and president of
the Romanian Academy. A. Manolache, Gh. Dumitrescu, and Gh. Pîr-
nuță, *Gîndirea pedagogică a generației de la 1848* (Pedagogical Thought of
the Generation of 1848) (București: Editura didactică și pedagogică,
1968), pp. 137-39. The purpose of *The Historical Magazine for Dacia*
was to facilitate the task of writing a real history of the Romanians by
publishing both original sources and historical dissertations relating to
the subject. See Bălcescu, "Prospectual pentru Magazinul istoric" ("Prospectus for the Historical Magazine), *Opere*, I, Pt. i., 99-104.

   3.   Nicolae Bălcescu, "Despre starea soțială a muncitorilor plugari
în Principatele române în deosebite timpuri" ("Concerning the Social
Conditions of the Land-tillers in the Romanian Principalities at Various
Times"), *Magazinu istoricu pentru Dacia* (The Historical Magazine for
Dacia) (București: Cu tipariul Collegiului National, 1946), II, 229-370
Hereafter cited as "Despre starea soțială." See also *Opere*, I, Pt. i, 185-
198. In the interval between 1844 and 1846 Bălcescu had published num-
erous other articles, including six in the first volume of *The Historical
Magazine for Dacia*.

   4.   Bălcescu, "Despre starea soțială," *Opere*, I, Pt. i, 187-88.

   5.   Ibid., pp. 188-90. For the views of present day Romanian historians on the question of Latin continuity and the origins of feudalism,
see A. Oțetea, "La formation des états féodaux roumains," *Nouvelles
études d'histoire* (Bucharest: Editions de l'Académie de la République
Socialiste de Roumaine, 1965), III, 87-104, and Valentin Al. Georgescu,
"La préemption et le retrait dans le droit féodal de Valachie et de Moldavie—Aspects de structure et de réception," pp. 181-203 in the same
volume.

   6.   Bălcescu, "Despere starea soțială," *Opere*, I, Pt. i, 190-93. The
quote is from p. 193.

   7.   Ibid., 192-193. The quote is from p. 193.

   8.   Ibid. The Phanariotes were Greeks from the Phanar or lighthouse
district of Constantinople. Originally prosperous merchants, they entered
the Ottoman bureaucracy and rose through the ranks winning important
positions in foreign affairs and the navy. From the early part of the
Eighteenth Century (1711 in Moldavia and 1718 in Wallachia) until the
Turkish occupation of the Danuabian Principalities during the Greek
Revolution of 1821, they served as governors of the Principalities. After

this time they were replaced by native hospodars. The period from 1711 to 1821 is generally known as the Phanariote regime.

9. Bălcescu, "Despre starea soțială," *Opere*, I, Pt. i., 194; the acts in question are contined in annexes xv-xvii.

10. Ibid., 194-195; the decree in question is contained in annex xviii.

11. Ibid., 195.

12. Ibid.

13. Bălcescu noted that in the year 1775 more than 10,000 peasants left the plough to become highwaymen. Ibid., p. 196.

14. Ibid., 197-198; the quote is from 198.

15. Ibid., 198.

16. In the late 1830s, Bălcescu became involved in revolutionary activities as a follower of Ion Câmpineanu, a leading member of the National Party in the Wallachian Assembly and the leader of a secret society in Wallachia. Câmpineanu was arrested in 1839, but revolutionary activity in Wallachia did not cease. In 1840, Bălcescu joined another secret society in which one of his former teachers, the French educator, J. A. Vaillant, played a principal part along with two young lawyers, Eftimie Murgu and Mitică Filipescu. This movement was discovered by the authorities and the principal members were arrested in October 1840. As a result of this involement, Bălcescu was sentenced to three years imprisonment at the Mărgineni Monastery. In 1843 Bălcescu, Ion Ghica (a friend and former classmate who had recently returned from Paris where he had completed his education) and Christian Tell (a major in the army) founded a new secret society, *Frăția* (the Brotherhood). Like earlier revolutionary groups, *Frăția*'s aims included the abolition of feudalism and achievement of national unity and independence. See Cornelia Bodea, *Lupta Românilor pentru Unitatea Natională, 1834-1849* (The Romanian's Struggle for National Unity, 1834-49) (București: Editura Academiei Republicii Socialiste România, 1967), pp. 12-18 and 49-51; G. Zane, "Mișcarea revoluționară de la 1840 din Țara Romîneasca" (The Revolutionary Movement of 1840 in Wallachia"), *Studii și materiale de istorie modernă* (Studies and Materials Concerning Modern History) (București: Editura Academiei Republicii Populare Romîne, 1963), III, 201-205 and 217-22, and Academica Republicii Populare Romîne, *Istoria Romîniei* (The History of Romania) (București: Editura Academiei Republicii Populare Romîne, 1963), III, 990-95. Hereafter cited as *Istoria Romîniei*.

17. In the summer of 1846, the year in which his article entitled "Concerning the Social Conditions of the Land-tillers in the Romanian

Principalities at Various Times" appeared, Bălcescu suddenly left Wallachia and made his way to Paris. The exact reasons for his departure are
shrouded in mystery. His friends Ion Ghica and Ion Voinescu II attributed
his departure to his desire to complete historical research in libraries and
archives abroad. However, many other explanations have been advanced.
See for example Dan Berindei, *Bălcescu* (Bucureşti: Editura tineretului,
1969), pp. 82-83; Cornelia Bodea, "Actions prérévolutionnaires roumaines avant 1848," *Nouvelles Etudes d'Histoire* (Bucureşti: Editions
de l'Academie de la République Socialiste de Roumaine, 1965), p. 285,
and Vasile Maciu, "Une centre révolutionnaire roumaine dans les annees
1845-1848: la Société des Etudiants roumains à Paris," pp. 250-53 in the
same volume. Other relevant references are found in P. P. Panaitescu,
Contribuţii la o biografie a lui N. Bălcescu (Contributions to a Biography
of N. Bălcescu) (Bucureşti: Tipografia "Convorbiri Literare," 1924), p.
61, and G. Zane, "Aspecte noi al vieţii lui N. Bălcescu în lumea unor documente inedite" ("New Aspects of Bălcescu's Life in the Light of Some
Unpublished Documents"), *Studii: Revistă de istorie* (Studies: The Historical Review), XIII, No. 1 (1969), 39. Whatever his motives, he remained
abroad, chiefly in Paris, until the outbreak of the Revolutions of 1848.
He became an important émigré leader and also maintained ties with
liberal leaders within the Principalities.

18. He began his journey back to Wallachia on March 12/24, 1848
and became an important leader in the revolution in that Principality
shortly after his arrival on March 28/April 9.

19. The "Proclamaţiunea revoluţiunii din Ţara Românească în
numele popurului Român" ("The Proclamation of Revolution in Wallachia in the name of the Romanian People"), which contained a twenty-
two article program, was commonly called the Islaz Proclamation since
it was first publically read at that site on June 9/21, 1848. For an analysis of some of the conflicting statements about the authorship of the
proclamation see Zane's notes in Bălcescu, *Opere*, Pt. ii, 270-281; the
text of the Islaz Proclamation may be found in ibid., pp. 145-56.

20. The provisional government was established in Bucharest on
June 14/26 after the abdication of Prince Bibescu. Bălcescu served as
a secretary in this government, which was recognized by revolutionaries
throughout Wallachia. An early attempt was made to enact the program
embodied in the Islaz Proclamation through the proclamation of laws
providing for such things as the abolition of the rank of boyar, the establishment of freedom of speech and freedom of the press, the establishment of a national guard throughout the country, and the abolition of

the death sentence and corporal punishment. However, as noted above, two days later it was decreed that the relationship between the peasants and the estates owners would remain unaltered until a constitutional convention had met: "Until then there is no right nor is there any excuse for ceasing to obey the proprietors or the leaseholders of estates indebted to proprietors except with regard to the infamous *iobăgie*." Bălcescu thought this last action was a mistake. For the above noted acts passed by the provisional government see *Anul 1848 în Principatele Române* (The Year 1848 in the Romanian Principalities) (Bucureşti: Institut de Arte Grafice "Carol Göbl," 1902-1910), I, 567-69, and 619-20. According to G. Zane, "*iobăgie* was not to be understood then, as it is understood today as servile obligations in general, but as *dîjma* (quitrent) in men." Bălcescu, *Opere, IV, Corespondenţă, scrisori, memorii, adrese, documente, note şi materiale* (Works, IV, Correspondence, Letters, Remembrances, Speeches, Documents, and Materials), ed. G. Zane (Bucureşti: Editura Academiei Republicii Populare Române, 1964), Zane's note, p. 490. Hereafter referred to as *Corespondenţă*. For a general survey of the events of the period under discussion, see *Istoria României*, IV, 87-89.

21.   Bălcescu to A. G. Golescu, Buzău, June 22, 1848, *Corespondenţă*, p. 89; see also Virgil Ionescu, *Contribuţii la studiul gîndirii economice a lui Nicolae Bălcescu* (Bucureşti: Editura ştiinţifica, 1956), pp. 89-90. Hereafter cited as *Contribuţii economice a lui Bălcescu*.

22.   Ionescu, *Contribuţii economice a lui Bălcescu*, p. 91; Gh. Georgescu-Buzău, *The 1848 Revolutions in the Romanian Lands* Bucureşti: The Meridiane Publishing House, 1956), pp. 54-55, and Apostol Stan, *Le problèm agraire pendant la révolution de 1848 en Valachie*, volume 34 in the collection "Bibliotheca Historica Romaniae" (Bucureşti: Editions de l'Academie de la Republique Socialiste de Roumaine, 1971), p. 96. Hereafter cited as *La problème agraire*.

23.   By this time the position of the Wallachian revolution in international affairs was becoming quite precarious. Partly because they feared being preempted by the Russians if they did not act, the Turks intervened. On July 14/26 Suleiman Pasha, a Turkish diplomat who was supported by an army of twenty thousand men, arrived at Bucharest. He demanded that the provisional government be replaced by a *caimacam* (regency) in accordance with the *Reglement organique* (see below, pp. 179-80). If the Wallachians did not submit to this demand Suleiman Pasha noted that he would use the armed force at his disposal to execute the sultan's wishes. If they did comply, he assured them that their complaints

would be considered in Constantinople. Although there was some discontent, a regency consisting of Ion Eliade Rădulescu, Neculai Golescu, and Christian Tell was elected on July 28/August 9. Bălcescu had been elected as the third regent, but he refused to serve because he disapproved of the policy of concessions that had been inauguarated. Nevertheless, he did agree to serve as a member of the commission sent to Constantinople to negotiate with the Turks concerning the rights of the Principalities vis-à-vis the Ottoman Government. He arrived in the Turkish capital on August 10/22. G. G. Florescu, "Misiunea diplomatică a lui N. Bălcescu la Constantinopol (august 1848)" (N. Bălescu's Diplomatic Mission to Constantinople (August 1848)"), *Studii*, XIV, No. 6 (1961), 1521-26; see also *Istoria României*, IV, 101-04, and 202-03.

24. Bălcescu, *Question économique des Principautés Danubiennes*, *Opere*, I Pt., ii., 67.

25. Ibid., pp. 68-72; see also Ionescu, *Contribuții economice a lui Bălcescu*, pp. 90-94, and Stan, *Le problème agraire*, pp. 96-112.

26. Ion Eliade Rădulescu (1802-1872) had been one of Bălcescu's teachers at the College of St. Sava in Bucharest. He was the dominant literary intellectual in Wallachia in the period before the revolution of 1848. He was one of the early leaders of the Revolution of 1848 and served as a member of the executive committee of the provisional government established on June 14/26 as well as of the *caimacam* elected on July 28/August 9. He recommended a moderate course of action at this time and temporized on questions relating to social reform. Although he went into exile for a while after the failure of the revolution, he later returned to Wallachia and again played an active role in politics.

27. Nevertheless, Bălcescu continued, before its dispersal the property commission recognized three rights: "the right of property, freedom of labor, and the expropriation for measures of public utility. There is the résumé of the works about which some have made so much noise and even had the foolishness and the notoriously bad faith to qualify, even in official acts, as communism." Bălcescu, *Question économique des Principautes Danubiennés*, *Opere*, I, Pt. ii, 73.

28. Bălcescu, "Despre improprietărirea țăranilor" ("On the Alloting of Land to the Peasants") may conveniently be found in *Opere*, I, Pt. i, 267-87.

29. Bălcescu, "Despre improprietărirea țăranilor," *Opere*, I, Pt. i, 271.

30. Ibid., pp. 271-73.

31. Ibid., p. 273.

32.   Ibid., p. 277.

33.   Ibid., p. 278.

34.   Ibid.

35.   Ibid.

36.   Ibid., p. 279.

37.   Ibid., p. 280.

38.   Ibid.

39.   Ibid., p. 281.

40.   Ibid.

41.   Ibid., p. 284.

42.   Ibid.

43.   Ibid., p. 285.

44.   Ibid.

45.   The Turkish intervention began on September 13/25, 1848 and the Russian intervention began two days later when tsarist armies under the command of General Lüders crossed the frontiers on the Milcov to support the sultan's army. See Georgescu-Buzău, *The 1848 Revolution in the Romanian Lands*, pp. 63-65.

46.   Bălcescu's activities in the intervening period of time are treated in detail in my article "Bălcescu and the National Question in 1849," *East European Quarterly*, XII, No. 2 (1978), 189-208.

47.   Bălcescu, *Question économique des Principautés Danubiennes*, *Opere*, I, Pt. ii, 1-90. This work first appeared sometime around May 1850. Bălcescu felt anonymity might help convey the impression that the ideas contained therein were not those of one man, but were shared by all the émigrés. In addition to the evidence supplied by Bălcescu's correspondence with Ghica, internal criticism supports the claim of Bălcescu's authorship. The ideas and some of the phraseology in the second to tenth chapters of this pamphlet are similar to those contained in "Despre starea stocială a muncitorilor plugari în Principatele Române în deosebite tîmpuri," and those in chapters twenty-two and twenty-three are similar to ones in "Despre improprietărirea ţăranilor." See *Opere*, I, Pt. ii, Zane's notes pp. 242 and also 234ff.

48.   Bălcescu, *Question économique des Principautés Danubiennes*, *Opere*, I, Pt. ii, 4-7; the quote is from p. 7.

49.   See above, pp. 1-5 and Bălcescu, *Question économique des Principautés Danubiennes*, *Opere*, I, Pt. ii, 7-25 *passim*.

50.   Tudor Vladimirescu was an educated Romanian squire who had served in the Russian army during the Russo-Turkish War of 1806. Later he also served the Russian consul in Bucharest. Vladimirescu unsuccessfully

attempted to form a national movement and led a revolt against the Phanariote regime in 1821. He as ambushed and assassinated in the attempt.

51. Bălcescu, *Question économique des Principautés Danubiennes,* *Opere,* I, Pt. ii, 25.

52. Ibid., pp. 25-26.

53. Ibid., pp. 27-40.

54. Ibid., p. 52.

55. Ibid.

56. Ibid., pp. 52-53.

57. See above, pp. 174-78 and Bălcescu, *Question économique des* *Principautés Danubiennes, Opere,* I, Pt. ii, 54-66 *passim.*

58. With regard to the question of usefulness of making the peasants proprietors he asked how one could speak of the advisability of introducing a system of large and small landowners in any country at a time when thousands of people were crying anathema to property and demonstrating the crimes and misery and desolation with which it has filled the world. But, he further questioned, if the abuse of a principle had produced the disasters, must one conclude that it is necessary to destroy the principle, in this case to decree the abolition of private property? His answer was negative. He felt that immorality in society and the excessive inequality were not derived from the principle of property owning, but from the nefarious laws which governed it. And he proceeded to make concrete recommendations for improving the situation, see below, pp. 181-82. He favored a mixture of large and small landholdings, feeling that different geographical conditions necessitated different agricultural approaches. Bălcescu, *Question économique des Principautés Danubiennes, Opere,* I, Pt. ii, 57-59.

59. Bălcescu, *Question économique des Principautés Danubiennes,* *Opere,* I, Pt. ii, 73-74.

60. Ibid., pp. 77-81.

61. Ibid., p. 86.

62. The Convention of Balta Liman also provided that the princes would once again be elected for seven years rather than for life, that the assemblies would be suppressed as dangerous and replaced by *ad hoc* divans, and that a joint Russo-Turkish occupation of the Principalities should continue until they had been pacified; see R. W. Seton-Watson, *A History of the Roumanians from Roman Times to the Completion of* *Unity* (Hamden, Conn.: Archon Books, 1963), pp. 227-28; see *Istoria* *Romîniei,* IV, 223-24 for all of the provisions.

63. Bălcescu, *Question économique des Principautés Danubiennes,* *Opere,* I, Pt. ii, 87-89.

64.   He may well have been influenced in his thinking on this point by the French socialist Pierre-Joseph Proudhon (1805-1865). Leonid Boicu noted that Bălcescu had read some of Proudhon's works. Leonid Boicu, "Istoricul Nicolae Bălcescu" (Nicolae Bălcescu the Historian) *Studii și articole de istorie* (Studies and Articles about History), XIV (1969), 41-49, see esp. p. 42. Bălcescu's work, *Question économique des Principautés Danubiennes*, was quoted and discussed in various books about the Romanian economy, especially those concerning the agrarian question, between 1850 and 1860. Although they do not specifically cite Bălcescu's pamphlet, its influence on I. Ghica and J. Michelet is evident in their respective books, *Dernière occupation des Principautés Danubiennes par la Russie*, and *Les legendes*. Among those who specifically cite Bălcescu's pamphlet is A. G. Golescu, *De l'abolition du servage dans les Principautés Danubiennes*. Elias Regnault, author of *Histoire politique et sociale des Principautés Danubiennes*, drew very heavily on Bălcescu's pamphlet to explain the history of the land-tillers and their relationships with their overlords. According to G. Zane, K. Marx in turn drew much on Bălcescu's material in Regnault to illustrate some of the theories put forth in the first volume of *Das Kapital*. See Zane's notes, esp. pp. 246-247 in Bălcescu, *Opere*, I, Pt. ii. Contemporary Romanian scholars who have stressed Bălcescu's role as a precursor to Marx include G. Zane and Sultana Suta-Selejam, G. Zane, "Marx și Bălcescu" ("Marx and Bălcescu") *Viața Românească* (Romanian Life), XIX, No. 1 (1927), 40-59, and Sultana Suta-Selejan, *Gîndirea economică a lui Nicolae Bălcescu* (Nicolae Bălcescu Economic Thought) (București: Editura Academiei Republicii Socialiste România, 1967).

Lloyd A. Cohen

THE JEWISH QUESTION DURING THE PERIOD OF THE ROMANIAN NATIONAL RENAISSANCE AND THE UNIFICATION OF THE TWO PRINCIPALITIES OF MOLDAVIA AND WALLACHIA 1848-1866

The period of Romanian national revival, 1848-1866, was an important one for the Jewish population in the Danuabian Principalities. In comparison with other events occurring then, the Jewish question was and should have remained a minor one. It did not. The question of the status of the Jews soon reached an importance equal to and with the other poliical issues of the new Romanian state under Prince Cuza. In order to understand this phenomena, some background on the revival of the Romanian national consciousness needs to be presented.

Like many of their Balkan neighbors, the three Romanian Principalities, Moldavia, Wallachia and Transylvania, waged an unsuccessful battle for independence against either the Turkish conqueror from the south or the Hungarian invader from the north. Colorful and prominent leaders such as Ştefan cel Mare, Petru Rareş, Vlad Ţepeş and Mihai Viteazul waged glorious battles against the foreign invaders. Mihai Viteazul succeeded briefly even in uniting the three Principalities but the final victory of the invaders was not to be forestalled.

As with their Balkan neighbors, the revival of national consciousness was a slow process. In the Principalities it took the dual form of a political struggle against the Turks and their Greek agents (Phanariotes) and an intellectual one against the dominance of Slavonic and then Greek language, literature and ideology.

One key political event in this process was the Revolution of 1821. The lesson for the Romanians was that their destiny did not lie with the Greeks, but rather they had to find and to make their own way into history. Hence, the struggle centered on rediscovering their past in order to discover their unique identity so that they could develop a separate course for the Principalities.

The intellectual revival started in Transylvania and soon spread into the other two Principalities. It focussed upon the discovery of the Romanian past and the development of a Romanian language and literature to offset Slavonic and Greek cultural and religious dominance.

While it would be impossible to outline the events that led to the Revolution of 1848 and the double election of Prince Cuza to the throne of both Moldavia and Wallachia in 1859 in this short space—the reader is referred to, for example, Cornelia Bodea, *The Romanian Struggle for Unification, 1834-1849*, and T. W. Riker, *The Making of Romania*,—it should suffice to say that many of these new intellectuals now aware of Romania's past, tried to combine a revival of national consciousness with definite political aims. This led to the various movments that culminated in the Revolution of 1848 in the Principalities. When they failed, many of the leaders of 1848 fled abroad, where they worked to gain foreign friends for the cause of the Principalities. Napoleon III, that supporter of national causes, was soon swayed to their side in spite of fierce opposition by Turkey and Austria who had strong interests in the *status quo*. His involvement led to the interest of the other Great Power's in the fate of the Principalities. Moldavia and Wallachia were united under the sham title of United Principalities of Moldavia and Wallachia with the aid of Great Power intervention. After a series of crooked and scandalous elections for princes of the two Principalities, which the Great Powers overturned, the revolutionaries compromised and surprised the Great Powers with their own form of unification by electing Cuza prince of both Principalities in 1859.

The new prince, Alexandru Ioan Cuza, was relatively unknown Though from a boyar family and participant in the 1848 revolution, Cuza was elected because he seemed a safe candidate for an interim period until a suitable foreign prince could be found. His successful candidacy was based upon these premises. Cuza faced several serious domestic problems: the unification of both administrative systems of Moldavia and Wallachia, achieving acceptance of the new *de facto* political status of the Principalities, the acceptance of his dual election by the Great Powers and Turkey, financial reform, judicial reform, agriarian reform, the status of the dedicated monasteries, as well as, of course, the Jewish question. Plus Cuza soon decided he wanted to remain prince and did not want to surrender his throne to a suitable foreign prince. During the first few years of his administration, Cuza and the Legislative Assembly quarrelled bitterly and accomplished little. Cuza, who had designs for his own personal rule, took a bold and daring step to end the deadlock by a coup on

May 14, 1864. He, thereafter, ruled by himself with the cooperation for a period of time of Mihai Kogălniceanu and initiated many major reforms until another bloodless coup overthrew him on February 23, 1866.

Of the major issues that Cuza had attempted to resolve during his brief administration, it could be safely said that the Jewish question was the least important in scope. However, by the time of his downfall, it had grown out of proportion relative to the other major issues in the two Principalities. There were several factors for this phenomenon: First, there was the nature of the Jewish question and its increased complications owing to the massive influx of East European Jews during the period of national renaissance. Second, there was the inability of any native Romanian administration—with the exception of Prince Cuza in December 1864—to find a viable working solution that covered all phases of the issue and pleased the majority of those involved. Finally, there was the active interest of foreign Jews in the fate of their Romanian bretheren and the pressure on the Great Powers to intervene on behalf of the Romanian Jewry. The Powers, for one reason or another, became interested in the question and, hence, a national issue requiring a national solution was complicated by international intervention aimed at finding a national solution that might not have been in Romania's national interest.

The nucleus for the solution to the Jewish question at the end of the period of national renaissance did not come from those who had been in power, but, rather, from the new generation of Romanians such as Cuza and Kogălniceanu who had helped to make the Revolution of 1848 and later to unify the two Principalities. Much of their liberalism and revolutionary zeal was applied to many of the domestic issues they faced, and many of the programs of 1848 would find themselves adopted in one form or another by the new administration of the just unified Romanian state. However, whoever dealt with the Jewish question soon found that this issue was complicated by above key factors each of which had to be resolved in one form or another in order to achieve any satisfactory solution.

At the time of the national renaissance in the Principalities, the political position of the Jews was in flux. For most of the period, all Jews remained classified as foreigners subject to expulsion. This despite the fact that the Jews had well established communities with their own religious, social, political and economic organizations and institutions, and they were and had been very active in the economic life of Moldavia and Wallachia. Some weak distinction between native or long term resident and recent immigrant Jews was made in the 1850s; this was often ignored.[1]

The reason for this was the impact of recent Jewish immigration into the Principalities of Moldavia and Wallachia. Jewish immigration had been occurring since the Jews first entered the Danubian region. During the first half of the nineteenth century and especially during the reign of Mihai Sturdza, 1834-1847, Jewish immigration into the Principalities had increased in tempo.[2] This occurred for numerous reasons: It was part of the parallel population movements throughout Europe which featured a strong Jewish movement. Plus the anti-Semitic politics of the Russian and Austrian governments both at home and in their administrations of Bucovenia, Galicia, Poland and Bessarabia forced many Jews to flee to lands such as the Danubian Principalities which seemed to them to offer at that time a refuge from vicious anti-Semitic persuecution.[3]

This new immigration created problems which were not insurmountable, but rather of the nuisance variety and a consistent source of irritation to the successive governments which had to deal with them. Many of the recent Jewish immigrants lacked proper credentials, passports, and other documents. This raised the legal question of dual nationality as those for the most part continued to remain under foreign protection and appealed for foreign protection as well. For example, in 1825, Jews who were Austrian subjects, refused to pay liquor taxes, and they requested foreign protection and assistance from Austria and France.[4] The Principalities found themselves, therefore, involved in diplomatic dialogues with other countries such as Austria over regulation of this stream of immigrants and over the question of which government held legal sovereignty over these Jews. This question was never resolved to anyone's satisfaction.[5]

The governments of the Principalities of Moldavia and Wallachia claimed they held legal suzerainty over the Jews, who, because of their continued residence in the area, had become subject to the regulations of the Principalities *de facto* and *de jure*. It had become an accepted right for the host government to subject a citizen of subject of one nation, such as the one who carried on commercial enterprise under rule and protection of the other, to be subject to the state in which he conducted his business; and, therefore, he would be liable to all regulations and political vicissitudes of the country.[6] The Jews, on the other hand, claimed that the Principalities did not have any *de jure* rights over them because not only were they not given the opportunity to obtain the rights of citizenship but were actually denied them. Hence, they remained *de facto* and *de jure* under the regulation of the country of origin. When persecution increased, these Jews would appeal to their country's foreign representative for protection; other Jews registered with agents such as those of Britain and France claiming their protection.[7] The Jews based their appeal for foreign aid on the international legal principle that if a person suffered an injury to himself or to his property interests and was denied an opportunity to acquire or dispose of same, and if there would be no remedy under local law, he could then seek redress under international law.[8] For this claim the Jew's foreign protectors could intervene under conditions of denied rights and increased persecution. It had become an accepted fact and the right of a country to protect its nationals in course of international law and diplomatic relations even though the nationals might have renounced this right. The validity of this waving has been an open question.[9]

To complicate this matter, these foreign Jews were not officially accepted into the main stream of Jewish life owing to their vague legal status. For example, local community organizations often had to obtain local governmental permission to aid foreign Jews as, by illustration, was discussed in a letter from the Botoşani Jewish community in September 1864.[10]

As so often in their tragic history, the Jews proved to be their own worst enemies as they soon abused many of the privileges granted to them.[11] For example, Vasile Alexandre, the well-known poet, in a letter of September 18, 1864, to Baligot de Begne, Prince Cuza's personal secretary, expressed concern about the condition and future development of Romanian agriculture and the peasantry because the Jews had a definite impact—to the negative he implied—upon the agricultural sector as money lenders and as financiers.[12]

The physical presence of the Jews created many economic problems and helped to give rise to the belief that the Jews constituted a threat to the Romanian people and lands by their actual physical presence and their economic activity. The official census listed the population as 4,424,961 Romanians and 135,000 Jews in 1860.[13] Owing to their continued immigration, the Jews had changed the demographic nature of the cities and the countryside where their presence would have a considerable impact.[14] In the following cities, the amount of Jewish families residing there was as follows: Bucharest—2,400; Ploeşti—200; Brăila—500; Craiova—350; Iaşi—6,500; Botoşani—4,000; Falticeni—1,000; Galaţi—1,500.[15]

Already active in the economic affairs of the Principalities, this new wave of immigration could not help but to have a further impact upon the region's economic and social development. Further, many of these Jews, especially those from Russia, arrived impoverished. These Jews were at first an economic and social problem until they could establish themselves in their new surroundings.[16] On the other hand, more importantly, many influential Romanians, such as I. C. Brătianu, feared that these Jewish immmgrants would exploit the populace, especially in Moldavia where most of them seemed to have settled, through specualtion, financial manipulation, liquor selling, land holdings and so forth. Hence, they reasonsed that Jewish economic influence could only have a negative impact, and therefore, would be detrimental to the future economic development of the newly united Romanian state.[17]

It should be pointed out that these Jews never become completely assimilated; rather they followed the example of their co-religionists in countries like France who did not integrate wholly into society though they spoke the language and participated in national affairs. Their presence consistently reminded the Romanians that they were a different and an unassimilated minority active in their country's life.[18]

All of this caused the Romanians to look unfavorably upon the Jews and to give credence to many anti-Semitic charges, Alan, the deputy from Iaşi, for example, saw the current Jewish immigration as a definite threat to the well-being of the Danubian lands; he proposed more restrictive measures against the Jews in order to protect the interests of the Romanian lands and people. He admired and wanted to emulate the Russian example concerning these people.[19]

The second key factor was the extension of the Jewish question from a purely national one into an international one. This helped to blow a small issue into a large complex one and made it almost impossible to find a workable solution that would not only fulfill the domestic needs of the country involved but also fulfill the demand of those foreign interventionists interested in resolving this question as well. Nevertheless, throughout this epoch, the Jewish question remained still a national question requiring a national solution; the attempt to impose an international solution to a national problem was bound to encounter numerous difficulties.

This process began simply enough when the Jewish foreign co-religionists became interested in the fate of their Romanian-Jewish bretheran. The Romanian Jews believed that, with the aid from foreign prominent Jews, they would be able to obtain political and civil rights that they had been previously denied. Therefore, they encouraged foreign intervention on their behalf by their fellow co-religionists.[20]

Jews from abroad mounted an intense appeal on behalf of their co-religionists believing that their intervention would bring beneficial results. They therefore, in turn, petitioned the Moldavian and Wallachian governments to grant Romanian Jews political and civil rights. Foremost among several prominent and powerful Western Jews who took up Romanian Jewry's cause were the Rothschilds. They had always been active in aiding the cause of persecuted Jews. Among the Rothschilds were Baron James Mayer de Rothschild (1792-1862), Leopold de Rothschild (1845-1917), Baron James Jacob de Rothschild (1792-1868) and Baron Lionel de Rothschild (1808-1879); the last was especially influential in this question. He used his great influence with the Emperor of France, Napoleon III, for the cause of the Jews in the Danubian Principalities, and he paid as well a personal visit to Prince Cuza.[21] The Rothschilds cooperated with the famous Sir Moses Montefoire (1774-1885) who was active in aiding world Jewry. He sent many personal appeals on behalf of Jewish causes to world statesmen, and he travelled to the various countries where the Jews were persecuted in order to aid them and to remove the causes of their persecution.[22] These prominent Jews were joined by Sir Francis Goldsmid (1808-1878) and the Anglo-Jewish Committee. The former belonged to the Romanian Committee which centered its activity upon the improvement of the conditions of Jews in the Danubian Principalities; Sir Francis Goldsmid maintained an active correspondence with British leaders concerning the fate of Romanian Jews.[23]

When these prominent foreign Jews failed to obtain from the various administrations of the Principalities what they regarded as a satisfactory solution to the Jewish question, they turned to and requested from their respective governments action for the cause of Romanian Jewry. This was what transformed the Jewish question from a national one into an international one and made a solution so difficult to obtain. At one time or another, the Jewish question in the Principalities involved the active intervention of England, France, Austria, Italy, Germany, Turkey, Belgium, Holland, Switzerland, Russia, Greece and the United States. They all urged the Principalities to practice a policy of toleration and moderation in dealing with the Jews and to grant to them citizenship with political and civil rights.[24]

What motivated these countries to intervention must remain a moot question. Perhaps they were induced by a genuine humanitarian desire to aid the Jews; perhaps their consciences disturbed them because of their own treatment of their Jews; perhaps, they saw the Jewish question as a wedge with which to gain a political foothold into Balkan politics.

In the period between 1848-1859, the Jewish question had developed into a complex one. For example, in 1852, when Gregory Ghica prohibited Jews from residing in the countryside and obtaining vineyards, the Jews protested. They claimed that, in accordance with religious laws, only Jews could be allowed to handle wines used for consumption and religious purposes. When they obtained no relief from the local government, they then appealed to their foreign co-religionists for aid. It took the active intervention of the Chief Rabbi of Constantinople to remove this restriction.[25] Yet, at the same time, the Jews were regarded as residents of the Principalities in that they were given the same obligations as the other inhabitants; i.e., regarding taxation and subject to the draft according to a law of April 2, 1852.[26]

What added to the further confusion was the fact that no one group of political leaders of one administration could settle on a single unified policy with established purpose to resolve the Jewish question over a long range period of time. While in 1848 many leading revolutionaries and influential Romanians such as I. C. Brătianu and Rosetti had favored granting Jews political and civil rights with few qualifications as part of their revolutionary program, their viewpoint had changed by the time of Cuza's double election. They now favored numerous restrictive measures against the Jews.[27]

What brought about this change and finally forced the issue was the activity of the Jews. Beginning in 1856, an active minority of Jews began to undertake an extensive campaign to acquire political and civil rights. Their drive for rights included such politically difficult issues as mass naturalization, economic privileges and social and professional integration.[28] The Jews wanted to be part of the new emerging Romania, but how much did the new state want them? When petitions and appeals to the local governments failed, the Jews sought the aid of their foreign co-religionists in their drive for political and civil rights. This active minority continued to press for rights and proclaimed that they would take advantage of any given them even though the majority of Jews remained indifferent to this question concerning rights. Starting in 1856, a series of articles appeared in newspapers and journals debating what course should be adopted for the Jews in the Principalities.[29]

At the same time that the Jews residing in the Principalities began their campaign for rights, the Great Powers appealed to by the non-Romanian Jews took up the cause of the Jews and began to actively intervene into the affairs of the Danubian Principalities. This occurred when the Great Powers discussed the organization of the two Principalities at Constantinople in January 1856.[30] They made their intentions known that the fate of the Jews would become their concern. The Protocol of Constantinople, Articles 15 and 17, stated that there should be equality for all and no religious discrimination. Foreigners should be allowed to own property and they should be given equal civil and political rights unless they remained under the protection of a foreign power.[31] Further Articles 22-27 of the Paris Peace Conference of that same year provided for reform of the constitution by which two assemblies would be convoked where all classes would find their interests represented.[32]

The initial appeal for aid by prominent foreign Jews from the Great Powers seemed to have achieved results when the Rothschilds took up the cause of the Moldavian Jews. Baron Lionel de Rothschild urged Count Walewski, Napoleon III's foreign minister, to initiate immediate action on behalf of the Jews in the Danubian Principalities. In a letter dated July 24, 1858, Count Walewski replied that Napoleon III's government, which had always been interested in the fate of persecuted people and in line with its policy of supporting religious toleration, would do what it could for the Oriental Jews at the forthcoming conference to be held in Paris.[33] At the Convention of Paris, 1858, the Powers added Article 46 which stated that in Moldavia and Wallachia all religious groups had equal rights:

> All Moldavians and Wallachians shall be equal in the eye of the law with regard to taxation, and shall be equally admissible to public employment in both Principalities.
>
> Their individual liberty shall be guaranteed, no one can be detained, arrested or persecuted but in conformity with the law.
>
> Moldavians and Wallachians of Christian confession shall equally enjoy political rights. The enjoyment of these rights may be extended to other religions by legislative agreement.[34]

Even though Baron Lionel de Rothschild's act of intervention with the French foreign minister, Count Walewski, did have some influence on the French position at the 1858 Conference,[35] the general results of the Convention of Paris disappointed the Western Jews because they felt that the declaration did not include sufficient guarantees to safeguard the rights of their fellow Jews in the two Principalities.[36] They did not realize that any attempt to solve or to impose a solution on a national level to a national question would be feasible only if the nation involved accepted such a solution dictated by the interventionists or if the powers used force to impose and to maintain their views. On the other hand, the Jews in the Principalities were grateful for any assistance that they received. In a letter of August 15, 1858, the Jews of Bucharest thanked the French Consul for the aid that his government had given the Jews at the Convention and in the Principalities. They praised France because she had aided the Jews in every country when possible, and France was the first to emancipate the Jews and carried on this tradition ever since.[37]

The intense activity emanating from men like the Rothschilds, Montefoire, Goldsmid and others, together with the reports of the conditions
of the Jews of Moldavia and Wallachia helped to tip the scale in favor of
the Great Power's decision to intervene.[38] Ion Bălăceanu, the representative to France, wrote to Ion Ghica, from Paris in June of 1858,
that European interest had been aroused concerning the fate of the Jews
in the Principalities; and, that the recent reports of persecution and discrimination during the 1850s together with the Jewish drive for citizenship had intensified their attention to this problem. In France, he reported, this issue had become a well-known subject of written polemical
works that placed the Danuabian Principalities in a bad light.[39] It was
with this that Paris brought to the attention of Victor Place, its representative in Moldavia, the condition of the Jews, their status and their
need for protection.[40] Further, the minister of foreign affairs for the
Ottoman Empire, Fousaid, wrote the newly elected Prince of Moldavia,
Prince Ion Cuza, early in 1859, that the representatives of the Great
Powers had expressed to his government their interest in the affairs of
the United Principalities. They wondered whether the Principalities
were living up to their commitment as outlined by the treaties regarding subjects under foreign protection; i.e., the Jews and other minorities.
They concluded from the recent events that the United Principalities
had been remiss in their obligations:

> . . .in consideration of the disposition of the treaties regulating
> the subjects of foreign powers located in the Ottoman Empire.
> The residents of Ibraila (Austrian subjects), had been molested,
> their shops closed and several of them imprisoned.[41]

Thus, in the immediate period before the dual election of Alexander
Ion Cuza as prince of both Moldavia and Wallachia in 1859, the Jewish
question had begun to expand in scope and importance as far as the participants were concerned. What occupied those Romanians who dealt with
this issue was not the international aspects of it; rather, the impact of
recent immigration into the Principalities and its possible effects upon
the future Romanian development. They were in agreement with the
foreign Jews and the Great Powers that an answer should be achieved,
but there remained the unsolved question of the kind of solution owing
to the unknown thrust that these newly arrived Jewish immigrants as
citizens would have. In other words, the crux of the problem for the
Romanians was that of the rights and privileges all foreigners had in the

Principalities and on the process, if any, of naturalization for them would take without endangering what they considered to be *pro bon publice* of Romania.[42]

The first attempt to deal with this issue occurred at the ad hoc Divan held in Moldavia in October 1857. Many prominent Romanians, such as Mihail Kogălniceanu, who would become Prince Cuza's prime minister and would be instrumental in aiding the implementation of his reforms, and Costache Negri, who would become Cuza's representative in Constantinople, were not adverse to conferring citizenship with political and civil rights on the Jews, but they drew the line in regard to recent Jewish immigrants.[43] Kogălniceanu's reports on the rights of foreigners "Libertatea cultelor in România," [Liberty of Cults in Romania] brought forth a mixed reaction. He argued for the granting to certain "resident Jews" political and civil rights. Kogălniceanu and Negri advocated the position that this would strengthen the two Principalities by bringing into the political and economic life of Wallachia and Moldavia an active minority who would contribute greatly to the future development of the Principalities.[44] On October 29, 1857, the ad hoc Divan decied upon "rights for all Romanians."[45] However, many members opposed bestowing political and civil rights to the Jews and to any other minority. They saw these people as a threat to their vested interests as they feared that they would unite with the liberal faction and threaten their political and economic predominence in the life of the Principalities through initiation of "liberal reform" such as land.[46]

In spite of this, by the time of Cuza's dual election in 1859, no viable solution or policy toward the Jewish question had been adopted and implemented. Cuza's new administration was confronted with numerous monumental difficulties: dedicated monasteries, agricultural reform, financial and administrative unification, the acceptance of his dual election and the building of a foundation for the future economic and social development within the community of nations. The Jewish issue at this time was a minor one in importance to the others.[47]

The initial reaction of Cuza's new administration to the Jewish question had been to follow the historical precedent of the past and to impose a series of restrictions on the activities of the Jews;[48] i.e., in Wallachia measures were passed in 1861 limiting Jewish activities as controllers of hotels and caberts, as tenant farmers; they lost as well the rights to sell tobacco in 1862, and the government imposed a tax on kosher meat.[49] Cuza soon discovered that this anti-Jewish policy had three serious drawbacks which adversely affected his position as prince and his administrative

policy. First, this policy provided no viable solution; and, therefore, had
no real chance of succeeding in the long run. Second, the Jews, themselves, had begun to actively protest against their mistreatment and began
to petition for rights. Finally, this policy brought about increased foreign
intervention urged by the Romanian Jew's co-religionists, and Cuza was
looking for all the foreign friends he could find at the time in order to
bolster his candidancy for permanent residency on the Romanian throne.

Panu, a member of the parliamentary chambers and the cabinet pointed
out that Cuza's anti-Jewish policy failed for this key reason: It was aimed
at ending the exploitation of the peasantry by limiting Jewish activity in
the rural areas as landholders and leasers. The major fallacy of this theory
was that it only took into consideration one factor of the rural problem
and did not provide any remedies for other items that caused peasant ex-
politation.[50] Further, restricting Jewish activity ignored the issues of
naturalization and the question of granting them political and civil rights.
In spite of the fact that the Jewish question was minor in comparison to
the other issues of the day, having no solution for it magnified its importance out of scope. Cuza soon realized that if he was to accomplish his
program for reform, to build the foundation for the modern Romanian
nation, to unify the two principalities into one viable nation, to bring
progress to the countryside and to secure his throne, he could not allow
this question to go unsolved, thereby giving his enemies a weapon to use
against him.

Meanwhile, the Romanian Jews had not ceased in their campaign for
the acquisition of political and civil rights. By 1863 they became more
vocal in their demands. The issue soon became part of an open debate in
newspapers and journals.[51] The famous Rabbinical Scholar and Chief
Rabbi of Bucharest, the Malbim, took up the cause. He sent Prince Cuza
a petition in 1862 asking him to grant to the Jews citizenship and political and civil rights:

> By this you will be illuminated amongst your people
> As the "right" is your sogan
> And the love of G-d and country
> Live beneath your standard
>
> Inspiring all to odes of praise
> By certain legislation
> As liberty, equality and unity will be enjoyed
> On the basis of your rule

> Lead you nation with joy and prosperity
> And be with progress and energy
> Be the throne of your Majesty always secure
> And in the eternity well spoken about.[52]

The intervention of foreign Jews and the Great Powers had already complicated this national issue. Before the election of Cuza, this intervention had a relatively minor effect on the Jewish question and the internal affairs of the Principalities. However, with the election of Cuza in 1859, the action of the interventionists became more prominent with the Great Powers threatening to continue their activities until a "satisfactory solution" would be found.[53]

During the first years of Prince Cuza's reign, reports of the persecution of the Jews of Galați in the semi-official newspaper, *Le Journal de Constantinople*, brought forth a hostile response from the foreign ambassadors in the two Principalities.[54] The *Monitorul Oficial al Moldaviei*, of November 22, 1861, ridiculed this charge and claimed that toleration did exist in the Principalities.[55]

Meanwhile in Paris in 1860, the Alliance Israélite Universelle was founded with the purpose of aiding fellow Jews, obtaining their emancipation and gaining equality for them while improving their general life conditions. The Alliance Israélite Universelle had the support of all the Jewish organizations including the famous Anglo-Jewish Association as well as the Romanian community associations, Baron and Mrs. de Hirsch and the Hilfaverein des Deutschen Juden. The Alliance sponsored vast eduction projects for East European Jewry as well.[56]

The key figure and one of the founders of the Alliance Israélite Universelle was Isaac-Adolphe Crémiuex (1796-1880). A lawyer and active member of the French Legislative Assembly, he took part in the revolution of 1834. He became a member of the Central Consistory of the College of Notables in Paris. In 1840 he travelled with Sir Moses Montefoire to Damascu to aid his fellow Jews. In 1842 he was elected to the Chamber of Deputies; he participated also in the 1848 Revolution and became minister of justice in the Provisional Government. While he supported the election of Napoleon III as president, he opposed the latter's crowning himself emperor. For this Crémieux was imprisoned and forced into retirement. After Napoleon III's downfall, Crémieux participated in the government of National Defense. Throughout a long and distinguished career, he defended world Jewry from persecution and discrimination. He had as his personal goals the achievement of political and religious equality, moral progress for the Jews and an end to their sufferings for their religion. Crémieux relied upon the enormous influence he had built up during his years of public service to bring forth active French intervention on behalf of Romanian Jewry. He visited the Principalities twice, in 1864 and 1866, and later became an active figure in diplomatic relation with them.[57]

Cuza, who wanted international recognition and acceptance of his double election as prince of Moldavia and Wallachia, had no intention of weakening his domestic and international position owing to international agitation over the Jewish question, especially when the question of Dedicated Monasteries already had involved the interests of several foreign countries. Encountering tremendous internal opposition to both his position as prince and his internal reform program, Cuza did not want to have an unresolved Jewish question which might become a *cause celebre* for the opposition. Thus for both domestic and international considerations, he felt it would be best to find a viable solution to the Jewish question before it grew out of control and was used against him by his political enemies. Further, he could then concentrate his energies on other more pressing domestic problems including solidification of the throne. Cuza had no desire to surrender his throne to a foreign prince even though it was a condition for his dual election; he wanted to increase his claim and support to the throne no matter how shakey it seemed at the time.

Thus, when on January 1, 1864, a group of Jews presented a petition to Prince Cuza requesting the granting of citizenship, he expressed sympathy for their cause and stated that he favored the process of gradual naturalization for them:

> This year the Jews have been soliticiting for a number of rights. Having received a petition from them we have for some time decided on gradual emancipation, seeking little by little to accord civil rights and political equality to those other classes. I have long wanted to give to you all; I have not been able to do so. You will receive gradual emanciaption. Everywhere I have been I have liked you and I have not made a distinction because of religion.[58]

In 1864 the Assemblies, urged by Cuza's prodding and initiative, decided to grant limited naturalization to qualified Jews. Article 26 of the Comunal Law of March 1864 stated that native Jews who had hitherto held to Romanian customs and sentiments could obtain naturalization and the exercise of communal rights under one of the following provisions:

1. He had served in the army and obtained the rank of non-commissioned officer;
2. He had received a degree from a Romanian lyceum or college;
3. He had obtained a foreign degree such as M.D. that the Government recognized;
4. He had founded a manufacturing plant which employed at least fifty workers.[59]

This code provided a sharp contrast to past laws, especially the *Reglement Organique*, which had denied the Jews the opportunities to obtain citizenship.[60]

In spite of such gains for the community, the Jews took the opportunity to ask Prince Cuza for further political and civil rights. In a letter in *Reforma* dated December 8, 1864, the author, Marcus, a supporter of Jewish causes, stated that the Romanian Jews had proved to be loyal citizens interested in the moral, spiritual and economic progress and welfare of the country. He urged Prince Cuza to grant to the Jews naturalization and included a statement attributed to the Prince to prove that it was now time for the naturalization of the Jews: "After due consideration, my government has taken and would continue to take proper measures to hasten the emancipation of Romanian Jewry."[61]

At the same time, Jews abroad continued to agitate for more comprehensive political and civil rights for Romanian Jewry. In his report to Prince Cuza, Costache Negri, a long time friend and his personal representative to Constantinople, reported that the Turkish branch of the Alliance Israélite Universelle had a strong campaign in progress to convince the Turkish government to intervene on behalf of those Romanian Jews excluded from the recent legal improvements in the Jewish status.[62] As a follow up to Negri's report, A. Commondo, President of the Turkish Committee of the Alliance, wrote to Prince Cuza to register his organization's protest against any possible exclusion of Jews from the rights given to others: ". . . I do not hesitate to doubt the seriousness of the correspondence, and I seriously hope to see official statements which clarify the relative position of my co-religionists."[63] Finally, when Crémieux wrote to Prince Cuza on behalf of the Malbim asking for his reinstatement—he had been expelled from his pulpit as Chief Rabbi of Bucharest for opposing the introduction of the reform ritual—he also requested as well an end to the anti-Jewish measures of the 1850s and the 1860s and full citizenship for all Jews. Romania would benefit from this notion, Cremieux concluded, owing to the fact that the Jews would be excellent citizens; hence, they would not be an active minority excluded from future national development of the Romanian state.[64]

Opposition by senior boyars such as Lascar Catargiu and other members of the Chamber against his budgets, fiscal policy and other reform programs prompted Cuza to take increasingly important role in policy and decision making functions in order to promulgate his reform program. Cuza's relationship with the Chambers had deteriorated over a period of time since his dual election and legislative action had ground to a standstill by early 1864, a condition for which each side blamed the other. Taking the initiative, Cuza began a period of personal rule in 1864.

Cuza continued his program for the Jews. In addition to the Comunal Law of 1864, he recognized that Jewish financial talent could aid his administration when he appointed Adolphe Buchner as inspector of finance.[65] Towards the end of the year in 1864 Cuza acted decisively to end the Jewish question in Romania with a solution designed to please all parties concerned yet at the same time to protect the interests of the Romanian state. His plan was to bring into the mainstream of Romanian life the Jews and yet provide safeguards for them and the Romanians. In this he was influenced strongly in the heritage of the 1848er's to whom he had belonged. Much of his ideas had been adopted from their program for the 1848 Revolution.

On December 4/16, 1864 Prince Cuza issued his Civil Code and one of the issues resolved by this code was the Jewish question. In one stroke he solved the question of naturalization for the Jews as well as successfully handling the burning issue of the recent immigrants whom many Romanians feared and did not want to have the benefits of citizenship:

Article 7: All Romanians have civil rights.

Article 8: Those born in Romania but yet grown many obtain citizenship within a year after reaching maturity providing that they are not under foreign protection.

Article 9: Non-Christians and foreigners may obtain rights under the conditions of Article 16.

Article 10: All Chirstians born in Romania are citizens.

Article 16: A foreigner may become a citizen after ten year's residence and renunciation of all foreign protection. He must submit a documented petition to the Prince for this purpose to be acted by the Council of State.[66]

In one step Prince Cuza resolved both the Jewish question and the touchy issue of granting rights to foreigners. He recognized the distinction between native and non-native Jews; he granted citizenship to native Jews and made provisions for the non-native persons to become citizens. In this respect, he was carrying on the tradition of 1848 and the program that those men had envisioned as a foundation for the new united Romanian state. In his other domestic programs such as land reform, educational improvements and fiscal soundness, Cuza had the strong tradition of 1848 as a viable guide.

The Jewish community enthusiastically endorsed this new code and joyfully praised Prince Cuza for his enlightened act. Telegrams of gratitude, praise and support came from the various Jewish communities in both Principalities.[67] The telegram from Iași community of December 13/25, 1864 praised the Prince for his enlightened actions:

> ...with the thrill of pleasure, with respect and with unlimited devotion, the United Jewish Community of Iași came to offer at the feet of your Highness profound homage for the work that your government has done to hasten the emancipation of the Jews in Romania. Father of our country, you have become and will continue to be a light, may you live many years.[68]

The Piatra's community's telegram of December 15/27, 1864 echoed this statement of praise and gratitude: "He has acted by the principles of the pure heart, affection and kindness Hurrah! It is through the work of his justice that Jews too are emanciapted. Long Live Romania! For this justice glory to our Ruler, Hurrah."[69] Other telegrams from various Jewish communities were similar in context praising and thanking Cuza for his progressive steps in granting the Jews the opportunity for citizenship.

A leading contemporary Jewish writer on this question, Brociner, stated that Prince Cuza's proposals in the December 1864 Civil Code recognized that the Jews were entitled to and had rights.[70] These measures, he claimed, would help to bring the Romanians and the Jews closer together for the benefit of all and for the benefit of the newly united country.[71] Finally, one of the outstanding modern Romanian historians, Constantin C. Giurescu, in his work on Cuza, recognized that not only was Prince Cuza friendly to the Jews and an enlightened monarch concerning this issue, but that this step was one of the most progressive measures granted to the Jews regarding political and civil rights at that time, especially for any East European country.[72]

Of all possible actions to take regarding the Jewish question, why did Prince Cuza select this one? Xenopol pointed out that as late as

February 1864 Cuza came to realize that he had to do something about the Jewish question and that the policy of repressive measures had failed.[73]

After dealing with this issue, Cuza attempted to resolve other problems as the budget, administrative reform, electoral reform, the land question, fiscal reform and the strengthening of his position as prince. His reforms did much to put Romania on the road to modern development and toward gaining her place in the community of nations. However, he did not remain in power long enough to carry out his programs and to make whatever adjustments would be necessary.

Also he faced strong opposition to his reforms, for example, the land-owning aristocracy worked actively to undercut the efforts of his land reform program. His reforms and his high-handed manner plus his desire to be prince for life had united a coalition of upper class boyars against Cuza. They overthrew him on February 11/23, 1866, in a bloodless coup and sent him into exile for the remainder of his life. The reasons for Cuza's downfall are many and complex. Evidence does indicate, however, that the granting of naturalization to the Jews had little tangible influence on the boyar's decision to depose him.[74]

NOTES

1. Joseph Berkowitz, *La Question des Israélites en Roumaine*, Paris, 1923, pp. 225-30.

2. Anastase N. Hâciu, *Evreii în Ţările Româneşti*, Bucureşti, 1943, p. 154; March Borchard, *Intolerance et persecutions religieuses*, Paris, 1868, p. 8.

3. Bernard Stambler, *L'Histoire des Israélites Roumains et le droit d'intervention international*, Paris, 1913, p. 58; G. Panu, *Chestiunii politice, sufragiul universal, chestiunea Evreilor*, Bucureşti, 1893, pp. 96-97.

4. No. 34, Corespondenţa despre conflictul dintre Ovrei şi Consul Austriac şi despre celorlaiţi Consuli, Iaşi, November 26, 1825; No. 7 Corepondenţa din Iaşi adresata lui Huget, despre opreirea arendării moşiilor şi supunerea lor le un impozit, despre un incident cu Hahamii Ovrei, şi altiul cu falşificări debanî, Iaşi, February 27, 1825, see also No. 15, Memoriul lui Bois le Compte despre Molsava, Bucureşti, May 14, 1834, *Documente Privitore la Istoria Românilor*, Hurmuzaki, (ed.), vol. XVII, 1825-1846, Bucureşti, 1887-1922, pp. 9, 34-6, 362-3.

5. Le Ministre des Affaires etrangers, Kogălniceanu, a l'agent diplomatique de Roumanie à Vienne, October 22/ November 3, 1877, *Aderatele documente din correspondenţa de la 5 Octobre 1877 pînă la 15*

Septembre, 1878, n.p.n.d, p. 4; the editors in Panu, *Chestiunii politice,* pp. 96-7.

6. Geltrunk (U.S. vs. Salvador) U.S.–Salvador Arbitration Under an Exchange of Notes in 1902, (Foreign Relations, U.S. 1902, 873, 877) in Milton Katz and Kingman Brewster, Jr., *International Transactions and Relations, Cases and Materials,* Brooklyn, 1960, p. 118.

7. Stambler, *L'Histoire des Israelites,* p. 58.

8. Katz, *International Transactions,* p. 114.

9. North American Dredging Company, (U.S. vs. Mexico) Claims Commission, U.S. and Mexico Under Convention of September 8, 1923, March 31, 1926, in ibid., pp. 146, 155, 158.

10. Arhivele Statului din Botoșani, *Prefectura Județului Botoșani,* No. 9, September 29, 1864, *344/1864;* see also Arhivele Statului din Piatra-Neamț, *Primăria Patria-Neamț,* No. 16, 26, *5/1870.*

11. Verax, (pseud. for Radu Rosetti), *La Roumanie et les Juifs,* București, 1903, p. 6.

12. Scrisoare lui V. Alexandre, 18 Septembre 1864 către Baligot de Beyne privitoare de leges rurală, Mircești le 29 Auot 1864 as quoted *in* A. D. Xenopol, *Domna lui Cuza-Vodă,* 2 vols., Iași, 1903, vol. II, pp 365-6.

13. Isidore Loeb, *La Situation des Israélites en Turquie, en Serbie et en Roumanie,* Paris, 1877, p. 95.

14. Br. *Invasiunea Jidaniloru pe Țările Române, dedicata adeverâtiloru patrioti Români,* Iași, 1864; Emanual Cretzulescu, ancien agent diplomatique de Roumanie à Paris, *Les Israélites en Roumanie,* Paris, 1879, p. 10; Verax. *La Roumanie et les Juifs,* p. 370; Hâciu, *Evreii în Țările,* pp. 158-60, 301-4.

15. Loeb, *La Situation,* pp. 97-8.

16. Bogdan-Duică, *Românii și Ovreii,* București, 1913, pp. 54-5.

17. Brătianu, Minister of Interior, Chamber of Deputies, Extract of Session of March 24/April 6, 1868, Arhivele Statului din București, *Casa Regală,* 9/1868; see also, I. S. Valentineanu, *Ebrei în România,* București, 1866, pp. 5-8; Victor Slavescu, *Domintorul Cuza și Victor Place,* București, 1942, p. 61; Marcel Emerit, *Victor Place et la politique Francaise en Roumanie a l'epoque de l'Union,* Bucharest, 1931, p. 9; the editors in Panu, *Chestiunii politice,* pp. 96-7; Alexandre A. C. Sturdza, *Regime de Michael Sturdza, Prince Regnant de Moldavia, 1834-1849,* Paris, 1907, p. 44.

18. Panu, *Chestiunii politice,* pp. 125-7, 130-5.

19. Ibid., pp. 100-1, 109-113.

20. J. B. Brociner, *Cestiunes Israeliților Români,* București, 1910,

pp. 24-7; Lucien Wolf, *Notes on the Diplomatic History of the Jewish Question*, London, 1959, pp. 18-23.

21. *The Jewish Encyclopedia*, New York, 1925, vol. X, pp. 490-504; Hâciu, *Evreii în Țările*, p. 225; *Encyclopedia Judaica*, Jerusalem, 1971+, vol. XIV, pp. 339-46.

22. *Jewish Encyclopedia*, vol. VIII, pp. 668-70.

23. Ibid., vol. VI, pp. 30-1.

24. Loeb, *La Situation*, pp. iv-v, 101.

25. Berkowitz, *La Question*, pp. 234-5.

26. Stambler, *L'Histoire*, p. 73.

27. Loeb, *La Situation*, p. iv; Hâciu, *Evreii în Țările*, p. 239.

28. Xenopol, *Domna lui Cuza-Vodă*, vol. I, pp. viii, 12-3, vol. II, pp. 168-9, 180; Hâciu, *Ervreii în Țările*, pp. 153-6.

29. Panu, *Chestiuni politice*, pp. 152-6.

30. Xenopol, *Domnia lui Cuza-Vodă*, vol. II, pp. 180-4.

31. Brociner, *Chestiunea Israeliților*, p. 28; Hâciu, *Evreii în Țările*, p. 238; Stambler, *L'Histoire*, pp. 75-6.

32. The General Treaty of Peace Between Great Britain, Austria, France, Russia, Sardina and Turkey, signed at Paris, March 20, 1856, *The Map of Europe by Treaty; Showing the Various Political and Territorial Changes Which Have Taken Place Since the General Peace of 1814, Four Volumes*, Edward Hertzlett, (ed.), London, 1875-1891, vol. II, 1260-2.

33. Berkowitz, *La Question*, pp. 268-9; Loeb, *La Situation*, p. 104.

34. Convention Between Great Britain, Austria, France, Prussia, Russia, Sardina, and Turkey, Respecting the United Principalities of Moldavia and Wallachia, Signed at Paris, August 19, 1858, *Map of Europe*, vol. II, pp. 1343-4.

35. Brociner, *Chestiunes Israeliților*, pp. 24-7.

36. Berkowitz, *La Question*, pp. 268-9; Wolf, *Notes on the Diplomatic*, pp. 18-23.

37. Adresa Israeliților din București către consului-general Francez în Valachia din 15 August 1858, București, *Acte și documente relative la istoria renascerei României, 1391-1859*, Ghenadie Petrescu, Dimitre A. and Dimitie C. Sturdza, (eds.), București, 1899-1909, vol. IX, p. 57.

38. Ion C. Filiti, *Domniile Române sub Regulamenul Organic, 1834-1848*, București, 1915, p. 346.

39. Ion Bălăceanu to Ion Ghica , Nice, June 16, 1858, *Documente privind unirea Principațelor, III, Correspondența politică*, (1858-1859), Cornelia Bodea, (ed.), București, 1963, pp. 384-5.

40. Emerit, *Victor Place*, p. 42.

41.   Minister of Foreign Affairs, for the Ottoman Empire, Fousaid to His Majesty Prince Alexandre Ion Cuza, Hospidar of Moldavia, December 14, 1859, *Arhiva Cuza-Vodă*, vol. I, No. 30-1; see also Ernest Desjardens, *Les Juifs de Moldavie*, Paris, 1867, p. 22.

42.   Xenopol, *Domnia lui Cuza-Vodă*, vol. I, pp. 124-9; R. V. Bossy, *Politică externa a României între anii 1873-1880, privita de la agenţia diplomatica din Rome, Bucureşti, 1928, p. 15.*

43.   Vice-Council St. John to Earl Granville, Bucharest, July 31, 1872, *Correspondence Respecting the Condition and Treatment of the Jews in Servia and Romania: 1867-1876, Presented to the House of Commons by the Command of Her Majesty, in Pursuance of Their Address Dated February 15, 1877*, London, 1877, pp. 265-6.

44.   Pericle, Martinescu, *Costache Negri*, Bucureşti, n.d., pp. 167-8.

45.   Ibid.

46.   Ibid.; Panu, *Chestiunii politice*, pp. 152-6.

47.   Xenopol, *Domnia lui Cuza-Vodă*, vol. I, p. viii.

48.   Bernard Lazare, *L'Oppression des Juifs dans l'Europe Orientale les Juifs en Roumanie*, Paris, 1902, pp. 20-1; Bernard Lazare, *L'Antisemitisme, son histoire et ses causes, editions definitive, two volumes*, Paris, 1934, vol. II, p. 24; Borchard, *Intolerance et persecutions*, pp. 10-1, 17.

49.   Lazare, *L'Oppression des Juifs*, pp. 66, 70; Loeb, *La Situation*, pp. 112, 120-1; Berkowitz, *La Question*, pp. 357-8; Eric F. Braunstein, *L'Oligarchie Roumanie et les Juifs*, Paris, 1927, pp. 41-2; X. D. Xenopol, *Istoria partidelor politice în România, de la orgini până la 1866*, Bucureşti, 1910, p. 450.

50.   Panu, *Chestiunii politice*, pp. 16-7, 172-3.

51.   Xenopol, *Domna lui Cuza-Vodă*, vol. II, pp. 180-4.

52.   "Rugacine, Manificestate de către Şefulu religie Israeliţiloru d-ni marele Rabinu M. L. Malbim în sinagoga cea mare pentru fericita d. a. Domnitorulu Principatelorul Unite Alexandru Ion Cuza, February 1862," *Arhiva Cuza-Vodă*, vol. XII, No. 120-1.

53.   Vice-Council St. John to Earl Granville, Bucharest, July 3, 1872, *C.R.C.T.*, pp. 265-6.

54.   C. Negri to Cuza-Vodă, Constantinople, April 8.20, 1859, in *Documente privind unirea principatelor*, vol. III, pp. 578-9.

55.   Negri C. Dmnitor, October 2, 1861, Corespondenţa as quoted in Xenopol, *Domnia lui Cuza-Vodă*, vol. I, p. 216.

56.   *The Jewish Encyclopedia*, vol. I, pp. 413-7; N. Leven, *Cinquante d'ans d'histoire l'Alliance Israelite Universelle, 1860-1910*, Paris, 1911, pp.

1, 71-3, 81-97, see this work for a fifty year history of this organization and its numerous activities. Paul Goodman, *History of the Jews, a New Edition*, London, 1939, pp. 199-200.

57. *Jewish Encyclopedia*, vol. IV, pp. 345-8; *Encyclopedia Judaica*, vol. V, pp. 1074-6; Gaston Dubocage, "Quelques personnalities et grandes families Cremieux," *La Question Juive, vue par vingt-six emenites personnalities*, Paris, 1934, pp. 166-9; Hâciu, *Evreii în Țarile*, p. 225.

58. As quoted in Berkowitz, *La Question*, p. 279.

59. Comunal Law of 1864 as reported in *Monitorul Oficial*, March 10/22, 1864, p. 245; also in Alliance Israelite Universelle, *La Question Juive dans les chambres Roumanies, compte-rendu des seances de la chambre des deptutes et du senat du mois de Mars 1879*, Paris, 1879, p. iii; Loeb, *La Situation*, p. 99.

60. Xenopol, *Domna lui Cuza-Vodă*, vol. II, pp. 177-8.

61. Hibat Allah Marcus, "Apelu catre co-religionarii me, December 8, 1864," *Reforma, Diaru politicu, comerciale, agricole și literariu*, December 10, 1864, pp. 543-4.

62. C. Negri to Cuza-Vodă, Constantinople, September 14/26, 1864, *Archiva Cuza-Vodă*, vol. I, No. 500-1.

63. A. Commondo to Monsieur le Charge d'Affairs, n.d., ibid., vol. I, No. 448.

64. Adolphe Cremieux to Prince Cuza, Paris, November 18, 1864, ibid., vol. XII, No. 233-4.

65. Berkowitz, *La Question*, p. 286.

66. Civil Code in *Monitorul Oficial*, December 4/16, 1864, p. 1287.

67. For the telegrams from the communities of Iași, December 4/16 and 13/25, Galați, December 15/27, Focșani, Bacău, Huși, Roman, Bîrlad, Tecuci and Piatra, December 17/29. Botoșani and Vaului, December 18/30, and București, December 14/26, 1864, in *Arhiva Cuza-Vodă*, vol. XVI, No. 136-147, and vol. XII, No. 233.

68. Telegram, December 13/25, 1864, ibid., vol. XVI, no. 136.

69. Telegram, December 15/27, 1864, ibid., vol. XVI, no. 145.

70. Brociner, *Chestineau Israeliților*, p. 85.

71. Ibid., p. 90.

72. Constantin C. Giurescu, *Viața și opera lui Cuza-Vodă*, 2nd edition, București, 1970, p. 320.

73. Xenopol, *Istoria partidilor*, p. 448; Xenopol, *Domna lui Cuza-Vodă*, vol. I, p. 4, vol. II, p. 178.

74. Paul Henry, *L'Abdication du Prince Cuza et l'Avenement de la dynastie de Hohenzollern au throne de la Roumanie*, Paris, 1930; Xenopol, *Domnia lui Cuza-Vodă*, vol. II, pp. 67-68.

George R. Ursul

FROM POLITICAL FREEDOM TO RELIGIOUS INDEPENDENCE:
THE ROMANIAN ORTHODOX CHURCH, 1877-1925

The years between the achievement of independence and the establishment of the Patriarchate constitute a formative period in the life of the
Orthodox Church of Romania. Still reeling from the radical changes
imposed on it by Cuza[1] the years between 1877 and 1925 witnessed
an intensification of Church-State relations, with a clear definition of
the roles and responsibilities of each, the creation of a national organizational structure and a system of operations. These were not easy years
for the Romanian Church as any narrative of events suggests. Political
parties, with strikingly different philosophies, interferred constantly
in its life and structure, either through the passage of laws in which the
Church had little input, or through the appointment of partisan hierarchs
whose views were sympathetic to the government or party in power. A
Roman Catholic king and a movement to win converts to Catholicism
proved to be a constant irritant to the Romanian Orthodox and generated an atmosphere of intrigue and bitterness, while ambitious politicians and churchmen used the Church to promote their own self-interest.
At the same time, there occurred a sharp decline in the moral authority
of bishops as a series of scandals ended episcopal careers and questioned
the integrity of the leadership of the Church. On the other side of the
balance sheet, however, the Romanian Orthodox Church emerged as an
autonomous, self-governing Patriarchate in the Orthodox world with all
the prestige that this conveyed. Its clergy and hierarchs were better educated, standards at seminaries were significantly raised, the fabric and
occupants of monasteries improved, while the appearance of a lively and
occasionally controversial press attested to a new vitality in the church's
life. There was a renewed interest in morality and social justice, especially
after 1907, and discussion about culture and its role in the nation's past,
present and future. The inescapable conclusion must be that despite the

217

often pernicious results of political interference the regulation and supervision of the Church by the State, particularly through the Department
of Religion and Public Instruction, was useful and helpful in updating
the Romanian Orthodox Church and allowing it to fulfill its respon-
sibiliites with greater dignity and skill.

The intensification of Church-State relations was the result of a series
of legislative enactments passed through these years with the intention of
bringing the Church under regular government control and daily supervision. As a national institution, deeply rooted in the nation's struggle
for ethnic survival and the single most important factor in the development of Romanian culture, the Orthodox Church exercised a powerful
influence and hold on the masses, particularly in the countryside where
the pace of change and progress was slow. While governments might range
from being anti-clerical to indifferent, or even reflect a pious acceptance,
no statesman could forget either the historic role of the Church or its
contemporary meaning for the masses and ignore its role in shaping
and developing the future nation. With the Civil Code of 1864 Cuza had
already initiated an attempt to create a national church organization corresponding to that of the emerging Romanian state, but considerable
refinement was necessary to achieve this goal. While assuring the liberty
of other religious communities the Constitution of 1866 proclaimed
vaguely that the Orthodox faith was "the dominant religion" of the
country and implied the benefits of state patronage and attention. Within
the spirit of Western European liberalism, then in favor among Romanians
of the upper classes and intelligentsia, the Government passed four statutes
between 1872-1908 designed to help the Church fulfill its destiny as
"the dominant religion" but also, realistically, to regulate and modernize
it. The first law, legislated in 1872, described the procedures in the selection of metropolitans and diocesan bishops as well as the composition and
responsibilities of a Synod. The second, in 1893, dealt with clergy and
seminaries in an attempt to upgrade the theological education of the
Romanian priesthood. In 1904, a third enactment established a Church
House with centralized authority to improve and maintain the fabric
of church properties. Finally, in 1908, the Superior Church Consistory
was created as a quasi-ecclesiastical parliament to provide a voice in church
affairs for the laity as well as clergy and monastics. Throughout this
period relations between the Government and Church were conducted
by a Ministry of Religion and Public Instruction. The concept of the
domination of the Church by the State was not new and had existed
from Byzantine days as a distinct caesaropapism. In the late medieval

period the voevodes of Moldavia had supervised church affairs through an appointed official or logofat. With the creation of a Ministry of Religion in the 19th century religious laws passed by the Government were enforced, standards of clerical education maintained, ecclesiastical discipline upheld and a general supervision of the Church imposed.

The 1872 *Law for the Selection of Metropolitans and Diocesan Bishops and the Composition of the Holy Synod of the Romanian Orthodox Church*[2] united the historic metropolitinates of Wallachia and Moldavia in a single Romanian Church, with a Holy Synod, as the governing body of the Church, being the symbol of this unity. The Synod included the two metropolitans, six diocesan bishops and eight arch-hierarchs or suffragan bishops. With the intention of raising the formal educational levels of the episcopate all candidates for elevation, after 1892, were required to possess earned academic degrees. All future hierarchs were to be chosen by an electoral college composed of members of the Synod as well as the national legislature, both the Senate and the House of Deputies; the Metropolitan of Ungro-Wallachia would bear the title "Primate of Romania" and reside in Bucharest. Within the Church there were many who criticized the Law, pointing to the exclusion of clerical and monastic participation from the selection process of their spiritual superiors, and warned of the dangers of an electoral college, made up of current members of the Holy Synod and all Orthodox deputies and senators in the national legislature, some of whom were only nominal Christians, or were prepared to use their position for party advantage. In vain it was pointed out that this would, unfortunately, open the selection of church leaders to political considerations and not to an objective consideration of the spiritual, administrative and intellectual qualities of candidates for hierarchicial elevation. Nevertheless, the Law remained in force. Meeting twice a year the new Synod undertook a thorough overhaul of religious life and institutions. From May 3, 1873 to June 13, 1875 it passed a series of far-reaching statutes dealing with ecclesiastical discipline, canonical violations and trials, seminarians, the election and role of arch-hierarchs, burials and memorial services, regulation and improvement of the monastic life, church publications, means of sustaining and maintaining the clergy, the priority and dignity of the Primate, religious services and standardized books of ritual. In 1909 and 1911, the Law was subsequently modified to reflect changed conditions and widespread criticism.

A far more extensive ecclesiastical regulation was to come. In 1893 under the proposal of Take Ionescu, then Minister of Religion and Public

Instruction, the Government introduced *The Law Governing Clergy and Seminaries,*[3] a measure which provoked considerable public controversy throughout the country. Intended to improve the material condition of the Romanian clergy by having priests' salaries assumed by the Ministry and urban town councils, widespread criticism[4] pointed out that this made the priesthood a salaried bureaucracy, subservient to the State and political interests. The Law also reorganized seminary education, although this was divorced from the leadership of the Church and brought under control of the Ministry of Religion and Public Instruction. Thus, a complete program of theological education was established with 2 upper seminaries, at Bucharest and Iaşi, requiring 5 years of study, and 3 lower seminaries at Roman, Rîmnic and Curtea d'Argeş, requiring 3 years of preparation. In time, the Minister founded others so that by the eve of World War I every diocese had its own seminary, although it must be emphasized that all functioned under the direction of the State. Protopopes, district supervisors or archdeacons, according to the Law were also to be named by the bishops; this authority came to be used to reward those who reflected the political philosophy of the day. So controversial was this Law that significant changes, reflecting national and church opposition, had to be made in 1896, 1900, 1906, 1909 and 1910.

In 1902 the Minister of Religion, Spiru Haret, established Church House. There had long been a desire for a central bureau to control and preserve the physical fabric of all church and monastic properties and possessions, to administer all funds derived from the national budget or contributions and to handle all personnel questions. But the direction by a government ministry created another possibility for political favoritism to occur. Staffed with a self-serving and contentious bureaucracy Church House only lasted until 1921 when popular opposition led to its abolition. Nevertheless, it stood for government control of the Church and the potential for the abuse of power. Government regulation occurred next in 1909 when Haret proposed a synodal reform, which involved the participation of laity and the lower clergy in vital synodal decisionmaking with lay representation able to outvote the clerical representation. When enacted the new law established a Superior Church Consistory, which included members of the Holy Synod as well as representatives of the Orthodox clergy and monastic communities, and created what was, in effect, a Clergy Parliament. It also reduced the authority of the bishops, who were now to be elected by both Houses of Parliament, with Orthodox and non-Orthodox casting their ballots on eposcopal candidates for the Orthodox Church. The project unleased a national frenzy and the country's press devoted considerable attention to the issue. With its extensive clerical and lay participation it seemed to many to have been influenced by Protestantism and was a foretaste of what might yet befall the Church. The *Telegraful Român*[5] echoed the feelings of many Romanians when it deplored the fact that "turmoil continues in the Church through reforms and para-reforms, which are sometimes venomous, and riddled with a spirit of inevitable party politics, as well as the resignation of metropolitans and the disciplining of bishops. . . . "

In the first meeting of the 1909 fall session of the Holy Synod[6] a fierce fight broke out over the Consistory, which the bishops realized would assume some of the responsibilities formerly the prerogative of the Holy Synod. Discussion prior to the vote was lively, led by Bishop Gherasim Serafim, Bishop of Roman, who argued that it was anti-canonical. A break cooled tempers, but when the Synod re-convened Bishop Gherasim presented a lengthy memorial, quoting generously from Orthodox sources to support his contention of the non-canonicity of the Law. He attacked other members of the Synod who had capitulated to the Government, castigating them for violating the canons by allowing the rights of the bishops over priests and deacons to be assumed by the civil authorities. He insisted that by supporting such a law that "Those who wish to celebrate services in the Church of God, contrary to the laws of the foundation of the Orthodox Christian Church, then I, Bishop Gherasim of Roman, anathematize them." The oath of anathema, by one of their own number, shocked the bishops and raised the question whether they could, even canonically, continue to exercise their episcopal functions. A fierce debate was waged. Partenie, former Metropolitan of Moldavia, announced that he shared Gherasim's opinion, that the Ecumenical Patriarch, whose spiritual authority the Romanian Church still accepted, should interfere to maintain respect for the canons, and that the anathema was in force and no prelate could officiate services. Minister of Religion Haret responded furiously that this opposition was a revolt against a law that had already been passed by Parliament, although he denied that the state controlled and regulated the Church. In this he was supported only half-heartedly by Metropolitan-Primate Mironescu. The Government refused to back down, however, and the Law remained in force. Gherasim was persuaded under duress to rescind his anathema, was deprived of office and allowed to find a monastery of his own choosing to settle in. So much for Haret's disclaimer of governmental regulation of the State Church!

The end of the 19th century witnessed further intensification of Church-State relations. To invoke God's blessing on the armed forces and inspire them to greater efforts on behalf of their homeland, chaplains were appointed to the army on a regular basis; the Church also took the

initiative to provide medical and hospital services. Even before the achievement of independence Cuza had established the principle of military chap-
lincies by including salaries for several clergy to be attached to the larger
military units in the national budget for 1860.[7] This was followed in 1870
·by a decree *The Rule Concerning Clergy in the Army* which provided
for the appointment of an Orthodox priest to every regiment (later broadened to include Roman Catholics). The military clergy were expected to
conduct religious services, preach sermons exhorting the soldiers to heroic
feats in defending Country and Throne, and when possible, to accompany
the troops to the battle fields to comfort the sick in makeshift hospitals.
In 1877 local parish priests attached to specific territorial units were replaced by chaplains attached to permanent garrisons and were expected
to accompany the troops on manuevers.

In 1877 when the war of independence broke out the Church shared in
the wave of patriotic enthusiasm which swept across the country, con-
ducting prayers nationwide for the success of the Romanian army, organizing religious processions through the streets of Bucharest and other
principal cities of the realm and commemorating those soldiers killed in
the war with memorial services. Thus, when the Romanians found themselves involved in the Bulgarian campaign of 1913 the Church immediately
assumed a forceful role. Metropolitan Pimen Georgescu of Moldavia met
with Ion Kalinderu, President of the Romanian Red Cross, about the
possibility of utilizing monks for medical purposes.[8] Consequently, Archimandrite Teoctist Stupcanu, the Abbot of the historic monastery of
Neamţ, and 16 members of that community, formed a hospital detail,
charged with maintaining equipment for surgery, X-ray, bacteriology and
all necessary medical and food supplies. Sent by King Ferdinand to Teliş,
where Metropolitan Pimen joined them, they aided in establishing the first
isolation ward for cholera victims. The monks worked there for the entire
summer until the cessation of hostilities and the withdrawal of Romanian
troops from Bulgaria.

The monastic involvement in the medical treatment of Romanian soldiers established a precedent that was continued during World War I. When
war was declared in 1914, Metropolitan Pimen took the necessary steps
to prepare the monastic communities of Moldavia for medical involvement
should Romania be drawn into the conflict. Establishing a medical training
school and hospital at the Cetăţuia Monastery in Iaşi he began to recruit
volunteers. The courses lasted six months and examinations were conducted by a three-man medical commission appointed by the Minister of Public
Health. In the first three months of 1915 alone 90 monks enrolled and by

1916 when Romania found itself involved in hostilities 100 monks had graduated from the intensive study programs. They were placed at the disposal of the Romanian Red Cross and sent to Bucharest. There they worked with the wounded brought back from the front, divided for service among five hospitals set up by the Red Cross; each unit included a monastic priest who was confessor for the spiritual needs of the wounded. The monks remained in Bucharest until the Government was moved to Moldavia when they were reassigned to Vaslui, Bârzeşti, Iaşi, Focşani, and Ruginoasa, the latter being installed in the fomer palace of Prince Cuza. Archimandrite Stupcanu of Neamţ served as the head of this monastic contingent and undertook frequent visitations to the five different groups. After the war the Abbot and seven monks were singled out for their tireless work and exposing themselves to infectious diseases by distinguished service medals, first rank. In fact, so many monks died at their posts from contracting cholera and other diseases that after 1918, seventy parishes they had served as monastic clergy prior to the outbreak of war, were without priests. In all, 120 monks participated in the medical services of the Romanian army. Equally involved during the war were Orthodox nuns. Under the leadership of Abbess Ana Ghenovici 20 nuns from Moldavia were sent to Bucharest at the beginning of the war, working in different hospitals in the capital, even remaining there during the German occupation, when they were complimented by the occupying authorities for fulfilling their responsibilities. A larger group of nuns trained in sick and operating room techniques at the hospitals throughout Moldavia. It is estimated that about 115 nuns were involved in this work, for which many of them were recognized with Red Cross decorations.

During the war while the monastic communities of Romania were busily engaged in medical services the military chaplaincy was expanded. In the three years of war involvement 253 priests were mobilized for service in the army;[9] of this number 46 were almost immediately released from duty and returned to parish life. Of the remaining number, however, 25 priests were taken prisoner or killed in duty while 6 were wounded. Only 10 of these clergy had graduated from a full 5 year theological program, with the equivalent of the Bachelor of Divinity degree; 135 were licensed in theology, that is they had completed course work without having take the qualifying examinations or written papers; 70 had completed a 3-year seminary program and 10 four years of seminary. These figures not only reflect the considerable number of clergy serving as chaplains but they also suggest education improvement in the Romanian clergy. They stand out in sharp contrast to the low theological learning that characterized the clergy in the late 19th century. Obviously the *Law Governing Clergy and Seminaries* was slowly but clearly transforming a clergy, devoted and pious but lacking in formal theological preparation, into a literate, more articulate and educated priesthood. This more cosmopolitan outlook and clerical literacy was clearly reflected in printed contemporary sermons.[10] A review of these does not depict Romania's enemies, even the Germans, as monsters or extinguishers of culture, evil in the eyes of God. Rather than tearing down the enemy they concentrate on building up the morale and patriotism of the Romanian soldier.[11] Appealing to the historic struggle of the Romanian people to survive, Constantin Nazarie, director of the military chaplains, emphasized the importance of the flag and what it represents. "Defending the Flag, you honor the Country and Romanian People. Defend it because in their turn: the King, the Country, the People and God, the Protector of Romanianism, will bless you from generation to generation."[12] In another sermon "What it means to be a Soldier" Nazarie described the responsibility of the man fighting for Romania. "You bear, with joy," he exhorted his listeners, "the holy burden of the military . . . because good soldiers are the shield, pride and glory of the Land, you are the leaders of the People, honored and loved by men and blessed by God."[13] Other chaplains echoed similar patriotic themes, the necessity of obeying "superiors," and how God's aid is abundant and available, drawing on scriptural passages and local images familiar to the hardy Romanian soldier, a stalwart peasant before being drafted, that evoked a love of God, country, and family. Since no specific services for war existed, aside from the Te Deum authorized by the Holy Synod, these priests began to develop and publish pamphlets with services for various personal moments of importance to the faithful in the army; these included the blessing of holy water, confession on the battlefield, communion in hospitals, prayers for wounded soldiers and services for the dead.[14]

It was inevitable that the emergence of a united Romanian state after 1877 and its elevation to a "kingdom" should also have stimulated a demand for religious independence. Having won their political freedom on the battlefield Romanians began to regard the dependence of their Orthodox Church on the Ecumenical Patriarchate as a national humiliation.[15] Situated in Constantinople, the capital of their former masters, it was itself a prisoner of the Turkish state. Agitation for autocephalicity, the right of self-government and control over all church appointments, began almost immediately. It was spurred on by the memory of the hated

Phanariot period, when many assets of the church had been siphoned off for over two centuries by the representatives and appointees of the Greek Church. This rankled Romanians and control of their own religious destiny became a national imperative. The result was a drawn out negotiation by both the Romanian Government and the Church Hierarchy with the Ecumenical Patriarchate in which the Holy Synod in Constantinople delayed and continuously prolonged the discussion. But the Romanians were not to be denied their ecclesiastical independence and after five years of fruitless negotiation finally took the initiavtive. On March 25, 1882 Metropolitan Calinic Miclescu celebrated the service of the Blessing of Holy Oil for the first time in the history of Romania in the Metropolitan Cathedral in Bucharest.[16] Previously the oil, used in the consecration of churchs, annointing and religious services, had always been sanctified by the Holy Synod in Constantinople and then brought to Romania. In a dramatic sense the service was the first step in a religious declaration of independence and marked the bringing home of control over services and church personnel. Although the Ecumenical Patriarch, Ioachim, denounced Calinic and dismissed his action "as the type of disorder which merits the judgment of blasphemy" there was no turning back. On the occasion of a courtesy call to the Patriarch and Holy Synod during his visit to Constantinople in October 1866, Carol I had already discussed the issue. He now directed the Minister of Religion, D. A. Sturdza, to press on with negotiations. To this purpose Metropolitan Calinic lent his enthusiastic support, convening a commission that, in addition to himself, also included Metropolitan Iosif of Moldavia, and the great 19th century scholar, Bishop Melchisedec of Roman, to prepare a study on the historic traditions of the independence of national churches within Orthodoxy. Examining earlier synodal and conciliar decisions these apologists for the Romanian Orthodox Church published their report in October 1883,[18] emphasizing how the Romanian Church had always faithfully adhered to Orthodox canon law and dogma and that its desire for autocephalicity and self-determination rested firmly on the traditions and past practices of the Eastern Orthodox Church. The combined offensive of Church and State, with carefully veiled hints of retaliation if this were denied, finally impressed the Phanar and on April 13, 1885 Patriarch Ioachim and the ten members of the Holy Synod unanimously issued a Tomos of Autocephalicity recognizing the Romanian Orthodox Church as an independent, self-governing Church, under its own Holy Synod with the Metropolitan of Ungro-Wallachia as Primate.[19]

The publication of the synodal commission's report constituted a significant landmark for the writing of Romanian ecclesiastical history. It

sparked a general interest in and enthusiasm for church history and theology among churchmen and concerned laity throughout the kingdom.
Serious research into the origins and development of the Romanian
Church and an impressive output of publications began in the years following 1883. While the earliest books on the religious history of Romanians were written in Transylvania by the Uniates Clain and Maior early
in the 19th century, and a short study by Arch-hierarch Filaret Scriban
was published in 1871,[20] it was not until the controversy over autocephalicity that significant publications about the Romanian Church began
to appear. There were several studies on the "universal church" that included chapters on Romanian Orthodoxy, but these were brief and were
quickly supplemented by a number of significant monographs on church
history. St. Calinescu published his researches on ecclesiastical literature
(1895)[21] and Dumitru Stanescu on the influence of religion on the public
life of Romanians (1906).[22] G. M. Ionescu drew the attention of his
countrymen to the early adoption of Christianty by the Romanians and
its history to the end of the 5th century (1905)[23] as well as the history
of the Metropolitanate of Ungro-Wallachia (1914),[24] while in Cernauţi,
Eusebius Popovici, related through his wife to the first Metropolitan of
Bucovina, Eugene Hacman, was delivering his thoughful and well research-
ed lectures on the Romanian Church.[25] Almost inevitably the stage was
set for Nicolae Iorga's two volume *History of the Romanian Church and
the Religious Life of the Romanians* (1908-9),[26] the first comprehensive
survey of the Church. Simultaneously there were hundreds of pamphlets,
textbooks for secondary schools, articles or chapters in books that drew
the attention of Romanians to their religious history. Callist I. Ialomiteanu,
Fathers Simion Popescu, V. Pocitan, D. Georgescu, I. Mihailescu, Dominic
Ilonescu and C. Erbiceanu, and especially Nicolae Dobrescu, all contributed to an expanding literature which went far in popularizing knowledge about Orthodoxy and developing the interest of the educated.

The domination of the Church by the State, with constant interference
by political interests, took a heavy toll and contributed to the instability
of the hierarchial leadership. The example of Cuza removing Metropolitan
Sofronie of Moldavia in 1860 and replacing him with a *locum tenens*, to
secure a quiescent churchman who would acceed to the Prince's wishes,
established an unfortunate precedent, repeated with unfortunate frequ-
ency in the years between 1877 and 1925. Thus, Metropolitan-Primate
Iosif Gheorghian was forced to resign by Junimist Take Ionescu for his
opposition to the 1893 *Law Governing Clergy and Seminaries*, but resumed his office with the return to power of the Liberals three years

later. Ghenadie Petrescu, Bishop of Agreş, supported by Conservatives and Junimists, replaced Gheorghian and endorsed the 1893 Law. His accession to the primatial see provoked an uproar from the Liberals, whom he had not sufficiently cultivated. Petrescu, however, only lasted 3 years before he found himself in opposition both to the Government and the Crown. He was abruptly removed from office and banished to Căldăruşani Monastery for his opposition to the proposed Catholic baptism of the future King Carol II. According to the marriage agreement of Ferdinand, heir to the throne of Romania, and Roman Catholic, and Marie, an Anglican, all children were to be baptized and raised in the Catholic faith. In 1896, however, when the baptism of the young king-to-be appeared imminent a wave of Orthodox opposition to the possibility of another Catholic monarch swept the nation and was crystalized in the thundering denunciation of the Metropolitan-Primate. Issuing a public condemnation of the baptism and performing a service of blasphemy against King Carol I in the Paraclis, or patriarchal chapel, Ghenadie Petrescu became the storm center of a political crisis that eroded Orthodox support for the king and threatened to undermine the stability of the dynasty. The Government was obliged to persuade the King that the future Carol II be baptized in the Romanian Orthodox Church, but extracted a penitent Petrescu's resignation as the price.[27] After an interim of 11 years, when Gheorghian returned to the primacy with Liberal endorsement, the process was repeated. Athanasie Mironescu, his successor, barely survived three years when his opposition to Haret's proposed synodal changes in 1910 evoked such middle class hostility to the Government's action that out of retaliation it used charges of plagiarism, sexual immorality and heresy to force the hierarch from office.[28] He was replaced with the aged Konon Aramescu-Donici whose primacy became controversial. Chosen because of his advanced years and scholarly disposition by politicians who felt that he could be manipulated, he earned their opposition during the German occupation of Bucharest by his leniency and behavior toward the enemy. In 1916 he capitulated to German authorities and appointed Marius Theodorian as Director of the Metropolitiante, a position made vacant by the withdrawal of its incumbent D. G. Boroianu to Iaşi with the Romanian army. The Germans hoped that Theodorian, a Uniate from Transylavania, could manipulate the aged prelate to use the immense influence of his office to reduce Romanian participation in the war. He also sought to intimidate Konon to sign a document by which the Romanian Orthodox Church would accept the pope as head of the Christian Church while preserving the independence of the Orthodox position. This was only prevented by the bold initiative of Father George Negulescu, priest of the historic and socially prominent Batişte Church[29] and responsible for ecclesiastical discipline in the Metropolitanate, who ousted Theodorian and bolstered the Primate's will to resistance. The Germans, however, did not give up their hope of forcing Romania out of the war and hit on the idea of having a number of distinguished citizens who had remained in Bucharest sign a simple statement stating that the occupying German forces were treating the captive civilian population well and that no recriminations were launched against the families of soldiers in the Romanian army. The Germans, who intended to distribute it throughout captured areas and even smuggle it into Moldavia for circulation among the Romanian troops, however, altered the statement by adding clauses calling for Romanian soldiers to lay down their arms and return home because German victory was inevitable. Hundreds of thousands of copies were distributed and some desertions were attributed to them. Upon the cessation of hostilities all of those who had signed the statement, political figures, intellectuals and churchmen, including the Primate and the dynamic Archimandrite Iuliu Scriban,[30] were indicted and brought to trial. Despite his protest of innocence and German duplicity, Konon was forced to resign his see and retired to monastic life in disgrace.

Through these tempestuous changes of leadership the Romanian Church found its role as "the dominant religion" being challenged. At a moment of weakness and demoralization the growth and increasing militancy of a variety of Protestant sects and Roman Catholics directly challenged its position as the undisputed State Church. Among Protestants, the Baptists and Seven Day Adventists were the most energetic in their campaign of proselytization. Beginning in the mid-19th century the Baptists had become more visible and from an initial handful of converts had grown by 1924 to 30,000.[31] Funds from the Baptist World Alliance fueled an intensive propaganda campaign and financed a variety of religious publications, journals, newspapers, brochures and pamphlets. Many of these publications were flagrantly anti-Orthodox and reviled Romanian priests as "evil and drunken" while assailing Orthodoxy as a faith "imposed upon the people without involving liberty of conscience and consent." The editor of *Farul Mântuiriei*, the main Baptist newspaper, was I. R. Socaciu, a Romanian from Transylvania who had graduated from an American Baptist theological school. The Seven Day Adventists had only begun in 1870 with one convert in Piteşti; and although the Church grew painfully slowly it extended its operations to Bucharest by

1900 using German Adventist missionaries rather than native Romanians. Translations of denomination literature, originally in English, and pamphlets which set forth their theology were published. By 1924 their numbers had reached 4,000[32] and by actively spreading their ideas and seeking converts they had attracted the unfavorable attention of government authorities. Many of these Baptists and Adventists were not ethnically Romanian but were Hungarians in Transylvania, Russians in Moldavia, Germans who had left the Crimea in 1892 and settled in the Dobrogea,[33] or even Serbians in the Banat, and had strong relations with American and Western European religious communities from which they derived a considerable portion of their funding; they were usually working class, at lower cultural and educational levels and may have included many who felt neglected or even abandoned by the State Church.

This activity occurred while the Romanian Church was passing through the difficult period of leadership changes and reorganization, but it did not go unnoticed. Orthodox churchmen and laity slowly became increasingly aware of the gradual growth of Protestantism in the country and the active process of attracting converts. As early as 1904 Professor Nicolae Cotos was drawing attention to Adventist teaching and belief and pointing out the threat that they posed to the religious *status quo*.[34] Complaints about Adventist attempts at proselytization increased as priests reported the activities of Adventist missionaries in their parishes and Orthodox families began to lose members to this active campaign. Orthodox protests mounted until 1912 when the Minister of the Interior authorized the collection of brochures published in Romanian by the Adventists in order to assess their beliefs. Despite the repeated protests of the hierarchy for decisive state action against Protestant and Catholic initiatives, the Government was uncertain and unwilling to take action. It was quite prepared to regulate and use the Church when it wished for its own purposes, but when it came to upholding the role of "the dominant religion" and maintaining its privileged status it was much less enthusiastic. Moreover, it was reluctant to implement those laws which would restrict or suppress Adventism from fear of provoking the international press of accusing Romania of religious persecution. Although repeated requests were made by Primate Konon that the law be upheld the Ministry of Religion was loath to intervene and avoided the dilemma by informing the church hierarchy that "Because it is said that the sect is spreading not through force, but through doctrine, its progress can only be stopped and its existence curtailed also through doctrine, through good example on the part of the Orthodox clergy."[35]

It was in vain that Constantin Nazarie tried to impress on the Ministry the threat posed by Adventism, particularly that it threatened the stability of the realm by its vicious attacks on the Orthodox Church. "It directly attacks the national-religious life of the Romanian, who finds in the Orthodox Church the key factor for his life now and his future happiness."[36] He pointed out how Adventists refused to take the oath of allegiance to the Country and Throne and refused to be conscripted into the army. Analyzing and explaining Adventist beliefs Nazarie sought to demonstrate that this sect did not constitute a proper Christian church or religion "with the right to be recognized and neither can it have in this manner of pretension to be one which has teachings contrary to the order of the state and the comon sense which approved it." But the Ministry had resolved not to be drawn into the issue and abrogated its responsibility of upholding the laws. It was left then to the Orthodox Church to meet the challenge as best it could with its own resources. Consequently, Primate Konon issued a circular order to the clergy of the country on October 31, 1913. He advised them that' "A religious and national danger is felt more and more through the appearance among us of heretical Adventists who have secretly and furtively gone through the cities and villages catching some weak souls in their nets."[37] The best way of contending with the spread of Adventism seemed to be the example and vitality of the parish clergyman. ". . . the surest weapon against these 'spiritual wanderers' can only be the word of God coming from the mouth of priests on all occasions, in church, at home, on the street, or wherever there is an opportunity." He counselled his clergy that if they showed spiritual warmth and devotion they would succeed in combating Adventism because "our people is faithful and holds strongly to its law." If gentle persuasion could not win back converts from Orthodoxy to Adventism, and the example of dedicated priests not deter "the doubting soul" from leaving the ancestral faith only then were the clergy admonished to "address with insistence the judicial authorities, that they judge and punish these revolutionaries, in conformance with Article 181 of the Penal Code."[38] The Article specified fines from 300 to 5000 lei, and imprisonment from one month to two years for those who provoked "rebellion to the laws or constituted authorities, or contempt for the dominant religion. . . . " Although the number of Adventists and Baptists continued to grow, the Government was reluctant to act, even when confronted with documentation of examples of zealous Adventists stopping Orthodox en route to church services, insulting Orthodox clergy and publishing invective criticisms of the State Church. The creation of a

Greater Romania in 1918 heighted the problem swelling the ranks of all Protestant communions by adding large numbers of sectarians along the frontiers of the vastly expanded nation. It was largely a rearguard action that was waged throughout this period between Orthodox and Protestants with the Ministry of Religion unwilling to apply the law against sectarians.

The publication of a two part article "Papism and the Orthodox Church in the Kingdom of Romania" in the official church publication *Biserica Ortodoxă Română* in 1883[39] indicated the extent to which the State Church felt challenged. Its author, Bishop Melchisedec of Roman[40] traced historic attempts to convert Romanians in Moldavia and Transylvania to Roman Catholicism, the abortive Council of Florence (1438), coercive methods by which the Uniate Church had been established and the mounting contemporary campaign waged by Catholics. *The Religious Almanac for 1868* listed 45,152 Roman Catholics in Romania with 40,000 in Moldavia alone. While the Apostolic Vicar, Anton Ioseph Pluym, based in Bucharest, had only 8 churches and 4 chapels under his jurisdiction his counterpart in Iași, Iosef Sendari, titular Bishop of Marcopolis, had 99 churches and 11 chapels, served by 26 priests. Integral to Catholic activities was the establishment of a quality educational system that admitted Catholic and non-Catholic students. Thus, in 1886 the Apostolic Vicar, Vasil Laurezzi, an Italian, reported that in the Latin Archdiocese of Bucharest, founded only three years before, there were 29 Catholic schools with 2602 students of both sexes; in the girls' school with 976 students only 400 were Catholic.[41] These schools as well as one each in Iași, Galați, and Craiova were operated primarily by the Sisters of Notre Dame de Sion, a foreign Catholic community. In 1888, for example, the school in Galați was administered by 54 nuns, teaching 479 students of whom only 60 were Catholic. The nuns themselves were not Romanian but came primarily from Alsace and Germany, with a few from Poland, Holland, Italy, Austria and even Ireland. There was not a single Romanian among them! The expansion of this education system which came to be regarded as a means of converting the young daughters of Romania's more affluent Orthodox families, the construction of the imposing gothic Cathedral of St. Joseph, the Catholicism of King Ferdinand and the crisis that was precipitated by the baptism of his children, the conversion of a number of wealthy and socially prominent Romanians, including Iuliu Maniu, the visit of the Romanian Prime Minister to the Papal Nuncio in Vienna in 1902, and the appearance of French monks expelled from France in 1902, who put great pressures on the Romanian government to allow them to establish schools in all of the large cities of the country, all suggested a papal offensive to Orthodox Romanians.

These challenges spurred the Orthodox Church into activity. In the absence of strong governmental assistance and support church leaders resolved that they would have to assume the full burden of defending the Church by revitalizing Romanian religious life and creating new institutions to help it fulfill its mission. Approved by the Holy Synod on May 6, 1910, a series of national conferences for priests and deacons was inaugurated.[47] These ranged from a few days a week with refresher courses, lectures on how to cope with religious and social problems and to exercise a more active personal ministry. Attention to the proper conduct of services, the use of standardized service books throughout the country, monastic reform, more careful selection of candidates for ordination, the holding of youth conferences, all assumed a new importance. To stimulate the interest of the young and "inspire noble sentiments" it was recommended that "The giving of blessed icons to school children is a powerful way of attracting their attention to sacred history. . . . Colored icons are preferred to uncolored ones because they stimulate much more the imagination and happiest feelings."[43] A more active church press appeared with the installation of printing presses for the two metropolitinates and even most of the dioceses. These produced a stream of colored icons, pamphlets, books on church history, religious services for use at home, in the schools, before setting out on journeys, and a broad range of daily personal concerns. Diocesan publications tended to reflect more profound spiritual concerns and were directed to various levels of the reading public.

From the energetic Bishop of Rîmnic, Vartolomeu S. Bacaoanul, came a thoughtful output of religious articles through the Society "Renaşterea." The Clergy Society of Bucharest published *Ajutorul,* while at Piteşti *Pastorul* was the new publication of the Society of Brotherhood of the Clergy of the Argeş district. The Diocese of the Lower Danube published *Solidaritatea* while the Metropolitan of Moldavia put out *Ocrotirea.* Indeed, by 1920 every diocese had its own weekly or monthly journal. In addition to the official organ of the Holy Synod, *Biserica Ortodoxă Română,* begun in 1874, there was a lively and privately printed popular religious press. The weekly *Innoirea* examined cultural and national politics from a religious perspective; there was *Noua Revistă Bisericească,* edited by Teodor Păcescu, *Solidaritatea,* with a Christian socialist philosophy, and *Viaţa Creştină* which dealt with problems of religious culture in an age of materialism. There was also *Daruri, Crucea* and *Duminica Orthodxă.* Very popular and highly readable was the publication of the Ministry of Religion *Cuvantul* begun in 1923 and distributed gratis to the clergy. Accompanying this flurry of religious printing was the founding of parochial libraries. Proposed as early as 1875 it was not until the 20th century that the dream of a library attached to every parish church came close to realization. By 1909, 3,032 village parishes had libraries, mostly with 150 volumes or less; the 398 city parishes surveyed in 1919 revealed holdings of 500-2,000 volumes, some of them housed in their own buildings and providing facilities for lectures and conferences.[45] By 1920 as the result of an active church press and the parish library movement, 123 societies of a religious and cultural nature had been established and were conducted by priests.

Clergy and lay Orthodox self-help societies sprang up. Beginning in the cities they spread to the villages and by 1925 there were 40 organizations, with thousands of members, concerned with Christian charity or involved in the defense of the national church. Many of these were not content to hold religious services or publish newspapers but extended their concern into daily philanthropic activity. Thus, "Dragostea Creştină," founded in the village of Ştefăneşti by Father T. Bălăşel, built a small hospital for local use, while other groups of the faithful erected old-age homes and orphanages, a serious problem after the destruction of the war, and established parish pharmacies to bring down the costs of medicine for the rural population. The periodical Amvonul sought to rehabilitate prisoners by technical training and prepare them for employment after being released; it also cared for their children during imprisonment. Metropolitan Repta of Bucovina created a foundation in 1908 to raise and educate orphan children and personally solicited contributions. For the clergy "Mântuitorul Hristos" was a self-aid society designed to enhance its standing and remuneration by providing aid to infirm members, burial expenses and supplemental payments to widows and minors, while in Sibiu "Oastea Domnului" began to stimulate the moral awakening of the individual.

Of a more defensive nature the "Asociatunii ortodoxe române" was founded in 1885 to defend the Romanian Orthodox Chruch from "foreign propaganda." One of the first speakers it sponsored was Bishop Melchisedec of Roman, who warned of "those propagandists" distributing "hundreds of thousands of Protestant catechisms gratis" throughout the country and denounced a papal attempt to establish a Concordat with Romania. Probably the best known group that came into existence was the "Societatea ortodoxă naţională a femeilor române" (National Organization of Romanian Women).[46] It originally developed as a response to what was felt to be a Roman Catholic offensive of developing superior educational facilities, especially for girls, who, through being taught Catholic dogma, might convert and influence their families to follow them into the new faith. Thus, the society was born to create educational institutes and guarantee an Orthodox Christian upbringing for Romanian children. The first president was Ecaterina Cantacuzino, the wife of the Prime Minister, and it was supported enthusiastically by many distinguished public figures. The Society, which instituted Mother's Day in Romania and championed temperance, began its activity by establishing a series of pre-schools and kindergartens. Under the guidance of trained staff the courses proceeded with such success that Spiru Haret, as Minister of Relgion, ultimately determined to entrust the Society with all state kindergartens in Bucharest. It also inaugurated conferences[47] that attracted large numbers of people. The most decisive conference leader was Archimandrite Iuliu Scriban, then Director of the Central Seminary and member of the Society's Executive Committee. Efforts were made to organize a branch in every parish in the capital; even in the provinces an extensive attempt was made to make the work of the Society better known as well as attract new members and to solicit funds for a central treasury and endowment. Under the presidency of Veturia Triteanu, the Society developed in new directions, and went public, symbolized by a religious patriotic concert in the Great Hall of the Ateneul Roman on December 15, 1910. Conference leaders addressed the capacity audience outlining the reasons for the foundation of the Society, its concerns, activities and future plans to insulate Romanian students from the threat of "foreignization" posed by "the education of Catholic institutions."[48] Within three years, when it next met in Iaşi, the Society could point to 10 large schools for children, 18 popular libraries, 2 secondary schools for girls in Bucharest and Iaşi, several conferences and significant contributions to widows and orphans of soldiers who fell in the Bulgarian campaign.

The regeneration of the Romanian Orthodox Church was not limited to the practical activities of these societies but can be found in the awakening of a deep rooted concern for the amelioration of society based on the basic principles of Christian morality. In 1904 Princess Alina Stirbei offered a prize of 8,500 lei in the General Session of the Historical Section of the Romanian Academy for the best manuscript about "Moral and Christian Principles" which would be used by parents to help them in the education of their children.[50] The winner was also to have 1000 copies of his work published. Attention focused increasingly on religious values, the sanctity of marriage and the importance of the family unit as a symbol of the Holy Family. Thus, on June 28, 1914, Primate Konon opposed the widespread custom of a dowry being given by a bride's parents to the bridegroom to assist with the initial costs of establishing a home after marriage. By the beginning of the 20th century many people were unable to pay an adequate dowry. While peasants were not required to have dowries many wanted or insisted on having them; the problem was greater for a member of the lower ranks in the army for whom the pay scale was low. The higher the rank, the greater the dowry and since many prospective brides lacked the prerequisite amount, until they did, marriage was prohibited. This was in accordance with a Government decision based on its desire to fortify upper class elitism in the army where the control of society rested. The result, however, were thousands of couples who lived together as common law partners, produced families, but were not lawfully wed in civil or religious ceremonies. The Church was troubed with this state of affairs and did everything it could to induce these couples to marry. To regularize social arrangements and emphasize the sanctity of family bonds the Primate pressured the government authorities to intercede and force the offending couples into wedlock. In fact, the Government was as concerned as the Church that the basic unit of national life was the family; strong family life, with the authority of the Father, seemed important for social discipline as did the lawful propagation of future citizens and soldiers to defend the country. As a result of the Primate's action in the Archdiocese of Ungro-Wallachia alone, there took place 2520 marriages of common law couples and "the legitimatizing of thousands of bastard children, who will have the honor and generate the future family of Romanian society."[51] The couples went through a civil ceremony first and then later were married in mass church weddings with as many as 30-60 couples at a time being joined in matrimony. At the same time, however, Metropolitan Konon sought to get to the root of the problem and through a number of circulars to the Ministers of the Interior and Justice pleaded for a relaxation of marital pre-conditions and a reduction of legal and dowry complications that had created the common law situation. Konon's arguments carried weight and in following years the state showed sympathy in gradually eliminating them. The Romanian Church emerged from this issue with enhanced moral leadership in the country.

Another major social problem on the Church's docket was alcoholism. Throughout the 19th century this had been a continuous problem, stimulated by the harshness of life and offering a temporary escape for those who felt downtrodden. Continuing into the 20th century, when wage increases, especially after 1907, boosted family income, all too often spent on alcoholic beverages, alcoholism assumed the proportions of a national epidemic. In Maramureş, Bessarabia and Bucovina the increase in the number of establishments dispensing liquor after World War I was astonishing. In the district of Bălţi, the number of pubs increased from 6 in 1914 to 698 in 1923, in the district of Orheiu from 6 to 712 and in the district of Hotin from 7 to 700. Within 200 meters of the center of one Transylvanian village there were no fewer than 11 pubs for a total population of 800! Two-thirds of these establishments, mostly unlicensed, were owned by foreigners.

To confront this mounting problem Primate Miron Cristea undertook a national crusade against alcoholism.[52] He preached against the evils of excessive drink, pointing to the effects of liquor on the body, quoting statistics that related excessive consumption to suicide, death, medical problems, accidents, lost or reduced productivity and an increase in crime. At his initiative the Holy Synod on November 5, 1923 unanimously voted to launch a national campaign against the evils of drinking. "Alcoholism," its proposal lamented, "which has begun to ravage villages and cities, and often effected whole districts, has led to the ruin of numerous families."[53] Parliament endorsed the Church's stand "on such a great national interest" and approved laws designed to curb alcoholism based on social and moral principles, and a future healthy population, rather than lost income derived from state control of the production of alcohol. Subsequently, bishops composed model sermons against excessive drinking to be delivered by all priests in their dioceses. Clergy conferences included discussions of means of combatting alcoholism on their agendas and proposed practical and, if necessary, radical solutions. All directors, professors and teachers were to lecture, write and speak about the problem, work with alcoholics and try to help people overcome addiction. Parish priests were to use their influence, provide pastoral counseling for chronic drinkers and help to supervise and patrol local pubs and bars. The Romanian Church was determined to justify its role as the "dominant religion" and provide clear evidence of its special relationship with the State.

Amidst the formation of church societies and signs of religious renewal there was also considerable moral and intellectual ferment within the Romanian Orthodox Church, especially its clergy, after the Peasants' Revolts of 1888 and 1907. Many priests in the countryside shared the same precarious existence and grinding poverty of their parishoners.[54] Where villages were poor, priests were poor. Thus, when the peasants, burdened under ruinous taxes, payments and the corvee, and living in a depressed condition, burst into revolt against the boyars and great landlords, whom they felt were exploiting them, it was inevitable that many parish priests should have joined them. In 1907 some priests blessed peasants when they took up arms and even accompanied them on their campaigns. When the government had finally put down the rebellion, dozens of priests were arrested and and jailed on charges that "in sermons delivered in church they incited and instigated the peasants to revolt" or that some even "appeared in front of the peasant revolters dressed in their sacred vestments, a cross in their hands."[55] Three priests were shot for their role, without even a formal trial or official judgment. Among the 11,000 who lost their lives in the suppression of the revolt the clergy had made their own sacrifice for a better and more just future.[56] After 1907 seminarians and professors at the theological school in Iaşi expressed their horror at the viciousness with which the revolt was suppressed. They drew attention to the conditions provoking the outburst and, before being suppressed by the local authorities, who closed the school and discharged several of the faculty, began to agitate for government charity and the need for reform.

At every level of church operations political involvement may be seen, but it would be incorrect to deduce, however, that government direction was without ultimate benefit. The Church, which in 1877 had been unable to organize itself into a national unit, adequately train its personnel or maintain either the fabric of its buildings or the vitality of its mission, had emerged as a self-governing organism. The *Law Governing Clergy and Seminaries* was beginning to have its desired effects. Hierarchs were increasingly well educated and interested in scholarly and academic discussion, theology, church history and spirituality and from their pens began to issue forth a steady stream of significant publications. The educational attainment of the average priest also improved particularly in urban communities. In 1888 there had been 1000 churches without priests; by 1924, given a remarkable population increase, the number of vacant parishes had fallen to 621. Moreover, the clergy ordained since the Law showed great improvement in academic levels, with an increasing number passing through a full theological school program. The consequence was a new generation of clergy, like the young Archimandrite Iuliu Scriban, who combined traditional religious concern for society, morality and the family with a new awareness of the effect of industrialization, the advent of a growing urban, industrial population and the impact of radical economic changes on an essentially rural, agrarian society. Scriban, the scion of an old and influential Moldavian family, was related to several public figures and stands out as one of the most energetic and active Romanian Church figures in the early 20th century. Articulate, persuasive, intellectual, with a highly developed social and religious consciousness he was continuously excluded from episcopal appointment. He was too independent and the Government doubted that he could be controlled or even restrained. Moreover, his signature to the same document signed by Metropolitan Primate Konon during the war provided a convenient excuse to exclude him from the church hierarchy. Nevertheless, he helped stimulate spiritual renewal and through conferences, sermons, lectures and publications helped to make the postwar Romanian Church more vital and active. In this he was joined by the perceptive and forthright hierarch, Vartolomieu S. Bacaoanul, and Father Pişculescu-Gala Galaction who expressed profound thoughts and reflections on Orthodoxy and whose writings inspired several generations of Romanians with their insight, observation and inner enlightenment. The thrust of Scriban's reflections at pastoral conferences in the Diocese of the Lower Danube in 1907 and 1908, were summed up in his statement "The country is now asking from the priest for things' which he had never thought of before. . . . How do we fulfill them?"[57] This sentiment was echoed by many other church writers such as Father Marin Ionescu, who argued that, "We live at a moment when the Church must begin to descend from abstract formulas. . . and the time of the formulation of dogmas. . . and show more energy for social activity, for eliminating moral and material misery for many. . . . The Church is not simply a deposit of forms and formulas, an asylum for liturgical symbols, but rather the great outpost of inexhaustible moral energies bent for the improvement of society."[58]

The uprising of 1907 had, in fact, raised social consciousness and was a catalytic agent provoking a re-examination of traditional theology and the role of Christianity in the modern world. This dealt with definitions of culture, national and international life and how one might relate the Gospel of Christ to conditions of life in a new century. Increasingly, these questions began to be taken up in books, pamphlets and as topics of conferences and public addresses. The earliest and most original texts on morality and the moral implications of contemporary social problems began to be penned by D. G. Boroianu (1900), Scriban (1915), and I. Mihalescu (1916), while Arch-Hierarch Vartolomeu S. Bacaoanul began to write about Christian socialism (1913),[59] N. Petrescu-Comnen on the regulation by the state of capital and labor, I. D. Barza on the financial and social problems born in the agony of war that produced widespread suffering and Father Constantin Provian on cultural and social issues in light of the Gospel. Even Ioan Gh. Savin, Inspector General of the Ministry of Religion and the Arts, wrote that the involvement of priests in banks, cooperatives, educational and charitable organizations that constructed orphanages, old-age homes, hospitals and pharmacies, was part of their priesthood; they were not extra-ecclesiastical or supplemental to their regular roles, indeed, they constituted the essence of the Gospel. "Without these activities the Church would remain inactive, limited only to the sacraments. The cultural and social activities of the priest among his parishoners must be considered at the same level as the celebration of the Holy Liturgy . . . ."[60] There was no doubt in the minds of these Orthodox clergy and laity that the Christian faith could and must play a dominant role in life since morality "the ultimate fruit of Christian conviction" could only exist within a religious framework. Thus, Archimandrite Scriban could speak out against those in Romania "without conscience and feeling of responsibility, who prevent the possibility of a human and Christian life in people, perpetuating only vice and corruption." Despite state control the outcome of its domination of the Orthodox Church of Romania was producing a new and strange fruit! If the Church was the national Church it was also becoming the national conscience.

As one reads Scriban one senses a powerful new current loose among churchmen, demanding that the Orthodox Church put itself back at the center of national life by returning to its role of teacher, uplifting morals and causing men to focus on a higher vision, that of God, with whose help they believed improvement of society alone can be accomplished. In this process Scriban acknowledged the role of the priest, who must shed a lethargy and pledge himself to a new order. The opportunity of 1907 for rejuvenation of the clergy's role had been allowed to slip past, but it was still not too late to re-examine old customs and question if they should be continued because of tradition or whether new courses of action and solutions be devised. For Scriban the catalytic agent for social improvement was the priest, since his inspiration is not a material one but inspired by the highest spiritual authority "which springs not from culture, but from living contact, complete and daily with the Lord God and with His saints. Although patriarchal life no longer exists, the priest, however, through his life, through his behavior, through his thoughts, must be for Christians an icon of the time which tells us of a holy past and which also kindles in us the desire to taste the emotions of heaven. Living on earth, the priest must be the man who brings down the fragrance of heaven on the vast expanse of earth."[61] Accompanying this conception of the priest, as a Christian icon for believers, was a strong concern for social activism, for ecclesiastical involvement in the national economy and society, where motivated by the highest moral principles, the kingdom of God might be brought closer to mankind. Scriban's plans are not well defined, his ideas for national salvation are often unclear and repetitive, the intellectual musings of a spiritual visionary, but through his groping for a new role for the Orthodox Church there were flashes of light. But there were too few like him; political appointment of bishops was to guarantee that the Church would be governed by those who were politically sound and not religious reformers. The 20th century required a new and fresh approach of the Church and this is the promise of what might have been.

After 1885 all attempts to elevate the Romanian Church to the rank of a Patriarchate had fallen on deaf ears and the Great Church of Constantinople steadfastly rejected petitions and resisted all attempts, until after World War I, that would lead to its establishment. The appearance of a Greater Romania, however, and the integration of millions of Romanians who had lived beyond the borders of the Old Kingdom meant that the Orthodox Church claimed 14,000,000 adherents.[62] The second largest Church in the Orthodox world, after that of Russia, it seemed appropriate and inevitable that its status be enhanced. The decline of the prestige and influence of the Ecumenical Patriarchate, following the departure of hundreds of thousands of Greeks from the Turkey of Ataturk, made the legitimacy of the Romanian intentions more compelling. With the approval and compliance of the Government the Holy Synod took the initiative and without further reference to the Phanar unanimously voted for the establishment of the Romanian Orthodox Patriarchate. Three weeks later, the Government sanctioned the measure by legislation and it received immediate royal assent.[63] A special opportunity to commemorate this momentous event was provided by the 1600th anniversary of the First Ecumenical Council of Nicea (325-1925). Thus, from October 11-13, 1925 church services, lectures and festivities in Iaşi and visits to the monasteries of Bucovina were held. The presence of King Ferdinand and Queen Marie in the great Metropolitan Cathedral of Romania's second city for a solemn Te Deum, with the Metropolitan of Moldavia, Pimen Georgescu, and the newly confirmed first Patriarch of Romania, Miron Cristea,[65] did more than symbolize the integral relationship between Church and State. More importantly it signified to the world the full independence of Romania. The country, which had won its political independence was now master of its own Church and a dream of centuries had been realized!

NOTES

1. G. V. Niculescu, *Cuza Vodă și Biserica romîna*, (Rîmnic Vilcea, 1912) and C. Grăgusin, "Legile bisericești ale lui Cuza Vodă și lupta pentru canonicitate," *Studii Teologice*, Vol. 9 (1957), pp. 86-103.

2. N. Nicolescu, *Positiunea și Derpturile Mitropoliților Romani* (București, 1915), pp. 116-117.

3. Take Ionescu, *Legea Clerului*, (București, 1893).

4. *Privire asupra Proiectului de Lege Pentru Cler de un Preot* (București, 1893).

5. *Telegraful Român*, Iunie, 1909. *Politics and Political Parties in Romania*, (London, 1936) provides a brief description of party history and programs.

6. *Candela*, (1909), p. 396.

7. Gheorghe Moisescu, *Istoria Bisericii Romîne*, (București, 1957), Vol. II, p. 526.

8. *Viața Monahala*, (Iași: February, 1934).

9. Constantin Nazaire, *Activitatea Preoților de Armata in Campania din 1916-1918*, (București, 1921); Grigore N. Popescu, *Preoțimea Română și întegirea Neamului*, (București, 1940); Const. N. Galeria, "Preotul profesor Constantin Gh. Nazarie, Cinciseci de ani de la moartea sa," *Studii Teologice*, Serie II-a, Anul XXIX, Nr. 1-2, (București, 1977), pp. 175-180.

10. Marin Radulescu, *Zece Cuvântări pentru Ostași*, (Simleul-Silvaniei, *1920)*.

11. Constantin Nazaire, *Cuvantari Pentru Ostasi și Ragciuni pentru Rege, Oaste, și Popor in vreme de Razboiu*, (București, 1916), p. 40.

12. Nazaire, *Cuvantari Pentru Ostasi.*

13. Ibid.

14. Dimitrie Lungulsecu, *Datorile Preotului la Armata în Timp de Pace în Timp de Razboi*, (Craiova, 1915).

15. Simion Popescu, *Legăturile Bisericei Noastre cu Patriarchia de Constantinopl*, (București, 1915).

16. Moisescu, *Istoria Bisericii Romîne*, Vol. II, p. 530.

17. "Ioakim: Epistola I. S. S. Patriarhul de Constantinopol," *Biserica Ortodoxă Română*, Anul VI, (1882), p. 736.

18. *Studiu despre Ierarchia și Instituțiunea Sinodală în Biserica Orthodxă a Resaritului în genere și despre Ierarchia și Instituțiunea Sinodală*, (București, 1883).

19. "Acte, privitore la autocefalia Bisericei ortodocse a României; Documente; Act priviore la autocefalia, etc.," *Biserica Ortodoxă Română*,

Anul IX, (Bucureşti, 1885), pp. 333-354, pp. 553-557, pp. 921-933.

20. Moisescu, *Istoria Bisericii Romîne*, Vol. I, pp. 17-18; and Mircea Pacurariu, *Istoria Bisericii Ortodoxe Române*, (Bucureşti, 1980), Vol. I, pp. 39-48.

21. St. Călinescu, *Incercari de Literatura Bisericescă*, (Bucureşti, 1895).

22. Dumitru Stănescu, *Viaţa Religioasa la Români şi Influenţa ei asupra Vieţei Publice*, (Bucureşti, 1906).

23. G. M. Ionescu, *Istoria Bisericii Românilor din Dacia Traiană*, (Bucureşti, 1905).

24. G. M. Ionescu, *Istoria Mitropoliei Ungrovlachiei*, (Bucureşti, 1914).

25. Eusebiu Popovici, *Istoria Bisericeasca Universală şi statistica bisericească*, (Bucureşti, 1928).

26. N. Iorga, *Istoria Bisericii Românesti şi a Vieţi Religioase a Românilor*, (Bucureşti, 1928, 1932), 2nd edition.

27. *Petiţia Mitropolitului Primate Ghenadie câtre Majestatea Sa Regele*, (Bucureşti,1896); *Judecata şi Judecatorii Mit. Primate Ghenadie*, (Bucureşti, 1896).

28. *Apărarea Mitropolitului Athanasie*, (Bucureşti, 1911).

29. Matei Cazacu, "Istoricul Bisericii Batişte din Bucureşti ," *Glasul Bisericii*, pp. 777-882. The war years and harshness of German occupation are described by I. Ooaca, "Aportul slujitorilor Bisericii Ortodoxe Române la lupta contra regimului de ocupatie," and G. Vasilescu, "Din Suferinţele Bisericii noastre în teritoriul vremelnic ocupat," *Biserica Orthodxă Română*, Anul CXVI, Nr. 11-12, (Bucureşti, 1978), pp. 1284-1290 and pp. 1291-1301.

30. I. Scriban, *Acte si Mărturi privitoare la chestiuni si Fapte Bisericesti din timpul ocupatiunii germane in Romania*, (Bucureşti, 1919).

31. "Sectele Religioase din Romania," *Nouă Revistă Bisericeasca*, (Bucureşti, 1924), pp. 7-13; I. Grigorescu, *Biserică Ortodoxă i Sectele Rationaliste*, (Campulung, 1935); and, Oreste Tarangul, *Metodele de Propagandă practicate de sectari. Cum trebuie organizata lupta misionară în Condiţiunile Actuale*, (Chisianu, 1929).

32. "Sectele Religioase," pp. 15-19.

33. Metodie R. Popescu, *Scopul Sectei Adventiste*, (Bucureşti, 1940), p. 3.

34. Nicolae Cotos, "Din invătăturile sectarilor nostri—Adventiştii de ziua saptea," *Candela*, (Cernauti, 1904), pp. 358-364.

35. Inocentiu Ştefănescu, *Pericolul Propagandei Adventiste şi Combaterea Concubina jului din Jedeţul Prahova*, (Ploeşti, 1915), p. 23.

36. Constantin Nazarie, *Combaterea Principalelor Invataturi Advent-iste*, (București, 1921), p. 6.

37. Ștefănescu, *Pericolul Propagandei*, p. 17.

38. Ibid., p. 25.

39. Bishop Merchisedec, "Papismul și starea actuală a Bisericei ortodoxă în Regatul României," *Biserica Orthodoxă Română, Anul VII*, (1883), pp. 260-400, 565-573.

40. Gherontie Nicolau, *Melchisedec. Zugrăvit de câțiva dintre ucenicii săi*, (București, 1939).

41. *Candela*, (1888), p. 50.

42. *Regulament pentru Conferințele Pastorale ale Preoților și Diaconilor din România*, (București, 1910).

43. *Candela*, (1911), p. 340.

44. Ioan Gh. Savin, *Biserica Română și Nouă ei Organizare*, (București, 1925), p. 99.

45. Savin, *Biserica Română*, pp. 97-99.

46. *Candela*, (1911), p. 230.

47. Ibid.

48. Nifon N. Ploeșteanu, *Patru Conferințele Religioase*, (București, 1905).

49. I. Popescu-Malăesti, *Legi Creștine de Educație*, (București, 1924).

50. *Candela*, (1906).

51. Ștefănescu, *Pericolul Propagandei*, p. 7.

52. Miron Cristea, *Impotriva Beției*, (București, 1923).

53. Ibid., p. 3.

54. "1907—Marea răscoala a taranilor din Româniă," *Mitropolia Moldovei și Sucevei*, Anul LIII, Nr. 1-3, (Iași, 1977), pp. 14-124 includes a series of articles on the involvement of the Orthodox clergy and an impressive bibliography on the revolt in both Romanian and foreign languages.

55. Moisescu, *Istoria Bisericii Romîne*, Vol. II, p. 595.

56. To soften the Government's treatment of the Orthodox Church for the participation of the clergy in the rebellion Spiru Haret published a pamphlet, *Raport adresat Majestătii Sale Regelui asupra Acțiuni invătăturilor și a Preoților Rurali în Răscoalele Țărănești din 1907*, (București, 1907) in which he drew attention to those priests who had maintained public order and restrained, with some success, their own parishoners.

57. Iuliu Sriban, *Chemarea Preotului studiu îndrumator pentru Activitatea Pastorală a Preotului*, (București, 1921), p. 8.

58. Marin C. Ionescu, *Preotul și Armonizarea Claselor Sociale*, (București, 1925), p. 17.

59.   Vartolomeiu S. Bacaoalnul, *Scurte Incercări de Creștinism Social*, (București, 1913); also, Constantin Provian, *Curente Culturale și Sociale în lumina Evangheliei*, (București, 1921).

60.   Savin, *Biserica Română*, pp. 102-103.

61.   Scriban, *Chemarea Preotului*, pp. 27-28.

62.   Miron Cristea, *Principii Fundamentale pentru Organizarea Unitară a Bisericii Ortodoxe Române*, (București, 1920). For the role of the Church in the achievement o the Union of 1918 see Mircea Păcurariu, "Contributia Bisericii la realizarea actului unirii de la 1 Decembrie, 1918," *Biserica Ortodoxă Română*, Anul CXVI, Nr. 11-12, (București, 1978), pp. 1250-1263.

63.   Titu. Simedra, *Patriarhia Romaneasca: Acte si Documente*, (București, 1926) contains all documents, correspondence and records relating to the establishment of the Romanian Patriarchate.

64.   C. Dron, *Amintirea Soborului de la Nicea: Serbările de la Iași*, (Neamț, 1926).

65.   See R. Candea, *Patriarhul Miron Cristea* (Cernauti, 1925) and the issue of *Biserica Ortodoxă Română*, (November, 1925) with a biographical statement of the new patriarch and his installation.

SOME AMERICAN OBSERVERS OF THE RUSSO-TURKISH WAR

"The Russo-Turkish War" is generally assumed to mean that of 1877-78, next to the last of ten Russo-Turkish wars, almost all of which involved Romanian lands.[1] Strictly speaking it might be called the Russo/Romanian-Turkish War, even though the Romanian effort hardly compares with the Russian.[2] But it was, after all, Romania's War of Independence. It has also been called "The Balkan War." It is true that Serbia and Montenegro got reinvolved, and even Greece briefly at the end. But it was not only Balkan, there was a second front in the Caucasus. In any case, the whole war was fought on Ottoman territory.

Like all wars this too has underlying and immediate origins. Even after, a century, this is still a moot question. The prelude was the Hercegovinian revolt of 1875, the crushing by the Turks of the Serbs and Montenegrins in support of it in 1876, and Russia's bailing out of their little Slav brothers. More immediate was the "April" (actually May) 1876 uprising in Bulgaria. The disclosures of the barbaric Turkish atrocities in suppressing the revolt, for which Americans were largely responsible, raised such a stink in Britain and throughout Europe that British Prime Minister Disraeli's Turcophile and Russophobe hands were tied. At the same time public opinion in Russia was raised to a feverish pitch.[3] When the Turks, with underhand British support, rejected the reform proposals of the Great Power Constantinople Conference, which included a large autonomous Bulgaria, and produced a constitution which reaffirmed Romania's subject position, privileged though it was, the high-placed Russian hawks won over the doves, even though the latter included the Emperor.[4] In a few months the Russo-Turkish War was on. When the imperial manifesto was read on April 24 to the troops drawn up at Kishinev, the Emperor wept and the troops shouted hysterical approval, according to the American observer, MacGahan.

Scholars are still debating Russia's real grounds for war, or better, their relative weight, including the Straits outlet, bleeding Panslav hearts, Great Power rivalry with Britain and Austria-Hungary, and the requirements for

245

being the greatest Slav power. But what made it into a Russo/Romanian war against the Turks? Romania was in the way as usual, especially as Russia's naval power on the Black Sea had not yet recovered from the neutralization imposed by the Treaty of Paris (1856), though the Russians across Romania to the Danube, which supposedly guaranteed Roman- the two countries signed an agreement providing for the passage of Russian across Romania to the Danube, which supposedly guaranteed Romania's territorial integrity. Romania's subsequent participation in the war on the Turks was not an act of hostility but of self-defense against Russia, against the perhaps remote possibility of another Russian occupation— but also a hedge against the more than likely forced retrocession of Southern Bessarabia, which everyone knew was a Russian ambition. Nor were the Romanians particularly hostile toward the Turks. Lastly, it was Prince Carol's war: he needed it to bolster his shaky position by winning recognition of Romania's independence.[5]

Romanian independence, when it actually came, was almost an anticlimax. The paramount Romanian goal, both before and after independence, was union. Unlike that of other Balkan countries, liberation was less climactic because the Romanians had never been as subjected to the Turks. Professor Riker concludes (*The Making of Romania, 1856-1866*): "We shall now end our story on the making of Roumania, leaving to others to tell of the steps by which Charles was able to get rid of the hated Capitulations, secure the independence of Roumania in the Treaty of Berlin, and elevate his principality to the status of a kingdom. Independence, while often thought of as the ultimate destiny of this nation, had never been a paramount object of Roumanian nationalism during the critical and formative years which we have described."[6] Thus, war with the Turks, in reluctant alliance with the Russians, was to keep Southern Bessarabia, get rid of Ottoman suzerainty and therefore of the European protectorate, will full independence and keep Carol on his throne. Having exchanged cannon fire across the Danube with the Turks, who looked on the Romanians as rebels, the Romanian Assembly by a bare majority voted to go to war and ten days later voted itself independent.[7] But to achieve these objectives something more was needed—a baptism of blood.

Romania's war against the Turks was, one might say, a technicality, a question of *de jure* independence. With Turks, as such, they had no quarrel. At one time the Russians had to put a stop to fraternization between Romanians in Grivitsa Fort I and Turks in Grivitsa Fort II.[8] The Romanians went to war against the Turks to defend themselves against the Russians, against Russia's designs on Romanian territory. The Romanians were in the war not for the Russians or for the Bulgarians but for the Romanians.

Romania won its independence on what was to become Bulgarian soil. But the Bulgarian connection goes much deeper. The left bank of the Danube had acquired a considerable Bulgarian coloration; cultural and revolutionary centers and committees flourished in Braila, Giurgiu, Bucharest and others; the abortive revolt in Bulgaria in May 1876, which nevertheless ultimately brough about the Russo-Turkish War, Bulgarian liberation and Romanian independence, was hatchted in Bucharest. The Bulgarian Question aborted the Constantinople Conference. Eventually Romania was forced to give back to Russia Southern Bessarabia, where there was a sizable Bulgarian colony, for the more watery and less Romanian portions of Dobrudja, which had been included in Bulgaria at Constantinople. Bulgarians naturally make much of Romania's contribution to their liberation. Actually the Romanians had a specific objective in addition to those mentioned above. When the war ended the Romanians were still trying to take the Vidin area, technically part of the Ottoman Empire.

The American connection with the Russo-Turkish War, and therefore with Romania, began with the American Protestant missionary discovery of the Bulgarians half a century earlier. When the Bulgarian revolt erupted in the spring of 1876 (which an American missionary in Constantinople described as "the maddest freak that ever led men to death"),[9] and was drowned out by the Turks with the slaughter of ten to twenty thousand old men, women and children and the burning of dozens of towns and villages, it was a handful of Americans who converted a dismal disaster into a smashing success by publicizing the so-called "Bulgarian Horrors" (Gladstone's phrase), the effects of which escalated into the Russo-Turkish War.[10]

The London *Daily News* sent out a special correspondent, the American journalist J. A. MacGahan, who arrived in Constantinople in time to set off for Bulgaria with his old acquaintance, the U. S. Consul-General Eugene Schuyler, recently transferred from St. Petersburg. Thus began a teamwork which was to open the door to the Russo-Turksih War and Romanian independence. Of MacGahan it was said: "it fell to a war correspondent to write what still stands as one of the major exposures of history, one that became directly responsible for a war and eventually led to the independence of Bulgaria."[11]

MacGahan had already distinguished himself as roving correspondent for the New York *Herald:* among other assignments he had covered the seige of Paris from inside, a polar expedition, and the Carlist was in Spain.

He had made his mark in the Russian field, with a 900-mile ride through forbidding and forbidden Russian Central Asia, chasing a Russian military expedition against Khiva, described by Archibald Forbes as "the most remarkable and daring exploit in the annals of war correspondence," in the course of which he had travelled with Schuyler. He also met the Tsar's brother, Grand Duke Nicholas, whom he was to see again as commander-in-chief in the Russo-Turkish War. MacGahan married a Russian, Varvara Elagin.[12]

It seeemd as though the war would never start. For two months after its declaration the Russians waited for the extra-high Danube to subside. There was relatively little Turkish opposition to the four-pronged Russian invastion: occupation of the Dobrudja left flank; an army under the Tsarevich, the future Alexander III, facting the fortress quadrilateral: a premature dash by General Gurko via Tirnovo over the Shipka Balkan Pass; and the main force under the commander-in-chief, Grand Duke Nicholas. Suddenly the picture changed with the unexpected occupation of strategic Pleven on the Russian right flank by a large Turkish force from Vidin under Osman Pasha. Because the Russians had invaded the Balkans with insufficient and divided forces they were repeatedly thrown back by Osman. As long as Pleven held out the whole Russian advance was paralyzed. This is why the Russians reluctantly called on Prince Carol for help. Osman's stubborn resistance for more than four months, and the enterprise and fearlessness of the war correspondents, especially MacGahan, made Pleven, today one of the dullest towns in Bulgaria, in its day perhpas one of the best known names in the world. And it gave the Romanians their baptism of fire, their hour of glory, their passport to independence.[13]

The Russo-Turkish War has been dubbed "The Breakfast War," because every morning at breakfast Londoners got the latest newspaper reports from the front.[14] This was the last great war in which artist-correspondents had a field-day cooly sketching amid a hail of bullets. Though the Turks were wary of war correspondents, especially those representing the liberal British papers such as the London *Daily News*, the Russians gave them free rein right up to the front lines. Press coverage was so good that Constantinople, St. Petersburg and even Osman in Pleven got the news from the London papers.[15] Each had an armband, and his picture in a central portfolio, which at one time contained 82 mug shots. But over half never left the armchairs and fleshpots of Bucharest. Some who did quickly returned "to recruit their damaged health." Only five made it to the end of the line, San Stefano. Of these three were Americans. Correspondents were honor-bound not to report up-coming troop movements;

only one was kicked out for doing this.[16] Telegrams had to be translated and sent from Bucharest in Frnech because no one in the Romanian telegraph office knew English! In reaction correspondents gave vent to exceedingly long literary masterpieces by letter.[17] In Bucharest, Mac-Gahan's Russian wife, Barbara, helped with getting horses and supplies and with French and Russian versions of her husband's dispatches. The latter were sent to the St. Petersburg *Golos*.[18]

There were half a dozen Americans observing and reporting the war.[19] Officially, there was First Lieutenant Francis Vinton Greene, U. S. military attache in St. Petersburg, appointed to observe the war; Januarius Aloysius MacGahan and Francis Davis Millet were on the London *Daily News* team, which had a tie-in with the New York *Herald;* Jackson represented the New York *Herald;* Edward King the Boston *Gazette;* Colonel E. M. Grant reported for the London *Times.* On the Turkish side was Wentworth Huyshe, an Englishman for the New York *Times* and Henry Dwight, arm-chair correspondent of the New York *Tribune* in Constantinople.[20] Lieutenant Greene outranked by all other military observers, naturally was attached to headquarters, which gave him access to reports to and from all quarters. His official *Report on the Russian Army and its Campaigns in Turkey in 1877-8,* was published in 1879.[21] The main part, *The Campaign in Bulgaria,* was reprinted in 1903. Until interest in the Russo-Turkish War was superseded by bigger and better wars, Greene's work remained a standard text in military academies.[22] Being in the Engineer Corps, Greene included in the *Atlas* part of his work meticulous maps, fortification plans and even diagrams of entrenching tools. A more personal account is his *Sketches of Army Life in Russia,* actually half in "Bulgaria."[23]

Lieutenant Greene, a keen observer and student of military history, is critical of both Russians and Turks, but in the end the Russians won the war and his approval. He has nothing but admiration for the super-human endurance of the Russian and Turkish soldier. It was the generals on both sides, with a few brilliant exceptions, who goofed. The Turks tried to run the war with a committee from the palace in Constantinople, whereas the Russian GHQ was within spitting distance of the front lines. But there were too many Russian generals (and Grand Dukes and the Tsar himself during the Pleven seige) and not enough soldiers. At one time the Turkish Commander-in-Chief in Bulgaria was an ex-German, Mehmed Ali Pasha. There were three virtually independent commanders. One of the last commanders-in-chief, Sulieman Pasha, got court-martialed and fifteen years for the defeat at Plovdiv. Mainly Turkish strategy and lack of offensive action were at fault. On the other side, according to Greene, was "the

overweening contempt for the enemy which induced the Russians to open
the campaign with half the force which was found necessary to conclude
it; the lack of experience which resulted in such ignorant attacks, without
reconnaissance . . . as that at Plevna; the dispersion of the army into de-
tachments scattered over an enormous extent of territory; the assault of
entrenched camps with inferior forces; the lack of tactical ensemble in
the assaults—these are some of the faults which characterized the first two
stages of the of the war, and brought delay . . . and death to many a brave,
willing man."[24] It also brought General Todleben of Sevastopol fame
out of retirement to take command of the Siege of Pleven, and brought
in Prince Carol and his 37,000 combat ready but inexperienced troops
while the Russians waited for reinforcements from Russia. In the end,
there were more than 120,000 troops investing Pleven. Carol had been
waiting in the wings to come in on his own terms: the Romanian army
to remain a separate entity. This the Russians finally accepted. In addition, Carol was appointed commander-in-chief of the combined Western
army at Pleven, but this was "to a certain extent nominal."[25] General
Cernat commanded the three Romanian divisions, but Carol had a Russian
general as chief-of-staff who actually gave the orders (first Zotov, then
Todleben).

Greene concludes somewhat prematurely that "even after all the criticisms . . . of the Russians at the beginning of the war and around Pleven,
still the campaign as a whole must be judged to be the equal in brilliancy
and the solidity of its results of any in recent history."[26]

Other American observers had harsh things to say about the Turks.
Dwight, sitting in Constantinople, concluded that "the Russians have
better officers. It is the lack of brains in high quarters which has ruined
the Turkish army," defeated by its own commanders. Another American
(MacGahan) wrote that the Turks "leave no mistake uncommitted that
perversity, ignorance and stupidity can commit." Dwight is particularly
caustic about the Turkish handling, or mishandling, of the news. Turkish
papers were forbidden to publish anything "to trouble men's minds."
The surrender of Pleven was first reported as a great Turkish victory;
then nothing for ten days.[27]

The *Daily News* had two of the greatest war correspondents in its
stable, which comprised seventeen in both theaters and on each side of
the lines: Archibald Forbes, the Englishman, and MacGahan, the American. There was also another American on the *Daily News* team, Frank
Millet, orignally sent by the New York *Herald*. Forbes organized a "syn-
dicate" between the *Herald* and the *Daily News*. At the suggestion of the

American, Jackson, thinking no doubt of the Pony Express, Forbes set up relays of horses. Carrying the news of the great Russian repulse at Pleven (September 11), Forbes literally rode his horse to death. To avoid censorship he continued to ride from Bucharest to Brashov in Transylvania. On another occasion he got the news of a Russian victory at Shipka to the Emperor before the Russians got it from their own people.[28]

At Pleven operations were at a standstill, except on the Romanian sector. If the third battle for Pleven (September 7-12), was a "criminal" disaster for the Russians (the allies had over 18,000 casualties), it was the high point of Romania's participation in the war, the heroic but costly capture, with Russian support, of the redoubt Grivitsa I.

Unfortunately, the existence of Grivitsa II, 300 yards north, which dominated Grivitsa I and which the Romanians were unable to take, could not be seen and was not on the maps given the Romanians. So Grivitsa remained a bloody monument to Romanian valor but little else. The general verdict was that "the storming of this section had no further results."[29] MacGahan's verdict on Third Pleven was that "the whole business was one stupid, blind, reckless muddle, relieved only by Skobelev's skill and daring."[30] The view from inside Pleven was that "in exchange for the sacrifice of 20,000 men is one small redoubt, of no strategic value, the possession of which did them subsequently more harm than good."[31] According to MacGahan, "the Romanians are pushing forward their works against the second Grivitsa redoubt with a perseverance and pluck worthy of all priase, and which is the more remarkable as the Russians are doing absolutely nothing on their side. . . . The Romanian soldiers seem to be stout fellows. . . . Were the Russians advancing as rapidly on their side Plevna would fall before two weeks."[32] By this time most bored foreign correspondents had left. Forbes, off to London and St. Petersburg, left Pleven to MacGahan and Millet. On the way he reported, "Bucharest was a ball-room wherein Mars, Venus and Bachus were dancing the can-can in frantic orgies."[33] So the two American correspondents and Greene watched the fall of Pleven.

Though Lieutenant Greene thought it was a blunder, to MacGahan from the sidelines Osman's last forlorn sortie was a terrible and sublime spectacle. As the long lines neared the Russian trenches, the bugles sounded "Storm" and with cries of "Allah" thousands of Turks swept like a tornado into the Russian lines. But an unexpected event dashed the Turkish hopes. Osman was wounded. As the rumor of Osman's supposed death spread rapidly, the Turks fell back in disorder. The Turkish sortie was over.[34] With the surrender of Osman Ghazi the Victorious, 40,000

Turks were herded into captivity, on a mid-winter death march through Romania to Russia. Most never reached their destination.[35] Pleven had been costly for both sides.[36]

Millet entered Pleven a few days after its capture. This is what he found: "The most active imagination cannot picture the thousandth part of the frightful suffering, misery and wretchedness... nor draw the faintest outline of the panorama of ghastly horrors."[37] Or, to quote MacGahan, "Pleven is one vast charnal-house, surpassing in horror anything that can be imagined."[38] Conditions got worse before they became better. Greene severely criticized Osman for allowing himself to be boxed in at Pleven. He also characterized his last-ditch sortie as "one of the maddest, fiercest, least hopeful onslaughts ever made."[39] But in the last analysis he felt that "the Turkish defense of Pleven is the one thing which relieves their whole campaign from a charge of complete incompetency."[40]

After Pleven the big question was: to hibernate, perhaps north of the Danube, with risky political consequences; or to cross the Balkans in the dead of an unusually bad winter. The Turks counted on Generals December and January. Siding with Generals Gurko and Skobelev, Grand Duke Nicholas chose to cross. The passage, one of the great feats of military history, was made at two points: one, by General Gurko, went over the western, Araba Konak Pass to Sofia; a few days later, General Skobelev crossed at Shipka to the east. Millet went with Gurko.

Millet, had served in the Civil War, and had been an artist in Paris. He combined art and journalism. Henry James, the novelist, wrote, "He has made pictures without words and words without pictures." Later he became illustrator for the London *Graffic*. This is how he described the Christmas Day crossing of the Western Balkans: "The sun rose on a scene of wonderful picturesqueness and a landscape of serene beauty. Generals and aides-de-camp lay there in the snow huddled about the fires.... As I recall the thirty hours I spent in the mountains without shelter and scanty food...it seems a time full of touching incidents and dramatic events...."[41]

MacGahan, with a game leg injured a third time, hobbled after Skobelev over the Balkans near Shipka Pass to which the Russians had clung for five months. Snow was ten feet deep and the temperature zero. Thousands froze to death. But a three-pronged Russian attack again caught the Turks off balance and 30,000 surrendered. This is how MacGahan pictured the Russian crossing: "When I crossed the whole road was full of artillery and munition wagons.... Each gun had twelve horses and from twenty to fifty soldiers dragging it. The northern slope is many feet deep in snow. The southern slope, which is very deep . . . is a mass of ice, so that it takes as many men to hold the cannon back on this side . . . as it does to drag them forward on the other."[42]

Four victorious Russian armies now converged on Adrianople, where the armistice was signed on January 31, and on to Constantinople. One of the sorriest aspects of the war was the plundering and atrocities on both sides, military and civilian, and the surging of hundreds of thousands of refugees—Christians fleeing north, Muslims going south. With the war virtually over, the horrors endured by the panicky Muslim population continued in the mad mid-winter flight of 200,000 refugees as seen by Millet for thirty-five miles along the Adrianople road: ". . . women and infants, children and old men, both Turkish and Bulgarian, fallen . . . half buried in the snow . . . but while many of the bodies bore marks of violence and showed ghastly wounds, the great proportion of the women and children were evidently frozen to death."[43] Millet could only see a fraction of the sickening holocaust.

The end finally came with the signing of the peace treaty at 5 p.m. on March 3, at the village of San Stefano within sight of Constantinople, where Grand Duke Nicholas was staying in a house opposite the one in which the first U.S. minister to the Porte, Admiral Porter, had lived and died—the first time Russians had seen Tsarigrad since the eleventh century. Lieutenant Greene was there. MacGahan and Millet were also on hand jointly to chronicle the official end of the Russo-Turkish War:

> About four o'clock the Grand Duke mounted and rode to the Diplomatic Chancery where he asked at the door, 'Is it ready?' and then galloped toward the hill where the army was drawn up. . . . After riding between the lines the Grand Duke halted and formally made the announcement: 'I have the honor to inform the army that, with the help of God, we have concluded a Treaty of Peace.' A shout burst forth from 20,000 throats. . . . As we rode down into the village we could hear the joyful shouts still ringing in the air. . . . So ends the War of 1877-78.[44]

And now a post morten of some of the dramatis personae. MacGahan went to visit his friend Lieutenant Greece, down with typhoid in a Constantinople hospital. Greene lived but a week later, MacGahan died of spotted typhus (June 9, 1878). Eight years later his body was brought back to the United States by a warship and reburied in his home town, New Lexington, a few miles east of Columbus, Ohio. Of MacGahan, Greene

said, "no man of his age in recent years has done more to bring honor
on the name of America. . . ."[45] Another wrote: "The Army of the
Czar gave the Bulgarians their freedom, but it was the American correspondent who put the army in the field."[46]

Lieutenant Greene acquired three Russian and two Romanian decorations, became a general and a noted military historian; he resigned to go
into the asphalt business, but resurfaced in time to receive the Spanish
surrender in Manila. He lived long enough to write *Our First Year in the
Great War.*

Frank Millet was decorated by both the Russians and Romanians. He
was probably the only correspondent who covered all parts of the Balkan
front. He started out with Zimmerman in Dobrudja, was with the Tsarevich, saw Shipka, was in on the fall of Pleven, crossed the Balkans with
Gurko, and followed him all the way to Adrianople. He was with Mac-
Gahan at San Stefano. Millet became one of America's most distinguished
and versatile artists, hung in Europe and America, noted for his murals
in American public buildings and banks. A writer and inveterate world
traveler, on April 15, 1915, he went down with the *Titanic.*

Eugene Schuyler (1840-1890), who had helped, with MacGahan, to
blow the whistle on the Turkish atrocities in Bulgaria in 1876 and, with
Prince Tseretelev, to outline the blueprint of a large Bulgaria, was in the
dog-house in both Constantinople and in Washington. He was recalled
in 1878 for meddling in the internal affairs of a friendly country (Turkey)
but after a decent interval, in 1882 he was appointed first U. S. minister
resident and consul-general in Bucharest (simultaneously in Belgrad and
Athens) but his arrival there was delayed because his credentials were
addressed to "Prince" instead of "King" Charles.[47] Carol had retained
his throne, acquired independence for his country, losing Southern Bessarabia in the process but getting North Dobrudja, and had been voted king
and crowned with a piece of Turkish cannon from Pleven.

The Russo-Turkish War, romanticized as it has been, was horrible,
needlessly and badly fought and fateful in its ultimate consequences.
It brought untold death and suffering to soldiers and civilians. Sequel to
the "Bulgarian Horrors" were the vastly greater Russo-Turkish War horrors. It also produced some unparallelled exploits by American journalists
and astonishing feats by Russian, Romanian and Turkish soldiers.

NOTES

1.   A. D. Xenopol wrote about those from 1711 to 1877, *Resboaele
dintre Ruşi şi Turci* (Iaşi, 2 vols., 1880); see also F. S. Russell, *Russian*

Wars with Turkey (London, 1877). For the War of 1877-78, J. F. Clarke, "The Russo-Turkish War, 1877-1878," *Modern Encyclopedia of Russian and Soviet History*, with selected bibliography.

2.   Wtih pardonable pride Romanians tend to exaggerate their contribution. For example, "La participation directe de la Roumanie a la guerre de 1877-1878 avec un armee important ce qui a modifie du tout la situation politique dans les Balkans." (C. Velichi, "La Roumanie et les mouvements nationaux des Balkans (1840-1877)," *Actes du premier congres international des etudes balkanique et sud-est Europeenes* (Sofia, 1969), IV, 310.

3.   An excellent historiographic appraisal is David MacKenzie, "Russia's Views of the Eastern Crisis, 1875-1878," *East European Quarterly*, XIII (No. 1, 1979), 1-24.

4.   Barbara Jelavich, *St. Petersburg and Moscow. Tsarist and Soviet Foreign Policy, 1814-1974* (Bloomington, Ind., 1974), 172 ff.

5.   Barbara Jelavich, *The Ottoman Empire, the Great Powers, and the Straits Question 1870-1880* (Bloomington, Ind., 1973), 71.

6.   T. W. Riker, *The Making of Roumania* (London, 1931), 565-56. See also Dan Berindei, *L'union des principautes roumaines* (nd, np.).

7.   For chronology, I depend on C. C. Giurescu, ed., *Chronological History of Romania* (București, 1972).

8.   W. V. Herbert, *The Defense of Plevna, 1877. Written by one who took part in it* (London, 1895), 329-31î n. 97, p. 459.

9.   H. O. Dwight, *Turkish Life in War Time* (New York, 1881), 22.

10.   James F. Clarke, "Americans and the April Uprising," *East European Quarterly*, XI, 4 (1977), 421-28.

11.   Phillip Knightly, *The First Casualty. From the Crimea to Vietnam: The War Correspondent as Hero, Propagandist and Myth Maker* (New York, 1975), 50.

12.   Schuyler, then chargé d'affaires in St. Petersburg, headed for an investigation of Russian administration in Central Asia, and MacGahan, on assignment for the New York *Herald*, had travelled together for a while. MacGahan wrote *Campaigning on the Oxus and the Fall of Khiva* (New York, 1874) and Schuyler, *Turkistan. Notes of a Journey in Russian Turkistan, Kokand, Bukhara and Kuldja* (2 vols., New York and London, 1876; abridged ed., New York, 1966). On Schuyler see M. B. Petrovich, "Eugene Schuyler and Bulgaria, 1876-1878," *Bulgarian Historical Review* (Sofia), VII, 1 (1979), 51-69; on MacGahan T. D. Dimitrov, *Ianuari Makgahan. 1844-1878* (Sofia, 1977) and F. L. Bullard, *Famous War Correspondents* (Boston, 1914), ch. IV.

13.   Pleven and the Russo (Romanian)-Turkish War is a favorite topic

of Romanian historians. G. Giurescu is no exception. He edited and wrote
a number of things on this subject. See Frederick Kellogg, "The Historiography of Romanian Independence," *East European Quarterly*, XII, 3
(1978), 369-77.

14.   Rupert Furneaux, *The Breakfast War* (New York, 1958; in London, *The Siege of Pleven*), vividly describes the work of the correspondents.

15.   C. and B. Jelavich, eds., *Russia in the East, 1876-1880. The
Russo-Turkish War and the Kuldja Crisis* (Letters of Jomini to Giers),
(Leiden, 1959), 58. See also Herbert, *The Defense of Plevna*, and Dwight,
Turkish Life.

16.   Fred Boyle, *Narrative of an Expelled Correspondent* (London,
1877).

17.   F. V. Greene, *Sketches of Army Life in Russia* (New York, 1880),
ch. 7, describes the Russian handling of the correspondents.

18.   Barbara (Varvara Elagin) MacGahan, "Her Life and Times. A
Short Autobiography" (c. 1897), unpublished, 42 pp.

19.   Beatrice Marinescu and Şerban Rădulescu-Zoner, "American
Consular Reports about Romania's Struggle to Win Independence (1877),"
East European Quarterly, XII (1978), No.3, 349-58, quote dispatches of
U. S. vice-consul Adolph Stern; and Cornelia Bodea, "Contemporary
American Recordings of Romania's Unity and Independence," Ibid.,
359-67, quotes N. Y. *Times'* Carroll Tevis from Bucharest.

20.   Wentworth Huysche, *The Liberation of Bulgaria. War Notes in
1877* (London, 1984), including second-hand material from other correspondents.

21.   The *Report* was also published as *The Russian Army* (etc)., New
York, 1879; London, 1880). It includes a separate *Atlas* vol.

22.   *The Campaign in Bulgaria* (London, 1903), 201; was published
as a text book. Others are J. H. Anderson, *The Russo-Turkish War 1877-
78. In Europe* (London, 1910); F. B. Maurice, *The Russo-Turkish War.
1877. A strategical Sketch* (London, 1905), both using Greene; and General H. Langlois, *Enseignements de deux guerres recentes. Guerres Turco-
Russe et Anglo-Boer* (3rd ed., Paris, 1904).

23.   New York, 1880, 1881, 1885; London 1881. None of the book
concerns army life in Russia; about half is not concerned with army life.

24.   Greene, *Campaign*, 250.

25.   Ibid., 131. There were instances of one side refusing to take orders
from the other.

26.   Ibid., 251.

27. *Turkish Life in War Time*, 204. Dwight is merciless in his criticism of the Turkish conduct of the war.

28. See F. L. Bullard, *Famous War Correspondents* for chapters on Forbes, MacGahan and Villiers (another British artist-correspondent in the Russo-Turkish War). See also Furneaux, *The Breakfast War*.

29. *Kriegsschauplatze der Russisch-Turkischen Krieges. 1877-1878* (Zurich, 1879), 61. Colonel Ott, an engineer, was on an official Swiss mission. A Romanian historian, N. Banescu, believed that the capture of Grivitsa I forced Osman's surrender (*Historical Survey of the Roumanian People* (Bucureşti, 1926).

30. Quoted in A. Forbes, *Czar and Sultan* (New York, 1894), 173.

31. Herbert, *The Defense of Plevna*, 269. See also n. 97, p. 459. Without Grivitsa II (which the Turks called *Bash*, or Head redoubt), Grivitsa I (which the Turks called *Kanli*, or Bloody redoubt) was more than useless. Lieutenant Herbert was stationed in Grivitsa II.

32. The unsuccessful Romanian attack on Grivitsa II (October 19) was "the last assault made upon any of the Turkish redoubts" (Greene, *Campaign*, 145).

33. Forbes, a prolific writer of books as well as dispatches, wrote *Czar and Sultan* (New York, 1894), a slightly fictionalized account of his Russo-Turkish War experiences.

34. Many of MacGahan's and Millet's (and several others) dispatches and letters are in *The Correspondence of the Daily News*, vol. I, 1877; vol. II, 1877-78 (London, 1878), a narrative made up of spliced and coded correspondent's reports. MacGahan on Osman's surrender is in II, 146-51. T. D. Dimitrov has calculated that MacGahan's contribution totals 250 pp., "MacGahan as Correspondent of the Russo-Turkish War," J. F. Clarke and G. A. Tabakov, eds., *MacGahan and Bulgaria, 1878-1978. A Centennial Commemoration* (New Lexington, Ohio, 1979), 59-65. A useful source for correspondents' accounts is H. M. Hozier, *The Russo-Turkish War* (2 vols., London, nd).

35. On the morning of December 10, the Turks evacuated most of their positions opposite the Romanian sector. The Romanians were the first to enter Pleven, engaging the Turks northwest of the town. According to Romanian sources Osman offered to surrender to Colonel (later General) Mihail Cerchez. See Report of General Cernat to Prince Carol, November 29, 1877 (o.s.) in D. Berindei, et al., eds., *Războiul pentru independenţă naţională, 1877-1878* (Bucureşti, 1971), no. 481, pp. 491-94. See also C. Căzănişteanu and M. Ionescu, *Războiul neatîrnării României* (Bucureşti, 1977), 243. Russian and most other sources have Osman surrendering to

General Ganetsky, commander of the break-through sector. For this controversy, see General R. Rosetti, "Roumania's Share in the War of 1877," *Slavonic and East European Review*, XIII (1930), 577, n. 83; and Tsonko Genov, *Osvoboditelnata voina 1877-1878* (Sofia, 1978), 177-78.

36. At the Centennial of Romanian Independence confernce at Ohio State University, 1977, Ilie Ceauşescu, in a paper "The Military Effort of Romania in the War of Independence," stated that the Romanian losses at Pleven were equal to the Russian. This is nonsense. According to Rosetti (p. 578, n. 93) Romanian casualties (all categories) south of the Danube, not just at Pleven, were 26,612, of whom 19,093 were sick. Todleben's estimate for Russian casualties at Pleven was 30,000. (Letter to General Brialmont, Brestovets, January 18, 1878). Greene estimated Pleven cost "nearly 40,000," presumably including Romanians (*Campaign*, table p. 197). At the third and bitterest battle for Pleven, September 7-12, after the arrival of the Romanians, the Russian losses were 13,179, the Romanian, 2564 (Rosetti, "Romania's Share," 574, n. 55). Greene gives 15,702 and 2511, respectively (*Campaign*, 130). A recent Romanian account gives 10,000 killed or wounded south of the Danube, with the last battle for Pleven costing the Russians 2000, the Romanians 250 and the Turks 4000. (Căzănişteanu and Ionescu, *Războiul*, 262, 244). Herbert's rather high estimate for total Pleven losses was Russians 55,000, Romanians 10,000, Turks 30,000 (*Defense of Pleven*, 407). Perhaps out of ideological gratitude, Bulgarians credit the Russians with 200,000 casualties in liberating Bulgaria, which is almost equally absurd (Boris Chalpanov, "In the Footsteps of the Liberators," *Slavyani*, February, 1978, 15). Half that would be more likely. Not long after the Russians and Bulgarians met they became mutually disenchanted.

37. Quoted in Furneaux, *Breakfast*, 214.

38. *Daily News Correspondence*, II, 196.

39. Greene, *Sketches*, 76.

40. Greene, *Campaign*, 191.

41. *Daily News Correspondence*, II, 295.

42. Ibid., 370-71.

43. Quoted in Furneaux, *Breakfast*, 225.

44. *Daily News Correspondence*, II, 581.

45. Greene, *Sketches*, 161.

46. Bullard, *Correspondents*, 117.

47. Evelyn Schuyler Schaeffer, *Eugen Schuyler, A Memoir* (New York, 1901), includes letters to his sister.

Gh. Buzatu

ORIGINS OF ROMANIA'S OIL POLICY

In Romania, as in all countries possessing "black gold," petroleum was not always given continued attention by the leading political, economic and financial circles. Thus, during the Middle Ages, petroleum, like most of the resources of the Romanian subsoil, was not the object of written provisions stipulating ownership rights, exploitation conditions, and the like. The earliest written stipulations on mining rights only date back to the 19th century.[1] In Moldavia the Callimachi Code of 1817 laid down that mining property belonged to the state (Articles 382 and 509)[2] while in Wallachia the Caragea Code of 1819 established the right of occupancy (Part II, Chapter 1, Article 1).[3] The two codes were in force until 1832, when they were suspended by the *Règlements Organiques*. After the Russian model, the *Règlements Organiques* established in mining law a single ownership system in the two Principalities, the subsoil was the property of the superficiary.[4] Differences persisted only in the conditions laid down for mine working; for example, in Wallachia as well as in Moldavia, the owners were entitled to work their mines, but if they delayed working them for 18 months or five years respectively, the ruling prince conceded them to a third party. It was in the interest of the ruling prince that the mines should be worked for in Moldavia, for example, he levied dues amounting to one tenth of the profit derived thereform.[5] The last differences between Moldavia and Wallachia in the mining system were abolished after their union in 1859: on November 26, 1864, Al. I. Cuza's Civil Code introduced *a single system* to be enforced throughout the territory of the young Romanian state.[6] Article 489 stipulated in this respect: "Land ownership includes superficiary and subsoil ownership."[7] With regard to working conditions article 491 stipulated that the owners of the subsoil were to submit to the (unspecified) prescriptions of a future mining law.[8] The Constitution of 1866 also pointed to the necessity of issuing a mining law in Romania (article 131).[9] At the same time, the mining system ruling in the subjugated historical Romanian provinces (Transylvania

Bucovina, Bessarabia and Dobrudja) was the system in force in the great neighboring empires, which held sway over them.

During the latter half of the 19th century, mining resources (petroleum included) were given greater attention owing to the part they played in the economic development of the modern Romanian state, for which reason they were at the time the object of special stipulations in the mining laws. It should be noted that no fewer than six mining bills were tabled in the Bucharest Parliament during the last decades of the 19th century, namely in 1863, 1870, 1873, 1881, 1886 and 1895.[10] From among them only one—which had been worked out by P. P. Carp, a Conservative minister, in 1895—came into effect. The bill, subsequently named the P. P. Carp law, was significant in three respects: it established a mining system for the first time in Romania, it made an important reform in the field of mine ownership, and inauguarated a state policy in the mining industry.[11]

During the modern period, petroleum has held an ever more important role and place in Romanian mining enactments, proportionally to its increasing economic importance. To begin with, the stipulations relating to petroleum were restricted to a few articles incorporated in the 1895 law. Subsequently, special laws were issued on petroleum, also described as "black gold," which was also given preponderance in the general mining laws. Such is the case of the 1924, 1929 and 1947 so-called *mining* laws, which were primarily *petroleum laws*.

The mining law of 1895 was passed following a vehement confrontation between the Conservative and the National-Liberal parties. The bill submitted by P. P. Carp, Minister of Public Property in the 1891-1895 Conservative cabinet, incorporated a significant innovation respecting mine ownership. Carp had adopted a number of stipulations included in western regulations, had adjusted them to suit Romanian conditions, and had thus established a *sui generis* mining system, which was a compromise between the different existing systems of subsoil ownership (accession, dominial, occupancy, regalian). In consequence, the Carp law was an "inextricable labyrinth" winding its way between all the aforementioned systems.[12] For example, article 489 of the *Civil Code*, which laid down that superficiary ownership was inseparable from subsoil ownership, was maintained. Nevertheless, this principle was not adopted when it came to a *mining subsoil*, which was separated from superficiary ownership.[13] For most of the subsoil resources (gold, silver, iron, coal, etc.), the regalian ownership system was adopted, the law stipulating that, should the superficiary be unwilling to turn to account the deposits occurring in his subsoil, the state was to step in, being entitled to grant the right of working the deposits to another interested person for a term of 75 years at most. In that case the superficiary was to receive from the operator of the mine a rent for the plots of land he had taken over, an annual royalty amounting to four percent of the net income, and an indemnification for any damage cuased to the surface area. The royalty due to the government amounted to two percent. Article 7 stipulated that a mine once opened with the agreement of the Ministry of Public Property, became an asset which was "distinct from superficiary ownership."[14] Most Romanian experts in mining legislation regard P. P. Carp's reform as "audacious," considering the time when it was made. For example, one of them observes that the reform was striking a blow "at the then dominant concepts of the sacred and inviolable right of ownership."[15] And indeed, it was one of the most serious reasons for which Carp's bill was energetically opposed by the landowners and by the Liberal opposition in Parliament. On January 31, 1895, D. A. Sturdza, leader of the National-Liberal Party, declared in the Senate that the bill was "a most daring attempt on the Constitution" for the reason that, *inter alia*, "the principle of the sacred and inviolable right of ownership was contested thereby."[16]

The law of 1895 allowed two important exceptions from the principle of separatability of a mining subsoil from superficiary owenership: one, where by the stipulations of the law of April 3, 1882 were maintained— that law laying down that the subsoil was state property in Dobrudja, which had been returned to Romania four years previously; the other exception concerned the *oil problem*, with serious consequences for its subsequent evolution. It was specified that under the Carp Law the subsoil had been separated from superficiary ownership in the case of mining substances (gold, silver, etc.). But the distinction did not involve *bituminous substances* (petroleum, asphalt, ozokerite), which, in pursuance of article 65, and notwithstanding the present law, remained at the disposal of the superficiary."[17] Consequently, for petroleum and the other bituminous substances, the superficiary was entitled after 1895 to proceed as he deemed fit, without any constraint from the state as to the turning to account of the deposits or the failure to turn to account, as to working condition and the like. The law merely obliged the superficiary to observe the obligations concerning the mining policy, the relations between workers and concessionaires and payment of the mineral rights duty to the state.[18]

Later, the principle admitted by article 65 of the P. P. Carp law gave rise to two distinct mining and petroleum enactments: 1. the laws on petroleum occurring on private property; 2. the laws on petroleum on state-owned land.[19]

In the case of *private land* the rights of the superficiary had been specified in article 65. Subsequent stipulations proposed to bring under regulation the relations between the superficiary (in his capacity as assignor of an area of land) and the concessionaire (who took over the respective area in consideration of a royalty). The 1895 law had failed to define these relations,[20] and for a time the concessions of oil-bearing land were juridically insecure. In order to obviate this drawback, on May 22, 1904, the D. A. Sturdza cabinet promulgated "the law on the regulation and consolidation of the rights to exploit petroleum and ozokerite and private land" (the I. Stoicescu law).[21] Article 1 of the law stated that the right of the concessionaire of an oil-bearing area of land was "a real personal right" opposable to all and preserved by entering the deed of concession in special registers, which were created at the time and were kept at the offices of the so-named mining regions.[22] The law of 1904 was reinforced by the N. Xenopol law of June 21, 1913.[23]

Oil deposits on *state-owned land* came under the system established by the Carp law (article 70) as regards prospecting and working conditions, mining police rules and the manner of constituting the areas and granting concessions and so forth. Up to 1900 the Romanian state had a single policy regarding the oil-bearing land under its control; it consisted in granting concessions in consideration of ever more considerable financial advantages. During the interval from 1895 to 1900 three *sets of regulations* were issued on granting concessions of state-owned, oil-bearing land, viz, in 1895,[24] 1899[25] and 1900.[26] As a number of experts have pointed out,[27] the changes had become necessary as a result of the state's fiscal needs. Thus, in 1899 the royalty due to the state for oil rights on land owned but it increased from four percent to 8-14 percent, further to go up to 10-15 percent in 1900. At the same time, the areas for which concessions could be granted were extended from 40 to 100 hectares.

In 1903 Vintilă Brătianu, one of the leading members of the National-Liberal Party, pointed out that the Romanian state had "sinned" grievously in its capacity as owner of oil-rich lands. From 1895 to 1900 concessions had been granted for an oil-bearing area totally 3,653 hectares (102 concessions),[28] and most of the land had come under the control of companies founded and controlled by the big international oil trusts. The concessions had been granted following the filing of an application to which a 30 bani stamp had been affixed! Apart from that, the applicants "had had no condition imposed on them as to the mode of working (the spring), nor any guarantees that the working would be done properly."[29]

We conclude that up to 1900 the Romanian state did not carry out a far-sighted, consistent policy where petroleum was concerned. It is fair to say this was a difficult thing to achieve as long as the mining law of 1895 was in force, but it is impossible to overlook the fact that the Romanian state showed little concern for the oil-bearing land it owned and failed to envisage the consequences of granting concessions for such extensive areas on terms that were most advantageous for the applicants, and primarily for the foreign capitalists. The results soon became apparent for the oil companies controlled by international trusts gradually took over most of the oil-bearing land both private and state-owned—thus building up a safe reserve for the development of an industry that relied almost exclusively on foreign investments.

It was the events of 1900 that compelled Romania to insist on the necessity of a definite, far-sighted petroleum policy, and she was among the first countries in the world to do so.[30] At the time such a necessity was rather a natural *reaction* to the exigencies of some of the international oil companies and only in the second place a result of the intimate conviction of the Bucharest leading circles regarding the part to be played by, and the benefits to be derived from, the development of a national oil industry.

What was it that occurred in 1900? That year, with P. P. Carp's Conservative cabinet in office (July 1900-February 1901), Romania went through an acute agricultural and financial crisis. The budget deficit amounted to 74 million lei, a considerable sum. The *Standard Oil Company* tried to take advantage of Romania's financial difficulties and launched an offensive in order to be granted concessions for the oil-bearing land owned by the state. On November 25, 1900, an envoy of the American trust, Porter by name, submitted to the then Romanian Minister of Finance, Take Ionescu, the text of a draft convention. The trust engaged to pay the Romanian government 10 million gold francs in cash through the agency of *Disconto Gesellschaft*, in exchange for a 50-year concession of state-owned oil-bearing land totalling 15,000 hectares. The sum that was offered was not a loan; it was an advance on the 8 percent royalty the Romanian state was to collect from the trust for working the land that had been the object of the concession.[31] The draft convention, moreover, contained some other provisions that the Romanian state could not have accepted (among other things, the obligation to conceded the monopoly of pipe lines). Consequently, the National-Liberal Party in opposition at the time, found it easy to rouse public opinion in the country by pointing out the dangers likely to result from the conclusion of a convention with the American concern.[32] That was not all. Barely two days after Porter's offer, i.e., on November 27, 1900, the *Disconto Gesellschaft* itself asked to be granted a concession for the same 15,000 hectares, in consideration of an advance amounting to 6.4 million gold marks.[33] How did such a situation arise? According to certain sources of information,[34] divergences had risen between the two—German and American—competing groups and cooperation between them was no longer possible. Furthermore, Charles I, King of Romania, *vetoed* the agreement with the Americans and favored the deal with the *Disconto Gesellschaft* group where the Hohenzollerns were shareholders.[35] As to the Liberals, their energetic stand against the convention with the Standard Oil Company was the result of several factors.[36] The stand taken by the National-Liberal Party as a whole was primarily due to reasons of political expediency. Moreover, some of the leading liberals were pro-German, the Party leader, D. A. Sturdza, among others. Both in 1900 and during the years that followed, the latter had repeatedly declared for cooperation with the German financial and economic groups in order to enable the European market "to shake off" Rockefeller's domination.[37] Finally, a view had begun to take shape in the ranks of the National-Liberal Party according to which the national capital ought steadily to increase its participation in the oil industry.[38] This view was mostly upheld by a group which rallied round the Brătianu family and whose positions in trade, industry and banking were on a steady ascent. The tendencies apparent in the Liberal group did not chime in with the conceding en bloc of the state-owned oil-bearing land to foreign trusts. If that party had had to choose between the Americans and the Germans, it would have undoubtedly chosen the latter for the reasons shown above. Moreover, the *Standard Oil Company* was in bad repute in Europe, mostly by reason of its methods of conquering and controlling the production and sales markets. When the promoters of the aforementioned trend in the National-Liberal Party decided on cooperation with the German groups, they thought they would have to deal with more tractable partners and could consequently bank on obtaining a participation—even if slight to begin with—of the national capital in oil-extraction in Romania.[39]

Under the circumstances what were the chances of success of the two oil-conceding conventions proposed by the American and the German groups? The American proposal having no chances of success was shortly withdrawn by Porter. And although he convention submitted by *Disconto Gesellschaft* had found favor with the king and with some of the Liberals, it was rejected by the Conservative cabinet, which could not but resent the failure of the negotiations they had engaged in with the Americans.[40]

The attempts made by the powerful international companies in 1900 to obtain the conceding en bloc of the oil-bearing land owned by the Romanian state were not without weighty consequences. It may with good reason be stated that the 1900 offensive of foreign capital was a main factor in *impelling* the Romanian state to evolve an oil policy under the domestic conditions prevailing at the time. The most outstanding Romanian experts in this field are at one in stating that Romania's oil policy dates from 1900. Its inception is ascribed to the reaction cuased in Romanian public opinion and in political and economic circles by the proposals submitted by the international companies, and also to the decision made, consequent upon those proposals, by the P. P. Carp Conservative cabinet to reject both the American and German offers.

Thus from 1900 the petroleum issue became a main concern of Romanian political parties and of the government in Bucharest. Before long the two "historical" parties—the Conservative and the National-Liberal—which competed for power, made their stand on the liquid fuel issue clear. Or rather they sought to put into practice the ideas they had put forward while in office. The only exception was the 1905 "agreement" between the Conservative and the National-Liberal parties whereby the granting of concessions of state-owned oil-bearing land to international trusts was ruled out. Later the two parties drew steadily apart in their policy regarding "black gold." Gradually but unquestionably, the National-Liberal Party asserted itself in proportion to its political, financial and economic consolidation. In 1911 it submitted what may be described as a survey-program entitled *The State Policy in the Oil Industry*,[41] which Maurice Pearton considered to be "a manifesto of economic nationalism concerning oil resources."[42] The principles set forth at the time were to be subsequently developed and to be put into practice by the I. I. C. Brătianu Liberal cabinet (1922-1926), which nationalized the mining subsoil in 1923 and elaborated the mining law of 1924,[43] the P. P. Carp Law of 1895 being thus abrogated.

NOTES

1.   See Stefan Chicoş, *Legislaţia minieră* (Mining Legislation) in *Romania's Encyclopedia*, III, Bucureşti, 1943, p. 120. There were no special stipulations concerning petroleum at the time, petroleum being included in the comprehensive category of "mining property."

2.   Cp. Romania's Geological Institute, *Legiuirile miniere vechi şi noi ale României. Legiuirile din Vechiul Regat pînă la 4 iulie 1924*

(Romania's Mining Enactments, Old and New. Enactments in the Old Kingdom (Wallachia and Moldavia) up to July 4, 1924), VII, Bucureşti, 1925, p. 3-4.

3.   Ibid., p. 3.

4.   Ibid., p. 4-8; I. Tănăsescu, *Sistemele de organizare a proprietă-ţii miniere şi politica minieră în diferite state* (Mining Property Organization Systems and the Mining Property in Various States), Bucureşti, 1916, pp. 74-75.

5.   Cp. *Legiuirile miniere vechi şi noi ale României*, VII, Bucureşti, p. 8.

6.   Stefan Chicoş, op. cit., p. 122.

7.   *Legiuirile miniere vechi şi noi ale României*, VII, p. 9.

8.   Ibid.

9.   Cp. I. G. Vântu, *Proprietatea zăcămintelor miniere în România* (Mine Deposit Ownership in Romania), Bucureşti, 1938, p. 10.

10. Ibid.; N. I. Moruzi, *Le regime juridique du sous-sol minier en Roumanie (Loi des mines de 1924)*, Paris, 1926, p. 36; G. G. Anagnoste, *Legislaţia minieră şi petroliferă română* (Romanian Minining and Petroleum Legislation), Ploieşti, 1924, p. 15.

11. See M. Plătăreanu, *Politica economică şi socială a României în trecut şi în cadrul legislaţiei actuale* (Romania's Economic and Social Policy in the Past and as Part of the Present Legislation), Bucureşti, 1936, pp. 169-170.

12. Cp. Dr. G. N. Leon, *Politica minieră în diferite state şi raporturile ei cu politica minieră în România* (The Mining Policy of Various States and its Relations with Romania's Mining Policy), Bucureşti, 1915, p. 191.

13. See *Legiuirile miniere vechi şi noi ale României*, XI, Bucureşti, 1925, pp. 26-27.

14. Ibid., VII, p. 12.

15. Th. Ficşinescu, *Legislaţia minieră în România* (Mining Legislation in Romania), I, in *Moniteur du Petrole Roumain* (Bucureşti), No. 20/1. 10.1925, p. 1.613. See also Dr. F. C. Gerretson, *History of the Royal Dutch*, II, Leyden, 1955, p. 288.

16. *Legiuirile miniere vechi şi noi ale României*, VII, pp. 27-28.

17. Ibid., XI, p. 39.

18. Ibid., VII, pp. 27-28.

19. Tănăsescu, op. cit., p. 78.

20. Anagoste, op. cit., p. 48.

21. *Legiuirile miniere vechi şi noi ale României*, VII, pp. 207-212.

22. Ibid., p. 207.

23. Ibid., pp. 221-231.

24. Ibid., pp. 113-122.

25. Ibid., p. 188.

26. Ibid., pp. 123-141.

27. Tănăsescu, op. cit., p. 82.

28. Vintilă, I. C. Brătianu, *Scieri şi cuvîntări, 1899-1906* (Writings and Speeches, 1899-1906), Bucureşti, 1937, vol. I, pp. 138-139.

29. Ibid., p. 239.

30. Vintilă I. C. Brătianu, *La politique d'Etat de petrole en Roumanie a la suite de la nouvelle Constitution et de la Loi des mines*, Bucureşti, 1927, p. 4.

31. See the text of the proposed convention in D. Sturdza, *Cestiunea petroleului în România* (The Oil Question in Romania), Bucureşti, 1905, pp. 3-5.

32. Cf. ing. Stelian Ionescu, *Asupra concesiunei "Standard Oil Company" în România* (Regarding the Standard Oil Company Concession in Romania), Bucureşti, 1900, passim.

33. See the text in Sturdza, op. cit., pp. 6-7.

34. Cf. Gh. Ravaş, *Din istoria petrolului românesc* (From the History of Romanian Petroleum), Bucureşti, 1955, pp. 67-68.

35. Ibid., p. 68.

36. Cf. Vintilă I. C. Brătianu and ing. C. Hălăceanu, "Politica de stat în industria petrolului," (State Policy in the Oil Industry) in Vintilă I. C. Brătianu, *Scrieri şi cuvîntări, 1907-1911*, Bucureşti, 1938, vol. II, pp. 302-303.

37. Cf. D. Sturdza, *Petrolul românesc* (Romanian Petroleum), Bucureşti, 1904, passim.

38. Cp. Vintilă I. C. Brătianu, op. cit., I, pp. 106-107.

39. Ibid., p. 107.

40. Gh. Ravaş, op. cit., p. 69.

41. See Vintilă I. C. Brătianu and C. Hălăceanu, Dipl. Eng., in Vintilă I. C. Brătianu, op. cit., II, pp. 299-438.

42. Maurice Pearton, *Oil and the Romanian State*, Oxford, 1971, p. 66.

43. See Gh. Buzatu, *Problema petrolului românesc şi naţionalizarea sobsolului minier în 1923* (The Problem of Romanian Oil and the Nationalization of the Mining Subsoil in 1923), in the Yearbook of the A. D. Xenopol History and Archaeology Institute, Iaşi, t.V/1968, pp. 145-159; idem, *Unele aspecte privind lupta pentru acapararea petrolului românesc. (Legea minelor din 1924)* (Sidelights on the Struggle to Corner Romanian Oil—the Mining Law of 1924), in the Yearbook . . . , Iaşi, t.VI/1969, pp. 67-94; idem, *The Place of the Oil Problem Within the Evolution of Romanian-English Relations (1880-1929)*, in the Yearbook . . . , Iaşi, t. XV/1978, pp. 59-78.

Victoria F. Brown

THE ADAPTATION OF A WESTERN POLITICAL THEORY IN A
PERIPHERAL STATE: THE CASE OF ROMANIAN NATIONALISM

INTRODUCTION

From the achievement of political autonomy in the late 1850s, until the late 1930s and the establishment of royal dictatorship, the National Liberal Party (NLP) was a pre-eminent factor in Romanian politics, and its programs were governmental policy during much of Romania's existence prior to 1918.[1] Its ideology became the official credo of the Greater Romanian state not long after the war. Yet, although the insistence of the present regime on the primacy of ideology has led to much analysis of the relationship between Marxist theory and its recent East European incarnations, it has been far too readily assumed that the ideological commitment of earlier politicians, who called themselves Liberals or Conservatives, is not to be taken seriously.

The customary treatment of Romanian liberalism provides an excellent illustration of just this point. Was the NLP's ideology really liberalism? Romanian liberalism, like East European liberalism in general, usually has been dismissed by Western writers since World War II as a mere travesty, if not an open contradiction, of liberalism as conceived in the West. Carlton Hayes, for example, calls Balkan liberalism "hardly more than a slogan."[2] L. S. Stavrianos writes that "Rumanian politics consisted to a large degree of barren squabbles between 'Liberals' and 'Conservatives'— meaningless labels without underlying principles."[3] Joseph Rothschild judges the interwar Romanian National Liberal Party to have been "'liberal' only in the historical sense of being the heirs of the revolutionaries of 1848 and of the revokers of the serfdom of 1864."[4]

Recent Romanian historians give even shorter shrift to the question of the Western theoretical roots of Romanian liberalism.[5] Although writers do some analysis of the social composition of the NLP, they normally ignore completely the question of ideological underpinnings. Even authors

269

such as Mircea Muşat and Ion Ardeleanu,[6] who devote several pages to "Doctrina şi programul Partidului naţional liberal," do not progress beyond a vague listing of the points used as propaganda by the NLP to deal with the post-World War I democratic challenge.

Both the "liberal-in-name-alone" school and those who eschew all discussion of liberal ideology sidestep an essential issue.[7] Factional infighting and personal squabbles in the NLP could never entirely obscure the very real questions of how Romania was to meet the political, economic, social and international difficulties of the modern world. In outlining appropriate theoretical and practical responses to these underlying problems, politicians could not avoid taking some stance toward liberalism which was a major influence on East European national movements from the early nineteenth century. Liberalism was an extremely powerful and progressive force in Western Europe's development. The economically advanced societies emulated by Romanians and other East Europeans were, in large measure, the products of triumphant liberalism. It stands to reason, then, that the NLP might not merely have picked up the liberal attitude toward national liberation and a few slogans, but fervently desired to implement liberal economic and political programs in the sincere belief that liberalism was a universal recipe for rapid development and subsequent prosperity. The lack of success of Romanian liberalism and the self-serving disingenuousness of many of its programs should not blind us to the reality and importance of the attempt nor to the significance of the causes for its failure.

For in spite of their deviations from classical liberalism (for reasons to be considered later), Romanian liberals did share a number of assumptions, aims, methods and class loyalties of Western liberalism. This paper will attempt to show that the Romanian NLP was a genuine, if rather disreputable, offspring of West European liberalism, adapted to local conditions. The poor showing of the special Romanian form of liberalism, in its attempt to pull the country up by its bootstraps, was not due simply to the venality and hypocrisy of Romanian liberal leaders (qualities at least partly shared, as we shall see, with their Western counterparts). Rather, what often has been viewed as a peculiarly Romanian, or East European, betrayal of "true" liberalism, was largely the result of limitations inherent in the generally practiced forms of European liberalism as a principle of political-economic organization for a poor, underdeveloped country.

The articulation of any political concept is liable to take place on several levels, to serve a variety of purposes, and on each of these levels the concept in question will have a rather different meaning. At one end of the spectrum, political philosophers seriously seek to develop and exprsss a coherent set of principles which embody their notions of how state power should be used and in whose name it should be wielded. Such writers speak to a very limited intellectual élite about general, "lower case" concepts—liberalism, socialism, conservatism. At the other extreme, propagandists churn out slogans, think up electoral tactics and distill party wisdom into terms easily digestible by the unsophisticated masses. Between disinterested and unaffiliated political thinkers and ideological hacks is an intermediate group which translates abstract theory into political programs. Its audience is that body of reasonably well-educated state officials, politicians, lawyers, doctors, businessmen, teachers, and prosperous artisans and farmers or peasants whose opinions may have a significant influence on political decisionmaking.

In a discussion of initial French reactions to English liberalism, Bertrand Russell enunciates what he calls "a general principle: [that] a philosophy developed in a politically and economically advanced country, which is, in its birthplace, little more than a clarification and systemization of prevalent opinion, may become elsewhere a source of revolutionary ardour, and ultimately of actual revolution. It is mainly through theorists that the maxims regulating the policy of advanced countries become known to less advanced countries. In the advanced countries practice inspires theory; in the others, theory inspires practice." Russell's "general principle" clearly applies to Romania.[8] Thus, the logical starting point for an analysis of Romanian liberalism is the body of theoretical assumptions which it borrowed from Western liberalism. Section I will consider this liberal theory.

In both East and West, however, theoretical beliefs were modified sharply, with the passage of time, by day-to-day political exigencies. It was the "intermediate" level of abstraction, not that of high theory, at which the effects of liberal ideas on political and economic practice were most strongly felt; so it is the intermediate level which must be of primary concern here. Sections II and III will look briefly at the historical development of Western liberalism and explore the characteristic deviations made from "pure" theory by what might be called "practical ideology" or "operational theory." Sections IV and V will do the same for Romania and will contrast the variety of liberalism practiced there with Western forms.

The discrepancy between liberal talk of freedom and Liberal Party tendencies to hedge it in with restrictions ultimately contributed in the

West to a lessening of liberal influence around the turn of the century. Section VI will be devoted to a comparison of the "crisis" which beset Western liberalism at the end of the nineteenth century with that from which Romanian liberalism suffered in the 1920s.

I. THE LIBERAL TEMPER

Most theoretical discussions of liberalism begin, as the theory itself did historically, with the concepts of "liberty," "the individual" and "reason." From John Locke forward, people who have called themselves liberals have championed the emancipation of the individual person from the traditional fetters of birth, custom, and autocratic government. They have extolled the right and duty of the individual to think for himself and have trumpeted the value of loosening the arbitrary bonds in which he was held by temporal and spiritual authorities and communities. The manner in which liberals have argued for these general cuases have varied greatly, however, with historical circumstances.

In its original form in the late seventeenth century, and during most of the eighteenth, liberalism was, as Bertrand Russell succinctly describes it, "opposed to everything medieval." In temper, it was "optimistic, energetic, and philosophic, because it represented growing forces which appeared likely to become victorious without great difficulty, and to bring by their victory great benefits to mankind." He continues: "For a hundred years, nothing occurred to dim these hopes: then at last [the liberals] themselves generated the French Revolution, which led directly to Napoleon and thence to the Holy Alliance. After these events, liberalism had to acquire its second wind before the renewed optimism of the [later] nineteenth century became possible."[9]

In the process of gaining its "second wind," liberalism worked out more closely some of the implications of its premises, took on a more somber view of the world, acquired a close alliance with the bourgeoisie and became the ideology of many political parties throughout Europe. It was from this new late eighteenth and early nineteenth century strain now known as "classical" liberalism—that the Romanian National Liberal Party's developed. Hence it is this strain in liberalism which largely will concern us here.

Classical liberalism, though it shared the earlier liberalism's general libertarian goals, was both more narrow and more grim and pessimistic in temper. It was, as Sheldon S. Wolin points out in his excellent and provocative chapter, "Liberalism and the Decline of Political Philosophy," in *Politics and Vision,* "a philosophy of sobriety, born in fear, nourished by disenchantment, and prone to believe that the human condition was and was likely to remain one of pain and anxiety."[10] Absence of pain, rather than pleasure, was what classical liberal man most sought. "The chief, if not only spur to human industry and action is uneasiness,"[11] John Locke had written bluntly in 1690. This same uneasiness, felt even more acutely later, was identified as "The first Spring and Cause of All Action" by Benjamin Franklin, who went further to say: *"Pleasure* is wholly caus'd by *Pain....* The *highest Pleasure* is only Consciousness of *Freedom* from the *deepest Pain."*[12] Adam Smith too asserted that pain "is in almost all cases a more pungent sensation than the opposite and corresponding pleasure."[13]

There appear to be three sources for this dismal view, all stemming from the underlying fact that liberalism was (throughout at least the first sixty or so years of the nineteenth century in the West and far longer than that in Eastern Europe) a philosophy of limits. First, in a purely theoretical, epistomological context, Locke and the other empirical philosophers had emphasized that man's own capacity for knowledge was limited to what could be garnered by his senses or derived by reason from logical propositions. There was no guarantee at all that the human intelligence was capable of comprehending the universe fully or deeply or that divine inspiration would fill the gaps in its understanding.

Second, as Wolin points out, contrary to our current view, "the liberal tradition contained very strong reservations about the controlling function of reason in human nature."[14] "It is by hopes and fears," wrote Bentham, "that the *ends* of action are determined; all that reason does is to find and determine the means."[15]

Third, and most important for the purposes of this paper, the material goods of the world were also perceived as severely limited, so that many people could not hope for prosperity or even a poor but decent living. This idea of physical scarcity, only touched on by the original wave of liberal writers, was strongly reinforced by the economic writings of Thomas Malthus, the early John Stuart Mill, Nassau Senior and others in the early nineteenth century. The physical scarcity notion, in fact, became central to the classical liberal view and was closely related to the idea of prevention of pain as the aim of human actions. If there is not enough to go around, one is always exposed to fears for one's own material security and well being. It takes only a short additional step to identify the absence of physical want with the absence of pain and hence the pursuit of wealth with the pursuit of happiness. This materialistic view, this preoccupation

with economic ends, became one of the identifying badges (though not
the exclusive property) of nineteenth century liberalism, even after its
raison d'etre, the fear of scarcity, lost much of its terror in the wake of
the industrial revolution. "Anyone who had taken part in extended discussions of social problems knows that, invariably, some reference is
made to human nature," writes H. K. Girvetz. "Moreover, the conception of human nature involved is usually fundamental to the whole argument."[16] For the nineteenth century classical European liberal, man was
"Economic Man" whose essential nature and most characteristic behavior
were manifestations of his "propensity to barter, truck and exchange
one thing for another."[17]

To recapitulate, classical liberals did not believe universal truth was
either revealed by God or discoverable by man. Likewise, they thought
man could not be relied on to act rationally, for the general good. Therefore neither the traditional Christian morality nor the self-evident natural
law was, for liberal thinkers, a reliable cement to hold society together.
What, then prevented the degeneration of society into murder, theft and
general chaos? The answer of the classical liberals stemmed from their
conviction that man acts in his own interest. There may be many possible
principles of actions, but, wrote Bentham, "The most powerful, most
constant, most uniform, most lasting, and most general among mankind"
is "personal interest," what he called the "utility" or "self-preference
principle."[18] As a rule, people do not work consciously for the communal
welfare. Instead each person acts to assuage a private "itch after honour,
prestige, power and riches,"[19] as Locke had phrased it and, *mirabile dictu*,
the world is so designed that the sum of countless individual acts of self-
interest is the greatest good for society as a whole, so long as the natural
order of things is not upset by those trying to fix matters permanently
by legislation. Thus, the glue which keeps society from breaking apart is
the lucky coincidence (or perhaps divine design) that unfettered self-
seeking produces the optimum amount of happiness possible in this
world. The classic exponent of this view is, of course, Adam Smith:

> As every individual, therefore, endeavours as much as he can both to
> employ his capital in the support of domestic industry, and so to
> direct that industry that its produce may be of the greatest value;
> every individual necessarily labours to render the annual revenue of
> the society as great as he can. He generally, indeed, neither intends
> to promote the public interest, nor knows how much he is promot-
> ing it. By preferring the support of domestic to that of foreign indus-
> try in such a manner as its produce many be of the greatest value, he

intends only his own gain, and he is in this, as in many other cases, led by an invisible hand to promote an end which was no part of his intention. Nor is it always the worse for the society that it was not part of it. By pursuing his own interest he frequently promotes that of the society more effectually than when he really intends to promote it. I have never known much good done by those who affected to trade for the public good. It is an affectation, indeed, not very common among merchants, and very few words need be employed in dissuading them from it.[20]

It would seem that the classical liberal creed, based on such a convenient dovetailing of desire and result, must be an extremely optimistic one. The dark and anxious view appears, at first, inconsistent with the rosy world of the invisible hand. This contradiction disappears when the role played by the notion of physical scarcity is taken into account. Because the world's resources are "not increasing in proportion with what men need or covet, . . . It is impossible for anyone to grow rich except at the expense of someone else."[21] The best of all *possible* worlds is by no means a fair, good or benign world. This line of reasoning leads to an extraordinarily passive, negative and fatalistic creed for mankind as a whole. Men are created equal or possess equal "natural rights" only in the sense that they are equally entitled to work for their own good. Only particularly fortunate individuals can hope to escape the general fate, while for the generality of mankind, life, even in society, continues to be nasty, brutish and short. Human progress is no foregone conclusion, and there is no built-in moral law which necessitates an equal sharing of limited resources. Accidents of birth—one's nationality, social class, intelligence, talents, wealth, and the like—largely determine how one will do in the struggle for survival (a later term, of course, but one which, as vulgarly understood, would fit in beautifully with the pre-existent classical liberal world view). The political implications of such a philosophy are distinctive and far-reaching, even more so when those acting on them are a small minority in a poor country.

II. LIBERALISM AS AN IDEOLOGY IN THE WEST

Any political theory becomes dynamic and powerful only when it reflects the desires and serves the interests of some significant group. Liberalism, like other grand ideas put into practice, has taken on a variety of forms, and cannot be fully understood without consideration of those who tried to live by it.[22]

Liberalism in Western Europe had become, by about 1860, the quintes-
sential ideology of those urban merchants, industrialists, financiers and
professionals whose contributions to society appeared to themselves, in
the years after 1815, to be much greater than their share in power and
social standing. These practical bourgeois movers and shakers found in
the ideas just discussed an ideal theoretical justification for that curious
combination of smugness and ruthlessness typical of the nineteenth
century entrepreneur. For the classical European liberal, the people
whose efforts were crowned with material success were those who in
fact had given the most to society as a whole. Because their prosperity
and society's coincided most fully, it was merely common sense that they
also should wield the most power and enjoy the greatest prestige within
the social-political order. In practice, this sanguine view of their own usefulness was often used, when liberals attained a degree of power, as a
rationalization for the unbridled reign of self-interest.

Classical liberalism as just defined is an exceedingly narrow and disingenuous ideology. Yet historically, liberalism, during the first half of
the nineteenth century was anything but a simple, cynical support of the
status quo. On the contrary, the period between 1815 and 1848 in particular was characterized by an epic struggle on the part of disenfranchized
liberals against traditional privilege and obstructive legislation which they
believed was hindering the efficient workings of the unseen hand and
denying their rightful place in the sun.

In the first years after 1815, classical liberalism was a fervent and
idealistic creed with broad appeal. It was the most progressive of political theories, and its ties to eighteenth century liberalism was very clear.
In England, liberals worked vigorously for the cautious expansion of the
suffrage and the repeal of the Corn Laws which were stifling the economic
life of the country. On the continent, liberals tried in various ways, often
illegally, to weaken the stranglehold of the old agrarian aristocracies on
political and economic life. Students and political exiles from Eastern
Europe eagerly adopted a philosophy whose passion for destroying obstacles to the smooth and natural functioning of societies everywhere
was accepted as a shining beacon of hope by peoples whose national
development had long been smothered under the rigid restrictions of
foreign oligarchies.

Having suffered frequently from the arbitrary exercise of unlimited
power, liberals of all lands and varied social strata labored strenuously
for the definition and limitation of authority, convinced that only artificial restraints were preventing the just redistribution of power and

prestige. Liberal desires for a freer, more fair and natural society were embodied concretely in demands for parliamentary government, greater economic liberty, a broader suffrage, extension of education, and national self-rule in order that those who contributed positively to the general welfare could have a share in power commensurate with their productivity. The question of precisely who were to be the real inheritors of aristocratic power was left for the moment unspecified.

At this stage, while liberal spokesmen were attacking the established powers and were fairly general in their demands, the generous, freedom-loving aspects of liberalism dominated. The degree to which liberalism could and would become the protective, exclusive ideology of one class was not yet evident. As the century progressed, however, the divergence of interests grew between urban middle-class liberals and others who at one time had shared with them a common underdog status. The mid-century saw a more narrowly bourgeois liberal viewpoint beginning to crystallize. Given their own often self-made background, their preoccupation with economic improvement, and some recent successes in fighting the aristocracy and throne, it is not at all surprising that members of the prosperous bourgeoisie should have become the most vociferous partisans of political liberalism. They also stressed the necessity of industrialization and of modernization in every realm of human endeavor. In so doing they spoke almost exclusively in the name of the urban entrepreneur, not that of the factory laborer, the dependent artisan or anyone in the agricultural sector.

In the West, whether it was achieved gradually as in England (Huskisson's reforms of commerce, the Corn Law of 1828 and the Reform Bill of 1832), or by a sudden, revolutionary takeover as in France (1830), the growing power of liberalism and its advocates in the two decades before 1848 modified the nature of liberal demands and diminished the willingness of most middle-class liberals to ally themselves with their less fortunate neighbors. In the 1820s, the radical "Doctrinaires" Royer-Collard, Victor Cousin and François Guizot spoke in the name of mankind. In the 1830s and 1840s, however, Guizot and his fellow liberals were themselves in power and devoted their talents and inspirational forces to the worldly policy of "enrichessez-vous."

The 1848 revolution in France, as elsewhere in Europe, foundered on the inability of liberal reformers—even the more radical generation which had succeeded the Doctrinaires—to make common cause with the "lower orders." Likewise in England, the enthusiastic liberal indignation of the 1830s and 1840s against agricultural and political restraints became strangely muted when demands for the right of free assembly for the working-men or a truly democratic suffrage began to claim public attention as the century wore on. In the transition from abstract theory to practical politics there is always a tendency to simplify and even to falsify ideas to some extent—in the West as well as in the East. Local consistency tends to be sacrificed to political expediency. In the history of liberalism after 1848 this tendency becomes especially noticeable.

III. "SECTARIAN" LIBERALISM IN THE WEST

By about 1860 there were signs everywhere in Western Europe that some of the broad principles of liberalism in the original sense (constitutional, parliamentary government; religious toleration, etc.) had been woven into the basic political fabric of most political parties. It was only a rather eccentric and narrow vision of classical liberalism, however, which usually called itself Liberalism (with a capital L). This specialized form of liberal ideology—which took credit for the general liberalizing of society and embodied most precisely the spirit of its quintessentially bourgeois era—had usefully beed dubbed "sectarian liberalism" by Carlton Hayes, who describes it thus:

> This fateful 'sectarian liberalism' was grounded in peculiar developments in the 1860's and 1870's, particularly the speeding and spreading process of industrialization, the vogue of materialistic philosophy, and the stirring triumph, in international as in national affairs, of *Realpolitik*. Its main props were bourgeois promoters of big business: bankers, speculators, builders of railways and steamships, coal and iron magnates, proprietors of expanding foundaries and factories. Supporting them, somewhat in the nature of a flying buttress, was an embellishing array of intellectuals: . . . scientists, engineers, physicians, lawyers, professors, and literary men. . . . [Sectarian liberalism's] central stress was upon economic liberty, upon the paramount importance of encouraging individual initiative and private enterprise.[23]

Since this "sectarian" sort of liberalism was the model most closely followed by the National Liberal Party of Romania, it needs a closer look. A political theory explicity based on self-interest obviously will be particularly vulnerable to distortions of its original ideas. However, commited in theory "sectarian" Liberals were to individualism, parliamentary government (a later term of course), *laissez-faire* economics and (sometimes national self-determination, Liberal parties and governments in the 1860s and 1870s seldom stood for complete individual freedom, the full, unqualified right of all citizens to participate equally in political life, total lack of governmental economic intervention, or self-government for every nationality in the world.

For mid-nineteenth century European Liberal parties, individual liberty did not include legal equality for women; government was to be based on suffrage determined by property-ownership, while the right to vote was to be cautiously extended only to those groups which had demonstrated their social respectability; governmental economic restraint did not extend to refraining from breaking strikes organized by legal or illegal trade unions; and the English Liberals supported national liberation more enthusiastically for Greece, Serbia, and Italy than for Ireland, India, or Romania. Whenever groups of people pressed too hard for the logical extension of certain principles underlying liberal theory, they were branded subversive and stalwartly resisted by those who called themselves Liberals.

During the 1860s and 1870s Western "sectarian" Liberals saw several issues in the same light, irrespective of where they lived, although only some of these positions taken by Liberal Parties were consistent with traditional liberal views.[24] In classical fashion Liberal parties were vigorously opposed to governmental regulation of commerce and industry, as well as to inherited privilege, high taxes, trade barriers, strong labor associations and church influence, especially in education. They staunchly defended limited, constitutional, parliamentary government and a free press, as long as they remained in the hands of the "responsible" propertied classes. Those whose property was merely inherited or had accrued as the "unearned increment" of rentiers were as suspect, in their way, as those who owned nothing and worked for a daily wage. Neither large landowners nor laborers were viewed by the typical Liberal of these decades as productive, responsible members of society. The form of property favored was that produced by a modern, technically advanced, urban, industrialized economy.

The characteristics so far listed were implied by classical liberalism or at least consistent with it. Several other common Liberal party attitudes and policies, however, deviated from classical liberal theory. For example, in their general attitude Western Liberal parties deviated markedly from the grim, scarcity-based classical liberal view of the human condition. The early conviction of the inexorability of poverty and want was very much tempered by a new Liberal confidence in the ability of mechanization, standardization and mass production to improve the general standard of living. Malthusian pessimism gave way to the self-help optimism of Samuel Smiles. In Russell's phrase liberalism had got its second wind.

Other steps, too, were taken away from classical liberalism. For example, loath as they were to involve the government in any activity, since they felt the market would regulate better and more cheaply, Liberal parties nonetheless approved of governmental involvement in certain necessary public works—roads, bridges and sometimes museums, libraries and even railroads—and state funded public education was enthusiastically championed by Liberals all over Europe. Likewise, while Liberal leaders continued to speak of their libertarian support for local self-government, their actual programs frequently involved enthusiastic administrative centralization and nationalistic unification, in clear violation of the concern for independent individualism normally associated with liberalism. During the same period, nationalist-economic considerations sometimes dictated departures from the original liberal support of national aspirations and caused a divergence in views among the Liberal parties of Western Europe. Thus Liberal Great Britain buttressed the sagging Ottoman Empire, while French Liberals, with less at stake economically, championed the cause of national liberation as a solution to the Eastern Question. Another common feature of "sectarian" Liberalism, which certainly was not implied by classical liberal theory, was the chronic corruption which hauted Liberal Party governments across Europe. To quote Hayes again:

> Some of the most influential elements in the Liberal parties were not virginal; they evinced no qualms of conscience about playing the stock market, consorting with shady promoters and jobbers, resorting to bribery of electors, legislators, and newspapers, and using public office for private gain. Corruption was, of course, no novelty of the 1870s. It was a chronic and hydra-headed manifestation of human nature. But now it was freer—more liberal. . . . Not that those who practiced corruption called or even recognized it by that name. They called it, in economics, "promoting progress," or, in politics, "assuring the triumph of liberty." . . . The association of sectarian Liberalism with economic and political corruption was not isolated in time or place. It gradually assumed the aspect of a set and almost universal pattern.[25]

In practice, then, in Western Europe the broad humanitarian principles of liberalism sometimes proved incompatible with adherence to the dictates of self-interest (also a venerable liberal principle) and, not surprisingly, the "utility principle" generally won. Classical liberal approval of modernization, secularization, and industrialization dovetailed so neatly with middle-class self-interest that these ideas remained central to Liberal Party theory and practice. Yet one must not forget that Liberal parties, however cynical and worldly they became, did remain true to their original Lockian heritage in one crucial respect: in the final analysis they accepted the limits of their power and never developed the authoritarian or paramilitary solutions in dealing with opposition which would become all too usual among extremists of both right and left after World War I.

IV. LIBERALISM IN ROMANIA

Because of the intensely political nature of Romanian society and the perceived urgency of the need to solve its problems, writers who stood completely above the fray were rare indeed. Much more common, and certainly more useful for understanding the realities of Romanian politics, were writers of the intermediate sort who chose a quasi-academic, "objective" style to express partisan ideas. Among Romanian Liberal ideologues, such writers as Ştefan Zeletin, I. G. Duca, and D. Draghicescu contributed to the National Liberal Party cause in the area of "operational theory" or "practical ideology."[26] They frequently cited Western thinkers and pointed to Western developments in support of their positions. Yet, although they also usually wrote with a concrete set of local circumstances in mind, they, and the party which they served, consistently failed to give sufficient weight to the agrarian nature of their country and the inapplicability of standard liberal remedies to the problems which beset it. An analysis of Romanian Liberal writings and NLP sponsored legislation reveals a movement which adapted central assumptions, attitudes and historical tendencies of nineteenth and early twentieth century Western Liberals in several ways and at several stages. The manner in which Western Liberal ideas were applied was also critically affected by the discrepancies between Eastern and Western development, even when the Romanian exponents of liberalism did not realize this.

After the mid-nineteenth century in the West, as indicated, the early pessimism of Malthus and company tended to loom less large in the minds of well-to-do and influential liberals. One of the striking characteristics of the Romanian variety of liberalism, by contrast, was that in general mood it never lost the classical liberal uneasiness and preoccupation with material scarcity. The continued anxiety of the Romanian Liberal was neither surprising nor unwarranted since he found his late-starting land at a sizeable disadvantage, economically and politically, compared to the advanced nations of the West. This telling difference in tone is manifested in each of the major areas of similarity between Romania and the West.

The basic positions which the Romanian National Liberal Party shared with its Western counterparts were: a commitment to national self-determination and a fierce devotion to the interests of the modernizing, urban bourgeoisie and the cause of "Economic Man."[27] Further, in spite of the NLPs high-handed attitude toward political niceties, the party showed, from its inception until its demoralization in the mid-1930s, a basic faith in parliamentary constitutional government and an unwillingness to stretch its tactics beyond a fairly well-defined level of chicanery and coercion.[28] As to the root meaning of the word "liberalism," i.e., "liberty," although it certainly was used universally to justifiy liberals' views, in practice liberty always has been, as noted earlier, a highly relative and equivocal notion. ("Abstract liberty, like other mere abstractions" remarked Edmund Burke, "is not be be found.")[29] It was, in fact, the changing interpretations of liberty in the real world that finally led, in both East and West, to the major crisis of liberalism to be discussed below.

A. Romanian Liberalism and Nationalism

On the face of it, the "National" rather than the "Liberal" part of the Romanian National Liberal Party's title seems to characterize the party more accurately. Certainly it is true that the National Liberals always dearly wished to minimize external influences in Romanian affairs. Nonetheless, although the term "National" certainly points up the focus of much of NLP liberalism, the term "Liberal" itself is also not inaccurate, in part (though only in part), because nationalism is historically the first link between Romanian and Western liberalism.

Paris was, for at least a century and a half, the spiritual home of educated Romanians.[30] In the 1830s and 1840s many of the future national leaders of the Principalities lived in the French capital, attending lectures at the Sorbonne and the College de France and participating with great ardor in the revolutionary doings of those years. It was there, under the varied liberal and romantic influences of Guizot, Cousin, Quinet, Ledru-Rollin, Lamartine, Michelet and Lammenais (as well as of the liberal Polish prince Adam Czartoryski), that Romanian hopes of national independence, unification and parliamentary government were nurtured.

While national self-determination had to be a central object of liberal party policy only among those nationalities which could not yet take for granted the existence and/or independence of their own national states, European liberals universally approved it. A prosperous and truly sovereign state under national leaders was a common and unexceptional liberal goal everywhere.

The sort of Western liberalism which initially most inspired Romanian liberals was of the rather diffuse and theoretical pre-1848 variety. Since they were all too aware of the Principalities' underdog status, Romanian leaders—in Paris in the 1830s and 1840s and at home at least until the achievement of autonomy in 1859—took up a high-minded strain of national liberalism requiring generous and humanitarian actions on the part of others.

Gradually the romantic and idealistic generalities of Herder and Quinet started to give way under the influence of anxieties and doubts, to a still rather naïve but more stridently chauvinistic national feeling in the spirit of Michelet. As the century wore one Romanian nationalism became ever more shrill and exclusive in its attitudes toward neighboring states and minorities within Romania.[31] Yet in their dealings with Western powers, Liberal Romanian diplomats continued to insist unfailingly on the humanitarian duties of the rest of the world to recognize—purely out of a sense of justice—Romanian rights and independence.

Because of their fear of scarcity Romanian liberals—unlike the steely-eyed purists of classical English liberalism—considered the problem of material limits from the viewpoint of the dispossessed in their relations to other countries. In was anxiety about Romanian fitness in the international struggle for existence which led Romanian liberals toward their major deviation from Classical Western liberalism, toward their belief in the need to supplement the workings of the invisible hand and their modification of their economic philosophy in the direction of Listian protectionism.

This inconsistency of attitude paralleled the equivocal reactions of Western "sectarian" Liberal parties to issues involving the national aspirations of others.[32] Often the decisive factor for Liberal parties all across the continent was national interest rather than liberal theory, though the discrepancy between theory and reality was greater in Eastern than in Western Europe. Thus, the Liberal Party's nationalist detestation of foreign economic power in Romania produced an extreme "prin noi înșine" (by ourselves) policy which treated the need for industrialization as a perennial national emergency requiring full national mobilization by the state. "The mirage of national self-sufficiency," writes David Mitrany "appears to have been so bewitching as to convince statesmen and business men that an extensive industry could be created without capital, and the currency at the same time revalorized into the bargain. Foreign holders were bought out at almost any price."[33]

B. Romanian Liberalism and the Bourgeoisie

In East European countries, where national and class oppressors were both of a different nationality from those seeking liberation, social issues (primarily land reform) early became part of liberal programs. Old King-dom Romanians—like Hungarians and Poles and unlike, say, Bulgarians, Slovaks and even Transylvanian Romanians—still had an indigenous nobility, however, which was the first source of its national leaders. The Romanian liberal-national leaders came typically from the less wealthy landed nobility, and had received their education in the West.[34] They were predisposed by both economic interest and training to favor econo-mic modernization, after the Western paradigm. Like the supporters of liberalism in the mid-nineteenth century West, the Romanian NLP was the "permanent representative of the bourgeoisie and the banking in-terests, being led by the directors of the National Bank and of the prin-ciple credit institutions and industrial enterprises."[35] Its supporters also included members of the small urban bourgeoisie of more modest means as well as "intellectuals belonging to the lower and middle levels of the towns and villages,"[36] and landowners with commercial and industrial interests.

In the same way as in the West, though to an even greater degree, class interests prevented Romanian Liberals from allying themselves with the masses. In its identification with the developing bourgeoisie, Romanian Liberalism was modelling itslef closely on the "sectarian" Liberalism of the West. A desire for personal recognition and national progress also put Romanian Liberals in direct conflict with the semi-feudal great landlords who were represented by the Conservative Party. This pattern of alliances and rivalries echoed that of the West, but it was telescoped into a much shorter time period since Romania only became autonomous in 1859 and its regular party political life only began in the 1860s. The Romanian Na-tional Liberals, like their Western counterparts, tried to defend them-selves against enemies from above and below them. Agriculture, especi-ally in the period of Liberal supremacy after World War I, openly was made to pay for industrialization, while industrial workers, a tiny minority, were effectively ignored, though much ink was spilled on propaganda to convince them of NLP concern.

On the third front as well, however, Romanian Liberals left the need to battle constantly, in typically non-Western fashion, to rid their country of foreign political hegemony and economic monopoly. Yet, entirely consistently with classical liberal principles, foreign domination, though feared and detested by the NLP, was not attacked either as reactionary or exploitative in a class sense. On the contrary, Ştefan Zeletin, the most frank and zealous of Romanian Liberal spokesmen, explicitly credited foreign capital and enterprise with bringing to Romania the very sort of modernization he saw as essential to Romanian economic and, in the long run, political prosperity. His quarrel with foreign traders and investors really comes down simply to one of national personnel. It was time Romanian capitalists got their share of the pie; the Romanian bourgeoisie must defend (and in fact create) itself.

Like Liberals in the West, Romanian liberals were convinced that the coincidence of political and economic power, i.e, the running of the government by those who contributed the most to economic prosperity, was the best possible guarantee of national well-being.[37] But the great lag in Romanian historical development radically changed both practical and theoretical implications of this calculation. In the West, middle class economic growth had preceded and spurred on the desire for political power. In Romania, however, a handful of wishfully thinking liberals— who already had a large share of political influence and wanted commensurate economic power—ignored the overwhelmingly agricultural basis of their own country and swallowed whole the Western notion that the commercial-industrial bourgeoisie was necessarily the most productive class of society. They then proceeded to try to turn themselves into such a bourgeoisie, as though to justify *ex post facto* their own pre-eminence in the political sphere.

The connection between Liberalism and the industrializing bourgeoisie is most explicitly explored for Romania by Ştefan Zeletin. In his two political books, *Burghezia Romăna* and *Neoliberalism*, Zeletin identifies the terms "liberal," "bourgeois," "modern" and "capitalist" with one another and asserts that these terms describe a group of people in Romania, the "oligarchy," who, quite properly, according to him, are the country's real rulers. He maintains that in the West liberalism gained its influential political position because it was the ideological justification of the historically necessary upward thrust of the commercial-industrial bourgeoisie. "The logic of history," a Marxist concept, borrowed "for purposes that were certainly not Marx's"[38] is the core of Zeletin's argument. The bourgeoisie is for Zeletin, what the proletariat is for Marx, the ultimate agent of change, the vehicle of human progress.

In Zeletin's analysis, whereas free trade furthered English bourgeois prosperity by opening up Eastern Europe, African and Asian markets to already well-developed English manufacturing interests, the small countries of these backward regions could themselves only develop their own bourgeois capitalist prosperity by subsidizing industry and raising a barrier of protective tariffs to shield their native industries in their infancy. Romanian Liberals were certainly aware of the theoretical objections to this line of argument: "Perhaps," wrote one, "it appears to some that the 'liberal' party has been at bottom a protectionist party in its national economy and would thus contradict its basic 'liberal' conception."[39] A characteristic answer to such doubts was given by Mihai Manoilescu: "Par contre, le libre echange en empechant les pays d'elever leur niveau de productivitie, constitue pour eux un regime de contrainte. On peut dire en un mot: La protection c'est la liberte. La libre-echange c'est la contrainte."[40] If this epigram is not simple doubletalk, perhaps its meaning lies in the nature of governmental intervention in the Romanian economy. Governmental involvement in industry came almost exclusively in the form of *aids* to industrial development—subsidies, protective tariffs and other incentives—which were financed largely at the expense of agriculture. On the other hand, regulatory governmental "interference" with industry— in the form of worker legislation, anti-trust activity or controls on quality or quantity—was kept at a minimum.[41] Thus industry was given as much freedom to expand as its limited capacity to find capital would allow.

By Romanian Liberal logic, if protectionist or interventionist policies could obtain for Romanian the bourgeois freedom of action to which *laissez-faire* capitalist development led in the West, these policies could legitimately be called "Liberal." That this argument is self-serving is obvious, but that it is also an accurate expression of National Liberal philosophy should be equally evident. What the position of Zeletin and his colleagues boils down to is an unusually frank attempt to rationalize a choice made to some extent by "sectarian" Liberals everywhere: when asked to decided between behaving passively with consistent faith in the invisible hand, and defending actively one's vital national or class interests, Liberal parties tended to choose the latter course. The conviction that one's own nation and its middle class will in the long run be the agents of history is cold comfort in the face of present oppression or poverty. Therefore, argued Romanian liberals, it is better to admit that *some* regulatory legislation can help to speed things along, than to sit idly by waiting for one's interests to be served in the fullness of time.

V. "SECTARIAN" LIBERALISM IN ROMANIA

The Romanian NLP did not believe in *laissez-faire*, as Western liberals of all sorts mostly did, though, as we have seen, the Romanians argued that this was a violation of the letter rather than the spirit of liberalism. Whatever the merits of this argument, the spiritual kinship of Romanian with Western "sectarian" Liberalism on a variety of other important issues is manifest. Romanian NLP leader Ion C. Brătianu, as succinctly described by R. W. Seton-Watson, was an Eastern version of the typical sectarian liberal politician:

> He himself was a man of high character and wide sympathies, but he considered that the somewhat doctrinaire ideals of his brother Dimitrie and their old associate C. A. Rosetti were ill adapted to the iron age upon which Romania was entering; he attached great value to the rapid creation of a new middle class, strongly nationalist in feeling and able both to hold the Jews at arm's length and to outstrip in economic development the more primitive and less wealthy communities of the Balkan peninsula: and he therefore, like more than one statesman in contemporary Europe, while maintaining his own private standards, found it convenient to encourage the "spoils system" and to build up his party organization on the basis of "Enrichissez-vous."[42]

Neither Brătianu nor any of the other NLP leaders gave any credence whatever to suggestions that there might be another possible or desireable path for Romania than that of Western liberal industrialism. They always spurned with the utmost indignation suggestions for a peasant state (as in Stambuliskii's Bulgaria) or planned, centralized government ownership and regulation of industrial development on the Marxist model. Traditional Romanian Liberals also would view with great suspicion Carol II's Mussolini-style corporatism of the 1930s as pushing government intervention too far to the detriment of (their own) individual enterprise.[43]

Belief in national self-determination, acceptance of definite limits to state and party powers, and, especially, support for the nascent bourgeoisie and its program of urbanization and industrialization were major ways in which Romanian liberalism thought and acted in the spirit of classical liberalism. Likewise, Romanian Liberals shared their Western counterparts' objection to high taxes, inherited privilege, labor associations, industrial regulation and church influence in government and education.[44] They also supported mass education, a free press and parliamentary government in responsible middle class hands—though they gave an even more flexible definition to "responsibility" in journalism and government than did the more high-handed among Western "sectarian" liberals.[45]

The Romanian liberalism of the NLP also imitated the most typical departures of Western "sectarian" Liberal parties from the broad, Lockian conceptions of early Liberalism. As already noted, in the West here was a pronounced reluctance of Liberal parties to expand the application of general preclassical emancipation in truly democratic fashion whenever emancipation threatened to conflict with more narrow, classical liberal concerns for the protection of the property and interests of society's "responsible" sectors. In Romania too, it was not until 1913 that the Liberals formally espoused the causes of sweeping land reform and universal manhood suffrage, while collusion between entrepreneurs and politicians was one of the basic facts of Romanian public life from the beginning.

In a rather different context, Romanian and Western "sectarian" Liberals alike indulged in certain characteristic deviations from classical liberalism—such as support for state-funded public education and public works—which harkened back to the spirit of the earliest, humanitarian sort of liberalism. Finally, in a few areas, both Western and Romanian Liberal parties, because of their strong class commitment and national loyalties, behaved in ways quite counter to any earlier version of liberalism. The passage on Western Liberal corruption quoted earlier also precisely describes the flavor of Romanian Liberal political life. The cavalier Romanian treatment of national minorities after 1918 and the NLP's consistent centralizing policies (embodied most strikingly in the 1923 constitution) also parallel directions taken by Western Liberal parties in the 1860s and 1870s.[46]

Of course, in all these matters there was a wide gradation of views and practices among Liberal parties, ranging from the quite close adherence to classical liberal views in highly industrialized, urban England and Belgium, through the looser, less precise interpretations in semi-developed Italy to the more extreme Eastern variations, as in Romania, where modernization was just beginning. The dates of the heyday of Liberalism vary also from the 1860s and 1870s in Britain[47] to the 1920s in Romania.

Yet is is essential that, through the welter of local interests and grievances, one not lose track of that underlying kinship of attitudes, desires, loyalties and programs, which made up "sectarian" Liberalism all over Europe.

VI. THE CRISIS OF LIBERALISM

The particulars varied across the continent but the pattern was similar everywhere. Self-interest, the prime mover in the liberal world view, had come to the fore, more or less blatantly, as the central tenent of Liberal Party ideology all over Europe and in its least edifying incarnation was responsible for a series of scandals implicating Liberal Party leaders in cases of political corruption. Defensive strategies had begun to take the place of assaults on the old order. As liberalism gained influence, it gained caution and inevitably compromised with reality. The fight against absolutism waned and the "golden mean," the "juste milieu," increasingly came to stand for an intense bourgeois struggle against the radical demands of the "have-nots." The growth of movements representing the underprivileged challenged the easy self-satisfaction into which liberalism had sunk in the eyes of many. In the West, the last two decades of the nineteenth century and the early twentieth century witnessed a marked decline of liberal influence and a splitting apart of some Liberal political parties. The same critical stage was also reached by Romanian liberalism, but not until the 1920s and 1930s.

Karl Polanyi graphically describes the reasons for which crisis grew out of the very nature of classical liberalism:

The middle classes were the bearers of the nascent market economy; their business interests ran, on the whole, parallel to the general interest in regard to production and employment; if business was flourishing, there was a chance of jobs for all and of rents for the owners; if markets were expanding, investments could be freely and readily made; if the trading community competed successfully with the foreigner, the currency was safe. On the other hand, the trading classes had no organ to sense the dangers involved in the exploitation of the physical strength of the worker, the destruction of forests, the pollution of rivers, the deterioration of craft standards, the disruption of folkways, and the general degradation of existence including houses and arts, as well as the innumerable forms of private and public life that do not affect profits. The middle classes fulfilled their function by developing an all but sacramental belief in

the universal beneficience of profits, although this disqualified them
as the keepers of other interests as vital to a good life as the further-
ance of production.[48]

In Western Europe feudal society had evolved gradually into bourgeois,
capitalist society, urban, industrialized, rapid in pace and technologically
advanced. The tensions leading to and caused by the political enfranchise-
ment of the masses followed in the wake of economic development. The
underprivileged groups who attacked time-honored liberal ideals were
mostly composed of urban workers and women. In most of Eastern Europe, however, an almost feudal society existed side-by-side with modernizing tendencies, multiplying social, economic and political troubles. In
countries like Romania, where the peasantry became a potential political
force *before* large-scale industrialization, the process of modernization
was confused and complicated, and the resulting ideological explanations
and rationalizations based on Western models became correspondingly
tortuous. The pre-war Liberal-Conservative debate in Romania on the
proper degree and kind of development was increasingly supplemented
by the insistent rumblings of emergent peasant spokesmen as well as by
the small but shrill clamor of the urban working classes. Thus, although
the fundamental liberal crisis and the attempts to resolve it show striking
similarities across the continent, the identity of the challengers to the liberal order varied between Romania and the West.

Whenever it occurred, the period of crisis gave rise to much theoretical redefinition, to searching for the "real" meaning of liberalism and
attempting to reconcile the idea of freedom with the perceived need of
the middling groups of society (always liberalism's major support) to
defend property, order and social stability.[49] In Western Europe Liberal
parties relented from their earlier stands against imperialism, worker
legislation, democratic suffrage and even government intervention to some
extent, but still they lost votes as the lower classes gained an increasing
vote, while the substantial burghers, who had always been the basic supporters and *raison d'être* of classical liberalism, began to see some of the
disadvantages, even to themselves, of a totally economic society and hence
began to desert the Liberal Parties.[50] By the 1920s Western European
liberalism had well passed its prime, while many of its former supporters
now adhered to the conservative parties of the revitalized right. In many
places (especially Germany) vast interlocking enterprises had formed and
were beginning to look more favorably on the possibilities of alliance with
the state. Because there was considerable political flexibility and a wide

distribution of power in the West, middle class entrepreneurs and professionals who questioned the premises of classical liberalism could forge alternative political allegiences. New or revitalized parties of the right grew up and were thought to be more capable of serving bourgeois interests than classical liberalism.[51] In the other direction, people of more democratic views, who would have been liberals fifty or a hundred years before, were now looking to the new labor-oriented parties.

As was usual in Eastern Europe, the telescoping of economic and industrial phenomena into a much shorter period of time than in the west had a vital effect on events and attitudes. The Romanian National Liberal Party scarcely had been challenged from below at all before the outbreak of World War I since political participation was strictly limited until the institution of universal manhood suffrage in 1918. But after the war in Romania the new mass parties, (the large Peasant and Transylvanian National and small Socialist parties) with their democratized and radicalized constituencies, did not hesitate to lump both of the traditional parties together as tools of the exploitative privileged classes. For the Conservatives this new opposition posed no particular ideological problem. For years they had been fighting a rear-guard action against all comers. One more enemy simply corroborated their beliefs about the pernicious and infectious nature of modern life. In any case they were fast fading away as a serious political force in parliament.[52]

The Liberals, on the other hand, used to thinking of themselves as the guardians of freedom and defenders of progress, were now being called to answer for behaving as just another wing of the ruling élite. With the postwar loss of the traditional right and the burgeoning of new, more egalitarian parties, the Liberal Party, though its own ideological position had scarcely changed, became the only viable defender of the old social-political order.[53] The chief ideological task for the National Liberals was therefore to create a new party image and a new interpretation of their party's role, both to attract new adherents among the masses and to reverse the outflow of intellectuals and prosperous peasants who were now deserting the NLP for the peasant-oriented views of the new parties. Although National Liberal Party dominance was re-established fairly quickly in the 1920s, party ideologues continued to feel much more keenly than ever before the need to articulate and justify the theoretical bases and underlying aims of Romanian liberalism producing the spate of writings on liberal philosophy in the 1920s.

The job of rationalizing Liberal Party actions and intentions was an exceedingly complicated one because the goals of Romanian liberals had always been contradictory and inconsistent: their assumptions (the sort of society they wanted and their view of human nature) were vintage Manchesterian liberal, but their methods (the casting-off of *laissez-faire* and tendency to use the political process for economic ends) were more akin to the doctrines for which classical liberalism was being deserted in the West. The justifications and rationalizations, which were engendered by the soul-searching attempts of Romanian liberals, can, therefore be divided into two main groups. Some authors like Ştefan Zeletin and Mihai Plătăreanu, tried to fit the liberal shoe to the Romanian foot. They attempted to demonstrate, with a certain amount of contortion, that the NLP really was true to the liberal heritage, but at least they were honest about who was served by their version of liberalism. Others, such as Mahai Manoilescu, chose to jettison classical liberalism in favor of a vague, corporatist "neo-liberalism" which purported to foster social harmony and the end of class warfare, while at the same time they supported policies which could only prove socially divisive.[54] By the mid-1930s, the Zeletin school of old-style liberals had been largely superceded by the neoliberals, and theoretical classical liberalism was for all intents and purposes dead in Romania.

The differences in developmental timing between Romania and the West have been mentioned repeatedly and it was this discrepancy which in the end was fatal to the hopes of Romanian classical liberalism. The smallness of the middle class and the economic backwardness of the country conspired, in spite of the wishful thinking of Zeletin and Co., to prevent bourgeois liberalism from being the agent of progress to transform Romania into a fully modern state.

The major flaw in the Romanian liberal position was that it could not point convincingly to the pre-existing productivity and service to society of the industrializing middle-class for the simple reason that the benefits of industrialization for Romanian society were in the future.[55] The bourgeois self-interest strain of classical liberalism, when not justified by the existence of a large middle class, became a mere defense of privilege, and traditional liberal freedoms were consequently sacrificed to the more selfish elements of "sectarian" liberalism. The opponents of liberalism in Romania could (and often did) argue that direct industrialization, led by the bourgeoisie, was fine for the West but highly inappropriate for an overwhelmingly agrarian country like Romania which ought to aim for an agriculture-based, peasant economy.[56] They could maintain, alternatively, that since the National Liberal Party already was far too powerful economically and politically for Romania's good, industrialization, when it takes place, must be directed by the presently dispossessed proletariat (and peasantry) whose energies still lie untapped beneath the yoke of oppression put on their shoulders by generations of self-seeking Liberals and Conservatives.[57] The crisis brought on by such challenges (which traveled faster than modernization) was then quickly reinforced by factional quarrels, the rise of fascism, depression, renewed Great Power meddling and war, and the NLP never got another opportunity to try to serve as the great positive factor which liberalism had been in the West.

FINAL REMARKS

The foregoing analysis has suggested several conclusions about liberalism and Romania.

First, by carefully comparing the Western and Romanian versions of liberalism one discovers that there are a number of uniquely liberal assumptions, aims, methods and class attitudes which Romanian liberal politicians did share, as indicated both by their theoretical writings and by the political-economic programs they attempted to implement.

Second, the corruption and narrow self-absorption which are such ubiquitous accompaniments of Romanian liberalism do not constitute sufficient evidence that Romanian liberalism was a mere sham. The Liberal Parties of many Western countries also vulgarized liberal theory and took advantage of a position of power in ways strikingly parallel to what happened in Romania. Yet no one suggests that theirs were not genuine forms of liberalism.

Third, certain characteristic positions taken by the Romanian NLP and its theorists appear to be fundamentally inconsistent with Western liberalism, theoretical or practical. Romanian liberals rejected *laissez-faire* and encouraged governmental intervention in the economy. It is probably for this reason, more than any other, that students of Eastern Europe have concluded that Romanian liberalism was nothing but a snare and a delusion from the beginning. This conclusion is too simplistic because a clear pattern can be discerned in the points at which Romania deviated from classical liberalism. Domestically, the Liberals supported state aid to industry because it argued that the Romanian economy was still too underdeveloped to engender, without government help, the capital necessary for rapid industrial growth (the classic infant industry argument). Externally, protectionism was invoked because in the international context Romania was among the "lower orders," not in the "bourgeoisie" of the nations, to which the developed nations of Western Europe belonged.

These points of deviation are of critical importance because they demonstrate that Romanian liberalism departed most significantly from classical liberalism not out of mere ignorance or cyncial self-interest, but because the classical *laissez-faire* method of achieving liberal goals would not work in the Romanian context. When a choice had to be made between liberal ends and liberal means the NLP chose what they perceived to be the former.

The most curious thing about Romanian liberalism was that it swallowed whole the market mentality, the notion of making everything, including land and labor, into saleable commodities, but it did *not* accept what Polanyi calls "the most startling peculiarity of the system . . . that, once it is established, it must be allowed to function without outside interference."[58] The key to the fundamental dilemma of Romanian liberalism lies in the phrase "once it is established."

As Kenneth Jowitt observes:

> . . . almost without exception Romanian intellectuals noted that Romanian economic development occurred under very different auspices than those that characterized nineteenth-century Western Europe. Romania, East Europe, and the rest of the non-Western world 'skipped' the nineteenth century in the sense that, unlike Western Europe, no revolutionary reversal [Polanyi's 'Great Transformation'] took place. Only in Western Europe—particularly in England—did a 'market society'—as opposed to a society with markets—come into existence.[59]

Because Romania was backward compared to Western Europe, her society and economic life, to which the NLP tried to apply liberal principles, had not reached that comparable stage of development at which classical liberalism appeared in the West. There was no real middle class; manufacturing was still in its cradle; the economy was distorted by the preponderance of foreign investors whose interests did not necessarily correspond with those of Romania. For these reasons the positive elements of classical liberalism—its energy, invention and interest in creating a freer society and more equitable distribution of power—were unable to operate effectively in Romania. The dangers of classical liberalism, on the other hand, its propensity to be preempted as the narrow and short-sighted program of one sector of society, could not be avoided. In reality these negative aspects were greatly accentuated by the small size of the minority to which classical liberalism could appeal in Romania and by the crucial fact that this minority achieved political dominance *before* instead of after it had earned its position through transformation of the soceity and economy.

The tragedy of Romanian liberalism was that the necessary conditions for its success simply did not exist. Its timing was wrong, its resources were inadequate, and its supporters were too few. Still, its leaders did not or would not see how decisive these obstacles were, and so deluded themselves into expecting what could only have been accomplished by a series of true economic miracles—events occurring in contradiction of objective facts. Yet, in spite of all these problems a real yearning for and attempt at liberalism did exist in Romania. The failures of Romanian liberalism were largely due to its inappropriateness to the context and limitations of classical liberal doctrine itself. National Liberal leaders were guilty of historical and cultural näiveté and selfishness, but their vision of the kind of urban, industrialized, "marketized" society they wanted and their fervent belief in the bourgeoisie as the agent of progress were a thoroughly classical liberal vision and belief.

NOTES

1.   The National Liberal Party began as the National Party in Wallachia and the Liberal Party in Moldavia. After unification of the Principalities the two coalesced into the group known as "Reds" which soon became known as the Liberal Party. The final change of title to National Liberal Party came after the 1907 revolt.

2.   Carlton J. H. Hayes, *A Generation of Materialism, 1871-1900* (New York, 1941), p. 72.

3.   L. S. Stavrianos, *The Balkans Since 1453* (New York, 1961), p. 483.

4.   Joseph Rothschild, *East Central Europe Between the Two World Wars* (Seattle and London, 1974), p. 293.

5.   See, for example, Mircea Iosa and Train Lungu, *Viaţa politică în România, 1899-1910* (Bucharest, 1977); Anastasie Iordache, *Viaţa politică în România, 1910-1914* (Bucharest, 1972); Mihai Rusenescu and Ion Saizu, *Viaţa politică în România, 1922-1928* (Bucharest, 1978); and Emilia and Gavrila Şonea, *Viaţa economică şi politică a României, 1933-1938* (Bucharest, 1978).

6.   Mircea Muşat and Ion Ardeleanu, *Viaţa politică în România, 1919-1921* (Bucharest, 1976), pp. 89-131.

7.   Henry L. Roberts, in *Rumania: Political Problems of an Agrarian State* (New Haven, 1951), is more aware than most of Romanian Liberalism's connections to Western liberalism when he writes:

> Although the National Liberal Party was pleased to trace its origins
> to the group of young Romanian intellectuals who had been inspired
> by the ideals of the French Revolution of 1848, the temper of the
> Brătianu Party in the early 1920s bore a far greater resemblance to
> the rigid and narrowly conceived liberalism of Guizot in the latter
> years of the July Monarchy,

p. 108. Even he does not explore the comparison in full detail, however.

8.   Bertrand Russell, *A History of Western Philosophy and Its Connection with Politics and Social Circumstances from the Earliest Times to the Present* (New York, 1945), p. 601. Similarly, his conclusion—that "this difference is one of the reasons why transplanted ideas are so seldom successful as they were on their native soil"—will be borne out fully in the conclusion of this paper.

9.   Ibid., p. 597.

10.   Sheldon S. Wolin, *Politics and Vision, Continuity and Innovation in Western Political Thought* (Boston, 1960), pp. 293-94.

11.   John Locke, *An Essay Concerning Human Understanding*. 2 Vols. (Oxford, 1894), Vol. I, p. xviii.

12.   Benjamin Franklin, *A Dissertation on Liberty and Necessity, Pleasure and Pain* (New York, 1930), pp. 16 and 20.

13.   Adam Smith, "Theory of Moral Sentiment," in *Works*, 6th edit. (London, 1812), Vol. I, pp. 208-9.

14.   S. Wolin, op. cit., p. 332.

15.   Jeremy Bentham, *Handbook of Political Fallacies*, p. 213, cited by ibid.

16.   H. K. Girvetz, *The Evolution of Liberalism* (New York, 1963), p. 27.

17.   Adam Smith, *An Inquiry Into Nature and Causes of the Wealth of Nations* (New York, 1937), p. 13.

18.   Jeremy Bentham, *An Introduction to the Principles of Morals and Legislation* (Oxford, 1907), p. 3.

19.   John Locke, op. cit., II, p. xxi.

20.   A. Smith, op. cit., p. 423.

21.   John Locke, *Essays on the Law of Nature* (Oxford, 1954), p. 211.

22.   For comparative analyses of liberalism in Western Europe, see: J. Collins, *Liberalism in Nineteenth Century Europe* (London, 1957); R. D. Cummings, *Human Nature and History: A Study of the Development of Liberal Political Thought*. 2 Vols. (Chicago, 1969); Theodore Meyer Greene, *Liberalism, Its Theory and Practice* (Austin, 1957); David Harris, "European Liberalism in the Nineteenth Century," *American Historical Review*, 60, 1955, No. 3: 501-26; H. J. Laski, *The Rise of Liberalism, The*

Philosophy of a Business Civilization (New York, 1936); Guido de Ruggiero, *The History of European Liberalism* (Oxford, 1927); J. S. Schapiro, *Liberalism and the Challenge of Fascism: Social Forces in England and France, 1515-1880* (New York, 1949) and *Liberalism, Its Meaning and History* (New York, 1958); and F. Watkins, *The Political Tradition of the West: A Study in the Development of Modern Liberalism* (Cambridge, Mass., 1948).

23.   Carlton J. Hayes, *A Generation of Materialism, 1871-1900* (New York, 1963), p. 49.

24.   For discussions of liberalism in particular countries, see, for England: Crane Briton, *English Political Thought in the Nineteenth Century* (New York, 1931); Elie Halévy, *The Growth of Philosophical Radicalism* (New York, 1928); H. J. Laski, *Political Thought in England from Locke to Bentham* (London, 1920); J. Plamenatz, *The English Utilitarians* (Oxford, 1949); for France: Kingseley Martin, *The Rise of French Liberal Thought: A Study of Political Ideals from Bayle to Condorcet* (New York, 1964); J. P. Mayer, *Political Thought in France from Sieyes to Sorel* (London, 1943); Roger H. Soltau, *French Political Thought in the Nineteenth Century* (New Haven, 1931); for Germany: L. Krieger, *The German Idea of Freedom* (New York, 1957); F. Frederici, *Der deutsche Liberalismus: Die Entwicklung einer politischen Idee von I. Kant bis T. Mann* (Zurich, 1946); F. C. Sell, *Die Tragödie des Deutschen Liberalismus* (Stuttgart, 1953); R. H. Thomas, *Liberalism, Nationalism and the German Intellectuals* (Cambridge, 1952); for Italy: K. R. Greefield, *Economics and Liberalism in the Risorgimento, 1814-48* (Baltimore, 1934); C. Marandi, *I partiti politici nella storia d'Italia* (Florence, 1965); and L. Salvatorelli, *Pensiero politico Italiano, 1700-1870* (Turin, 1943).

25.   C. J. H. Hayes, op. cit., pp. 79-80. This passage reads like nothing so much as a precise description of life under the National Liberals in Romania.

26.   Because of the challenge to Romanian Liberal power in the 1920s, that period is the most prolific in ideological tracts. Among Liberal writers Ştefan Zeletin, *Burghezia română, originea şi rolul ei istorice* (Bucharest, 1925) and *Neoliberalism: Studii asupra istoriei şi politicii burgheziei române* (Bucharest, 1927) was one of the few who openly argued theoretically in justification of dominance by the sort of bourgeois oligarchy whose interests NLP policies in fact consistently supported, hence the space is devoted to him here. Some Liberal supporters, such as Mihai Plătăreanu, *Politica economică şi socială a României în trecutul şi în cadrul legislaţiei actuale* (Bucharest, n.d., probably 1930) explicityly adopted Zeletin's point of view without themselves discussing Liberal theory at any

length. Others, such as D. Draghicescu, *Partidele politice și classie sociale* (Bucharest, 1922) militated for a truly democratic program, in the tradition of old-fashioned idealistic liberals Mihai Kogălniceanu, C. A. Rosetti and Spiru Haret, as the only means for the NLP to maintain its preeminence in Romanian political life. Finally, writers such as I. G. Duca, "Doctrina liberală" in *Doctrinele partidelor politice* (Bucharest, n.d.), pp. 103-110 and numerous articles in NLP journals; Mihai Manoilescu, *Neoliberalismul* (Bucharest, 1923) and "Neoliberalismul" in *Doctrinele partidelor politice*, pp. 143-161; and P. P. Negulescu *Partidele politice* (Bucharest, 1926) tried to formulate a new sort of liberalism to deal with the ideological crisis of post-World War I Romanian liberalism.

27.   It is the continual association with the characteristics of Western liberalism which demarcates the ideas and policies of the party of Romanian liberalism from those of the other parties in Romania throughout the history of Romanian liberalism. The NLP's fascination with industrialization separated it definitively from the Conservative, Peasant and Transylvanian parties, and even from Averescu's People's League (later Party) which often acted as a Liberal surrogate, but was stocked with erstwhile Conservative landowners. The Socialists were in favor of industrialization, but of course had the opposite class orientation.

28.   Where a party of more totalitarian leanings would not have hesitated to use force and even to overthrow the parliamentary system entirely, the old style Romanian Liberals sought other methods of getting their own way. Even in the 1920s and early 1930s, instead of forming subversive paramilitary groups or rousing the army, NLP leaders used their considerable influence with the king and arued their case in parliament and in the press. They differed fundamentally in this approach from Russian revolutionaries, Italian fascists and members of many parties in Romania and elsewhere.

29.   "On Conciliation," in *The Works of the Right Honourable Edmund Burke* (London, 1854), I, p. 464.

30.   See Cornelia Bodea, *Lupta românilor pentru unitatea națională, 1834-1839*, (Bucharest, 1967), pp. 111-130 and 141-152, and Appendices. Paris was, in particular, the major source of new ideas about the rights of nationalities. In Paris too, young Romanian patriots learned to associate liberal nationalism with the desire for economic development and the creation of a responsible middle class capable of governing in the modern spirit.

31.   NLP theoretists tried to justify their exclusive nationalism by attacking internationalism, maintaining that "by failing to account for the specific characteristics of each nation, by the theoretical leveling of

the races with their distant mentalities and traditions, it impedes true progress." I. G. Duca, op. cit., p. 105.

32.   See p. 000, above.

33.   David Mitrany, *The Land and the Peasant in Romania* (London, 1930), p. 447.

34.   Preliminary data I have collected for a study of the economic and educational background of National Party members indicate that the usual assumption that Liberals were educated in France and Conservatives in Germany will be borne out by more detailed evidence. See, for example, George Nicolescu, *Parlamentul român* (Bucharest, 1903), and the biographical sketches in *Politics and Political Parties in Rumania* (London, 1936).

35.   Constantin Argetoianu, "Pentru cei de mîine, Amintiri din vremea celor de ieri," manuscript in *Arhiva Comitetului Central al Partidul Comunist Român*, pp. 734 and 857; cited in M. Mușat and I. Ardeleanu, op. cit., p. 92.

36.   M. Mușat and I. Ardeleanu, op. cit., p. 90.

37.   A constant theme of NLP parliamentary speeches and such party organs as the newspaper *Viitorul* and the periodical *Democrația* is the fitness of the Romanian middle class, as represented by the National Liberal Party, to protect the welfare of Romanian society as a whole. Party programs from the 1880s through the 1930s strike the same theme.

38.   H. L. Roberts, *Rumania, The Political Problems of an Agrarian State* (New Haven, 1951), p. 114.

39.   Mihai Plătăreanu, op. cit., p. 16.

40.   Mihai Manoilescu, *Theorie du protectionisme* (Paris, 1929); cited in ibid., pp. 16-17. See also, I. N. Angelescu, "Increase of Production and its Influence on the National Currency of Romania," *Correspondance economique romaine* (Jan.-Feb., 1924).

41.   This was scarcely surprising as the ties between government, the NLP and Romanian financiers and entrepreneurs were intricate and pervasive. See Al. Gh. Savu, *Sistemul partidelor politice din România, 1919-1940* (Bucharest, 1976) for documentation of some of these connections.

42.   R. W. Seton-Watson, *A History of the Romanians from Roman Times to the Completion of Unity* (London, 1934), p. 355.

43.   The long and debilitating debate between the old-style parliamentarian Liberals (bătrînii, led by Constantin Brătianu after the death of I. G. Duca and Ion I. C. (Ionel) and Vintilă Brătianu) and the new authoritarian-minded faction allied with King Carol II (tinerii—under Gheorghe Tătărascu) spelled the end of the sense of limitations in Romanian Liberal politics. See Emilia and Gavrila Șonea, op. cit., and ibid.

44. See the small pamphlets of party programs published every few years which are currently kept at the Biblioteca Academiei Republicii Socialişte Române, Bucharest.

45. Prefects' reports (available in the Ministerul de Interne section of the Arhiva Centrală de Stat Bucureşti); the formal protests of members of parliament registered with the Minister de Interne and in the *Dezbateriile parlementare Adunării Deputatilori* opposition newspaper articles; and periodic reports in Western papers such as the *Manchester Guardian* provide a myriad of examples of how the NLP ran roughshod over its opponents, when it was in power. The tradition, though certainly not in the original spirit of liberalism, was a very old one in Romania and was followed to some degree by every governmental party.

46. See pp. 000, above.

47. Even in England, however, as the century passed, "laws limiting the free use of property and the free right of contract multiplied at an increasing rate, principally in connection with factory legislation." Robert C. Binkley, *Realism and Nationalism, 1852-1871* (New York, 1935), p. 39.

48. K. Polanyi, *The Great Transformation* (New York, 1965), p. 133.

49. The account of the crisis of liberalism in Western Europe by Guido de Ruggiero, op. cit., pp. 417-433, though published in 1927, is still very clear.

50. See George Dangerfield, *The Strange Death of Liberal England, 1910-1914* (London, 1935) and Michael Bentley, *The Liberal Mind 1914-1929* (Cambridge, England, 1979) for the decline of the English Liberal Party.

51. Charles S. Maier, *Recasting Bourgeois Europe, Stabilization in France, Germany, and Italy in the Decade After World War I* (Princeton, 1975) is an extremely thorough and well-written study of the new direction taken in bourgeois self-defense after World War I in France, England and Germany.

52. There has been no separate study of the decline of conservatism in Romania after World War I. David Mitrany, however, includes valuable information on the effects of the wealthy agrarian class, the land reforms, in his *Land and Peasant in Roumania*, while Muşat and Ardeleanu, op. cit., devote a chapter to the two Conservative party branches and make some useful contributions to our knowledge of what, politically, happened to former Conservatives.

53. Averescu's People's Party, as suggested earlier, was the haven of disaffected Conservatives, but the General was not politically astute enough to marshal the disaffected middling groups of Romanian society

nor strong enough simply to dispense with parliamentary government as Carol II did in 1938.

54.   See I. G. Duca, op. cit., and Mihai Manoilescu, *Neoliberalism*.

55.   Liberal insistence that the NLP had been the first to call for universal manhood suffrage and extensive land redistribution did not much impress the peasants, who supported, largely, the new Peasant Party which was naturally prepared to go much further than the NLP in instituting a real peasant democracy.

56.   See, V. Madgearu, writings of the principle Peasant Party theorist, *Doctrina țărănistă* (Bucharest, 1923); *Evoluția economiei românești după războiul mondial* (Bucharest, 1940); and *Țărănism* (Bucharest, n.d.).

57.   For the views of Romanian socialists, see, for example: Lucrețiu Pătrășcanu, *Problemele de baza ale României* (Bucharest, 1974); Serban Voinea, *Marxism oligarhic* (Bucharest, 1926); and C. Dobrogeanu-Gherea, *Neoiobagia* (Bucharest, 1910).

58.   K. Polanyi, op. cit.,

59.   Kenneth Jowitt, "The Sociocultural Bases of National Dependency in Peasant Countries," in *Social Change in Romania, 1880-1940: A Debate on Development in a European Nation* (Berkeley, 1978), p. 18.

Paul Cernovodcanu

CONSTANTIN C. GIURESCU, PROMOTER OF ROMANIAN-
AMERICAN SCIENTIFIC AND CULTURAL RELATIONS

The celebrated "poly-historian" Constantin C. Giurescu, author of an important synthesis of the history of the Romanians and of countless works that tackle a great variety of subjects opening up new trends in research, also came out as an active promoter of scientific and cultural relations between Romania and the United States of America during the last decade of his life.

The historian's ties with United States scientists dated back to the period preceding World War II; when the first volume of his *History of the Romanians* appeared in 1935 and 1937, it was also sent to some American universities and a eulogious review[1] was published by the well-known Professor Charles Upson Clark (1875-1960), who had a extensive knowledge of our past history and had been an honory member of the Romanian Academy since 1923.[2] Later Professor Giurescu met the American historian during the latter's visit to Romania in the spring of 1940, when he arranged for him to deliver lectures in the towns of Iaşi, Cluj and Timişoara. Subsequently, the two historians kept up a correspondence.[3]

After more than two decades, the Romanian historian resumed his friendly relations with his American colleagues, though the latter were of a younger generation this time. Thus, as of 1964, after the political and economic relations between Romania and the United States had improved, with beneficial effects also on culture and science, our country was successively visited by a number of professors from the United States who came over for documentation and resarch into the history of Southeastern Europe. Aware of the prestige Professor Giurescu enjoyed among Romanian historians, they got in touch with him. From among them, we will mention in the first place Professor Peter F. Sugar of Washington University in Seattle, Charles and Barbara Jelavich, both professors at Indiana Univesity in Bloomington, and finally Radu Florescu and Raymond McNally, professors at Boston College. The subjects tacked by the

303

Romanian historian with his American friends were many and varied. They illustrated the wide range of their interest, which went from Balkan history to the Dracula myth—a literary misrepresentation of the personality of the gallant Voivode Vlad the Impaler—the American scientists being informed of the achievements scored in Romanian historiography after World War II. The foundations were thus laid for closer cooperation between the historians of the two countries, and after the mutual summit visits in 1969-1970 and the agreements subsequently concluded, a Romanian library was opened in New York City and an American one in Bucharest, and regulations were agreed upon in order to ensure mutual social-economic documentation visits, which were handled by the International Research and Exchanges Board (IREX) in the United States and by the Ministry of Education and the Academy of Social and Political Sciences in Romania. Already in 1968, on the initiative of Radu Florescu, American professor of Romanian origin, C. C. Giurescu was invited to deliver lectures on Romanian history in a number of American university centers. From September 30 to November 3 that year, the Romanian scholar was the guest of ten institutions of higher education,[4] where he successively lectured on Transylvania's importance in the history of our people[5] and on the completion of Romania's state unity,[6] and to satisfy the curiosity of the public at large, he outlined the real personality of Dracula, i.e., Vlad the Impalter, a Wallachian voivode of note.[7] The journey was for Professor C. C. Giurescu an opportunity to extend his contacts with the American scientific world[8] and also to spread sound information on Romanian history among United States professors and students, rousing the interest of many of his listeners in the study of the Balkan area and of our country.[9] At the same time, as from 1968 Professor Giurescu established close connections with some of the outstanding representatives of the Romanian groups in the United States, scattered over various cities, thereby helping to maintain spiritual and affective ties with their country of origin.[10] For the Romanian public the fruitful results of Professor Giurescu's first visit to America after World War II, materialized in the publication of a travel diary in 1971.[11] The diary, which was a best-seller at the time, aroused great interest, the broad masses of readers thus became acquainted not only with Professor Giurescu's activities in the United States, but also with the facts of contemporary American life as seen by the Romanian scholar.

The favorable results of the 1968 visit prompted the American university circles to ask Professor Giurescu to visit them again. In consequence, in 1972, he was again invited to the United States, this time by

Professor Istvan Deak, in the early months of the academic year, as visiting professor and holder of the *Nicolae Iorga* chair, recently created at Columbia University in New York City, to lecture on Romanian history and civilization. On the occasion, the Romanian historian not only came into direct contact with the teaching activities of American establishments of higher education, but also extended his ties with the American faculty,[12] at the same time attending numerous scientific events which were then taking place at the university centers in Dallas, Urbana-Champaign, Chicago, Detroit and Seattle. The opening lecture at Columbia University,[13] published in New York City in 1972 by the Romanian Library, is the first printed work Professor Giurescu devoted to the relations between the two countries; furthermore, it is an important contribution to historical research, being considered by experts as a work of reference. The author starts with the earliest intellectual contacts and the first translations of American classics into Romanian, and proceeds with his analysis to the contemporary period, giving a most suggestive picture of the significance and scope of those relations in our century and more particularly during the last decade.

During the years that followed, personal contacts with American scholars and the post-graduate students who came to Romania to prepare their theses on Romanian history, continued in Bucharest and also abroad on the occasion of the international congresses and symposia. Professor Giurescu fostered the activities of the American Library in Bucharest, where he delivered a number of lectures,[14] and encouraged his colleagues and younger researchers whenever they showed an inclination for American history.[15]

In 1975 the Romanian scholar, who had become a member of the Academy the previous year (1974), again went to the United States on two occasions: in May, as a guest of Harvard, Brown and Boston universities, to attend a seminar on "The Evolution of the Peasantry in Eastern and Southeastern Europe" initiated by Professor Albert B. Lord (Harvard), where his paper on "The Evolution of the Romanian Peasantry from the XIII to the XX Century" was a great success; the second time was in August, as an outstanding member of the delegation of Romanian historians attending the XIV International Congress of Historical Sciences held at San Francisco. Here Professor Giurescu submitted a report on "Nomadic Populations in the Euro-Asian Area and the Party they Played in the Formation of Medieval States,"[16] after which, at Section III (History by Chronological Periods, subdivision "Europe and the U.S.A.") he read a summary of his paper on the "Influence of the New World in the

Field of Economy."[17] This was the second inroad of the Romanian historian into Romanian-American relations in the past, this time viewed from an economic perspective.

For the American people 1976 was a jubilee year for they commemorated the bicentenary of the American Revolution and their independence. Romania was the only socialist country to attend the special session of lectures that was devoted to this event in the United States. A delegation of historians headed by Professor Giurescu represented Romania at the symposium on "Independence Movements" held at Wayne State University in Detroit in June 1976 on the initiattive of Professor Richard V. Burks. The Romanian historian submitted two greatly appreciated papers, dealing with subjects of great importance in our national history, namely "Romania's National Independence—A Result of the Will and Fight of the Romanian People" and "The Creation of the Unitary Romanian National State as a Premise of the Developments of the Romanian Nation and of the Utilization of its Material and Spiritual Resources," laying stress on the struggle of our people for the preservation of the political entity of the Romanian states during the Middle Ages and at the outset of the modern period. The second stage of the journey took place at the University of Colorado in Boulder, where the debates of the second symposium of Romanian-American history were held under the aegis of Professor Stephen Fischer-Galați.[18] At this prestigious scientific event Professor Giurescu again submitted the papers mentioned above, which were given as warm a reception as at Detroit. In 1976, the Romanian historian attended the session organized by the Academy of the Socialist Republic of Romania in Bucharest on July 12-13, to commemorate the bicentenary of the American Revolution. The guests included Professors Richard V. Burks, Radu Florescu, Kemal Karpat and Walter C. Bacon.

In September of that year, Professor Giurescu published the second edition of his Travel Diary, to which had been added an account of the visits he had paid in the United States in 1972, 1975 and 1976. The book came out in the spring of the following year[19] and aroused as much interest as the first edition.

The Romanian historian last visited the United States from March 30 to April 21, 1977, when he headed a delegation to the event staged there to celebrate Romania's independence—a courteous response to the attention given by the Romanian colleagues to the bicentenary of the American Revolution. Scientific events were then organized at Columbia and Northeastern universities as well as at the Romanian Library (New York), and also at the following universities: Rutgers, Rochester, Ohio State, Wayne State, Oregon and Washington. On the occasion Professor Giurescu read the following papers: "The Nature of the Romanian State. Sidelights on its Unity" and "Historical Origins of Cooperation in Southeastern Europe," both of which enjoyed a well-deserved success. At Columbus (Ohio) the Romanian delegation was given an impressive document signed by the Governor of the state and with the latter's seal imprinted on it, laying stress on the significance of Romania's independence, on the "unique role" our country has played in the world and also on its endeavour to achieve cultural, economic and political independence. A similar document was handed to the delegation of Romanian historians in Detroit. Here the document was signed by George E. Gullien, Jr., President of the University.[20]

The six journeys made to the United States for scientific purposes during a nine-year interval in the course of which Professor Giurescu read numerous papers and took part in various sessions organized in American university centers from the Atlantic to the Pacific coasts; the many contacts he established with overseas colleagues and with a number of representatives of the Romanian groups in the United States; the impulse he gave to the development of scientific and cultural ties as well as of the traditional friendship between the peoples of the two countries, make of him the most prestigious and at the same time the most dynamic promoter of Romanian-American relations to date.

Over and above his historical works, his lectures and the other activities designed to foster friendship between Romania and the United States, Professor Giurescu has left a priceless travel diary where, by means of day to day notes, he has outlined some of the significant features of the very complex American world. The author gave therein not only pertinent appreciations of the general political, economic and social situation in the United States, but also a vivid and picturesque description of the everyday life of the man in the street, his eye ranging from important state problems to the minor details of everyday, apparently nondescript, facts. Special attention should be given to his suggestively described impressions of the Amerian population centers, from the great metropolises to the humble habitations in Indian reservations. The diary at the same time show the remarkable scientific activities carried on by the author in American university centers, and his contacts with historians, students and post-graduate students, moreover reflecting the special attention he was giving to the Romanian-American groups in the United States, which he considered as an essential factor in the promotion of spiritual links between Romania and the United States.

When reading, even cursorily, a few pages of Professor Giurescu's Travel Diary, one becomes sharply aware of the endeavors of the Romanian historian to understand the American world and to depict Romanian realities to American audiences, untiringly militating for a rapprochement between the two peoples. For which reason, even though it may actually come under the head of fiction, the diary carries great weight among Professor Giurescu's works, for it faithfully illustrates the efforts he made in the promotion of Romanian-American scienfitic and cultural relations, which should rely on mutual respect and consideration.

We will quote here the author's profession of faith as made in the Foreword: "It seems to me . . . that to endeavor to show what I have seen in that overseas country, might be useful, as a contribution to improving the Romanians' knowledge of the most important industrial country in the world . . . I am writing as a scientist would; I am neither an apologist of the United States nor a critic at any cost, as the case is, unfortunately, with some of those who visited and judged that country with preconceived ideas. I will show the bright aspects—because there are such aspects in numbers; and I will also show the unfavorable aspects because, as in every nation, whether big or small, there are also dark and semi-dark spots. I will endeavor to show them all *sine ira et studio*, according to Tacitus' old-time formula. But what I can say from the very beginning is that the bright spots are more numerous than the dark ones, for otherwise the extraordinary development of this nation and the part it now plays in the world would be unaccountable."[21]

A visit to George Washington's home at Mount Vernon bringing to Professor Giurescu's mind the birth of the American nation, he points out in his Diary: "The American War of Independence was fought by farmers, craftsmen and tradesmen of town and village; and it was fought against heavy odds for England's regular armies were well armed and well equipped. And the Constitution issued on 4 July 1776, prior to the French Revolution, was the first solemn written statement to the effect that *'all men are endowed . . . with certain inalienable rights, that among these are life, liberty and the pursuit of happiness.'* The significance of this document, on which the democratic regime relies and which marks a decisive moment in mankind's history, cannot be overstressed."[22]

It was only natural that Professor Giurescu, in his capacity as historian, should be struck by the interest the Americans took in history. After his visits to American universities and colleges, and following the contacts he made there, he noted that "all over the United States, there was *growing interest in history*, in the local American past to begin with, but also

in the past of Europe and even of the whole world. It is undoubtedly a
sign of maturity; the young American nation, for it is young compared
with the nations of Europe, is becoming increasingly *aware of its personality*, of the many springs nurturing it and at the same time of its
responsibilities in world history. For after a stage during which the nation
was built up and was consolidated—a stage which lasted up to World
War I and which is bound up with the Monroe Doctrine (December 1823),
a doctrine advocating that American interests should be confined to the
Western hemisphere, with its effects continuing to make themselves felt
even after that War, as proved by the American Senate's disapproving
President Woodrow Wilson when he made the League of Nations Pact—
a second stage followed during which the United States asserted itself
throughout the world."[23] The author further asks himself what are the
characteristic factors during the world-wide stage of United States policy,
more particularly after 1945, and seeks to answer the question, even
though "there is not yet enough *remoteness in time*, enough *perspective*
for the guiding lines, the causes and effects to become apparent." In his
political estimations the Romanian historian considers the basic element
of the present world-wide stage of American policy to be "*the concern to
find outlets for the products of its industry*, which takes first place in the
world in terms of quantity as well as of technique—an ever more advanced
technique. American life *centers* on industry, giving, whether directly or
indirectly, the means of existence to the majority of the population; commerce is closely bound up with it, and so is the network of railway, naval
and air communications, and also that part of higher education which
assumes the form of scientific and technical research institutions. . . . As
. . . American life centers on industry, which is its representative element,
it is obvious that the sale of industrial products is its number one problem.
. . . The negotiations carried on in recent times with partners in Europe
and outside Europe are aimed at ensuring maximum freedom in the goods
movement and removal or lowering of the customs barriers impeding the
movement. On the other hand, American industry relies on the "free
enterprise" principle, on competition, which, in theory as well as in practice, is part of the American "way of life" and which accounts for the remarkable development of industry. It is consequently no exaggeration to
state that, in the last analysis the present world-wide stage in United States
policy is guided by the will to promote the spreading of the American
"way of life" for the purpose of providing a maximum number of outlets
for the products of American industry. Whatever goes counter to the
American way of life, which relies on an industry based on the principles

underlying the American way of life, is for the typically American citizen a real or potential danger against which, as he appreciates, measures of defense and control should be taken."

According to Professor Giurescu this accounts for the weight given to the military-industrial complex in the United States during the last decades; for the military service becoming compulsory in a country where it has for long been usual to recruit only volunteers for the army; and finally for the widespread military bases the world over. As seen by the Romanian scholar, all the above elements are designed "to promote the development of American industry and the introduction of American products in the greatest number of markets." The author, however, admits that this is but a sketchy explanation for "reality more complex," other factors, to his mind, "of lesser importance,"[24] bolstering the essential one. For example, he does not dwell on the rivalry and competition between the great powers and on the impact of the various ideologies on the conditions prevailing at present in the world and in the United States.

The social problems that confronted the United States in the 1960s and the 1970s did not go unobserved by the Romanian scholar, nor did the part played by the "hippies" in contesting the traditional values of American society. A considerable part of public opinion—more particularly the intelligentsia and the youth—was affected by "the Vietnamese syndrome," and the "violence climate" had reaching alarming, nationwide proportions. Professor Giurescu in his capacity as historian, endeavors to examine and at least partially to account for the causes of the traumas that affected the United States during the last decade. Dealing for example, with the disturbances prevalent among students, he intuitively sensed that the unrest had "more complex foundations than the material and vocational claims they made. There is no denying," Professor Giurescu goes on to say, "that some of the university regulations are old-fashioned and should be updated, that the scholarship and the loan systems could be improved and extended; it is furthermore beyond question that the war in Vietnam, whereby death walked into more than 30,000 American homes, was one more reason for unrest; the war raises professional problems for the young people, who instead of seeking employment after graduation, are enlisted and, after training for a time, are sent to the battlefield. It is also unquestionable that black students with good reason demand that due attention be given to the problems specific to the black population. But there seems to be something that goes beyond these demands: part of the youth calls in question the contemporary way of life the way of life of the consumption society, the rush for profit, the nerve-racking rush of everyday life which induces neurosis. This is "the great refusal" Professor Herbert Marcuse of San Diego University speaks about. This is how concepts at the opposite pole cropped up, and the "hippies" put in an appearance, leading a contemplative life, disdaining work, adorning themselves with flowers and living on alms." But Professor Giurescu realized that the "hippies" were a transient phenomenon, and indeed it is obsolete today—a crisis in the consciousness of the youth of the 1960s, who have now reached maturity. The author of the Diary concludes that "advancing in age and having to earn their living, the hippies are likely to change their minds. When work is not performed reluctantly and is not excessive, when it is creative, it is the central element of life, making for balance and a sound body and mind."[25]

Pointing to the existence of a "climate of violence," more conspicuous in the United States than elsewhere, the Romanian historian sought to account for it. He considered that "several elements should be taken into account. In the first place, the westward drive and the occupation of the whole continent from the Atlantic to the Pacific occasioned much fighting with the native population, the Indians; it was a ferocious fight of extermination which could also be accounted for by the cruel treatment inflicted on the prisoners by the Indians. As they made their way westward, the settlers—men and women, boys and girls—were armed and were able to use a gun. Weapons—rifles and also, quite frequently, pistols and revolvers—were the inseparable companions of the gold seekers in California, in the Rockies and in Alaska; of the cattle breeders on the out-of-the-way ranches; of the farmers whose house was in the center or on the border of their allotment, hundreds of yards and sometimes miles away from the nearest habitation." Professor Giurescu then reverts to present-day facts and observes that "according to data collected by research institutions, about three million firearms of every type are being sold annually in the United States. With the frame of mind now prevailing, it would be impossible to forbid the sale of such arms, as has lately been suggested; controlling measures have however been taken, though of limited scope. The prevalance of fire-arms partly accounts for the climate of violence. . . . The third reason, especially as far as young people, school children and undergradutes are concerned, lies, as I think, in the very great publicity made of scenes of violence. . . by means of motion pictures, T.V. shows and the radio." To the aforementioned reasons the author of the diary adds the existence of gangs of criminals, of the shiftless black youths, more particularly from among the unemployed. And he concludes: "All these elements put together, plus the age-old will to get on in life, inherent in man, which here assumes more flagrant forms and which went unchecked by scruples in the 19th century, account, as I think, for the climate of violence."[26] Nevertheless the Romanian historian soon makes a qualification so as not to leave the impression that America is the paradise of delinquency. He adds that "there should be no exaggeration. The overwhelming majority of the American population sides with public order and the law, yearning for a climate of lawfulness, in the shelter which allows them to lead a quiet life and look after their affairs. They do not want war; they make war only if it can't be helped. . . . They have no propensity for war as a means of settling international disputes. The Americans are first and foremost a people of industrialists, merchants and farmers and show a preference for the methods used *in these pursuits*, that is negotiations, compromise and arrangements, and not military methods."[27] It was in estimating the relations between the United States and China at the time he wrote the Diary (1968), relations that had been "frozen" as a result of the cold war, that Professor Giurescu showed the remarkable intuition of an investigator of politics. He then stated that "for American industry the 750 million Chinese may build up a first rate market while for the Chinese an understanding with the United States, China holding the place due to her at the United Nations, would mean full recognition of her status as a great world power and freedom of action in working for her own purposes in Asia. This, to me, is logical and would, as I see it, lead to an understanding between the two great powers on the two sides of the Pacific. It is true I have taken into account economic considerations only and not political ones as well. But so great is mankind's yearning for a lasting peace enabling it to lead a quiet life without any fear for the morrow that politics might at long last yield to economic factors and to the popular feeling. Is this a dream? A scholar's ideal? History has shown that what is today an ideal is tomorrow's reality."[28] And indeed Professor Giurescu's premonition was correct for today we can see that the relations between the United States and the People's Republic of China had been brought back to normal.

There are in the Diary of the Romanian historian a number of interesting appreciations of a general nature such as, for example, the part to be played by women (p. 132-133); the problem of racial integration of the colored population (p. 135-140); of the American Indians (p. 166-167) and of the assimilation of foreign immigrants. Concerning the latter process, Professor Giuresuc wrote: "This huge 'melting pot'—for this is the suggesting phrase that described American society—quickly assimilates by its civilization and culture, and its way of life the various ethnical elements that settles here. In the second generation, the third at most, all these elements are assimilated; the children and grandchildren of the immigrants can hold the most exalted positions. . . in the American economy, administration and cultural life, and feel proud to belong to the American nation."[29]

As was only natural, in his Diary the Romanian scholar devotes a fairly extensive space to the Romanians established in the United States, giving particulars about their life and pursuits, their cultural activities, church organization, etc. (p. 220-230). Professor Giurescu tells us that the most important centers of Romanian immigrants are to be found in Detroit and in the satellite town of Dearborn in Michigan, with 10 to 12,000 families of Romanian Americans; next came Cleveland, Boston, Cincinnati, New York, St. Paul and, in smaller numbers, some cities in the states of Wisconsin, Nebraska, Indiana, Florida, Illinois, North Carolina, Pennsylvania and Washington. The greatest number are settled in the states of Michigan and Ohio, most of them descending from the emigrants that came from Transylvania at the time when that province was under the domination of the Austro-Hungarian monarchy; they had left their native land "because of the hard life they led. . . in poverty and oppression." After an unpretentious beginning as factory workers or farmers, "by dint of assiduous work and economy, they gradually rose to a higher station, with houses, stores or workshops of their own, and today not a few of the descendants of the immigrants of two generations ago have handsome positions not only financially speaking but also with a name in the educational system among the professional classes, as teachers, engineers, physicians, lawyers, etc."[30] The author furthermore observes American customs and the cultural traditions inherited from the past generations as well as the reactions to shows and festivals. He took interest in the cultural associations initiated by the U. S. Romanians in order to forge closer links between Romania and the United States; mention is thus made of the American-Romanian Research Institute set up at McKeesport (not far from Pittsburgh) in February 1968, with John Halmaghi of the Pittsburgh University Library as director and George Rusu, a clergyman, as secretary, and of the American-Romanian Cultural Foundation created in the summer of 1976 on the initiative of Barbu Niculescu, a New York lawyer.

As was to be expected, most of the Diary deals with life in the United States universities and with the cultural centers he had visited, with particulars concerning their organization and activities, the professors and students, the organization of libraries and the works dealing with the history of Romania and of Southeastern Europe they possess, etc. There are entire paragraphs recording the professor's participation in various scientific events, congresses, and symposia, the lectures he then delivered, and the papers he read, with stress laid on his contacts with his American colleagues. The Romanian professor shows his great satisfaction with the hospitality and warm reception given him when invited by American historians, the names of various professors—Radu Florescu, Stephen Fischer-Galaţi, Istvan Deak, Peter Sugar, Robert Burke, Richard V. Burks, Frederick Kellogg, Albert Lord, John Campbell, Keith Hitchins and others—occurring repeatedly, with flattering remarks throughout the Diary. Finally, part of his daily notes are devoted to his moments of diversion—visits to various places, to museums, to public monuments and institutions, to beauty spots, parks and the like. There are suggestive pictures and impressions of Boston, Washington, New York, Pittsburgh, Dallas, Chicago, Detroit, San Francisco and Los Angeles, and also of smaller places such as Urbana-Champaign (Ill.), Cohassett (Mass.), Boulder (Col.), Santa Barbara (Cal.), Sedona and Flagstaff (Ariz.), to name a few.

As the author observes in a chapter of his Diary, "it is very difficult for anyone to imagine the complexity and variety of the physical structure of the immense country which is the United States of America, where all forms of imaginable geographical features can be met, from the widespread sun-drenched southern beaches to the tall mountain peaks above the snow- and ice-line, from the black earth of the fertile Illinois and Iowa plains to the Death Valley of eastern California, from the orange, tangerine and lemon plantations of California to the great salt desert west of Salt Lake City. Not to mention the immeasurable frozen expanse of Alaska and the tropical splendour of the Hawaii archipelago. And it is just as difficult for anyone to imagine the wide range of the country's natural resources of every kind, of a vegetable, animal or mineral nature. With an area of 9,363,353 square kilometers, the United States is the fourth largest country in the world after the U.S.S.R., Canada and China; but it ranks first as far as production and the wealth of resources are concerned."[31]

To conclude, we should not overlook the fact that Professor Giurescu has been Romania's messenger in the United States, for he brought to the experts' knowledge and popularized in his addresses to wide audiences, the most important moments of her history and of the fight she waged for unity and independence over the centuries, and he also pointed to present-day achievements. By the scientific and cultural activities he carried on in the United States, the Romanian scholar undoubtedly rendered great services to his homeland, while at the same time unswervingly militating for a spiritual rapprochement and for friendship between the two peoples.

To conclude, I will take the liberty to add a few personal disclosures. Having been the professor's student and later an investigator in the fields of research he so successfully dealt with (Romanian feudalism, socio-economic and local history, Bucharest in the past, etc.), I was among the habitual visitors to his home, consulting with him whenever necessary. His house was always open to me and his hospitality was generous. I wish to point out that my bent towards the study of American history is partly due to Professor Giurescu's promptings. He welcomed my idea to investigate, together with Ion Stanciu, a younger colleague, the early Romanian-American relations and to write a book on the image of the New World as built up in the Romanian countries before 1859. The gracious assistance of the greatly appreciated historian helped us to print the book[32] and we voiced our gratitude to him.

I last met our lamented professor at his home in Bucharest on November 3, 1977. I had come to inform him about the results of my visit to the United States, where I had recently attended the symposium Professor Kemal Karpat had organized at the University of Wisconsin to commemorate the centenary of Romania's independence. Professor Giurescu was in capital form, optimistically making plans for the future. He cherished the hope of another visit to the United States the following year and had thought of me as one of his companions.[33] But an unrelenting destiny was to decide otherwise ten days after. I visited the United States again in 1978, but *alone* . . . .

NOTES

1. In *The American Historical Review*, vol. 44 (1939), pp. 866-868.

2. Cornelia Bodea, *Romanian-American Academic Relations in the Past* in *Revue roumaine d'histoire*, XVIII (1979), No. 4, pp. 822-824.

3. Constantin C. Giurescu, *Jurnal de călatorie* (Travel Diary), București, Sport-Turism Publishing House, 1977, p. 9.

4. Namely at the Russian and East-European Study Center of Boston College and at the universities of Pittsburgh, Illinois, Indiana, Arizona, Colorado, California at Berkeley, Washington and Wayne State.

5. A compendium of *Transylvania in the History of Romania. An Historical Outline*, London, Garston Press, 1969, 138 p. +32 plates +1 map.

6. A more extensive version of it was printed in book form in an English translation under the title *The Making of the Romanian National Unitary State*, București, 1975, 174 p. +1 map.

7. The lecture was printed in a Spanish version under the title *Dracula historico, origen de una legenda* in the "Historia y vida" review, Barcelona-Madrid, VI (1973), No. 60, pp. 54-69.

8. It was then that he met Professors R. Pipes and M. K. Dzewanowski of Harvard, Father W. Seaway Joyce of Boston College, Professor Stavro Skendi of the School of International Affairs of Columbia University, Irina Lynch and Anthony Oldcorn of the Wellesley College, James Clarke and Janet Chapman of the University of Pittsburgh, Paul Schroeder of the University of Illinois, Stephen Dandi and Maurice Friedberg of Indiana University, Gregory Oswald, Boyd Breslow and J. Donohoe of the University of Arizona, Stephen Fischer-Galați, Howard Dougherty and James Jankowski of the University of Colorado, William Slottman of the University of California, Berkeley, Donald W. Treadgold, Imre Boba and Marc Szeftel of the University of Washington and Alfred H. Kelly of Wayne State University.

9. From among whom we will mention Victoria Brown (University of Washington), Paul Shapiro (Columbia University) and Paul Michelson (Indiana University), who chose subjects concerning Romanian history for their dissertations.

10. From among whom we should mention Mircea Eliade, writer and professor at the University of Chicago, Professor George Palade, physician, the Nobel Price winner of a latter date, Professor Anghel Rugina, Northeastern University, Dr. Mircea Fotino of Harvard Atomic Reactors, Professor Nicolae Iliescu of Harvard, George Ursul teaching at Emerson College, John Halmaghi, head of the bibliographical department at the University of Pittsburgh Library, lawyer Barbu Niculescu, and Titus Podea, Diplomat. Eng., of New York City. From among clergyman Professor Giurescu mentions Glicherie Moraru, parish priest of the Detroit Orthodox church, and Alexandur Moisi, theologian and professor at Boston College, among others.

11. *Jurnal de călătorie. Impresii din Statele Unite, Paris și Londra* (Travel Diary. Impressions from the United States, Paris and London), București, Cartea Românească Publishing House, 1971, 209 p.

12. For example with Professors Eugene Rice, Andrew Cordier, Voitech Mastny, Bela Kiraly, Robert Austerlitz, Zbigniew Brzezinski, all of Columbia University, also with Professor George Hoffman of the University of Texas, Professor Kemal Karpat of the Univerity of Wisconsin,

Dimitrije Djordjevic of the University of California at Santa Barbara, Professor Wayne Vucinich of Stanford University, Professor G. B. Kovici of Portland University, Professor Paul McCoy of East Texas State University, Professors Eric Hamp, William McNeill and Gregory Campbell of the University of Chicago, Professors James Augerot, James Algeo and Frank Warnke of the University of Washington, Professor Adrian Jaffe of Pomona University, and others. It was also in 1972, more precisely on February 5, that Professor Giurescu attended the commemoration at Columbia University of the pro-Romanian, American historian Philip Mosely, who had passed away shortly before, and read a paper titled *Mosely and Romania*, cp. *In memorian Philip E. Mosely (1905 1972)*, in *South-Eastern Europe*, Pittsburgh, 1 (1974), pp. 112-114.

13. *On Romanian-American Cultural Relations*, New York (1972), 20 p. (Romanian Library, New York City).

14. We will only mention the lecture headed *From the History of Romanian-American Cultural Relations*.

15. From among whom we will mention the lamented Sergiu Columbeanu, Ioan Stanciu and myself from the *N. Iorga* History Institute, Cristian Popişteanu, editor-in-chief of the *Magazin istoric*, Radu Toma, reporter of *Agerpress* and later of *Lumea* (The World), etc.

16. Printed as a separate pamphlet by CISH AHA, XIV International Congress of Historical Sciences, San Francisco, August 22-29, 1973, 62 p.

17. Published as a separate study under the title *Influence of the New World in the Field of Economy. I. Plants of American Origin in the Carpatho-Danubian Area* in *Nouvelles études d'histoire*, Bucureşti, V (1975), pp. 269-279. Professor Giurescu also made a general survey of the XIVth International Congress of Historical Sciences in San Francisco in *Tribuna României* (Romania's Tribune), IV (1975), No. 71 (15 October), p. 10.

18. See my report on the Boulder reunion headed *Second Romanian-American History Colloquim* in *Revista de istorie* (History Review), 30 (1977), No. 2, pp. 340-342.

19. *Jurnal de călătorie* (Travel Diary), Bucureşti, Sport-Turism Publishing House, 1977, 366 p. + plates + 1 map.

20. Professor C. C. Giurescu was interviewed by Petre Ghelmez, chief editor of the *Tribuna României*, VI (1977), No. 109 (15 May), p. 10.

21. *Jurnal*, p. 7-8.

22. Ibid., pp. 70-71.

23. Ibid., pp. 190-191.

24. Ibid., pp. 191-193.

25. Ibid., pp. 155-156.

26.   Ibid., pp. 278-279.

27.   Ibid., pp. 279-280.

28.   Ibid., p. 280.

29.   Ibid., p. 174.

30.   Ibid., p. 226.

31.   Ibid., pp. 145-146.

32.   *Imaginea Lumii Noi în țările române și primele lor relații cu Statele Unite ale Americii pînă în 1859* (The Image of the New World in the Romanian Countries and their Early Relations with the United States of America up to 1859), București, the Socialist Republic of Romania Academy Publishing House, 1977, 177 p. + plates.

33.   I owe my first visit to the United States in 1976 to Professor Giurescu's initiative to co-opt me as a member of the delegation he headed to the commemoration of the bicentanary of the American Revolution.

Glenn E. Torrey

THE DIPLOMATIC CAREER OF CHARLES J. VOPICKA
IN ROMANIA, 1913-1920

The appointment in 1913 of Charles J. Vopicka as "Minister to the Balkan States, a collective post encompassing Romania, Bulgaria, and Serbia, was in the best tradition of the American spoils system. Born in Bohemia in 1857, Vopicka emigrated to the United States in 1880, settling in Chicago a year later. He enjoyed almost immediate business success in real estate and banking. Later, with a partner, Vopicka founded the Bohemian Brewing Company but, curiously, he refused to drink his own beer and would allow none of it in his own home.[1] Vopicka's genial and outgoing nature caused him to become active in the civic and social life of Chicago, as well as in local Democratic politics. He ran for Congress on the Democratic ticket in 1904 and was defeated. But, as an influential and wealthy party supporter, Vopicka was eventually compensated by being suggested by President Wilson on June 25, 1913, for the post as minister to the Balkan States. Secretary of State William Jennings Bryan responded almost immediately in the affirmative: "Am willing to consider Vopicka settled on for the Balkan States as you wish—but it might be well to *see* him first."[2] Despite a deluge of protests from anti-liquor organizations, Vopicka was formally appointed on September 11.

Vopicka's outspoken and colorful personality, permeated by strong bias, combined with his lack of experience in diplomatic practice, caused his career to be marked with notoriety and controversy from the start. Enroute to take up his post in the autumn of 1913, Vopicka paid a visit to his homeland to savor the applause due to a native son who had made good. He was, in the words of an experienced observer, "The idol of the Czech people of Bohemia."[3] The Bohemian National Council in Prague, by its own confession "the largest and most intelligent association in Bohemia" scheduled a reception for Vopicka and telegraphed President Wilson their "thanks and gratitude . . . for the honor conferred upon their countryman . . . ."[4] But the American consul in Prague, Frank Deedmeyer was alarmed by Vopicka's behavior.. He criticized the diplomat's failure to pay a courtesy call on the imperial governor before "associating publicly and privately with the local Czechic and Pan Sclavonic [sic] political agitators." He faulted Vopicka for taking up lodgings "at a small, inferior, cheap hotel, owned by a conspicuous socialist Czech politician, a member of the Imperial Parliament and one of the leaders in opposition to the national Austro-Hungarian government." After explaining the policy of Vienna in maintaining a balance between Czech and German in Bohemia, Deedmeyer stated that "it is generally regarded here and especially in official and imperialistic circles, that Mr. Vopicka's course and more so the uses to which local politicians did put him, have seriously distrubed this nicely poised equilibrium. . . . " After failing by personal intervention to modify Vopicka's behavior, Deedmeyer visited the Imperial Governor of Bohemia, Prince Thun-Hohenstein, where he reportedly found Vopicka's activities and those of his Czech admirers received with "seriousness, it might almost be said with apprehension. . . . " He told the State Department that he heard that Vopicka intended to continue his triumphal tour in Vienna and Budapest. Deedmeyer advised Washington that Vopicka "be directed by the Department of State [to] depart Prague at once and proceed without stops to his post of duty."[5]

Although Deedmeyer's assessment gave evidence of animosity and exaggeration, the Department of State was alarmed and Bryan ordered Vopicka "to avoid any receptions or entertainments that emphasize racial or national differences and proceed at once to Bucharest." Deedmeyer delivered this message 20 minutes after receiving it and Vopicka departed the next day.[6]

The whole episode reached the public a few weeks later in a *Chicago Daily News* page one story entitled "Blunder Laid to Vopicka."[7] The Bohemian-American Press Association of the United States leapt to Vopicka's defense and quiried both the State Department and Deedmeyer, including a veiled threat against the latter.[8] Vopicka himself angrily denied he had done anything of a political nature in Prague, demanded to know who made the charges, and aksed that the Department of State issue a public denial. The Department decline to comment,[9] but the issue would not stay dead. In April, 1914, Frederic Penfield, the American Ambassador in Vienna, wrote a "confidential—for Secretary of State only" letter: "the subject is the old one of the Minister of the Balkan States." Deedmeyer had forwarded reports that Bohemian nationalists were preparing for another Vopicka visitation. Penfield asked

Washington to instruct Vopicka to avoid Austria-Hungary in his travels. Bryan obliged.[10]

The Czech furor had hardily died down before Vopicka again gained public notoriety. In his inaugural audience with King Ferdinand of Sofia, at a time when the guns had hardly cooled from the Balkan Wars, Vopicka was reported in the American press to have told the monarch, in a confidential tone, "I have met Kings Charles [Romania] and Peter [Yugoslavia] and understand there has been some difficulty in the Balkan states. If there is any more trouble, come to me. I think I will be able to arrange matters."[11] The report of this gaffe caused the Schenectady, New York, branch of the Womens Christian Temperance Union to write the Department of State expressing its "condolences at the actions of Charles J. Vopicka, Minister to the Balkan States. No less might have been expected from a brewer. . . . Our protest was registered, with others, against his appointment. . . . We can only pray that his course may prove a lesson to all departments of our government preventing appointments from a similar class of citizens in [the] future."[12] Vopicka again vigorously denied he had made such a *faux paux* in Sofia and forwarded Romanian press clippings which, quoting Bulgarian press reports, said that Vopicka had behaved with an attitude of "perfect correctness and dignity."[13] Again the Department of State refused to pursue the issue.

Reports of Vopicka's diplomatic naivitee and social maldroitness continued to surface. Sometime after arriving in Bucharest, according to one such report, Vopicka received a formal invitation from Queen Elizabeth to an afternoon tea. On the morning of the reception, he called the palace on the telephone and asked to speak to the Queen. Told she never answered the telephone, Vopicka insisted and said that the American minister had to speak to her. Whereupon Her Majesty came to the phone and Vopicka reportedly said: "Good morning, Queen. This is Mr. Vopicka, the American Minister. I can't come to your tea this afternoon but I will drop in soon."[14] Vopicka's midwestern American style of entertaining at Legation functions was the source of much amusement to the Romanians and the diplomatic community.[15]

An incident of a more serious nature arose in the summer of 1914. On July 30, Mr. Alex Colin, manager of the Roumanian Ford Agency in Bucharest wrote an irate letter to Secretary of State Bryan, complaining that Vopicka had refused to pay 300 francs due on the latter's purchase of a new Studebaker automobile. Charging Vopicka with using "chicanery which a mere tradesmen would shun," Colin explained that upon purchasing the automobile, the American Minister had requested a discount of 300 francs as a commission for bringing another customer, a commitment on which he failed to deliver.[16] Vopicka, asked by the Department of State to respond to these charges, identified Colin as "a Jewish Roumanian agent of Bucharest" who demanded the 300 francs in question after Vopicka stopped housing his vehicle in Mr. Colin's garage where the latter was showing it to prospective customers. According to Vopicka, Colin had offered to drop his claim for 300 francs if he was able to sell one or two cars to Vopicka's friends.[17] The Department of State sidestepped the issue by making no response to Colin's letter, on the technicality that it lacked a personal signatue.![18]

The notoriety which surrounded Vopicka continued throughout his career in Bucharest and caused him to be seen as somewhat of a Don Quiote at the Department of State. It did not, however, prevent Vopicka from becoming genuinely popular with the Romanian people and serving as an important, positive influence on the developing relations between the two countries.[19] The quality which endeared Vopicka to his hosts was the sympathy he expressed for the achievement of their national aspirations. Vopicka had a deepseated hostility toward the Austro-Hungarian Empire, born no doubt of his Czech origin, and, as the war progressed, he agitated ceaselessly for the application of national self-determination to its subject peoples, especially the Czechs, the Yugoslavs and the Romanians. A retrospective comment, written in 1920, summed up his attitude: "for years the obstacle to European peace was Austria-Hungary and I believe that by the division of that Monarchy the main source of trouble for peace in Europe was removed."[20]

After the outbreak of war in 1914, Vopicka became in effect a fulltime, resident American Minister in Bucharest. He made several visits to Bulgaria and Serbia, chiefly in a humanitarian role to inspect prisoner of war camps or to distribute relief supplies, but his contact with his two additional charges was slight, especially after 1915 when Bulgaria entered the war and the Serbian army and government retreated to Corfu. Special agents stationed in Sofia and Corfu were officially attached to his Legation in Bucharest but were, in practice, independent.[21]

Until the autumn of 1915, Vopicka's political reporting was not well informed regarding the intentions of King Ferdinand and Prime Minister Brătianu, erroneously implying that they were willing to sell Romania's services to the Central Powers.[22] But after the intervention of Bulgaria in October 1915, however, Vopicka gave evidence that he understood Romania's firm but prudent policy of preparing to achieve the national ideal by joining the Entente in order to participate in the division of the Habsburg lands. In the spring and summer of 1916, he was much more accurate in reporting these intentions than were his more experienced German and Austrian colleagues.[23]

With the outbreak of the war between Romania and the Central Powers on August 27, 1916, Vopicka's antipathy toward the Germans and Austrians increased. He was sharply critical of their bombing of Bucharest with zepplins and although he had been left temporarily in charge of Austro-German affairs, he cooperated with Romanian authorities in the famous investigation of the premises of the former German Legation. The results were sensationalized and resulted in charges that the previous occupants had hidden caches of explosives and germ cultures. The State Department, upon learning of the affair, vetoed further American involvement.[24] But, at the same time as he demonstrated a pro-Romanian attitude, Vopicka showed an active and compassionate interest in the welfare of Austro-German prisoners of war and civilian internees, making repeated visits to their places of detention and pressing for the upgrading of their living conditions.[25] After the Romanian defeat and the occupation of Bucharest by the armies of the Central Powers (December 6, 1916), Vopicka stayed on in Bucharest rather than following the Romanian government to Iași and exhibited even greater initiative in protecting the welfare of the Romanian population. He worked in a tireless and fearless manner, intervening to secure the release of innocent persons arrested or detained by the military authorities, demanding the return of property looted or requisitioned by the occupation forces, and using his influence and resources to provide more adequate food, fuel, and medical supplies for the suffering civilian population. Vopicka became a symbol of hope to the residents of Bucharest and crowds numbering in the thousands gathered regularly in front of the American Legation.[26] The German Military Commander, General August von Mackensen, and his Chief of Staff Colonel Hentsch, the targets of many of Vopicka's complaints, resented the American's actions and sent to Berlin charges of 61 counts of improper or unneutral behavior.[27] German State Secretary for Foreign Affairs, Alfred Zimmermann asked Washington to recall Vopicka, specifying that he had unlawfully placed on American flag over a Romanian house to prevent the entry of German occupation authorities, provided safe-keeping for documents belonging to the Romanian Germanophobe Take Ionescu and made hostile remarks in public against Germany: "I hate these Germans; now at last they will get flicked out of their boots; they have no troops anymore."[28] All these actions, especially the latter, were quite in character for Vopicka, but the American denied to Lansing that they were true as stated.[29] Meanwhile on January 10, 1917, the German military authorities ordered Vopicka to leave Bucharest immediately, arguing that he could no longer remain when the Court to which he had been accredited had moved elsewhere. The U.S. government acquiesced.[30]

Vopicka left Romania on January 13 and traveled via Berlin where he had a long conversation with Hilmar von dem Bussche, a former colleague in Bucharest and now German Undersecretary for Foreign Affairs. The German government, which was in the process of reacting to Wilson's peace moves and which had been commited unwillingly by the High Command to resuming submarine warfare just days before, had no desire to exacerbate relations with Washington needlessly. Backing away from the action of the military authorities in Bucharest, Bussche professed that he did not believe the charges and would accept Vopicka's explanation of his behavior. He withdrew the request that Vopicka be recalled. Bussche also made a personal gesture of reconciliation by inviting Vopicka to the christening of his daughter, to be held that afternoon. Vopicka, gregarious and curious, accepted.[31]

Vopicka continued on to New York, arriving on March 19, 1917 and began to work immediately on behalf of Romania. He described to reporters the "pitiful conditions" of the German occupation and related that the "Romanian people believe that America is the only friend to whom they can turn."[32] Going on to Washington, he urged Wilson, who at that time was preparing to declare war on Germany, to take similar action against Austria-Hungary. Wilson, however, was laboring under the hope that Austria-Hungary could be separated from Germany and had not yet accepted the idea that she should be dismembered.[33]

Vopicka spent three months in the United States, making forty speeches on behalf of Romania and the allied cause before he was instructed to return to Romania and take up his post, now at the temporary capital of Iaşi, in Moldavia.[34] But in Vopicka's absence, the charge at the American Legation in Iaşi, William H. Andrews, succeeded inadvertently in negating whatever positive influence Vopicka may have had in advancing the Romanian cause in Washington. In a dispatch sent to the Deparment of State to explain the arrival of an unofficial Romanian mission to the United States in the summer of 1917, Andrews not only slandered members of the mission but discredited Romanian claims to Transylvania.[35] According to a leading authority on the subject, Andrew's biased and inaccurate reporting, made possible by Vopicka's absence, contributed to the reluctance of the American leaders to give serious consideration to Romania's claims until the war war virtually over.[36] This attitude created a serious divergence between the official United States position against endorsing Romania's irredentist claims and Vopicka's strong opinions to the contrary. This issue remained a point of tension throughout his career.

Upon Vopicka's return to Romania in the fall of 1917, he found himself occupied with the effects of the Russian Revolution upon that afflicted nation. Although the Romanian army had recovered from its defeat of 1916 and was fighting magnificently, the Russian army on the Romanian front was in full process of disintegration, involved in fraternization with the enemy, indiscipline to the point of anarchy, and even in criminal acts against the Romanian army and population. Vopicka's reports to Washington describe the Russian activity in lurid terms: "They are delivering their war material to our enemies in exchange for alcohol, and they are committing murder, arson, robbery, and unspeakable crimes against women. Having used the greater part of the resources of their country, they are extending famine conditions by wontonly destroying food depots in Moldavia and Bessarabia."[37] Vopicka did his best to convince the Russian soldiers to continue fighting. He made repeated trips to the front to exhort them, speaking to as many as 70,000 at a time according to a *New York Times* report. The *Times* reporter commented: "There was a great demonstration at the conclusion of the speech, the enthusiastic soldiers carrying the minister about on their shoulders."[38] Vopicka, always convinced of his own importance, later bragged that his speechmaking helped delay the Russian armistice by "over two months."[39] Vopicka likewise had no sympathy for Bolsheviks seeking aid from the United States. One Ukrainian delegation sought to soften his hostility by claiming that Jesus Christ was the first Bolshevik "because he said that nobody should own anything more than his neighbor." Vopicka, good capitalist that he was, dismissed this argument by replying that the idea might have been alright in Christ's time but that it was impossible now.[40]

In the fall and winter 1917-18, Vopicka did everything possible to keep Romania in the war and to revitalize the Russian army on the eastern front. He was successful in convincing the American government to extend financial credit to the Romanians. He tried, but in vain, to move Washington to endorse the Entente's commitment in the treaty of 1916 to support Romania's aspirations to Austro-Hungarian territory. He repeatedly suggested the dispatch of Allied troops, especially Japanese and American units, to Russia to "suppress anarchy" and enable the Romanian army to keep fighting. In a unique solution, he promoted the idea of recruiting members of the disintegrating Russian army into a special unit of the

United States Army which would continue fighting on the eastern front. As a last resort, he supported a French plan that the Romanian army and court forsake Moldavia and retreat into South Russia where they could link up with pro-allied forces and continue to resist the Austro-German invaders.[41] Vopicka's efforts to persuade Romania to fight on were undercut by the refusal of his government to endorse Romania's territorial aspirations. The best that Washington would do was to reiterate in November that it would support the restoration of Romania's territorial integrity.[42]

Stuck in a hopeless military situation by Russia's defection and without assurance of Entente help, Romania attempted to stall for time by signing an armistice with the Central Powers on December 5. For the next two months a debate raged in Iași over the options of waging war or seeking peace. Lloyd George's speech of January 5, 1918 which mentioned reassessing the secret treaties and stated that "the breakup of Austria-Hungary is no part of our war aims," together with Wilson's 14 Points (January 8), several of which communicated the same message, tipped the scales in favor of those advocating peace.[43] Vopicka was deeply disappointed over the president's handling of Romania in the 14 Points and, hoping that his version of them might be in error, asked the State Department to repeat to him its text.[44] But the snub given Romania's full aspirations in the 14 Points accurately represented Wilson's views and Vopicka had no reply when the pro-Allied Brătianu first, and later the pro-German Marghiloman, told him that in view of their allies' position there was no purpose in fighting any longer. Additional sacrifice would bring no territorial gains.[45] The best Vopicka could do was to tell the Romanians to "read between the lines," an implication of American support he was not authorized to communicate.[46] After the Romanian decision to sign a separate peace early in 1918, Vopicka concentrated his efforts on preventing an American backlash against Romania for deserting the Allied cause, arguing that her action was solely the result of *force majeure*.[47]

During the remainder of the war, while the Central Powers were ascendant in Romania, Vopicka maintained a low profile. But he privately supported the Romanian annexation of Bessarabia even though he hesitated to make a public pronouncement without instructions from Washington. He also continued to repeat to Washington the requests of Brătianu and other Romanians that Wilson publicly endorse the territorial promises made to Romania by the Entente in the Treaty of 1916.[48] On November 6, 1918, while attending a celebration in Chișinău marking the first anniversary of Bessarabia's declaration of autonomy, Vopicka became carried away in a public speech and endorsed Romania's full aspirations, a position his government had not yet authorized him to take. The speech caused a sensation as it was reported in Romanian newspapers that Vopicka had pledged "in his official capacity" the support of the United States government for the national aspirations of Romania to Transylvania, the Banat, Bukovina, and Bessarabia. The Romanian Chamber of Deputies and the Romanian Senate voted expressions of gratitude for Vopicka. Fortunately for Vopicka, Wilson's attitude on this issue had just changed and a telegram was on its way which established an identity between Vopicka's personal views and those of his government.[49]

After the ending of hostilities, Vopicka worked tirelessly for the sending of American relief supplies to Romania, arguing later with characteristic hyperbole that his aid literally saved Romania from starvation and Bolshevism.[50] Vopicka, as might be expected, was also an outspoken champion of the Romanian position in the dispute with Hungary over Transylvania.[51] Vopicka's partisanship caused William Rattigan, the British charge in Bucharest to question his American colleague's judgment to the degree the Britisher refused to participate with Vopicka in a fact-finding mission to Transylvania.[52] Likewise, Frank L. Polk, acting secretary of state, recalled Vopicka to Paris in 1919 for consultation over what he considered an excessively pro-Romanian attitude. Polk wrote to another American: "Vopicka is far too enthusiastic in his admiration for the Romanians; I may let him go next week, but by that time he will be sufficiently educated not to be too enthusiastic every time the Romanians' name is mentioned."[53]

Although Vopicka may have been viewed by his American diplomatic colleagues as naively and annoyingly Romanophile in 1919, he was at the peak of his popularity and influence among not only the Romanians but the Czechs and Yugoslavs as well. Traveling home from Romania that summer he was feted in Prague by President Masaryk and provided with a special railway car for his convenience.[54] His support of the awarding of Fiume to Yugoslavia made him appear the champion of the third nation that was to become the Little Entente. Among his awards were the Serbian "Grand Cordon of the White Eagle—First Class" as well as the "Grand Cross of the Star of Romania."[55] His arrival in New York, at which he emphasized the need for the United States to live up to its image as the "savior" of these people, occasioned an editorial in the *New York Times* which praised Vopicka as an expert and advocated America's active involvement in Europe.[56]

But already Vopicka was entering into personal activities which, although never fully known publicly, would besmirch his reputation and end his diplomatic career under a threat of criminal prosecution. While on leave in the United States during the summer of 1919, Vopicka was active among American banking circles, undertaking to negotiate a loan for Romania. American officials, none too favorably disposed toward Bucharest because of the exacerbating behavior of the Romanians in Hungary and at the Paris Peace Conference, were angered. The Treasury Department requested the State Department take steps to see that Vopicka's activities ceased.[57] The State Department promised to inform Vopicka.[58]

Exactly what type of warning, if any, was given Vopicka is not known. But whatever it was, it apparently did no good. By the end of 1919, reports began to accumulate at the State Department, indicating that Vopicka was engaged in commercial ventures in Bucharest. "Under the very transparent camouflague of interposing one or another of his sons-in-law, he is importing shoes, foodstuffs, steel products, etc. He has played much politics and is generally discredited. Some of his transactions are much criticized even by Romanians whose code of ethics is certainly not strict." So ran the report of an American businessman active in Bucharest.[59] In another report, from the same period (December 1919), Allan Dulles, attached to the American Commission to Negotiate Peace, passed on to Leland Harrison, Assistant Secretary of State and personal assistant to Joseph Grew, Secretary General of the Commission, a summary of statements made to him by two of Herbert Hoover's representatives in Bucharest. Citing a Major Green, formerly in charge of Hoover's work in Romania, Dulles reported that "it was notorious that Minister Vopicka was engaged in trade on his own account, using largely one of his son-in-laws." He added that Green had, on a number of occasions," surprised Mr. Vopicka in the act of checking out invoices. . . . Major Green stated that if a clever man should be sent to Bucharest to investigate Mr. Vopicka's actions he would be able to 'get the goods on him' in the way of documentary evidence of his commercial activities within a month."[60] In a marginal note marked "secret," Harrison recommended "that a Consulate or Consulate General be created at Bucharest. . . and that the Consul or Consul-General be directed to make a secret report to the Department on the question as to whether Mr. V. is or is not engaged in trade on his own accounts, under cover of a member of his family."[61]

Throughout the early months of 1920, the complaints against Vopicka were investigated by the Chief Special Agent of the Department of State and his staff in several cities.[62] On September 24, 1920, charges against

Vopicka were summarized in a Department of State memorandum:[63] "That Mr. Vopicka is personally involved in commercial dealings incompatible with his official position . . . " and guilty of "general charges of incompetence and unfitness as the American representative in Romania." As evidence against Vopicka on the first count, the memorandum linked him to the importation of goods into Romania through the Trans-Occanic Commercial Corporation and William Stephenson, Jr., his son-in-law who stood to realize a profit of $150,000 on the deal. It also alleged that Stephenson made his business headquarters at the American Legation. On the second count it reiterated the complaints accumulated in 1919 (cited above) and added the witness of several American diplomats. "A representative of the Department of State who was recently in Bucharest" wrote: "Vopicka is an absolute disgrace to America and it would be terrible to let him return. . . . His conduct of the Legation is not his concern but that of the nation. It has been merely a shop and an office where business is transacted. Vopicka's son-in-law opens all telegrams and letters, and is under no oath of secrecy as he is here only to make money. And to do this he uses the American Minister—greatly to that individual's pecuniary advantage. . . . The whole business of Vopicka's actions is common talk here and makes me ashamed. And to be ashamed of anything done by an American, in Romania of all places, is going some."

The memorandum added the testimony of "a former consul at Bucharest" who charged that Vopicka neglected the official affairs of the Legation as well as allowing it to be used in the business of his son-in-law and that of "two or three German-American banking men, who live at the Legation or make it their headquarters as representatives of an exporting company." The incumbent charge in Bucharest wrote "During my long experience in the diplomatic service I have never seen a legation so poorly organized, so lacking in business methods and so short of dignity as this one. It has been a target of criticism from almost every quarter. Since my arrival here many people have jested with me about the demoralized condition of our legation. These jests have not only been made by American but by foreign diplomats and by some of the best citizens of the country."

The memorandum also summarized charges that Vopicka was then in the United States to promote the formation of a large banking institution in Bucharest to be called "Lex American-Romano." One of the principle aims of this bank would be to open long term credits for Romanian purchases of American agricultural machinery and to finance the exportation of Romanian oil. A prominent Romanian was to be president and the vice-president was General Dumitriu Iliescu, already in discredit because of his derelection as director general of the Ministry of War 1914-1916 and his unsavory record in Paris as head of the Romanian Military Mission there 1916-1918. Vopicka's role in the operation was to interest American investors in the deal.[64]

On September 25, 1920, the day following the writing of this memorandum, Bainbridge Colby, the successor to Robert Lansing as Secretary of State, ordered Vopicka to delay his return to Romania because "the Department desires to consult with you concerning the affairs of your mission. . . ."[65] Exactly what passed between Vopicka and the Department of State is not known but a few days later James Hamilton Lewiş, Senator from Illinois, intervened with Colby asking that Vopicka be allowed to sail for Europe early in October, because "there are advantages in the messages he will communicate to certain heads of nations who have great numbers of voters in this country."[66]

It appears that Colby, not unconcerned with the approaching election, consented to some sort of arrangement whereby Vopicka would be allowed to return to Bucharest and then resign. Word spread that Vopicka would be removed from office and Senator Lewis complained bitterly to Colby early in November.[67] On December 9, Vopicka, back in Bucharest, submitted his resignation, for "personal considerations" of family health and business.[68] Later in the month, Ellridge Greene, charge in Bucharest upon Vopicka's departure, forwarded to the Department of State samples of sales merchandise of the Trans-Oceanic Commercial Corporation which he found in the "upper apartments of the Legation" and which he presumed were the property of Vopicka or his son-in-law William Stephenson, Jr. These samples consisted of soda, several samples of rice, a number of samples of belting, nails of assorted sizes, cloth samples, house-furnishings stuff, pine lard, edible tallow, "Pine City" tallow, and "Advance Compound." Greene added: "it appears to be the impression of many business persons in Bucharest that Mr. Vopicka was the agent for the firm of importers and exporters known as the Trans-Oceanic Commercial Corporation and that the offices of the Company were considered to be at the Legation. Reference has often been made in my presence to the sums alleged to have been invested by the Minister in the Company and of the manner in which he conducted his business."[69]

In February 1921, just before the change of administrations, the question arose as to whether or not to prosecute Vopicka for direct violation of the statutory inhibition that no diplomatic officer "shall, while he holds his office, be interested in or transact any business as a merchant, factor, broker, or other trader, or as an agent for any such person, to, from, or within the country or countries to which he or the chief of his mission, as the case may be, is accredited, either in his own name or through the agency of any other person. . . . "[70] Assistant Secretary of State Merle-Smith quiried Under Secretary Davis, who decided not to pursue the matter any further.[71] It seems hard to avoid the conclusion that the outgoing administration did not relish the prospect of a prominent political appointee being indicted for corruption The physical "evidence" against Vopicka was retained by the Department until 1932 when it was destroyed.[72]

Vopicka, his reputation tarnished within the Department of State, if not publicly, set about to defend the conduct of his mission. His book, *Secrets of the Balkans*, published in 1921, was intended to uphold his record against State Department critics, who had often leaked their dissatisfaction to the press. Vopicka's mission was also praised in a letter of acknowledgment from King Ferdinand to President Harding,[73] and in 1929 when Vopicka's alleged incompetence was the butt of a jest in the Bucharest daily *L'Independence Roumaine*, the latter's competitor, *La Roumanie*, defended Vopicka. "He was one of Romania's greatest friends in her darkest hours. He worked for us at Jassy where he insisted on following us, with cheerfulness and ardor that had not been forgotten."[74] Despite the charges of corruption (which were difficult to evaluate because the investigation was never ajudicated) it was *La Roumaine's* evalution of Vopicka that has prevailed in Romania. Likewise in the United States, where the charges against him were never made public, Vopicka preserved his public image as a prominent business and civic leader in Chicago. When he died in 1935, throngs attented his funeral and Democratic luminaries Harold Ickes and Otto Kerner were among his honorary pallbearers.[75]

NOTES

* The research and travel underlying this study were supported in part by grants from the International Research and Exchange Board, the American Philosophical Society, and the Faculty Research Committee of Emporia State University.

1.   Arthur S. Link, *Wilson: The New Freedom* (Princeton, 1956), p. 106, note 40.

2.   Wilson to Bryan, 25 June 1913; Bryan to Wilson, c. 25 June 1913, Arthur S. Link, ed., *The Papers of Woodrow Wilson, vol. 28 (1913),* (Princeton, 1978) pp. 4-5.

3. Frank Deedmeyer (Consul-Prague), to Secretary of State, 10 November 1913. National Archives, Department of State, decimal files 1910/ 1929, 123 V 89.

4. Bohemian National Council to Wilson, 3 November 1913, ibid.

5. Deedmeyer to Secretary of State, 8, 10 November 1913, ibid.

6. Bryan to Vopicka, 10 November 1913; Deedmeyer to Secretary of State, 14 November 1915, ibid.

7. *Chicago Daily News*, 30 January 1914.

8. Bohemian-American Press Association to Bryan, 2 February 1914; Bohemian-American Press Association to Deedmeyer, 2 February 1914; Department of State, decimal files 1910/1929, 123 V 89.

9. Vopicka to Secretary of State, 14 February 1914; Department of State to Bohemian Press Association, 16 February 1914; Department of State to Vopicka, 16 March 1914. Ibid.

10. Penfield to Secretary of State, 21 Arpil 1914; Bryan to Vopicka, 5 May 1914. Ibid., Vopicka denied he intended to visit Prague in the near future. Vopicka to Bryan, 7 May 1914, 9 May 1914, ibid.

11. Quoted in Vopicka's obituary in the *New York Times*, 5 September 1935, p. 26.

12. Mrs. Maude H. Flickinger to Bryan, 9 April 1914, Department of State, decimal files 1910/1929, 123 V 89.

13. Vopicka to Secretary of State, 15 April 1914, ibid. Robert Lansing (Counselor, Department of State) told Vopicka that the Department of State gave no credance to the original newspaper reports. Lansing to Vopicka, 13 May 1914, ibid.

14. *New York Times*, 6 January 1917.

15. Victor S. Mamatey, *The United States and East Central Europe 1914-1918* (Princeton, 1957), p. 122, note 99.

16. ⸱ Colin to Bryan, 30 July 1914, Department of State, decimal files 1910/1929, 123 V 89.

17. Vopicka to Bryan, 6 August 1914, ibid.

18. Lansing to Vopicka, 8 October 1914, ibid.

19. On Romanian-American relations, see Stelian Popescu-Boteni, *Relații între România și S.U.A. pînă în 1914* (Cluj, 1980); Arackel Thomas Devasia, "The United States and the Formation of Greater Romania 1914-1918 (Dissertation, Boston College, 1970); Ion Stanciu, "Aspecte ale relațiilor româno-americane în anii neutralității României (1914-1916)," *Revista de Istorie*, 1976 (6), pp. 921-34; Boris Rangheț, *Relațiile româno-americane în perioada primului război mondiale 1916-1920* (Cluj, 1975).

20. Charles J. Vopicka, *Secrets of the Balkans* (Chicago, 1921), p. 320.

21. United States, Department of State, *Papers Relating to the Foreign Relations of the United States. 1915. Supplement.* (Washington, D.C., 1928), pp. 70-71; ibid., *1916. Supplement.* (Washington, D.C., 1920), p. 135 note no. 1.

22. Vopicka to Secretary of State, 12 October, 19 October, 27 October 1915, *Foreign Relations of the United States. 1915. Supplement,* pp. 63, 66, 68.

23. Vopicka to Secretary of State, 18 July, 22 July 1916. Ibid. *1916. Supplement,* pp. 39-40.

24. Vopicka to Department of State, 6 October, 8 October 1916; Lansing to Vopicka, 14 October 1916; Ibid., pp. 824-25; Alexandru Marghiloman, *Note Politice 1897-1924.* Vol. II (Bucharest, 1927), p. 211.

25. Vopicka, *Secrets,* p. 91; Vopicka to Department of State, 8 September 1916. *Foreign Relations of the United States, 1916. Supplement,* pp. 50-3; Marghiloman, p. 349.

26. Vopicka, *Secrets,* p. 115.

27. Ibid., pp; 121-25.

28. Gerard (Berlin) to Lansing, 28 December 1916, Department of State, decimal files, 123 V 89; The Dutch minister in Bucharest, Vredenburch, talked freely of Vopicka's alleged involvement in illegal currency speculation. Marghiloman, p. 349; See the memorandum by the German Under Secretary of State for Foreign Affairs, 17 January 1917. Germany, Auswaertiges Amt, *Archives of the German Foreign Ministry,* 1867-1920, filmed for St. Antony's College, Reel 2.

29. Vopicka to Lansing, 9 January 1917, ibid.

30. Devasia, "Greater Romania," pp. 138-39; *New York Times,* 7 January, 16 January 1917; Vopicka, *Secrets,* pp. 105, 118 ff; Similar charges were used to secure the recall of the Dutch minister. Marghiloman, pp. 374-75.

31. Gerard to Lansing, 17 January 1917, Department of State, decimal files, 123 V 89; *New York Times,* 18 January, 20 January 1917; Vopicka, *Secrets,* pp. 125-26.

32. *New York Times,* 20 March 1917.

33. Devasia, "Greater Romania," p. 150. Vopicka, *Secrets,* p. 128.

34. Ibid., pp. 128-29.

35. Ranghet, *Relaţiile,* pp. 29 ff.

36. Mamatey, *East Central Europe,* pp. 123-26.

37. Vopicka, *Secrets,* p. 163.

38. *New York Times,* 17 October 1917.

39. Vopicka, *Secrets,* p. 138.

40. Ibid., p. 312.

41. Vopicka to Secretary of State, 17 November 1917, *Foreign Relations of the United States. 1917. Supplement 2, Vol. I,* (Washington, D.C., 1932), p. 309, 457-59; Vopicka, *Secrets,* pp. 157-59, 164, 168.

42. Lansing to Vopicka, 28 November 1917, *Foreign Relations of the United States. 1917. Supplement 2, Vol. I,* p. 325. For a survey of the evolution of Wilson's attitude see Keith Hitchins, "Woodrow Wilson and the Union of Transylvania with Rumania, 1917-1918," *Revue roumaine d'histoire,* 1979 (4), pp. 803-10. Also, Rangheț, *Relațiile,* pp. 65, 99 ff; Devasia, "Greater Romania," pp. 168-174.

43. Devasia, "Greater Romania," pp. 179-80; Rangheț, *Relațiile,* pp. 106-09; Mamatey, *East Central Europe,* pp. 202-05.

44. Vopicka to Department of State, 12 January 1918, *Foreign Relations of the United States, 1918, Supplement 1, Vol. I* (Washington, D.C., 1933), p. 752.

45. Vopicka, *Secrets,* pp. 197-99.

46. Vopicka to Department of State, 9 February 1918, *Foreign Relations of the United States, 1918. Supplement 1, Vol. I,* p. 757.

47. Vopicka to Department of State, 1 March 1918, ibid., p. 760.

48. Vopicka to Department of State, 21 October 1918, ibid., p. 783. Vopicka, *Secrets,* p. 246.

49. Dennis (Charge-Bucharest) to Department of State, 16 February 1924, Department of State decimal files 123 V 89. (Paraphrases articles from the Romanian press recounting the incident at Chișinău.) Lansing to Vopicka, 5 November 1918, *Foreign Relations of the United States, 1918. Supplement 1, Vol. I,* p. 785. Vopicka, *Secrets,* pp. 262-63.

50. *New York Times,* 4 May 1919, 9 July 1919; Vopicka, *Secrets,* p. 298.

51. Vopicka, *Secrets,* pp. 300-2.

52. Sherman David Spector, *Rumania at the Paris Peace Conference* (New York, 1962), p. 312.

53. Ibid., p. 306.

54. *New York Times,* 9 July 1919.

55. Ibid., 5 June 1919.

56. Ibid., 10 July 1919.

57. R. C. Leffingwell (Treasury) to Breckenridge Long (Assistant Secretary of State), 16 August 1919, Department of State, decimal files 123 V 89.

58. Long to Leffingwell, 21 August 1919, ibid.

59. J. A. Moffett, Jr. to Commander Hugo Koehler, 3 December 1919, ibid.

60. Allan W. Dulles to Harrison, 8 December 1919, ibid.

61. Marginalia on Dulles to Harrison, 8 December 1919, ibid.

62. Special Agent in Charge (New York) to J. M. Nye, Chief Special Agent, 31 March 1920, ibid.

63 "Memorandum regarding Mr. Vopicka," 24 September 1920, ibid.

64. In addition to the memorandum cited in footnote 63, see also, Wallace to Secretary of State, 23 September 1920, ibid.

65. Colby to Vopicka, 25 September 1920, ibid.

66. Lewis to Colby, 2 October 1920, ibid.

67. Colby to Lewis, 12 November 1920, ibid.

68. Vopicka to Colby, 9 December 1920, ibid.

69. Greene to Colby, 29 December 1920, ibid.

70. Salmon to Merle-Smith, 31 January 1921, ibid.

71. ? to Merle-Smith, 19 February 1921, ibid. (Author's signature unreadable.)

72. Marginalia on Greene to Colby, 29 December 1920, ibid.

73. Ferdinand to Harding, 1 July 1921, ibid. (The original, in French, was sent to Harding but he complained that he could not read it and sent it back to the Department of State for a translation.)

74. *L'Independence Roumaine*, 29 June 1929; *La Nation Roumanie*, 30 June 1929, ibid.

75. *Chicago Tribune*, 8 September 1935.

Gerald Bobango and Ion Stanciu

ROMANIAN-AMERICANS AND THE UNION OF 1918

De astăzi România la sînul ei te chiamă,
Răsune'n toate lumea fanfarele în vînt,
Și clopotele toate cu glasul lor de-aramă
S'anunțe libertatea pămîntului tău sfînt!

These lines by Viorica I. Bantunoiu are to be found, not in a Transylvanian gazette prior to the First World War, as one might expect, but in Cleveland, Ohio, in the pages of the *Calendar America* for 1920.[1] While at the
outbreak of the great conflagration of 1914 large circles of public opinion in Europe were fairly well acquainted with the national aspirations
of the Romanian people to complete their national territorial unity by
incorporating Transylvania into the Old Kingdom, people in the United
States of America had little knowledge of such things in Eastern Europe.

There is, however, some evidence that the major milestones in the long
struggle waged by Romanians for their national cause were not entirely
alien to Americans. They had learned of the 1848 revolution, largely its
Transylvanian episodes; the 1859 union of the Danubian Principalities was
less well-known, but the gaining of Romanian independence in 1878 found
identifiable comments and reactions in American official circles and in the
Eastern press.[2] Nonetheless, it can hardly be said that on the eve of World
War I Romania as a country and the Romanian people as a nation were
part and parcel of the American public's general knowledge. The few press
articles during 1912-1913 occasioned by the Balkan Wars did discuss long-
term objectives of Romanian diplomacy with respect to the national issue,
but had little impact on the hazy images of far-away Southeastern Europe
which Americans in the still-provincial days of Theodore Roosevelt and
William Howard Taft continued to hold. Without major events such as
wars to generate news stories, much of American information on Romania
was that provided by the various Austro-Hungarian consular offices in the
United States, which were hardly impartial sources. Most information
received dealt with the endemic peasant revolts and the depressed condition of the rural population, or else centered on the frivolities of court
life. As for Romanians living beyond the kingdom, and their struggle for

337

unification with the mother country, such problems were understandably ignored in the Dual Monarchy's official press releases, especially those for foreign consumption. Moreover, bilateral political relations were limited between Romania and the United States, and until the mass migrations of the Transylvanian peasantry between 1895 and 1924, cultural contacts were few.

There is a further element operative as well—even after the outbreak of the war, public opinion in the United States continued to conceive of the Austro-Hungarian Monarchy as the true "melting pot" of people in Central and Eastern Europe, investing it with a civilizing mission. Thus Romanians, Czechs, Poles, and South Slavs had to counter this image if they were to win ground for their national ambitions.

The outbreak of the war increased America's interest in European affairs without, however, doing much specifically to. increase any public concern for Romanian aims. This was due primarily to the fact that for the first two years of the war, during which Romania remained neutral, the impression was quickly formed in the West, aided by Bulgarian and Magyar propaganda, that Romania was trading its neutral stance for promises of later gains from the Central Powers. Besides, the Romanian government at first tended to overlook the political potential of American public opinion, and made few efforts to influence it before 1916. This left as the main source of American contact and information about Romania the colonies of Romanian-American immigrants themselves, especially as organized in their beneficial societies and church congregations. Yet even this potentially influential force was vitiated by the apparently unclear and seemingly contradictory aims of Romania's policy in the period 1914-1916. This notwithstanding, the contributions of these Romanian-American communities to the Romanian war effort and to the fulfillment of national state unification in their mother country was to prove large and important during the era which climaxed at Alba Julia on December 1, 1918.

By the time the vote for Union was registered within the walls of the massive fortress built by Charles VI in the heart of the ancient Dacian Kingdom, there were in the United States at least 85,000 Romanians who had been born in Romania, with another 5,400 or so having one or both parents born in the old country, the vast majority of this population being Transylvanian in origin.[3] To these might be added another 20,000 Romanians in Canada, mainly from Bucovina.[4] Beginning about 1895, great numbers of the rural peasantry of Transylvania, seeking economic opportunity and freedom from what can only be termed an oppressive political and economic regime centered in Budapest, had swelled the ranks of the "new immigration," contributing their labor, skill, and love of freedom to the making of America. They arrived with Austro-Hungarian passports; they listed "Ungaria" as their country of origin; but questions as to their ethnicity brought inevitably the response, "Sînt Român." Most of them upon arrival were unlettered or semi-literate and had no skills but those of agricultural laborers. Of intellectuals there were few, and priests they sorely lacked. Nevertheless, for many of them America acted as a "school of nationality," as a result of the communal institutions which they founded, the Romanian-language press, and the greater awareness of their own ethnicity fostered by the multifarious ethnic milieu of Pittsburgh, New York, Chicago, Indiana Harbor, Detroit, Erie, and Youngstown. Some evidence suggests that they learned to speak and write a better Romanian than they ever did at home,[5] while in many cases it is also true that this largely Transylvanian population learned more than ever before about the politics and culture of Romania proper, due to the greater accessibility of information and printed material available in America, much of which had been denied to them under the Hungarian regime at home.

The net result, then, of this increased sense of personal and ethnic identity, and a concomitant of Romanians' rapid upward mobility and increased literacy in American society relative to those of other ethnic groups,[6] was that by the time of the Great War the Romanian-American community as a whole was likely more aware of events in Europe, and specifically in Romania, than its members had been before their migration. This knowledge, combined with the greater freedom of expression enjoyed in the New World, led to their taking an active and vocal role in promoting the accomplishment of Romanian national unity. With their money, their press, and even with their blood, Romanian-Americans added to the configuration of events climaxing at Alba Iulia.

THE ROLE OF THE ROMANIAN-AMERICAN COMMUNITY

Even before the war, Romanian-Americans took a keen interest in events transpiring in the Regat, one of the earliest actions of each local Romanian society being to build a library of Romanian books, journals, and newspapers as soon as possible after organizing.[7] On July 2, 1912, the bimonthly journal *Steaua Noastră* in New York reported on the recent dedication of the statute of Alexandru Ioan Cuza in Iași, noting that "Romanians in Arizona, in the South and West, in Montana," throughout the land, "unite in one soul," in honoring the memory of the Prince of Union.[8]

More prophetic for the future, however, was the editorial in the Cleveland weekly *Românul* in 1913 commenting on Romania's performance in the Second Balkan War:

> Poate cît de curînd, mai curînd decît ne aşteptăm, mai curînd decît ne închipium, România va fi chemată să aducă la îndeplinire năzuinţele noastra, desrobirea întregului neam românesc.[9]

The Romanian-language press, then, did not confine itself solely to news of Romanian-American affairs, but consistently reported Romanian and European affairs.[10] Moreover, from its inception it undeviatingly took a stand favoring Romanian territorial ambitions and irredentism. More room was afforded in the annual *Calendars* published by the newspaper *America's* press in Cleveland than in the four-page bimonthly papers. Thus one 1914 *Calendar* devoted two-thirds of its 141+ pages to extensive coverage of the Balkan War and Romanian affairs, while lauding the acquisition of Dobrogea.[11] Along with *Românul*, *America*, and the *Calendari* published in America and Romania, Romanian-Americans also received *Calicul român* between 1906-1916, and *Libertatea*, begun in 1917 in Cleveland by the priest Ioan Moţa from Orăştie, whose mission in America was to propagandize for union of the Ardeal with the mother country.[12] While *Libertatea* lasted only two months, *Foaia Poporului* started in Cleveland in 1913 and eventually became the organ of the Romanian-American National Committee, first headed by Rudi Nan of the *Liga şi Ajutorul*. Other newsheets uring the Romanian cause were *Renaşterea Română* in Cincinnati, *Deşteptarea* from 1914 on (which gave way to *Românul-American* in Detroit), and *Deşteaptă-Te Române* in Hamilton, Ontario. In Youngstown, Ohio, was the weekly *Transilvania*, first printed in the summer of 1917, and a most important publication was *Roumania*, written in both Romanian and English and appearing in Chicago. *Roumania* was the work of the Bucharest professors Paul and Gogu Negulescu who used the monthly review to make known Romania's goals to Americans, during the year which it lasted. Paul Negulescu raised significant sums of money for Romanian war relief also through his series of visits and conferences at American universities.[13]

Along with this extensive press activity, the major forums for Romanian-Americans' concerted activity with regard to Romanian affairs were the two major beneficial organizations created well before the war. The earliest was the Union of Romanian Societies of Assistance and Culture (USRA) founded in Homestead, Pennsylvania, on July 4, 1906, as primarily a working-class beneficial association, and the later group, the Romanian-American Association of Alliance and Assistance (*Liga și Ajutorul*) was incorporated in 1914 by the merger of two separate groups and oriented around the smaller circles of the Romanian-American intelligentsia.[14]

The USRA was by far the more widespread and popular body. In the autumn of 1917 it could claim 76 member societies and perhaps 13,000 members,[15] while as late as 1924 the *Liga* included only 14 societies with 1,643 members enrolled.[16] Along with these, by the 1920s, there were five or six societies calling themselves "independent," the *Farșarotul* organization of Macedo-Romanians in New York City, and the most sizeable association outside USRA, the Union of Romanian Greek-Catholic Societies of the United States, with sixteen local clubs.[17] In 1913-1914 appeared the Federation of the Romanian Socialist Workers of the United States, which affiliated with the International Workers of the World and the United States Socialist Party of Eugene V. Debs. The Socialists, however, remained a relatively small group.

In their official newspapers, local society activities, and especially at the annual conventions and sessions of the Supreme Executive Committee of the USRA during the war years, these Romanian-American organizations showed themselves to be concerned not only with the effect of the conflict on Romania, but with the realization of Romania's legitimate national aspirations. As such, then, Romanian-Americans in general strove to be of one mind with their brethren in Europe.

During the first two years of the war, as Romania struggled to remain neutral amidst the havoc of the Eastern Front, there was naturally much speculation in America as to her future course. Yet most members of the Romanian immigrant community, as former subjects of Austria-Hungary, could not conceive any course which would place Romania on the side of the Central Powers. On August 15, 1915, Francis M. L. Radich, Secretary of the Romanian National Club "Dacia" in New York, disputed recent claims many by correspondent Solomon Șufrin that Romania would not join the Allies. Reviewing the history of persecution by Austria, noting that Romanian representation for Transylvania in the Hungarian Diet was a mere 25% of what Romanians' numbers entitled them to, Radich urged his opponent to consult the 75,000 Transylvanian Romanians in America, banded in ninety societies, as to where their hearts lay. "Everyone is sighing for the day when they shall be united with the mother country," he stated. "Every society is the proud possessor of a Romanian tricolor banner (no Hungarian at all). . . . " These, he concluded, are the sons and daughters of the Romanian irredenta, and no foreign influence is likely to conflict with their national aspirations, the strong German influence in Bucharest notwithstanding.[18]

The war had its impact on the USRA, especially in the declining proportion of new members. Those who might have joined the Union instead diverted their money overseas to assist friends and relatives caught up in the struggle. Others returned home to Europe to replace brothers or fathers or uncles killed in the war, as the extended family system of the Balkan village demanded. Members themselves felt the economic pressures in America brought by the war. Declining wages for a time meant they could not pay their monthly dues, and they withdrew from the societies. Yet on the whole, and despite these setbacks, the Union continued to grow, from 3,400 members at the end of 1914 to 5,162 by 1916 and a claimed membership of 13,000 by the end of 1917, with a national treasury reported as containing $15,719.27 by the time America entered the war. This significant jump in membership may be explained by several possible factors. Many immigrants, knowing that their people back home were faced with great difficulties, hastened to join Romanian societies and name their families in Transylvania as their beneficiaries under the insurance policies. Or, those planning to volunteer for the armed forces, especially after the United States entered and the use of conscription began, saw the need for insurance protection more than before. Finally there were many who were certain, or at least hopeful, that the money they had saved in America would go farther once Transylvania belonged to the Old Kingdom, and they joined groups such as the USRA to help bring this about.

Moreover, despite the modest wages earned by many Romanian workingmen during 1915, fourteen local societies of the USRA convened popular assemblies between March and August of that year to collect funds for war relief for Romania. By the time the final assembly, that of the "Armonia" Society in St. Louis, completed its drive, the campaign had gathered $5,000. As the battles went on in Europe, both interest and concern as well as donations increased. A peace congress in Cleveland in May saw 2,000 delegates present. *America*, which had increased its size from four to eight pages after July 1, 1915, sought to use Romanian-Americans' patriotic zeal for their homeland and their humanitarian feeling to inspire new membership in the USRA, stating that only those who knew how to fulfill their call, who were moved by national and cultural affairs while others "slept in ignorance," could be called "true Romanians." The more members the USRA could enroll, the more relief funds might be sent to Europe, and "the more our voice will be heard by the powers fighting for the rights of subjugated nations," wrote Secretary-General Gheorghe Salca in the 1916 *Calendar*.[19]

As 1916 dawned and pressures on Romania to enter the war intensified, Romanian-Americans increased their attention to the European
situation and their contributions to relief of war widows and orphans
of those conscripted into the Habsburg armies. *America* on February 6
took a strong stand favoring the proposed Jones Act then before Congress, which would grant increased self-government to the Philippine
Islands. The situation of Transylvania was held up as an obvious comparison. Later in the month came an appeal to all Romanian societies
and parishes in the Canton, Ohio area to help "our relatives who call
us" in the homeland by attending a big rally at the local hall, a gathering which produced a collection surpassing all expectations.[20]

March 5 brought *America*'s initial call to "100,000 Romanians" to
give one dollar each for an orphanage in Sibiu, and this notice continued
for weeks.[21] That October, with Romania now in the war against the
Central Powers, the Executive Committee of the USRA voted to give
$1,000 to the National Romanian-American Association for War Relief,
newly formed in Cleveland.

This association had already collected nearly $19,000 by mid-February
and its campaign produced an eventual $31,000 by July 1.[22] As the war
entered its final year, a Romanian Women's Committee of the Red Cross
was added in Cleveland.

In the meantime Romanian-Americans became more visible to the
American public. On May 30, 1916, a mammoth flag-consecration celebration was staged in New York City, organized by the Avram Iancu
Society, with more than sixty societies from various cities represented.
E. Borcea, a member of the Romanian commission buying supplies in the
United States, was a guest at the Palm Garden banquet, at which a Russian
band played *Deşteapta-te Române*. It was the first Memorial Day celebration ever held in the United States by the Romanians.[23] Two months
later the USRA convention in Detroit sent a telegram of congratulations
to Woodrow Wilson on his renomination for the presidency.[24] While part
of the Romanian-American press had been decidedly anti-Wilson in 1912,
it was time to mend fences.[25] Only a month later Romania declared war
on Austria and many already sensed that America's moral leadership
would strongly influence the war's outcome. Not only did Romanians
in America, in any event, wish to be considered good citizens of their
adopted country (although few had taken out citizenship papers) but
henceforth they actively sought the good will of the American government and public to gain support for Romanian goals. Wilson's message of
December 1916, to the belligerent powers, showing him to be favorable
to the solution of national problems, solidified this intent on the part of

Romanian-American organizations,[26] and the President's message to the Senate on the self-determination of peoples, given on January 22, 1917, produced telegrams of accord and felicitations from *America, Românul,* the USRA, and the Romanian Red Cross.[27]

As the winter wore on, *America* sold buttons inscribed *pentru neam și țară* and told Romanian immigrants to wear them to prove they were Romanians.[28] The notice occurred several times in the issue of February 15, 1917, all in capital letters, and added, "anyone not wearing them is afraid to show they're Romanian."[29] In some cases there was reason to be hesitant. The growing outrage over Germany's unrestricted submarine warfare, the atrocity stories spread by the British press on the depredations of the Hun, combined with the increasing pressures for "100% Americanism" of the day, had a more than subtle effect by 1917 on native American's views of those of their fellow citizens stemming from the Austro-Hungarian realm. In March, *America* reported some Romanians in Harrisburg were beaten on the street for their war sentiments.[30]

All this, combined with the entrance of the United States formally into the war on April 6, 1917, made it all the more imperative for Romanian-Americans, along with other Central and Eastern European immigrant folk, to cultivate an image of loyalty to their adoptive country, while simultaneously promoting the cause of their mother country.

The impact of Wilson's war message was immediate. *America*'s circulation increased by 1,000; by April 15 it claimed some 11,800 circulation and in August began to publish daily. Moreover it now began to receive contributions from such Romanian illuminati as Nicolae Iorga.[31] Society No. 96 of the USRA was founded in April 1917, also, in Lansing, Michigan, naming itself "Woodrow Wilson."[32] In July *America* waded into the polemics of irredentism, attacking the Cleveland-based Hungarian paper, *Szabadsag,* for its assault on the newly-arrived Romanian mission to Washington. *Szabadsag*'s notions of Magyar claims to the Ardeal were made, *America* noted, "in a totally perverse manner," and "motivated entirely by illogic, with no basis of right."[33] This was premature, however, for the Romanian "mission" turned out to be merely a group of three priests, who had unofficially come to Washington to lobby for Romanian interests. They called themselves the "M.P.R.," or the *Misiunea patriotică română,* and a San Francisco newspaper erroneously labeled them an offical body. *America* subsequently lamented the fact that an occasion was even given for Hungarians to denigrate Romanians, but offered no apologies for its precipitous sensitivity in the matter.[34]

Now the rhythm of propagandizing for Transylvania increased apace. August 1917, found popular assemblies being held in Romanian clubrooms from New York to Chicago, demanding a *România Mare*, while *America* ran a series of full-page editorials on the history of Transylvania, with the theme, "Documents, Not Arguments."[35]

At the General Assembly of the USRA that summer an amendment to the General Statutes was unanimously passed providing that any member of the Union serving in the United States armed forces who was killed or returned home an invalid was entitled to full insurance benefits and was exempt from his monthly dues. Those returning unharmed were to be received back into their former societies without paying a new entrance fee.[36] In addition the book *Istoria Americei*, by Ilie Martin Salișteanu, which the Union had been selling for some years, was to be sent free to all Romanian prisoners of war.[37] Romanian-Americans were already volunteering to serve. In Youngstown, Ohio, was formed a Legion of Romanian Volunteers, led by the prominent official of the *Liga*, Rudi Nan. These men would shortly see the fields of France.[38] By the end of the war, the Union had 428 men in the United States Army, and eight of these never returned.[39] On the final day of the 1917 Convention, Paul Negulescu appeared to ask support for his forthcoming review, *Roumania*, intended to counterbalance Hungarian and German attempts to discredit Romania, and to propagandize in the Allied nations. He was received with "an outburst of prolonged applause, a fact which moved Mr. Negulescu deeply."[40]

Not only did the USRA support such literary efforts, but it continued to aid the Allied war effort with its funds. In October the Union bought $2,000 worth of bonds from the Second Liberty Loan, raising its purchases thus far to $7,000.[41]

America appealed to its readers to "choose between President Wilson and the Kaiser" and to "buy bonds only if you're a good American."[42] Interestingly, this call was launched in English. Not only was this a solid way to display one's patriotism, but indirectly such contributions, it was believed, helped the war effort on the Romanian front, especially now that America was in. Ion Păcurar, President of the USRA, urged all members to take part in a major fund drive, to raise an estimated $75-100,000 from the societies alone, and perhaps an equal amount from individuals.[43]

Not only financial support, but emotional and ideological purity was proclaimed by *America* to its readers. Early in October it reprinted the "American's Creed" which originally appeared in the *New York Herald:*

> I believe in one god, architect of the universe and father of man. I believe in my country as the most beautiful work of his hands. I believe in President Wilson as the interpreter of his divine intentions and as the embodiment of American ideals.[44]

America's entry also produced the beginnings of an organized propaganda effort developed by the hard-pressed Romanian government. On June 29, 1917, Vasile Stoica, Captain of the Romanian Army, and the renowned Transylvanian memorandist Vasile Lucaciu (father of one of the leading Romanian-American priests, Epaminonda Lucaciu in Trenton, New Jersey) arrived in Washington, and four days later met with Secretary of State Robert Lansing, who, Stoica later wrote, promised to support Romania's cause.[45] Not only did the two seek to enlighten American public opinion on the issues of the war in Central and Eastern Europe, but they hoped to organize a volunteer corps of Transylvanian Romanians from America, far more extensive than the Youngstown group, to fight in the American or French army.[46]

Many difficulties had to be overcome, not the least of which was the lack of an official Romanian mission in Washington. Until the arrival of Dr. Constantin Angelescu on January 15, 1928, as the first Romanian minister to the United States, spokesmen for Hungarian territorial claims had the advantage of little competition, for the ears of American officialdom. Moreover, the United States did not declare a state of war against Austria-Hungary until December 7, 1917, which meant that, despite the favorable reception by Lansing, Wilson's government could not really commit itself in advance on the question of the Ardeal. Stoica and Lucaciu set to work energetically, publishing a series of articles in the *Washington Post* and the *New York Times,* calling assemblies of Romanian-Americans, dealing with journalists and politicians. During the summer of 1917 they laid the basis of a Romanian National Committee, headed by Epaminonda Lucaciu. The popular assemblies at Romanian centers which had produced much excitement and newspaper coverage during August were repeated toward the end of the year in Cleveland, Trenton, and Detroit. Stoica succeeded in gaining an interview with Secretary of the Interior Franklin Lane, and in August the two Romanian emissaries met with Theodore Roosevelt. This had perhaps the greatest impact on American public opinion, for the belligerent ex-president agreed to sustain Romanian national aspirations. In editorials published in the *Kansas City Star,* Roosevelt steadfastly advocated the dissolution of the Dual Monarchy, and upheld the right of Romanians and other peoples to dissociate from the Empire. In speeches in September, October, and December, Roosevelt attacked Wilson's "fifty-fifty attitude" toward Vienna and Budapest and urged revindications for the Austro-Hungarian minorities.[47]

Although Wilson continued to state that he would not undertake the reorganization of the *Monarchie*, the Romanians sent numerous memoranda to Lansing and continued to proselytize. When the Fourteen Points were announced on January 8, 1918, the tone of Romanian propaganda began to suggest the need for increased democratization of Romanian life after the war, for this is what the President liked to hear. In the weeks following, discussions with American businessmen also served to make the prospect of a Greater Romania more attractive, by stressing commercial advantages to be gained by the penetration of American capital into the country; 1919 saw a Romanian-American Chamber of Commerce materialize in New York.[48] Nevertheless, March 1918, brought a cooling off of official American interest, as Romania was forced to sign a separate peace with the Central Powers at Buftea on the 5th of the month. In April, after ten months of intensive activity in the United States, Lucaciu left for Paris, leaving Stoica to sustain the campaign.[49]

Efforts now focused not only on continued relief funds, but on the formation of a Romanian-American volunteer legion. The USRA began to work closely with E. Lucaciu's Romanian National Committee. In April the Executive Committee of the USRA approved the administration by the National Committee of all war relief funds collected by the Union and its locals.[50] A delegation headed by Ioan Păcurar and Ioan Șufana, and including the editor of *America*, C. R. Pascu, traveled to Washington to confer with the Romanian legation.[51] On May 13 a large representative meeting of Romanians from all over the United States took place in Cleveland "to organize the Romanians on the political terrain,"[52] and on July 7 at the closing session of the annual USRA convention in Youngstown, the National Committee won the collective approval of the Romanian societies for a plan to raise 20,000 men for a Romanian Legion to be recruited in the United States and the Allied nations for service against Germany. Headquarters for this work were to be in Cleveland, where the National Committee had established its permanent offices.[53]

This particular convention, more than any other during the war years, dealt with events relative to the hostilities. On the first day the treasurer's report showed that bonds of the Third Liberty Loan were selling quickly among the membership.[54] Due to the interruption by the war of the reception of payments to members' beneficiaries living in Romania, these monies were ordered put into a special fund.[55] The problem of those evading the draft for the United States army, or refusing to serve on particular fronts once conscripted, was dealt with strongly. On July 2 the resolution passed unanimously declaring such individuals removed from the USRA and its member societies. Membership might be reinstated

should a man decide to serve without protest, or voluntarily enlist in the
American armed forces or any Romanian Legion force in an Allied nation.[56] The following day the Union pledged $1,000 annually to the
Ecaterina Theodoriu Orphanage, a sum which would support twenty
orphans a year. Numerous individuals also promised $50 annually to
sustain children of those killed on the battlefields.[57] Finally, needless
to say, the meeting adopted a firm resolution urging freedom for the
4,100,000 Romanians living under foreign rule in Transylvania, Banat,
and Bucovina.[58]

Thus through their press, through their formal organizations, with their
savings laboriously acquired out of workingmen's wages, Romanian-
Americans helped the war effort and provided relief for those suffering
abroad. Many went off to France and Italy where by October 1918,
Romanian Legions were being organized and had received official government sanction. The 112th Trench Mortar Battery at that moment, made
up almost entirely of volunteers of Transylvanian Romanian origin, was
fighting in France. On October 6, 1918, Vasile Stoica received prominent
space in the *New York Times* with his call for an American-Romanian
Legion of 10,000 volunteers, one which could be quickly organized on
the order of the Slavic Legion already formed under the American Army
High Command, and in which Serbs, Czechs, Ruthenians, and Ukrainians
were fighting. Stoica offered the services of the Romanian National Committee in the drive for recruitment.[59]

For a number of reasons, however, such a Legion never materialized,
largely because the war was fast approaching its end. Dissolution of the
Austro-Hungarian Monarchy was already openly spoken of, as Emperor
Karl vainly promised reforms. The National Committee, seeing that moral
fervor and diplomatic persuasion were now to replace military coercion,
bent its efforts to counteract Hungarian propaganda and influence the
coming peace negotiations. On October 19 the Committee responded in
the *New York Times,* in terms of foreshadowing what was to become
standard rhetoric in the Bucharest-Budapest dialogue, to what it called
"renewed efforts of the Hungarians to falsify history and truth," and
protested with all its energy Magyar attempts "to hoodwink the good faith
of the democracies of the world." Hungary's intention to appoint Count
Apponyi delegate to the Paris Conference was seen as an example of the
utmost cynicism, considering that Apponyi was "the most ferocious
tryrant of the subject races of Hungary."[60]

FROM THE AMERICAN SIDE

Besides all this activity initiated by Romanian-Americans, the first of April, 1917, saw a group of Americans headed by Tileston Wells found in New York the Romanian Relief Committee of America. Calling on the public to contribute to the relief fund for the population of Moldavia so severely beset by the ravages of war, the RRCA ultimately gathered over a million dollars which resulted in deliveries of medicines and food supplies to Romania. The mailing of direct contributions by Romanian-Americans was also facilitated by the RRCA, which worked in conjunction with the American Red Cross to this end. The latter organization itself played a major role in Romanian assistance. After initial efforts to create a volunteer ambulance section for Romania in August 1917,[61] in the fall of that year the Red Cross sent a mission to Moldavia, composed of thirteen doctors and eleven nurses led by Colonel H. Anderson. Despite great hardships, the group remained from September 1917, to March 1918, in Romania, and both civilian and military circles praised its laborious and dedicated activity. Altogether the mission supplied foodstuffs and clothing, along with medical aid, to the value of $2,527,000.[62] Romania thus received the third largest allocation of American assistance, exceeded only by France and Armenia.[63] A larger American Red Cross mission returned to the country to pursue successful relief work during 1919.

Such efforts naturally produced better knowledge in the United States of Romania's war aims, and testimony sent back by American volunteers and medical personnel as to the sacrifices of the Romanian people and the strength of their resistance during the months of 1917 undoubtedly helped to modify earlier impressions and strengthened the work of Stoica, Lucaciu and others. While in 1916, the Hearst newspapers depicted Romania in the darkest terms, the *New York Tribune* was severely critical of Bucharest's policies and the *New York Times* and the *Washington Post* generally ignored Romania's situation,[64] by mid-1917 stories filed by Associated Press correspondents accompanying General Hugh Scott who headed the American military mission to Jassy reported the high morale of the Romanian troops who were eager to return to the battle.[65] At the same time political discussion of Romanian irredentist goals became more noticeable in American newspapers.[66]

As articles appeared in the *New York Tribune* by the American military critic and historian Frank M. Sismond, pieces which also found their way into the McClure press and the *Review of Reviews* by September 1917, American opinion on the worth of the Romanian army improved.

Senator Elihu Root's fact-finding mission to Romania in the summer and autumn helped to confirm the usefulness of bolstering Romanian forces financially and materially, while General Scott urged the War Department to assist any army to whose valor he could personally testify. Very influential in this vein were the reports filed by correspondent Stanley Washburn, who had witnessed the battles of September-November 1916 and became something of an authority on the Romanian military scene.[67] Charles Vopicka, American plenipotentiary to Bucharest since 1913, returned to the United States from February to August 1917, also to urge timely support for Romania,[68] while the testimony of two American Red Cross eyewitnesses in Romania, Gideon Wells and Bernard Flexner, made audiences of Romanian-Americans "unspeakably enthusiastic" as they lectured in various cities.[69]

Although the American government delayed a declaration of war on Austria-Hungary until nearly the end of 1917,[70] several elements of the American press establishment sought to inform public opinion on the real situation in the Dual Monarchy. Thus Ira Bennet, manager of the important daily *Washington Post*, showed himself to be a partisan of the Romanian cause from the fall of 1917 on, while a manager of the *New York Times*, Louis Wiley, facilitated Vasile Stoica's access to the columns of the paper. After the failure to obtain official consent for a Romanian Legion, Stoica continued to publish in the *Times* many political, historical, and ethnographic articles, along with current news on Romania's struggle to incorporate all her historic territory within one national state. A series of English booklets also followed, along with press conferences and interviews with American newspapermen.[71] The solemn Carnegie Hall Meeting of the "oppressed nationalities," held on August 12, 1917, in which such leaders of the Czechoslovak movement as M. R. Stefanik took part, brought the American public into direct contact with the centrifugal forces operating on the polyglot empire on the Danube, and brought such prominenti as Senator Gilbert Hitchcock, Chairman of the Senate Foreign Relations Committee, along with Wilson's friend S. M. Lewis, into the circle of those interested in the Romanian cause.[72]

By December 1917, with the United States' declaration of war on Vienna, actions in support of the Romanians entered a new phase, with efforts aimed at attaining American approval for Romanian revindications. Constantin Angelescu's work here was important, for United States government circles required assurances in regard to Romania's future democratic tendencies. Two things were important to stress in this connection: the projected Romanian land reform which would follow the war, and the plebescitary nature of all proposals put to Romanian inhabitants of Hungarian lands. To this end, the "Separation Congress" of Romanian-American churchmen and lay faithful in Youngstown, held on March 9-10, 1918, was important, when religious separation from Austria-Hungary and hierarchical affiliation with the Metropolitanate of Ungro-Valahia in Bucharest were proclaimed symbolically on behalf of one hundred and fifty thousand Romanian-American immigrants and their organized churches.[73]

While Angelescu had to leave the United States by the end of March 1918 (after the Buftea-Bucharest armistice led to Romania's withdrawal from the war), he was not wrong in his assessment that much had been done to change American public opinion about Romania in the previous couple of years. Perhaps this opinion "wishes to make up for the injustice with which it treated us at the beginning," Angelescu noted.[74] In fact the American press, at least, by the time Romania left the hostilities in June 1918, seemed to show clear understanding of the *cul-de-sac* which forced Bucharest to sign a separate peace. Numerous commentaries in the *New York Times,* in the *Sun,* the *Globe,* and the *New York American,* absolved Romania from blame for her actions.[75] In the same month, while the U.S. Senate voted a resolution allowing the organization of a Legion of Slavic Volunteers to fight Austria-Hungary, the *Washington Post* urged that the Buftea Treaty should not be a reason for denying Romanian-Americans the same permission.[76]

Throughout 1918 the Romanian Red Cross relief campaign continued zealously in its work, promoted by Tileston Wells, John Riddle, Livingston Seaman, and Right Tight. Even an American Women's Red Cross Committee was set up with the same end in view.[77] Public meetings in New York, Baltimore, Boston, Cleveland, Chicago, and Pittsburgh were well attended.[78] Outstanding personalities such as Louis Brandeis, the Supreme Court Justice, and Professor George Herron, Wilson's reliable diplomat in Europe proved to be efficacious supporters of Romanian self-fulfillment. 1918 also saw the members of the *Inquiry* panel, charged with establishing postwar ethnic and geographic frontiers, hold a series of consultations with Vasile Stoica, and apparently the Romanian emissary favorably impressed chairman Isaiah Bowman and his colleagues Major Douglas Johnson, Professor Charles Seymour, James T. Shotwell, and others toward a pro-Romanian settlement of the Transylvanian question.[79] It was testimony to the herculean task carried out by Romanian spokesmen during 1918 that by the time of the Paris Peace Conference American public opinion lay generally on Romania's side, considering the relatively unknown quantity which this small country represented to Americans in 1914, and the equally limited size of the Romanian-American ethnic community relative to those of other Central and Southeastern European groups. Indeed, in mid-1918, the territorial causes of the Poles, Italians, South Slavs, and Czechoslovaks had all more or less been formally endorsed by the United States—the Romanian issue alone remained moot. The propaganda campaign of the summer and autumn of 1918, then, remains singularly impressive when only six months later, on November 6, came the announcement from the State Department that the American people would support at the coming peace negotiations "the just political and territorial rights. . . " of the Romanian people.[80] It was the brilliantly successful climax of the Romanian and Romanian-American cause in the United States.

Within a matter of days, the war to end all wars was over, and Romanian-Americans, like their brethren overseas, looked to the future. Upon the outcome of the great gathering in Paris depended the prospects of many tens of thousands of immigrants. A goodly number of those would at last return home to a Romanian Transylvania, their sojourn in the United States over. Some would hasten to visit relatives and villages long cut off by the restricted travel of wartime. The delay in receiving news from home did not end with the cessation of the hostilities. The major American papers did not carry the announcement coming out of Berne on December 9 until two days later, when Romanians in the United States read of the action of the Transylvanian National Assembly on December 1 and the celebration at Alba Iulia.[81]

Thus the centuries-old process of national unification of the Romanian people had completed itself, in many ways independently of the dictates of the Great Powers; as in 1859 and 1877, Romanians had taken matters into their own hands and used the international configuration of events to their own advantage, had channeled the historic force of nation-building in the desired direction.

Romanians far to the west of the Carpathians, those who had traveled across mountains and ocean to the new world, far from the mountain pastures and green valleys sounding with the shepherd's pipe—these, like their fellows in the motherland read the news of those fateful weeks of 1918 with pride and satisfaction, knowing that they, too, had contributed to the making of *România Mare*, to the final creation of the Romanian national unitary state.

NOTES

1. *Calendarul Național al Ziarului "America,"* 1920 (Cleveland, Ohio: Editura Companiei di Publicitate a Soc. Romîne, 1920), p. 114. "Ardealul" by Viorica I. Bantunoiu. (Hereafter, *Calendarul America*).

2. Gerald J. Bobango, "Romanians in America," in *Harvard Encyclopedia of American Ethnic Groups,* 1981, Harvard University Press, 1980. The centenary of Romanian independence in 1978 produced a number of original works dealing with American-Romanian relations: Serban Radulescu-Zoner, "American Consular Reports About Romania's Struggle to Win Independence (1877)," in *East European Quarterly,* XII, No. 3 (1978), 349-358, and Cornelia Bodea, "Contemporary American Recordings of Romania's Unity and Independence," in the same issue, pp. 359-367, as well as the ground-breaking work of Paul Cernovodeanu, "The Image of the United States of America as Viewed by the Romanians in the 19th Century," in *Revue Roumaine d'Histoire,* XVII, 1 (1978), 141-151, and Ion Stanciu, note 67, *infra.*

3. See Christine Avghi Galitzi, *A Study of Assimilation Among Roumanians in the United States* (New York: Columbia University Press, 1929).

4. C. R. Pascu, "Românii din Canada," *Calendarul America,* 1921, p. 156.

5. Galitzi supports this hypothesis, and it is reinforced in Gerald J. Bobango, "The Union and League of Romanian Societies in America: An 'Assimilating Force' Reviewed," *East European Quarterly,* 12, No. 1 (1978), 85-92.

6. On this see Josef J. Barton, *Peasants and Strangers: Italians, Rumanians, and Slovaks in an American City, 1890-1950* (Cambridge: Harvard University Press, 1975), *passim.*

7. C. R. Pascu, *Istoria Uniunei și Ligei Societăților Române de Ajutor și Cultura din America, 1906-1931* (Cleveland: Tip. Ziarului "America," 1931), p. 104.

8. *Steaua Noastră,* I, No. 7, July 2, 1912, p. 1.

9. N. Iorga, *Istoria contemporană de la 1904 la 1930* (București, 1932), p. 162.

10. Stephen Fischer-Galati, "The Romanian-American Press As a Source of Information on Romania," Paper given at the Romanian Library, New York, November 24, 1976, pp. 10-11. (See following article.)

11. This Calendar, without cover or indication of publisher, although obviously originating in Romania, was found by one of the authors among

the materials of the *Ulpia Traiana* Society in Erie, Pennsylvania. Assistance in its identification would be welcomed.

12. Ştefan Meteş, *Emigrări Româneşti din Transilvania în Secolele XII-XX*, ed. a 2-la (ed. Ştiinţifica şi Enciclopedica, Bucureşti, 1977), p. 458.

13. *America*, XII, August 5, 1917, p. 1. *Roumania* was published monthly from August 1917, until the summer of 1918. As of October, 1917, Negulescu raised from his conferences and public meetings some $20,000 most of which was used on medicine sent to Romania (cf. Library of the Academy of the Socialist Republic of Romania, Manuscript Div., Fund Ion I. C. Brătianu, MS 53022, Brătianu to Dr. C. Angelescu, 8/21 October, 1917).

14. Sofron S. Fekett, *Istoria Uniunii şi Ligei Societăţilor Româneşti din America* (Cleveland: Tip. Ziarului "America," 1956), pp. 24-48.

15. *America*, XII, October 24, 1917, p. 1.

16. Fekett, p. 50.

17. Şerban Druţu and Andrei Popovici, *Românii în America* (Bucureşti: "Cartea Românească," 1926), pp. 199-204.

18. *New York Times*, 15 August 1915, II, 12: 7-8.

19. For details of membership, funds, and a chronological list of the local club assemblies, see *Calendarul America*, 1916, *passim*.

20. *America*, XI, February 24, 1916, p. 4, and March 2, 1916, p. 2.

21. Ibid., XI, March 5, 1916, p. 1ff.

22. *Proces Verbal Comitetului Suprem Executive al U.S.R.A.*, 28-29 October 1916, p. 5.

23. *New York Times*, 31 May 1916, 22:3.

24. *Proces Verbal Adunarea Generală a U.S.R.A.*, 1-6 Iulia 1916, p. 5.

25. See the issues of *Steaua Noastră* for the summer and autumn of 1912. Taft is called a friend of immigrants, while Wilson is labeled a racist, full of class bigotry in an editorial of 30 July 1912, p. 2. On 11 September is the comment, "Yes, they're for Wilson, the power of money, put in action by the trusts and centers of great finance" (p. 1). Interesting is the contrast between this, and the attitude toward Wilson once the President espoused self-determination for Transylvania six years later.

26. Miron Constantinescu, Ştefan Pascu, et al., *Desăvîrşirea Unificării Statului Naţional Român: Unirea Transilvaniei cu Vechea România* (Bucureşti: Ed. Academiei Republicii Socialiste România, 1968), p. 134.

27. *America*, XII, January 29, 1917, p. 1.

28. Ibid., XII, February 15, 1917, p. 3.

29. Ibid., pp. 3-5.

30. Ibid., XII, March 8, 1917, p. 1.
31. Ibid., XII, April 15, 1917, p. 1ff.
32. Ibid.
33. Ibid., XII, July 5, 1917, p. 1.
34. Ibid., XII, August 2, 1917, p. 2.
35. Ibid., pp. 1-2, and following issues.
36. *Proces Verbal U.S.R.A. Luat in Adunarea Generală*, 1-5 Iulie 1917, p. 10. The convention actually met through July 6.
37. Ibid., p. 18.
38. Fckett, p. 131.
39. *Calendarul America*, 1920, p. 197.
40. *Proces Verbal U.S.R.A. Luat in Adunarea Generală*, 1-5 Iulie 1917, p. 19.
41. *America*, XII, October 23, 1917, p. 1.
42. Ibid., XII, October 24, 1917, p. 1.
43. Ibid.
44. Ibid., XII, October 3, 1917, p. 3.
45. V. Stoica, *America pentru cauza noastră* (București, 1926), p. 7.
46. Ibid.
47. Constantinescu and Pascu, op. cit., p. 170.
48. *New York Times*, 5 April 1919, 20:5.
49. Stoica, p. 10.
50. *Proces Verbal Comitetului Suprem Executiv al U.S.R.A.*, 20-21 Aprilie 1918, pp. 3-4. Although the funds would remain in the bank accounts of the USRA.
51. Ibid., p. 3.
52. *Calendarul America*, 1919, p. 218.
53. *New York Times*, July 8, 1918, 2:3.
54. *Proces Verbal U.S.R.A. Luat in Adunarea Generală*, 1-5 Iulie 1918, p. 7. The total bonds held by the USRA now equaled $8,000—from the First, Second, and Third Liberty Loans, the Union had purchased $5,000, $2,000, and $1,000 respectively.
55. Ibid., pp. 7-8.
56. Ibid., p. 14. Ioan Păcurar had already removed them on his own authority earlier in the year at the meeting of the Supreme Executive Committee.
57. Ibid., p. 19.
58. *New York Times*, 8 July 1918, 2:3.
59. Ibid., 6 October 1918, III, 5:1-4.
60. Ibid., 19 October 1918, 3:4.

61.   Stoica, p. 19. Its establishment was supported by the American Captain L. C. Doyle and Henry Sleeper, with the assistance of the Romanian Adrian Miclescu, head of the supplies sub-commission of the Ministry of War who came to the United States to contract for materials and munitions. Since the military situation prevented the delivery of ambulances to the Romanian front, those obtained were subsequently directed to the Italian front.

62.   Hoover Institute on War and Peace Archives, Furlong Charles Wellington Collection, Booklet, *The Work of the American Red Cross*, no. 2, p. 80.

63.   See *Neamul românesc*, December 2, 1917. The mission was recalled after the Peace of Buftea. Cf. also Henry P. Davison, *The American Red Cross in the Great War* (New York, 1919), 233-251, and E. P. Bicknell, *With the Red Cross in Europe* (Washington, D.C.: The American National Red Cross, 1938), 489-490.

64.   C. Chirițescu, *Istoria războiului pentru întegirea României, 1916-1919* (București, 1922), 465.

65.   Library of Congress, Manuscript Division, Hugh Scott Papers, Box 71, Correspondence and Reports on the Mission to Russia, 1917, Press Material of August 23, 1917. Worthy of note also was the publication of *Rumania's Sacrifice* by Gogu Negulescu, translated by Mrs. C. de S. Wainright (New York: The Century Co., 1918).

66.   Ibid.

67.   Cf. Stoica, p. 13, and the recent study of Ion Stanciu, "Stanley Washburn, An American War Correspondent on the Romanian Front, September-November 1916," *Revue Roumaine d'Histoire*, XV, No. 2 (1976), 293-304.

68.   Charles Vopicka, *The Secrets of the Balkans, Seven Years of the Diplomatic Life in the Storm Center of Europe* (Chicago: Rand McNally and Company, 1921), p. 128. Vopicka also lent his support to Romanian representatives Gogu Negulescu and Colonel Adrian Miclescu in obtaining supplies and contracts with American firms, and gaining access to financial circles. See Library of the Academy of the Socialist Republic of Romania, C. Angelescu Fund XIX/9, Miclescu to the Ministry of War, 17/30 July 1917.

69.   Foreign Ministry Archives, Fund 71/1914, E2, Part II, vol. 302, Constantin Angelescu MS Memorandum, March 28, 1918.

70.   A state of war against the Austro-Hungarian Empire was declared only on December 7, 1917.

71.   Stoica, pp. 14, 16, mentions 2,300 such booklets, along with the

pamphlet "Greater Romania" by David Mitrany, and A. V. Leaper's *The Justice of Romania's Cause.*

72. Stoica, p. 16.

73. Foreign Ministry Archives, Fund 71/1914, E2, Part II, vol. 302, C. Angelescu's Memorandum, March 28, 1918, and Stoica, p. 25. For a full discussion of the Youngstown Congress, see Gerald J. Bobango, *The Romanian Orthodox Episcopate of America: The First Half-Century* (Jackson, Michigan: The Romanian American Heritage Center, 1979).

74. Foreign Ministry Archives, Angelescu Memorandum, *supra.*

75. The *New York American* in its issue of May 22, 1918, observed that the treatment accorded to Romania by the Peace of Bucharest clearly indicated how far one might count on Austria-Hungary's sincerity.

76. *America,* July 1, 1918, p. 1.

77. Library of the Academy of the Socialist Republic of Romania, MS 53631.

78. Stoica, pp. 38-39.

79. Stoica, pp. 60-62, and see Mitchell Pirrie Briggs, *George D. Herron and the European Settlement* (Stanford: University Press, 1934), 74-75.

80. Stoica, pp. 50-51.

81. *New York Times,* 11 December 1918, 4:4-5.

Stephen Fischer-Galati

THE ROMANIAN-AMERICAN PRESS AS A SOURCE
OF INFORMATION ON ROMANIA

According to recent Americana the first link between Americans and Romanians was forged by Captain John Smith who fought on the side of Transylvanian and Wallachian princes against the Turks in the seventeenth century. Smith was captured by the Turks but escaped to England wherefrom he sailed to Jamestown to become one of Virginia's founding fathers.[1] More direct contacts were established in later years but it was not until 1903 that the first Romanian newspaper appeared in the United States, the *Tribuna* of Cleveland, Ohio.[2] Two years later, another Romanian newspaper—*Românul*—appeared also in Cleveland and in 1906 the most-widely-read of all Romanian papers, *America*, was published in the very same city.[3] In 1914, the Cultural Association of Romanian Workers founded the newspaper *Deşteptarea* in Detroit, Michigan.[4]

There were other papers published at one time or another since 1903. In the long run, only *America* and *Deşteptarea* (renamed *Românul American* in 1939) survived. And of these two it was the latter which consistently provided information about Romania and Romanians in Romanian at the expense of primary concentration on the affairs of Romanian-American communities and community affairs in Cleveland, Detroit, New York, Los Angeles, and a few smaller centers in which men and women of Romanian origin and their descendants congregated.

The following brief study on the Romanian-American press as a source of information on Romania will focus on contents analysis of *Deşteptarea* and *Românul American* over a period of nearly fifty years, from 1924 until the dissolution of *Românul American* in 1968. The latter chronological limit is self-evident; the former corresponds to the growing concern of the Romanian-American workers' movement with that of the Romanian movement following the outlawing of the Romanian Communist Party and the corollary political developments in Romania. Our analysis will be concerned exclusively with matters related to Romania avoiding consideration of polemics with other Romanian-American newspapers, primarily with *America*, on issues only peripherally related to Romanian affairs. This procedure seems justifiable because all Romanian-American papers other than *Deşteptarea* or *Românul American* devoted little space to Romanian problems and events and such space as was devoted was reserved for information derived from the *New York Times* or from papers published in Bucharest. *Deşteptarea* and *Românul American*, on the other hand, were politically-oriented papers whose sources of information on Romania were far more diversified and whose coverage of Romanian affairs was indeed extensive. These two papers relied on the news disseminated in the principal Bucharest dailies, on the socialist and communist press, whether published in Romania or abroad, and on occasion on firsthand reports received from ad hoc correspondents in Romania proper. Whether it is justifiable in terms of the papers' effectiveness in reaching large audiences concerned with Romanian affairs and in promoting a clearer understanding of events and developments in Romania among their readers is another question. The question may, however, be judged relevant since interest in Romanian affairs was ajudged to be at best marginal even among Americans of Romanian descent.

An analysis of the press coverage of Romanian matters in the period 1924-1944 reveals that only the *New York Times*, and on rare occasions major papers published in urban centers, carried any news regarding Romania.[5] More significant perhaps is the lack of coverage manifest in *America* and other Romanian-American papers, a lacuna which becomes even more striking upon reflection on the fact that a considerable part of *America* was printed in English on subjects unrelated to Romanian affairs. Circulation figures are obscure and often exaggerated.[6] It is believed, however, that *America*'s daily circulation reached 20,000 copies by the end of the 1920s which, if true, would give credence to the oft-repeated argument that *America* has always been the primary Romanian-American paper in the United States. Be this as it may, it is doubtful that *America*'s readers learned much about Romania at any time if that was their purpose in reading the paper in the first place. Whether the readers of *Deşteptarea* or of *Românul American* were concerned with news about Romania to a comparable extent as that of news about the working class movement in the United States and elsewhere is unknown. It could be surmised from the nature of the papers that their primary purpose was not dissemination of news about Romania as such. Romanian affairs were subordinated, at least until 1948, to general problems of the international workers' movement and, by extension, of the international communist movement led by the Soviet Union. The circulation of these papers is believed to have been quite small. In the absence of exact figures an educated estimate, based on extrapolation of data provided periodically by the publishers, would place the weekly distribution at not more than 2,000 copies.[7] This by itself provides no clues as to the number of readers who were actually concerned with Romanian affairs. It does, however, seem justified to assume that the readers of *Deşteptarea* and of *Românul American* were more motivated than those of *America* to try to keep abreast of developments in Romania and, in any event, had the opportunity to secure such information as they might have wished to secure if for no other reason than that such information was in fact provided in considerable detail.

Deşteptarea and *Românul American*, no matter how extensive their readership during the years of their appearance, remain an invaluable source of information on Romania as such and as depicted in the United States by Romanian-Americans. In this lies their greatest significance.

Two separate stages are evident in the evolution of the two papers. The first, lasting roughly until 1945, is characterized by the securing and disseminating of information from a variety of sources as indicated above. The second, starting with the establishment of the Groza regime in 1945 and ending with the discontinuation of publication of *Românul American* in 1968, is characterized by almost exclusive reprinting of articles from the Romanian press or of paraphrasing or translating of materials published in *Scînteia* and other Romanian papers. Inasmuch as the Romanian press became available to interested readers in the United States after World War II there is little need for our analyzing the contents of *Românul American* since 1945 as a source of original information or as an instrumentality of the Romanian-American community in the United States. But this is evidently not the case for the twenty years antedating the end of World War II.

During the interwar years and until the defeat of the Axis powers became apparent, *Deşteptarea* and *Românul American* were concerned with roughly the following aspects of Romanian developments: (1) General news from and about Romania; (2) News about the Romanian workers' and revolutionary movements with special emphasis on the role of the Romanian Communist Party; (3) The history of the Romanian Communist Party and details of its activities and of those of its leaders; (4) Relations between the USSR and Romania and relations between the Communist Party of the Soviet Union and the Romanian Communist Party; (5) Problems related to Bessarabia and to the Moldavian Socialist Republic; and (6) Articles on certain aspects of Romanian history.

The most banal feature of the papers was the dissemination of news of general interest on Romania. Within this category the stress was on political developments centering on the rise of fascist tendencies and manifestations in the 1920s and 1930s. *Deșteptarea* provided considerable coverage of anti-Semitic manifestations directed by Corneliu Zelea Codreanu and A. C. Cuza in the 1920s, on political assassinations and other acts of violence directed or committed by the Iron Guard in the 1930s, and on corollary persecutions of Jewish and other minority groups ondoned, if not actually encouraged, by the several political parties which succeeded each other in power in the 1920s and 1930s.[8]

In short, *Deșteptarea* alerted its readers to the realities of the political crisis of interwar Romania at a time when most other sources of information distributed in the United States ignored Romanian problems or minimized the significance of key events.[9]

Far from banal, however, was the coverage of the programs and activities of the workers' movement in Romania in both its benign and revolutionary aspects. *Deșteptarea* was in fact the only paper published in the United States which provided extensive coverage of political trials ranging from those following the Tatar Bunar events to those of progressive leaders such as Professor Constantinescu-Iași in the mid-1930s.[10] The greatest emphasis was placed on the several trials related to the Grivița Strike of 1933 and to those involving anti-fascist workers and intellectuals in following years.[11] Closely tied to these political manifestations was *Deșteptarea*'s constant concern with the mistreatment of political prisoners in Romania and the accompanying requests for liberation of such prisoners. Almost every issue of the paper condemned conditions prevalent in Doftana and other political prisons and provided vivid descriptions of the inhuman treatment of prisoners, which on occasion, led to the death of inmates.[12]

Statistical data on the misery of workers and peasants were provided from time to time but such materials were secondary in emphasis to other political events.[13] The direct link between workers' and peasants' unrest and despondency and the expectations of a better life in the future was, in the columns of *Deșteptarea* and *Românul American*, the work of the progressive political forces in Romania, particularly that of the Romanian Communist Party. And it is in this rubric that these two Romanian-American papers provided their readers with the most thorough and original information.

The work of the Romanian communists and of their party in Romania was covered primarily through biographic information of leaders although periodically accounts of Party conferences and resolutions were published in extenso. In the 1920s the most heralded leaders were Max Goldstein, Boris Ştefanov, Marcel Pauker, and particularly M. Gheorghe Bujor.[14] In the 1930s the emphasis shifted somewhat with Ştefanov, Constantin Doncea, Gheorghe Gheorghiu-Dej, and Ana Pauker assuming ever greater significance.[15] Numerous interesting details on the political activities of these leaders and of other important communists were revealed with special emphasis on their plans, programs, and actions from the time of their first joining the communist movement until their imprisonment.[16] The material on formal Party activities was less ample but of at least equal significance. The Resolution of the Political Secretariat of the Executive Committee of the Comintern on the Romanian Party, of 1930, was published in full as were the proceedings of the Fifth Congress of the Romanian Communist Party in 1932, Draganov's report on the Party to the Seventh Congress of the Comintern in 1935, and the Resolution of the Sixth Plenary Session of the Romanian Communist Party in 1939.[17] Although the data have since become known they were novel and crucial for understanding the work and activities of the communists in the interwar years. And similar data were provided on other occasions as well.

As the 1930s progressed, *Deşteptarea* devoted many a page to two major activities of the Romanian communists: their attempts to mobilize the anti-fascist forces in Romania with a view to establishing a United Front and their participation in the Spanish Civil War.[18] The information provided on the Spanish Civil War, particularly that regarding the work of individual units, was frequently unobtainable through other sources of information accessible to American readers. It is noteworthy that the Romanian contingent periodically sent messages directly to *Deşteptarea* calling for united political action by anti-fascist forces in the United States and Romania.[19] This was all the more significant since the efforts toward the establishment of a united anti-fascist front, comprising all groups concerned with peace and freedom, resulted in the creation of a united organization of Romanian-Americans in the spring of 1939 and the adoption of the name *Românul American*, in lieu of *Deşteptarea*, for the organ of the new organization.[20]

As may be expected of newspapers concerned with the international labor and revolutionary movements substantial coverage was given to the policies of the Soviet Union toward Romania. In this rubric *Deşteptarea* and *Românul American* focussed on two major aspects: general political and diplomatic relations between the USSR and Romania, with special emphasis on the treatment of the Romanian Communist Party by the

rulers of Romania, and corollary developments in the Moldavian Socialist
Republic. The former encompassed primarily articles originally published
in the Soviet or Romanian press normally critical of official Romanian
actions.[21] Articles elogious of the work of Nicolae Titulescu both at the
League of Nations and in promoting better relations between the Soviet
Union and Romania and factual statements such as the Russo-Romanian
agreement on the establishment of formal diplomatic relations in 1934
did, however, also appear on occasion.[22] After the establishment of the
royal dictatorship of King Carol II in 1938, and particularly after the
German entry into Romania in 1940, the number of items of Soviet origin
increased with the notable exception of the one year period dating from
August 1939 until October 1940.[23] Following the invasion of the USSR
by the Romanian armies in the summer of 1941 *Românul American* became an invaluable source of data provided by the Soviet press on the
war and corollary relations with Romania.[24]

On the related, and much emphasized, Bessarabian question and status
of the Moldavian Socialist Republic *Deșteptarea* and *Românul American*,
at least until 1940, frequently stated that Bessarabia rightfully belonged
to the Romanian workers and working peasantry.[25] In 1940 *Românul
American* altered its position to take into account the realities of the political situation ensuing from the occupation of Bessarabia.[26] It is not
entirely clear whether the two newspapers regarded the Romanian workers
and working peasants of Bessarabia as Romanians or as "Moldavians" at
any time before 1940. The imprecision may be ascribed to the ambiguity
regarding the nationality of the Romanian-speaking inhabitants of the
Moldavian Socialist Republic which permeated the articles devoted to that
republic which appeared so frequently in the colums of *Deșteptarea* and
Românul American.[27] Be this as it may, meaningful information on Bessarabia and the Moldavian Republic was unobtainable anywhere in the
United States except in the two newspapers under review and, as such,
Deșteptarea and *Românul American* did yeoman service in keeping their
readers abreast of developments in Eastern Romania and on Soviet policies
affecting Romanians living in Bessarabia and in the Moldavian Socialist
Republic itself.

Deșteptarea and *Românul American* also shared the unique function of
offering their readers contributions to the history of the Romanian workers' and revolutionary movements at a time when such historical material
was inaccessible elsewhere. Among the studies published were articles on
Horia, Cloșca, and Crișan, on Tudor Vladimirescu, on the Bobâlna Uprising of 1437, and on the workers' movement in Romania, the last ones

representing a serialized version of the exhaustive study of the subject produced by M. Roller.[28]

It is evident that for readers concerned with Romania and Romanian problems during the years in which little information was available, *Deşteptarea* and *Românul American* were an essential source of information and commentary on matters Romanian. And, to a definite extent, the value of *Românul American* as a source of information did not decrease in the years following the defeat of fascism and the ensuing changes which occurred in Romanian and world history.

During the years immediately following World War II *Românul American* emerged as an American edition of *Scînteia* and, after the formal establishment of the Romanian People's Republic in 1948, also of other publications appearing in Romania. Its originality as a source of news thus declined because *Scînteia* and other Romanian publications were available to readers concerned with Romanian affairs. Nevertheless, *Românul American* added two important features during the last twenty years of publication: publication of substantial parts of its contents in the English language and publication of original articles on Romanian problems and issues written by members of its editorial board.[29] It is fair to assume that the coverage in English was prompted by the changing character of its readership. The number of individuals of Romanian origin who could read Romanian declined in the 1930s and 1940s and the second and third generations of Romanian-Americans were at best deficient in their knowledge of Romanian if not altogether ignorant of that language. This waning proficiency in Romanian was also evident in the articles written by Romanian-Americans who comprised the editorial board. Their commentaries on Romanian affairs, written in archaic and frequently Americanized Romanian, illustrated the linguistic realities which afflicted writers and readers alike. In fact, the commentaries were as a rule mere *explications de textes* in simplified idiom for broader understanding.[30]

The ultimate demise of *Românul American* in 1968 reflected the objective conditions of the late 1960s. The readership had dwindled because of the death of the older generation, including most of the editors, and because of the availability of extensive information on Romania through the Romanian press, the American press, and an ever larger number of books and periodicals published in both Romanian and English in Romania and in the United States. Nevertheless, historically *Deşteptarea* and *Românul American* had performed invaluable services in making available

information on Romania to the Romanian-American community and to
other individuals interested in Romanian affairs for over half-a-century
when such information was generally unavailable in the United States.
Students of Romanian-Americans, of Romania, of the Romanian workers'
and revolutionary movements, of Romanian communism, and of international relations owe a debt of gratitude to the publishers c᷄ ᷄.e now
defunct papers. A chapter in the history of Romanian-American relations
and of the Romanian-Americans ended in 1968; it was valuable in many
respects.

NOTES

1.   Vladimir Werstman, Ed., *The Romanians in America, 1748-1974*
(Dobbs Ferry, 1975), p. 2.

2.   Ibid., p. 4.

3.   Ibid., pp. 4-5.

4.   Ibid., p. 6.

5.   The *New York Times Index* provides a complete listing of al
materials on Romania published in the *New York Times*.

6.   Werstman, op. cit., pp. 6, 15.

7.   *Deşteptarea*, 16 December 1933 (The paper appeared weekly.)

8.   Typical of the coverage was the series of articles entitled "Asasin-
atele fasciste: procesul uciderii ministrului Duca" which began with the
5 May 1934 issue of *Deşteptarea*.

9.   Relevant in this regard are the several articles denouncing other
Romanian-American papers for hiding or distorting the truth about conditions and events in Romania. See especially *Deşteptarea* of 11 November
1933 and 3 March 1934. See also the several articles entitled "Situaţia din
România," signed by N. Grigorescu, which were published seriatim started
with the issue dated 1 December 1934 as well as the rubic "Din România"
which appeared in almost every issue following that of 13 July 1935.

10. For instance: *Deşteptarea* 8 November 1925; 2-30 September
1933; 15 June 1935; 18-25 April 1936.

11. Ibid.

12. *Deşteptarea*, 15 November 1925; 20 May 1929; 10 October 1929;
16 November 1930; 3 May 1931; 21 October 1933; 27 October 1934; 22
February 1936; 3 July 1937; 30 October 1937; 20 November 1937.

13. See note 9 and also *Deşteptarea*, 17-24 September 1938; 25
February 1939.

14. *Deşteptarea*, 15 November 1925; 20 December 1925; 4-11 March
1928; 15 July 1929; 15 September 1929; 3 May 1931.

15. *Deşteptarea*, 2 September 1933; 10 March 1934; 22 September 1934; 27 October 1934; 28 January 1936; 27 February 1936; 1 May 1937; 30 October 1937; 1 January 1938; 20 April 1938. Also *Românul American*, 16 December 1939.

16. *Supra*, notes 14 and 15.

17. *Deşteptarea*, 28 December 1930; 10-25 January 1931; 4-15 Sept-1932; 2-30 October 1932; 16 February 1936. Also *Românul American*, 29 July 1939.

18. *Deşteptarea*, 12-19 June 1937; 3 July 1937; 31 July 1937; 6 November 1937; 5 February 1938; 23 July 1938.

19. *Deşteptarea*, 23 July 1938; 4 February 1939.

20. *Deşteptarea*, 1 April 1939; 27 May 1939.

21. See for instance *Deşteptarea*, 15 September 1929; 1 October 1929; 24 March 1934; 8 September 1934; 30 April-18 June 1938.

22. See especially the summary statement published in *Deşteptarea* of 8 September 1934.

23. *Românul American*, 4 December 1940; 12 April 1941; 24 May 1941 and every issue thereafter.

24. Ibid.

25. *Deşteptarea*, 16 April 1926; 1 April 1927; 8 September 1934; 17-24 September 1938.

26. *Românul American*, 6-20 July 1940; 28 September 1940.

27. *Deşteptarea*, 16 August 1925; 8 November 1925; 21 February 1926; 1 February 1927; 28 October 1933; 26 October 1935; 16 February 1936; 8 January 1938; 23 July 1938. Also *Românul American*, 30 December 1939.

28. *Deşteptarea*, 7 September 1935; 16 February 1936; 15-22 January 1938; 9 July 1938; 17 September 1938-25 January 1939. Also *Românul American*, 28 September 1940; 12 April 1941.

29. For typical items see *Românul American*, 1 January 1948; 21-28 May 1949; 7 July-31 December 1949 and almost every issue published thereafter.

30. Ibid.

Paul D. Quinlan

THE UNITED STATES AND THE PROBLEM OF TRANSYLVANIA DURING WORLD WAR II

During the period between the two World Wars one of the most complex and controversial issues of territorial ownership involved the bitter dispute between Hungary and Romania over the picturesque land of Transylvania. Situated between Hungary and the Romanian lands of Wallachia and Moldavia, from the tenth century to 1918 (except for a period of Turkish domination from 1526 to 1699) Transylvania had been controlled by Hungary and Austria. In 1865 it was fully incorporated into the Kingdom of Hungary. Yet it has been estimated that since the eigh teenth century the Romanians formed an absolute majority of the population. In spite of this they were treated as second class citizens at best by the ruling Hungarians, with little voice in politics. This, combined with the Hungarian policy of magyarization and the growing national self-consciousness of the Romanians in the latter part of the nineteenth century, eventually helped to bring about their joining with their co-nationalists in the Old Kingdom in the forming of a united Romanian state. The ramifications of this controversy spread far beyond the borders of Romania and Hungary and involved not only the European Powers, but also to a limited degree the United States. Utilizing unpublished and published American and British documents, the purpose of this chapter is to outline the role of the United States in the dispute over Transylvania during World War II.

Prior to World War I the United States government showed no interest in the question of self-determination for Romanians living outside the Old Kingdom, including those in Transylvania. It was not until the very end of the war, as a result of the disintegration of the Austrian Empire, as well as the constant pressure in Washington by Romanians under the leadership of Vasile Stoica, that the United States finally recognized, in principle, the idea of Romanian unification.[1] On November 5, 1918, Washington announced that "the Government of the United States deeply sympathizes and will not neglect at the proper time to exert its influence that the just political and territorial rights of the Roumanian people may be obtained and made secure from all foreign aggression."[2] This was more than two years after the governments of Britain, France, Russia, and Italy had specifically recognized Romania's right to annex the eastern parts of the Hungarian plain, Transylvania, Bucovina, and the Banat in the Treaty of Bucharest of 17 August 1916.

At the Paris Peace Conference the United States supported Romania's claim to historical Transylvania. Since a clear majority of the population were Romanians this presented no problem for the Americans. Even according to the Hungarian census of 1910 Romanians made up fifty-five percent of the population while the Hungarians only thirty-four percent.[3] Moreover, during the war Romania was an ally and Hungary an enemy. On the other hand, the "Inquiry," a group of scholars working under Colonel House on American territorial proposals, recommended to Wilson in January 1919, that several border regions, comprising parts of the Banat, Crişana, and Maramureş, including the predominatly Magyar cities of Oradea (Nagyvárad), Satu Mare (Szatmárnémeti), and Arad, not be given to Romania.[4] Basing their policy on the principle of national self-determination, the Americans hoped to erect the best possible ethnic frontiers between the two countries. Unfortunately for Hungary, the majority of Hungarians in Transylvania lived in areas so far to the east that any attempt to restore these districts to Hungary would place an equal, if not larger, number of non-Magyars under Hungarian rule. In the end the United States was only able to prevent Romania from getting the entire Banat. Both the British and the French opposed the American objections in Crişana and Maramureş on economic and military grounds. Economically such a division would have created great confusion as it would sever the cities of Oradea, Statu Mare, and Arad from their economic hinterland, as well as cut the main north-south railway at several points so that trains would have to crisscross international frontiers going from one city to another. At the same time, the entire area was under the control of the Romanian army, and on 1 December 1918 a huge assembly of Romanians at Alba Iulia voted for the union of these lands with Romania.[5]

On June 4, 1920 Hungary signed the Treaty of Trianon. Hungary, like the other vanquished nations, had to accept the peace terms drawn up by the victorious Allies. As with the Treaty of Versailles, the United States never ratified the Trianon Treaty. Instead, in August of the following year the United States signed separate peace treaties with Hungary and Austria, thereby recognizing Romania's acquisition of lands from the now defunct Austro-Hungarian Empire, including Transylvania.[6]

As a result of the war and the peace treaties, Romania acquired more land and people in comparison to her prewar size than any other state, while Hungary lost more than any other state. Romania more than doubled the size of her territory and population, from 53,244 square miles to 113,918 square miles and from a population of 7,626,945 at the beginning of 1914 (including Southern Dobrogea) to that of 15,541,424 in 1920.[7] Of this increase approximately 39,500 square miles consisted of Transylvania and adjacent areas with a population of 2,800,073 Romanians. Unfortunately this also meant that 1,704,851 Hungarians now found themselves living within the new enlarged Romanian state.[8] According to the Romanian census of 1930 Romanians numbered 57.8 percent of the people in Transylvania (including the Banat, Crişana, and Maramureş), while Hungarians made up 24.4 percent.[9] Hungary, however, having lost most of her non-Magyar subjects was reduced to 28.6 percent of her prewar area, having now a total size of less than what she lost to the Romanians alone.[10]

As a result bitterness between Hungary and Romania reached a new high, and would continue almost unabated throughout the interwar period. Although the new rump Hungarian state was for the most part made up of those with Magyar as a mother tongue a dominant goal of successive Hungarian governments was to restore her lost territories. Little of this involved the United States though. During the interwar years United States relations with both countries were friendly, centering mainly around economic and financial matters.[11] The only unresolved territorial settlement between the United States and either country involved Romania's possession of the former Russian province of Bessarabia, which historically was a part of Moldavia and had a predominantly Romanian population.[12] In 1933 the United States gave *de facto* recognition to its union with Romania.

With the outbreak of World War II, the United States became gradually involved again in the question of Transylvania. In the summer of 1940, trapped in the middle of the power struggle between Nazi Germany and the Soviet Union, Romania was forced to give up more than a third of her territory and population. On June 26, Romania was given a twenty-four hour ultimatum by the Russians to cede Bessarabia and Northern Bucovina. Because of Romania's annexation of Bessarabia, Romanian-Soviet relations had remained poor during the interwar period, with formal diplomatic relations not restored until 1934. Soviet-Hungarian relations were no better, with formal relations being re-established in 1934, then broken and restored again in February and September 1939 respectively. Nevertheless, probably in an effort to bring greater pressure on the Romanians, the Soviets told the Hungarians that they agreed with their claims for Transylvania, and even urged them to take military action.[13] The Hungarians needed little encouragement. With Romania's cession of Bessarabia and Northern Bucovina, Budapest began demanding Transylvania back, going as far as mobilizing her troops and threatening armed intervention.[14] In order to avoid a war in the Balkans, Hitler and Mussolini intervened, forcing both sides to agree to the so-called Second Vienna Award of August 30, 1940.[15] Under this Hungary acquired the northern half of Transylvania, 16,792 square miles, and containing about a million Hungarians. Yet as before the ethnic problem defied a reasonable solution—more than one million Romanians were now brought back under Hungarian rule.[16] The United States did not go along with any of these changes, following her general policy of not recognizing any territorial changes that had been made since the war began.[17]

The United States also had adopted the policy of not entering into any commitments involving territorial changes in the hope that all such issues could be settled after the war at the peace conference.[18] A somewhat similar through less dogmatic view was adopted by the British. On September 5, 1940, the Foreign Secretary, Lord Halifax, stated in the House of Lords, that Britain would not "recognize territorial changes unless they have been evidently and freely agreed between all the parties concerned." In the same statement Halifax also pointed out "that we are unable to accept the settlement now announced of the Hungarian-Romanian dispute over Transylvania since that settlement is the result of a dictation by the Axis powers imposed on Roumania under duress."[19]

During the years 1942 and 1943 the question of the future status of Transylvania was largely an academic one for the United States government. In spite of the fact that Washington never recognized the Vienna Award, the State Department was undecided as to what Transylvania's future status should be. One State Department memorandum stated that "our own studies have pointed to the conclusion . . . that probably some form of autonomy for the entire Transylvanian area may prove to be the solution best suited to serve the interest of international security and of future collaboration and peaceful relations among the Danubian states."[20] The British also engaged in this kind of speculation. One idea called for "the creation of an independent Transylvanian state cantonised on Swiss lines."[21] On the other hand, the British, who were taking the lead over the Americans at this time in the Balkans, utilized the issue of Transylvania in their broadcasts to Eastern Europe. London tried to use Transylvania to stir up further animosity between Romania and Hungary, both enemy states, in an effort to force them to keep more troops at home instead of on the eastern front. In addition, as the war progressed, Britain, and to a lesser extent the United States, became involved with the question of Transylvania in dealing with "peacefeelers" from Romania and Hungary. But both London and Washington rigidly avoided making any commitments to either enemy state.

Actually after 1941 the Western Powers were severely limited in dealing with Transylvania. Like the Western Nations, the Soviet Union did not recognize the Vienna Award. Nevertheless, in the following summer Molotov seems to have suggested to the Hungarian ambassador that if they stayed out of the war they could count on Soviet support in regaining the rest of Transylvania.[22] But this effort was to no avail, and in the following December during Anthony Eden's visit to Moscow, Stalin indicated that Romania should have all of Transylvania and perhaps more.[23]

As the war progressed with the Red Army doing all of the fighting on the eastern front, it became evident that the Soviets would have the final say on Transylvania. Yet, in spite of what Stalin told Eden in Moscow, subsequent events show that the Russians had not completely decided on its future status, especially since they could use it for their own purposes. Although in June 1943, Molotov stated in a memorandum to the British that the Soviet Union did not recognize the Vienna Award, two months later the Russians told Ferenc Honti, the Hungarian Consul in Geneva, that they might allow an autonomous Transylvania to remain within the Hungarian state.[24] But this attempt to entice Hungary away from Germany got nowhere, and by October they apparently had reverted back to favoring the Romanians.[25]

As the Soviets pushed closer to Romania during the winter of 1943-44 the United States and England began to draw up preliminary armistice proposals for Romania. Washington hoped that all of the Romanian territorial issues, including the ultimate fate of Bessarabia and Northern Bucovina which the Romanians had reconquered in the summer of 1941, could be postponed for the postwar peace conference. But the British, believing that the Russians would have a free hand in Romania anyway and fearing that such an injection might wreck any chance of Western participation in a Romanian armistice, let Washington know that they were against raising the question of frontiers at this time.[26] At the beginning of April, as the Red Army began to cross the Pruth river into the Romanian province of Moldavia, the Kremlin issued a press release, which among other things, stated that they intended to reincorporate Bessarabia and Northern Bucovina into the Soviet Union.[27] Several days later the Russians handed the Americans and the English their preliminary armistice

terms for Romania. Besides reiterating their stand on Bessarabia and
Northern Bucovina, the Soviets announced that they considered the
Vienna Award "unjust" and were "ready to conduct operations in common with Rumania against the Hungarians and the Germans with the
object of restoring to Rumania all of Transylvania or the major part
thereof."[28] Apparently the Russians hoped to compensate the Romanians with Transylvania for their loss of Bessarabia and Northern Bucovina.
Moreover, from a military point of view, the Russians were anxious to
get the Romanians to change sides.[29]

The Soviet terms, including those on territories, disturbed the State
Department. One memorandum pointed out that "although there is no
disposition to consider the line established by the Vienna Award of 1940
as being satisfactory or definitive, the whole complex Transylvanian
problem should be left for postwar consideration."[30] In a telegram to the
American Ambassador to the Yugoslavian government-in-exile, Secretary
of State Hull wrote that "our objection . . . was on grounds of principle
rather than an evaluation of the relative merits of the claims to Transylvania." We "question whether any line that might be drawn while the war
is in progress would afford a basis for the eventual stability of the region."[31] Hull also noted that "the same considerations would apply" to
Bessarabia and Northern Bucovina. Perhaps this objection was connected
also with their growing fear that Eastern Europe was about to come under
Communist control. But the Department backed down on its political
views in light of the significance that the American Joint Chiefs of Staff
placed in getting Romania to change sides. Moreover, in order not to
delay the armistice negotiations as well as to gain some compensation,
the State Department agreed to Churchill's request that the words "subject to confirmation at the peace settlement" be added to article four on
Transylvania.[32] The Soviets accepted this addition.[33]

In spite of these setbacks, the State Department was by no means
ready to completely abandon its objective of postponing a final settlement on Transylvania until after the war. Shortly after Romania changed
sides in the following August during the discussions of the detailed armistice terms, Hull notified American Ambassador Harriman to recall to
the Soviets Washington's desire to postpone territorial settlements.[34]
The State Department also hoped that the armistice would place limitations on the use of Romanian troops in disputed areas so as not to further
prejudge their ultimate disposition; but this was ignored by the Soviets.
The final article of the armistice on Transylvania merely reiterated what
the Russians had already stated in their preliminary terms including the
additional request by Churchill.

Shortly after the Romanians signed their armistice, negotiations began among the Big Three for an armistice with Hungary. In article two dealing with the withdrawal of Hungarian forces from areas occupied since 1937, the State Department tried to have inserted the phrase "without prejudice to ultimate settlement of disputed territorial claims."[35] An indication of another line of thinking of the State Department was manifested in the proposal that "Hungary might be assured that an attempt will be made to establish a more just ethnic boundary between Hungary and Rumania."[36] Molotov, however, opposed the "without prejudice" phrase, claiming that "this would cause concern on the part of Czechoslovakia and Yugoslavia." Yet at the same time he told the Americans and the British that neither article two nor article nineteen (which declared the Vienna Award null and void) "would be interpreted as relating to final boundary settlements." With this ambiguous assurance Washington agreed to drop the phrase.[37]

Even as late as this it still cannot be said for certain that the Soviets had completely made up their minds on Transylvania. More certain, however, was their willingness, unlike that of the Western Powers, to use it for their own immediate ends. In April 1944, and once or twice in the following September, the Russians indicated to the Hungarians that they would insure Hungary's existing frontier if they would change sides and declare war on Germany.[38] Moreover, in November 1944, shortly after Northern Transylvania had been liberated by Soviet and Romanian armies, the recently reinstalled Romanian administration was ousted by the Russians and a proto-Communist Hungarian government was set up in Cluj under Soviet auspices. In part done in order to weaken the new non-Communist Sănătescu government in Bucharest, it also seems to indicate that Moscow was still giving some thought to some kind of an autonomous or independent Transylvania.[39] But this apparently came to an end when on March 9, 1945, in an effort to win popular backing for the new Communist controlled Groza government, the Russians announced, with much fanfare, that they were turning over administrative control of Northern Transylvania to the Romanians.[40]

As far as the State Department was concerned, this ended any lingering hopes that they still might have had of keeping the overall question of Transylvania alive. Not desiring "to make an issue of this point," the State Department simply informed the Soviets that "prior notification should have been given." Acting Secretary of State Grew explained to the American political representative in Romania Burton Berry that "it is difficult to argue that a decision of this kind should not be made by the power having primary military responsibility in the area in question."[41] Furthermore,

Washington was already in the midst of one of its first serious disagreements with the Russians over the latter's forceful installation of the minority Groza government.[42] In the same telegram to Berry, however, Grew pointed out that in order to minimize friction between Hungary and Romania in the future it "is the Department's view that the precise location of the final boundary is a matter which should be given detailed study . . . at the time peace treaties are signed."[43]

When discussions began amongst the Allied Foreign Ministers on the peace treaties in London in September 1945, the only remaining question involving Romanian territory was Transylvania. Realizing the importance that the Soviets placed in getting Bessarabia and Northern Bucovina back and the uselessness of further opposition, the United States had already agreed to this change.[44] In order to provide for a "detailed examination" of the precise boundaries between Hungary and Romania, American Secretary of State Byrnes submitted a proposal which called for restoring the whole or the greater part of Transylvania to Romania "after examining the respective claims of the two states."[45] In arguing for this Byrnes explained that he "thought that by a slight change in frontier it would be possible to restore half a million Hungarians to Hungary," and that "the change he had in mind would not affect more than 3,000 square miles."[46] This involved essentially the same area that the United States tried to prevent Romania from acquiring in 1919. Byrnes was supported by the British and French. But the Russians strongly objected, proposing instead that "the whole of Transylvania . . . be restored to Rumania." Molotov claimed that the different nationalities were so "closely intermingled" that "it was impossible to draw a line which would not leave many Roumanians in Hungary and many Hungarians in Roumania."[47] Unable to agree, in the end it was decided to consider the question at a future meeting.

With the development of the Cold War the problem of Transylvania became increasingly wrapped up with East-West political objectives. The Russians and the Romanian Communists publicized the American stand on Transylvania in order to discredit them in the eyes of the Romanians. At the same time American officials in Budapest called on Washington to utilize its position to help strengthen the pro-Western Hungarian government. In order to help the Communists in Hungary, along with strengthening their own position, Soviet officials in Budapest, as well as local Communists, talked about the possibility of Soviet support on Transylvania if they "behaved well."[48] Probably in part for the same reasons, during a visit of Hungarian government leaders to Moscow in April 1946, Stalin and

Molotov indicated that they would support some territorial adjustments and advised them to open direct negotiations with the Romanians.[49] Shortly afterwards the Hungarians sent a high Foreign Office official to Bucharest. But the Romanians refused to discuss the issue. No further signs of encouragement came from Moscow either. Although one can only speculate if Stalin was serious or not, in London and Paris, as John C. Campbell, an American delegate at the Paris Peace Conference, pointed out "the Soviet delegation never changed its position of full support for Rumania."[50]

In any case, by this time the United States had all but given up on gaining any border changes in Hungary's favor. In a telegram on April 5 to Berry, Byrnes cabled that the "Soviet position appears fixed." Moreover, the British, feeling that a slight border adjustment would only anger the Romanians without satisfying the Hungarians, now seemed "less enthusiastic" for the American proposal than they had been in the previous September.[51] Perhaps most important State Department studies showed that apart from a large-scale compulsory exchange of populations, which the United States felt was too drastic, it was unlikely that frontier adjustments would reduce "those under alien rule" by "as much as 100,000." The "Transylvanian question," Byrnes concluded, "cannot be solved by trimming frontier [sic]."[52]

There was little for the Americans to do but to acquiesce to the Soviets. In order to reduce the large number of questions in dispute between the Americans and the Russians, when the Allied Foreign Ministers met in Paris on May 7, Byrnes quickly dropped the last American proposal, which would have left open the possibility of Hungary and Romania bringing about frontier changes amongst themselves, and agreed to that of the Soviets which restored Romania to her pre-World War II borders.[53] For all practical purposes this ended the issue of Transylvania as far as the United States was concerned.

With the Paris Peace Conference about to open shortly the disappointed Hungarians made several last ditch attempts to alter the situation. In June Hungarian officials flew to Washington, but the most they could get out of the Americans was a promise to support them if the Russians would reopen the issue.[54] They received even less encouragement in London. Shortly afterwards in Paris when the Hungarians approached Molotov on what the Americans had said, the Soviet Foreign Minister clearly let them know that they were not going to change their minds.[55] Although in essence the question of Transylvania already had been settled, in August the Hungarians presented their case before the peace conference. Due to the efforts of the Australians, the Hungarians also were given a chance to present their views before a special territorial commission. It is interesting to note that even the Hungarains could not come up with a convincing alternative solution for Transylvania. Under their first proposal Hungary would recover 8,494 square miles with a population of approximately 500,000 Magyars—as well as over 850,000 Romanians![56] Their second proposal called for the returning of a much smaller border region, 1,544 square miles, where the Hungarians outnumbered the Romanians two to one. But here as in 1919 the economic arguments favored Romania, and as far as the United States could determine this would not reduce the number living under alien rule anywhere near enough to solve the minority problem.[57] In the end the commission, including the United States, voted for the Soviet position, which was later approved at a plenary session of the conference on October 15, 1946.[58]

In conclusion, as far as the Americans were concerned the question of Transylvania was one of many secondary problems that they became involved with as a result of World War II, and one whose outcome they did not entirely agree with. In order to prevent Transylvania from continuing to be a major source of friction in Eastern Europe, first the United States hoped that the entire question of its future status could be postponed for the postwar peace conference. Unable to achieve this, the United States then hoped that a more equitable frontier could be redrawn between Hungary and Romania. But the whole area came under the military control of the Red Army and in the final analysis this was what really counted. The Soviets imposed their solution, which, regardless of their motives, restored the frontiers to those originally worked out by the Western Powers themselves at the time of World War I, and viewing Transylvania as a whole in accordance with the principle of national self-determination. Perhaps one surprising outcome is that since World War II, because of Soviet hegemony in Eastern Europe, the question of Transylvania has been largely dormant. But it would be foolhardy indeed to say that the question has been finally solved.

NOTES

1. I. Gheorghiu and C. Nuțu, "The Activity for the Union Carried Out Abroad," *Unification of the Romanian National State*, eds. Miron Constantinescu and Ștefan Pascu (București, 1971), pp. 127-141 *passim*; Victor S. Mamatey, *The United States and East Central Europe 1914-1918* (Princeton, 1957), pp. 375-378.

2. U.S., Department of State, *Papers Relating to the Foreign Relations of the United States, 1918*, 2 vols. (Washington, 1933), 1, 785;

Vasile Stoica, În America pentru Cauza Românească (București, 1926), p. 49.

3. Annuaire Statistique Hongrois 1912 (Budapest, 1914), XX, 24. Historical Transylvania is the region lying between the Apuseni Mountains and the Carpathian chain. According to the Hungarian census of 1910 out of a total population of 2,678,367 the Romanians numbered 1,472,021, and the Magyars 918,217. Ibid., 12, 24.

4. Sherman D. Spector, Rumania at the Paris Peace Conference (New York, 1962), p. 99. At the Peace Conference Romania acquired not only Transylvania proper but also the eastern edge of the Hungarian plain consisting of Crișana, Maramureș, and two-thirds of the Banat. In this chapter the word Transylvania will be used to include all of those territories that Romania acquired from Hungary.

5. The Allies unanimously agreed that most of the predominantly Magyar areas of Békés and Csanád would remain with Hungary, even though they had been promised to Romania in the Treaty of August, 1916. Spector, p. 104. See also U.S., Department of State, Hungary-Rumania Boundary, International Boundary Study Pubn. 47 (April 15, 1965), pp. 4-7.

6. The United States signed a separate peace treaty with Austria on August 24, 1921 and with Hungary on August 29, 1921.

7. Anuarul Statistic al României 1915-1916 (București, 1919), 183-184; Anuarul Statistic al României 1935 și 1936, 31.

8. These population figures are based on the Hungarian census of 1910, the last one taken before the war.

9. Anuarul Statistic al României 1937 și 1938, 60. According to the Romanian census of 1930, the number of Romanians had increased to 3,207,880 from that of 2,800,073 given in the Hungarian census of 1910, while the number of Magyars dropped from 1,704,851 to 1,353,276. This was due to a number of factors, such as the emigration of Magyars and immigration of Romanians, and changes in the classification practices of the different regimes. C. A. Macartney, Hungary and Her Successors (London, 1937), pp. 252-253.

10. Hungary went from 125,402 square miles before the war to 35,870 square miles after the war. League of Nations, Health Organization, Statistical Handbooks Series: The Official Vital Statistics of the Kingdom of Hungary, No. 10 (1927), 111, No. 3, p. 10.

11. Paul D. Quinlan, Clash Over Romania: British and Amercian Policies Towards Romania, 1938-1947 (Los Angeles, 1977), pp. 19-23.

12. Ibid., pp. 22-23.

13. Documents on German Foreign Policy 1918-1945: The War Years,

June 23-August 31, 1940 (Washington, 1957), Series D, X, 76, 132, 566; C. A. Macartney, *October Fifteenth: A History of Modern Hungary, 1929-1945*, 2 vols. (Edinburgh, 1956-57), 1, 404-405; Stephen D. Kertesz, *Diplomacy in a Whirlpool: Hungary Between Nazi Germany and Soviet Russia* (Notre Dame, 1953), p. 50; John Flournoy Montgomery, *Hungary: The Unwilling Satellite* (New York, 1947), pp. 138-139.

14.   A. Simion, "Les conditions politiques du diktat de Vienna (30 août 1940)," *Revue Roumaine d'Histoire*, XI, no. 3 (1972), 450-460 *passim*.

15.   For a recent Hungarian study see Dániel Csatari, *Dans la tourmente: les relations hungaro-roumaines de 1940 à 1945* (Budapest, 1974). For two Romanian studies see Traian Bunescu, *Lupta poporului român împotriva dictatului fascist de la Viena (august 1940)* (București, 1971); Aurică Simion, *Dictatul de la Viena* (Cluj, 1972).

16.   The statistics for the ceded area vary considerably depending on their sources.

1910 Hungarian census		1930 Romanian census	
Romanians	919,690	Romanians	1,176,433
Hungarians	1,123,216	Hungarians	911,550
Others	142,640	Others	307,164
Total	2,185,546	*Total*	2,395,147

1941 Hungarian census	
Romanians	1,066,353
Hungarians	1,347,012
Others	163,926
Total	2,577,291

17.   Cordell Hull, *The Memoirs of Cordell Hull*, 2 vols. (New York, 1948), 11, 1168.

18.   *Foreign Relations 1944*, IV, 176, 173, 143-144; Hull, 11, 1168.

19.   Parliamentary question, 9 March 1943, F.O. 371/37389, R2190/2190/37, Public Record Office, London; Minute by Rose, 3 December 1942, F.O. 371/33257, R8370/22/37. See also Bunescu, pp. 188-189.

20.   *Foreign Relations 1944*, 111, 851.

21.   Memorandum by Sargent, 1 June 1942, F.O. 371/33134, R3793/43/67; Admiral Miklós Horthy, *The Confidential Papers of Admiral Horthy*, ed. Miklós Szinai and László Szücs (Budapest, 1965), 264.

22.   Antal Ullein-Reviczky, *Guerre allemande paix russe* (Neuchâtel, 1947), p. 101; Kristóffy's widow in *Studies for a New Central Europe*, 111,

no. 2 (1972), 70; Mario D. Fenyo, *Hitler, Horthy and Hungary: German-Hungarian Relations, 1941-1944* (New Haven, 1972), pp. 2-3. But see also Elek Karsai, *A budai Sándor—palotabán törtent* (Budapest, 1964), p. 472.

23.   Llewellyn Woodward, *British Foreign Policy in the Second World War*, 5 vols. (London, 1970-76), 11, 223.

24.   Molotov to Clark Kerr, 7 June 1943, F.O. 371/34449, C7263/155/18; Macartney, *October Fifteenth*, 11, 176-177.

25.   Peter Gosztony, "Die ungarische antifaschistische Bewegung in der Sowjetunion währed des Zweiten Weltkrieges," *Militärgeschichtliche Mitteilungen*, IX (1972), 101; Nikolai I. Lebedev, *Rumyniia v gody Vtoroi Mirovoi Voiny* (Moscow, 1961), pp. 158-159.

26.   Minute by Strang, 8 February 1944, F.O. 371/43992, R2835/294/37; Minute by Sargent, 8 February 1944, F.O. 371/43992; Minute by Rose, 12 February 1944, F.O. 371/43992; Foreign Relations 1944, IV, 145.

27.   Ibid., 165-166.

28.   Ibid., 170.

29.   See for example Sargent's minute, 3 April 1944, F.O. 371/43996, R5133/294/37.

30.   Foreign Relations 1944, IV, 173.

31.   *Foreign Relations* 1944, IV, 174. See also State Department memorandum, Hull to Roosevelt, 26 August 1944, Map Room, Box 164, Naval Aides Files, Franklin D. Roosevelt Library, Hyde Park, New York.

32.   Moyne to Foreign Office, 11 April 1944, no. 906, F.O. 371/43998, R5776/294/37; Foreign Office to Washington, 11 April 1944, no. 3074, F.O. 371/43998, R5776/294/37; Halifax to Foreign Office, 11 April 1944, no. 1839, F.O. 371/43998, R5786/294/37; Foreign Relations 1944, IV, 173-174.

33.   Molotov to Churchill, 10 April 1944, F.O. 371/43998.

34.   *Foreign Relations* 1944, IV, 199-200.

35.   Ibid., 111, 945-946.

36.   Ibid., 886.

37.   Ibid., 962-963, 953-954.

38.   Fenyo, pp. 146-147; Macartney, *October Fifteenth*, 11, 349-350, 353-354, 373-374. See also Elisabeth Barker, *British Policy in South-East Europe in the Second World War* (New York, 1976), p. 262.

39.   R. V. Burks, *The Dynamics of Communism in Eastern Europe* (Princeton, 1961), pp. 155-157; Bela Vago, "Romania," *Communist Power in Europe 1944-1949*, ed. Martin McCauley (New York, 1977), p. 115; Vojtech Mastny, *Russia's Road to the Cold War* (New York, 1979), p. 206.

R. V. Burks reported that the Russians allegedly suggested to Count Istvan Bethlen, whose ancestors had ruled Transylvania in the seventeenth century, that "he assume the governorship of a new 'independent Transylvanian' state." Bethlen supposedly rejected the offer. Burks, pp. 156-157.

40. Ştefan Lache and Gheorghe Ţuţui, *România şi Conferinţa de pace de la Paris din 1946* (Cluj-Napoca, 1978), p. 158. In an article published in 1946 Romanian Communist Party Secretary, Vasile Luca, pointed out that "the Rumanian people will never forget, that only by removing Maniu-Bratianu followers from the commanding posts of the country, it has [sic] been possible to restore Northern Transylvania to Rumania, even previous to the peace conference." Vassile Luca, "The Vienna Verdict and the Solution of the Problem of Nationalities," *Rumanian Review*, 1, no. 2 (June, 1946), 28.

41. *Foreign Relations* 1945, V, 527.

42. See Quinlan, pp. 122-130 *passim*. So as not to give the impression that they approved the new Groza government, American and British officials in Romania did not participate in any of the festivities celebrating the return of Northern Transylvania. See *Foreign Relations* 1945, V, footnote 38, 524; The Diary of General Cortlandt Van R. Schuyler (unpublished), p. 83. (Copy xeroxed from the original in 1974 then in the possession of the author.)

43. *Foreign Relations* 1945, V, 527.

44. Ibid., 1944, IV, 177. Not having much choice, the new Romanian government did not protest this.

45. Ibid., 1945, 11, 266.

46. Ibid., 280.

47. Ibid., 279.

48. Kertesz, p. 175; John C. Campbell, "The European Territorial Settlement," *Foreign Affairs*, XXVI, no. 1 (October, 1947), 211; Philip E. Mosely, *The Kremlin and World Politics* (New York, 1960), p. 233.

49. Ferenc Nagy, *The Struggle Behind the Iron Curtain* (New York, 1948), p. 210; Kertesz, pp. 181-182.

50. Campbell, *Foreign Affairs*, XXVI, no. 1 (October, 1947), 211. Robert R. King in his book on minorities in the Balkans feels that "apparently Stalin was willing to permit frontier adjustments" but "only if Rumania approved." Robert R. King, *Minorities Under Communism: Nationalities as a Source of Tension Among Balkan Communist States* (Cambridge, Massachusetts, 1973), p. 39.

51. *Foreign Relations* 1946, VI, 587; Campbell, *Foreign Affairs*, XXVI, no. 1 (October, 1947), 212.

52.   *Foreign Relations* 1946, VI, 587.

53.   Ibid., 11, 259-260.

54.   Nagy, pp. 228, 236-237.

55.   Ibid., p. 237.

56.   Kertesz, p. 181.

57.   *Foreign Relations* 1946, IV, 851-852; Lache and Țuțui, p. 264. John C. Campbell concluded that the number of Hungarinas living in Romania would still be "over one million strong."

58.   U.S., Department of State, *Paris Peace Conference 1946: Selected Documents*, ed. Velma H. Cassidy, Pubn. no. 2868 (1947), 1345. The vote was ten in favor with two abstentions (Australia and South Africa).

Robert Forrest

ROMANIAN-AMERICAN ECONOMIC RELATIONS, 1947-1975

Romanian-American economic relations are a study in political toleration. The years of worst intoleration were 1947-1962, during which the
United States tried to embargo Eastern Europe. After 1962 relations
between the two countries gradually improved. The main reason Romania
became more tolerant of the United States was the Romanian need for
economic assistance in order to maintain its independence within the
CMEA. The United States gradually discarded its Cold War conception of
the socialist states as a scourge that must be controlled or eradicated for
two main reasons. First, in the later 1960s, many Congressmen came to
believe that America's export controls were not damaging the socialist
countries' economic growth and became more receptive to the presidential
policy of using reductions in export controls for political reasons; especially as divisions appeared in the Soviet "bloc" which the United States
could exploit. Previously the desire of Congress for strict export controls
had conflicted with the presidential policy of having flexible export controls which could be selectively relaxed for political reasons. The second
reason for increased American toleration was economic. Many American
industrialists began to complain during the 1960s that Eastern Europe
contained a large potential market, but American corporations were losing
sales to their European and Japanese competitors due to export controls.
In this way, businessmen were supporting the presidential policy of reducing export controls, but for economic rather than political reasons. By
1969, the President, the Congress and the business community stressed
the importance of East-West trade as a means to alleviate America's serious balance of payments deficit. In short, American export controls
were perceived as more harmful to the United States than to the socialist
states for both political and economic reasons. However, agreement between the President, the Congress and the business community was tenuous
as the Jackson-Vanik Amendment soon revealed. This problem was unable

to destroy the improved relations between the United States and Romania, although it did expose the fragility of the increased tolerance created by these improved relations.

Subsequent to Romania's 1947 nationalization of industrial property, including all direct foreign investments, America's economic relations with Romania were frozen by the Cold War. However, little was lost to either country, as neither country had ever been of significant economic interest to the other. It is characteristic of this early period that American oil investments were not confiscated by the Romanians, but by the Russians during the fall and winter of 1944-45. American Cold War economic machinery was aimed directly at the USSR, which was believed to be the leader of a monolithic bloc of communist states threatening the West. This machinery may be described as an embargo which had two goals. First, it was believed that an embargo of Russia by the West would produce economic hardship in the weak communist states and cause internal rebellions or make the Soviet leaders compromise with the West.[1] Economic restrictions were also part of America's recently formulated containment policy. They would reinforce this policy "by depriving the socialist world of military and strategic goods, which it was believed would keep the Soviet Union in a position of relative military and economic inferiority, thereby minimizing Soviet flexibility in foreign affairs."[2] When the Soviet Union failed to collapse or seek cooperation with the West and grew stronger by pursuing a policy of autarky that included economic and political domination of Eastern Europe (minus Yugoslavia), it became necessary for the United States to alter its Cold War economic policies. It is the task of this study to trace the creation of American Cold War economic policies and their alterations in the case of Romania during the 1960s and 1970s.

The years between 1947-54 were the low point in Romanian-American economic relations. Total trade between the two countries fell from $2,291,000 in 1950 to $448,000 in 1954, a 76 percent decline. During the entire year of 1952, the United States imported less than $500 worth of goods from Romania. Romania's economy had either been destroyed during the war or was under Soviet control, consequently Romania had nothing to sell the United States. At the same time Americans were in no mood to buy, as they were occupied with their own economic problems and between 1948-54 with creating their Cold War embargo legislation. Immediately after World War II, the Truman administration used export controls under the authority granted to the President by Section 6 of the Act of July 2, 1940.[3] The purpose of these controls was to prevent inflation developing in the United States from the abnormal export demand for materials temporarily in short supply from countries reconstructing their war ravaged economies. The Congressional concern about this short supply issue remained significant until 1949,[4] indicating that export controls only gradually came to be directed at the socialist countries for political reasons.

The deepening of the Cold War during 1947-48 caused Truman to extend export controls on March 1, 1948 to the licensing of all short supply and strategic materials destined for export to continental Europe.[5] This was the beginning of United States economic warfare against the socialist states. The major policy alternation of March 1, 1948 was from the economic consideration of short supply to the political goal of denying the Soviet Union and its allies strategic American materials. Initially both Congress and the Truman administration felt export controls were for an emergency that would be of short duration. However, the communist takeover of Czechoslovakia in February 1948, the Berlin Blockade of 1948-49, the success of the communists in China and the numerous violations of the export control program during 1948[6] resulted in the formalizing of the existing informal export control program by the passage of the Export Control Act of 1949 on February 26, 1949. Despite these discouraging events, Congress was still optimistic that export controls would not be needed very long.[7] However, the act remained in effect for twenty years, and formed the cornerstone of American Cold War economic machinery designed to isolate the socialist states from the West. This goal was based upon a moral determination that communism was a vile disease that must be controlled. Control was to be achieved by weakening the military potential of the Soviet bloc by restricting the bloc's economic growth.[8] The Export Control Act of 1949 also continued the administrative procedures created during 1948. The Office of Export Control of the Department of Commerce was required to continue its custom of consulting with other appropriate executive departments concerning applications to export a given commodity or commodities to a communist country. Consequently, a hierarchy of interdepartmental committees was created that included representatives of the Departments of Commerce, Defense, State, Treasury and various other regulatory agencies such as the Atomic Energy Commission and the Central Intelligence Agency.

A Commodity Control List (CCL), consisting of 1,300 items, was prepared by the Office of Export Control to facilitate its adminisration of export controls. No product listed in the CCL could be exported to a communist country without first obtaining permission in the form of a validated license from the Office of Export Control.[9] All items not on the CCL could be exported without governmental permission under the category of a general license. However, the Office of Export Control also adopted the policy that all items, destined for a communist country, not on the CCL required a validated license until proven to be non-strategic. In 1965 the Office of Export Control shifted its emphasis to selecting specific designations of items and requiring only them to have a validated license.[10] The licensing regulations developed by these inter-departmental committees has been a source of controversy especially since the mid-1960s. As with most legislation, it is not the legislation but the administration of it which is most significant. The central problem relating to the Export Control Act has involved the President's authority derived from Section 3 (a) to use discretion in executing the Act. The various administrations since 1949 have desired to apply export controls selectively for foreign policy reasons; however, Congress has taken the position of maintaining more stringent export controls, because Congress, reflecting the anticommunist stance of the American people, has desired only the barest minimum of trade with the socialist states. This issue has been very important for the socialist states of Eastern Europe. The Presidential use of selective export controls has caused the creation of what amounts to different CCLs for different socialist countries. The CCL has been shortened, as in the case of Romania, to indicate presidential favor for Romania's improved relations with the West, or raised as in the case of Cuba, to indicate presidential disfavor with a socialist state's western policies.

That portion of the business community interested in East-West trade consisting of industrial manufacturers using advanced technology demanded by socialist states, has been very vocal in its support of the presidential policy for controlling exports and for a general reduction of the CCL based on a narrow definition of what constitutes a strategic commodity. The major complaint of business about the administration of export controls has been that delays of several months or more were common before the Office of Export Control ruled upon their applications for an export license.[11] If the application was refused no reason was given. At times a license application for a particular commodity would be granted, but at other times a license application for the same commodity would be denied. This difficulty in understanding the regulations and their application cause some firms to renounce the possibility of a sale by refraining from making an application.[12] These delays were also criticized for causing American firms to lose sales to foreign competitors offering similar or inferior products.[13]

The Secretary of Commerce was ordered to reduce the number of commodities on the CCL by the Export Administration Act of 1969 and the Equal Export Opportunity Act of 1972, which also directed that business must be consulted for their advice involving questions that affect application processing procedures.[14] The Export Administration Amendments of 1974 also attempted to reduce the time for processing applications for validated licenses to ninety days, however the delays have not been shortened much for products utilizing sophisticated advanced technology.[15] The bureaucratic problems business experienced with their validated license applications were caused by the vague standard of controlling exports to socialist countries that threatened the national security of the United States, which Congress created in the Export Control Act. The vagueness of this standard subjected the Office of Export Control to the possibility of criticism from Congress or right wing groups anytime they approved an export application or reduced the CCL; therefore, it was easier to refuse applications and refrain from reducing the list. This political pressure and the large number of agencies involved in processing an application also accounts for the delays in reaching a decision. Finally, once a decision had been reached, fear of criticism helps explain the bureaucratic reluctance to publish the reasons for an approval of a license for a particular commodity so that a precedent would not be developed which could prevent denial of similar cases under different conditions.[17] In short, the political pressures enveloping the administration of export controls forced the Office of Export Control to adopt a conservative posture with respect to East-West trade which until 1969 conformed more to the foreign policy goals of Congress than to those of the President.

The conservative administration of the Export Control Act of 1949 has severely restricted Romania's opportunity to purchase industrial products utilizing the advanced technology needed by Romania's ambitious economic development program. Romania has also been restricted in fulfilling its needs by the Mutual Defense Assistance Control Act of 1951, commonly called the Battle Act, and a regulation made under the Export Control Act that foreign subsidiaries of American corporations are subject to the export controls of the United States, if the commodity the foreign subsidiary wishes to export to a socialist state is of United States manufacture, contains controlled American components, or is based on restricted technology developed in the United States.[18] This extraterritorial application of United States legislation on export controls, which makes illegal transactions that are legal under the domestic laws of a foreign state, so irritated foreign governments that numerous problems were created for the State Department.[19] The justification for this regulation has been that the United States can not permit American businesses to destroy its export control program by simply selling the socialist states controlled strategic materials from their foreign subsidiaries. The Battle Act, administered by the Department of State, attempts to extend United States export controls into a more complete multilaterial export control system by threatening the loss of foreign assistance to any country which sells strategic materials "to any nation or combination of nations threatening the security of the United States, including the Union of Soviet Socialist Republics and all countries under its domination."[20] Foreign assistance has never been terminated to any country despite occasional Congressional pressure to apply the sanction.[21] The State Department in deference to diplomatic necessity has liberally interpreted the act over the years which has caused the Coordinating Committee or COCOM[22] export control list to contain fewer items than the American CCL. The other COCOM members have kept their national lists coextensive with the COCOM list. The result has been that Romania and the other socialist states were able to obtain imports from Western European and Japanese firms which were prohibited to them by United States' export controls. The difference between the CCL and the COCOM lists is the cause of American business complaints about loss of sales to their foreign competitors.

The financing needed to sell exports to Eastern Europe was also ended when the socialist states were denied access to Export-Import Bank financing by a 1945 Congressional Act which prohibits use of the bank's facilities for any communist country unless the President determined that it was in the national interest to permit the Export-Impact Bank to participate in the financing of trade between the United States and a communist state.[23] Private American firms or banks were also prohibited from extending credit to Romania by the provisions of the Johnson Act of 1934 which bans long-term credits to countries that have defaulted on their debt obligations to American citizens.

The Export Control Act of 1949 and its multilateral extension, the Battle Act, provided the basic machinery for the economic embargo against the Soviet Union and its satellites in Eastern Europe. The purposes of this embargo as it existed after the passage of the Battle Act, have been very succinctly summarized by Josef Wilczynski as intended to slow down the military build-up of socialist countries, to slow down the development of the military-supporting capabilities of socialist countries, to slow down economic growth by causing dislocation in key socialist projects and to pre-empt key materials in short supply considered necessary for the Western defense effort.[24]

These political objectives were formulated under the assumption that the socialist states formed a monolithic bloc under Soviet domination by a Congress captured by the anticommunist hysteria characteristic of this early phase of the Cold War. The charged intellectual atmosphere of this period also led many Congressmen and private citizens into the fallacy of being extremely conscious of the economic, military and political power of the United States in relation to that of a much weaker Soviet bloc and at the same time contending that anything less than a total embargo of the Soviet bloc would immediately jeopardize the national security of the United States.[25] Little recognition existed that East-West trade in non-strategic goods could benefit both parties and that this trade coupled with the normal economic growth of the West would continue the "power gap" in the West's favor despite the fact it would become smaller. In this sense, Congress displayed a curious lack of confidence in the capitalistic system it was so determined to protect. This attitude continued nearly unaltered until the later 1960s and survives to some extent to the present day.

American economic relations with Romania received a further blow on August 1, 1951 when President Truman terminated the most-favored-nation status (MFN) of all the socialist states in accordance with Section 5 of the Trade Agreements Extension Act of 1951. In Section 5 Congress denied MFN status to the Soviet Union and to "any nation or area dominated or controlled by the foreign government or foreign organization controlling the world communist movement."[26] However, Congress permitted the President discretion to determine which countries were dominated by the world communist movement, and President Truman determined that all the East European states would lose MFN status despite the fact that such action would unilaterally abrogate United States treaties with Poland and Hungary and violate American obligations to Czechoslovakia under the GATT. The moral implications of these actions implemented during 1951 and 1952 were outweighed by the American need to extend Cold War restrictions to imports from the socialist states, in order to isolate the Soviet Union and its allies from the United States. The cancellation of MFN status subjected Romanian exports to the United States to the very high tariff rates of the Smoot-Hawley Tariff of 1930.

The Cold War embargo policy of the United States was only partly responsible for the low levels of trade between the United States and Romania in the early 1950s. Soviet dominance of Romania was so complete between 1950-55 that Romania was effected very little by American trade restrictions. During these years, Gheorghiu-Dej depended upon Soviet power to preserve the power of the Romanian communist party against the anti-communist and anti-Russian sentiments of the Romanian populace.[27] The Romanian people, and to some extent the communist leadership of Romania, were bitter about Soviet exploitation of Romanian resources and industrial production for the repair of the Soviet's war damage.[28] Russian exploitation of Romania's economy was not ended until 1956.[29] The relaxation of the Cold War which followed the end of the Korean War and Stalin's death caused some lessening of licensing restrictions for exports to the socialist countries in August 1954.[30] At the end of the 1955 Geneva Summit meeting Eisenhower indicated that his administration was not opposed to "trade in peaceful goods."[31] In fact, Eisenhower had advocated trade in peaceful good as early as March 1954, and he continued to support such trade as "the greatest weapon in the hands of the diplomat" throughout his tenure as president.[32]

Romanian officials were encouraged enough by Eisenhower's stance on East-West trade to visit the United States in October 1956 in an attempt to sell cement and petroleum to the United States in exchange for American agricultural machinery and high-grade fertilizers.[33] While the Romanians received no special concessions as a result of this visit, Romanian-American trade did realize significant gains between 1957-59 (see Chart 1). More importantly for the future, was the Romanian offer in May 1956 to negotiate a settlement of claims by United States citizens for property nationalized by the Romanian communists in exchange for improved trade relations. A settlement of these claims was achieved on March 30, 1960,[34] which marks the turning point toward closer American-Romanian economic relations.

The promise of the American government, as a consequence of the 1960 claims settlement, to seek Congressional authority to ease export license restrictions for Romania was quickly lost in the wake of the Berlin Crisis of 1961 and the American problems with communism in Cuba which culminated in the Cuban Missile Crisis during the fall of 1962. This heating up of the Cold War was reflected in a renewed Congressional attempt to tighten export controls against the Soviet bloc, thereby erasing the loosening of economic restrictions achieved by the

Eisenhower administration. President Kennedy believed the Soviet bloc theory to be a myth. He was critical of Congress for continuing to base legislation on it which limited presidential discretionary powers to use East-West trade as a diplomatic tool to maintain an open dialogue on all questions of mutual interest that could help and the state of permanent political belligerency that characterized the Cold War.[35] The nuclear test ban treaty of August 5, 1963 and the sale of wheat to Russian in October 1963 were a means to that end.

The legislation which concerned Kennedy, were the amendments to the Export Control Act passed on July 1, 1962 and the Trade Extension Act of 1962 which removed the President's discretionary power regarding MFN and expressly denied MFN to all communist countries. Congress refused a Department of Commerce request to make the Export Control Act permanent rather than renewable every two years, because Congress wished to maintain its close surveillance over the administration of export controls.[36] The need for this watchfulness resulted from the findings of the House Select Committee on Export Control, Paul A. Kitchin—Chairman, that the Department of Commerce had been too liberal in granting validated licenses for exports to Eastern Europe.[37] Representative Kitchin considered the liberality of the Department of Commerce to be serious because:

> the Economic base of this prolonged tense cold war is becoming more important each day. As our military posture and that of the Soviet bloc approach a clear stalemate due to the absolute destructive power of each to annihilate civilization in a nuclear military conflict, the economic phase attains the status of a prime and strategic operation.[38]

In view of this changing situation, Kitchin led the successful drive to restrict the export not only of materials having a potential military significance, but also of materials having a potential economic significance which "may adversely affect the national security of the United States."[39] This amendment not only broadened the scope of export controls to reflect Kitchin's emphasis upon the political significance of trade, but it also stigmatized those American firms engaged in East-West trade as being unpatriotic, since Congress had declared that virtually any trade with socialist nations was harmful to the national interest. This Congressional action came at a time when American businessmen were beginning to display a renewed interest in East-West trade in non-strategic goods. The

The 1962 amendments to the Export Control Act and the removal of the President's discretionary authority to grant MFN status to socialist countries constitute the Congressional response to Khrushchev's doctrine of peaceful coexistence. These acts also reveal the increased Congressional moral and political commitment to sterilizing the United States from the communist virus. Congress at this time was building its own Berlin Wall of legislation.

If Kennedy felt precluded from spending his political capital to increase East-West trade, Lyndon Johnson had no such feelings of confinement. His use of trade as a means of reducing the animosities of the Cold War gradually became a part of settled policy. From his first State of the Union Message on January 8, 1964, Johnson continued to develop a policy which would liberalize East-West relations. A policy which denied the Soviet bloc theory and strongly urged an end to Congressional attempts to isolate East from West, Johnson's policy, known popularly as building bridges, was clearly stated in an address at the dedication of the George C. Marshall Research Library on May 23, 1964. The President claimed that a Soviet bloc no longer existed, as evidenced by the attempts of East European nations to assert their national identities. Consequently, he announced that "we will continue to build bridges across the gulf which has divided us from Eastern Europe. They will be bridges of increased trade, of ideas, of humanitarian aid." The purpose of building bridges was:

> to open new relationships to countries seeking increased independence yet unable to risk isolation, to open the minds of a new generation to the values and the visions of the Western Civilization from which they come and to which they belong, to give freer play to the powerful forces of legitimate national pride—the strongest barrier to the ambition of any country to dominate another, to demonstrate that identity of interest and the prospects of progress for Eastern Europe lie in a wider relationship with the West.[40]

It is clear that Romania, which had promptly paid the United States the $2.5 million required to discharge its obligations under the terms of the 1960 claims settlement agreement, was to be an example of what the United States and the East European states could gain from building bridges. The Romanians had adopted a foreign policy that was very independent of the Soviet Union. They had openly defied the Soviet Union in refusing to subordinate their economy to the coordination plans of the

CMEA. Instead, Romania had been steadily increasing its economic ties with the West. Johnson hoped to encourage Romania's independent policies and to foster an internal liberalization of Romania's communist regime by relaxing trade restrictions. At the same time as Johnson's May 23 speech, a Romanian delegation was in Washington negotiating for a trade agreement. The negotiations took place between May 18 and June 1 and resulted in the U.S.-Romanian Agreement of June 1, 1964. This accord represents the first major step in liberalizing the American export control program for Romania.

The agreement included the establishment of a General License List for Romania, such as had been established for Poland, that permitted Romania to import most American commodities without the need for a validated license. When a validated license was required, it would remain valid for 24 months. Previously, a new validated license was required for each shipment. The United States also agreed to grant Romania licenses for the sale of several complete industrial facilities in which the Romanians had expressed an interest. In conjunction with the liberalizing of licensing regulations both parties agreed to protect each others industrial rights and processes and not to re-export each other's technology. This clause reveals the Export Control Office's constant concern to insure that American exports, especially exports of technology, were not re-exported to unauthorized third parties. The 1964 trade accord also included an agreement to establish a United States Trade Office in Bucharest, and to give continuing consideration to MFN treatment for Romania. At that time, it was generally believed that if Romania persisted in its independent course, Romania would soon receive MFN treatment. MFN treatment for Romania was necessary if relaxation of export controls were to increase American exports to Romania, because the Romanians needed to sell more to the United States if they were to buy more.

Finally, the accord included the political agreement for mutual settlement of consular problems, including the negotiations of a new consular convention. The United States Legation was raised to an Embassy in accordance with this portion of the accord as a symbol of the improvement in American-Romanian relations and of America's approval of Romania's independent foreign policy.

Parallel to the agreement, the United States also received official high-level oral assurances that Romania would begin to allow the emigration to the United States of many dual nationals, as well as Romanians desiring to join their families in the United States. Thus, the issue of freer Romanian emigration policies, so crucial to the 1975 bilateral commercial agreement with Romania, had been discussed first in June 1964 and was presumably discussed throughout the intervening eleven years.[41]

The first positive result of the U.S.-Romanian Agreement of June 1, 1964 was a Presidential determination enabling the Export-Import Bank to extend credit and guarantee loans to Romania for periods up to five years; the Attorney General also determined at this time that the Johnson Act of 1934 applied only to long-term loans. Consequently, private banks could grant loans to Romania which represented the normal terms of commercial credit without being in danger of violating the Johnson Act. It also facilitated the sale of complete industrial installations by making the financing of them possible. This action also complimented the Presidential determination in February 1964, to allow Commodity Credit Corporation guarantees for credit sales of American agricultural products to Romania. The purpose of these determinations was to make possible the desired increase in exports to Romania by providing the Romanians and American business firms the necessary financing to permit increased exports of American goods to Romania. The one is inextricably tied to the other. In short, these financial concessions encouraged American companies to trade with Romania.[42] In this way the Johnson administration by executive action was thwarting the Congressional policy of sterility.

These concessions only required executive action on the part of President Johnson; and the Johnson, Nixon and Ford administrations have remained committed to them. Congressional assent was another matter. In fact some of the concessions were delayed until after the 1964 elections, because of administration fears of Congress. This was true of the selling of whole plants to the Soviet bloc, and the Johnson administration remained somewhat divided upon this point.[43]

However, the Johnson administration did grant licenses to Firestone and Universal Oil Products of Chicago to sell complete industrial plants to Romania. Universal Oil Products agreed to build a $25.5 million fluid catalytic processing unit near Ploesti. Firestone was to construct a $40-50 million synthetic rubber processing plant that was to use raw materials produced by Universal Oil Products's installation. The financing for both installations was guaranteed by the Export-Import Bank. The Romanians had been trying to purchase a synthetic rubber plant in the United States since 1960, but the sale had been blocked by the Defense Department, which considered the technology too advanced to export to Romania. However, the Romanians specifically asked to be permitted to purchase a synthetic rubber plant during their negotiations with the American government in May 1964. The Defense Department dropped its opposition at that time because the technology had become widely known, and it also capitulated to administration pressures that the sale would encourage Romania's independent course.

Unfortunately, Firestone and the Johnson Administration had not sufficiently considered the unpatriotic stigma that the 1962 amendments to the Export Control Act had placed upon East West trade. Firestone was finalizing the sale when the Goodyear Tire and Rubber Company in December 1964, denounced the sale of a synthetic rubber plant to Romania as unpatriotic. A conservative college age organization, the Young Americans for Freedom (YAF), turned the controversy into an anti-Firestone crusade in February 1965, by picketing Firestone's plants and retail stores and urging people to boycott Firestone's products. The YAF was assisted by Goodyear which instructed its salesmen to distribute to their customers, two right wing publications attacking Firestone's Romanian venture. Goodyear claimed it had never seriously considered selling synthetic rubber or a synthetic rubber plant to Romania and was not attacking Firestone because it was disgruntled at losing the project to its competitor. This is probably true, but Goodyear did seem to utilize the controversy to damage a major competitor. Whatever were Goodyear's motives, the resulting adverse publicity, coupled with the Johnson administration's reluctance to support Firestone in the controversy caused Firestone to withdraw from the venture in April 1965. Romania did not lose the synthetic rubber plant, as Italy's Pirelli Company built the plant for Romania. Universal Oil Products finished their project with only minor harassment from conservative groups.[44]

The Firestone episode was a severe blow to Johnson's building bridges policy, but it was not an isolated incident. It was part of a general campaign against trading with Eastern Europe which began during the heightened Cold War tensions of 1961-62. The campaign by conservative groups included threats to boycott businesses which engaged in East-West trade, the picketing of stores selling commodities manufactured in Eastern Europe and the passage of ordinances requiring merchants to purchase expensive licenses before communist goods could be sold in their stores. Both Presidents Kennedy and Johnson had denounced these practices, but nothing was accomplished until the public uproar over the Firestone episode. After that controversy, the Johnson administration strongly defended the right of American business to engage in authorized East-West trade, the licensing ordinances were declared unconstitutional and the decline of East-West trade due to the escalation of the Vietnam War caused the issue to die away, but not before it had caused considerable damage.[45]

Johnson's building bridges policy received another blow when Wilbur Mills refused to hold committee hearings on the President's East-West Trade Relations Act of 1966. The bill would have removed some of the unpatriotic stigma attached to East-West trade but more importantly, it would have restored the President's discretionary authority to grant MFN status to communist countries thereby ending the asymmetrical American policy of liberalizing exports to Romania while continuing to discriminate against imports from Romania. This part of the bill reflects the conclusions of the Miller Report of April 1965, that East-West trade is a diplomatic weapon, but it cannot be effectively used to gain concessions until the President is given the flexibility to negotiate commercial agreements and to grant MFN treatment to socialist states. After this defeat, due to the continued growth of the Vietnam War, Johnson gradually dropped his building bridges policy. Finally, the failure of the East-West Trade Relations Act of 1966 and of the Firestone contract to build a synthetic rubber plant in Romania, caused Ceausescu, Romania's leader, to shift his interest in the West from the United States to West Germany, France and Italy.[46]

If the Firestone episode had a depressing effect on American trade with Romania, it did not destroy the growing interest of American businessmen in East-West trade.[47] Few American companies were willing to risk investing in Romania between 1965-68. Only Pepsi Cola in 1966 and American Machine and Foundry Company, permitted their transactions to be published. There was no question of a soft drink being an aid to the enemy, and AMF's business only consisted of the construction of one twelve lane bowling ally for approximately $200,000.[48] When American Metal Climax, Inc. announced in 1971 it would supply $10 million worth of technology to construct an aluminum sheet-rolling plant in Romania, President Nixon sent a public letter endorsing the AMAC investment to forestall another Firestone episode.[49]

American firms that desired to trade with Romania found two means of avoiding the danger of public protest. The first method was to use the facilities of Tower International, Inc., which was established in Cleveland, Ohio by Cyrus Eaton, a long-time advocate of closer ties with the Soviet bloc. Eaton founded the company in 1964 as a venture capital corporation, to promote trade between the U.S., Canada and Eastern Europe.[50] All transactions would be kept secret if the American companies desired secrecy, and all those companies using Tower International during the 1960s desired secrecy.

The other method used by American companies to avoid adverse local publicity was to negotiate sales through their European subsidiaries. Litton Industries is an excellent example of this practice. Through their Swedish subsidiary, Sweda, Litton sold cash registers in Eastern Europe.[51] Copee Rust a Belgian company jointly owned by Copee and Cie. of Belgium and the Rust Engineering Company of Pittsburgh, a Litton division, has signed five contracts with Romania since 1964 for various manufacturing plants. The last was for an $8 million urea plant.[52] The largest European subsidiary transaction which has been published is that of Badger Company, Inc. of Cambridge, Massachusetts, a subsidiary of the Raytheon Company. This was a $15 million monomer plant built by a Dutch subsidiary. The Badger Company transaction was done as much for financial reasons, as to avoid adverse public reactions. Badger combined with the Schneider Company, a well known French machinery manufacturer, to be eligible for French financing, which permitted eight to ten year loans at 6 percent interest. Many American firms have used their European subsidiaries to obtain access to the financial sources of Western Europe, because they granted more favorable terms than American banks were permitted to offer. A major problem caused by this practice and the secrecy of Tower International is that they render any attempt to discover the total value of American trade with Romania impossible. It has been estimated that for every dollar exported to Eastern Europe from the United States, four or five dollars are exported by foreign subsidiaries and affiliates of American corporations.[53] It must be stressed again that these sales by foreign branches of American firms did not consist of items that could not be exported from the United States. Validated licenses were obtained when necessary. The distinction is that the exports were manufactured and shipped to Eastern Europe from Western Europe rather than the United States. European firms producing their own products could often legally export them to Eastern Europe, whereas American firms operating in Western Europe were prohibited by United States laws from selling such materials to East Europe. Branches of American corporations located in Europe could not utilize their foreign locations to avoid United States export controls.

Romania's condemnation of America's involvement in Vietnam was the mildest of all communist nations. At no time were American companies discouraged from trading with Romania, but the atmosphere of 1966-68 was not conducive to trade. American-Romanian trade declined about 29 percent in 1967-68 from its 1966 level, but it has increased steadily since 1969.[54] The 1968 Congressional withdrawal of Export-Import Bank and CCC financial programs from Romania also depressed

American-Romanian trade, but this was the only concession granted Romania in the 1964 trade agreement that was removed during the Vietnam War.

Romania's attitude toward America's Vietnam involvement and its increased interest in cooperation with the West were rewarded by President Nixon when he displayed America's favor of Romania's policies in 1968 by making Romania the first Warsaw Pact state to be visited by an American president. Nixon's visit also gave trade with Romania the stamp of respectability, as most American firms were still nervous about getting involved in another Firestone episode. In December 1970, Ceausescu returned Nixon's visit when he traveled to Washington, D.C. This exchange of state visits underlined Nixon's determination to continued encouraging Romania's independent policies and emphasized that Romania continued to be interested in improved relations and increased trade with the United States, despite the problems Romanian-American trade relations had encountered between 1965-69.

The Nixon-Ceausescu visits also occurred in the more favorable atmosphere for East-West trade which surrounded the passage on December 30, 1969 of the Export Administration Act of 1969. This Act represented a major shift in Congressional export control policy. The movement to alter the Congressional export control policy was led by Senators Muskie and Mondale after hearings they held on East-West trade in 1968. These two senators, as well as many other members of Congress had concluded that the American economic embargo of the socialist states had not been effective in retarding the growth of either their military or economic power.[55]

The only notable result of American restrictive trade policies had been to reinforce the doctrinal belief of the socialist states in autarky and to give an indirect subsidy to Western European industry at the expense of American corporations and their foreign subsidiaries. American business had become quite concerned about the growth of Common Market economic power. Western European sales to Eastern Europe were permitting West European producers to grow while American companies were legally barred from entering the East European market, which appeared to be potentially vast to many American businessmen.

The economic concerns of business also coincided with the economic concerns of Congress. The balance of payments deficits of the later 1960s had become critical and Congress desired to alleviate this strain on the American economy by encouraging American corporations to export more of their products. It was believed that the trade surplus the United

States enjoyed with Eastern Europe would be increased if American businesses were "on a more equal competitive basis with the businesses of our allies."[56] The economic reasons for reducing the export control program were considered more important than political reasons; however, the political reasons were also very important. The myth of the Soviet bloc was rejected and Congress moved towards the opinion that the relationship of the Soviet Union and its allies was changing, as was the relationship between the United States and these countries. To take advantage of these changes and to lessen tensions the hostile language of the Export Control Act, appropriate in 1949, was changed to encourage trade, which reflected the attitudes of 1969 that sought to reduce tensions.[57] This policy change also removed the unpatriotic stigma and moral condemnation that the Export Control Act and its 1962 amendments had placed upon American firms which traded with the communists. Trade would not be considered as mutually beneficial. In short, Congress was moving away from its policy of insulating the United States from communism.

These goals, embodied in the Export Administration Act of 1969, removed much of the negativism that had surrounded export controls. The act declared that it was United States policy:

> (A) to encourage trade with *all* countries with which we have diplomatic or trading relations, except those countries with which such trade had been determined by the President to be against the national interest, and (B) to restrict the export of goods and technology which would make a *significant* contribution to the military potential of any other nation or nations which would prove detrimental to the national security of the United States.[58]

Conspicuously absent in the language of the act is any reference to controlling exports that have an economic effect upon the socialist states. However, the labyrinth of regulations and licensing requirements remained as a legacy of the Export Control Act.

Despite the fact that the Nixon administration at first opposed the Export Administration Act of 1969, the act's goal of reduced East-West trade barriers became part of Nixon's detente policy.[59] After 1969, foreign policy considerations and diplomatic initiatives, not explicit national security considerations, dominated East-West trade policy and this caused a continual relaxation of national security export controls.[60]

Romania was particularly favored by the relaxing of trade restrictions following the passage of the Export Administration Act of 1969. The CCL for Romania was again reduced on May 1, 1971, following an official visit to Romania by Secretary of Commerce, Maurice Stans in April 1971; thus only 10 percent of United States exports to Romania required validated licenses. Export Controls for Romania were now reduced to a level very comparable to that of Yugoslavia. Next, government financing was made available to American businesses trading with Romania. When in 1971 Congress again allowed the president discretionary authority to extend Export-Import Bank and CCC services to East European countries if he determined this to be in the national interest. President Nixon made this determination for Romania in November 1971. Overseas Private Investment Corporation programs were also authorized for Romania in April 1972. OPIC programs would guarantee any direct investments American firms made in Romania as a result of Romania's 1971-72 joint venture decrees. Finally, Romania joined the International Monetary Fund in April 1973, which made the Johnson Act private credit restrictions inapplicable to Romania.[61] The extension of these government financing programs once again provided American corporations with the credit and guarantees needed to attract American business to Romania.

At this point, the United States had dismantled 90 percent of its export control program and all of its financial restrictions directed at Romania. The removal of financial restrictions was an extremely important step in normalizing Romanian-American economic relations. Romania's national currency, the leu, is not convertible, and consequently may not be used to pay for the purchases in the West needed to finance its program of rapid economic development. Since 1959, Romania had reduced its trade from 79 percent with communist countries to around 50 percent by the early 1970s, causing Romania's supplies of hard currencies to become increasingly important. The only means Romania had to earn hard currency were tourism and exports to the West. Tourism brought in little hard currency, and the annual balance of trade was negative between 1958-72 except for the years 1959, 1960 and 1965. Romania's trade surplus with the other socialist states and the developing countries had not solved Romania's financial problems, as these currencies were most nonconvertible. Western firms had been willing to accept Romanian credits with developing countries as partial payment for some of their sales, but the practice was not large enough to offset Romania's cumulative Western debt, which was estimated in early 1970 at between $1 billion and $1.5 billion.[62] At that time, 25 percent of Romania's hard currency earnings were required to meet the interest and principal payments on this debt.[63]

To help solve this balance-of-payments problem, Romania has become the only CMEA state to join the GATT in 1967 and the IMF and IBRD in in 1972. Membership in these international institutions has been reinforced by Romania's domestic economic reforms. Romania tired to increase its exports by improving the quality of Romanian products, and by bringing Western buyers together with Romanian plant managers so that these plant managers could learn from their Western buyers how to manufacture products that would be competitive in Western markets. Exports to the West were also subsidized [64] Romania did not consider these reforms to be very useful, unless the United States would end its asymmetrical treatment of Romanian exports by granting most-favored-nation status to Romania. Romania's first formal request for MFN status came during its negotiations with the United States in May 1964, but Lyndon Johnson was unable to obtain the authority from Congress to grant this treatment. Nixon had called for MFN treatment to be extended to Romania during his 1969 visit to Bucharest, but the Nixon administration did not push Congress to grant it until February 1972. At that time, Nixon supported legislation before Congress specifically designed to grant Romania MFN status.[65] However, this attempt was blocked in Congress over the Soviet Union's restrictions on the emigration of Russian Jews.

In spite of this setback, Romanian-American relations continued to improve. Ceausescu visited Nixon in Washington, during the first week of December 1973. This state visit resulted in the signing of several agreements, the most important of which was the Joint Statement on Economic, Industrial and Technological Cooperation. In this document the two presidents reaffirmed their desire to continue expanding and developing relations between their two countries. These expanded relations were to include trade expansion as well as encouragement for direct American investment in Romanian enterprises. The issue of MFN treatment for Romania was conspicuous by its absence, despite a pledge by Nixon to secure MFN status for Romania. However, a Joint American-Romanian Economic Council was established through a separate agreement by the Chamber of Commerce of the United States and the Romanian Chamber of Commerce to promote the expanded economic relations called for in the Joint Statement.[66]

The discretionary power of the President to grant MFN status to socialist states was finally restored by the Trade Act of 1974. However, Section 402 of the act stipulated that no nonmarket economy country would be eligible for MFN treatment, government credits or guarantees, if that country denied the right or opportunity of its citizens to emigrate. This section, known as the Jackson-Vanik amendment, had the immediate effect of cancelling access to Export-Import Bank, CCC and OPIC financial programs for American business transactions in Romania. The

President was given authority to waive by executive order the restrictions of Section 402 and to enter into negotiations for a bilateral commercial agreement with a socialist state if he determined that such waiver would "substantially promote the objectives" of Section 402; and if he "received assurances that the emigration practices of that country will henceforth lead substantially to the achievement of the objectives of this section."[67]

The Soviet Union rejected the Jackson-Vanik amendment and renounced its commercial agreement with the United States in January 1975; all other eligible Eastern European countries which could have been effected by the waiver provision, except Romania, indicated that they were also unwilling to accept the terms of Section 402.

The American-Romanian Economic Council had been preparing for negotiations for a bilateral commercial agreement between the United States and Romania. When Romania agreed to negotiate on the basis of Section 402, negotiations on a government to government level began in January 1975. The administration was very careful to keep Congress fully informed of the progress of the negotiations. The successful negotiations were concluded with the signing of the United States-Romanian Trade Agreement on April 2, 1975. President Ford transmitted to Congress on April 24, 1975 a proclamation extending MFN treatment to imports from Romania which is included in Article I of the Agreement.[69] The same day, the President issued an executive order waiving Subsections (a) and (b) of Section 402 which restored Exim Bank, CCC and OPIC financial programs to Romania. President Ford also submitted the required report to Congress indicating that his waiver would subsequently promote the emigration objectives of Section 402. This report is based on a clause in the December 5, 1973 Joint Statement on Economic, Industrial and Technological Cooperation which stated that "they will contribute to the solution of humanitarian problems on the basis of mutual confidence and good will . . . . I have been assured that if and when such problems arise, they will be solved on a reciprocal basis, in the spirit of the Declaration."

The vagueness of President Ford's report concerned many members of Congress, especially in the Senate. Most senators considered Romania's compliance with the free emigration requirements of Section 402 to be the key issue involved in accepting or rejecting the trade agreement. Arthur A. Hartman, Assistant Secretary of State for European Affairs informed Congress that the emigration issue posed serious problems for Romania after the Soviet Union had rejected Section 402; therefore the understanding that the United States had reached with Romania on the meaning and implementation of Section 402 could not be publicly discussed. Congress reluctantly accepted this explanation and relied suspiciously on the increased emigration which Romania had allowed in the spring of 1975.[71]

The Ford administration and the House of Representatives placed greater emphasis upon the necessity for the United States to continue encouraging Romania's independent foreign policy. In fact, they feared that if the commercial agreement were rejected, American-Romanian relations would begin to deteriorate. Members of the House emphasized Romania's continued good relations with Israel and its membership in the GATT, IMF and IBRD as evidence of Romania's independence and Western orientation.[72] These members of the American government felt that the United States-Romanian Trade Agreement would meet the requirement of encouraging Romania's independence from the Soviet Union and within the CMEA, because Romania's economic viability was the key to its strategy of independence. The underyling objective of the United States' policy of encouraging Romania's independence as a means of dividing the Warsaw Pact shines through these debates.

Most of the opposition to the United States-Romanian Trade Agreement in addition to the political argument that Romania's emigration policies were not acceptable, centered on the economic issue that American labor would be unable to compete with low-priced Romanian imports. They maintained that the agreement would only cause more unemployment for an American economy already suffering the highest levels of unemployment since the Depression of 1929. However, the danger was lessened by Romania's centrally planned economy. A significant increase in the exportation of any product depended on the extent that the increase was included in the investment allocations and the production goals of the economic plan.[73] The draft trade agreement also contains a provision that allows either party to impose restrictions considered necessary on imports from the other party to prevent or remedy actual or threatened market disruption. It would also be possible to suspend or terminate the agreement at any time for national security reasons. Consequently, the American market was not considered to be threatened by a flood of Romanian exports to the United States.[74]

The United States-Romanian Economic Agreement also contains articles designed to promote American exports to Romania. There are extensive provisions on business facilitation to assure American businessmen the conditions necessary to conduct successful commercial negotiations with the Romanians. A goal of tripling bilateral trade is linked to Romania's

5-year plan through Romania's accession protocol to the GATT. This protocol provides that Romania will increase its imports from GATT members at the same rate as its overall imports as projected in its 5-year plan.[75]

Congress easily passed the agreement in July 1975, and it became effective on August 3, 1975 during President Ford's trip to Romania. At this point, the United States achieved the goal of normalizing American-Romanian economic relations which had been desired by Presidents Johnson, Nixon and Ford. The significance of this achievement was lessened somewhat by the fact that the United States-Romanian Economic Agreement must be renewed annually. Nevertheless, the agreement recognizes that the Cold War animosities which existed between the two countries had been solved. In fact, Romania announced in May 1975 that it had reached a settlement with the Bondholder's Protective Council of $750,000 to be paid American claimants for defaulted Romanian bonds and guarantees, thereby settling the last economic issue separating the two countries.[76] Most importantly, the agreement preserved the increasingly good relations between the United States and Romania. This was achieved by permitting Romania to obtain the financing necessary to increase its imports from the United States. It also granted Romania MFN treatment so that Romania could sell more to the United States in order to buy more from the United States.

Extending MFN treatment to Romania meant that the Congressional policy of insulating the United States from contacts with communism had been discarded for the Presidential policy of using trade as a diplomatic tool to encourage Romania's independence from the Soviet Union. The bureaucracy would no longer be under pressure from Congress to deny export licenses to Romania to maintain the isolation of Americans from Romanians.

However, Congress was just catching up with the business community which had been establishing closer relations with Romania since the early 1960s. Romania's demand for Western products coupled with its shortage of hard currency forced Romania on March 17, 1971 to become the first CMEA country to permit private direct investment. Under that decree a foreign firm may own as much as 49 percent in any joint enterprises formed with Romanian companies.

Control Data Corporation announced in April 1973, that it had formed a joint venture with Romania in which Control Data owned 45 percent of the firm's equity. The joint venture is to last 20 years. The significance of this joint venture is that it creates a situation in which capitalists and communists must work together on a daily basis to achieve a common goal—the success of the business firm. No other project, resulting from East-West relations, requires such close cooperation for such an extended period of time. It will be extremely interesting to see how the partners adjust to the ideological differences separating them and it will be even more interesting to observe what impact the adjustment has on ideology, whether the liberalizing of American-Romanian economic relations wil generate closer personal contact and exchange of ideas and contribute to the ability of each society to tolerate the other's existence?

NOTES

1. Josef Wilczynski, *The Economics and Politics of East-West Trade* (New York: Praeger Publishers, 1969), pp. 275-78.

2. Thomas A. Wolf, *U.S. East-West Trade Policy, Economic Warfare Versus Economic Welfare* (Lexington, Mass.: Lexington Book, D.C. Heath and Company, 1973), p. 48. (Hereinafter cited as Wolf, *East-West Trade Policy.*)

3. Act of July 2, 1940 (54 Stat. 714).

4. U.S. Congress, Senate, *Congressional Record*, 81st Cong., 1st sess., 1949, 95, pt. 1: 949-56.

5. U.S. Congress, Senate. *The Administration of Export Controls*, S. Rept. 1775, 80th Cong., 2nd sess., 1948, p. 3.

6. Ibid., pp. 5-19.

7. Export Control Act of 1949, Section 12 (63 Stat. 9) limits the termination date of the act to two years or "upon any prior date which Congress by Concurrent resolution or the President may designate." Some members of Congress were also worried that export controls would have a negative effect on the economy, that export controls were contrary to traditional American trade policies and that export controls concentrated too much power over business in the hands of the executive. U.S. Congress, Senate & House, *Congressional Record*, 81st Cong., 1st sess., 1949, 95, pt. 1: 949-56, 1368-71. These reasons contributed to the hope that export controls would be of short duration.

8. Anthony M. Soloman, "The Revival of Trade Between the Communist Block and the West," *Annals of the American Academy of Political and Social Sciences*, CCCLXXII (July, 1967), 106.

9. "Multinational Report," *Fortune*, October, 1970, pp. 47-49.

10. U.S. Congress, Senate, Committee on Banking and Currency, *East-West Trade, Hearings,* before the Subcommittee on International Finance

of the Committee on Banking and Currency, United States Senate, on S.J. Res. 169, 90th Cong., 2nd sess., 1968, Part 1, pp. 205-6. (Hereinafter referred to as *East-West Trade.*)

11.   U.S. Congress, Senate, Committee on Foreign Relations, *East-West Trade, A Compilation of Views of Businessmen, Bankers and Academic Experts Hearings,* before the Commitee on Foreign Relations, United States Senate, 88th Cong., 2nd sess., 1964, pp. 9, 29, 31-32, 133, 163. (Hereinafter referred to as *East-West Trade,* Committe on Foreign Relations.); *East-West Trade,* Part I, pp. 149-56.

12.   *East-West Trade,* Part 1, p. 298; U.S. Congress, Senate, Committee on Banking and Currency, *Export Expansion and Regulation, Hearings,* before Subcommittee on International Finance of the Committee on Banking and Currency, United States Senate, on S. 813 and S. 1940, 91st Cong., 1st sess., 1969, pp. 94-118. (Hereinafter cited as *Export Expansion and Regulation.*)

13.   *East-West Trade,* Part III, pp. 1039-41; *East-West Trade,* Committee on Foreign Relations, pp. 22, 27.

14.   Export Administration Act of 1969, Section 4 (a) (1) (83 Stat. 842); Equal Export Opportunity Act, Sections 104 (2) and 105 (86 Stat. 644-46); more than 1700 commodities were decontrolled between 1969 and 1972; U.S. Congress, Senate, Committee on Banking, Housing and Urban Affairs, *Continuation of Authority for Regulation of Exports, Hearings,* before the Subcommittee on International Finance of the Committee on Banking, Housing and Urban Affairs, United States Senate, on S. 1487, 92 Cong., 2nd sess., 1972, p. 4. (Hereinafter cited as *Authority for Regulation of Exports.*)

15.   U.S. Congress, Senate, Committee on Banking, Housing and Urban Affairs, *Extension of the Export Administration Act, Hearings,* before the International Finance Subcommittee on the Committee on Banking, Housing and Urban Affairs, United States Senate, on S. 3084, 94th Cong., 2nd sess., 1976, pp. 308-316. (Hereinafter cited as *Extension of the Export Administration Act.*)

16.   *Export Expansion and Regulation,* p. 181.

17.   *Extension of the Export Administration Act,* p. 5.

18.   *East-West Trade,* Part 1, p. 390; *Extension of the Export Administration Act,* pp. 58-59.

19.   *Export Expansion and Regulation,* pp. 364-365.

20.   Mutual Defense Assistance Control Act of 1951, Section 101, (65 Stat. 645).

21.   For example, see *Public Papers of the Presidents of the United States, Harry S. Truman.* Jan. 1, 1959-Jan. 20, 1953, (Washington, D.C.: U.S. Government Printing Office, 1966), pp. 288-89, 439-40.

22. *Extension of the Export Administration Act,* p. 4; The highly secret Coordinating Committee or COCOM meets in Paris annually to formulate multilateral export control policy. It is composed of all the original NATO members except Iceland plus Japan. That is, all the major industrial countries of the West with the minor exceptions of Sweden and Switzerland. For discussions of the Battle Act and COCOM see Josef Wilczynski, "Strategic Embargo in Perspective," *Soviet Studies,* XIX (July, 1967), 74-86 and Gunnar Adler-Karlsson, *Western Economic Warfare, 1947-1967, A Case Study in Foreign Economic Policy* (Stockholm: Almquist and Wiksell, 1968).

23. U.S. Department of Commerce, Bureau of International Commerce, *Overseas Business Reports,* "Basic Data on the Economy of Romania" (Washington, D.C.: Goverment Printing Office, 1971), p. 20.

24. Wilczynski, "Strategic Embargo," op. cit., 75.

25. See the numerous articles in the *Congressional Record* for 1950 and 1951.

26. Trade Agreements Extension Act of 1951, Section 5 (65 Stat. 73), U.S. President, Proclamation, "Giving Effect to Sections 5 and 11 of the Trade Agreements Extension Act of 1951." *Code of Federal Regulations,* title 3, the President, 1949-1953, pp. 121-22; loss of MFN benefits became effective August 31, 1951.

27. Stephen Fischer-Galati, *The Socialist Republic of Romania* (Baltimore: John Hopkins Press, 1969), p. 1.

28. Ibid., p. 40; Kazimierz Grzybowski, "Foreign Investment and Political Control in Europe," *Journal of Central European Affairs,* XIII (April, 1953), 13.

29. John Michael Montias, *Economic Development in Communist Rumania* (Cambridge, Mass.: M.I.T. Press, 1967), pp. 50-52.

30. "East-West Trade," *The New Statesmen and Nation,* September 4, 1954, p. 251; *Public Papers of the Presidents of the United States, Dwight D. Eisenhower, 1956* (Washington, D.C.: U.S. Government Printing Office, 1958), pp. 296-297.

31. U.S. Department of State, *Department of State Bulletin,* Vol. XXXIII (August 1, 1955), 175.

32. *Public Papers . . . Dwight D. Eisenhower, 1955* (Washington, D. C.: U.S. Government Printing Office, 1959), p. 517 and ibid., *1957,* p. 442.

33. Welles Hangen, "Rumania Offers More Oil to West," *New York Times,* October 23, 1956, p. 19.

34. Dana Andrews Schmidt, "Rumania Offers to Settle Claims for U.S. Property," *New York Times,* May 2, 1956, p. 1. U.S. Claims were

estimated at $88 million and nearly half of this belonged to Standard Oil of New Jersey and other oil companies that had large holdings in the Ploiesti oil fields. The U.S. settled for $24,526,370. Of this amount $22,026,370 consisted of Romanian assets blocked in the United States. The Romanian government paid the remaining $2,500,000. See U.S. Department of State, *United States Treaties and Other International Agreements*, Vol. 11, pt. 1, "Settlement of Claims of United States Nationals and other Financial Matters, " TIAS No. 4451, March 30, 1960.

35.   *Public Papers. . . , John F. Kennedy, 1962*, (Washington, D.C.: U.S. Government Printing Office, 1963), p. 782 and ibid., *1963*, p. 94; Samuel Pisar, *Coexistence and Commerce* (New York: McGraw-Hill Book Company, 1970), pp. 62-3.

36.   See the testimony of J. N. Behrman, Assistant Secretary of Commerce for International Affairs, in U.S. Congress, Senate, Committee on Banking and Currency, *Extension of Export Control Act–1962, Hearings*, before the Committee on Banking and Currency, United States Senate, on S. 3161, 87th Cong., 2nd sess., 1962, pp. 3-18; and U.S. Congress, House, *Extension of the Export Control Act of 1949*, H.R. Dept., 2nd sess., 162, pp. 5-6.

37.   U.S. Congress, House, *Investigation and Study of the Administration, Operation and Enforcement of the Export Control Act of 1949 and Related Acts*, H.R. Rept. 1836 to accompany H.R. 11309, 87th Cong., 2nd sess., 1962, pp. 22, 31.

38.   U.S. Congress, House Committee on Banking and Currency, *Extension of the Export Control Act of 1949 and Issuance of Gold Medal to Bob Hope, Hearings*, before Committee on Banking and Currency, House of Representatives, on H.R. 11309, 87th Cong., 2nd sess., 1962, p. 21.

39.   Act to Provide for Continuation of Authority for Regulation of Exports and Other Purposes, Section 2 (76 Stat. 127).

40.   *Public Papers. . . , Lyndon B. Johnson, 1963-64*, Book II (Washington, D.C.: U.S. Government Printing Office, 1965), p. 709.

41.   The sources for this discussion of the U.S.-Romanian Agreement of June 1, 1964 are: Kurt Neubauer, ed., *Doing Business with Eastern Europe* (Geneva, Switzerland: Business International S.A., 1972), p. 160; and especially the testimony of William A. Crawford, U.S. Minister and Ambassador to Romania from 1961 to October 1965, in U.S. Congress, Senate, Committee on Finance, *Romanian Trade Agreement, Hearings*, before Committee on Finance, United States Senate, on S. Con. Res. 35, 94th Cong., 2nd sess., 1975, p. 80 (hereinafter cited as *Romanian Trade Agreement.*)

42.   This information is from Tad Szule, "U.S. Acts to Spur Romania Trade," *New York Times*, June 2, 1964, pp. 1, 12; *Wall Street Journal*, June 2, 1964, p. 6; "East-West Trade Gets a Lift," *Business Week*, October 15, 1966, p. 39; *East-West Trade*, Part 2, pp. 910-911, 923.

43.   Max Frankel, "U.S. Assays Stand in Red Bloc Trade," *New York Times*, April 19, 1964, p. 14.

44.   This material is from U.S. Congress, Senate, *Congressional Record*, 89th Cong., 1st sess., 1965, 111, pt. 8: 10678-80; pt. 13: 18226-34, 18256-57; pt. 14: 19508-09; pt. 15; 19753-56; *Wall Street Journal*, January 6, 1965, p. 17; *Business Week*, July 26, 1965, p. 51, 74 and July 31, 1965, p. 71; *Business Abroad*, September, 1969, p. 32; *The New York Republic*, November 12, 1966, p. 8. The division within the Johnson administration over sales of turnkey projects to Romania is evident in its refusal to strongly support Firestone during the controversy. The reason was probably fear of losing political support for Great Society programs.

45.   See U.S. Department of State, *Department of State Bulletin*, Vol. LV (September 26, 1966), 449-52; "Ordinances Restricting the Sale of 'Communist Goods'," *Columbia Law Review*, LXV (February, 1965), 310-18.

46.   The sources for his material are: *East-West Trade*, Part 2, pp. 793-818; *East-West Trade*, Part 3, p. 1110; U.S. Department of State, *Department of State Bulletin*, Vol. LIV (May 30, 1966), 838-844.

47.   Marshall I. Goldman and Alice Conner, "Businessmen and East-West Trade," *Harvard Business Review*, XLIV (January-February, 1966), 26.

48.   *Wall Street Journal*, January 27, 1966, p. 14; *Wall Street Journal*, April 14, 1967, p. 18.

49.   "A Communist Comes to Talk Business," *Business Week*, October 31, 1970, p. 28.

50.   *Wall Street Journal*, November 25, 1970, p. 13; "Going 50-50 in East Europe," *Business Week*, January 16, 1971, p. 41.

51.   *Forbes*, June 15, 1970, p. 70; "Nobody Here but us Marxists?" *Forbes*, July 15, 1971, p. 48.

52.   "Copee Rust's Long-Term Strategy Pays Off in East European Sales," *Business Europe*, April 2, 1971, p. 107; "Rumania Tries the Hard Sell on Trade," *Business Week*, July 26, 1969, p. 76.

53.   *Authority for the Regulation of Exports*, p. 18.

54.   "East-West Trade and More Western Firms Travel a Joint Venture Route to Bloc Markets," *Business Abroad*, August, 1968, p. 11. Some of this decrease was not due to the war in Vietnam, but from a scarcity of hard currency held by Romania in 1967.

55.   See *East-West Trade*, Parts 1-3; U.S. Congress, Senate, *Export Expansion and Regulation Act*, S. Rept. 336 to accompany S. 2696, 91 st Cong., 1st sess., 1969, pp. 2-5; Export Administration Act of 1969, Section 2 (83 Stat. 841).

56.   U.S. Congress, Senate, *Export Expansion and Regulation Act*, S. Rept. 336 to accompany S. 2696, 91st Cong., 1st sess., 1969, p. 4.

57.   Ibid., p. 3.

58.   Export Administration Act of 1969, Section 3 (83 Stat. 841). Emphasis added.

59.   *Export Expansion and Regulation*, p. 272.

60.   *Extension of the Export Administration Act*, p. 5.

61.   See U.S. Department of Commerce, Domestic and International Business Administration, *Overseas Business Reports*, "Trading and Investing in Romania" (Washington, D.C.: Government Printing Office, 1973); U.S. Department of State, *United States Treaties and other International Agreements*, Vol. 24, pt. 1, "Investment Guaranties," TIAS No. 7627, April 28, 1973.

62.   Ibid., p. 4.

63.   *Business Week*, December 1, 1973, p. 40.

64.   Harriet Matejka, "Foreign Trade Systems," in *The New Economic Systems of Eastern Europe*, ed. by Hans-Herman Hohmann, Michael C. Kaser and Karl C. Talheim (Berkeley and Los Angeles: University of California Press, 1975), p. 464; See also Iancu Spigler, *Economic Reform in Romanian Industry* (London: Oxford University Press, 1973).

65.   Wolf, *East-West Trade Policy*, p. 111; *Public Papers . . .* , *Richard Nixon, 1972*, (Washington, D.C.: U.S. Government Printing Office, 1974), p. 231.

66.   U.S. Department of State, *United States Treaties and Other International Agreements*, Vol. 24, pt. 2, "Joint Statement by the President of the United States of America and the President of the Council of State of the Socialist Republic of Romania," TIAS No. 7746, Dec. 5, 1973.

67.   Trade Act of 1974, Section 402 (C) (1) (a) (b) (88 Stat. 2057).

68.   *Romanian Trade Agreement*, p. 102.

69.   U.S. Congress, Senate, Committee on Finance, *Background Materials Relating to the United States-Romanian Trade Agreement*, 94th Cong., 1st sess., 1975, pp. 10-11, 14. (Hereinafter cited as *Background Materials.*)

70.   Ibid., p. 11.

71.   U.S. Congress, House, Committee on Ways and Means, *United States-Romanian Trade Agreement, Hearings*, before the Subcommittee

on Ways and Means, House of Representative, on H. Con. Res. 252, 94th Cong., 1st sess., 1975, p. 38. (Hereinafter cited as *U.S. Romanian Trade Agreement.*) U.S. Congress, Senate, *Congressional Record*, 94th Cong., 1st sess., 1975, 121, pt. 19: 24936-24948, *passim;* U.S. Congress, House, *Congressional Record*, 84th Cong., 1st sess., 1975, 121, pt. 20: 25204-25216, *passim.*

72.   *U.S.-Romanian Trade Agreement*, pp. 126-130.

73.   U.S., International Trade Commission, *Special Report to the Congress and the East-West Foreign Trade Board on Impact of U.S. Imports of Granting Most-Favored-Nation Treatment to Romania.* (Washington, D.C.: Government Printing Office, 1975), p. A-16.

74.   *Background Materials*, pp. 15-23.

75.   Ibid., pp. 14-15.

76.   U.S. Congress, House, *Extension of Nondiscriminatory Treatment to Products of Romania*, House Rept. 359, to accompany H. Con. Res. 252, 94th Cong., 2nd sess., 1975, pp. 6-7.

UNITED STATES–ROMANIAN FOREIGN TRADE
(thousands of US dollars)

Years	Total Trade	U.S. Exports to Romania	U.S. Imports from Romania
1950	2,291	2,009	282
1951	712	390	322
1952	683	(1)	683
1953	379	7	372
1954	448	66	382
1955	461	191	270
1956	841	464	377
1957	1,440	966	474
1958	2,244	871	373
1959	3,025	1,820	1,205
1960	2,423	962	1,461
1961	2,743	1,404	1,339
1962	1,428	802	626
1963	2,038	1,245	789
1964	6,428	5,156	1,272
1965	8,221	6,385	1,836
1966	31,712	27,057	4,655
1967	22,971	16,795	6,176
1968	22,233	16,680	5,553
1969	40,360	22,394[2]	7,966
1970	79,824	66,399[3]	13,425[3]
1971	66,176	52,532	13,744
1972	100,462	69,051	31,411
1973	172,210	116,510	55,700
1974	407,640	277,120	130,520
1975	322,200[4]	189,300[4]	132,900[4]

1. Less than $500.
2. U.S. Department of Commerce statistics vary between 22,394 and 32,000.
3. United Nations lists imports as 59,767 and imports as 13,417. The UN statistics are based upon Romanian statistics.
4. Rounded off to the nearest thousand.

Sources: United Nations, Department of Economic and Social Affairs, *Yearbook of International Trade Statistics; Statistical Pocket Book of the Socialist Republic of Romania,* 1970; U.S. Department of Commerce; Paul Marer, *Soviet and East European Foreign Trade, 1946-1969: Statistical Compendium and Guide.* Bloomington and London: Indiana University Press, 1972. Tables F-7.